THE BRITISH EMPIRE 1558–1995

SECOND EDITION

T. O. LLOYD

OXFORD
UNIVERSITY PRESS

*This book has been printed digitally and produced in a standard specification
in order to ensure its continuing availability*

OXFORD
UNIVERSITY PRESS

Great Clarendon Street, Oxford OX2 6DP

Oxford University Press is a department of the University of Oxford.
It furthers the University's objective of excellence in research, scholarship,
and education by publishing worldwide in

Oxford New York

Auckland   Cape Town Dar es Salaam Hong Kong Karachi
Kuala Lumpur Madrid Melbourne Mexico City Nairobi
New Delhi Shanghai Taipei Toronto
With offices in
Argentina Austria Brazil Chile Czech Republic France Greece
Guatemala Hungary Italy Japan South Korea Poland Portugal
Singapore Switzerland Thailand Turkey Ukraine Vietnam

Oxford is a registered trade mark of Oxford University Press
in the UK and in certain other countries

Published in the United States
by Oxford University Press Inc., New York

ISBN 978-0-19-873133-7

PREFACE

LOYALTY and thrift were the principles that shaped the British Empire, and, now that they survive as private virtues rather than as forces to shape public policy, the British Empire has passed from the scene. Until quite recently loyalty to an often distant monarch, rather than a geographical or linguistic devotion to a nation, was the force that held states together. Great empires could expand over vast distances and encounter no long-lasting resistance at anything more than a tribal level. Patriotic resistance would now make such expansion far more difficult than in the past, and can dissolve away all but the most ruthless of empires.

Until 1500 the empires created in this way were confined to single masses of land, and could only be continent-wide. About 500 years ago empires began to spread across oceans and became world-wide. Although the British Empire came closer than any other empire to establishing itself in every region of the globe, there were clearly occasions at which it might have expanded more vigorously. The restraint on expansion was the pressure of thrift: the great empire was ruled from a country whose citizens had as much freedom as anyone in the world, and one use they made of their freedom was to keep taxation low. As a result the imperial rulers could at times have stood amazed at their moderation in taking so little.

The British Empire was the creation of a system of political values that we now have a little difficulty in understanding, but in many ways and for many peoples it served as a bridge between old and new. The period of greatest expansion was also the period in which the ideas of nationalism and of elected representative government were becoming accepted in Europe and began to spread throughout the world. Between them, nationalist commitment in the colonies and acceptance of the legitimacy of national feeling by the imperial powers brought the transoceanic empires to an end peacefully and quickly.

Ever since Sir John Seeley published *The Expansion of England* a hundred years ago, only the most scholarly and specialized studies of tiny portions of the imperial subject have avoided putting forward proposals of one policy or another. All sorts of different points of view have been advocated in the guise of history as well as in the simpler form of direct recommendation: the empire should expand, the empire should become united in a more formal and better organized way, the empire should be defended against its (usually German) enemies, the empire should be turned into a commonwealth of independent nations, the empire should be attacked and overthrown, the empire should be dissolved into its component parts, and so on. That stage of history-writing is now over. The emotions have hardly cooled enough to allow anyone to accept the advice of a (fallen) imperial commander:

> Nothing extenuate,
> Nor set down aught in malice

and historians will go on making explicit recommendations about what should be done about empire, or giving their readers emotional relief from the new problems of the post-imperial age by writing about a period that may possibly now look simple. But there are limits to the amount of good advice they can give, and perhaps there are limits to the amount of moralizing they can do.

Moral standards change: things have been done in the twentieth century that might leave Genghis Khan or Timurlane feeling outclassed in mass slaughter, but on the whole we tend to be ready to apply to people of the past standards of judgement rather higher than those accepted (or at least lived up to) by modern states. Part of the difficulty is that the world has changed so much. Four centuries ago slavery was natural: four centuries from now people may very well have given up our habit of eating meat and may have great difficulty in thinking about most of us without a shudder of inbred and almost uncontrollable revulsion. They may be all the better people for it, but it will not be the way to understand the history of the twentieth century, and moral revulsion is not the best way to understand the path of empire.

The end of directly political writing about the empire has other results. For over a hundred years the American colonies that became the United States were normally discussed as if their development was an aberration in imperial history, while other colonies followed the natural line of progress that ought to be taken in a well-conducted empire. This was often accompanied by attempts to show that anyone could have followed a more sensible American policy than George III, usually with the idea in mind that relations between the British Empire and the United States ought to be closer. Now that it can be seen that there is nothing very special about the American experience, the United States can be treated as an early example of the development of the spirit of national pride that is incompatible with imperial connections. The Commonwealth can do a great deal of good, but it can hardly be the uniquely strong influence on its members' foreign policies which was assumed, at least implicitly, by writers who thought the American colonies were a peculiar (and a peculiarly deplorable) case.

The word 'imperialism' invokes such a triumph of political commitment over historical precision that it will not be used in this book. Its meaning and its emotional overtones have changed a great deal in the last hundred years, but it has all the time been used to recommend one line of policy or another. Richard Koebner and Dan Schmidt explained in *Imperialism: the History and Significance of a Political Word* (1965) how its meaning changed from an aggressive foreign policy to imperial enthusiasm and on to imperial expansion, closer imperial unity, an imperial economic policy, a process of exploitation of imperial subjects, the last stage of capitalism, and many other things besides. Each of these concepts is relevant to the story, and can be called by its own more precise name, which is clearer than saying 'imperialism' and leaving the reader to work out which meaning is being used (there was a time when Marxist historians tried to impose a taboo on one meaning, saying that no Communist country could pursue an imperialist policy, but there are signs that even this slightly arbitrary limitation on its use is being abandoned).

Attempts have recently been made to remove the word 'discovery' from historical writing almost completely. The objection is that the word ought to mean that 'the geographical feature in question was seen for the first time by human beings', but was misused to mean 'it was seen for the first time by Europeans', so that 'Columbus discovered America' was seen as a phrase that degraded the original inhabitants of the Americas to a level at which they were fit only to be conquered by the Spanish. This is a humane attitude, but it misses the point of the word and obscures one of the great changes of the last 500 years. The unified map of the world which enables mankind to see the relationships between every place on earth could not have been drawn 500 years ago, and what the 'discoverers' were finding was the way that the scattered pieces of human knowledge of separate areas fitted together. If we are not to say 'Columbus discovered America', we can at the very least say 'Columbus discovered, in a way that other people could use, the geographical relationship between Europe and America', and thus helped to put together the map of the world in a way that the calm existence of the original population did not. So the word will be used occasionally, and will be used in this map-making sense of finding the geographical relationship between one part of the world and another.

Everyone knows that abstract nouns can cause trouble, but proper nouns can be even harder to manage. Transliteration raises insoluble difficulties. Is Siraj-ud Daula (which seems to be the way to spell the name which is accepted at present) or Surajah Dowlah (a common eighteenth-century form) the better way to ensure that twentieth-century readers of English come as close as possible to pronouncing the name of the last independent ruler of Bengal in the way that his subjects would have done? In the absence of tape-recordings of eighteenth-century speech it is very hard to say. The quest for accurate transcription of primarily oral languages can confuse rather than help the reader, even if it performs the secondary purpose of establishing the greater wisdom of the writer.[1] The verbal anarchy defended by T. E. Lawrence in the Introduction to *Seven Pillars of Wisdom* probably goes too far, but anyone who thinks that certainty can be reached ought to consider his argument.

Apart from these linguistic problems, political changes affect the names of places and, most often and most confusingly, the political units. In the last four centuries the name 'Canada' has referred to a variety of geographical areas: the boundaries have changed a dozen times with the curtailment of New France and then the steady expansion of Canada until it now includes the whole of what was 'British North America'. Many countries have changed their names on becoming independent or a little later, often for very obvious reasons: Belize could hardly remain British Honduras for ever. In the past countries like Sverige, Suomi, and Magyarország have been happy to allow English names for them to be used which have little or nothing in common with the native names, but less self-confident countries becoming independent recently have wanted their native names to be adopted in English as well. An example from history after independence (at least, independence from Britain) will show the sensible attitude for the historian to take to changes of name. For twenty years after the end of British rule the two states now known as Pakistan and Bangla Desh were the single state known as Pakistan. It would be very confusing, when writing about those twenty years, to refer to Pakistan as if it simply meant the present-day state of that name and to obscure the fact of political union by giving the name Bangla Desh to what was then called East Pakistan. So states and colonies will be given the names in use (applied to the appropriate geographical areas) at the periods under discussion, though there may be some references to the present-day situation to make the geographical position clearer.

There remains the question of giving a name to the large political unit in the British Isles that ruled the empire from London. The name changes from England to Britain in 1707, and perhaps should change again to the United Kingdom in 1801, but this is a little clumsy. Scots law was not united with English law, the cricket team plays under the name England, and nobody refers to the King of Britain after the days of King Lear. What about the people who make up such a large part of the story? 'Britishers' has overtones of a very distinctive imperial approach and, despite the well-meant efforts of George III to publicize the word (and some arguments put to me skilfully and persuasively), 'Britons' still has too much of a suggestion of woad about it to be entirely satisfactory. Phrases like 'British emigrants' often make sense but some of the time 'Englishmen' is the only way to avoid

[1] 'Ngomi is of course simply the eastern Bantu variant of the southern Bantu name Ngumi', in J. D. Fage, *A History of Africa* (1978), 314–15, may remind older scholars of Potter's correction 'but not in the South' in S. Potter, *Lifemanship* (1950), 43.

the awkwardness of saying 'people from England, Ireland, Scotland, and Wales'. English women, and smaller minority groups, may feel that they have been excluded by the tyranny of words.

Though its name was altered the identity of the political unit at the centre of the British Empire changed very little. And some centre to hold it together has to be found: it was a very large empire but at times it does seem to have been even more confusing than was absolutely necessary. Perhaps there really was a rule at the Colonial Office that no colony should have a constitution exactly like that of any other colony; if so, it was enforced with an entirely untypical uniformity. Loyalty to the monarch was a common factor, but not a uniform factor: a monarch who was committed to professing different religions in England and in Scotland would have relatively little difficulty about being the ruler of the vast majority of Hindus and of a large proportion of the world's Muslims. Nations rest on the belief that everyone is a citizen and everyone must be treated the same but empires do not have to make any such concessions to equality and can perfectly well have laws for each different group under the monarch.

While his subjects saw the monarch as a distant but supreme ruler, the monarch was to an increasing extent controlled by the free (and thrifty) people of the British nation. The unifying legal structure was that of an empire, but one great force for change was the influence of Britain on all of its colonies. This cultural influence never turned into anything like complete assimilation, and may in the future turn out to have been only a matter of linguistic unity among the prosperous classes, but it certainly means that at the present day the rulers of an astonishing diversity of countries can communicate very easily. It also means that unity for the historian is inevitably London-based: equal time for all could only be managed in a very long Oxford history of the modern world, a Canada-centred history would do full justice to the colonies settled from Britain but might find it hard to fit India in properly, and an India-centred history might have the same trouble with colonies of white settlement. So this history emerges as a London-centred story, written from a point of view that occasionally feels like a cross between that of a well-informed leader writer on *The Times* and a rather passive official at the Colonial Office. It is divided – as administrators' affairs are always divided – on a chronological basis; there may be a slight overlapping between chapters, but on the whole periods of time rather than divisions of space or contrasts of constitutional form mark the divisions. The introductory section to each chapter tries to knit together what follows, even at the risk of imposing too tight a logical pattern on it; chapters are subdivided, but it does no harm for readers to be reminded that the troubles of the East India Company helped precipitate the American War of Independence and that the problems of settling new territory in western Canada were not entirely different from those of occupying eastern Africa.

These are small problems. The greatest problem for a historian facing this subject is one brought out by people who respond to hearing about writing the history of the British Empire, by saying that the British Empire is dead. And that forces the author to face the fact that possibly the greatest work of classical history and possibly the greatest work of modern history were written about empires that were dead. Anything, however unintentional, that puts a historian into the same field of endeavour as Thucydides and Gibbon is a little alarming. Comparison or competition are hardly sensible responses to such a challenge. All that can be done is to say that the subject of the British Empire is one entirely worthy of the genius of such men, and to confess that it will be a long time before it meets a historian who can match its greatness.

But all of us can be courteous: it has been a pleasure to work in the libraries of the Royal Commonwealth Society (often at a durable table inlaid with the letters R.E.S.) and of the London Library, and there is no need to mention less pleasant libraries; I have received generous and welcome hospitality in the all-too-short visits I have made to a few Commonwealth countries; Ivon Asquith has been very patient in waiting for a somewhat belated manuscript; Kate Hamilton has been dextrous enough with the word processor to keep that lateness to a minimum; John Roberts has been a trusting, encouraging, and helpful editor; and my brother Ifan has been very helpful in reading earlier drafts and providing information and advice, which has often been useful and has always been stimulating. This book is dedicated to him.

CONTENTS

MAPS

TABLES

1. *Colonies and Distant Monarchs 1558–1649*

When Elizabeth I came to the throne of England in 1558 she and her government in London ruled less land than her predecessors had done for hundreds of years. For about four centuries the rulers of England had been trying to conquer and rule France, Scotland, and Ireland, but they had just lost their last foothold in France at Calais, their position in Ireland was as insecure as it had ever been, and the Scottish problem had taken an altogether new turn because Mary the Queen of Scotland could present a good claim to the English throne. By the time of Elizabeth's death in 1603 Englishmen did not rule any more land outside the British Isles than they had done 45 years earlier but their seafaring position had been transformed. Hakluyt was exaggerating when he said that Englishmen had excelled all the nations and people of the earth in their explorations, but he was quite right when he asked:

Which of the kings of this land before her Majesty had ever their banners seen in the Caspian Sea? Which of them hath ever dealt with the Emperor of Persia. . . Who ever saw . . . an English leiger [subject] in the porch of the Grand Signior at Constantinople? Who ever found English consuls at Tripoli, at Aleppo, at Babylon, at Basra and who heard of Englishmen at Goa before now? What English ships did pass and repass the Strait of Magellan, traverse the mighty breadth of the South Sea [the Pacific], enter into alliance, with amity and traffic with the princes of the Moluccas and the Isle of Java, double the famous Cape of Bona Speranza and return home most richly laden with the commodities of China, as the subjects of this now flourishing monarchy had done?[1]

None of this suggested that the English would go forward to build up the most wide-ranging empire that the world had ever seen, and even if Hakluyt had added that the English had made some attempts to settle in North America and had organized themselves for trade in the East Indies he would not have much altered the case. But at least a dream of empire was not as impossible as it had been in 1558. These steps into a wider world were part of a great process of expansion by western Europe that had already been going on for decades. A hundred years before Elizabeth came to the throne no

---

[1] This quotation from Hakluyt is taken from A. L. Rowse, *The Expansion of Elizabethan England* (1955), 161–2.

member of the human race had ever been in a position to make a map of the whole world; civilizations had risen and flourished in different regions of the world but they had little or no idea of their geographical relationship to one another. By 1558 the Portuguese voyages around Africa and into the Indian Ocean, and the Spanish voyages to America which led on by way of the Philippines to the circumnavigation of the globe had made it possible to draw maps which, though they were wrong in important details, showed what the world was really like. The English had not taken any important part in this; voyages from Bristol at the end of the fifteenth century had reached a few points in North America and had opened up cod fisheries off Newfoundland, and in the 1550s London merchants had used the northern searoutes to start trading with Russia, but most of the nation's energies overseas in the first half of the sixteenth century had been devoted to the last and least rewarding of the attempts to conquer France. Rivalry with France was one theme in the centuries of empire to come, but after the loss of Calais the English concentrated on capturing French colonies or in restraining French attempts to dominate Europe rather than on trying to make anything substantial out of the nominal claim to the French crown that English kings asserted until 1801.

During Elizabeth's reign the English had been concerned, as Hakluyt explained, with trade and with opening up new lines of commerce. They looked along the Atlantic coast of North America for places in which to settle, and they might have been more successful in founding colonies if they had not at the same time been engaged in what they saw as a desperate struggle to save their religious and political liberties from Catholic Spain, although the Spanish would have said the war was to some extent intended to check the rather aggressive interpretation the English placed on the idea of the freedom of the seas.

It was only when this war was settled, and England embarked on a period of forty years of almost unbroken peace, that settlement began in North America and in the West Indies, and that trade with India became regular and organized enough for the English to set up trading posts there. By the death of James I in 1625 the English had laid foundations for colonies in Virginia, in New England, and in some of the small West Indian islands that the Spaniards had not considered worth settling. At the same time they had established bases in India in which they exercised some degree of local political authority, though only in the way that trading companies normally did when away from home, and with no idea of challenging the authority of the Great Moghul, the ruler of India. During the reign of Charles I there was a great flood of emigrants to North America and the West Indies, and a third type of colony appeared in addition to the colonies for English settlement and the trading posts which needed political power to function effectively: the colonies which were emerging in the West Indies were beginning to turn into plantations in the modern sense in which Englishmen directed the labour of other people.

Almost all the colonies the English ever acquired were of one or another of these three types, and in a number of other ways the overseas activities undertaken between the 1550s and the 1640s laid down the pattern for all that was to come. The government's main response to the world outside the British Isles was to build a strong navy. This was not done for imperial purposes, but once the navy had been developed it affected everything that happened in English policy. The government certainly had no money to spare to help the colonies, and this introduced the general rule that English colonies had to cover their own costs, both in the sense that the government of a colony had to raise enough revenue to pay its own bills and in the sense that there were no subsidies to encourage people to stay in a colony where they could not earn their own living. The result of these rules of practice was that the English set up colonies only in places where it was relatively easy to do so, at first because the places they went to were thinly populated, then because political disintegration in India enabled them to advance there, and because in the last phase of imperial expansion they had the sort of technological superiority needed for bringing most African rulers under their control.

Because it was easy to launch them, a great diversity of colonies sprang up and usually they were neither compelled by any external danger nor persuaded by any liking for their neighbours to come to closer terms with one another. In fact, it was much more common for colonies to break up into a number of separate units as they grew larger. This happened in New England over religious issues; it was to happen in a great many other places, usually for less solemn reasons, over the next three centuries. The tendency to split up was strengthened by another result of the absence of involvement of the government in London: the colonists had to work out how to handle their local problems of administration and, while there was virtually no idea of challenging the power of the monarch in England, policies had to be decided much faster than the royal government could ever manage. As a result it was accepted by the 1630s that English colonies could take most decisions for themselves, and this meant they developed the institutions which, over the course of time, grew in a way that enabled them to become self-governing and then independent by stages which could be so small as sometimes to be imperceptible. Because they had to run their local affairs, English colonies were quite different from those the Spanish, the Portuguese, the Dutch, and the French established between 1500 and 1650, and at the time all the other European empires looked more durable than the English.

European Expansion Begins

Other European countries had entered the field distinctly earlier. The decisive decade for exploration had been the 1490s: Columbus reached the West Indies (which at first he took to be a part of Japan), Vasco da Gama sailed around the Cape of Good Hope into the Indian Ocean, and Pope Alexander VI recognized that Spain's new interest in expansion would clash with Portugal's existing claims unless they were defined quickly. The Treaty of Tordesillas of 1494 embodied his division of the world between them along a not-very-precisely defined meridian line running about 45° West. This division, which quite unintentionally put the uncharted territory of Brazil into the Portuguese section, encouraged the Spanish and Portuguese to believe that they had a right, backed by a religious authority recognized by every country in western Europe, to all land that did not have a settled and effective government, and that they were entitled to monopolize the trade of these new territories. European powers claimed monopoly rights over the trade of their colonies for centuries to come, though other Europeans defied these claims whenever possible, but nobody launched such world-wide claims as the Spanish and the Portuguese, and the Spanish claims became even more all-embracing when Philip II of Spain secured the crown of Portugal for himself in 1580. These claims were never universally accepted; the destruction of the unity of Christendom by the Reformation helped to undermine the authority of the Pope to allocate territory, but it was Catholic France that first challenged Spain's position in the West Indies and that conflict had been going on for some years when in 1559, at the end of one round of European wars, France and Spain included in the peace treaty a clause which stated that fighting in regions west of the Azores or south of the Tropic of Cancer was not to be taken as a reason for resuming hostilities in Europe. This clause, crisply abbreviated to the phrase 'no peace beyond the line', recognized that the Spanish were not going to admit that anyone was entitled to contest the Papal award and also that nobody else was going to take it seriously.

For over a century any non-Spaniards who entered the area claimed by Spain were likely to be called pirates. Some of them undoubtedly were pirates in the straightforward sense that they were ready to seize and plunder any passing ship without regard to the religion or nationality of its owners, but Spanish charges ranged much more widely. So far as they were concerned traders and sailors who had been blown off course were pirates; and in the range of activity between purely peaceful traders and pirates who were ready to attack ships of any nation there were some traders who were prepared to use force to make Spanish ports deal with them, and others who were willing to appear to use force in order to provide Spanish settlements with an excuse for trading. The word pirate was perhaps not so strong a term

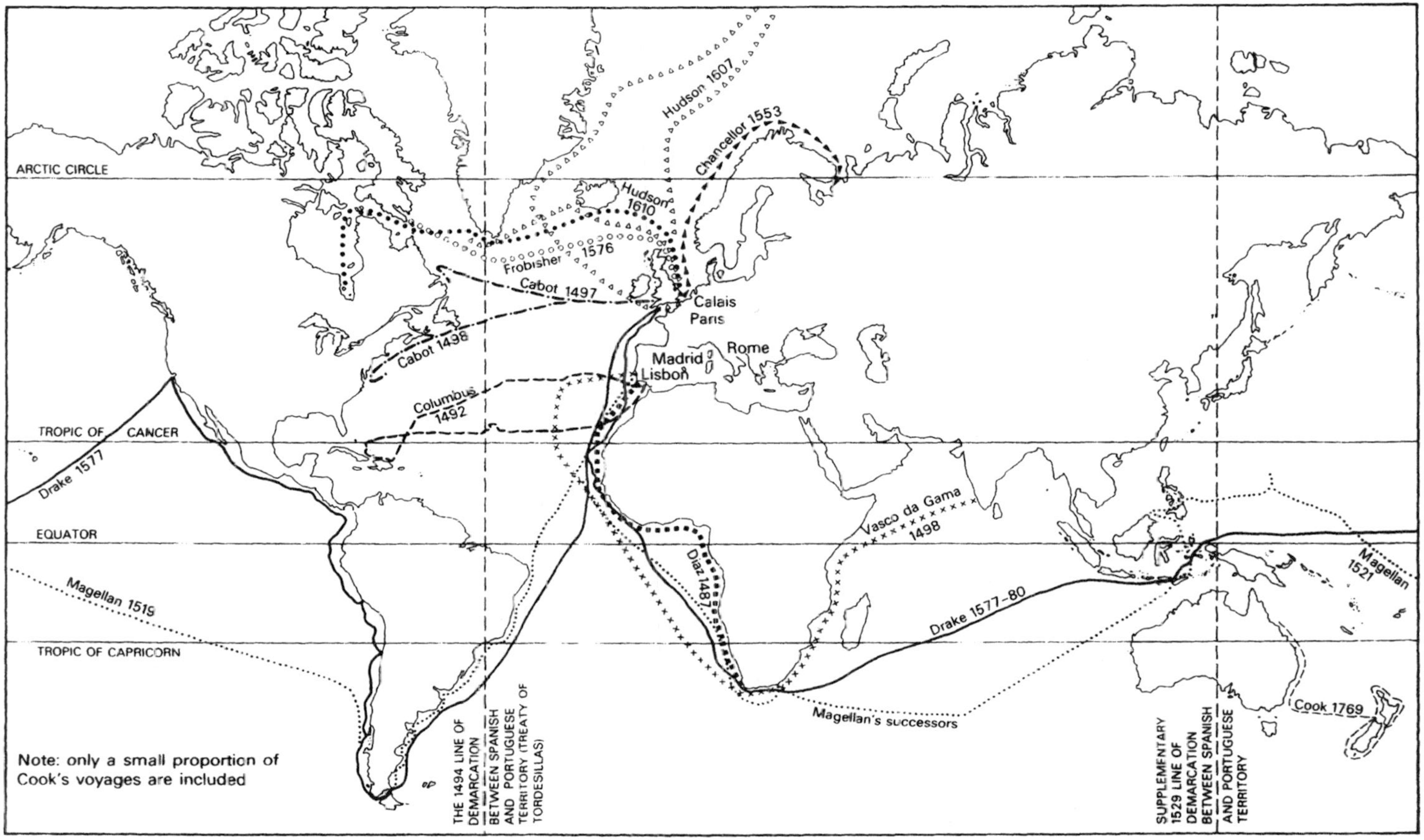

Map 1 Voyages of Discovery

Note: only a small proportion of
Cook's voyages are included

SUPPLEMENTARY
1529 LINE OF
DEMARCATION
BETWEEN SPANISH
AND PORTUGUESE
TERRITORY

THE 1494 LINE OF
DEMARCATION
BETWEEN SPANISH
AND PORTUGUESE
TERRITORY (TREATY OF
TORDESILLAS)

ARCTIC CIRCLE

TROPIC OF CANCER

EQUATOR

TROPIC OF CAPRICORN

Magellan
1521

Cook 1769

Drake 1577-80

Magellan's successors

Vasco da Gama
1498

Chancellor 1553

Hudson 1607

Hudson
1610

Frobisher 1576

Cabot 1497

Cabot 1498

Columbus
1492

Diaz 1487

Calais
Paris
Rome
Madrid
Lisbon

Magellan 1515

Drake 1577

of condemnation as in later centuries: European rulers were only just beginning to acquire for themselves, on behalf of their states, a monopoly of the use of force. By comparison with the rest of the world in the sixteenth century, some parts of western Europe might look like well-organized nations but it was still true that the main bond holding countries together was the personal loyalty that a local military leader felt to his sovereign. By the end of the period of imperial expansion, in the middle of the twentieth century, it was widely believed that everyone in the world should be a citizen of an independent and sovereign state and should have the same rights as all the other citizens in the state, but in 1500 very few people would have understood such a notion. The crumbling of the old idea of a state based on obligations and obedience may have helped increase the dynamic force that enabled European countries to spread their authority over most of the world; the very widespread acceptance of the new idea of a state based on independence and equality gave people outside Europe political principles which helped them in the later struggle to dismantle the European empires.

Military leaders in the sixteenth century who could not find wars to fight elsewhere might turn on their own sovereigns and fight at home; there had been some decades of civil war in England after the English had been driven out of France in the middle of the fifteenth century. But an out-of-work military leader more often found a war-ridden frontier where he could operate without needing to consult his king. Subjects of the King of England had been doing this in Ireland ever since Strongbow's invasion in 1169. By the fifteenth century the King of England was Lord of Ireland, though his new territory was separate enough to have its own parliament, whose power was reduced but not eliminated by Poyning's Law of 1495, which forbade it to pass any law that had not been approved in advance by the King and his council. Centralization of royal authority went further in Wales, which in 1536 was put under English law (and language) and given a couple of dozen seats in the House of Commons. For some centuries Wales had been an area where rather independent lords raised private armies to hold the Welsh down, and sometimes turned these armies against the king. One of the classic formulations of the feelings of settled but militarily powerful people on the quiet side of a frontier about their neighbours on the less settled side is to be found in a nursery rhyme:

> Taffy was a Welshman, Taffy was a thief,
> Taffy came to my house and stole a piece of beef.
> I went to Taffy's house, Taffy was in bed;
> I picked up a marrowbone and hit him on the head.

This simple account of cattle-raiding followed by an expedition to punish the thieves explains the situation on frontiers all over the world, and of course these punitive expeditions (which sometimes took the form of pre-emptive strikes by people who wanted to get their retaliation in first) were carried out without consulting any central government.

The most striking activity undertaken on a frontier without consulting royal authority – perhaps the most striking event in the whole history of European expansion – was the conquest of most of the American continent south of the Tropic of Cancer in the space of a single generation by a succession of Spanish military leaders. Overseas expansion was often led by men with no clear instructions or with instructions that they ignored, but the Spanish conquistadores like Cortes and Pizzaro took this further than most. Their sovereign was immensely puzzled by the process and strongly suspected that some of them intended to secede and set up independent states in South America, but the conquests attracted special attention and gained retrospective approval because they opened up a great wealth of silver and gold for the treasury of the King of Spain. They gave the ruler of Spain, more often referred to as the Holy Roman Emperor, Charles V, possessions of a type previously unknown. Charles's territories could already have been described as an empire, in the sense that he ruled over a collection of different political units held together by the allegiance his subjects felt they owed him rather than through a sense of common institutions or common language which could serve as the foundation for a unifying national spirit. The powerful states of the time normally were empires, and had been for many centuries, though a few shadowy forerunners of the nation state could be seen by 1500. England was something like a nation by the closing stages of the Hundred Years War with France in the mid-fifteenth century, and France was certainly much more like a nation at the end of the war than she had been at the beginning. England had probably lost in international importance during the fifteenth century, partly because of her defeat in the Hundred Years War, partly because of the success of the Habsburgs in building up their empire on the basis of dynastic marriages. At the time empires were normal enough; it was nationalism that was unusual and, if it did develop, it might easily break Charles's empire into fragments because of the absence of linguistic or geographic unity.

Acquiring land across the sea added a new complexity to an empire. It was unlikely that even a common language could create a common national spirit to unite Spanish-speaking people divided by the salt, estranging sea, but as long as empires based on the principles of allegiance to a monarch were the dominant form of political organization they were very well adapted to face the problems of expanding and then of ruling new subjects. The expanding European states often brought the energy of incipient nationalism to their forward march, but more or less all the states they encountered outside Europe were organized on the principle of allegiance or loyalty to the ruler. All that the Europeans had to do was defeat the existing ruler and proclaim that their own ruler had filled the vacant throne. When rights of conquest or hereditary rights had placed two or more territories under a medieval ruler, he was quite accustomed to finding that they were ruled under different constitutions and he would not think of trying to impose a uniform system of government on them; Queen Elizabeth had rights and duties in England that were rather different from the rights and duties she had in the Channel Islands, which were all that was left of William the Conqueror's Norman territories, and it was perfectly natural for each new English acquisition overseas to be won on terms that differed from what had happened previously.

In the sixteenth century the word 'empire' did not usually refer to a state with transoceanic possessions of this sort. When Henry VIII and his Parliament said that England was an empire they simply wanted to say that it was a sovereign state independent of the Pope's judicial authority. But when Dr Dee (a scientist too aware of his Welsh descent to want to use the word 'English') wrote about the British Empire in the 1570s he was discussing the prospect of possessions beyond the seas, which were likely to be linked to England by the bond of allegiance to the sovereign more than by anything else. There were limits to the range of territory that could be held together in this way in the sixteenth century: towards the end of his life Charles V abdicated and retired to a monastery, leaving his German lands and his title of Holy Roman Emperor to the line of his brother Ferdinand, even though he would probably have preferred to keep the entire empire together and leave it to his son Philip. Despite the partition, Philip received Spain, the Netherlands and 'the Indies', or South America, which meant that he inherited most of Charles's revenues. Kings wanted to build up reserves of bullion for the very practical reason that it would enable them to recruit armies, and it was also true that gold and silver had a great power to dazzle men's minds. It was one of the magnetic forces that drew them overseas, and led them to disappointment quite as often as to wealth.

The leaders who went out to any area of European expansion had to make all their own decisions because it would take months, if not years, for their sovereign to reply to any request for instructions. So leaders, and their followers on the frontiers of empire, often looked like disobedient and violent men. An understanding monarch reflected that disobedient and violent subjects were also to be found much closer to home. At a time when important people wore swords as a matter of course, the assumption that the strong ruled the weak was natural enough. It was an attitude of mind which had existed long before the sixteenth century; the great change was that an attitude which could be found in a number of separate societies was suddenly turned by the expansion of Europe into a force that altered the way that the whole world ran its affairs.

The English Commercial Offensive

In a world like this, merchant ships went around armed against pirates, and non-Spanish merchant ships which sailed to South America found that citizens of towns on the 'Spanish Main' (the mainland area which is now the coast of Venezuela) would ask to be forced to trade. This ambiguous situation led to the first English clash with Spain. Hawkins, a Devon merchant, had seen that the demand for slaves from Africa was increasing in South America, and in 1562 he sailed – in the way many Englishmen were to do in the seventeenth and eighteenth century – to West Africa, bought slaves, took them to the Caribbean ports, and sold them at a profit. When he did this again in 1564 he was received less amicably, and in 1568 he found a visiting fleet at San Juan de Ulloa hostile enough to alarm him. The tension rose, and in the fighting that followed he was very lucky to get out alive. Hawkins withdrew from this dangerous line of business, though he felt his enterprise in trying to open up a new line of trade deserved recognition and he put a black slave on his coat-of-arms. His cousin, Francis Drake, who had also been among the survivors of San Juan de Ulloa, took a more aggressive attitude to the Spanish empire; as an uncompromising Protestant he felt that his country ought to be at war with Spain and, if it would not do this, he would fight on his own account, looking round for people prepared to invest in a private attack on the wealth of Spain. If he had had any doubts about this, the Queen's attitude must have set his mind at rest: she had invested, on a commercial basis, in Hawkins's slave-trading and, less openly, she invested in Drake's plans for a non-governmental attack on Spain. Between 1577 and 1580 he sailed around the world – the first Englishman to carry out the feat originally achieved by the survivors of Magellan's voyage 60 years earlier – plundering Spanish ships and towns of their gold and silver as he did so. Officially England was at peace with Spain, and Elizabeth expressed official regret at Drake's activities. But she and the other investors received 4,700 per cent on their investment, and she made Drake a knight. England and Spain remained nominally at peace for another half-dozen years, but disputes about trading and commerce-raiding in South America were among the reasons why Philip II tried to invade England in 1588. The Spanish Armada was defeated so decisively that the English often reckoned that their command of the sea began then, although it was never secure until the end of the seventeenth century. Without the naval strength established during Elizabeth's reign, imperial development would not have been possible; and the foundations of that strength had been laid earlier. Fishing boats crossed the Atlantic for most of the sixteenth century, and in the middle of the century Henry VIII set out to encourage an artillery industry. The manufacturers were very successful at making guns out of Sussex iron,

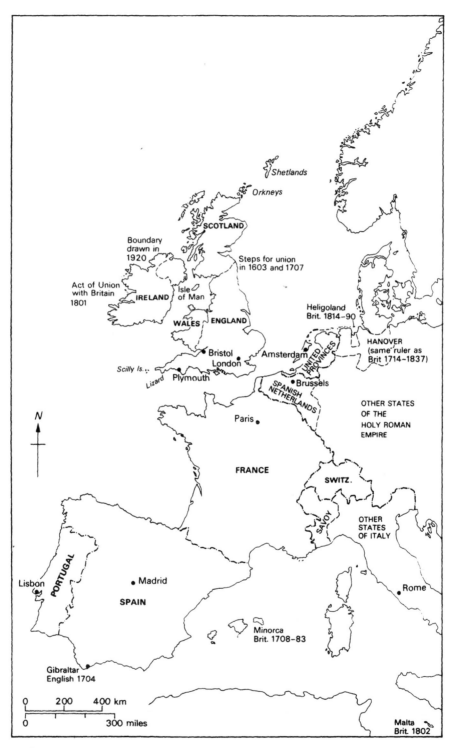

Map 2 Britain in Early Modern Europe

which affected naval tactics for many years. The sea powers around the Mediterranean used bronze cannon which were much more elegant and probably more accurate but cost about four times as much. English ships could equip themselves with a heavy weight of broadside relatively cheaply. so that they were built simply to carry guns without worrying too much about anything else. Other navies might stick to the old tactics of trying to board enemy ships and capture them, or concentrate on firing at the masts and rigging in the hope that successful shooting would disable the other side, but the English preferred to shoot into the hulls of their enemies because they knew that with enough time and enough shot they would destroy their opponents.

The war between England and Spain went on for sixteen years after the defeat of the Armada, with a good deal of the English effort being under-taken by private ventures like Drake's (though they were easier to ack-nowledge once war had begun officially). It became clear that neither country could win a victory that would compel the other to surrender. This failure to defeat England and a number of other setbacks showed that the power of Spain was declining, which was one of the major political changes of the first half of the seventeenth century. But while England was coming to be seen as a reasonably important power after having looked very weak in the middle of the sixteenth century, a more conspicuous change was the emergence of the Netherlands. The United Provinces, as they were then known, had been under Habsburg rule and began a 40-year war with Spain for their national independence in the 1570s. In the early stages England had given them a certain amount of help, partly out of sympathy for their Protestant religious beliefs and partly to check the power of Spain – it was this war in the Netherlands, more than the troubles in South America, which convinced Philip that he should try to invade England. By the 1590s it was clear that the Netherlands would become independent and would be very powerful at sea. Even before the war with Spain ended in 1609 the Dutch were preparing to attack various parts of the empire the Portuguese had built up in the Indian Ocean in the previous hundred years, stretching as far east as Java and the other Spice Islands near it, and later on they also attacked the Portuguese possessions in Brazil.

When English merchants moved out into the world beyond Europe, it was natural enough that the Spice Islands became their ultimate objective. Transport cost so much that it was virtually impossible to make a profit by importing anything that could be produced locally; although salt cod was brought across the Atlantic, in general nothing but luxury goods like gold, silver, furs, and spices would yield a reasonable return after paying for a costly ocean voyage. Because transport costs were so high, trade could add a good deal to the national income of any country which was successful at it. Once goods had been brought to a European port, they could be re-exported at a higher price to other European countries that had no direct trade across the sea, so a good many of the calculations about trade were concerned with re-exporting goods which had not been processed into an improved form but were simply being sent to a place where they commanded some additional scarcity value. Spices suited this situation very well: they had a high value in proportion to their weight, they could not be produced in Europe, and they were always valued by rich people who used them to mask the taste of the not-too-well preserved meat which was the best that anyone could hope for in the winter.

Going to the Spice Islands was only the last stage of increasingly ambitious ventures. In Russia English merchants had gone some way south of Moscow, and trade was also being carried on in the Eastern Mediterranean or Levant. These steps into new territory were too big and too risky to be undertaken by individual merchants. In the sixteenth century the right to import commodities, or to process them domestically, normally rested on a grant of a monopoly. Granting a monopoly was the easiest way for the monarch to encourage a trade or an industry, and was also a way to reward courtiers, who did not get salaries and hoped for substantial favours of just this sort. Because grants to courtiers came to be seen as an abuse, monopolies to individuals were prohibited in 1624, but corporations could still receive them and they continued to be the basis for trade outside Europe in the seventeenth century. It seemed obvious that the best form of organization for overseas trade was the one that was used first in exporting wool and then by the cloth traders, who still accounted for three-quarters of English exports in the first half of the century: all the merchants involved would sell together at a 'staple' town, usually in Belgium or the Netherlands, where they could avoid competing with each other and so increase their bargaining strength.

Merchants trading overseas had to cover the diplomatic and even military expenses which in later centuries would be met by their governments. To deal with this, a group of merchants who wanted to trade in a particular part of the world would ask the monarch for a charter allowing them a monopoly of bringing goods from their chosen region into England, giving them rights to defend themselves against pirates and bandits with their own armed force, and letting them settle legal problems that would otherwise have to wait years until they got back to England. This sort of approach suited the violent attitudes of the age: as much money was invested in expeditions for private warfare against Spain as in all the trading and land-settling companies of the sixteenth and early seventeenth centuries. Against this background merchants, or factors, trading a long way from their home base realized that the safest form of organization was to set up a factory or small enclave for merchants of the type that the Hanseatic League had maintained in London up to 1598. A base like this could not resist the authority of the host government but it could protect merchants against local hostility or the attacks of other traders. Members of the merchants of the wool staple traded as individuals, but in 1552 the Muscovy Company was launched on a joint stock basis, allowing people to sell their shares without weakening the Company, and it began trading with Moscow by going north-east to the White Sea. In the 1580s the Turkey Company and the Venice Company were founded, and in 1592 they combined to form the Levant Company, which learned enough about the riches of the Indies for various members of it to organize the East India Company, which had about £68,000 trading capital for its first voyage and a charter granted on 31 December 1600. Its first governor, Sir Thomas Smith, had been to Russia for the Muscovy Company and was active in the Levant Company, and remained governor of the East India Company with two brief interruptions until 1621.

The Dutch launched their much larger East India Company with about £500,000 of capital two years later, and when the English company tried to trade with the Spice Islands the Dutch opposed it fiercely. Its base at Amboyna was overrun in 1623 and some of its garrison tortured to death in an episode Dryden reckoned would still be remembered when he wrote a play about it in a period of anti-Dutch feeling 50 years later. The English East India Company held a substantial base in the East Indies at Bantam until 1682, but very early in its history it decided to concentrate on the western Indian Ocean. In 1605 it began trading at Surat, which was convenient for the Persian trade already developed by the Muscovy Company and also for diplomatic contact with the Moghul capital at Agra. The Company devoted itself to building up a substantial trade in pepper which, while not as valuable as the most expensive products of the Spice Islands like nutmeg and cloves, still commanded a very steady market in Europe. The problem was to find exports with which to pay for it; English woollens and iron products were not luxurious enough for the ruling class in India and were far too expensive for the vast majority of the population. Living standards for most of the population were lower in India than in western Europe and silver bullion, which was the nearest thing to a common international currency at the time, had a higher purchasing power in India than in Europe, so that anything made by people who were paid European wages would be expensive in terms of silver in India. The Company, from its very first voyage, exported bullion rather than English products and, when economists complained that this would lead to a loss of bullion which would cause deflation and depression in England, the Company replied that it exported between 50 and 90 per cent of its pepper to countries in northern Europe which paid four or five times as much silver as the Company paid in India, so that on balance its activities substantially increased the amount of bullion in the country. Transport costs cut into that favourable balance; the Company reckoned it had to sell Indian cotton textiles at 2½ to 3 times their

Indian price to cover costs, and dividends were not normally above 7 or 8 per cent a year.

The Moghul Empire, which at that time covered the northern two-thirds of the Indian subcontinent, was at its most impressive; these were the decades of the Taj Mahal, the Red Fort at Delhi, and also of an attempt by the Muslim rulers of India to conciliate the Hindu majority. When the Company retained a courtier, Sir Thomas Roe, to strengthen their position at Agra in 1616, he advised them that their factories need not be fortified because the Moghuls were perfectly able to keep the peace that traders needed, and could capture fortified towns if they set their minds to it. On the other hand, strength at sea would help displace the Portuguese who had gained control of the Indian Ocean a century earlier, and this would please the Emperor; accordingly the East India Company armed its ships heavily enough to hold the sea against the Portuguese and against the local pirates.

Because the Company was intended to provide an opportunity for all English merchants interested in the Indian trade to take part, it did not treat shareholdings as permanent commitments. Members of the Company put their money down on a separate basis for a distinct and limited series of enterprises; profits from the voyage would be divided in proportion to capital invested, but capital as well as dividends could be withdrawn when the enterprises were complete and all the goods brought back had been sold off. Despite this somewhat unstable basis the Company did quite well until 1630 when trade was dislocated by a famine in Gujerat, and in the next few years its legal position was undermined because Charles I allowed the Courteen family – whose interests in the West Indies had suffered because he had given away their rights in certain islands inadvertently – to trade with India without any regard for the Company's charter. The bases in India, of which Surat founded in 1611 and Madras founded in 1642 were the most important, kept going even when the Company in London was at its lowest ebb and the current stock had sunk to 60 per cent of its original price. This gave continuity to the English connection with India, but by the middle of the century India was not at the centre of English overseas activity. The eastern trade never disappeared, but trading posts were being closed down and the Indies were losing their hold on people's attention. Poets had referred to the riches of the east for many years, but in the early seventeenth century 'My America, my new-found-land'[2] seemed a more effective phrase to represent emotional force and involvement.

The Tobacco Colonies

One of the attractions for Englishmen in the long wars with France had been the prospects of conquering and ruling new territories. The end of the wars drove them back to the British Isles, and some of them turned to fight for

---

[2] John Donne, 'To his mistress going to bed'.

land in Ireland. The struggle there in the sixteenth century became more embittered than ever because Ireland had remained Roman Catholic when England had become Protestant in the middle of the century. The conquest of Ireland was the largest military undertaking of Elizabeth's reign, costing over £1m., or the total royal revenue for three years, which was far more than any other military or naval activities, and a new wave of English landlords was able to gain estates if they could hold the rebellious Irish population in subjection. Some of the men who took part in this, like Sir Walter Raleigh and his brother-in-law Sir Humphrey Gilbert, were also attracted by the idea of getting lands on the other side of the Atlantic, and the success of the Spaniards encouraged them in the widespread belief that an immense amount of gold and silver was waiting to be discovered all over the Americas. When Frobisher sailed to the north of America in 1576, inspired by hopes of finding a north-west passage to India or China in the way that hopes of finding a north-east passage had led to the voyage that opened up the Muscovy trade, he and his backers were excited to find what they thought was gold on the route. More voyages were made in 1577 and 1578 to bring ore back, but the whole enterprise collapsed when the ore turned out to be only pyrites. The fishing fleets that had gone to Newfoundland since early in the century indicated another possible area for settlement, and Gilbert lost his life in 1583 on the way back from inspecting the prospects for a colony there.

The first full attempt at establishing a colony was Raleigh's colony of Virginia, named for Elizabeth the virgin queen and located in what is now the Roanoke district of North Carolina. After a voyage of investigation in 1584 a colony that was intended to be permanent was launched in 1585. Although it was evacuated in 1586, new settlers came later in the year, and were reinforced in 1587. In the next few years all of England's maritime energies were concentrated on resisting Philip of Spain's attempt at invasion, and by the time one of Raleigh's associates was able to visit the colony again in 1590 it had disappeared. No further colonization could be attempted while the war with Spain went on, partly because ships bound for the North American seacoast were forced by the prevailing winds to go uncomfortably far north or dangerously close to the Spanish settlement in the south, but interest revived after peace was made with Spain in 1604. By then Raleigh was in prison, charged with planning to drive the new king (James VI of Scotland, who in 1603 succeeded Elizabeth and became James I of England) off the throne, but the idea of a colony in Virginia attracted merchants from Plymouth and from London. They got in touch with commercially-minded courtiers, including Roe, and in 1606 persuaded the king to issue a charter to the Virginia Company, dividing the North American seacoast from about 35 °N to 45 °N into a section for the Londoners including Sir Thomas Smith, who went south to the region of

Raleigh's original settlement, and a section for the Plymouth men who followed their fishing interests further north. In the event the Plymouth group did very little after 1609 but in 1607 the Londoners committed themselves more fully than before and launched an expedition which founded a settlement at Jamestown in Chesapeake Bay. Only then did it emerge that the settlers did not really know what they intended to do. They knew only two ways to make money out of territorial expansion: to find gold and silver, or to make themselves into landlords with plenty of tenants to cultivate their new estates. There was clearly no gold to dig up, and the Indians did not look like becoming docile tenants – the question was whether they might not instead drive the newcomers into the sea. Perhaps the Indians would have done so if they had been conscious of any pressure of numbers on the land, but North America was not crowded and the Indians assisted the new settlers and showed them how to grow the local crops.

When the settlers got to Virginia, everyone expected the gentlemen of the party to run things, just as in England. But being a gentleman in England was not just a matter of giving orders; it required considerable wealth, spent lavishly and in a way that commanded respect. The gentlemen in Virginia were in no position to do this; they had very little money to spend in a gentlemanly way and no particular experience of colonization to give them any other claims to respect and obedience, as nothing got done and about 60 of the 100 initial settlers died in 1607. A military man, Captain John Smith, pulled the colony together in 1608 but it became all too clear that the colonists were not even able to feed themselves; 1609 was remembered as 'the starving time' and the settlers were preparing to give up and leave for England when Lord De La Warr arrived with fresh supplies and new settlers in June 1610. The difficulty for the Company in England was that establishing someone who had crossed to North America took an initial investment equal to about a year's wages, so the investors had to keep on providing supplies without seeing any sign of how the colony would repay them. Francis Bacon who put money into an unsuccessful company to colonize Newfoundland wrote in his essay On Plantations (the word used then and for most of the seventeenth century for what would later be called colonies) 'You must make account to lose almost twenty years profit, and expect your recompense in the end.' The dynastic change from Tudors to Stuarts in 1603 is sometimes said to have been accompanied by a shift from optimism to gloom, and Bacon certainly took an unusually sober approach.

Because John Smith's period of office had been reasonably successful, the Company put the colony under military discipline, which stabilized the situation and provided a more efficient system of government than trying to transplant a peculiarly English way of running things. The first signs of a solution to the financial problem began to appear; the settlers started growing tobacco and by 1611 they were exporting it to England. It sold at a high enough price per pound to cover the cost of carrying it across the Atlantic, and Jamestown enjoyed a tobacco boom, though the increase in exports from 20,000 lb. in 1617 to 350,000 lb. in 1621 was not enough to enable the Company to show a profit, because the (wholesale, pre-duty) price fell from four or five shillings a pound to a shilling a pound at the same time. Bacon, as an advocate of really long-term investment, said the concentration on tobacco was 'to the untimely prejudice of the main business', though it is not easy to see what he thought the main business of a plantation ought to be – his essay was full of sensible advice, much of it showing signs of the influence of the Virginia experience, but he never explained why people should want to support this sort of enterprise, unless it was to be part of a programme for sending people abroad to reduce overpopulation.

In 1619 Sir Thomas Smith, who had been treasurer of the Company since 1609, was pushed into retirement and the new directors led by Sir Edwin Sandys brought about two important changes. One problem for the Virginia planters was that tobacco could be grown in England; James I agreed to help the company by making tobacco-growing illegal in England and, although people broke the law and tried to raise tobacco for much of the rest of the century, the American monopoly was eventually made effective. This was not just a matter of helping a company and a colony in trouble; imports were easy to tax, governments found that luxury products were particularly satisfying because their sales were not depressed by high import duties, and tobacco paid duty at a shilling a pound or about 100 per cent of the wholesale price. In theory an excise on home production of tobacco could have produced the same revenue as a tax on imports but in practice it took a strong and efficient government to levy an excise, while almost any government could find private businessmen who would pay a lump sum of cash in return for the right to collect the official rates of customs duties at a port. Over three-quarters of the taxable imports into England came through the port of London, so that collecting the London duties provided a chance to become very rich; this was how Sir Thomas's father had gained his fortune and his title of 'Customer' Smith. Other ports dealt very much in the coastal trade; if sea transport was expensive, land transport was prohibitively costly, and very slow, so that a number of small ports could flourish on goods being taken from one part of England to another. Checking their activities to see that they were confining themselves to local products, and were not turning to smuggling was very difficult until improvements in transport and in the structure of government meant that the vast majority of imports paid duty. So James had good reason not to trust a local market in tobacco, and to believe that he would do better if he kept it as a commodity to be imported and to pay duty accordingly, mainly at London and Bristol.

As soon as he had gained control, Sandys brought about another change in the Virginia Company's way of running things; he told the Company's governor in the colony to have an assembly elected from among the colonists to give him advice and to act as the legislative body to pass any local laws needed inside the colony. This was a third form of government, after rule by gentlemen and rule by military discipline had turned out not to be very successful, and most Englishmen would have found it rather less usual than either of the earlier types of government. A few of the larger towns in England had the right to elect a council to run their own affairs, but the great majority of Englishmen lived in the countryside where Justices of the Peace ran things in the way that gentlemen had always done. Companies like the Virginia Company ran their affairs through elected committees, and this may have suggested to Sandys that the colonists could run their end of the business with the aid of an elected system as well. Virginia had no property qualifications to limit men's right to vote until 1670, and this was a little more like the usual arrangements in a company, where all shareholders were able to vote, than the position in parliamentary elections, where property qualifications for voting went on for hundreds of years to come.

Elected assemblies were uncommon enough in English life to encourage the Virginia assembly to treat the House of Commons as the natural parallel to its own position and to look to Commons precedents as a guide to its rights and duties. This did not necessarily mean that they took a very exalted view of their own importance. They could not easily have found any other body with which they could compare themselves, and in any case the House of Commons of the 1620s was itself not very important. Passing new laws was not a common occurrence, and the Commons usually left the conduct of day-to-day policy, especially in foreign affairs, to the King and his council, with complete certainty that this small body was better informed than the Commons or even the average members of the House of Lords. In Virginia, the Governor, appointed by the company and sent out from London, kept executive authority in his own hands. He had a council to advise him on these policy decisions, and he and his council recognized the great similarity between the powers of the assembly and those of the House of Commons in passing laws and imposing new taxes.

Basing the structure of authority upon a governor, a council for day-to-day affairs, and an assembly to pass legislation, vote taxes, and express the trend of public feeling was an arrangement that would seem natural to anyone who knew about the English system of King, Privy Council, and Parliament. The structure turned out to be very durable; most of the colonial constitutions set up by the British in the next three-and-a-half centuries show similarities to the Virginia Company's way of doing things, though there were sometimes refinements, such as a legislative council created as an upper house to work with the assembly; and in several cases – especially when the majority of the population was not of British descent – the legislative body was appointed rather than elected.

This success in constitution-making did not bring success for the Virginia Company; Sandys was able to keep up emigration, but death and discouragement meant the population hardly rose above 1,000. An unexpected Indian attack on Good Friday 1622, in which a large number of colonists were killed, dealt the final blow to the Company. Spanish hostility was obviously a handicap to it, but when the charter was declared void in 1624 it was mainly because the Company was bankrupt; the Spanish objection was to the colony rather than to the Company, and the colony was allowed to survive. Something permanent had clearly been created in Virginia and, shortly after coming to the throne in 1625, Charles I did what he could to stabilize the situation by declaring it a royal colony and taking into his own hands the power to appoint the governor. This did not involve the King's government in any expense; if people went overseas, presumably they did it in order to make money, and the King could see no reason why he should provide any of his not very plentiful revenue to enrich them faster, though he might invest money of his own if he thought he had a reasonable chance of getting a dividend. Economists were afraid that the country was over-populated and believed that the problems of poverty and unemployment would be reduced if the surplus hands and mouths would go overseas, but it did not follow that the government was going to pay for them to go. All that the King could do was to provide some sort of legal foundation of government for Englishmen going to unsettled and thinly populated areas, which he did by linking the legitimacy of their governments to the legitimacy of his government. He did not have the military power to offer protection to Englishmen overseas; if the Spanish from the south were to attack English colonies, they would have to defend themselves or rely on English diplomacy, because Charles could send neither ships nor troops across the Atlantic for help. Most colonists remained loyal subjects of the King, but they paid very little money to him and his government and they received very little help, financial or military, from it. The legal status provided by the King carried various legal implications with it. The colonists remained subjects of the King of England and had to obey English law. They were also subject to the English Parliament, which put them on a different footing from the King's Scots or Irish subjects, who had Parliaments of their own that were not subordinate to the Westminster Parliament in the way that the Virginia assembly was. Parliament did not often pass laws with any wide-ranging implications, and the most wide-ranging recent laws, the religious legislation of the Reformation, were never applied at all precisely in America, but no legal framework could have been imagined for the colonies which gave them a legitimate position under English law without putting them under the legislative supremacy of Parliament.

By the time Virginia became a royal colony it was no longer the only English settlement in the Americas. The Virginia Company had itself produced a subsidiary company which occupied the islands at first known officially as Somers Islands – though when Shakespeare wrote *The Tempest* some people already called them the Bermoothes, and Bermuda it remained for posterity. The subsidiary company did better than the Virginia Company, kept going for another sixty years, and in the 1640s provided most of the settlers who moved on to the Bahamas. But there were more important developments in the North American seacoast and at the east end of the Caribbean. At the time the Caribbean islands seemed the more attractive prospect, and in the first generation of migration more Englishmen went there than to the American colonies that developed north of Virginia. There had been unsuccessful attempts even further south; the unfortunate Raleigh got himself out of the Tower by promising to find James I a supply of gold in Guiana, but he found no gold and he irritated the Spanish so much that they pushed James into having him executed in 1618 on the 1604 charge of treason. But this had been an attempt to land on the Spanish Main, and the Spanish felt much less concerned about the long string of small islands in the Lesser Antilles at the eastern end of the Caribbean. English merchants felt confident that money could be made out of settlements there, if only they could acquire enough influence at court to secure a charter to launch them. They did not hope for any tangible support for their undertaking, but a charter would give them some standing in England, allow them to create a legal government, and possibly convince any enquiring Spaniards that they were not simply setting up a pirate base. The Spanish were sometimes justified in thinking that a pirate base was precisely what English companies had in mind; in the 1630s the Providence Island Company was set up by determined Protestants who thought that plundering Catholic ships would be rewarded in this world and the next, though other Englishmen, who settled informally on the east coast of central America, were concerned with felling trees and exporting logwood as a dye-stuff. Charles was not inclined to look too hard at what he was giving away in the charters he issued, and he issued two charters, one to the Earl of Carlisle and one to Sir William Courteen, which covered the same islands, probably because people in England did not know much about the geography of the area and possibly did not much care. To resolve the question, Lord Carlisle was given a charter that covered the whole area and the Courteen family were given, by way of compensation for their neglected rights, the permission to trade with India which caused the East India Company so much trouble in the 1630s. But a colony which depended on a patent-holder in England was not likely to do very well, and Carlisle was among the least active of the patent-holders. The desire to get land to cultivate as a farmer and proprietor or simply to get work as a landless labourer drew people to the islands in large numbers. Apprehension about the Spaniards turned out to be unjustified; they had serious problems with the Dutch, who were moving forward in the West

Indies, and also with the trade winds, that blew from the east and made it very hard for ships from the Spanish Main or from the larger islands like Cuba to reach the smaller islands. In any case occupying them was of little interest to the Spanish authorities, for the islands the English settled had a much smaller area than Jamaica, the smallest and least developed of the Spanish islands; later on, after it had been taken from the Spanish, Jamaica was the most important of the English Caribbean islands, but this only serves to show how small the English settlements were. The newcomers were not able to brush aside the native Carib population with quite the contemptuous ease with which the Spaniards had conquered the mainland; attempts to settle in earlier years had been resisted successfully and in some islands the English settlers had to remain at least as careful about the risk of native attack as any community in North America. This sort of pressure, combined with fear of the Spaniards, made it easier for the English to work with the French who were settling in the same region of islands than earlier or later generations would have thought possible. The first effective English settlement in the West Indies, founded in 1624, was on the island of St. Christopher (later called St. Kitts) which was shared with the French, informally at first and then by a formal partition worked out a couple of years later which lasted until the British gained the whole island in 1713. In 1627 a settlement was made on Barbados, which had two additional attractions: it was uninhabited, so the dangers of warfare with the Caribs did not arise, and it was so far to the east of the island chain that it was even better protected by the trade winds than any of the other islands. In the course of two centuries of wars and battles and scuffles, in which all the other islands were invaded and many were conquered, Barbados remained untouched. But the flow of immigrants went on, with very little space to receive the new settlers, so in 1628 some of them made the easy move from St. Kitts to Nevis, and a couple of years later made a slightly longer move and occupied the islands of Antigua and Monserrat, laying the foundations of English settlement in the Leeward Islands.

Almost all this expansion was based on tobacco. Virginia's success had shown what could be done, and the West Indian settlement spent very little time considering any other commercial prospects for some years. Conditions of work were not pleasant; landowners tried to get their estates cultivated by indentured labourers who had come out under a contract to work for some years for the man who paid for the journey or anyone to whom he sold the right to command their services. The passage cost £6, or something like a year's wages and for repayment the indenture might run from four to seven years – though they would, of course, have to be fed and clothed in that period. To encourage rich men to bring out poor settlers like this, a 'head right' system was used to give land – 50 acres a head in the case of Virginia – to the landowner for each immigrant he had brought across the

Atlantic. The indentured labourers hoped to be able to set up as independent farmers once they had worked off the costs of their passages, but the islands soon became so crowded that they were unlikely to be able to do this. Many of them found it easier to move on to the North American mainland after their indentures had expired. New labourers came out, many from Ireland where pressure on land was unusually severe; they came from southern Irish ports, so they could not have been directly affected by the English conquest and the Scottish settlement of Ulster at the beginning of the seventeenth century, but possibly Irish landlords felt that it no longer made sense to keep up private armies and turned men out of service for this reason. The steady flow of emigrants from the British Isles meant that landowners in the West Indies did not need to look further afield to find workers for growing tobacco, for which they needed a relatively small labour force working all the year round.

In the 1630s the tobacco boom showed signs of having reached its peak. Prices were falling and far-sighted men were looking for something else to cultivate. The islands could hardly survive without an export crop: some progress was being made in establishing cotton-growing when, in the 1640s, English politics and Dutch commerce worked together in a way that decided the course of the West Indies for centuries. Charles I and his Parliament quarrelled, and this led to the Civil War of the 1640s which ended with the defeat and execution of the King and, in 1649, the establishment of a republic. While the civil war raged, the English government could not maintain even the rather shadowy control it had exercised previously. The tobacco growers had been accustomed to trading practically exclusively with their home country for reasons of language and sentiment, because it was safer, and because England and the London re-export trade provided an adequate market for all the tobacco they could grow. At just the time when the Civil War was weakening this commercial connection, the Dutch were trying to conquer the Portuguese colony of Brazil. In the end they failed, but during their period of dominance they entered the sugar trade very successfully and persuaded the English in the West Indies to grow sugar to take the place of tobacco; at first they thought they could absorb the English islands into the Amsterdam trading system, but while it quite soon turned out that this was not the case and direct Dutch influence did not last very long, the commitment to sugar dominated the islands for at least two hundred years and remained important long afterwards.

Growing sugar and preparing it for shipping to London was harder work than growing and curing tobacco, and a much larger labour force was needed for the process of harvesting the cane and crushing it which had to be done in a very short period of time. Much the easiest way to assemble a larger labour force was to buy slaves, and the Dutch were ready to help with this, giving the fairly long credit that anyone who wanted to become a planter would need in order to finance his purchases of slaves and of machinery to crush the cane and take the first steps in refining it. Sugar leaped forward to dominate the market and to transform life socially and racially first in Barbados and then in the other English West Indian islands. The smaller landlords who could not find cash or credit to equip themselves as sugar planters quickly sold out; land prices in the 1640s rose to heights which showed that the profits of sugar were being anticipated and capitalized generously. This was pleasant for the small landowners, who could move on to Virginia and resume tobacco growing there, but less prosperous white men in the West Indies lost almost all hope of working up the scale to become modest farmers on their own land. So small an area of land was available in Barbados when it turned to sugar in the 1640s that land prices were pushed up to ten times the level at which it had been sold for growing tobacco. The island no longer gave men without much capital the economic opportunity sometimes to be found on a frontier, where land can be acquired cheaply by anyone prepared to make the great effort needed to clear it and plant the first crops.

It took fifteen or twenty years for the prosperous white planters to see the dangers of a community in which the vast majority of the population were slaves from Africa and there was no room for any white man below their own level of prosperity. By the 1660s all the islands were committed to sugar and the white planters were taking drastic steps to prevent their white employees from leaving the islands and tilting the population balance still further towards the black slaves, but this of course made white employees all the more determined to avoid going to the West Indies. A number of Royalist prisoners from the civil wars in England and Ireland were transported to the sugar islands in the 1650s as convict labour with the prospect of eventual release to become part of the white garrison, but this barely covered the losses from death and emigration. At the beginning of the switch to sugar there were about 25,000 Englishmen in the West Indies and the figure rose to almost 40,000 in the 1660s – partly because more islands were captured or settled – and then hardly moved higher for over a century to come. The black slave population increased quickly: by the 1660s the slave population exceeded the white population in the English West Indies taken as a whole, though this chiefly reflected the transformation of Barbados, which had turned whole-heartedly to sugar, reduced the number of small farmers, and established a slave majority by 1650. The other islands followed and had slave majorities by the 1670s, and once they had done so the process was irreversible; white men could not be persuaded to come to an area where wages were set by the cost of slave labour. In any case nobody wanted to reverse the process; tobacco had been a pleasant commercial curtain-raiser but by the second half of the seventeenth century people in England were convinced that the real attraction of possessions overseas lay in the sugar islands. If anything, these developments strengthened the links with

England: the sugar planters, just like the tobacco farmers, needed a market to which they could send their staple export product, and England was turning into a market that was always ready to absorb new products for domestic consumption or for re-export through its expanding commercial system.

The Religious Colonies

On the North American mainland there were no equally dramatic economic developments, though there were prospects for quite considerable political changes. The Plymouth merchants gave up the idea of founding a northern colony, though they were interested in the prospects for fishing and they traded with the Indians along the coastline. A group of Puritans who felt that the Church of England was too close to the Roman Catholic Church had left England and gone to the Netherlands; they noticed with regret that their children were becoming Dutch in speech and habits, and some of them decided that their best prospect of remaining both godly and English was to get in touch with the Plymouth merchants, obtain from them financial support and the legal right to found a colony, and go somewhere in America where English bishops would not interfere with them. They came back to England, recruited fellow-Puritans (so that the people from the Netherlands were only about one-sixth of the whole group), hired the *Mayflower* and sailed across the Atlantic to land at what they called Plymouth Rock in Massachusetts Bay. Saying that 'the Pilgrim Fathers will always hold a unique place among the venerated saints of mankind'[3] may be going too far, but their plain approach to life, the simple statement of belief they made on the voyage in the Mayflower Compact, and their peaceful settlements and good relations with the Indians among whom they settled were certainly in sharp contrast to what happened in most colonies. They started off, like most other overseas enterprises, on a commercial basis by raising money from investors who stayed in England, and it took them about a dozen years or so to pay the investors off and become entirely free to run their own affairs. They chose their own governor every year, though as they re-elected Governor Bradford thirty times in the next thirty-five years their policy suffered no lack of continuity. Neither Bradford nor his successors obtained a charter for the colony, and because of this it was absorbed into the much larger colony of Massachusetts in 1691.

The change involved no religious problems because the larger colony had been launched for much the same reasons: a number of Puritans, of whom the largest single group came from East Anglia, had formed the Massachusetts Bay Company and obtained a charter to settle there in a firm determination to cut themselves off from England and the elements of Roman Catholicism they detected in the Church of England. Most of the

[3] C. M. Andrews, *The Colonial Period of American History* (1935–8), i. 299.

people who went to Virginia or the West Indies were clearly looking for an opportunity to do better than they could in England, and if they made fortunes they would probably go back to England to enjoy their wealth, but the Massachusetts Bay Company was more concerned with escape from England or with the creation of a society that improved on its better aspects and rejected the worse.

Its charter, unlike most of the others, did not say that meetings of the directors of the Company had to be held in England. So after a year's preliminary investigation they moved the charter and their centre of government to Boston (Massachusetts, though named after the East Anglian port) in 1630 and made it clear that they intended to cut off all official connection with the English government. This was not as easy as they hoped; they knew that, however much it might disapprove of their activities, the English government certainly had no power to get its orders obeyed on the western side of the Atlantic, but their charter, which they hoped would make them independent of England, and on which they relied for the legal basis of their community, said – like all the other charters – that they must not pass laws that were not consistent with English laws. This later led to more troubles than they could have expected, but in the 1630s they seemed to be effectively independent.

They had not gone overseas out of a belief in religious toleration. Each one of them knew what he or she meant by true religion, and all of them were sure that the church and the government in England were wrong. It was probably natural that the community they set up was so convinced of its own religious ideals that it thought toleration was harmful, but it was also natural that the strong-minded people who had committed themselves to this Atlantic crossing were not able to agree among themselves what was the true religion to which they were so committed. Questions of religion mattered so much to the leaders of the colony that arguments in favour of religious toleration would have seemed to them simply a new onslaught on the purity of religion. By restricting the right to vote to fully accepted church members, political power in Massachusetts was placed in the hands of the godly men who had led the expedition; those who had joined the expedition merely in the hope of a better standard of living found their efforts justified by success because, despite some difficult times in the 1630s, the labouring population in the colony by the 1640s was fairly certainly more prosperous than they would have been if they had stayed in England, and about 20,000 people had settled in New England at a total cost of about £200,000. A more rigorous church system, which in any case allowed them a chance to work out their own salvation, may not have seemed too high a price.

Those who had come to New England to have an opportunity to practice their own approach to religion, and then found they did not agree with the views held by those who were in power, had a more serious problem.

Map 3 The Thirteen Colonies

Dissenting minorities were driven out by religious difficulties: Roger Williams left Boston within a year of arriving, though it was not until five years later that he made his way south through the dense woodlands to Rhode Island to launch the first settlement based on principles of religious toleration in 1636. Several other groups made their way south in the 1630s to establish new settlements on the south shore between the Plymouth region and the Dutch settlement of New Amsterdam at the mouth of the Hudson River. These settlements felt at least as detached from England as the Massachusetts Bay Company, and of course they had less of a legal foundation, because they had no charters of their own. They were new colonies which were produced by the existing colonies, even if in no friendly spirit, and the possibility that colonies could produce new colonies was likely to make the task of the government in London even harder if it ever tried to impose a unified colonial policy.

In the absence of charters, the new colonies on the south shore devised constitutions of their own: Connecticut's Foundations in 1639 were primarily concerned to bring a group of separate towns, each with a rural hinterland, together as one colony with a congregational approach to religion which would avoid the dangers of conflict and division, while the Constitution of Rhode Island, established in 1643, took a long step further towards complete commitment to the view that no particular variety of religion would be given a special position and that everybody would be allowed to carry on worship freely.

Toleration as wide-ranging as this would not have been acceptable in England, where hostility to Roman Catholicism had been building up for seventy years since Mary Tudor's attempt to wipe out Protestantism. Sir George Calvert, a politician at the Stuart court, had already shown his interest in colonization by trying to found a settlement in the Avalon district of Newfoundland, though this had failed partly because of the climate and partly because of the opposition of the fishermen who came from England every summer to use it as a base for fishing on the Grand Banks. Early in the 1630s Calvert announced his conversion to Catholicism and, though Charles I valued his services and asked him to stay at court, he decided it could only cause trouble if he did so. He set out to launch a North American colony to which Catholics could retreat to avoid the discrimination that seemed to have become unalterably established in England and in New England. When Sir George died unexpectedly Charles gave his son the title of Lord Baltimore and continued to support the scheme.

Although the 1624 Act against letting an individual hold a monopoly meant that no businessman could take the place of a trading company, there was no reason why an individual should not hold a charter as a great landlord. Some companies had suffered because their policies did not suit the King's diplomacy. The primarily Scottish Nova Scotia Company had established itself on the Atlantic seacoast north of Maine and the Canada Company had in 1628 captured the recently established French base at Quebec, but both of them had to give up their territory when peace was made with France in 1632, and they faded into financial oblivion. So land-holding companies were not in favour, while the idea that land should be held by a great individual landlord fitted the way people thought society ought to be run. The chartered company continued to be regarded as the best type of organization for carrying on overseas trade, but a grant to an individual proprietor began to be seen as the best way to set up a new colony to which settlers would come to cultivate the land. The proprietor would choose a governor for the colony, paying perhaps more attention to making sure he was acceptable to the King than the chartered companies did. While the Maryland charter gave the Calverts the same executive authority as the Bishops of Durham held on the Scottish border, it required them to make sure that the colonists had approved the laws of their colony before they came into effect; it may have been realized from earlier experience that an assembly was needed, or there may have been some feeling that a Catholic colony would have special problems. Emigration to the colony went on happily enough in the 1630s. The majority of the settlers were Protestant but the Calvert family influence, sometimes reinforced by having a member of the family go to Maryland as governor, was quite sufficient to protect the interests of the Catholic minority and secure religious toleration in normal times. A period of disturbance was bound to give the more zealous of the Protestants a chance to try to gain power in order to persecute the Catholics. When the Civil War broke out in England in the 1640s, it could be taken calmly enough in most of the American colonies because the colonists had no particular desire for changes; in Maryland the Protestants did want changes, and by 1655 they had taken power from the Catholic minority, though the new government was never completely in control of the situation and Catholics maintained a more satisfactory position than they could have in any other territory under English rule at the time.

Setting up so many colonies to give people a chance to practise religion in their own way had helped produce a great diversity among the English colonies. Maryland was organized as a late and formal version of the feudal system, the Virginian way of life was always expected to reflect some memories of the heirs of the Elizabethan gentlemen and seadogs who had launched it, and Massachusetts and the other New England colonies that emerged from it retained a moral earnestness that sometimes survived the loss of the faith that had initially inspired the earnestness. The attitude of the New England colonies was probably well suited to the commercial and industrial society that was emerging in the seventeenth century, but at the time they made less impression on the world than the others. Despite the higher standard of living they were offering most of their inhabitants, they were economically a little too isolated to attract much attention. People in Europe saw the advantages of colonies most easily when the colonies produced something valuable that was not produced at home. The southern colonies, in the islands or on the American mainland, offered tobacco and other products that could be exchanged for English exports or help the London re-export trade, but the agricultural products of New England were similar enough to those of England to mean that there were not many openings for trade, and this meant that the differences caused by religion were not healed by close commercial relations.

While the colonies looked to Englishmen like a widely diverse collection of territories with widely differing religious and economic foundations that had little in common, the other colonizing powers of Europe probably noticed their similarities rather than their differences. By 1640 all the British colonies in the New World had assemblies of elected representatives to look after local problems of legislation and taxation and, while some of them had been created with royal authorization, some had plainly been set up in order to make independence possible. By comparison with that of the rulers of France, the Netherlands, or Spain, the King of England's control over his colonies was very slight. The English colonies looked rather like colonies of the Greek type, where emigrants set out from their native city to launch a new city and, while often cherishing a deep affection for the city that they had left, did not acknowledge a political obligation to obey it. The other European countries acted much more like the Romans: they had conquered large existing populations in the territories to which they had gone, and had established substantial colonies that were ruled by the sovereign power at home much more directly than was the case in the English colonies. The loyalty to the Crown of English settlers was not matched by any comparable institutional framework; a well-informed observer on the continent of Europe might reasonably have expected that the execution of Charles I would lead to the disintegration of his empire overseas and that the Republic would be unable to assert any authority at all over emigrants whose political links with England were already so relatively weak.

2. Monarchs and their Colonies 1649–1714

The new government set out in 1649 to establish its position with a degree of success which must have surprised everyone who knew about its problems and had not realized the great energy that religious faith gave to its leaders. It transformed the way that the English dealt with the world outside Europe; even though Charles's son came back to the throne as Charles II in 1660, the Republic changed the direction of English imperial policy and set a pattern followed at least until the death in 1714 of the last direct descendant of Charles I to sit on the throne. Queen Anne died a year after the signing of the Treaty of Utrecht, which had brought to an end a cycle of wars which, while primarily concerned with the balance of power in Europe, had given English governments an opportunity to take colonies away from other European countries and increase their empire by annexation as well as by settlement. Annexation showed that the English government had much more power to take action outside Europe than it had possessed in the first half of the century.

This was one of the changes initially seen under the Republic: the capture of Jamaica in 1655 opened up a new road which encouraged rulers in the second half of the century to go forward and force other European powers to give up their lands on almost the whole of the North American coastline. Cromwell, the head of state in the Republic, encouraged a reorganization of the East India Company, with a new charter which put it on a firmer basis. The restored Stuarts also encouraged companies by giving them charters, and two or three trading companies did a lot to expand English interests, although settlement of land by commercial companies never regained its initial importance. The Republic also pointed the way to the future in its attempts to regulate English trade in a way that would help English shipping, though its efforts were not immediately successful; the monarchy took the same legislative approach, but was able to make its laws effective and on this basis set up a system of control of trade in the empire that survived until the middle of the nineteenth century.

One of the first problems faced by the Republic was that most of the colonies outside New England were loyal to the Stuart monarchs, and so in the early 1650s considerable effort had to be put into making them accept the new government. The restored Stuarts did not have to deal with any difficulty of this sort but they did have a general problem of making sure that the King's authority was accepted. The idea that the colonies might be told to go their own way was not considered; an administrative system was set up to make sure that the King's orders were obeyed on the far side of the Atlantic as much as in the more distant parts of the British Isles – it was realized that he could not expect complete obedience, and in some respects the system was losing its impetus even by the beginning of the eighteenth century, but the shift from the Greek pattern of virtual independence to the Roman pattern of general obedience in the colonies had been made and there was no reason to think it would be reversed.

Continuity in Republican and Royalist Policy

In 1649 the government of the Republic was not at all sure that it could assert its authority over distant colonies; it had too many problems close to home. Ireland had been in rebellion for eight years. After the Elizabethan conquest there had been the usual influx of people wanting land, but the landlords of the traditional type had been supplemented by London-based land-holding companies and also by peasant emigrants from Scotland. As a result the north-east corner of the island had become much more distinctly Protestant in population than the rest, though Protestant landlords owned property in a good deal of the rest of the island. In 1641 there was a Catholic rebellion against the Protestants of Ulster, and English authority over the island was shaken. However, much of the island remained loyal to the monarchy: the Republic was determined to subdue the Catholic Irish and the Royalist Irish, and it was not much concerned about any differences between the two. Cromwell took his army across St. George's Channel and led it forward ruthlessly and successfully, and by 1650 it was clear that the English government was going to be able to reconquer the island. For the next year or two Cromwell and his army were involved in the conquest of Scotland, and by May 1653 the Republic had more power to make itself obeyed over the whole of the British Isles than any monarch had ever had.

The Republic had then to face problems further afield. Many royalists had gone into exile in the colonies, especially Virginia, and the new government could not expect its orders to be obeyed on the other side of the Atlantic. The attractions of sugar-trading with the Netherlands reinforced the West Indian lack of enthusiasm for the new government. But most of the English fleet had been on Parliament's side during the Civil War, and in 1650 the Republic decided it was strong enough to impose an embargo on trade and send out an expedition to make Virginia and the West Indian islands acknowledge its authority. Deploying forces in America in this way was more ambitious than anything the monarchy had done, and the Republic's success in winning the obedience of the colonies and forcing the small royalist fleet to give up its privateering activities showed how much more effective England's power had become.

Because the new government had an effective army it could raise much more revenue from taxes than the King had done, and so was more powerful than the monarchy had been. It intervened to regulate trade; in 1651 the republican Parliament passed a Navigation Act which set out to protect the English shipping trade by laying down that imports could be taken to the ports of England or of English colonies only by English ships or by those of the country that produced the goods. Despite the traditional virtues of the local oak trees, English shipbuilders had to import so much of their material, from ropes to masts, that English sailing ships were never quite as good as the best European ships. Superior gunnery and, by the eighteenth century, larger fleets, gave the royal navy command of the seas, but merchant shipping needed a different type of help. Legislation had been tried before, from the late fourteenth century onwards, but more effort was made to enforce the 1651 Act than had been done in the past.

Its effect on colonial trade was, in the eyes of the English government, a secondary matter. Until the 1640s the colonies had taken it for granted that they would trade only with England, partly because Charles's government gave orders that they should, partly because the hostile Spanish colonies offered them no real alternative. The success of the Dutch in the West Indian sugar trade in the 1640s showed that this natural monopoly of the colonies' trade would not last any longer, so English shipbuilders were gratified to find that the Navigation Act would limit the colonial trade to English ships. The direct effect was to cut sharply into the Dutch carrying trade, by shutting re-exports from Dutch ports out of England (which compensated English colonies to some extent for losing their Dutch connections) and by forbidding the export of colonial products in Dutch ships. The legislation was resented bitterly enough by the Netherlands to lead to a war in which the English Republic was able to assert itself against the Dutch Republic. But when the great general of the Civil War, Oliver Cromwell, lost his temper with the Rump Parliament for trying to monopolize power, and made himself supreme instead, he regretted this war between Protestant countries and set out to make peace between them as soon as possible.

Cromwell's foreign policy has been called out-of-date, because he based it on the bellicose anti-Catholic and anti-Spanish feeling of the reign of Elizabeth. If the objective of his policy had been to maintain a balance of power by opposing the strongest nation in Europe, he was no doubt picking the wrong enemy; France was the rising power, and later in the century English policy was devoted to holding her in check. On the other hand an attack on Spain made very good sense for anyone who wanted to follow a policy of overseas expansion. Her empire had become unwieldly and, if its defences could be forced, it provided opportunities for trading and for snatching a few of the less well-defended colonies. In 1655 an expedition was sent out to attack Hispaniola (San Domingo); this was the first time the English government had sent a naval expedition to seize the colonies of another European nation, and lack of experience led to lack of success. Penn and Venables pulled their forces together and, very much as a consolation prize, captured the island of Jamaica. It was not thickly populated or well defended, but it was much larger than the islands the English already held in the Caribbean, so it provided land for English emigrants for some years. It was also the first colony gained by conquest. Until then the English had been sailing to places so far from effective Spanish opposition and so thinly populated that the government had not had to provide any help. Jamaica indicated another approach to the art of colonization, in which the government took valuable colonies away from Europeans who had reached them first.

With this interest in the western hemisphere went a renewed interest in the East: in 1657 the East India Company was given a new charter and put on a much more durable basis. Previously there had always been at least the possibility that it might be wound up after its current voyages were complete but under Cromwell the traders reorganized its joint-stock system so that, while individual owners might sell their shares, the Company was designed to go on trading forever; and almost all companies founded subsequently were organized in the same way. The East India Company's nominal capital of £740,000 would have been about 2 per cent of the national income, though in fact only half of it was paid up until calls for fresh capital had to be made in the 1690s. It still had its pepper trade and the factories in India at Surat and Madras, and at Bantam in the East Indies, with a number of smaller bases, and it was beginning to look for new opportunities.

After Cromwell's death in 1658 the republican system of government soon fell apart and in May 1660 Charles II returned peacefully to his father's throne. Cromwell had seen that while a monarch with some claim to divine authority could rule three separate kingdoms separately by virtue of his three separate crowns, a republic had to have a parliament that united all of the British Isles. Once he had acquired supreme power he created a House of Commons to which Scotland and Ireland elected members, though he ignored a request from Barbados for representation. Charles II returned to the old system of three separate kingdoms, united only because the same man was head of each of them. In religious matters the restoration of monarchy was followed by the decisive establishment of the power of the Church of England, and in constitutional questions Charles showed that he was much more resigned to the need to work with Parliament than either Charles I or Cromwell had been, but in colonial affairs there was no change of direction, though the new government may have been able to follow its policy with more continuity than its predecessor.

The restoration caused no trouble to the East India Company, which was quite soon able to turn itself into a distinctly royalist body and was given a rather wider range of political powers than it had possessed before. The relaunched company was primarily concerned with exporting textiles, and in particular Indian cotton goods, which continued to be its main line of business throughout the century and a half in which it traded with India. Muslins and calicoes became the fashionable fabrics, and under the determined leadership of Sir Josiah Child profits went up sharply if not always regularly in the 1670s and 1680s, so that the price of shares rose ninefold between 1660 and 1685. These above-average profits depended to some extent on the Company's political influence in England; in India it was not powerful enough to control the market, but its charter gave it a monopoly in England which let it push prices up further than would have been practicable if non-members of the Company (denounced as 'interlopers') had been able to import cotton goods into England freely.

In India the power of the Moghul Empire was rising to its zenith. The earlier Moghuls had ruled only the northern half or two-thirds of the subcontinent but Aurangzeb, who ruled from 1658 to 1707, set out to conquer the south and was almost completely successful in this. Naturally he encountered no opposition based on nationalism, but his fervent support of Islam led him to abandon the tolerant policy his predecessors had adopted towards the Hindu majority, and this probably intensified resistance to his advance. After the event it looks very much as if his campaigns overstrained the resources of his empire and made it impossible to hold together, but at the time he was seen as the greatest of conquerors. As a feudal ruler he could not concentrate all power in his own hands, and the East India Company saw that it had to deal with a hundred local rulers. The most that Aurangzeb could expect was to make the local rulers obedient to his authority, or else to replace them with deputies of his own who would be reasonably faithful vassals. He knew that he would be rash to expect everyone to obey him all the time; he had secured the Moghul throne for himself by the skill with which he had played off his brothers against one another, and he distrusted most of the people around him. The English were well informed about the manœuvres that had made him Emperor, and Charles II's Poet Laureate, John Dryden, wrote a play about the struggle for the succession in Delhi. It is a safe guess that no Indian thought of writing a play about the equally dramatic course of events that put Charles II on his throne.

Despite Aurangzeb's successful policy of expansion to the south, some Company employees suspected that his empire was not as powerful as it looked. In 1686 they declared war on him in order to establish a separate company state from which they could trade. The Emperor had no particular difficulty putting a stop to this, though the Company was able to re-establish its position by blockading shipping in the Bay of Bengal and the Emperor forgave the Company in much the same way as he would have forgiven any of his nobles who tried to rebel but who was so powerful that it was neither convenient nor practicable to destroy him. On land the Company was not really strong enough for such antics, but its naval superiority gave it a place in the third or fourth rank of powers in India, beneath the Emperor at the top and great rulers like the Nawab of Bengal in the second rank. Its encouragement of textile production for its export trade helped the imperial revenue. Even after the failure of the rebellion its position was secure enough by 1690 for Charnock to establish a trading station fairly far up the River Hughli, on the southern edge of the Bengal cotton-weaving district, and over the next hundred years Calcutta grew to be the effective capital of India and the second city in the British Empire.

Bengal textiles were vital to trade; after the founding of Calcutta they made up, taking one year with another, over 40 per cent of the Company's exports to England. The inland location of the new base underlined the fact that the Company did not operate simply by coming to India, buying things and sailing away again. Exports worth up to £0.5m. a year in the late seventeenth century were taken from India to England, often for re-export to the rest of the world, and this trade determined the flow of dividends. But this was only the last stage in the process. Acquiring the products to be exported from India was not so simple; the Company directors had to put down the 'investment', mostly in silver bullion though public pressure made them include some English products as well, and had to finance a good deal of the running costs of the textile production that they were encouraging. The trading employees in India were not paid salaries in the modern sense of income they could live on; they got small retainers, starting at perhaps £5 a year, and it was taken for granted that they would supplement their retainers by trading, sometimes acting as agents buying the goods that would eventually be exported by the Company (though this could easily lead to fraud), but more often dealing for their own account. While textiles were always the major item, the old trade in pepper was being displaced by the coffee trade with Arabia, and by the trade in tea, which then came exclusively from China.

As the fashion for silk and then for tea and a little later for porcelain developed, the Company looked for Indian products to export to China, and it began dealing in opium. The Chinese market for it already existed, and the Company also found a new market for it in England, where it was used as a narcotic and as a pain-killer, for which it was much more satisfactory than the only available alternative, alcohol. Apart from its own local trade in goods the Company covered some of its expenses by taking part in the carrying trade which flourished in the Indian Ocean, known at the time as the 'country trade'. Asian ships did not go round the Cape of Good Hope to trade with Europe, and East Indiamen, as the Company's ships were called, were so heavily armed and were so much safer from the risk of piracy that merchants found them useful carriers even though they did not sail as fast as local ships until the Company had its ships built of teak some decades later. This trade in India and the Indian ocean was one in which the Company had no legal basis for claiming a monopoly, so other Englishmen, as well as the Dutch, the Portuguese, and the Indians, could take part; when the Company complained of 'interlopers', it was entitled to complain only about Englishmen who brought eastern products to the English or European markets.

There was no corporation tax or income tax to absorb a proportion of its profits, and the Company contributed to the king's revenue partly by paying customs duties on imports brought into the country, and partly by making nominally voluntary contributions to the exchequer. All its imports could be seen as luxuries, and the Stuart government was very ready to see luxuries taxed; as James II put it to his Parliament in 1685, 'Lay it on Luxury, as chocolate, tea, coffee, East Indian commodities as not necessary for the life of man, and on wine.'[1] The Company did very well despite this attitude to its imports; in the 1660s it made a number of loans to the government, amounting altogether to £130,000, and in the 1680s it regularly paid 10,000 guineas a year, which came to about 1 per cent of the King's total revenue. It is hard to say how directly the King reminded the Company that it was doing well because it had been granted a monopoly of the English market.

Its profitable career showed that it was doing better than the trading companies launched in Charles's reign. After the failure of Hawkins's attempt to open up a regular slave trade with South America, the English had paid only infrequent visits to the west coast of Africa, though a company to trade with 'Ginny and Binny' (Guinea and Benin) had been launched in 1618. It had established a fort at Kormartin in 1631, but by the 1650s it was fading into bankruptcy. In 1660 the Company of Royal Adventurers had been formed to look for gold, but it very soon realized that the switch to using slaves in the West Indies to grow sugar had transformed the trading situation, and that the Dutch had done very well out of the new developments in the British West Indies. To get into this trade, the Company was reorganized in 1663 and added buying slaves and shipping them off to the sugar islands to its original objectives. The Company was not well organized, but even a strong company would have had difficulty resisting the attacks of the Dutch – now at the height of their power – on its forts in West Africa, which began before war had been declared in Europe. By 1668 the Company had collapsed; when its successor, the Royal Africa Company, was launched in 1672 it had to tidy up the debts outstanding as well as restore the trade in gold and slaves from West Africa.

The gold was very fine, and, when minted, affected the currency: the Company issued a guinea coin to pay its dividends and had it specially

[1] C. D. Chandaman, *The English Public Finances 1660–1688* (1975), 156.

stamped with an elephant to show that it came from Africa. The coin was meant to be worth a pound, but for all normal purposes the value of a pound was twenty silver shillings each weighing one-fifth of an ounce, and the golden guinea went to a premium above this. Even when it was declared to be worth twenty-one shillings in 1717 it was undervalued; silver coins were exported to India where their value was still high, or to Amsterdam where they could be melted down and exchanged for gold, and Britain moved inadvertently to a gold standard.

Gold made up less than a quarter of the Company's exports from West Africa; its charter recognized recent changes in trading patterns by laying down that the Company was to provide slaves for the English colonies in the Caribbean, and then giving it a monopoly of the trade. This monopoly was defended in the same way as that of the East India Company: the Royal Africa Company had to meet the expenses of building and manning forts on the West African coast as protection against other Europeans, and private traders could not have undertaken fixed costs of this sort. The Company was not powerful enough to go inland and kidnap slaves, and had great difficulty keeping up its coastal garrisons in the unpleasant and unhealthy conditions in which they lived, but in any case, military expeditions to capture slaves were unnecessary. As has been normal for most organized communities that are not based on a money economy, African society was based on slavery (in the sense of the life-long ownership of human beings who could be traded), which sometimes involved plantation work or even being used as a human sacrifice: there is no calculus to compare the disadvantages of local slavery with those of being taken across the Atlantic and used as plantation or mining labour. African states went to war with each other often enough to have a large number of captives to sell, and competition among the slave traders encouraged this and pushed them into searching aggressively for slaves among their neighbours or else finding themselves enslaved by their better-equiped rivals. There is a story that an African chief said to a trader 'You have three things we want, powder, musket and shot. And we have three things you want, men, women and children.' This was not the whole story of African trade, which included cotton cloth and metal goods as well as arms (and neither women nor children were much wanted by the slave traders), but European trade certainly made African states fight each other more often than before.

Getting the slaves across the Atlantic was always a difficult problem for the Royal Africa Company and for all the other traders. The conditions for the crossing were not much worse than for the criminals who were just beginning to be shipped across from England in the 1670s, and the death rates were not much higher. Financially, the slave traders had rather more reason to take care of the people they were carrying than the transporters of convicts or of indentured labourers did; all of these groups were being taken over as a speculative venture on which the shipper got no return unless he delivered live bodies, but the slave traders had already paid out cash to purchase their slaves. On the other hand the slaves were rather more likely to revolt at sea than anyone else, and they were much more likely to commit suicide or die of shock and despair. The Royal Africa Company did no worse than other traders in taking slaves across, but its commercial difficulties with its customers were probably worse than the average.

Launching a sugar plantation took a great deal of capital and the planters were always short of money; many of them had bought estates at the high land prices of the boom, and most of them felt they owed it to themselves to live in a gentlemanly way that ignored debts. The long credit that the Dutch had given the first planters to get them started in Barbados in the 1640s came to an end with the Dutch war of the 1650s, which made it harder for English planters to finance development when they wanted to grow sugar in Jamaica. The Royal Africa Company had to provide slaves for English colonists as a condition of keeping the charter which gave it the monopoly of the trade, and the colonists added to the injury of leaving their debts unpaid the insult of complaining that too few slaves were being delivered. This was true enough: the Company needed to sell about £100,000 of goods a year in West Africa to carry on enough trade to cover its fixed costs for shipping and for its forts; it was never able to manage this and in a good year it could only take about 6,000 slaves across, which might be worth £90,000. But selling more slaves would have done it little good if it could not get paid for them, and in the 1680s the planters owed the company money for two full years supply of slaves. The Company continued to hope for better times; its monopoly was left intact under Charles II and James II, and it did not realize how the deterioration of its forts in West Africa was eating up its capital and bringing closer the day when large sums would have to be spent on rebuilding them.

Another trading company with territorial interests was launched in 1670. Two fur traders from the French settlement of New France on the banks of the St. Lawrence had been trying to convince their employers that the best way to develop the trade was to set up bases on Hudson Bay to which the Indians could come in their canoes down all the rivers that flowed into the Bay. When they were unsuccessful in France they crossed to England and in 1668 an expedition was sent out to test their theory. It did so well that the King gave a charter to the 'gentlemen adventuring into Hudson's Bay' which allowed them a monopoly of trade in the whole area of the rivers and streams running into the Bay. The monopoly was normal practice, and the boundary chosen was intended simply to make sure that the Company did not go east of the Bay into areas claimed by New France; nobody had any idea that the river system of the Bay gave the Company an area – known as Rupert's Land after Prince Rupert, the Governor of the Company – that covered millions of square miles to the west. The Company did not send expeditions of its own into this area for over a century; like the East India and the Royal Africa Companies it established trading posts and waited for the local inhabitants to come and trade at them.

The Company's line of communication, which placed it fairly close to the centre of northern North America, was already long and was open only in the ice-free months. Stretching it further by setting up trading posts inland seemed neither necessary nor prudent, so a network of Indian traders grew up which took the Company's goods inland. The English products brought by the Company suited the Indians' needs; the woollen blankets and iron pots which had little commercial appeal in India or Africa were very appropriate for a cold climate in which metal was scarce. The Company sold guns to the Indians, but not as part of a process of political disturbance like that caused by the slave trade in West Africa; Indian hunters quite soon preferred guns to bows and arrows for hunting, and hunting was the basis for the Hudson Bay trade. For something over a century the major export item was beaver fur for felting and making into men's hats. Other furs were attractive as novelties or as luxuries but the beaver trade was steady and reliable until silk hats replaced felted beaver hair in the early decades of the nineteenth century.

The Company got on as well with the local population as any European settlers anywhere in the world, but it was very exposed to attacks from New France. Its bases around the Bay were staffed by a total of only a few hundred men. Bringing a force north-west from the French colony on the St. Lawrence to attack them would be very difficult but, if a force could be brought at all, it would not have to be very large to capture all the bases. This led to a great setback for the Company; by the early 1680s it seemed to have established itself, and paid its first dividends, at about 50 per cent a year, but it was then caught up in England's wars against France, the bases were captured, and no regular dividends could be paid until after it had got its property back under the terms of the Treaty of Utrecht in 1713. Part of the reason why the shareholders had to wait so long for a return was that the original capital had been only 10,000 guineas, and the Company financed itself by fairly short-term loans from the merchants with which it did business, so the shareholders stood at the end of a long line of creditors but could expect substantial returns on their money in the end if the Company survived.

Land in the New World

In the 1670s the Hudson's Bay Company must have looked like one of the least important overseas concerns that Charles II and his government had to handle. Much more attention was paid to the North American seacoast, where English colonies doubled in number and were treated more seriously by London than ever before. Charles's government was as concerned about trade as its predecessor and was not restrained by any deep Protestant sympathies, so it was naturally inclined to go to war with the Netherlands, and in the 1660s this was popular. Charles's own inclination was always towards a pro-French and anti-Dutch policy, though marriages between the Stuart family and the ruling Dutch House of Orange slightly restrained him and by the 1670s most Englishmen were beginning to be a little worried by the increasing power of France. Parliament never voted enough money for a naval war with the Netherlands to be decisively successful, so the most substantial result of the anti-Dutch policy was that in 1664 the English seized New Amsterdam, and kept it in the 1668 peace negotiations by handing over in exchange the English colony of Surinam in Guiana. The Dutchmen of New Amsterdam were the first community of any substance outside the British Isles to be absorbed into England's possession by conquest but they were close enough to the English in religion – the line of really intense division between groups in the seventeenth century – for there to be no prolonged resistance. They had no other Dutch communities to look to; they kept their own language for over a century and the switch of allegiance from one ruler to another was one that nobody at that time found at all difficult.

The new colony was divided among a number of courtiers; the largest section went to Charles's brother, James, Duke of York, who renamed New Amsterdam after his own ducal title, and just to the west two families from the island of Jersey, the Berkeleys and the Carterets, received a grant of land which they named after it. They divided the territory in two, though it was reunited thirty years later. West New Jersey, the southern part of the colony, which was owned by the Berkeleys, did not flourish and was sold to two Quaker families. Their purchase encouraged another courtier, of an unusual type, to ask for a grant of land. William Penn, a son of the admiral who captured Jamaica, was a friend of the Duke of York and had become a Quaker of the quieter second generation that followed George Fox in his beliefs but not in his attacks on all symbols of the established order. Penn wanted to set up an area of toleration for Quakers something like Lord Baltimore's Catholic colony of Maryland and, as the Stuarts owed his family money, they gave him the land grant as part of a financial settlement. In 1681 he launched Pennsylvania (which included three counties that in 1702 became Delaware) as an immense private estate to which settlers were welcomed and where they could buy land on relatively easy terms. Because of this and because the colony was committed to religious toleration for everybody, it attracted a great many immigrants. Within a dozen years Philadelphia, its capital, was among the half-dozen largest English towns in North America and, although it had a population of only a few thousand people, very few towns in England apart from London were much larger. Expansion south towards the nearby colony of Maryland went on fast enough for a pair of surveyors, Mason and Dixon, to have to draw a boundary between the two in 1702, though this line was not completely accepted for some decades.

Philadelphia stood on the edge of land that had never been occupied by Europeans, and so the Pennsylvanians had to work out their relations with the Indians. On the whole they managed this in accordance with Quaker principle, avoiding local warfare and paying a negotiated price for land. It would still have been very difficult to explain to the Indians that they were selling their land in perpetuity, and of course nobody could have had any idea of the immense flood of immigrants that was going to cross the Atlantic. In the seventeenth century North America was so thinly populated that it was hard to think that a particular piece of land had scarcity value. The most influential philosopher to think about the problem of the ownership of empty land, John Locke, served as a secretary and adviser to yet another of the courtier-backed expansion schemes of Charles II's reign; he was agent to Lord Ashley, who later on as Lord Shaftesbury became a famous Whig leader but in 1663 was a well-placed courtier and one of a group who got a charter for a colony south of Virginia to be called Carolina. The proprietors could not do much more than launch a rather fragile settlement around Charleston, and even this could not be occupied continuously until 1681. The northern section of the colony was settled by people from Virginia rather than emigrants brought out by the proprietors, and the southern section by emigrants from Barbados as well as from England. In 1691 the Company recognized this and set up two separate administrations, though they were run by the same governor until 1710.

Locke's argument about property started from a simple view of what he understood the siutuation to be in America: the land was empty, unclaimed, and ought to become the property of the first cultivator. This showed how very different everything was from the situation that had developed in England over the course of centuries, and colonial developments always gave Englishmen the idea that they were moving into empty land and seeing what could be made out of it. One odd aspect of the policy of the Carolina proprietors was their attempt to create in America a very formalized version of what had grown up in England. Locke could have learnt from his Carolina experience that the old English approach to property, based on the tenants' allegiance to the landlord, was no longer fully accepted and certainly was not suitable for export to a new territory. The original outline for settlement looks both feudal and foolish – foolish because the men of importance were to be ranged in a tidy hierarchy with outlandish titles like cacique and landgrave, and feudal because it rested on the assumption that the proprietors would get a permanent rental income from politically loyal and economically co-operative tenants.

Most of these schemes of settlement by proprietors which included half the mainland colonies in the seventeenth century, assumed that the proprietors would become great landlords of the old English type on a very grand scale. Charles II found land grants very convenient; he could give them to people who at the beginning of the century would have asked for monopolies and he could feel confident that these grants would not rouse the hostility in England that monopolies had caused. But the settlers who had come to America to look for land did not like the proprietors' form of ownership. The old feudal tenancy, with its claim to perpetual rents, had disappeared in England in the 1660s and in the colonies Americans wanted to avoid being tenants of any sort. With so much land to be disposed of, it was hard to make them put up with anything less than freehold tenure, and so it was almost impossible for the proprietors to make very much out of their estates. Locke's philosophy about property accepted the settlers' point of view: in his theory it is the man on the spot who is doing something to the land (though mainly by directing the labour of the people he has brought over at his own expense) who is justly entitled to ownership.

In the West Indies pressures on land had already become intense; the proprietors were replaced by royal governors, and external danger made the government's support for the islands essential. The French, the Dutch, and the Spanish were ready to attack them, and over so widely scattered a set of islands the attacker would always find some weak spot to invade and devastate. The successful invasions by the French in 1666 and 1667 inflicted losses on the Leeward Islands that the planters found hard to survive, and these attacks forced the authorities in the West Indies to realize the dangers caused by the shift in the population balance. They tried bringing out political prisoners after rebellions in Britain, they tried kidnapping new recruits, and they tried legislating to keep up the number of white men that planters must employ, but white men still left for England or went on to new parts of the Americas rather than compete against slave labour. This was only one of the disadvantages of a slave labour force. Assembling slaves required capital, or at least credit, to get started, and the slaves had to be trained and had to be watched in case they rebelled. On the other hand they were available, recruiting them was simpler than persuading workers to come out from England, and they could never leave to work elsewhere.

The English government maintained a small military force in the islands but it was not large enough to guarantee the English population against slave revolt or foreign invasion, and the settlers had to make an effort on their own account as well. This was not very difficult; the Spanish still did not recognize other colonies in the Caribbean and the old rule of 'no peace beyond the line' went on, so that West Indian governments could still recruit on an official basis men who were committed to fighting aginst the Spanish whether the governments thought they were at war or not. The Spanish naturally thought these irregulars were pirates and their position was certainly ambiguous. In the 1660s Henry Morgan, who had been recruited to help defend the islands, could be seen as the most outrageous of pirates or as a bold seadog who, in the course of active defence of the islands, led his men through extreme hardship to the capture of Panama, which was then brutally plundered. Charles II's response fitted the occasion. He summoned Morgan back to England in disgrace, and made him a knight. This happened at a turning-point in Caribbean affairs, for in 1670 the Spanish accepted the inevitable and by the Treaty of Madrid acknowledged the English colonies in the West Indies as legitimate settlements, though the logging settlements on the central American mainland were left in an ill-defined position.

After this the irregulars could no longer claim the benefits of an ambiguous position; either they were adventurous sailors who were willing to settle down and live peaceful lives once the Spaniards stopped harassing them (and Morgan showed the way by becoming Deputy Governor of Jamaica), or else they were straightforward pirates who were ready to plunder the ships of any nation including their own. The next fifty years were the classic age of piracy when men like Teach (Blackbeard) plundered in all directions and buried their fortunes on treasure islands, but after their main base in the Bahamas was brought under control by the British government in 1718 the Atlantic was made reasonably safe from this. The Indian Ocean was still far from safe and the East India Company went on building ships to resist attack.

Charles II managed to induce the Barbados assembly to grant him the revenue forever from a tax of 4½ per cent of the value of all sugar exported from the island, and the Leeward Islands settled on the same terms and were briefly united under the same governor as Barbados. The grant was voted more because Charles ended disputes over land titles running over the previous twenty years than because the West Indians believed they ought to support the English Exchequer, but a permanent colonial contribution to the home government was – at least for England – a new and interesting departure, though one that had no sequel. All sorts of small items of royal expenditure were charged to the Barbados and Leeward revenues but no other colony saw any reason to make a similar grant. Efforts were made to persuade Jamaica to follow Barbados, and a twenty-one year grant to cover the island's own expenses was voted in 1683, but this grant was not large enough to provide any surplus to spend elsewhere and was not much more than a recognition that the government in England was not going to spend its money covering the costs of local government for Englishmen who had gone overseas. The cost of keeping up a navy was already the really large item in the expenses of empire, but the English needed a navy for their own safety from invasion as well as to protect their trade, so the colonies – and perhaps particularly the West Indian colonies – got some benefit from money the English would have had to spend in any case.

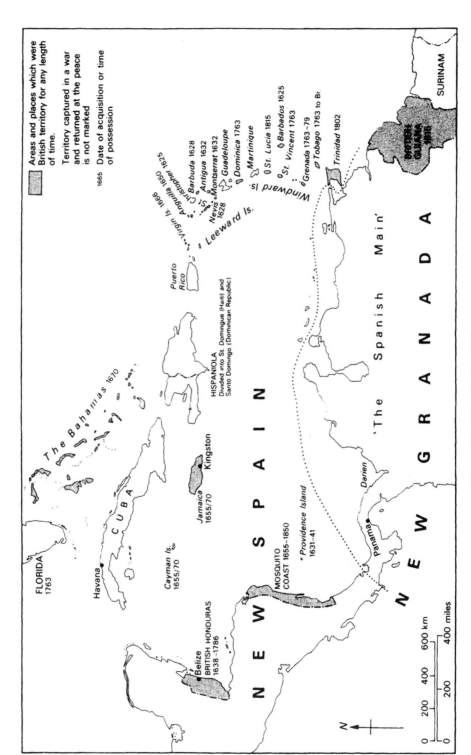

Map 4 The West Indies 1623–1815

While the King found it convenient to have a source of income that Parliament could not touch or question, people in England did not reckon the advantages of colonies in terms of the grants of revenue that they could make. The government had been thinking about ways for the administration to maintain some degree of control over the colonies since the mid-1650s; in 1675 Charles set up the first organization to establish any record of continuity, a sign that his possessions overseas were settling down into some sort of discernible order. The Lords Commissioners for Trade and Plantations, who quickly became known as the 'Lords of Trade', were the direct descendant of a committee of the Privy Council suggested by Ashley, on which Locke had served. By the time the new committee got its name, Ashley had left the court, and the court was losing touch with part of the merchant interest. The Lords of Trade were Church of England men, but this hardly entered into their ideas about possessions overseas. Most of the empire for which they were responsible had been settled by people outside the Church of England, of whom the majority were nonconformist Protestants, though there were a fair number of Roman Catholics in Maryland and in the West Indian islands to which Irishmen had gone.

As their title suggested, they were much more concerned with trade, and this probably reflected the general English attitude inside and outside the government. Only some large religious or political issue would induce people to take the very considerable step involved in emigration if they had any established position to keep them in England – younger sons, the poor, and those with nothing to lose might easily be more ready to travel, if they could get the financial backing needed, or were willing to go as indentured labourers. The sense of panic about over-population that had swept across England in the late sixteenth century, and had made emigration look like the answer to problems of poverty and disorder, had died down and there were even suggestions that a substantial population helped economic expansion. Nobody suggested discouraging emigration, but it was certainly not welcomed as eagerly as in earlier decades, and the flow may have declined a little.

By comparison with other European empires overseas, the English could feel they were doing well enough. The Spanish empire was still pre-eminent, it covered the larger part of the New World, and extended to the Philippines in the Pacific. This whole area had blossomed as a great region for settlement, in which the Spanish language was steadily being forced upon the survivors of the original population and to which Spanish emigrants went out as regular reinforcements to maintain the conquests of Cortes and Pizzarro. There had been virtually no further expansion after the fifty years of extraordinary growth in the first half of the sixteenth century. Spain stood very much where she had done when Philip II came to the throne, except that the Netherlands had broken free and had set up an empire based much more on trade than on overseas settlements.

The Dutch might have been willing to see a world without territorial empire, if only it had been possible to keep up a trading system on that basis. Their ports and forts in the Spice Islands or the West Indies or the West Coast of Africa were intended as supply bases for shipping and not as the starting point for territorial expansion. In 1652 they had established a very well-placed port at the Cape of Good Hope as a supply depot, but the Dutch East India Company was always a little worried when settlers at the base interpreted their responsibility to provide food for passing ships as a reason for pushing on into the hinterland. Other Dutch bases provided no such opportunities for settlers to move inland, and the directors preferred expansion to be restrained in this way. This was largely because the Dutch were conscious that they were operating on a narrow margin, and they did not want anything to distract them from their main purpose, which was to bring goods for trade and re-export to their great complex of ports, banks, and merchant houses around Amsterdam.

The French stood in sharp contrast to all this; their main energies were directed at expansion in Europe, with the Netherlands marked down as a particularly attractive target, but they were so rich, so dynamic, and so confident in the second half of the seventeenth century that they were quite willing – as asserted in the motto of their great king, Louis XIV, *nec pluribus impar* – to fight several enemies at once. They set out to develop an empire and wage European wars at the same time, though their empire was unlike any of the others: it cost them money. The King of Spain got money from his empire in the form of bullion from its mines and, after the 60-year period from 1580 to 1640 in which Spain ruled over Portugal, so did the Portuguese empire. Like the Spanish, the Portuguese had not made new acquisitions since the great days of the sixteenth century, and they had lost their possessions in the Spice Islands, but Brazil continued to flourish and was beginning to emerge as the world's main source of gold. The French settlements along the river St. Lawrence had no such attractions; the peasant farmers who settled along the river were probably better off than if they had stayed at home, but they could not produce enough revenue to support the fairly lavish military, civil, and ecclesiastical establishment that had been set up there as well. The Spanish could pay for such things out of their gold and silver; the English could not afford such things, and ran fairly frugal colonial administrations, whose pay was often in arrears whether it was supposed to be paid by the English government, the colonial taxpayers, or the company which had a charter to operate in the region. Only the France of the Sun King could afford the luxury of overseas development for its own sake, or at least for the sake of a distant and ill-defined future. In England the Lords of Trade certainly had no money to spend on the colonies; and would have been quite as surprised as any earlier generations at a suggestion that they ought to be spending money on them. People who had gone overseas had probably made a wise choice and were likely to be doing better than they could have done at home, so the government felt it had done enough for them already.

This of course helped make sure that people of established wealth did not go to the colonies. The Lords of Trade did not go themselves. Some noblemen went out as governors because they needed the money and, perhaps because they were habitually lavish about their spending, were usually rather popular. Governors were almost always sent out from England rather than chosen from among the men on the spot. Normally they were military officers, partly because the army provided a supply of trained talent, partly because they were likely to pay attention to orders from London, and mainly because the organization of defence was the crucial part of their work. The governors of royal colonies, appointed by the king, were expected to maintain a rather dignified and aloof attitude and it was thought that they might find it hard to do this if they had lived in the colony as subordinates or as private citizens in the past. The East India Company and other companies like the Royal Africa Company and the Hudson's Bay Company rarely brought in men like Roe to help with work at the top, and normally expected to promote people who had spent their lives working for the Company. When a colony was launched as the property of a single owner he, or one of his family, might go out to oversee the administration but he was unlikely to cut his links with England, if only because it was important to be able to maintain the court favour which was part of the political strength needed by anyone who wanted to run a colony on his own.

Stuart Rule in North America

In 1675 the Lords of Trade had ten colonies on the North American seacoast to think about, stretching roughly from Portsmouth (in what was still part of Massachusetts) to Charleston, a length of coast running about as far from north to south as that of Britain. The territory was not densely settled and while emigrants to America might be loyal subjects of Charles II, in Virginia, or might be deeply distrustful of him on religious grounds, as in New England, they were not certainly united with one another. If they ran into trouble they hoped – without too much justification – for help from England, and they knew they were most unlikely to get it from their neighbours. Their Lordships also had to look after half-a-dozen Caribbean islands, of which the newest, Jamaica, was much the largest and looked like providing the best prospects for the future. The shift from tobacco to sugar cultivation in the West Indian islands was now almost complete, and the cultivation of food crops was being steadily abandoned to leave more space for the specialist production of still more sugar. The Lords of Trade did not have to take such a close interest in the activities of the chartered companies, but the three large companies trading outside Europe were clearly providing London with trade that could not come in any other way. Trade with Russia might survive if the Muscovy Company went out of business, but it was not easy to imagine that trade with Hudson Bay (with all that it did for London furriers and re-exporters) could continue if the Company lost its trading rights, and the Royal African Company was believed to be necessary for the slave trade until the 1690s, and the East India Company kept its position in trade with India for over a century after that.

The duties of the Lords of Trade reflected the approach of their contemporary, Lord Halifax, who said 'we fight for trade, the fairest mistress men ever knew'. They made the Navigation Acts effective; in the colonies the legislation came to be known as 'the Acts of Trade', which expressed rather well the way that, while the Acts' main importance to England lay in their encouragement to shipping, their main impact on the colonies came in the way they affected the pattern of trade that was developing. The authority of government was still exercised more directly through the law courts than in later centuries, and the authority of the Lords of Trade was underlined when they received the power to hear appeals from courts in the colonies. This enabled them to control the activities of people who did not expect the Navigation Acts to be taken seriously. So many exceptions had been made to earlier Navigation Acts by royal licence that it had sometimes looked as if they were intended to raise revenue rather than to direct trade, and in the 1660s there had been a few signs that the legislation which Charles had inherited from the Republic and had then extended might still be treated in the same way. In the 1670s it became clear that this was not the case and that the English really did intend to have a network of trade among all English possessions to give the colonies a safe if restricted market in England and to allow England – and London in particular – the whole re-export trade from the entire empire. Parliament listed a number of goods, known as the 'enumerated articles', which the colonies were not allowed to send anywhere outside the empire, and which were to be carried out only in ships from England or from the country of origin. The 'enumerated articles' included most of the more important English imports from areas in the temperate zones and almost all the goods exported from the tropical and semi-tropical regions in which the colonies most committed to trade were to be found.

While England thus had a monopoly power to buy colonial products, the sugar and tobacco and other products of the colonies were more or less guaranteed the entire English market by a system of preferential tariffs. The tax on foreign sugar was well over twice that on English West Indian sugar in 1661 and the margin was widened later. Bounties, or subsidies, were paid to colonial producers of naval stores and of indigo dye. Measures like this gave the colonies a secure market and also provided larger supplies of tropical goods than could be consumed in England, so that English merchants could develop their re-export trade with the rest of the world. Their position was strengthened by the Staple Act of 1663, which prohibited the colonies from trading with European countries or their colonies. Most items produced in Europe paid practically no English duty if they were to be re-exported to the colonies, but a few, including iron and steel, were taxed at a rate which made continental products very expensive and thus gave English manufacturers a clear field in the colonial market.

On balance the trading aspects of what came to be known as the Old Colonial System probably favoured England more than the colonies, though the colonial monopoly of English markets was a substantial counterweight to English monopoly of colonial trade. Whatever its actual effect, the English wanted at least to make sure that they would not be out of pocket over expansion in America, and the fear that they would lose money was expressed by the economist Charles Davenant when he wrote in 1698: 'it cannot reasonably be admitted that the mother country should impoverish herself to enrich the children nor that Britain should weaken herself to strengthen America.'[2] By the second half of the seventeenth century English politicians realized that military and naval support of the colonies was going to cost money. The colonies had at first been left to look after themselves because the king had no money to spare for defending them nor any forces he could send across the Atlantic, but after 1650 it was accepted that the colonies had a right to expect to be protected against European attack, though not against Indian or other local problems. The Navigation Acts were not in the first instance devised to make up for the fact that some English revenue was devoted to colonial defence, but defending the colonies came to be seen as an integral part of the Old Colonial System.

The Navigation Acts were complicated and applying the regulations would have been harder if there had been a great deal of trade between the colonies, but in the seventeenth century most of the trade of each colony on the American mainland or in the West Indies was with England rather than with other colonies. In Virginia, dependence on a one-crop export trade led to trouble: the price of tobacco continued to fall after Charles's restoration, and thus was the main reason for Bacon's rebellion in 1675, which was put down by the government of the colony before royal troops arrived from England. Virginia like most of the mainland colonies consisted of a few ports with an extensive hinterland that was left untouched until the coastal sections had been fairly fully settled. Carrying anything by land was still expensive, even in settled areas, and was even more expensive when there were no roads – Roger Williams travelled only 50 miles from Boston to set up Rhode Island but this was a serious matter when it meant marching through uncut forest. Trade by water was easier; the sugar colonies had a

---

[2] This quotation from Davenant is taken from C. M. Andrews, *The Colonial Period of American History* (1935–8), iv. 336.

very saleable product close to the sea and as they concentrated more and more on sugar they imported their food, first from England, then from Ireland, and by the eighteenth century from New England and from the Carolinas. This was not what English food exporters wanted but, as it kept down the cost of provisioning the sugar plantations, it was supported by the sugar industry in England. Apart from this there was not much trade between colonies. Colonial merchants might not like the English monopoly of trade, but they wanted their markets in England, so there was unlikely to be opposition to the general principles of the Acts of Trade.

The Lords of Trade did not like colonies owned by a single proprietor. No new ones were created after Pennsylvania, and over the next fifty years the government bought out most of the proprietors' rights. The existence of separate colonies with separate governors was accepted with much less question. Perhaps because the problems of transport eroded their feeling of unity, colonies often split in two: the Three Counties separated from the bulk of Pennsylvania to become Delaware, and Carolina was reorganized as two separate administrations. The reunion of divided colonies was very rare; the reintegration of the two parts of New Jersey was the only successful seventeenth-century example. In the West Indies the original unity laid down in the Carlisle grant disintegrated as the Leeward Islands broke away from Barbados and Jamaica was set up with an entirely separate governorship. The Leeward Islands had tried to ignore Carlisle's lieutenant-governor as early as the 1630s, and when the islands became royal colonies in the 1660s they were treated for a short time as separate communities, with each island being regarded as an individual colony. Stapleton brought the Leeward Islands together again by 1682 and the Codrington family managed to keep them united until after the end of the seventeenth century, but the general tendency to fragment into separate colonies seemed irresistible to people on the islands, no matter how foolish it seemed to British administrators who saw them as tiny communities that on a map of the world looked very close together. None of this was the assertion of a separate nationality; they were all subjects of the King of England, and relied on this for their safety, but this reassuring English presence only encouraged them to manage their own local affairs in smaller and smaller units.

One instructive attempt at unification was made. For fifty years Massachusetts had behaved as if its possession of its own charter made it into something very like an independent state, and the Stuarts set out to reduce its power. In 1679 the territory of New Hampshire was carved out of it, and was established as a separate colony. Charles and his brother James also attacked the charter itself in the courts. The Stuarts liked using charters as a way to give royal encouragement of development and enterprise, as was shown by the large number of them they issued to trading companies and to colonies, including some like Rhode Island and Connecticut which they could not have found politically very sympathetic. But when the City of London emerged as the last centre of strength for the Whig opponents of royal policy at the beginning of the 1680s, it was asked by a writ of *quo warranto* to show that it was entitled to all the powers it had been exercising. The City turned out to have exceeded the authority given in the charter, which was then revoked and a new charter issued that sharply limited its powers. The same line of attack was used against Massachusetts; the charter had already been under examination, and in 1684 the courts ruled that Massachusetts had exceeded its authority and the charter was forfeited. No new charter was issued; James set out to create a Dominion of New England which would have united Massachusetts, Rhode Island, Connecticut, New Hampshire, and the New Jerseys with his own colony of New York. The constitution of the Dominion, which was to have a governor and council but no elected assembly, was a long step away from the normal pattern of colonial constitution-making, and showed how irritated Charles and James had become with elected parliaments and assemblies, and with disloyal Massachusetts Puritans, by the 1680s.

They were obviously much more concerned with problems of the world outside Europe than any previous rulers had been. One of Charles's most fruitful contributions to knowledge of the wider world was his establishment in 1675 of Greenwich Observatory, which was intended quite as much to assist sailors with the problems of navigation as to carry on scientific research. The great problem for any navigator was to know where his ship was: it was relatively easy to determine the latitude, which measures distance north or south of the equator, but it was much harder to find the longitude, or distance east or west of a fixed meridian – a line from pole to pole running through all the points at which the sun is at its highest at the same moment. All over Europe sailors had been accustomed to drawing a meridian through a point in their own country or through the furthest point to the west out in the Atlantic that they could determine with any certainty, and English sailors had usually taken their fixed meridian from a point west of the Lizard (the last promontory of land they could see as they left the English Channel).

Greenwich was set up as a new meridian which would suit the astronomers' convenience, and the government relied on them to make the new meridian into a suitable base-line for calculating the longitude. This meant either working out very accurate tables of the movements of the moon or devising a chronometer which could keep time for a voyage of months or years without relying on a pendulum that would be disturbed by the rolling of the ship. Progress was slow, but by the mid-eighteenth century success had been achieved in both methods of calculating longitude: the Greenwich astronomers had worked out the tables for the movements of the moon and an English watchmaker, John Harrison, had made a chronometer that kept such perfect time that it could meet the requirements of any sailor. Greenwich had begun producing a return on the money spent to launch it as an astronomical and nautical centre well before that: in the early eighteenth century French charts were still better than any others, but the table of wind movements, trade winds, and monsoons that Halley published in 1686 was a great help to navigation. In 1600 ocean voyages were a rarity in England, but by 1700 ordinary English ships were able to find their way around the Atlantic and Indian oceans with little difficulty, and the money that Charles spent on Greenwich was among the most useful items of government expenditure of his age.

Earlier monarchs had spent very little on such things and had not done much about the world outside Europe or about the development of their colonies. Even the Republic had felt far from confident about forming a long-term colonial policy; Cromwell's Council had invited merchants to say what should be done, but had not had time to do much more than conquer Jamaica and revive the East India Company. Charles behaved rather like a landlord who could take a long view of the future and expect his possessions to provide him with an income in the fullness of time. The term plantations, still applied to the colonies, indicated the way in which a return on investment was expected from them. The Lords of Trade asked merchants and other interests to give their opinions about policy; a number of ministers had grants of their own for settlements in North America and clearly expected to benefit as landlords, though they did not go out like the Penns and the Baltimores to take an active role in running their properties. James Duke of York was unusually deeply interested in colonial affairs and colonial investment: apart from his ownership of what had been New Amsterdam, he was a governor of the Hudson's Bay Company and of the Royal Africa Company, and several of the politicians at court invested in these companies and even held posts in them. Later on this might have led to complaints about the possibility of corruption; at the time it was simply seen as evidence that politicians were committing themselves fully to their work. Neither politicians at court nor governors in the colonies were expected to live on their salaries; having outside interests would not cause any trouble if it simply supplemented their salaries, though it would be used as an additional reason to attack them if they followed policies the king disliked.

Despite this increased activity the power of the kings of England in their colonies was still much smaller than that of the kings of France or of Spain. When James succeeded his brother Charles as king in 1685 he showed that he was willing to make the power of the Crown more effective in North America by pressing on with the creation of the Dominion of New England, but he had neither the surplus revenue nor the obedient bureaucracy needed to run a system like that applied by continental monarchs. James was by European standards a clear-sighted ruler who wanted to gain a little more of the authority over his subjects to which all kings were entitled, but by the standards of Englishmen he was a ruthless tyrant with the additional vices that he wanted to promote the cause of Roman Catholicism and was willing to infringe the rights of property. Late in 1688 he was overthrown by a revolt in which most of the powerful men in the country rose against him, though they would probably not have rebelled if William of Orange, the ruler of the Netherlands who became William III of England, had not organized an invasion.

The Struggle with France Begins

Once William and his wife Mary (who had a better claim to the throne than her husband) were established as joint rulers in England they had, like the Republic thirty years earlier, to bring the rest of the territories of the King of England into obedience to the new authority. In Scotland the resistance to the change was crushed quickly enough. William had to fight a much more serious war in Ireland, where the Catholic majority naturally saw James as their best hope for power; the successful defence of Londonderry and the victory at the Boyne in 1690 became immovable parts of the Protestant tradition; the Treaty of Limerick and the Protestant failure to honour the treaty's promises of religious toleration became unforgettable parts of the Catholic view of the history of Ireland. In North America these struggles were not so clear cut. James's Dominion of New England collapsed almost at once. There was so much hostility to his Catholicism and his attack on chartered rights that it might have been thought William and Mary would have had no difficulty establishing their authority in America, but this was not what happened. Whether because people really did not know how to interpret the revolution in England or because they wanted fairly complete independence and correctly suspected that William was going to exercise much the same overall powers as Charles and James had done, there was a revolt in New York that took some months to suppress and the colonists of Massachusetts at the beginning of the 1690s were no more reconciled to English rule than in the past.

The difficulties this attitude could cause the colonists were already becoming clear before William had completed the work of setting up governments in North America that would co-operate with him. As far as William was concerned, seizing the English throne was just one move in his struggle to resist the growing power of France that had already lasted twenty years and would take up the whole of the rest of his life. By the 1680s the power of France was beginning to alarm Englishmen as well. From 1066 to 1558 France had been the country that England would fight if she was going to fight anyone, but for over a hundred years that role of the perpetual enemy had been taken by Spain or – in the minds of a few people – by the

Netherlands. William's accession to the English throne marked a return to the attitude of hostility to France, and for almost all of the following 125 years England was either at war with France or preparing for war with France or recovering from war with France.

Most of these wars started over European issues. Englishmen were afraid that France might be able to dominate Europe and were determined to hold her in check. Of the seven wars with France that can be counted between 1690 and 1815, only one was indisputably a war about colonies, but of course all of them affected the colonies and their inhabitants. By the end of the struggle France had lost almost every single colonial possession she had, so that French imperial history had to begin all over again in the nineteenth century, but nobody in 1690 could have guessed at such a result. Colonies were very handy bargaining counters if a state wanted to concede something less important than territory in Europe, but it was hard to imagine that any country would want to take all of its rivals' imperial possessions.

The struggles in the West Indies in the 1690s were probably less devastating than those of the 1660s, and the French missed a chance to press home an attack on Jamaica when it was at its most vulnerable, just after the great earthquake of 1692 had destroyed the original capital of Port Royal. But on the North American mainland, colonies had been affected very little by the earlier wars among European countries; except for the brief clash that had led to the Dutch loss of New Amsterdam the colonies had fought only with ill-armed Indians and had won their little wars without help from England. After King Philip's War, a relatively serious struggle with Indians in New England in the 1670s, this had ceased to be any serious danger and the frontier had been reasonably peaceful. By the 1690s the northern colonies were spreading north and west in a way that was quite likely to lead to an eventual conflict with New France, though the distance between the English and the French colonies was still too great for a full-scale conflict to be possible. Bringing up supplies over long distances through dense woodland in King William's War (as the struggle of the 1690s known in England and Europe as the War of the League of Augsburg became known in America) was so difficult that launching an attack was more a matter of logistics than of strategy. The war was unlikely to become much more than a dispute over frontier posts, in which success would depend to a considerable extent on winning the support of the Indians who lived in the wide area between the colonies. The French carried out a successful attack on Albany, which was very close to the northern frontier of New York settlement up the Hudson Valley, but it was still not likely that they could reach the coastal towns which were the heart of English settlement. It would have been at least as hard for the English to move north and attack the St. Lawrence Valley. English forces and the New Englanders worked together reasonably well in operations on the seacoast to capture Port Royal in Nova Scotia, but this was a long way from the centre of French settlement and the port was returned at the end of the war.

Even this limited warfare showed the most independent-minded of the colonists that the English connection had some practical uses, and the English government did its best to live up to the implicit bargain that lay behind the Navigation Acts. The southern colonies did not contribute much to the war in America and though they were called on to help, there was no co-ordinated organization for strategy. The strain of conducting frontier warfare against the French and their Indian allies, without assistance from the south, forced the Massachusetts assembly to ask for help from England in terms that showed a reasonable willingness to co-operate with policy laid down in London. The English response to the pressure of war was to attempt to unify the system of government in much the way that Charles and James had tried. Lord Bellomont's position as Governor in New York, Massachusetts, and New Hampshire, and military commander in Connecticut, Rhode Island, and New Jersey was similar enough to the position held by the Governor of the Dominion of New England to show that unification was not just an eccentric idea launched by James II. No single administrator was appointed to hold these posts together after the death of Bellomont and the problems of unified defence in North America remained unsettled. The English government continued to think that the mainland colonies were much safer from attack than the West Indian islands, but the dangers of war in North America were becoming more obvious.

The men who overthrew James II denounced him for being an enemy of the type of established property that depended on charters like those of the City of London or the colony of Massachusetts. The new, limited monarchy of William III that replaced James was expected to show much more respect for established interests. But the new government could see the advantages of a unified system of empire, and the need for instruments of organization like Bellomont's extended governorship, just as its predecessor had done. The House of Commons was moving forward to assert a greater degree of control over the colonies than before; partly to evade this, William created a Board of Trade and Plantations, made up of civil servants and privy councillors, that was unlikely to pay much more attention to the Commons than its predecessor, the Lords of Trade, had done. In its first twenty or thirty years of life the new Board was rather more active than the Lords of Trade; between 1720 and 1760 effective executive power passed to the Secretary of State in charge of relations with France and southern Europe, though the Board still served as the main clearing house for the American pressure groups which could keep up London connections; in the last twenty years of its life, when Gibbon was a member, it was as complete a sinecure as he could have wished because power had now passed to the holder of a new Secretaryship of State. The original board (linked by the presence of John

Locke to the Carolinas and the colonies of the 1660s) helped to unite the two New Jerseys, and continued the policy of encouraging proprietors to sell or give up their special powers and turn their domains into royal colonies. This process had begun when James turned his own proprietorship of New York into a royal colony on becoming king, and over the next forty years Maryland, the re-united New Jersey, and the two Carolinas all became royal colonies. Charles II's expansion into North America had been a process of expansion by proprietors, but this was almost all dismantled in the following generation.

A certain amount of the Stuart expansion had been carried out by chartered companies, and the enemies of James II showed relatively little regard for the rights laid down in these charters. The companies had been closely linked with the King's court, and were also open to attack because they were monopolies. The Hudson's Bay Company was so deeply involved in the struggle with the French in North America, and came so close to being overwhelmed, that nobody stepped forward to try to take its place. The Royal African Company came under criticism from the West Indian sugar planters, who clamoured for more slaves to be supplied without explaining how they would be paid for, and also from other English merchants who thought they could do a better job of supplying slaves. As a result the Company lost its monopoly; after 1697 all English merchants could trade with West Africa, though they were supposed to pay a tax of 10 per cent of the value of goods exported from England, the proceeds of which went to the Royal Africa Company to enable it to keep up its forts on the West African coast. The revenue was never enough for this, and the Company began declining into bankruptcy much faster than before. Over the next ten years it kept going by making a succession of calls on its shareholders for additional funds; by 1708 it was fairly clearly insolvent, and after 1713 it almost completely ceased trading. The low price of sugar before 1690, the dangers of war after 1690, the Company's inadequate provision for depreciation, and the planters' unwillingness to pay their debts, might between them have ruined the Company in any case, but the end of the monopoly must have contributed something to the collapse. The claims of the opponents of monopoly turned out to be reasonably justified; more and more slaves were shipped across the Atlantic by the independent traders, and the government found itself drawn further and further into keeping up the forts that provided English traders with a base of operations in West Africa.

Challenging the East India Company was a larger issue. Nobody thought trade could be carried on in India without a network of factories and fortifications, which meant that there would have to be a company with a charter to run them – the idea that the government might provide them would have struck the merchants as inappropriate and would have alarmed the politicians who would have had to impose taxes to pay for them. A new

Company was organized from among merchants who had tried to trade with India on their own account, and from employees of the old Company who disliked Child's leadership. The open and public part of the contest between the two companies for the monopoly of the Indian trade (apart from the normal process of lobbying, in which it was said very large sums were spent on bribery) was devoted to finding which of them would lend more money to the government. These loans were much larger than anything known before, running into millions when hundreds of thousands had been the previous limit. The difference was that until 1688 loans had been made directly to the King: he ran the government as an extension of his private household and, although he was the richest individual in the country, he was in many ways just a private borrower like any other and a prudent lender would not trust him with a loan that would run for a long time.

After James II had been overthrown, a new system of government began to develop under which Parliament met every year and voted taxes annually, the King chose ministers who were acceptable to Parliament, the administrative departments became independent of direct royal intervention (though the King still had a great deal of authority over his ministers) and Parliament took responsibility for national financial policy. Loans were handled as the National Debt rather than the royal debt and it became possible to raise long-term loans with the authority of Parliament behind them, and even to float loans on terms which meant that the principal would never be repaid but that, because the interest would be paid regularly forever, it would be possible to treat the bond for the debt as an asset which could be bought and sold. The Bank of England began its career by lending the government £1.2m. in irredeemable bonds, and in return was given a pledge that no other joint-stock company would be allowed to open a bank.

Anyone else looking for commercial privileges would naturally be expected to provide an attractive loan, and in 1698 the new East India Company won the right to the monopoly of Indian trade with Britain by lending £2m. at 8 per cent. Parliament had some regard for the rights of property; the old Company was allowed to run in competition with the new one for a few years, and of course in India the old Company had advantages in organization, in diplomatic connections, and in possessing established forts and factories. The old Company invested heavily in the shares of the new Company, so that its shareholders would in any case not be totally excluded from Indian trade, and the companies moved towards a compromise. Working out the details took time, but the United East India Company came into existence in 1709, and combined the assets of the two existing companies, at the price of enlarging their loan to the government to £3.2m. and reducing the interest charged to 5 per cent.

During the dispute the political strength of the textile importers was reduced, and the English manufacturers of woollen and linen goods obtained some degree of tariff protection against Indian goods. No doubt they were helped by the government's needs for revenue in the period of the wars against Louis XIV, but neither this nor the nominal prohibition of textile imports from India in 1720 caused the Company or the Indian textile trade much trouble. Unprinted goods were given exemptions for the sake of the English textile printing industry, fashionable Indian muslins were smuggled in from the Channel Islands, and the re-export trade to the rest of the world was unaffected, so Indian exports rose steadily. In the first half of the eighteenth century the London trading turnover of the Company ran between £1m. and £2m. a year, of which about half went on bullion and other items to export, perhaps a sixth on transport costs, and a third for English customs duties. The establishments in India, with their low-salaried staff and their substantial share in the country trade, were self-supporting and profits on trade were about 5 per cent of turnover. The old Company had paid lavish dividends of about 20 per cent at first, which had led to calls on the shareholders for more capital in the 1690s; after 1709 the new company paid dividends starting at 8 per cent and declining as the years passed. The capital accounts were dominated by the loan to the government, which was increased by a further £1m. in the 1740s, and it was the decline in interest paid on the government bonds rather than a fall in trading profits that led to declining dividends.

This was a very modest setback compared to the disaster that overtook the only independent Scottish attempt at colonization. Scotland was an unhappy country in the late seventeenth century, partly for reasons beyond the control of politicians or merchants; the climate grew steadily harsher, for these were the worst years of the 'little ice age' that ran from 1500 to 1850 and must have had some general effect of encouraging emigration from Europe. But Scotland also suffered from internal religious differences, and from the effects of the Navigation Acts after 1660 that cut her off from a good deal of overseas trade. William III made sure that the crowns of his new territories stayed on the same head, but he still had separate governments in his different kingdoms. In the late 1690s the Scottish government gave its support to a proposal intended to enable the country to escape from all its economic problems: a trading company was to be launched which would set up a commercial centre at Darien on the Panama Isthmus. The idea attracted immense enthusiasm among all classes in Scotland, and led to disaster. However well placed the site might be for access to trade routes, it had an unhealthy climate and was in Spanish territory. For two years the colony staggererd along, with much the same problem as the early English settlements in Virginia which had failed to find any line of activity in the first three or four years that would bring in money. The English discouraged the colony, the Spanish first watched it carefully to see that it showed no sign of succeeding and eventually in 1700 they captured it.

Nothing was left of the hundreds of thousands of pounds – perhaps as much as half the floating capital of Scotland – that had been invested and over half the colonists were dead of hunger or disease. The English were blamed, and yet Darien was one of a number of events that convinced the Lowland Scots that they should try to reach better terms with England before attempting to become independent; in 1707 England and Scotland became united with a single government and a single Parliament, and one of the terms of the Union was that the Darien investors should be reimbursed for their losses. Lowland fear of the Highland Scots was another powerful motive for Union, but the effect was to give eighteenth- and nineteenth-century Scotsmen opportunities in the British Empire that had previously been closed to them. And these opportunities were very considerable; later generations might see the eighteenth-century empire as a monument to the constrictions of mercantilism, but at the time people saw it as the largest area of unrestricted trade in the world and it offered excellent prospects for men like the sugar and tobacco merchants of Glasgow.

Apart from developing a wide range of trading opportunities, the newly-United Kingdom was acquiring a position of great strength at sea and some military importance on land. After a quarter century of peace, broken by underfinanced wars against the Netherlands, England had undertaken a quarter-century of wars against France that ran almost without interruption from the day William III came to the throne until the death of Queen Anne. These wars were inspired by a belief that Louis XIV of France hoped to become the overlord of Europe, and that he wanted to restore the Catholic James II or his descendants to the throne. Particularly because of this latter fear, an effective navy meant a lot to the English in these wars and they spent money quite lavishly to keep it strong. This was no new departure: Charles I had wanted a strong navy, though his reliance on unparliamentary taxation to pay for it had led to trouble; the Republic had gone further afield than previous governments and had won some notable successes; and Charles II and his brother James had tried to build up a strong navy without becoming too caught up by the House of Commons and its desire to control policy by controlling finance. Charles's Navy had fought very well against the Dutch in the 1660s until the money ran out, and had kept going in the 1670s satisfactorily enough.

In the 1680s the navy had not succeeded very well in its primary purpose of preventing invasions. In 1685 two small-scale but embarrassing attacks, by the Duke of Monmouth in the west of England and the Duke of Argyll in Scotland, had been defeated on land but the initial landings had been carried out without the navy being able to stop them. William III, helped by the 'Protestant wind' that kept the English navy pinned in harbour while William's Dutch fleet could choose a convenient place to land, was able to carry out a successful invasion with quite a substantial military force, so the events of the 1680s underlined the possibility that James II might be able to make a successful return from exile. His prospects were obviously improved by the French navy's success at Beachy Head in 1690, and suffered a setback when the English won a battle off La Hogue in 1692. After this Louis XIV spent relatively little money on his navy; he had to defend his frontiers against the threat of invasion by land through Belgium, and naval supremacy was always for him a secondary consideration. Apart from the risk of invasion, English trade was also in danger; the interception of the Smyrna convoy in 1693 was said to have cost English merchants £2m. (which would have been something like 3 per cent of the gross national product). Much of this would have been intended for re-export, rather than directly for consumption, but as half of England's total exports by this time were re-exports rather than domestic products the commercial community suffered enough of a loss to show why the English had to be far more concerned about command of the sea than any other country except the Netherlands, and also how fragile that command was before 1700.

When the war came to an end England had spent about £40m. on it, or something like 10 per cent of the national income each year of fighting. Very few territorial changes were made at the end of the war, and none of any significance overseas. Politicians could see the peace was unlikely to last long because of the problems of the succession to the throne of Spain and her colonies. No solution was found: within a few years the European powers were at war again, essentially over the question whether Spain and her colonies were going to pass into the hands of a relation of the King of France or a relation of the Holy Roman Emperor; in the end they passed into the French line of descent, and in the eighteenth century policy towards France had always to be conducted in the light of the possibility that the French and Spanish government might ally for war. This might suggest that France won the War of the Spanish Succession but nobody in Britain and not many people in France saw the result this way; it was regarded more as a struggle in which the British asserted themselves militarily on the continent of Europe and began to show signs of a policy of taking over the smaller colonies of other European powers by conquest.

The fighting in Germany and in Belgium has always attracted more attention than other aspects of the war. Marlborough's campaigns have commanded the admiration of military analysts; his successes showed that Britain could conduct a war on land, and made it clear that the balance of power would be maintained and Louis XIV would not be able to establish France as the dominant power in western Europe in the way that had seemed probable in the 1680s. The attention of people in Britain was focused on the area where Marlborough was campaigning, particularly because this was the area of the greatest military and financial commitment, but this was not the whole of the struggle. Naturally enough, war raged fiercely in Spain; in 1704 the English captured Gibraltar and held on to it, initially as a base for their communications in Spain; a good deal of the naval activity of the war took place around Spanish waters and the English managed to stop the Bourbon forces from setting up any effective siege of Gibraltar. Moving further into the Mediterranean to protect the Habsburg lines of communication with Italy, they captured the island of Minorca in 1708. Gibraltar and Minorca remained in British hands throughout the war, and were formally transferred to Britain by the Treaty of Utrecht in 1713. Extracting this sort of consolation prize from the Bourbon candidate was the first stage of Britain's advance into the Mediterranean, which in the nineteenth century was followed by a series of acquisitions which led to control of the route to the east.

In America the war was not much more decisive than its predecessor, but British successes in Europe and claims to compensation to make up for the fact that the Bourbons had secured the Spanish throne meant that Britain kept her gains instead of returning them as she had done in 1697. An expedition sent north from New England captured Port Royal on the Nova Scotia peninsula, as in the previous war, but this time Britain retained the peninsula, which was the most settled and prosperous part of the region known as Acadia. The French kept the two substantial islands now known as Prince Edward Island and Cape Breton Island, just to the north of the peninsula, and also the area of the mainland between the peninsula and the St. Lawrence which is now known as New Brunswick. But there was still a French-speaking population on the peninsula itself; transferring a population to a new ruler in this way was common enough in Europe, and the only unusual thing about this transfer was that the British promised to let the inhabitants retain their Catholic religion without enforcing the laws restricting the civil rights of Catholics that had been passed at Westminster. Catholic priests came to the Acadians from New France, and tried to make sure that the Acadians would not become reconciled to British rule. The British also conquered the island of Newfoundland, and were not faced by any such problems there. The English had been fishing there for over a century, and had been settled for over fifty years, so they had a strong position for making the French give up any claims to settle there. The French retained fishing rights and rights to use the western shore as a base which turned out to be a source of dispute for almost two centuries, but the British were clearly establishing their control over the whole Atlantic seacoast. The Treaty of Utrecht was not the triumphant dictation of terms to a prostrate enemy that some Whigs would have liked, but it provided something for almost all overseas commercial interests in Britain and in her possessions overseas. These gains were the by-products of a war fought mainly for reasons connected with the balance of power in Europe, but they were attractive enough to encourage the British to think about further involvement outside Europe. Perhaps they helped persuade the British to follow a policy which kept them out of almost all the continental wars of the next quarter-century.

3. Peace and War 1713–1763

The long wars against France had left the British more confident about their position overseas than before, but not necessarily more interested in activity outside Europe. Between 1713 and 1763 they paid little attention to the colonies in America, and at least for the first half of the period it was hard to see what else could have been done. A framework for governing the colonies across the Atlantic had been set up but the British government of the early eighteenth century was not at all energetic in handling problems inside Britain and was most unlikely to exert itself about things further afield. Some people felt that choosing as Queen Anne's successor in 1714 a ruler from Germany, who might neglect British interests for the sake of his Electorate of Hanover, was already a warning that the British should be careful about any overseas entanglements. For twenty-five years Britain took little interest in the outside world and even managed to remain at peace with France. After 1739 this all came to an end, and Britain spent the next quarter-century at war with France, directly or by proxy in the colonies, with only a year or two of armed truce. This second set of wars was much more obviously concerned with colonial problems and ambitions than the wars at the beginning of the eighteenth century, and the result in 1763 was a dramatic conclusion to the overseas struggle which left no doubt of Britain's imperial supremacy, even though its effect on European affairs was less clear-cut. The overseas struggle had become closer to a world-wide contest; the fighting outside Europe before 1713 had been confined to North America, but between 1739 and 1763 the British went far enough afield to attack the Philippines and – what was much more important – the struggle had spread to India. Between 1690 and 1713 the weakness of the Europeans in India, and the power of the Moghul emperors, had kept the peace. By the 1740s the Moghul central government had grown too weak to impose peace on Europeans, in the 1750s the British and the French took an important role in struggles among Indians, and by 1763 the British had made themselves rulers of one of the most important regions of India, though they had not yet worked out a legal form to express the new reality in India.

Early Eighteenth-Century Britain
The British emerged from their wars against Louis XIV in a calmer frame of

mind than they had been in during the disturbed and excited seventeenth century. It was not necessarily a kindly mood – the number of types of crimes that carried the death penalty went up steadily in the early eighteenth century – but it was practical rather than cruel. Some of the increase in capital offences was perhaps due to a more precise and less summary handling of the law, which meant that in practice fewer people were executed; and certainly the more formal use of transportation to the colonies gave the authorities more flexibility in punishing crime. From the 1650s onwards, judges had ordered convicts to be transported, but they had only been able to do this by passing a death sentence and then getting it commuted. Prisoners offered the choice very rarely preferred death to the colonies but, because they were essentially treated in the same way as indentured servants, they could only go to America if a merchant was willing to take them on the basis of a calculation that he could sell their services at the other end. Particularly during the French wars, no merchant might be willing to take them, and then they had to remain in Newgate prison. But after the wars were over the government cleared off the backlog of prisoners by arranging, in the 1718 Act, to pay a subsidy to merchants to take them across the Atlantic, and it also gave the judges the right to impose a sentence of up to 7 years transportation. The old process of commuting death sentences also remained in effect, and the result of these arrangements was that about half of all eighteenth-century felons were transported, so that about 30,000 were sent to North America in the next 60 years.

This was greeted with mixed feelings in America, but treating the world outside Europe as a handy alternative to the gallows certainly showed a brisk and practical approach. A century earlier, in Shakespeare's day, that world had been a mysterious place; Othello could tell his travellers' tales of the men whose heads do grow beneath their shoulders and, while the references to Bermuda in *The Tempest* were up-to-the-minute, they came in a play that was a collection of fairy stories. When Defoe wrote about the world outside Europe for an early eighteenth-century audience, he could take a much more realistic approach. Robinson Crusoe was far too busy cultivating his island on the basis of hard work helped by all the capital goods he had salvaged from the shipwreck to have any time for fairy stories. *Gulliver's Travels* went back to telling fantastic tales, but Swift wrote the book in the same realistic style as Defoe, and took it for granted that his readers would find it quite natural that at the ends of the earth men were just the same as in England – petty, trivial, grasping, and generally unpleasant. Very few writers had actually been to the world outside Europe. The most successful writer who had lived in an English colony was Aphra Behn, who was brought up in Surinam before it was transferred to the Dutch in 1668, and her most important novel of American life, *Oronooko*, was so completely sympathetic to the Indian hero that it should be considered as an early contribution to the cult of the noble savage rather than a book which could help its English readers understand the wider world.

While writers simply reflected people's greater knowledge of the colonies and did not do much to increase it, the churches made quite substantial efforts to keep in touch across the Atlantic. Most British churches and sects had supporters in America. Even colonies which did not have direct religious origins would have religious commitments; Virginia had been launched in as secular-minded a mood as almost any colony but it remained firmly attached to the forms of the Church of England, though the lack of regular episcopal organization made its clergy more responsive to the wishes of their congregations than was usually the case in England. By the end of the seventeenth century the Anglican church in England was developing institutions to serve American needs: the Society for the Propagation of Christian Knowledge was launched in 1699 and the Society for the Propagation of the Gospel in Foreign Parts in 1701 so that the established church could help its brothers in the colonies who were exposed to much more competition from other Protestants. The early career of the great missionary John Wesley showed the problems facing Anglicans in an area without bishops; when he went to preach in the newly-launched colony of Georgia from 1735 to 1737 the Church of England made no provision for his activity, and he went out attached to the Moravians. The church was held back from full-scale episcopal organization by the thought of the expense and the political commitment involved at a time when 'a prince of the church' was a perfectly reasonable way to describe a bishop. The Bishop of London, who was responsible for church organization in America, suggested in 1749 that a bishopric should be created for the American colonies; nonconformist Protestants in England and in America opposed it strongly enough to lead the government to lay the idea aside. And Anglican laymen in America may have felt that a bishop from across the ocean would be harder to influence than the local clergy, many of whom were American by origin, though in several cases they had gone to Britain to complete their education.

These problems of religious organization were the concern of a minority. Many more people thought of the works outside Europe in a way that still reflected the idea of El Dorado, or at least of immense profits, and the idea was exploited in vast manipulations of the stock exchanges in France and Britain around 1720. Apart from her territorial gains, Britain got the right in the Treaty of Utrecht to sell 4,800 slaves a year in Spanish America which, at a normal profit of about £4 a head, might yield £20,000, and in addition one British ship a year would be allowed to visit Cartagena and trade there. It was fairly clear that there was going to be some smuggling as well but, even allowing for the often-repeated story that other ships lay over the horizon and sent boats in to add to the stock on board the single ship, the net profits from the ship could hardly have been much more than twice those of the slave-trading. In 1710 financiers in the City of London had formed the South Sea Company to bid for the right to use the privileges they expected Britain to get at the end of the war.

Even though the annual value of these rights could hardly have been as much as £100,000 a year, the Company was ready to outdo the Bank of England and the East India Company and take on £9½m. of the National Debt, which would have been about a quarter of the total outstanding after the Treaty of Utrecht. Under the scheme holders of government bonds could choose to exchange them for South Sea Company shares, and the government would pay interest on these bonds to the South Sea Company at a lower rate than it paid previously – the South Sea Company was doing much the same thing as the East India Company, providing the government with a loan at a reduced rate of interest in exchange for overseas trading privileges. There was no adequate trading base for this financial performance, and it is most unlikely that the promoters ever thought that there was. They expected to make their profit by pushing the price of the shares up, so that they could buy the government bonds for a relatively small number of shares. In France there had already been speculation, followed by disaster, when John Law persuaded the government to unite all the French colonies into a single vast Company for trading up the Mississippi and in the Indies, which was then used as the base for a wild expansion of the French currency. In the summer of 1720 the South Sea Bubble burst, and the dream that El Dorado might be found in the outside world faded a little further, though the Company went on endeavouring to use its Utrecht trading privileges for another thirty years.

Legislation had been passed, at the height of the bubble, to stop the creation of new joint-stock companies, which ruled out one of the ways in which the British had organized their expansion overseas, Walpole, the Prime Minister who picked up the pieces after the collapse, was first of all concerned to make sure that the King and his government did not run into any more trouble, which meant a programme of no new taxes, no wars, no new assertion of authority, and much less expansion than either before or after. This was a sensible policy which would bring stability to Britain, and took it for granted that stability would mean that relations with the colonies would remain unchanged. Neither of the kings whom Walpole served as Prime Minister was firmly seated at the centre of political power in the way their predecessors had been. George I and George II were Germans by birth and upbringing, and were on the throne simply because all the heirs with better hereditary claims were disqualified by being Roman Catholics. While they were accustomed to being absolute rulers in Hanover they realized that being King of England was more important than being Elector of Hanover and they spent most of their time in England, but they never felt entirely at ease in the forty-six years during which they ruled in London.

Before 1688 kings had been able to choose their ministers and to wield sufficient power to keep them in office unless the Commons used the exceptional procedure of impeachment to try to prosecute them for political misdemeanours. Between 1688 and 1714 monarchs had changed their ministers fairly frequently but they did not defy changes in public feeling and were always able to gain a majority in Parliament for the man they chose. After 1714 the balance shifted to a point where the King and the Commons had something like mutual vetoes: the King chose the ministers and could normally be sure of not having to put up with a minister he disliked, but the Commons could reject a minister they disliked by refusing to vote for the taxes he proposed, thus pushing the King into dismissing him. The King and his politicians were usually on good enough terms to avoid these extreme steps but as the decades passed the King found he was sharing more of his power with Parliament.

British and French Colonies in North America

Much the same pressures could be seen at work, in a less decorous way, in North America. The colonial assemblies saw themselves as bodies parallel to the House of Commons and they felt they could use their authority over finance to control the royal governors. They voted the local taxes for the governors' salaries which might be as high as £2,000 a year (a hundred times a labourer's wage, and 40 per cent of the Prime Minister's salary), and sometimes they felt governors should earn their salaries by letting the assembly have its own way. The pressure was less intense in the sugar islands, where British garrisons and naval support were visible, but life for a governor on the mainland was difficult and grew harder as memories of the wars against the French became dimmer. Seventeenth-century military men with a habit of authority and experience of command were succeeded by eighteenth-century gentlemen and noblemen whose family connections and political influence in London were less relevant to problems in the colonies.

Judges were as irremoveable in the colonies as in England, but colonial assemblies could apply pressure to them by declining to vote their annual salaries. The governor had other officials whose posts entitled them to sit in his executive council, but although they might have looked like potential ministers the legislative assemblies could not use them to control the governor and, as the governor had no automatic right to dismiss his councillors, he could not use them as his ministers either. A few posts were filled by the vote of the assembly but most office holders were appointed by the government in London. If the Secretary of State had regularly taken the governors' advice about appointments, patronage might have been used to control the assemblies – some governors, notably in Massachusetts, were able to get their own way in their assemblies much more often in wartime and, while this was partly due to patriotism and partly due to fear of the French, it does appear that war contracts could build support in what had not always been promising soil for the governors. But most of the time colonial appointments were made in a way that reflected friendships and pressures in London. Posts in Britain were normally filled in this way, and people in London would have said that appointing officials in the colonies in a different way would have implied that the colonies were not a normal part of the British structure of government. People in America would have replied that the colonial structure of government was different in one important way because the colonists paid the taxes for these official salaries. In Virginia and in the West Indies the assemblies voted a more or less perpetual grant of taxes; in New York and New England there were annual struggles over the revenue.

Because they had no way of driving out of office the men who ran the executive in their colonies, the colonial assemblies could not assert themselves in the same way as the Westminster Parliament, and had to fall back on using the seventeenth-century approach of saying that there should be redress of grievance before taxes were voted to run the government. Even when a governor accepted the assembly's idea of what was a grievance, his instructions from London limited his freedom of action, usually in the interests of uniformity of imperial policy – one problem was that some American colonial assemblies had Scottish rather than English ideas about divorce and the indissolubility of marriage, but the governors were instructed to veto bills allowing divorce, in order to reduce the difficulties foreseen if each different part of the empire had its own laws about marriage. The governors stuck reasonably well to their instructions on this and other matters and, while they did not always understand the new societies in which they were serving, eighteenth-century attacks on their competence were certainly on some occasions political propaganda that colonists were naturally tempted to launch against men who were carrying out the policy of a distant monarch and government.

'Salutary neglect' is a description that fits the colonial policy of the British government in the first half of the eighteenth century, particularly when it is compared with the fairly active government of the late seventeenth century. Governments in Britain in the eighteenth century did not do very much; some of the neglect of the colonies simply paralleled what was happening in the British Isles. But the royal power of veto over the legislation of the colonial assemblies was still active at a time when it was dying out in Britain, and it could be exercised either by governors on the spot or by the government in London. Apart from legislation which might break up the unity of imperial law, some colonial legislation was likely to affect the interests of people in Britain directly. For instance, coin and currency were always in short supply in the colonies and the British government in a mood of less than salutary neglect did nothing about it, so colonies sometimes passed laws to make bills of exchange into legal tender. These bills of exchange almost invariably sank to a discount in terms of sterling, which meant that British merchants exporting to America lost money if they were compelled by colonial legislation to accept them as payment. Even if the government neglected to veto legislation of this sort, the Westminster Parliament could in theory pass laws to repeal colonial legislation, but in practice Parliament did not legislate on issues that could be seen as internal concerns of the colonies and did not go round picking up loose ends left by the governors. It kept the Navigation Acts up to date, but under Walpole's premiership in the 1720s and 1730s it passed so little legislation of any general application even within Britain that it was quite natural for it to do nothing about the colonies.

The growth of the colonies was likely to force new departures in policy and legislation on the British government; the American population rose from about a quarter of a million at the beginning of the century to about two million by 1776. Something under half the increase in population consisted of white immigrants, about equally balanced between free settlers and indentured labourers, with the transported convicts forming a small minority of the total. The population was becoming less markedly English than it had been at the beginning of the century, with a large number of Ulstermen (who felt the operation of the leasehold system was squeezing them out of land they had conquered and settled in Ireland), Scotsmen, and Germans among the settlers. It was a prosperous community: going to America was a big step to take, and one that would not be taken by people with prospects at the top of English society unless they were going out to fill a government post, but for anyone else it was likely to lead to a higher standard of living than could reasonably be expected in Britain. There were no large cities to compare with London, but then London had no rivals in Britain either. New York and Philadelphia were rather like rich country towns. They were several weeks journey from London, but towns like Liverpool or York were several days journey from London, so that the colonists might feel distant but not uniquely isolated from the metropolis, and had closer ties with it than many parts of the English countryside. The colonists had enough newspapers to take any visiting Englishman aback, and were developing industries fast enough to disturb the balance of the integrated commercial system: in 1699 Americans were forbidden to spin woollens for export, even to another colony; in 1732 a similar limitation was placed on the manufacture of hats and caps; and in 1750 the Iron Act allowed them to smelt iron ore into pig iron but forbade them to go any further in processing it, though in the event the American colonies were producing more iron and steel than Britain by 1775. Nobody suggested that the Parliament at Westminster did not have the authority to pass such legislation, perhaps out of a feeling that Britain was paying enough for the defence of America to be entitled to impose a unified industrial policy, possibly more out of a feeling that it would be hard to enforce. When Parliament in 1733 passed the Molasses Act which tried to help planters in the British West Indies by imposing prohibitive duties on New England's imports of sugar, rum, and molasses from non-British colonies, the Act was not properly enforced and Americans came to speak of its having been 'nullified'. North America became more of a market for British manufactures, as part of a triangle of trade that financed increased British imports from the West Indies. In 1740 Britain exported about £0.7m. to North America and about the same amount to the West Indies, but twenty years later the West Indies took £1m. and the mainland took £2m., while imports from the West Indies ran at £1.8m. and from the mainland at £0.6m. Part of the deficit of the mainland colonies with Britain was covered by their exports to the sugar islands, part of it by increased indebtedness to British merchants.

In 1732 a new colony – the fourteenth British colony on the Atlantic seaboard – was set up in Georgia. The philanthropic General Oglethorpe intended it initially as a place where people released from debtors' prison could make a fresh start in life. In practice few debtors went out, but the settlers were helped liberally with private and public funds administered by the charitable trust created to run the colony. The trust ran it for twenty years as something like the proprietors' colonies of the previous century, but in 1752 it became a royal colony. The settlers complained that the trust tried to lay down too many rules about what crops to grow and when to grow them. These complaints may have been justified but the settlers had another dispute with the philanthropists; they agitated to be allowed to own slaves like their neighbours to the north and eventually they were successful. As slaves were to be found in all the American colonies and were an important, though perhaps not a vital, part of the economy of Virginia, Maryland, and the Carolinas, the Georgians were asking only that they should be allowed to do what everyone else did.

The British colonies were steadily filling up the Atlantic seacoast and populating the area fairly densely. The establishment of Georgia completed the process of coastal settlement, and it was close enough to the Spanish colony of Florida to open up a new area of conflict. Military costs were still well under control; the mainland colonies cost only about £20,000 a year, though the West Indies garrisons cost rather more. The French approach to North America had been rather different; they had penetrated to the interior by the two great river systems, the St. Lawrence and the Mississippi, and began developing them as a single communications route linked by the Great Lakes and running through the hinterland west and north of the British settlements. The French were few in numbers, depended on the support and sympathy of their home government, and aroused very little public enthusiasm in France. Two novels of the 1720s point the contrast in public attitudes to the American colonies of the two countries in an odd way: the Abbé Prévost's *Manon Lescaut* and Daniel Defoe's *Moll Flanders* are about prostitutes, both of whom are transported to the new world, but Manon dies from exposure in the arms of her faithful des Grieux after walking six miles from New Orleans, while Moll Flanders settles down with her fifth husband to reckon her net worth in cash and tobacco before returning from Virginia to London. The Abbé's morality may be more edifying, but Defoe's book is the product of a society that saw colonies as attractive and profitable places that people would like to move to (though, of course, pro-emigration literature had appeared ever since the Elizabethan plays *Westward Ho* and *Eastward Ho*).

But while the French did not feel encouraged to emigrate in large numbers, the 50,000 inhabitants of New France moved inland much more boldly than the Abbé Prevost might have made one expect. It is not clear whether this reduced their disadvantages or simply made them more alarming to the British. The Hudson's Bay Company went on trading at its posts on the shore of the Bay, and did rather well for its shareholders, but French fur traders moved out beyond the Great Lakes and by the 1740s La Verendrye had led them to places well west of the Bay. The Hudson's Bay Company would have had to change the way it did business completely if it wanted to convert its coastal settlements to which Indians came to sell their furs into bases from which fur trading parties went into the interior. For the French, who had to go inland to trade in furs at all, pushing on to the west was a matter of development by easy stages. Their enterprising approach brought them profits; the Hudson's Bay Company got 10 beaverskins for a gun at its posts on the Bay, but to the Indians this was the final stage in a complicated pattern of inland trade, so that when the French travelled out to the central hunting areas they were able to save the Indians all the transport and trading costs and could get 30 beaverskins for a gun. This competition made conflicts more likely and meant that in any conflict rival groups of Indians would be involved; those who traded with the French would support them, and their enemies would support the British, so that Indian skirmishing inland played a larger part in the fighting of the 1740s than in previous wars.

In the early eighteenth century the West Indian islands had established their position as the overseas area that meant most to Britain, and had become completely dependent on sugar and on slaves to grow the sugar. On the North American mainland the transportation of convicts meant that there was some non-free white labour to do much of the hardest work in growing rice and tobacco. In the islands almost all white men were part of a rigid structure that turned them into guards and gaolers. The progress of the West Indian colonies was particularly important to Britain because they were so closely linked to her economic development. By the eighteenth century growing sugar and carrying out the first stages of refining it were the main economic activities on the islands. The tariff structure strongly discouraged completing the work of refining the sugar until it reached Britain, and there the increasing flow of sugar transformed people's diet, provided revenue, and launched new industries. Sugar was one of the first imports to be reprocessed and used in new products made in Britain, such as jams or biscuits or sweetened drinks. Honey had been the only sweetener; sugar had been as expensive as cinnamon or cloves and it could be taxed as a luxury in the firm belief that this would not make life harder for the working classes who were not thought to be consumers of sugar, though this was clearly changing in the eighteenth century. By then sugar was fully established as the most important single item imported into Britain. In the seventeenth century it had been an important re-export, which may have irritated planters who would have liked to export directly to the eventual destination. In the eighteenth century British consumption, rising steadily at a bit over 2 per cent a year, was more buoyant than the re-export trade, which made the British preferential tariff more advantageous to the planters.

Another part of the economy was stimulated by the need to provide a labour force to grow this flourishing crop. When the Royal Africa Company collapsed under the weight of its fixed costs, the need for permanent bases on the West African coast — essential if only because half-a-dozen other European countries were setting up forts there — led the government first to try to organize the slave-trading merchants into a loosely organized company which would be responsible for looking after the forts, and then to provide a subsidy to keep them going. Previously the government had argued that the slave trade was so profitable that the traders could pay for their own forts, but by the mid-eighteenth century this attitude had changed to an acceptance of the fact that the trade was so necessary for the sugar islands (and the sugar islands so necessary for the British economy) that the trade would have to be supported if it could not afford to meet these overhead costs. Certainly the slave trade was expanding in the early eighteenth century; more slaves were being bought in Africa than before, and the wars among Africans to provide captives to sell had more of a disturbing effect on the states of West Africa. The planters might have been expected to see that slavery in the West Indies was wastefully debilitating, for the slaves died so fast that new ones had continuously to be brought in.

By degrees the British came to dominate this trade, partly because they were so committed to sugar that they were bound to make large purchases of slaves on their own account, partly because their increasingly dominant position at sea meant that they could take the place of the Dutch as general suppliers of slaves for planters in other European colonies who wanted to buy them. By the middle of the eighteenth century about 70,000 slaves a year were being taken across the Atlantic, half of them in British ships. About half of them went to British colonies, mainly to the sugar islands, and the rest were sold in other colonies in the Americas. Later in the century the number shipped may have risen to as many as 100,000 a year, and the British share of the total certainly became larger. The sugar plantations and the slaves on them were the first British overseas investment of any size, at a time when investment of this sort was unusual, and in several eighteenth-century wars the British fought to defend this property, though it was not a central cause of any of the wars in which they were involved.

After the Treaty of Utrecht Britain remained at peace for a generation, declining to join in the only important continental war of the period, the War of the Polish Succession. Openings for quarrels were bubbling up in several places in the 1730s. Macaulay was attributing rather too much blame to Frederick II of Prussia when he wrote 'in order that he might rob a neighbour whom he had promised to defend, black men fought on the coast of Coromandel, and red men scalped each other by the Great Lakes of North America.'[1] When Frederick attacked the Empress Maria Theresa in 1740 to snatch the province of Silesia from her, Britain and Spain were already at war, and there were two or three areas where France and Britain were likely to clash, though Macaulay was quite right to underline the world-wide dimensions of the struggle.

After its financial disaster in 1720 the South Sea Company had pulled itself together and had tried to trade with South America as though nothing had happened. It was perfectly clear to everyone that the company could carry on enough trade to flourish only if it supplemented its income by bringing in more goods than its treaty permitted, and the smuggling trade became large enough to disturb the Spanish authorities. Their coastguards used fairly brutal methods to discourage it: after intercepting one ship they cut off Captain Jenkin's ear – upon which, he later told a committee of the House of Commons, 'he committed his soul to his God and his cause to his country.' He had plenty of time to prepare this great phrase, for the outrage was said to have happened in 1731 and he was not asked about it until 1738, but the delay led to no awkward questions; by the late 1730s Parliament was growing increasingly annoyed with Spanish interference with British trade, and it was not willing to let Walpole go on with his peaceful policy.

War began with an unsuccessful attempt to return to the city-plundering strategy of the previous century, went on with a great commerce-raiding voyage round the world by Anson, and (not before it had at last ended the trading career of the South Sea Company) was swallowed up by the more far-flung clash of British and French. That struggle was still concerned more with European than with colonial questions. Frederick's aggression disturbed George II's position as Elector of Hanover and, because he tried to defend Maria Theresa's treaty rights and France joined in the attack upon her, Britain found itself at war with France. This side of the war was not especially popular: opponents of the king and of his ministers played on the

[1] T. B. Macaulay, 'Frederic the Great', in *Essays*, (Everyman 1946 edn.), ii. 134.

fact that a good many MPs felt too much money was spent on German commitments. George got financial support from Parliament for troops to defend his Electorate and they did well enough to maintain his position, but he could not establish in office the ministers he really wanted, who would have been committed to full-scale involvement in Germany, so that he had to put up with a government which was not completely devoted to fighting on the continent of Europe.

Outside Europe the struggle in the sugar islands was less destructive than it had been 50 or 60 years earlier. It led to no permanent transfers of territory, though some islands were made neutral at the end of the war, and the half-dozen years after the war ended in 1749 were one of the peaks of eighteenth-century prosperity in the sugar trades. On the American mainland French and British possessions were expanding and reaching the verge of collision. The point of contact between British and French colonies was still on the seacoast, and here the British regular forces and the colonial militia co-operated effectively and captured the fortress of Louisbourg, which the French had fortified at immense cost to command the entrance to the St. Lawrence and hold back the British in Nova Scotia. Nobody wanted to push the struggle any further; nobody in the 1740s imagined that a fight to the death was at hand.

From Commerce to Empire in India

The East India Company might have liked to have been able to take the same detached attitude as the Hudson's Bay Company. Its employees were afraid that the death of the expansionist Moghul Emperor Aurangzeb in 1707 would lead to disorder and disintegration, and events in the next half-century showed they were right. The Company felt very pleased when in 1717 it received an imperial decree giving it a good deal of the territorial autonomy for which its ambitious employees had hoped in the 1680s and, in return for an annual payment of 13,000 rupees, freed it from paying customs duties inside India, but there is no sign that the Company realized that developments of this sort showed the Moghul Empire was beginning to lose control of the country. Power was slipping into the hands of important feudal vassals, and men like the rulers of Hyderabad in the south and of Bengal in the east were emerging with much more power than they had enjoyed in the previous half-century. But they were still respectful to the Emperor; as fellow-Muslims they were part of the group that had dominated India for centuries, and it is unlikely that he was nearly as worried by their attitude as he was by the threat of Persian invasions like the one that led to Delhi being captured and plundered in 1739, or by the rebellious Marathas of western India, Hindu in religion and devoted to cavalry raids to plunder their neighbours. European traders were really no problem; they usually negotiated with his direct vassals or with princes lower in the scale.

This did not satisfy the French. After the collapse of Law's schemes his vast unified company was divided into its component parts again, but it still took some years for the French to recover in India. By the 1730s they were able to be more active. Though they were still doing less than half as much business as the British company, their rate of return on capital was higher. They realized that the loss of power at the imperial centre would allow them to strengthen their position by negotiating with the imperial vassals. In the 1740s the French in India would have been happy enough to ignore the war in Europe and remain neutral, as they had done during earlier European wars, mainly because previous emperors could maintain the peace. The British Company might have agreed to this, but ships of the French and British navies had sailed to the Indian Ocean and could not remain neutral. In 1746 the British squadron withdrew to Calcutta to refit; the French seized their opportunity and captured Madras, the main British settlement in southern India. In the 1748 peace settlement it was returned in exchange for Louisbourg, but nobody in India had any doubt that the French had demonstrated their superiority.

The next year Dupleix, the most dynamic of the Frenchmen in India, made his bid for supremacy in southern India. He made his candidate, Salabat Jang, Nizam of Hyderabad, and he also helped Chanda Sahib to become Nawab of the Carnatic, the region which lay inland from Madras. None of this necessarily involved fighting between French and British, but it came at a time when the British Company was revising its policy of relying on the Moghul Emperor and on the successes of Englishmen outside India to protect its position. It had always had a few troops in its settlements to defend property locally, but even when it had begun building up its own little army it had only about 3,000 men in 1749. When the Company entered the dynastic politics of southern India by putting forward a candidate of its own in the Carnatic, the French were soon able to drive him back to Trichinopoly and beseige him there. The best the Company could do was to send a 25-year old clerk and a force of 500 men off to Arcot, the capital of the Carnatic. The clerk, Robert Clive, was able not only to take Arcot by a surprise attack but also to inspire his little force to hang on to it during a 50-day seige in which a series of onslaughts on the citadel was beaten off. Next year the British candidate gained the throne of the Carnatic; the directors of the French Company decided that Dupleix had been wasting their shareholders' money, and in 1754 they recalled him, which must at the time have struck everybody as a prudent step to keep expenses down. The British Company had shown that it could play an effective role in the rougher sort of Indian politics, but there was no reason to think it would go on doing so. Clive had returned to England with his private profits from his trading and military activities, though he spent his money so fast (largely on an unsuccessful attempt to get into Parliament) that he was soon back in India, serving on

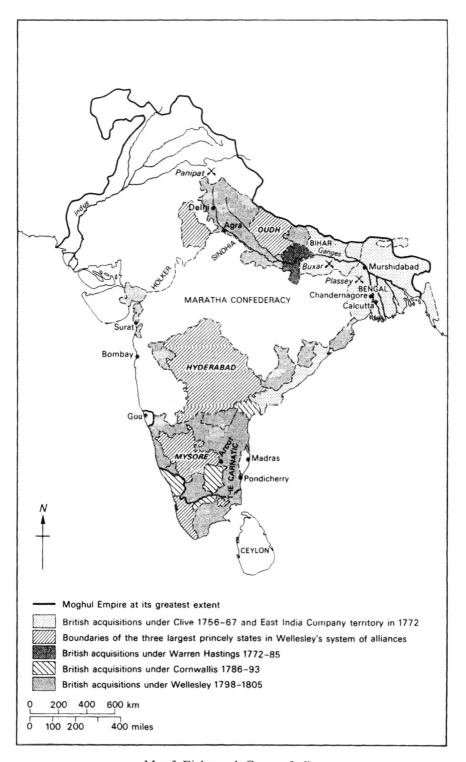

Moghul Empire at its greatest extent

British acquisitions under Clive 1756–67 and East India Company territory in 1772

Boundaries of the three largest princely states in Wellesley's system of alliances

British acquisitions under Warren Hastings 1772–85

British acquisitions under Cornwallis 1786–93

British acquisitions under Wellesley 1798–1805

| 0 | 200 | 400 | 600 km |
| 0 | 100 | 200 | 400 miles |

Map 5 Eighteenth-Century India

what was becoming recognizable as the military side of the Company's concerns.

One of the reasons for Dupleix's failure was simply that he was operating in a region of India where the profits from trade were not large enough to justify or even to support heavy military expenditure. Bengal was the real source of wealth, and Calcutta the centre of its export trade. When Alivardi, the Nawab of Bengal, died in 1756 and was succeeded by his grandson Siraj-ud-Daula, the Bengal scene appeared entirely peaceful. But, within a couple of months of coming to the throne, Siraj-ud-Daula marched on Calcutta, seized and plundered it after a few days of frantic but ill-prepared resistance, and allowed the few British survivors of the seige to be locked up in the prison of the fortress for the night. Because the cell was designed for only half-a-dozen prisoners, perhaps a hundred of the captives died in the night, and in later decades all Englishmen in India remembered the Black Hole of Calcutta as a dreadful atrocity. At the time the Company showed no signs of being intolerably offended; it sent a force under Clive to recover Calcutta, but negotiated amiably enough with Siraj-ud-Daula. He may have felt nervous about having plundered Calcutta or he may have thought he had done enough to show who was master in Bengal, but in any case he withdrew and paid the Company some compensation for its losses.

Clive's next concern was the French base at Chandernagore, a little to the north, and Siraj-ud-Daula allowed him to attack and neutralize it. While the British were doing this, they learnt enough about the political situation in Bengal to realize that in a few months of confused and contradictory policy (of which his aggressive and then conciliatory treatment of the East India Company was only one example) Siraj-ud-Daula had lost the confidence of the Hindu merchants and bankers who ran the financial system and of some of the Muslims who ran the Bengal army. Ten years earlier no Company official would have done much about this, and even in 1757 not many officials would have done the same as Clive: he joined the conspiracy against Siraj-ud-Daula, led his little army of 3,000 men against the Bengal army of 60,000, committed his troops beyond hope of withdrawal by crossing the Hughli (the lesser Ganges), and on 23 June 1757 held them steady at the battle of Plassey. His fellow-conspirators took no part in the fighting, and Siraj-ud-Daula's army disintegrated in the face of the determination of the Company's army. Siraj-ud-Daula could not have been defeated – if that is the word for the collapse of his army – and destroyed if he had not alienated his subjects by being unreliable and vacillating, without any signs of charm or kindness to make up for it, but the decisive fact was that the British had fought him, while his subjects had only deserted him and waited to see who would win.

Mir Jafar, who was made Nawab, had an adequate claim to the throne and might have been a good ruler under other circumstances, but it was quite clear that he was on the throne simply because the Company had decided to put him there. Anyone who became Nawab expected to be rich, and took it for granted that he should reward those who had helped him to the throne. Mir Jafar's generosity completely transformed the process by which the Company's employees conducted a certain amount of private business to supplement the Company's meagre retaining fee and enjoy a satisfactory income. The most ambitious of them could see that the largest gains were to be made in politics, and to politics they turned. Clive's estimate was that the Company and various private individuals made £3m. out of the change of rulers. He had been prosperous after the seige of Arcot; after Plassey the new Nawab gave him £234,000 in cash and the right to land rents of £27,000 a year, which made him as rich as a great territorial magnate like the Duke of Newcastle. Sixteen years later Clive was asked by a House of Commons committee about the way this had happened. He responded by explaining to the chairman of the committee, the fashionable playwright and military man John Burgoyne, how he had entered Murshidabad the capital of Bengal as a conqueror and how bankers and jewellers had rushed forward to thrust presents on him; and, he concluded, as he thought back to the moment of triumph, 'By God, Mr. Chairman, I stand amazed at my own moderation.' Clive returned to England almost immediately to go into Parliament and keep an eye on East India Company policy in London, but his followers – whose idea of moderation ran on much the same lavish lines remained in control of Bengal. If one man would pay generously to become Nawab, then so would another, and the atraction of gifts paid out upon a change of ruler led to the deposition of three Nawabs in rapid succession, which reduced the position to one which was obviously that of a puppet of the Company. The French in South India were eliminated as a political power in the 1760 and 1761 campaigns; the Moghul emperors were in no position to do anything about the rise of British power because, just a few months before the battle of Plassey, an Afghan army had marched south-east and plundered Delhi again. So, partly because of Siraj-ud-Daula's incompetence and partly because of the eagerness of the Company employees to supplement their incomes by plunging into Indian politics, the British began to move inland.

The Triumph of William Pitt

For quite different reasons settlers were also beginning to move inland in America. They were no longer so ready to see themselves as isolated settlements on the sea coast, unrelated to each other and uninterested in the interior. At the beginning of the 1750s very few Englishmen in America had pushed even as far inland as the East India Company had done when it founded its port up the Hughli river at Calcutta. George Washington, a Virginia gentleman whose home at Mount Vernon was quite close to the salt water of Chesapeake Bay, could ride off to the frontier with no difficulty and acquire land to sell to future settlers. The significant difference was that by the 1750s this speculation in land looked like making good sense. Washington had first seen the attractions of open land when working as a surveyor along a line running north-west to the Ohio valley and Lake Erie, and he could reckon that his survey was not going to remain as a simple tribute to the government's desire for information. If Englishmen in America were to push on to the west, it was fairly predictable that there would be clashes with the thinly scattered Indian population, and it was quite certain that if they went far enough either west or north they would meet the French.

In 1754 the Board of Trade ordered representatives of the mainland colonies to meet at Albany. A Philadelphia intellectual, Benjamin Franklin, back in his native land after a prolonged and enjoyable period in England, put down a statement of the need for political union which the conference accepted, but the colonial assemblies then rejected this plan for common defence, probably because it would have involved a good deal of extra spending. The failure of the conference underlined the absence of any instititions for co-ordinating policy on the western side of the Atlantic. The governors wrote to the Secretary of State in London, but as he was also responsible for a wide range of Irish, domestic, and foreign concerns allotted to the Southern Department, they could not feel sure of prompt attention. Other officials communicated with the Board of Trade whose President, Lord Halifax, managed during his dozen years in office after 1748 to make the department rather more effective than usual. Franklin placed his own hopes on the idea that the Westminster Parliament would pass legislation to set up a union.

Despite this absence of co-ordination the British government was eager to move against the French and make sure they could not endanger the American colonies. As part of the process of organizing Nova Scotia as a colony more seriously than before, the Acadians were pressed to take the oath of allegiance to George II in accordance with the Treaty of Utrecht, and those who refused were deported to the French settlement in Louisiana. After the failure of the 1754 conference Braddock had been appointed to the newly-created post of commander-in-chief in America, and he rapidly put together a force which marched north-west through the area Washington had been surveying towards Fort Duquesne, just to the south of Lake Erie. His force was ambushed a little short of its objective and he was killed by the French and their Indian allies. Washington, who survived the defeat, must have noted the possibilities for irregular warfare. Closer to Europe the British set up a blockade of Brest, a step which took them a long way towards war with France, and began looking for allies to protect Hanover against France in the event of a continental war. First they arranged an alliance with Russia and then, at the beginning of 1756, an alliance with Prussia. As

France made her preparations for war, it was relatively simple for her to make an alliance with Austria against Prussia and it also turned out to be surprisingly easy to draw Russia into this alliance. By the middle of 1756 Britain's conflicts with France outside Europe had turned quite unexpectedly into a war in which the three major powers of Europe were allied against Frederick of Prussia and so were preparing to attack George's Electorate of Hanover.

The British felt very confident of their position at sea; to reinforce the strength of their blockage they laid down unilaterally the rule of 1756 that neutrals could not take advantage of wartime conditions to enter upon trade that would not have been allowed in peacetime. But in fact they were so ill prepared that they lost their naval base of Minorca and seemed unable to organize any effective counter-measures. The Duke of Newcastle, an amiable obliging man whose sense of duty and failure to perceive his own inadequacies had led him to become Prime Minister in the last months of peace and to preside over the move to war, was now very well aware that things were falling apart. Pitt, who had led the attacks on a policy of commitment to Hanover during the war of the Austrian Succession, returned to the same line of denunciation. Newcastle still enjoyed the King's approval and still had a majority in the Commons, but he resigned because he realized that nobody could provide an adequate answer to Pitt's attacks.

This was not a period in which the British suffered defeats gladly, however much their lack of preparation in peacetime might seem to invite them. It was the great age of patriotic songs: 'Rule Britannia' was written in 1740 and 'God Save the King' was first published in 1742 and gained in popularity during the Jacobite rebellion of 1745. Lord Chesterfield, when discussing 'useful prejudices . . . which I should be very sorry to see removed' a little after the previous war, had declared that 'that silly, sanguine notion, which is firmly entertained here, that one Englishman can beat three Frenchmen, encourages and has sometimes enabled one Englishman in reality to beat two.'[2] People were very angry when Admiral Byng failed to attack the French at Minorca, and the decision to execute him for cowardice was exactly what the public wanted. Voltaire wrote satirically about the British arranging to shoot an admiral to encourage the others, but probably most Englishmen at the time would have taken the idea seriously.

So it was not surprising that George found that nobody would accept the dangerously exposed position of Prime Minister and that Pitt was indispensable even though he had no majority in the Commons. His first ministry was brief, but when his government was defeated it was clear that nobody could take his place: for three months George II had to run the administration without any parliamentary ministers – an operation that was not as

---

[2] *Lord Chesterfield's Letters*, ed. J. Bradshaw (1892 edn.), i. 195.

impossible as it would have been seventy years later, though not nearly as normal as it would have been seventy years earlier. During this period of political vacuum public opinion – or at the very least commercial opinion – made it clear that Pitt was indispensable. So many cities enrolled him as a freeman, usually by giving him a scroll of membership in a gold box, that Horace Walpole summed up his popularity in the phrase 'For some weeks it rained gold boxes', and the more prosaic Duke of Newcastle recognized that no government could survive if Pitt opposed it.

A coalition was formed in June 1757 in which Pitt ran the war, and justified his claim 'I know that I can save this country, and I know that no other man can', while the Duke of Newcastle made sure that the majority in the House of Commons realized that their business was to vote money for Pitt's military operations without too much fuss. Relatively little could be done for the first year or two; Pitt had a view of the war that stretched over the whole world, but it took some time to prepare the resources to give effect to this vision. In America the distances to be covered were so large that they were the major obstacle to effective operations. The colonies were encouraged to co-operate as actively as possible with British forces by promises of payments to cover the military costs, apart from clothing and pay, of any forces they could raise to support troops sent from Britain. On this basis the colonies spent about £3m. of which about £1.25m. was later refunded. In 1758 an expedition following a more northerly route than the one taken by Braddock was able to capture Fort Duquesne, which was renamed Pittsburgh by grateful Pennsylvanians who felt that at last a British politician had emerged who understood American needs. Louisburg was captured again, and by the beginning of 1759 British forces could close in upon the centre of New France in the St. Lawrence valley.

Earlier expeditions, in the wars against Louis XIV, had twice failed to make any progress up the narrow estuary of the St. Lawrence; the new expedition under Wolfe sailed up the river and established itself outside Quebec, the capital of New France: British troops took up positions east of the city and also on the south side of the river, but there was no attempt at a seige and the routes north and west of the city remained open. The British sailed up and down the river, trying to find an opening to land troops to the west of the city, and in September they were successful. Wolfe led his troops up the cliffs on to the Plains of Abraham which commanded Quebec from the west, and so there emerged the unusual sight of infantry lined up in the formal European manner on North American soil. Three sharp volleys and the French lines were broken. Wolfe and his opponent Montcalm were mortally wounded in the small-scale encounter of a few thousand men which affected the history of North America as decisively as Plassey affected the history of India. Fighting went on in New France for another twelve months, but after the fall of Quebec this was more a matter of moving forces over long distances than of confronting threats that the French might retrieve their position.

Their prospects were hopeless because the British had developed a command of the sea that was much more effective than anything seen in earlier wars. Between 1692 and 1747 the British had defeated the French at sea a number of times, but these battles could not eliminate the possibility that the French fleet would come out of port at a time of its own choosing and assist attacks on British colonies or an invasion of the British Isles. There had been invasions by descendants of the deposed Stuarts in 1715 and in 1745 and, though neither had been successful, both of them had been rather alarming. In 1759 the French were known to be preparing an invasion of Scotland in which French forces would sail and rouse any remaining Stuart rebels. The British response was to blockade the main French fleet in Brest, and all through the summer the Channel Fleet under Hawke stayed at sea waiting for the French to come out. In the end they did come out, were pursued to the south-east down the coast of Brittany, and eventually were overtaken in Quiberon Bay. The action that followed was one of the most bizarre that sailing-ships ever fought, for it took place in a November gale that might well have put the whole of both fleets on to the rocks, but it was a complete defeat for the French who lost nine ships while the British lost only two.

However important this battle might be for future power at sea, the decisive point for the current war had been that the blockade made it impossible for the French to reinforce their West Indian or North American possessions. They lost Guadeloupe, one of the most fertile of all the sugar islands, as well as seeing New France cut off hopelessly from the sea. Pitt was almost the only British politician ever to think that acquiring colonial possessions was the main purpose of European war; by 1759 he had reached a position where he could carry out his objective almost at will.

The war in Germany still went on. George II welcomed victories in India or America, but the safety of his family possessions in Hanover came first in his mind, and Pitt had to pay attention to this problem. He had taken his first steps forward in English politics by denouncing the emphasis on German politics; he was able to shift to a position the King found acceptable by adopting the policy he later described by saying 'America was conquered in Germany', and this approach suited Britain's position very well. As long as war went on in Europe the French would have to make it their main area of activity and could not concentrate on colonial or naval war. So far as Pitt was concerned, America came first, but he was as delighted as anyone when the English force protecting Hanover won a distinct success against France at Minden, which might have been decisive if Lord George Sackville had not disobeyed an order to charge in a way that exposed him to conspicuous, though not permanent, disgrace. The King of Prussia kept up a desperate defensive campaign against his other main enemies, Austria and Russia;

Britain contributed to this struggle not only by keeping up the army for the defence of Hanover and western Germany but also by supplying money, first as loans and then about £3m. in grants, to keep the Prussian army going. At a time when most German princes had small armies they would supply on a cash basis to the highest bidder who was not actually attacking them himself, the British subsidies to Frederick had a very direct effect in keeping the German campaign going and making sure that France was tied to the continent of Europe.

In 1759 Garrick had delighted London audiences by celebrating Quiberon Bay with his song 'Heart of Oak', and its lines 'Tis to glory we steer, To add something new to this wonderful year' fitted the mood of a steady succession of triumphs very well. But in 1760 George II died, and his grandson George III had a dispute with his ministers about the King's Speech to Parliament which revealed a new attitude. The King could say whatever he chose in the speech as long as he could find ministers to support it, and George wanted to say 'this bloody and expensive war'. His ministers persuaded him to say 'this expensive but just and necessary war', but even this was enough to show his feelings. The war's momentum was too great for George to stop it quickly, but when he said in his speech 'I glory in the name of Briton' he was stressing the fact that, unlike George I and George II, he had been born and brought up in Britain, possessed an overseas empire to be proud of, and saw no need to pay particular attention to the problems of Hanover. The kings of England continued to be rulers of Hanover for another seventy years, until the crowns were divided upon the accession of Queen Victoria because only men could rule in Hanover, but after 1760 the interests of Hanover were never of such importance in deciding British policy.

The new King brought a Scottish peer, Lord Bute, into the cabinet; he had a high opinion of Bute as a political thinker, and was willing to see Scottish opinion conciliated. Considering the fears of Jacobite invasion there was something to be said for such a policy but it was not popular, especially in London, which had become the centre of support for Pitt and the war. George and Bute set out to press for a policy of peace and lower taxes, which recognized the great strain the economy had been asked to bear. Pitt thought of new campaigns; he knew Spain was thinking of entering the war on the French side, and he prepared an expedition against Cuba and another against the Philippines. But cabinet pressure left him almost isolated and in 1761 he resigned. The way was now open for peace negotiations with France, and these negotiations inevitably looked rather like the negotiations which had ended the wars against Louis XIV in 1713 – sensible enough at a time of high expenditure but not fair to allies nor likely to allow the British negotiators to gain the largest possible amount at the bargaining table. Even so, the Peace of Paris of 1763 was bound to produce an immense number of acquisitions of territory for Britain. There was some slight discussion whether the British should keep Canada or should choose the large French sugar islands like Martinique and Guadeloupe; very few politicians close to the centre of power thought of giving Canada back to France, but the issue underlined the fact that Canada was unlikely to provide much revenue for the British treasury directly, and certainly would not provide the amount of revenue that sugar for re-export would give at a time when Britain used for consumption or for manufacture all that her West Indian islands could produce.

Canada was valued because it would bring peace and security to the American colonies and would allow them to continue to increase their imports of British goods in a much more tranquil continent. The French had to give up New France, surrendering the St. Lawrence valley and the east side of the Mississippi (except for a small area around New Orleans) to the British, and transfer to the Spanish what was left, so the Spanish empire in North America took a long step forward to the north-east from its base in Texas and New Mexico. But the Spanish paid a price in the peace settlement for entering the war on the French side. They entered so late that Pitt had had plenty of time to prepare to attack them, and his expeditions captured Havana and Manila; as a result Britain took the Spanish colony of Florida, an area with a loosely defined western frontier lying somewhere a little east of New Orleans. The British also took the small sugar islands of Tobago, Granada, Dominica, and St. Vincent in the Windward Islands at the southern end of the chain of the Lesser Antilles. In a way this was a compromise between the people in Britain who wanted more sugar and the established planters in the West Indies who would find the additional competition of new sugar colonies entirely unwelcome. The French, who kept the three fertile and relatively large islands of Martinique, Guadeloupe, and St. Domingue produced about as much sugar as the British did from their ten islands, where the soil was showing signs of becoming exhausted.

The Peace of Paris left France and Spain ready to look for revenge, and Britain's hasty departure from the war left Frederick feeling betrayed, so that Britain was quite likely to be involved in another war soon, and a war for which it would be hard to find allies. But this was a problem for the future; a more immediate problem was likely to arise because Britain was acquiring a new type of colony. Englishmen had been settling overseas for a century and a half but their colonies had been inhabited by people who, apart from the slaves who got no choice in the matter, had no particular difficulty in committing themselves to being loyal to King George: Englishmen, Scotsmen, Irishmen, or Germans would accept the King without question, and the Dutch of New York and the Acadians of Nova Scotia were almost the only people who had ever been asked to make a serious change of allegiance, which had been harder for the Acadians because of religious differences. But Bengal and New France were territories in which large numbers of people – in Bengal, perhaps 26 million people, or two to three times as many people as in all of George II's domain – were being asked to transfer their allegiance. Obviously a transfer of allegiance in the feudal way was much less of a strain than the submergence of a national spirit, and there was a great difference between the national spirit of Englishmen and the allegiance to the King of France or to the Great Moghul felt by the inhabitants of New France and of Bengal; if the inhabitants of Bengal had felt that they were citizens of the nation of Bengal it would hardly have been possible for them to change to feeling they were Englishmen, but for them to feel that they used to owe allegiance to the Nawab of Bengal and now owed it to the British businessmen who had conquered the Nawab was not such a difficult transition.

The English had not been acquiring new subjects in the first century and a half of their overseas expansion; for the next century and a half they acquired new subjects at a rate which would have been quite inconceivable if they had been dealing with men and women who thought about their political rights and obligations in terms of nationalism. But the process is not so hard to understand once it is remembered that nationalism is a political emotion that was not often felt before the old feudal leaders of countries outside Europe had been conquered and replaced by Europeans. The Spanish in South America had of course embarked on this course long before the British; the changes of 1757–63 mark the point at which the British moved on an appreciable scale into the imperial activity of gaining new subjects in the process of expansion. Gaining territory by right of conquest was an entirely acceptable way to expand an empire, but it remained to be seen if anyone had worked out any better methods than those of the Spanish for ruling the new subjects acquired in that way.

4. *War and Survival, 1763–1791*

When the Seven Years war came to its triumphant but controversy-stained end, the government was left to reckon its gains and count the cost. After forcing a slightly reluctant Parliament to accept the peace terms, Lord Bute retired, partly because he thought the London mob would lynch him. The danger to him was not just that the peace terms were unpopular in London but also that Scotsmen, of whom he was obviously the most conspicuous, were hated. This sentiment was focused and encouraged by John Wilkes, a politician who realized that people were growing more ready to respond to a call for liberty on several issues connected with the freedom of the press and the responsibility of MPs to their constituents. In an ill-formulated way he appealed to the emerging feeling in Britain and in America that the state ought to avoid making life difficult for its subjects and that subjects ought to be free to express their opinion about government policy and even to have some effect on what governments did. Wilkes was too disreputable to become a political leader, but he said a good many things for which there was a growing audience; in the early 1760s he struggled against the government's wide-ranging police powers, in the late 1760s he defended the right of constituencies to choose MPs whom the House of Commons found obnoxious, in the early 1770s he asserted the right of the press to report parliamentary debates, and later on he warned the British government that it was treating its American subjects most unwisely. George III would have been better suited to the rather more strictly controlled world of the early eighteenth or early nineteenth centuries: Wilkes fitted his own relaxed and libertarian age of sentiments and ideals, and George detested him.

The war had left the British government with imperial problems: an attitude of salutary neglect could not be applied to the recently conquered population of New France, would lead to serious trouble if adopted by the East India Company and its subjects in Bengal, and was much less likely to be maintained in the existing American colonies than it had been previously. It took almost thirty years before the government could feel it had worked out satisfactory forms of government for the British possessions in India and in Canada, and by the time the legislation of 1785 and 1791 had been passed the problems of the thirteen colonies on the Atlantic seacoast had led to rebellion, war, and American independence. Trying to find a tighter framework for imperial administration and trying to make the colonies provide direct contributions to the British exchequer were very natural steps to take, but they were undertaken in a way that led directly to conflict. Hindsight makes the American War of Independence look like a vast and decisive transformation, while the reorganization in India and Canada looks like a normal part of the process of absorbing new territory after the Seven Years War; at the time the British government was likely to think the three areas of activity presented problems that had to be handled at much the same pace, and in the event sensible arrangements for India and for Canada in the early 1770s had unexpected and provocative effects on the American colonies which demonstrated that the empire was more of a unity, and more difficult to manage, than had been realized. By 1791 the more libertarian aspects of the struggle against the existing form of government, for which Wilkes was so good a symbol, were passing beyond their peak; interventionism carried a message about duty as well and, as the government came to intervene more often, it did so with more of a sense of mission than it had possessed in the early eighteenth century. In 1763 the British had taken territories by right of conquest; by 1791 they were ruling their territories on the basis of a moral conviction that they were better than other rulers. Perhaps the change can be seen in Cowper's lines:

> Regions Caesar never knew
> Thy posterity shall sway
> . . . . . .
> Empire is on us bestowed.[1]

The Emergence of the American Question

If not a sense of mission, then certainly a sense of serious-mindedness had been brought into British politics immediately after Bute's resignation. His successor, George Grenville, was more worried by the war debts than exhilarated by the prospects for trade and expansion. Some people had clearly done well out of the war: the East India Company employees were making a great deal of money for themselves in Bengal, and the inhabitants of the British colonies in North America were free from the fear of French attack that had worried them for so long, so in both places the desire to move inland that had been seen in the 1750s could be given full expression. But the ordinary subjects of George III got practically nothing from the East India Company, and had to pay taxes for the National Debt and for keeping troops in the newly conquered territories. The debt had risen to twice what it was before the war, or about £150m., which was about the same size as the national income at the time, and the interest was about £4.7 m. About £10m. a year seemed to be needed to pay it and meet the other expenses of government, which would mean keeping taxes at something close to the

---

[1] These lines from 'Boadicea' were written in 1780, when the position of the empire might have raised doubts even in Olney.

level they had reached during the war. Grenville was far from pleased when his rhetorical question to the Commons, 'Tell me where money is to be found, tell me where money is to be found' led Pitt to sing the line 'Gentle shepherd, tell me where' from a popular song of the day, with the result that he became known as 'the gentle shepherd', but this did nothing to reduce the financial difficulties.

In America the end of the war brought an entirely new set of problems. Apart from the removal of the French threat, which may have made some colonists think British protection was needed less than in the past, the conquest of New France convinced every colonist who wanted to settle on new land, or wanted to speculate in new land, that it was time to press forward into the region between the Alleghenies and the Mississippi that had been taken from the French. The government saw in this westward expansion the seeds of a war with the Indians for which the British taxpayer would have to make a large contribution; a war with the Cherokees in South Carolina was just over, the first signs of an Indian rising to the west of Maryland and Pennsylvania organized by Pontiac were appearing, and in May 1763 it broke out. As part of its administrative arrangements for the new territories, and also as a step to reassure the Indians, the government drew a Proclamation Line along the Alleghenies and forbade Americans to move west of it. This was not popular, even though Pontiac's rebellion could be suppressed only by British forces. The colonies were not able to unite for defence, and certainly were not able to raise the amounts of money needed for one of the most serious of all the wars against the Indians. By 1764 the total cost of administering the colonies was about £350,000 a year, of which two-thirds was spent on providing a defence system against the Indians that the Americans considered over-elaborate.

Grenville decided that things were too serious to let Pitt's ridicule put him off: he kept taxes in Britain at a level that provoked constant demands for tax reductions, and he decided to extend part of the British taxation system to the North American and West Indian colonies by making them pay stamp duties. In Britain a fee had to be paid to the government for any legal document or business contract, or for printing a wide range of things from newspapers to playing cards, or for receiving a diploma or licence to run a business, and the paper was then stamped to show that the appropriate tax had been paid. This produced about £¼m. a year, and Grenville wanted to set up the same system in the colonies, where he reckoned it would yield a bit more than £50,000 a year. These taxes were a natural part of the way governments kept going and had the effect of obtaining revenue from the upper and middle classes. Preliminary enquiries suggested that they would not provoke much more than the grumbling that greets any new tax.

But the old-established British colonies on the North American seacoast were not easy communities to tax. They did not expect much from any level of government and they paid for very little. Because they spent nothing on a regular army or navy, and not much on their local militias, they paid less than £100,000 a year in taxes, while the population of Britain – only three or four times as large – paid about a hundred times as much. Seen from the British side, Grenville's stamp duties were a long overdue attempt to share the burdens of the wars against France and of defence against the Indians a little more evenly over the people of the Empire; seen from the American side, they meant that taxes were to go up by about 50 per cent without giving the Americans any chance to vote on whether to accept the new taxes or not. Americans accepted that the British Parliament had some financial authority over them, but in the 1760s they argued that what it possessed was the right to regulate the trade of the Empire as a whole by measures like the Navigation Acts and that taxes intended simply to produce revenue could be imposed only by the assemblies of the colonies themselves. Of course the colonial assemblies were most unlikely to vote an increase of taxes on the scale Grenville wanted, but was also true that they had never been asked to vote money for general imperial revenue in the past.

Grenville had been trying to make the Navigation Acts more effective, and to collect more revenue by doing so. To stop the smuggling trade between New England and the non-British sugar islands of the West Indies, he reduced the import duties by a new Molasses Act and made arrangements for the lower duties to be collected properly. This caused some irritation which was made worse by the fact that the regulations were applied by Admiralty Courts sitting without juries, but the government was able to make the changes effective and increased its revenue by about £50,000 a year as a result. On the other hand, the response to the stamp duties showed that the British government was virtually powerless when American opinion was united against its policy. Grenville did not have to face the problem: he introduced the stamp duties in March 1765 and then was pushed out of office in July because he drew up a Regency Bill in terms that offended the King.

Resistance to paying the new taxes or to using paper bearing the official stamp began in Virginia and spread quickly to Massachusetts, where officials soon had to give up trying to impose the use of the stamps and in some cases had their houses burnt. The other old colonies in North America then followed this lead, and a period of rioting and disorder from August to October showed how completely the British government had failed to master the American situation. Resistance may have begun because the Virginia tobacco planters, who depended on selling their crop to the British market, were heavily in debt to British merchants: resolute men like George Washington freed themselves from this by getting out of tobacco growing, but less conscientious planters, who owed over £2m. in London by the 1770s, sometimes behaved as if they thought a quarrel with Britain would justify repudiating these private debts by an even more direct method than thrusting depreciating bills of exchange upon their creditors. People in Massachusetts and in the rest of New England were afraid that the British government wanted to give the Church of England the same privileged position in North America that it enjoyed in England. So there were individual and local discontents in the background, but taxation imposed without the consent of the local assemblies of the colonies was the great issue which united Americans against the British government.

Until the resistance to the Stamp Act the colonies were not in any sense united: they occupied an unbroken stretch of the Atlantic seacoast but they called themselves Americans more as a geographical description than as an assertion of common political purpose. The assemblies of the colonies dealt directly with the British government in the Seven Years War, and had very little contact with one another; they had no organization through which they could work together, and no government department in Britain had the authority to co-ordinate policy towards America. The Stamp Act crisis changed all this: in October 1765 representatives of thirteen colonies from Georgia to New Hampshire met in New York and discussed the problems they faced in their relations with the British government. Resistance to the stamps became better organized, and plans were laid for a general boycott of imports from Britain.

The government led by the Marquis of Rockingham which had replaced Grenville's ministry was made up of people who had not been at all enthusiastic about the introduction of the stamp duties, and they began to look round for lines of retreat that would not look too humiliating or make the King feel he was giving up too much of his authority. In March 1766 the taxes were abolished, but a Declaratory Act passed at the same time stated that Parliament had the authority to pass any legislation that it thought appropriate for any part of the Empire; the colonists' doctrine that it had no right to impose taxes except to regulate trade was to be rejected. In practice the restrictions on trade imposed by the Navigation Acts formed no part of the later arguments, and were accepted by the Americans until fighting began. Franklin was living in England at the time and when he was consulted in the weeks before the repeal of the Stamp Act he upheld the view that Parliament could impose taxes to regulate trade upon the colonies but could not impose other taxes. By 1768 he was moving towards the opinion that it was very odd to say that Parliament could pass laws and could impose some taxes but could not impose others, and from this he concluded that Parliament could not pass laws for the colonies at all, which expressed the feelings of a good many other Americans.

While a return to the peace and quiet of the 1750s seemed to be the best that could be hoped for in America, the news from India in 1766 suggested that there a difficult situation had been put right in a way that promised relief for the taxpayer. The East India Company had become the dominant force

in Bengal politics after the defeat and overthrow of Siraj-ud-Daula but, as
Pitt would have nothing to do with Clive's radical suggestion that the British
government should take over the new territory, nominal power in Bengal
was left in the hands of the Nawab. Besides forcing the newly-established
Nawab to reward generously the men who had put him on the throne,
Company employees pushed to the limit the Company's exemption from
taxes on internal trade granted in 1717: the exemption was intended for the
Company, but employees insisted that it applied to their private transactions, and they allowed Indian traders to claim (if they paid enough) that
they were acting as agents for tax-exempt Company employees. As individuals these Company employees were in the same position as the Persians
or the Afghans who captured and plundered Delhi; they had conquered
Bengal and they wanted to take their loot home. In the eight or ten years
after Plassey dozens of men came back from Bengal to enjoy the profits of
political intrigue or tax-exempt trading. Although these 'nabobs' (from
Nawab) were regarded as coarse, vulgar, and likely to drive up the prices of
all luxuries from plovers' eggs to seats in the House of Commons, they could
have been tolerated easily enough if their sudden wealth had been the only
problem. But, unlike the Persians, the Company stayed on in India and once
it was seen that the employees' determination to build fortunes for themselves had led them to neglect the interests of the Company, politicians and
shareholders took the problem more seriously. The Nawab found it intolerable; he tried to reduce the Company's trading advantage by removing the
taxes on local trade and, when the Company objected partly because of the
damage to state revenue but mainly because the employees wanted to keep
their privileged trading profits, he made an alliance with the King of Oudh
and the Moghul Emperor to drive the Company out. The allied armies were
defeated by the Company at Buxar in 1764, a much harder-fought battle
than Plassey, in which the British won a second military triumph which
provided further plunder for the men on the spot but did not restore the
Company's finances. Large shareholders found some compensation for this
by securing appointments to potentially lucrative jobs in India for their
friends and relations; the others worried about their dividends.

Clive, who had been losing ground in the Company, was now able to
reassert himself and win the support of the shareholders with a programme
for ending corruption and indiscipline in India. In a final tour of duty in India
from 1765 to 1767 he made some progress with this policy: the Company
clarified the political position by pushing the Nawab into obscurity on a
pension of £400,000 a year and taking over responsibility for running
Bengal, while making annual payments of another £300,000 a year to the
Moghul Emperor; accepting presents for political services was forbidden;
and the senior officials of the Company in India were given shares in a
trading subsidiary run for their benefit so that they should not be distracted

from their work by dealing on their own account. The general problem of private trading was not overcome, because the Company would not pay its employees large enough salaries to let them live comfortably without it, but at least Clive's reforms ought to have meant that the political position of the Company would not suffer because senior officials were neglecting their duty in order to make money.

Change was swift, miraculous, and too good to be true. In 1766 the dividend was raised from 6 to 10 per cent, a level not exceeded until the 1793 charter guaranteed shareholders 10½ per cent, which remained the rate until the dissolution of the Company. Those who, like Clive, had invested in Company shares found their faith very well rewarded. This did nothing for the government: the Company paid very little to the exchequer and yet its successes had been to some extent due to the support of the navy in the Indian Ocean and to more general support provided by the government. The Company paid for royal soldiers when it employed them, its imports paid the same duties as any other legal imports, and there was the long-standing loan of £4.2m. which provided the government with money at slightly below market rates, but the 1766 profit suggested that the Company could make a larger contribution to national revenue. Most of the prospective profit was in any case going to come from the surplus made out of governing Bengal. When Clive suggested that the British government should take over Bengal he had predicted that tax revenues and rents would exceed government expenses by about £2m. a year, and the 1766 figures suggested that his estimate was roughly correct.

By the time Clive returned to England, prostrated by the nervous strain of imposing his reforms on recalcitrant Company officials, the directors in London had agreed to pay £400,000 a year to the government. This sort of annual licence fee was understandable enough in the days before there was a tax on company profits, but it did mean that the Company had to pay the money every year whether there were any profits or not. The 1766 revenue figures were based on a year when Clive's reforms had been cutting costs, and when there were no wars to pay for. In the south, which had been peaceful for a dozen years, Haidar Ali had been building up his power in Mysore and in 1768 he began the series of wars against the British position in Madras which broke out from time to time over the next thirty years. Bengal was safe from external attack after the Emperor had been defeated at Buxar and the Afghans had defeated the Marathas at Panipat in 1761, but from 1768 to 1770 it was devastated by famine which caused hundreds of thousands of deaths and also weakened the Company's financial base. So the government got very little from the Company, and in any case Company payments would not have solved the government's problems.

Lord Rockingham was forced out of the Premiership in July 1766, only four months after repealing the Stamp Act. The King turned to Pitt and persuaded him to return to office. Because his health was weak Pitt decided to run the government from the House of Lords, taking the title of Earl of Chatham. This was a mistake: Pitt's power had depended on his ability to dominate the Commons and on the public belief that he stood for the people rather than the king; taking a title looked like accepting royal favour, and ruling the House of Commons from the Lords was very difficult. Rockingham had not been able to manage it, even though he had a political group behind him which was distinctly more cohesive and better organized than the usual groups; Chatham explicitly said he did not rely on party discipline, and soon he found that this led to no discipline at all. His health collapsed, and for most of 1767 and 1768 the government had no unified policy and no effective leader. A Secretary of State for American affairs was appointed who combined the administrative responsibilities of the Board of Trade with the political authority of the Secretary of State for Southern Affairs, but he was not able to repair the damage caused to relations with America by impatient backbenchers and the irresponsible Chancellor of the Exchequer.

The backbenchers wanted the land tax reduced to 15 per cent from 20 per cent, which they regarded as a wartime rate, and they forced the government to accept this. The Chancellor of the Exchequer, Charles Townshend, had said he would make the Americans pay taxes, and the loss of revenue from the land tax forced him to justify his boast. He decided to take the Americans at their word and exploit their statement that Parliament could impose customs duties to regulate trade even though it could not levy taxes inside the colonies. Taking this literally he placed import duties on glass, paper, paint, lead, and tea going into the American colonies. Fairly clearly the Americans had meant that they would accept legislation like the Navigation Acts if it was intended to produce a unified system of trade and development within the empire, but Townshend's duties made no attempt to do this. The circumstances in which they were introduced made it clear that they were intended to produce revenue to cover British expenses in America, and it seemed very likely that he wanted to use the money to make the salaries of governors and their officials independent of the colonial assemblies.

The duties aroused something like the same sort of resistance as the Stamp Act, with customs officers being tarred and feathered, coastguard cutters seized and burnt, and very little revenue being raised. But, because they were indirect taxes, Americans did not meet them with quite such a unified protest as they had met the stamp duties with and, because the British government was paralysed by Chatham's illness, it could not change its position in the face of the American response. Opposition grew; in September 1768 the Boston town meeting passed a resolution which came very close to a small-scale declaration of independence, and in the following eight or nine months most of the colonial assemblies quarrelled with their governors and were dissolved. Public opinion in most colonies by this stage accepted

Dickinson's argument that Parliament could not impose taxes, though it could use the Navigation Acts to regulate trade. In Massachusetts opinion was moving towards denying Parliament any right to legislate for the colonies, though nobody would openly challenge the King's authority to make policy as the controller of the executive power.

America, India, and Lord North

Chatham's government had not managed to do anything about these problems. In October 1768 the Duke of Grafton took Chatham's place as Prime Minister but the new government was not able to make any more progress with its colonial difficulties than its predecessor. Carleton, the Governor of Quebec, came to London in 1768 to give advice about the constitution that was being drawn up for the newly-acquired French-speaking territories, but it was very hard to settle the questions raised by the existence of an overwhelming Catholic majority and by the continued presence of the traditional land-owning seigneurs in Quebec who might continue to lead them, so it took six years to work out new legislation. Lord Hillsborough kept his post as American Secretary, but he did not establish good relations with the Americans. After two years Grafton accepted the fact that, as a supporter of Chatham, he really had no good reason for being in office, and his place was taken by Lord North.

Despite the title given him by courtesy, North was a member of the House of Commons, and in fact a very cool, reassuring leader of the government forces there. He was more willing than most prominent politicians to let the King decide the main lines of policy, and thought of himself more as the government's principal representative in the Commons than as the leader of the administration. Because mastery of the Commons was essential for a government, North gained some strength from being the first Prime Minister there after three Prime Ministers in the House of Lords, and he remained Prime Minister for twelve years. He had been in favour of Grafton's proposal to reduce tension in the American colonies by removing most of the Townshend duties and just keeping the tax on tea to remind people of the principle of the thing. As Prime Minister he put this into effect; it was not a step that would completely conciliate the colonies but at least it meant that the situation became less dangerous. A Spanish threat to go to war over the ownership of the Falkland Islands was fended off without conceding any Spanish right to the islands, though nobody in office in Britain really wanted to hold on to them at the time. Lord Hillsborough was forced out of office by the combined pressure of some of his colleagues and some Americans interested in expansion beyond the Proclamation Line, so his departure improved relations with some colonists and provided better prospects for creating new colonies inland. In the early 1770s prosperity and improved customs administration were increasing the revenue in North America, and it was beginning to look as if India would be the scene of the next imperial crisis.

It had become clear that the 1766 figures overstated the prosperity of the East India Company, but working out a new policy took some years. The Company was in no position to keep up its annual payments of £400,000, and in fact wanted to borrow £1.4m. from the government to cover the cost of the unsuccessful war with Haidar Ali and the loss of revenue caused by the famine in Bengal. The government suspected with some justification that part of the loss was due to the undisciplined behaviour of Company employees after Clive had left; the employees did not realize how fragile the Indian economy was, which encouraged them to take as much as they could, and the government did not realize that famines were relatively common in India, so it believed that all would be well if only it could control the conduct of the employees. The Company got its £1.4m. loan but its dividends were held down to 6 per cent until the loan was repaid, and the government set out to regulate the Company's political activity.

It transferred power over the parts of India ruled by the Company from the governors of the three major ports to a single governor-general at Calcutta, appointed by the government and controlled by a government-appointed council in which he was simply one of the five voting members. The government accepted the Company's practice of choosing a governor with experience of India, but it intended that the councillors should remind him of the British point of view and represent the British government in India. The last Governor of Bengal appointed by the Company, Warren Hastings, was confirmed in office and became the first Governor-General of all British territory in India, but three of his councillors came from London with no experience of India and a deep suspicion of the Company's employees. Things had been changing in Britain: the attitudes of Company employees in India had reflected the pragmatic and non-too-scrupulous approach to life that flourished in Britain in the first half of the eighteenth century, but people there were becoming more concerned about the general moral good of the community than they had been for some decades. Sometimes this made them sentimental and sometimes, when it was blended with the increased religious enthusiasm that came from the Wesleyan revival of the late eighteenth century, the new mood made them priggish or self-righteous, but in many ways the change meant that administration would be more honest and durable and would give the subjects of the British Empire a chance of being better governed than before.

The government believed it could see a useful step to ease the Company's immediate financial problems. War in Mysore and famine in Bengal were not unique events but the Company had reached the very difficult situation of having bought 17 million pounds (8m. kg) of tea that it had not been able to sell. Tea imported into Britain, whether for local sale or for re-export to the colonies, had to pay a duty of slightly over 100 per cent when it was unloaded in London, and the government saw in this a chance to help the Company and at the same time assert its principles in a way that would not hurt the Americans and might even conciliate them: imports to be sold in Britain would go on paying duty but the Company could take 7 million pounds of tea – well over a year's consumption – direct to America so that the Americans would pay only the American tax and could buy it well below the price charged in Britain, and it was thought that on these terms they would hardly try to continue to boycott it. In this way the government expected to manoeuvre them into buying tea which had paid the vestigial remains of the duties Townshend had imposed.

The American opponents of British taxation could see the point, and organized to meet it. The tea was held up at the ports, and to underline the resistance Sam Adams, the local leader in Boston most committed to independence, organized a group of determined and disciplined men who disguised themselves as Red Indians, went on to a ship, and threw the tea solemnly overboard. The Boston Tea Party of 16 December 1773 was conducted soberly and seriously enough to show that it had to be considered as a long step towards rebellion. The British Parliament responded to the challenge by suspending the municipal government of Boston, arranging to close the port, and levying compensation payments on the population. American opposition to these pieces of legislation was more widespread than opposition to the cheap tea had been; they become known as 'the intolerable Acts', and in this denunciation was included an item that deserved a better welcome.

Carleton and the more tolerant of the British ministers won the arguments about what to do with Quebec and its almost entirely Roman Catholic and French-speaking population. The Quebec Act of 1774 gave the Roman Catholics the religious toleration promised when Britain conquered New France, and also allowed them some role in government because the governor of the colony was instructed to include Catholics as well as Protestants in his council. The governor's officials would hold the voting balance in the council and, as the council was nominated rather than elected, the French Canadians could not turn their majority in the population into a majority in the legislature. This was probably the best way for a British Protestant government to rule with a minimum of friction a colony 95 per cent of whose inhabitants were French-speaking Catholics, but the two or three thousand British Protestant merchants who had settled in Montreal and Quebec City claimed a monopoly of power in any Quebec assembly on the grounds that Catholics could not sit in a British legislature. Their objections were echoed by the New Englanders; no doubt religious prejudice entered into it, but there was a fear in New England that Quebec was being organized as a base for establishing some kind of absolutism in North America. This fear was encouraged by the provisions of the Act which greatly enlarged Quebec: instead of being simply the area of dense settlement along the St. Lawrence valley it was to include the triangle of land between the Mississippi and the Ohio rivers, some of which had been French until 1763. This was sensible enough, because the area had been explored by the French and the inhabitants spoke French if they spoke any European language, but it was seen as further proof that Quebec was to be used as a recruiting ground for an attack on English-speaking America. In practice Carleton was to have difficulty in raising a militia to defend Quebec itself, and invading New England would have been totally impracticable, but the Massachusetts opposition to the Quebec Act showed how suspicious the colonists had become about any step taken by the British government.

The other 'intolerable Acts' had the effect of convincing a good many Americans that the radicals were right and that Parliament's claims to authority had to be opposed; it was one thing to be a subject of George III, and something quite different to be the subject of a few hundred gentlemen sitting in London who had no connection with the colonies. In September 1774 the twelve colonies from South Carolina to New Hampshire held the first Continental Congress in Philadelphia; it rejected Galloway's plan for a federal union which would have provided some organization to enable the colonies to work together and at the same time given them a fairly well-defined link with Britain, and it accepted Jefferson's argument that the colonial assemblies stood on a basis of equality with Parliament. The British Parliament had rarely passed legislation that affected the local concerns of the colonies, as opposed to the general trade of the empire; the Congress asserted that this had been a proper recognition of the limits of the powers of the Westminster Parliament. This reduced relations between Britain and America to the connection between the colonies and the King, and it was most unlikely that this connection would stand much strain. The colonists talked as if they believed that British intervention in their affairs was inspired by Parliament and that the King was less likely to interfere. This was not the way the British eighteenth-century constitution, or George III, worked: Parliament wanted money but it was able to recognize how hard it was to get British legislation obeyed in America; the King wanted obedience and was rather less ready to recognize the difficulties. In the reign of George II it could have been argued that the King took the advice of his ministers so often that he really was controlled by Parliament, and this could have added strength to Jefferson's argument that the colonies through their assemblies should control their own governments. But under George III this made much less sense; he had found no ministers whom he was willing to accept as directors of policy in the way that George II had accepted Walpole or Pitt. As a result the King controlled policy, and continued to control it throughout the American crisis while North as Prime Minister made sure that the Commons followed the policy that the King wanted.

So there was no question of handing power from Parliament to the Americans. When Chatham suggested a scheme for recognizing the next meeting of the Continental Congress as the effective ruling authority in America, he received very little support. British officials in America knew that the colonists were building up stocks of arms as a response to the more rebellious of the statements of the 1774 congress, and in April 1775 British troops marched inland from their base in Boston and tried to seize a store of arms at Concord. The fighting that followed was confused and disorderly, but it can reasonably be taken as the beginning of the American War of Independence. When the Second Continental Congress met the following month it took steps to raise an army to send to Massachusetts, and appointed General Washington to command it. The Congress was not eager for independence but it was not willing to accept British authority: its Olive Branch Petition was expressed in amicable language but in substance it said the Americans would not leave George III any power in the thirteen colonies (now including Georgia) that were represented at the Congress and would not provide any financial contribution to the general expenses of running the empire. If the British wanted anything more substantial than this nominal sovereignty in America they would have to fight, and so they began to prepare for war.

The American War of Independence

At the end of 1775 the Americans were not emotionally committed to independence and Sam Adams's assertion that the revolution was complete in the minds of men before the fighting at Concord overstated the position in most of the colonies, though it may have reflected Massachusetts feeling accurately. British opinion was also divided: some politicians thought George III and his government were inclined to attack liberty all over the empire, and saw resistance in America as part of the same spirit that had led to the various phases of resistance in England that had become associated with John Wilkes, and some economists were moving towards the view that colonies brought practically no profit to Britain and were certainly not worth the expense and trouble of a war. In the past public opinion had been more or less united in thinking that colonies were an asset, though of course believing that there were limits to how much should be spent on them. The opposition in Britain to the American War of Independence was a new departure: the Whig opposition to George III's attacks on liberty produced a long line of intellectual descendants of Burke who said that Britain should retain her colonies by the bonds of the affection that they felt for her, and should allow them to become independent if they wanted to do so. Adam Smith's *The Wealth of Nations*, published in 1776, presented the general case for free trade, and drew the specific conclusion that holding colonies and distorting trade from its natural channels through the mechanism of the Navigation Acts could not enrich the public in Britain, whatever it might do for those fortunate enough to have tariff preferences or other privileges. So far as ordinary unprivileged people were concerned, trade with the colonies would be worthwhile if they produced exports at a good price, whether Britain ruled them or not, and no amount of British rule could justify trading with them if they did not offer sound products.

These restrained and reasoned arguments of Burke and Smith did not affect the situation in Britain in the way that the publication of Thomas Paine's *Common Sense* in January 1776 mobilized opinion in America. By April 120,000 copies of this formidable marshalling of the arguments for independence had been sold, and the book clearly influenced opinion as well as reflecting it. By the summer of 1776 the revolution in the minds of men had been carried a long way further, and on 4 July the Continental Congress published its Declaration of Independence. By then fighting had been going on for about a year. The Americans had invaded Canada, had not gained the popular support they expected there, and had been driven back. The British had been obliged to give up Boston; the main battleground seemed to lie between New York and Philadelphia, and by the end of the year Washington was having some difficulty in holding his army together. The American objection to paying taxes was not simply a matter of resistance to rule from overseas: Americans were as opposed to paying taxes to the Continental Congress as to the Westminster Parliament. Congress financed Washington's army by inflation, issuing the money first and hoping revenue would come in later. The revenue was never enough, and 'continental' currency collapsed in just the way that British governments had always thought American paper money would collapse. But Congress did not collapse; probably the American revolution was carried out by a minority and most Americans would have preferred peace under George III to a prolonged war, but the governors of the colonies never tried very hard to organize the loyalties to help the British forces in America, while the revolutionaries were ready to fight and on the whole the others were willing to accept Congress as a legitimate government which controlled most of the territory of the thirteen colonies in 1776. Florida and Nova Scotia, which could see the garrisons for which taxes had been asked and could get some benefit from them, stayed British. So did Bermuda and all the Caribbean islands, partly because of British naval power, partly because of their trading links with Britain, and partly out of concern about their slave population. The colonies in rebellion stretched from Portland to Savannah and covered an area not much larger than the British Isles (though it was becoming harder to define the western frontier), but Congress controlled nine-tenths of this area in 1776.

Pushing the British out of the remaining tenth, which was mainly the prosperous and densely-populated area around New York, was much harder. Washington was able to hold his army together under very difficult conditions but there seemed to be no reason why he could force the British out unless they made a mistake. And in 1777 a mistake was made: Burgoyne, who had reverted from being an MP to being a general, was instructed to march south from Canada to join troops coming north up the Hudson valley from New York. But this ambitious plan of Lord George Germaine (previously disgraced as Lord George Sackville) was not co-ordinated properly: the troops never came north and Burgoyne and his army, outnumbered 3 to 1 and very unskilled at forest warfare, were trapped at Saratoga and forced to surrender. Militarily the defeat was a severe shock, and it was even more of a blow to the British diplomatically. The French had been watching the struggle with obvious sympathy for the Americans, but they had no intention of getting into the war unless the Americans showed that they could be useful allies in an attempt to avenge the defeats of the Seven Years War, and Saratoga showed that they could. After the defeat North offered the Americans complete freedom from the authority of Parliament, merely retaining the king's sovereignty, but France entered the war on the American side before negotiations on these terms could begin. This was not decisive: the French treasury could provide only small amounts of money to stabilize American finances and the French army was even less suited than the British for operations on the other side of the Atlantic.

In 1779 the British turned their attention to the southern colonies, which had never been as enthusiastic about the war as the areas around Virginia and Massachusetts. It seemed more practicable to recapture the seacoast and cut the Americans off from trade and outside help than to face the problems of supply involved in moving inland, and in the course of 1780 and 1781 Cornwallis took the southern ports and coastal areas, penetrating as far north as Virginia. The danger in this strategy was that it left the British forces spread over a much wider area than the previous concentration on the New York–Philadelphia front had done, but it seemed fairly successful. By 1781 Washington was afraid that American independence could not survive for long and France seemed increasingly likely to have to withdraw for financial reasons. The war had so far been reasonably popular in Britain, though the expense was much more than the trivial amounts of taxation involved could ever repay. Altogether it cost about £100m. or £12m. a year which meant something of the order of 8 per cent of the national income. The annual cost was a little more than the annual cost of the Seven Years War and the struggle lasted much longer. There was no fighting in Germany and no European ally to pay for, but keeping an army containing a good many hired Germans in America cost even more. All the other eighteenth-century wars had some fairly direct European implications, whether it was a matter of defending the King's possessions in Hanover or of maintaining the balance of power. The American War of Independence was fought almost entirely over an imperial issue and yet it was for Britain a defensive war in the sense that, however successful it might be, there was no prospect of territorial or commercial expansion to reward success, though defeat would mean a less dominant position at sea and the loss (in addition to the American colonies) of territory taken from countries like Spain in 1763.

In the autumn of 1781 success suddenly vanished. The strategy of spreading British troops along the coastline left Cornwallis at Yorktown – perhaps twenty miles from where the story of British expansion had started at Jamestown – faced by a larger American army and cut off from supplies by the French fleet. In October 1781 he had to surrender, and North when he heard the news said 'It is all over.' Conceivably a completely united people could have gone on with the war even after this defeat, but the opposition at Westminster had throughout the war argued that fighting to restore British authority in America could do no good, and had even been afraid that victory would immensely strengthen royal authority over Parliament in Britain. At first the opposition had not made much impression, and early in 1781 it had seemed possible that North might triumph over past precedents and become the first Prime Minister to lead the country into a war and survive politically to lead it out as well. Yorktown ended all that: the Commons did not like the prospect of paying for an unsuccessful war and North's majority began to break up. In March 1782 he resigned just in time to avoid defeat, though he would have resigned earlier if the King had let him. George realized that it was impossible to find anyone else who could persuade the Commons to support the war, and that the departure of North meant the acceptance of American independence.

The Rockingham government that succeeded North not only accepted American independence but almost welcomed it. When peace negotiations began, ministers did not try to gain any advantage from the fact that Britain was going to give up the considerable stretch of American coastline that she still controlled, and they tried to make the separation as amicable as possible. On the other hand the war against France and Spain, conducted mainly in the West Indian islands, had gone very badly; some British islands had been captured, most had gone very short of food, and almost all of them had been attacked. But the government was lucky enough to have its diplomatic position strengthened by a decisive naval victory over the French at The Saints, off the island of Dominica, and this enabled it to keep its losses in the war against France and Spain to a minimum: the French recovered Tobago which they had lost twenty years previously but half a dozen smaller islands which they had captured were returned to Britain, the Honduras logwood settlement was accepted as a legitimate interest but Britain dropped claims on the Moskito coast and Florida went back to Spain. As this territory stretched out west to the Louisiana territory which France had given to Spain in 1763, it strengthened the foundations for the expansion of the Spanish empire in North America. The British were probably not in the least sorry to see that this might lead their former colonies to a quarrel with Spain, but they did take care to reduce the risk of conflict in the north. They withdrew their claim to the formerly French areas south of the Great Lakes which had been included in Canada by the 1774 Act; it was fairly clear that the Americans would want to expand into this area and that, as the Canadians would not be able to defend it, Britain would find herself fighting another American war, in an area that would be very hard to reach. From the point of view of the Montreal fur traders, confining Canada to the area north of the Great Lakes was a blow; seen from London or from the United States – to anticipate the name they took in 1787 – it was a prudent concession that left the way open to friendly relations. The actual cession was to be put off until the Americans had done their best to complete a financial settlement with the Loyalists who emigrated to Britain, the West Indies, or the British colonies in North America rather than live under a republican government, but in principle the question had been settled.

Lord Shelburne wanted to avoid war and to keep open the door to trade. He may also have accepted Smith's argument that colonies brought a country no benefits and that free trade in the best markets was the only road to prosperity, but, even if this was in Shelburne's mind, it was not a popular view in Britain at the end of the war. An attempt to arrange for America to remain within the British trade and tariff systems was defeated. The surrender of the land south of the Great Lakes may have been sensible enough, but it did Shelburne's political career no good, and he was sufficiently in touch with opinion to warn the American negotiators as soon as they asked for the cession of Canada that there was no point in discussing the idea. The direction of British imperial interests might shift, and a few people in Britain might question the worth of colonies, but there was no question of a general withdrawal. British trade with America could go on after the political separation and prosper without any special assistance, but this was the result of an entirely different development.

The British economy was undergoing a profound modification, and was becoming committed to industrial production on a scale that had never been seen before. It had already had a considerable capacity for producing certain industrial products in the field of textiles and iron work, but the level of activity in these areas went up quite sharply; the immediate result was that Britain became a customer for certain sorts of industrial raw material – iron, cotton, and, a little later, wool – on a scale never known previously, and soon afterwards she became eager for commercial expansion of a type that reversed previous roles: until the Industrial Revolution traders went out to look for valuable commodities that could be brought home and sold or re-exported, but by the end of the eighteenth century British merchants and manufacturers were in the unprecedented position of being able to produce what seemed like limitless quantities of their new products – cotton textiles, china, cannon – and their new problem was to find people who could afford to buy on the scale needed to reduce the costs of production as much as possible.

One result of this transformation was that the British demand for raw cotton rose very quickly. Supporters of free trade pointed to the immense increase in trade with America in the years just after independence as a sign that the old colonial system was quite unnecessary and trade could do just as well without it, but this was confusing two rather separate things: British demand for cotton would have increased as soon as it was clear that not enough cotton could be grown in the British West Indies to keep Lancashire cotton mills running, but this did not prove that other trade would flow along channels that were not affected by political changes. In any case, independence did not alter the essential features of American society: successful trade on a large scale required a government which could maintain an adequate level of law and order, and it was easy to see that the United States could manage this. It was not so obvious that it could be maintained in Canada without British intervention, and it was fairly clear that trade in India could be carried on profitably only if there were some effective authority like the Moghuls to control the situation. In Bengal the East India Company had replaced the Moghuls, but it was not at all certain that this was going to be enough to restore tranquillity.

Hastings and India

The East India Company's finances were not restored by the concession made to help it sell its tea in America. In India Hastings as Governor-General was for his first two years almost crippled by the three Council members who used their votes to reduce his authority, but he held on and the death of one of the three left him able to reassert himself after 1776 by using his casting vote to give himself and his one supporter a majority. Hastings would probably have been happy to spend his time improving the administration of Bengal, encouraging education, and providing a framework of government within which the Company could go about its business and earn its profits. He was much more interested in Indian languages and culture than the ordinary British official; he was concerned that Company employees should know something about India, for practical reasons and also because he found the Indian way of life in some ways attractive and worthy of respect, and he had some success in encouraging this approach.

As things turned out, he had to devote most of his time to military activities: all three of the main trading centres were under pressure, and because of the war in America it was less likely than ever that help would be provided from Britain. Hastings was able to defeat the French because he was told of the outbreak of war in a message that came by the Suez isthmus route and took only 68 days to arrive and because, as Governor-General over the three centres, he was able to lay down much more of a unified policy than had been possible in the past. The trading centres were far enough apart to mean that it was still hard for the Company to handle its resources as a single unit. The Marathas were divided over the question of the succession and the authorities in Bombay, the only major trading port close to them, supported one of the candidates. This claimant was not successful, and a little later the new Maratha ruler, Nana Farnavis, led them against the bellicose Bombay government. At first they were successful but before they could exploit this Hastings had marched an army across India to resist them. Bombay survived, but the power of the Marathas remained unbroken and it was unlikely that they and the Company could live together peacefully for long. Haidar Ali resumed his attacks on Madras and, though they were held off more successfully than before, this defensive position did not look any more permanent than the repulse of the Marathas. Because of their success in the American War, and because Admiral Suffren came closer to securing French command of the Indian Ocean than any of his predecessors, the French regained in 1783 some of the ports they had lost twenty years earlier. But they had not won any victories in India itself and as Pondicherry and Chandernagore were to be run exclusively as trading posts they did not open the way for the French to return to Indian politics.

Hastings's wars were concerned only with enabling the Company to hold on to what it had already acquired, but this defensive achievement was not enough: the Company wanted dividends. To make the profits needed for this, and to sustain his armies while they fought, Hastings had to concentrate on his Bengal base and the minor princes a little further up the Ganges valley with whom he had made treaties. Bengal remained reasonably safe through-out his period of office and was a haven of peace and good government compared with the rest of India, which was collapsing under the stress of war as half a dozen major powers struggled for large portions of the dissolving Moghul Empire and a great number of smaller powers took what local gains they could. The British position in India owed something to their capacity for military organization and their willingness to work together, but it also owed a great deal to Indian weakness. In the seventeenth century nobody would have said government in India was either much more effective or much less effective than government in Britain; by 1770 British government had become perceptibly better and Indian government was racing towards collapse. The structure of personal loyalty, which had been the normal basis of all government when the English arrived, had become an invitation for anyone of above-average military talent to set out to build himself a kingdom. It was perfectly natural to accept the fact that one of the ruling princes had been replaced by a trading company, which was entitled to some degree of loyalty, especially as it was able to stop other powers invading its territory, and the fact that the people who had replaced the Nawab of Bengal were not native Indians was not very relevant – the Moghul Emperors were not native Indians, and some of them had been much more ready to thrust their alien religion on the Hindu majority than the Company ever was.

The divisions between Hastings and his Council around 1775 must have puzzled Indians, and some of them allied themselves with the Council majority. One of them was unfortunate enough to have committed forgery, for which under English – though not under Moghul – law he could be executed; and executed he was. Among the British there was some argument about whether Nuncomar (Nand Kumar) should have been judged by English law; presumably the Indians drew the simpler lesson that, just as anyone who had offended the Nawab was liable to be executed, final power under the British system was in the hands of the Governor-General. And just as he maintained his position in Bengal by methods which must have seemed perfectly natural to the Indian population, Hastings secured some of the funds to keep the Company solvent by the sort of steps that a powerful Indian ruler might use. The Company's treaties with its allies west of Bengal up the Ganges valley made it clear that they were to some extent subordinate to the Company for diplomatic purposes. Hastings called on these allies for help, which they provided with no more reluctance than was natural under the circumstances.

While all this was normal in India, it looked in England like extortion and breach of trust. If Hastings behaved in a perfectly normal way in India, he was nevertheless liable to have his methods of government examined rigorously in Britain, and it was soon clear that there was something to investigate. In the past, unsatisfactory ministers, whose activities might be considered as crimes against the nation, had been prosecuted by the Commons, with the House of Lords judging the case as the final and highest court of justice in the country. This old-fashioned process of impeachment was used to try Hastings. After a trial lasting seven years that left him virtually bankrupt he was eventually acquitted. Neither side had a consistent position: Burke, the leader and the most dedicated member of the prosecuting team, first said that Indians must be governed by methods 'correspondent with their manners', and then objected to a 'geographical morality' when Hastings argued that he had behaved exactly like any other Indian ruler. Hastings won his case by producing witnesses (including some of the Indians he was alleged to have ill treated) to say that he had done nothing extraordinary or objectionable by Indian standards, but he then expected to be honoured by the British government. The response from London was to say that he had obviously been acting from good motives in a way that everybody in India thought reasonable, and that he had saved the British position there by doing so; but that, if this was how things were done in

India, Indian methods of government must be replaced by British methods. The legal framework of government had been changed before Hastings ever got back to Britain, and he must sometimes have felt that his impeachment was a roundabout way of explaining the need for the India Act of 1785. But changing the substance of government from a system designed for the enjoyment of the rulers into one that did its best not to make life any harder than necessary for its subjects was going to take longer.

In the later years of the American War of Independence the opposition became increasingly convinced that the structure of government in Britain and in what was left of the empire would have to be changed. Once North had fallen, they set about eliminating a good many of the posts which provided salaries without too much work that had been used to reward loyal supporters of the government. They changed the way civil servants were paid so that in future they would live on their salaries instead of being expected to supplement them out of fees paid to them for their services by people who wanted to register purchases of land or anything else for which a government stamp was required. The administration of the colonies was swept away; the newly-created Secretaryship of State for American affairs was abolished and so was the Board of Trade, which had acted as his advisory council. Colonial affairs were placed in the hands of the Home Secretary. The new government repealed the laws which made Ireland subject to legislation passed at Westminster and which prevented the Irish Parliament from passing any laws that had not been approved by the London government, so it now had all the freedom claimed by the American assemblies in the years just before the Declaration of Independence. The British Lord-Lieutenant in Dublin still held the legal powers of the monarch and this meant he continued to exercise active control of the executive, subject to the instructions of the government in London. His position in relation to the Irish Parliament was a little like that of an American colonial governor, though he was expected to manage his Parliament more effectively than the governors did.

Along with this went the need for change in India. Party loyalty at Westminster had been confused in the years before the American War, and the end of the war released the parties from the unity that had been forced upon them by the need to be either for or against it. Before the final treaties were signed it was clear that North, the leading defender of the war, and Fox, its leading opponent, had put together a new majority. The coalition may have been formed for perfectly honourable reasons, but enough people thought it was simply a grab for office at the expense of the not particularly popular Lord Shelburne to mean that Fox and North would have been wise to behave more scrupulously than most governments. The India Bill they proposed in 1783 did not look scrupulous: in effect it said that the British government would take over from the East India Company the task of ruling in India, leaving the Company to carry on trading, and that all the appointments to government posts in the British part of India would be made by a parliamentary committee staffed by seven supporters of Fox and North. These governments posts may not have been quite as lucrative as they were before Clive's attempts at reform but the rewards were still considerable – Hastings, who was not accused of using illegitimate methods for personal enrichment, brought £150,000 back to England. So these jobs were very attractive, especially at a time when the earlier reforms had reduced the number of attractive jobs in England. Every Member of Parliament with relations who needed jobs could think about this when voting on the Bill, and so could the King: George III had put up with the abolition of the sinecure posts in Britain, over which he still had a good deal of control himself, but he saw no need to create a whole lot of new posts in India over which he would have no control. He gave one of his supporters a note to show to individual peers which made it clear that 'he would consider any peer who voted for the measure his enemy'.[2] This was enough: the Bill was defeated, and George promptly dismissed the Fox–North government. Even in the eighteenth century this was a bold step, and George had ventured to take it only when he knew that William Pitt, the son of the great Lord Chatham, was ready to form a new government.

Empire without America

Pitt's government was confirmed in office in a general election the following year, and he could then turn his attention to the pieces of imperial business that remained to be settled. The most immediate problem was in the British colonies in North America. When the American War of Independence broke out, Canada was still a French-speaking area just emerging from military rule, with enough English-speaking merchants looking forward to trading in furs north and south of the Great Lakes to cause trouble; Nova Scotia was thinly settled; and Newfoundland still showed some traces of being a summer fishing base rather than a colony in which people lived all the year around. The aftermath of the war changed all this: thirty or forty thousand United Empire Loyalists left the newly established republic and fled to the north, some out of devotion to George III and some because they were being persecuted by their victorious neighbours. The Treaty said that the American government would try to get debts to the emigrants settled, but the governments of the separate American states would do nothing to help carry out the obligation, and the British government was left with a debt of honour to the Loyalists. It gave them about £6m. in cash and some fairly lavish land grants, filling up the territory north of existing American settlement fairly effectively. The area just north of Maine attracted many more settlers than the Lake Ontario region and was separated from Nova Scotia to

² A. Foord, *His Majesty's Opposition* (1964), 392.

form the new colony of New Brunswick, which emerged as a curious blend of devotedly British immigrants in the south and of the French-speaking Acadians, returning from an exile in Louisiana that had been imposed on them by the British government, in the north of the province. Hostility to the anti-monarchist, anti-Catholic Americans could hold them together, and could unite all British subjects in North America for as long as the United States was seen as a threat and Britain seen as a possible defence against the threat.

The pressure to move westward that had been felt in the American colonies could also be seen in Canada. The Montreal fur traders had stepped very quickly into the shoes of the French, and quite soon were moving further west than the French traders had ever gone. The Hudson's Bay Company noticed the new challenge, and changed its own methods; for a hundred years it had maintained its coastal trading posts without showing much interest in going inland, but in 1774 it started inland expeditions to meet the competition from Montreal. The peace of 1783 intensified the competition; the Montreal traders could see that their position south of the Great Lakes was not going to survive for long and, even though the Americans had not fulfilled the provision of the treaty that required them to pay their debts to the Loyalists, the British government gave up the southern territories in 1794 when a new war with France had broken out. The Montreal merchants had already organized to concentrate on the area north and west of the Great Lakes, forming the North-West Company in 1785, which committed them to intense competition with the Hudson's Bay Company, and at first the North-West Company was much the more active.

In 1793 Alexander Mackenzie from Montreal reached the Pacific at the head of the first group of men to cross North America; and if he had reached the ocean a few weeks earlier he would have had the unexpected pleasure of seeing a British ship exploring the coast. For the Montrealers were not the only fur traders in the region; and at the end of the 1780s the British found that they were once more moving towards war with Spain over claims that went back to the great days of Spanish empire. The British sailed up the west coast of North America in search of sea-otter pelts, for which there was an excellent market in China; the Spanish claimed that their rights in California stretched up the coast and that the British should not sail there. Pitt felt that Britain need not be deterred by the risk of a naval war with Spain, and in 1790 the Spanish gave up their claims in Nootka Sound and sea-otter hunting went ahead. Captain Vancouver surveyed the coastline between 1792 and 1794, and came just too soon to meet Mackenzie. Nobody thought of using the overland route for trading purposes for another dozen years or so and Vancouver Island remained for some years to come a base for furs taken at sea rather than on land.

The Montreal fur traders had accepted, without much enthusiasm, the system of government with a nominated legislative council that had been devised for Canada in 1774, but it was most unlikely that the Loyalists would do so. They had been accustomed to local autonomy, and to the steps towards restraining the London government about which Americans had been agreed in the 1760s. Some of the provisions of the 1774 Quebec Act had been included because the French were not accustomed to representative institutions and some because they were not trusted to be loyal; neither of these considerations applied to American loyalists. So a new system of government would have to recognize their claims and also acknowledge the differences between them and the French-speaking majority. Relatively few of the Loyalists had gone into the area of French agricultural settlement (though a small group in the townships east of Montreal held a special position for many years to come), and most of the land grants were made in Nova Scotia and New Brunswick, or in the area north of Lake Ontario and west of French settlement.

In 1786 New Brunswick was given the elected assembly that a colony of Englishmen would naturally expect. The major step was taken in 1791 when Canada was divided into two colonies, Upper Canada on the Great Lakes and Lower Canada on the shores of the St. Lawrence, both of which were given elected assemblies, a step which William Grenville, who drafted the Act, said was meant 'to assimilate the constitution of [Canada] to that of Great Britain', with the substantial difference that in Lower Canada a French-speaking Roman Catholic majority had been given a distinct political position. It was quite likely that the Governor, backed by his nominated Executive Council of notables, would there be seen as the main support of the English-speaking commercial minority, and it was also possible that his subordinate, the Lieutenant-Governor of Upper Canada, would be seen there as the upholder of specifically imperial interests. The colonial governors in British North America, and in other colonies as well, returned to the seventeenth-century pattern; they were usually military men, and they expected obedience to their orders because Britain was spending a good deal of money on colonial defence. By 1791 the colonies more or less paid all their own civil costs when the gain from the Barbados export duties was set against the loss shown in Quebec, but the military cost of keeping up forces in the colonies – quite apart from the general expense of the Navy – was running at about £¼m. a year.

Mainly because of the military spending and the risks of invasion and war with the United States, Britain kept tighter control over the colonies she had retained in British North America than she had exercised in America previously, but the general principles of government were closer to what had existed in America before 1776 than to anything else. In India it was not possible to follow former precedents because there were no precedents for what had happened. Pitt had to deal with the situation caused by the defeat of Fox's India Bill, and he wanted to make as few enemies as possible while doing so. He was determined that the government should control policy in India, but he saw no reason why it had to control patronage. So far as he was concerned the East India Company could appoint the civil servants – a phrase which at the time simply meant the employees concerned with civil questions, as opposed to the military servants in the army – to run the general administration of the territories it had acquired in India, as well as retaining its trading interests, so long as its employees in India followed the policy of the British government rather than a policy of their own.

The Company directors retained the right to make appointments in India for over half a century, and on the whole handled their task very well. Nobody thought of filling posts by competitive examination, and no politicians would trust other politicians to make appointments for anything other than partisan reasons. When jobs in India came to mean a well-paid career rather than a chance to get rich quickly, the pressure to get a position became less frantic and the directors could settle down to choosing candidates who would serve the Company. Henry Dundas, the politician most concerned with government relations with the Company in the 1780s and 1790s, sometimes asked for appointments to be made to help him reward his followers in Scotland, but the government rarely pushed its own nominations for positions except for the policy-forming jobs like the governors and governor-generals. These men at the top of the system were to be seen as representatives of the government, rather than promoted Company employees, and their executive authority was restrained only by their superiors in London. The Company's Court of Directors gave them instructions about the details of carrying out policy in India, but the directors were supervised by a committee of ministers known as the Board of Control, and the President of the Board of Control became in this indirect way the minister responsible for British policy in India.

The government, the Company and almost all the Company employees agreed that a period of peace and recuperation was badly needed, so conflict over policy was unlikely. Cornwallis, whose reputation for good sense had not been damaged by the surrender at Yorktown, went out to India in 1786 as the first governor-general who had not been an employee of the administration in India and so could represent the views of the British government to Company employees. A governor who had risen by devoted service to the Company might have become out of touch with opinion in Britain; from now on the men at the top in India would know what British politicians wanted, and Cornwallis knew that administrative reform was now wanted in India as in London. He carried out the work of professionalizing the political side of the Company which Clive and Hastings had attempted previously.

In the past Company employees were unlikely to think that good government was more important than making the largest possible amount of money out of governing, because they were employed by a Company which naturally was concerned to increase its profits as much as it could. But the 1785 India Act separated the trading operations from the work of governing, and Cornwallis altered the administration accordingly. Men who were running the military and the civil side of government – 'military servants' and 'civil servants' of the Company – were put on salary. The rates were generous: the best-paid civil servants at £5,000 or £6,000 a year were earning more than the Prime Minister. But this was to be all they got, except for reimbursement for well-defined expenses. Joining the Indian civil service was to be attractive and to provide good pay and pensions but it was no longer a way to make an enormous fortune. The civil servants exercised great power; they were not directly responsible to politicians, and so in British India the civil service was the government rather than being the body by which the government carries out its policy. In the last resort the government in London, nine months away by sailing ship, would be obeyed, but in all normal circumstances the bureaucrats in India would decide what had to be done. Because he reflected a change of attitude in Britain, Cornwallis was determined to set up an honest and a beneficient bureaucracy; so far as he was concerned that meant a British bureaucracy, and Indians were steadily replaced in the more important positions. Obviously Indians had to be retained for clerical posts and Cornwallis did not try to impose English law on the broad mass of the population; Englishmen and the Indians who acted as parts of the English community were subject to English law, but this was an exception made for a small minority, and justice for the vast majority continued to mean the existing systems of Indian law.

Cornwallis wanted the Company to prosper and, like most people who cared for its prosperity, believed the best way to achieve it was to keep expenses down by following a policy of staying at peace and avoiding expansion. The British rulers were an important factor in diplomacy in India, and their presence helped make it impossible for the Moghul emperors to restore their old position of authority or for anyone like the Maratha rulers to take the place of the Emperors and re-create the unity of the seventeenth century by a new career of conquest, but there was very little sign that the Company wanted to expand: expansion was bad for trade, bad for dividends, and led to debt. At the end of the American War of Independence and the campaigns of Warren Hastings, the Company's debt was about £20m. – perhaps a tenth the size of the National Debt and far larger than any other privately incurred debt. Cornwallis's peaceful policy satisfied the government because it meant that Indian policy would not cause the country any expense, and it satisfied the Company because it meant that dividends were safer. When Cornwallis retired he was succeeded in 1793 by Sir John Shore, a Governor-General of the old type who had served with the Company throughout his career. But despite his early career Shore made no attempt to change Cornwallis's policy either in the local organization of the administration or in the peaceful attitude to other powers in India. Plassey had been a great political turning-point and had established the British as one of the major powers in India, but it did not lead to any desire to dominate the other major states there. The company took over Bengal and was clearly going to hold on to it, but in the forty years after Plassey it carried out very little territorial expansion.

5. *The Stress of Revolution,* *1788–1826*

Shortly before Cornwallis retired from office in India, Britain had gone to war with France once more, and the long wars dominated British foreign policy and military activity from 1793 until the final defeat of Napoleon in 1815. Imperial affairs were not quite so deeply affected by the wars; the world outside Europe was changed much more by the pressure of forces building up inside Britain than by Pitt's attempts at imperial strategy. He was a child of his age in his free trade views on economics, but he was his father's son when it came to military planning, and in the 1790s he committed the country to a policy of attacking French colonies that was no longer effective. The French had lost interest in colonies; Napoleon showed a few flickers of concern about the world outside Europe, but they soon died away. There was some truth in the Gilray cartoon which showed the world as a plum-pudding with Napoleon hacking away at the portion marked Europe while Pitt carved up the rest of the globe in a more leisurely manner, but this result was not brought about by Pitt's strategy. His attacks on sugar islands were expensive and unsuccessful; what transformed the world outside Europe was the expansion and mechanization of the textile and metal trades in Britain that became known as the industrial revolution, and the accompanying growth of population. Colonial possessions of the old type would not be so useful in this new situation. Britain emerged in a powerful position at the end of the Napoleonic wars because she was the power that had been fighting most continuously and had been financing the efforts of her allies, but at the peace conference she showed little interest in annexing colonies from other European powers.

The expansion shown in Gilray's cartoon went forward in other directions, prepared – often by Pitt himself – in the years before the wars began. Australia had been launched as a convict settlement half a dozen years before the fighting broke out, and by the time it ended Australians had brought sheep to their country and had found their way from the narrow coastal strip to the limitless grazing inland. The French Revolution was already under way when a new constitution was enacted for Canada which made it more attractive to immigrants leaving the United States or sailing from Britain, and Canadian lumber development benefitted from the demands of the war. Cornwallis's reforms provided the administration to run the conquests made in a totally unexpected series of aggressive wars by which Lord Wellesley turned Britain from an important regional power in India into the dominant authority in the subcontinent.

The French Revolution and the Industrial Revolution

It is fair to guess that Pitt would have been quite as pleased by the development of the institutions, mainly financial and industrial, which were able to make use of this new empire as by the actual territorial expansion. Pitt had come to office as the first Prime Minister who really understood the new political idea that government ought to avoid making life more difficult than necessary for ordinary people. Governments had always got revenue by taxes which fell on the whole population, often – as in the case of customs duties on the necessities of life – taking a larger share of the incomes of the poor than of the rich; and they then spent the revenue on the salaries of the well-paid and sometimes under-employed civil servants who came from the richer part of the community. Rulers had behaved in this way for several millenia, but the late eighteenth-century reformers wanted to change things. They did not believe in taking positive steps to redistribute money to the poor (and did not have the bureaucracy needed for such a policy), but they thought that by avoiding war, reducing the expense of the government, and getting rid of taxes that increased the cost of living they could make life easier for everyone. Pitt had read the works of Adam Smith, the most prominent British advocate of this new approach to government, and had become committed to this policy of financial reform. During the first nine years of his premiership he continued the process of abolishing unnecessary positions in the government, and reduced a large number of import duties.

When the French Revolution broke out in 1789 Pitt was rather inclined to welcome it. The revolutionaries seemed to share some of his opinions. Their devotion to liberty suggested that they would support his opposition to the slave trade, and they appeared to agree with his fiscal views. At a more down-to-earth level, he believed that if France was engaged in a revolution she would have no energy for war, and he did not change his mind even when she went to war with several German states in 1792. He was not very interested when Burke turned aside from the prosecution of Hastings to argue that Britain should devote herself to crushing the principles of the Revolution, but he did become concerned when the government of republican France announced in 1793 that the principles of the Revolution were to be exported by force and, much more specifically, that the treaties about the use of the River Scheldt were to be ended.

Apart from the threat of increased competition with British trade, this step also suggested that the estuary might be used to assemble a fleet to invade the country. Pitt responded by declaring war, and widened the war to cover the whole issue of the expansionist policy the French Republic was following. With a brief pause of less than two years after the Treaty of Amiens in 1802, and an even briefer pause when Napoleon was sent to Elba in 1814, the war ran on from 1793 until the final battle at Waterloo in 1815. Other countries joined in and dropped out, usually because they had been overwhelmed by the Napoleonic onslaught, but Britain and France stayed at war continuously throughout the struggle. Both countries gained allies from time to time, but there was never any doubt that France dominated her supporters while Britain's partners were much more independent of her. They normally put much larger land armies into the field than Britain could muster, and suffered heavier losses.

Inevitably the wars affected imperial development, but the overseas issues involved were never as close to the heart of the question as they had been in the three wars between Britain and France between 1740 and 1783. No state had been likely to emerge from the mid-eighteenth-century wars in a position where it could dominate Europe, so the British treated those wars rather like Charles II's wars with the Netherlands which involved important questions of trade but did not threaten Britain's freedom or her constitution. The wars against the French Revolution were seen as something much more like the wars against Louis XIV, or against Philip II of Spain, because the British thought their survival as an independent nation was threatened and as a result they were ready to make as large a contribution as possible to the conflict in Europe. But the wars against Louis XIV had had imperial aspects, and in the wars against the French Revolution the British never forgot that they had an empire.

Though the intensity and the eventual purpose of the war was very different from that of the wars in the middle of the century, Pitt's strategy was very like that of his father. Continental enemies of France were encouraged to fight against her on land and were helped by the steady payments of subsidies: something like £60m., or perhaps 5 per cent of all the money Britain spent on the war, was devoted to providing this sort of financial help. Meanwhile the British established command of the sea and used it to attack French colonies. War was seen as closely connected with colonies; in 1794 Pitt created a new secretaryship of state of war, which in 1801 became 'war and the colonies'. It took over the colonial side of the work of the Board of Trade and the Plantations, which had been revived in 1786, leaving the Board of Trade to concentrate on domestic economic problems. For the first twenty years of its existence the holders of the new secretaryship had to concentrate on the war. Lord Castlereagh briefly combined the post with the Presidency of the Board of Control for running India and it looked as if he might be going to become a minister for the whole empire, but after this short experiment India became firmly established as a separate department, and after 1815 the secretaryship for war turned into the nucleus of the nineteenth-century Colonial Office.

The strategy of attacking colonies did very little good. By this time France had no large colonies that could easily be captured and, while her West Indian sugar islands looked very tempting, they were dangerous and expensive to invade. The largest and richest of the islands, St. Domingue (the island of Hispaniola or San Domingo, which had been French since 1697), was already in revolt against France; the slaves on the island had taken liberty, equality, and fraternity as a slogan that meant something to them as well as to Frenchmen and were conducting a successful rebellion by the time Pitt's expedition arrived, so it was never clear whether the British were trying to drive out the French or to suppress a slave revolt. In the latter task they failed; the slaves defended themselves desperately and successfully, and tens of thousands of British soldiers who might have been fighting in Europe were killed or were incapacitated by yellow fever. The British had the negative satisfaction of seeing the French lose their largest West Indian colony to the slaves, but this was no substantial benefit to any Englishmen except the West Indian sugar planters, and it certainly brought the end of the war no closer.

When the Netherlands were brought into the war on the French side by the Dutch republicans, the British made more substantial gains, taking part of the Dutch colonies in Guiana and the Cape of Good Hope and the island of Ceylon (and, for a short time, holding Java), but none of this had any great effect on the war. Britain's continental allies were defeated time and again, so the subsidy system cost more than expected. The French Republic was defeated at sea much more often and more seriously than France had been in earlier wars, and might have been content to confine the war to Europe, but in the early years of his rise to power Napoleon devoted a good deal of attention to the wider world. After establishing his reputation by his victories in Italy in 1796 and 1797 he invaded Egypt, a step which worried the British in India as much as in Europe, but his capacity to advance in any direction was sharply reduced when his fleet was destroyed by Nelson at the battle of the Nile. In 1800 he turned his attention to America and forced Spain to return to France the Louisiana territory beyond the Mississippi which had been given to her in 1763, but – perhaps because he was clearly not going to reconquer St. Domingue – he changed the direction of his policy again and in 1803 sold the territory to the United States for $15m. After this he treated the world outside Europe simply as a place to which Britain's attention might be diverted while he concentrated on the central issue.

The sale of Louisiana took place just when the war was beginning again after the Treaty of Amiens, and the second half of the war could be seen even more directly than the first as a struggle between Britain and France. In

1804 and 1805 Napoleon was planning an invasion of Britain until he had to turn aside to fight the Austrians, and in 1808 Britain committed herself to supporting Spain and Portugal against French invasion. For the next six years there was almost always a British army in the Iberian peninsula; not a large army by the standards of the time, for it was only about one-tenth the size of the army of 600,000 that Napoleon led to Moscow and to disaster in 1812, but it held the field continuously and was a much larger commitment to land war in Europe than Britain had made earlier in the struggle. The search for colonies no longer drew her away from Europe, but economic warfare spread further and further afield, affecting a great deal of the commercially active world: in 1806 Napoleon issued his Berlin Decrees which excluded British exports from the parts of Europe controlled by France and this attempt to undermine British industry by cutting it off from its markets succeeded in reducing its exports to this area from £10m. a year to £3m. The British responded by imposing on the countries which applied the Berlin Decrees their own increasingly strict rules for blockade, now summed up in the Orders of Council. Napoleon had diagnosed the way in which the British economy had become, as far as overseas trading was concerned, different from anything that had been seen before. Because her overseas trade had changed from being a matter of merchants going out to find things that were unobtainable at home to the pursuit of markets for exports, the Berlin Decrees affected Britain more than they would have done previously.

A generation later Disraeli put forward a simple social analysis of the groups in society which had pushed the economy forward. 'A couple of centuries ago a Turkey Merchant was the great creator of wealth; the West India planter followed him. In the middle of the last century appeared the Nabob . . . the expenditure of the revolutionary wars produced the Loan-monger who succeeded the Nabob, and the application of science to industry produced the Manufacturer.'[1] Disraeli's first three inspirers of commercial development had been primarily concerned with importing goods, though often goods for re-export; as Britain industrialized, foreign trading became concerned with selling the goods – virtually unlimited by all previous stand-ards – that could be produced by machinery. The immense expansion of production, and the sharp reduction of costs that accompanied long produc-tion runs, were seen first in cotton textiles. By quite definable stages, British manufacturers first drove all but the finest Indian products out of the British market, competing on price rather than on quality, and then went on between 1790 and 1810 to win a large number of the other markets to which Indian textiles had been exported by the East India Company. Unlimited production accompanied by a need for new markets soon transformed the market in woollen textiles and in a variety of metal products as well. The process of industrialization changed life in Britain in a way that made a

[1] B. Disraeli, *Sybil* (1904 edn.), 100–1.

profound impact on everyone who lived through it, and transformed the thinking of those who realized that this was the way the whole world was going to develop.

The change affected the structure of British trade even more deeply than Britain's domestic economy. In 1780 Britain's trade still involved a great deal of re-exporting in virtually unchanged form goods that had been brought from outside Europe, but by 1810 re-exports had dwindled to a much smaller fraction of the stated figures than they had been thirty years earlier. Cotton textiles were taking their place, and by the end of the Napoleonic Wars made up about 40 per cent of all exports produced in Britain and exceeded re-exports in value. In one sense cotton textiles were themselves a re-export, though of an almost entirely unprecedented type; a few developments in the sugar trades had dimly foreshadowed the new process of importing a commodity from overseas, working on it and transforming it, and then sending a good deal of the finished product overseas again in its new form that was at the heart of the expansion of the cotton industry. A large enough percentage of the population was involved in cotton spinning to attract attention, but obviously it was nothing like as large as the place of cotton exports in total exports; cotton textiles solved the problem of what the British could export in exchange for their wide-ranging imports, only to open up the new question of finding markets large enough to absorb all that was produced.

The wars coincided with and stimulated some of the most dynamic phases of industrialization. Ship-building, metal-working for armaments, large-scale production of clothing for soldiers, and grain-growing to keep up with an expanding population at a time when importing food would have been difficult were all driven forward at a great rate. This was not pleasant for the working population, who had to endure the reduction of living standards that inevitably went with war at the same time as the proportion of national income devoted to investment was rising at the expense of consumption. Britain was in the unusually uncomfortable position of entering the process of industrialization without being able to borrow from any other country which had industrialized earlier. By the end of the war Britain had a well-established industrial base, but one which was too large for the level of demand existing after 1815. For the next fifteen years or so, until the coming of railway development provided work for the metal trades, British industry was searching frantically and unceasingly for markets all over the world, cutting the price of textile exports to a quarter of the 1814 level, and increasing its share of all export trade steadily although export earnings in 1842 were only 14 per cent higher than in 1817.

Although Britain's army was small by the standards of the time, her naval expenditure and her contributions to her continental allies meant that the war was far more expensive than any earlier struggles. Eighteenth-century wars had cost about £10m. a year, but the wars against the Revolution and Napoleon cost about £60m. a year, or perhaps 25 per cent of the national income. The pressure of war and of debt led prices to rise sharply and irregularly, and Napoleon's system of excluding exports had some success in dislocating the British economy: in the last eight or ten years of the war the standard of living of a large part of the population fell because prices had risen faster than their incomes. They tended to blame their troubles on the introduction of machinery and to gather in groups to break machines under the leadership of the apocryphal Ned Ludd, but many of their problems were clearly caused by the demands of the war. The increase in domestic grain production, which depended on opening up marginal land, was profitable only because of the high wartime prices, and when the war came to an end these prices looked like collapsing when imported grain could be brought in. Britain would then have become a country which lived on imported food bought by exporting manufactured goods, a most unusual type of economy in the early nineteenth century, and the farmers and landlords who had been growing grain would have been in a very exposed position. Britain's general fiscal policy, at least since the time of Pitt, had been to move in the direction of free trade; in 1815 this was reversed, and heavy tariffs were imposed on imported grain. Progress towards free trade resumed with Huskinson's reductions of tariffs and ending of some of the prohibitions on trade a few years later, but the Corn Laws of 1815 affected commercial policy for thirty years.

The World After the Wars

The Napoleonic Wars changed and simplified the map of Europe. The largest of all the transfers of authority that followed the convulsions of the long wars was the movement to independence of all Spanish territory on the American mainland and the emergence of over twenty successor states. When France invaded Spain in 1808 the authority of the monarchy was weakened and distant areas like Argentina declared their independence in the next three or four years. It was clear that the other South American territories would have to be ruled in a new way. The Spanish government was no more able to do this than George III had been, so the Spanish possessions gained their independence in a struggle that went on for fifteen years partly because the Spanish governors were much better at organizing the loyalists than anyone had been in the British colonies. As a result of the long struggle and the immense size of the Spanish empire, it turned out not to be possible to keep the Spanish territories together in the way the Thirteen Colonies had become united in the 1780s. The different administrative units of the Spanish empire had enough of a political organization and of a sense of their own identity to be able to survive as independent nations, so that it would have been hard to restore imperial rule and even

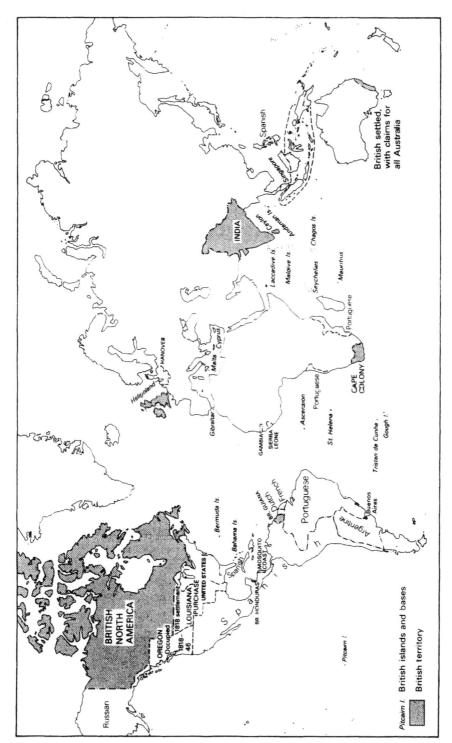

Map 6 Overseas Empires in 1815

Russian

BRITISH NORTH AMERICA

OREGON
Occupied
1818–
46

1818 settlement

LOUISIANA
PURCHASE

UNITED STATES

Bermuda Is.

Bahama Is.

Spanish

BR HONDURAS

MOSQUITO COAST

BR GUIANA
Dutch
French

Portuguese

Argentine

Buenos Aires

Pitcairn I.

Gibraltar

GAMBIA
SIERRA LEONE

Ascension

Portuguese

St. Helena

Tristan da Cunha

Gough I.

Heligoland

HANOVER

Malta
Cyprus

CAPE COLONY

INDIA

Ceylon

Andaman Is.

Laccadive Is.

Maldive Is.

Seychelles

Chagos Is.

Mauritius

Portuguese

Singapore

Spanish

British settled, with claims for all Australia

Pitcairn I. British islands and bases

British territory

harder to unite the Spanish-speaking states on any basis except the old loyalty to the monarch. Later on the United States absorbed states in Texas and California which broke away from Mexico, but this was more of a demonstration of the vitality of the expanding American frontier than an example that other countries could prudently follow. But the political cohesion that made it impracticable for other European powers to think of taking them over – as had been shown when a British expedition to Buenos Aires failed miserably in 1807 – also made it unnecessary to consider doing so. Britain's main concern was to be allowed to sell manufactured products to South America, and the end of Spanish political authority was accompanied by the end of Spanish commercial restrictions. The successor states followed free trade policies for some decades and maintained an adequate degree of law and order for trade to go on successfully.

The Spanish overseas possessions were reduced from the largest of the European empires to a collection of islands, and Portugal parted company with the largest of her colonies, Brazil, at just about the same time, though with much less fighting. The transfers of territory outside Europe at the end of the Napoleonic Wars were by comparison very small; the French had little enough to lose, and the British acquisitions from the Netherlands of the Cape of Good Hope, Ceylon, and part of the Dutch possessions in Guiana were not thought to be of much importance. The Dutch kept their large and valued possessions in the East Indies, which were returned at the end of the war, and in the next few years exchanges of territory were carried out to simplify the position and avoid disputes there. The British East India Company had maintained a not very successful base at Bencoolen on the south coast of Sumatra for over a century, and in the 1780s had begun moving on to the Malay peninsula by setting up a base at Penang. In the territorial transfers of the decade after 1815 the British Company gave up Bencoolen and committed itself to staying on the Malay side of the Malacca Straits, and the Dutch undertook to confine their operations to the islands.

While British gains in the 1815 peace settlements were small, British expansion in areas more or less unaffected by the war had gone ahead at a rate that suggested that a great force was pushing the country forward in a way that the war in Europe could not deflect. The expansion was in most cases based on steps taken before the war began, though the fact that the war did not noticeably affect these activities outside Europe reveals something of the pressure encouraging overseas activity at the time.

Australia had been launched as a colony before the war began, but its establishment on a sound footing went ahead between 1793 and 1815 as little affected by the wars as Jane Austen's heroines are always said to have been. One of the minor uses of the thirteen colonies had been as a convenient exile to which to send criminals. This had been becoming less acceptable to American opinion before 1776, and after the war convicts were not sent to the remaining colonies in North America. The government did not care to invest in Jeremy Bentham's idea of building a new style of prison in which to lock criminals up, even though he said that forced labour by convicts could be made to pay for the whole operation. Keeping prisoners locked up in the hulks, or disused ships moored off the coast, was thought harsh and not very secure; the government turned instead to consider the implications of the voyages of exploration Captain Cook had made in the Pacific between 1768 and 1779.

Cook had been noted as a navigator and a chart-maker ever since the operations in the St. Lawrence in 1759, and his Pacific voyages were great feats of seamanship and naval discipline, but a number of his findings were purely negative: going through the Bering Strait to the Arctic Ocean he found that there was no ice-free North West Passage, and sailing round the world in the high latitudes of the southern seas he found that people had been wrong in believing a large, virtually undiscovered continent existed there. On the other hand he charted a great many of the islands of the south Pacific, he sailed all the way round New Zealand, and all the way up the eastern coast of Australia. Previously only the north and north-west coasts had been discovered; they were taken to be part of the hypothetical great southern continent, but nobody thought they were attractive enough to be worth exploring. Cook reported that Australia was an island, and an island with an attractive and fertile coastline that reminded him of South Wales.

This seemed a very satisfactory place to which to send criminals. The government may possibly have been encouraged to choose this destination for them by some hopes of getting flax and tall trees for masts from Pacific settlements, but the transportation of convicts went ahead completely unaffected by the impracticability of any plans of this sort that there may have been. Captain Phillip's instructions told him to take the first fleet of convicts to what Cook had named Botany Bay; on arrival early in 1788, he decided that Sydney Cove would be much better, but Botany Bay remained the popular name for the fate of those condemned to be taken to the other end of the world. No entirely new settlements had been launched for over a century, and the government did not look back to the early days of settlement in North America (or even to the establishment of Georgia) to remind themselves how difficult it was for a colony to become self-supporting. As a result the whole colony came close to starving to death; a ship had to be sent to the Dutch at Cape Town, following the prevailing winds and sailing right round the world to get a few months' food.

The arrival in 1790 of a second fleet, with more convicts, brought relief just like the 1610 voyage to Virginia, but its supplies were barely adequate; and the government began to realize that, while Australia met the need for a place a long way from Britain to which convicts could be sent, it was not going to be able to survive without a reasonable flow of support for Britain.

Sydney was such an excellent harbour that it soon became the centre for the south Pacific whaling trade. Ships from England and New England, as well as a few owned locally, did very well out of providing whale oil – or train oil, from the Norwegian for whale – for Europe and America, but this was not enough to pay for all the imports that the infant colony needed. By 1800 Australia had cost the British government about £1m. which showed that colonization was cheaper than European warfare but also showed that the colony was not self-sufficient. Some of the money had been spent on building a port and roads running a short distance inland, but there were only about 5,000 convicts in the colony and it might easily have been cheaper to keep them in Britain. On the other hand it did get the colony started, and without the convicts it would have been very hard for anyone to launch a settlement so far from centres of trade and population, so the transportation of the convicts could be seen as the first of many schemes for government assistance to build up the population and labour force of Australia.

Most of the convicts were released after some years of forced labour, sometimes on public buildings and roads, sometimes working for private employers. They had great legal difficulties (not to mention financial problems) in returning to Britain, so they provided a base for the future population, though it was not very likely to grow because women were transported in much smaller numbers than men. Officers who had gone to Australia to serve in the garrison and some released convicts set up as private employers, with all the advantages of having unemancipated convicts assigned to them as a servile labour force. The governors who succeeded Phillip were not officers of great distinction; perhaps it was only natural that the best men were taking part in the wars against Napoleon. Captain Bligh, whose talent for getting on men's nerves had led to his being put into a small boat by the mutineers on the *Bounty* in 1789 and whose skill in seamanship enabled him to bring the boat 3,600 miles in 41 days to a safe harbour, was made Governor and decided to raise the moral tone of the colony by breaking up the officers' dealing in rum, which had become the normal currency for paying wages. Instead he was in 1808 for a second time the victim of a mutiny, and his officers imprisoned him. Local rebellions against a governor were not unprecedented, and the mutineers were not punished as severely as might have been expected.

When MacQuarie was appointed Governor in 1809 there was no sign that the government thought that he was particularly talented or that Australia needed a governor of outstanding qualities. He may have shone the more brightly by comparison with his predecessors, or Australia may have reached the point at which the previous investment of time and money was going to produce a return. Under MacQuarie the work of development went ahead so that Sydney emerged as a reaonably attractive town at the centre of a well-cultivated area in the coastal plain, and the two foundations of Australian development were laid during his governorship that determined the course of the colony at least until the discovery of gold in 1851. For its first quarter-century the colony had been checked in any westward movement inland by the eucalyptus-covered Blue Mountains. In 1813 a way through the mountains was found which meant that New South Wales could expand if any use could be made of the new land. In the area round Sydney stock-breeders were already applying themselves to building up herds of merino sheep from Spain which could provide meat for the colony but would primarily be intended to provide wool. When they moved on to the plains beyond the Blue Mountains the Australians found themselves committed to a diet of mutton and the British government learnt to its relief that the colony was within sight of covering its costs.

While the wars against France went on Britain's population had been increasing fast enough to cause alarm. The classic statement of the argument that the world would not be able to feed all its people was presented in the gloomy calculations to which Malthus, a lecturer at the East India Company's staff training college, was led by the obvious pressure of population of the 1790s. But there was the more cheerful view that the forces of famine and disease which he feared would be strengthened by the current expansion of population had already been holding growth back for centuries, and that the real novelty was that improved agriculture and the opening up of so many jobs in industry had partly overcome these traditional checks on growth. While the wars went on, emigration from Britain was relatively restrained; the new industrial jobs and the army and navy absorbed a very large proportion of the increased population. But while the tide of emigration was at nothing like the post-war level, it had begun to rise and helped the growth of the new colonies of white settlement by the early years of the new century. Australia began to receive voluntary emigrants as well as convicts, a few people went to the Cape of Good Hope even before the formal cession to Britain at the end of the war, and the colonies in North America which had remained British attracted settlers as the lumber trade began to thrive.

The Boundaries of British North America

Upper Canada had been set up under the 1791 Act as a home for United Empire Loyalist emigrants from the United States, and its first capital was in an exposed position very close to Niagara Falls on the American frontier. But in the mid-1790s courts and assemblies moved to York (named after the noble Duke of York who led his ten thousand men to the top of the hill, until, in an early example of renaming for ideological reasons, the city changed its name to Toronto in the 1830s to show it had cast off its links with what was seen as the corrupt British aristocracy).

Upper Canada began to show its power to draw together the exiles in the

Niagara Peninsula and the settlers moving west from Montreal to Lake Ontario. In Lower Canada the assembly showed some readiness to challenge the Governor: it said something for the restraint of the two sides that the Governor did not charge the assembly with favouring the French side in the long wars in Europe, and the assembly did not do anything that would have justified such a charge. The wars brought some prosperity to both Canadas. Britain needed to build as large a navy as possible, and the naval supplies she usually bought from the Baltic region were not plentiful enough and at times not secure enough from French attack for the government to rely on them. So Canadian wood was chosen instead; wood from the Baltic was certainly cheaper so the Canadian suppliers had to be helped by a favourable tariff, and for the first half of the nineteenth century the imperial preference helped Canadians find a market for the wood they cut as they cleared the land near the St. Lawrence and the Great Lakes system of water communication. The steamships which were being developed in the first years of the century were at first used for navigating rivers, which was something they could obviously do better than sailing ships, but they had not yet opened up the Mississippi, and so land on the Great Lakes was more attractive than almost any other land in the interior of North America.

In the later years of the long wars with France, the British blockade of French territories led to increasing irritation in the United States, and so did the British practice of taking seamen off American ships and pressing them to serve in the Royal Navy if it could plausibly be claimed that they were subjects of George III. The annoyance at this expressed by New England maritime interests was taken up by people who lived further inland, and pushed to a much more extreme level; when the enthusiasm for war shown by people who lived inland, led by Senator Henry Clay of Kentucky, is compared with the dislike of the idea of fighting shown by the New Englanders – who were the only people with genuine grievances – it seems fair to conclude that the blockade was adopted as a pretext by sections of the country that really wanted to take over land in Canada.

Once this desire for land is seen as the motive force behind the war, it is easy to understand why New England took very little part in the war and why the fighting was concentrated at the western end of Lake Ontario where Clay's war-hawks were closest to the land they wanted to acquire. But they made very little progress; the British kept an army in North America about one-third the size of their land army opposing the French in Spain and Portugal, and this was quite enough, with the Canadian militia, to hold back the American attack. The Americans had naval superiority on the Lakes, and used this to land an expedition at York, capture it, and burn it. The British saw the possibilities of this tactical innovation, and used their command of the sea to land a force in Chesapeake Bay, march inland, capture Washington, and burn it in turn. When an American attack from New York threatened Lower Canada the French Canadians made it clear that, while they wanted to reduce British influence, they knew quite enough about the way French-speaking Catholics were not being allowed any separate religious and linguistic rights in Louisiana to feel that they would be much safer under British rule. In this spirit of qualified loyalty they helped resist the American invasion. Late in 1814 the British tried to repeat their Washington success further south by making an attack on New Orleans from the sea. They were defeated, but before the Americans could be encouraged by this news they learnt that their diplomats had made peace with Britain.

The Treaty of Ghent did not look like a definitive settlement. It referred most of the points at issue to committees, some of which were never heard of again, but it acknowledged that the essential issue had been decided: an American attack on Canada was not practicable, and it was clear that the area of the St. Lawrence and the Great Lakes would not become American. One of the committees created under the Treaty laid down another feature of North American political geography. In 1818 its report drew a frontier across most of the west of North America along the 49th parallel of latitude from Lake Superior to the Rocky Mountains, and thus provided a basis for peaceful division of land as people moved out and settled the western half of the continent.

There was more need to define this boundary than anyone would have expected twenty years earlier. Jefferson's purchase of Louisiana had given the United States claims to land that ran west of the Lakes, and the greatly increased activity of the Hudson's Bay Company had meant that it was taking its territorial claims to Rupert's Land – the land whose rivers flowed into the Hudson Bay – more seriously than before. The 49th parallel served very well as a rough dividing-line between the Hudson Bay and the Mississippi river systems. But forty years earlier the Hudson's Bay Company had shown no interest in the further limits of the territory assigned to it under the 1670 charter and nobody took its claims to enormous areas of land very seriously. Competition from the Montreal fur-traders forced the Company to change its ways of working and to send its traders inland to meet the Indians who caught the beaver and other furred animals which were the foundation of trade. In the early decades of the commercial struggle the North-West Company was much more energetic, much more prepared for the conditions inland, and perhaps a little more unscrupulous than the Hudson's Bay Company. It needed all of these qualities if it was to overcome the immense disadvantage imposed on its traders by the fact that they had to go up the St. Lawrence and the whole length of the Great Lakes before they had got as far west as the rival trading posts on Hudson Bay. For a couple of decades the North-West Company adapted better to the conditions and was more successful; it survived divisions in its Montreal organization, the emergence and then the reabsorption of rival companies, and the risk of attacks from the south. In the opening stages the Hudson's Bay Company kept going only because between 1720 and 1770 it had piled up large financial reserves which it could draw on and had acquired a position in London that meant it could hope for friends to rally from outside. And so, in a most unexpected form, they did.

The Earl of Selkirk could see that the Scottish clan system was doomed by the last decades of the eighteenth century; as leader of the clan he wanted to do something to mitigate the shock for his people, and he believed the Hudson's Bay Company could help do this. When they saw that the days of private armies of retainers had gone for ever, most Scottish landowners got rid of the surplus tenants in what became known as 'the Highland Clearances' (or evictions), turned the land over to sheepfarming, and let the tenants go anywhere they chose as long as they got out of their old homes. Their old homes were rough and crude enough to mean that leaving them need not have been an unmixed disaster, but many of the evicted clansmen – whether they went to Glasgow, or to Nova Scotia, or to a wide range of other places – had no way to put their communities back together again. Selkirk did not want this to happen to his people. Emigration to Canada seemed to make good sense, but he thought it should be organized and the emigrants be able to stay with people they knew.

Working of these lines Selkirk established settlements in Prince Edward Island and in Ontario, and then considered the possibility of a larger settlement further west. He bought enough shares in the Hudson's Bay Company to gain a commanding position in it, and acquired a land grant of about 116,000 square miles in the area west of Lake Superior and running from Lake Winnipeg towards the southernmost part of the basin of the Bay, so that part of it lay south of the 49th parallel. In 1811 he began taking steps to colonize this area, and the life of the North-West Company was at once threatened. A grant of this sort, made on the basis of the 1670 charter, would establish the legal position of the Hudson's Bay Company as a great land-owner, and if Selkirk's Red River settlement survived it would lie across the desperately overstretched line of communication between Montreal and the North-West. If the area had not been so thinly populated, the scuffles that broke out in the next ten years all the way from Lake Superior to the Great Slave Lake in the Athabaska region around the 60th parallel might have been called civil war. While the 49th parallel was established as the frontier by the 1818 settlement (and the southern portion of Selkirk's land grant was transferred to the United States as a result), the area the fur-traders really wanted was far to the north of the frontier, and the flat, open, and unwooded land held by Britain just north of the new frontier was ignored because it had no furred animals.

After years of struggle that did nobody any good, and probably harmed the Indian population more than anyone because the two firms competed in providing distilled spirits to win their support, a merger was worked out in 1821 and confirmed by imperial legislation which extended the area in which the Company had exclusive trading rights. The superiority of the Hudson Bay route was accepted, and trade was conducted by sea rather than by the lake route for Montreal. The old Hudson's Bay Company's financial resources and its position in the London market left it as the main force in the new company, which kept the name of the Hudson's Bay Company, while the Montreal firms which had banded together to trade as the North-West Company were forced off the stage. The bankruptcy of the McGillivray, Thain firm in 1824 was the clearest sign that power had shifted from Montreal to London, but it was not known for many years whether this meant that British North America had failed to unite itself around a single trading system and that Rupert's Land had been saved from being dominated by Montreal.

The fact that after the merger the fur-trading system was based on London probably helped it in its next struggle, because it could mobilize British strength behind its negotiating position more easily than the Montreal-based North-West Company could have done when it was faced by problems on the Pacific Coast. The expansion of Russia across Siberia in the eighteenth century had moved on across the Bering Straits into Alaska, so a frontier had to be worked out between the Russian interest in catching the sea-otter along the coast 600 or 800 kilometres north of Vancouver and the Company's position inland. In 1826 the British and Russian governments worked out a rough boundary line that gave the Russians the fur-catching coastline they wanted but meant they had to co-operate with the Company to keep their supply-lines open. Further to the south, the Anglo-US frontier between the Rocky Mountains and the Pacific had been left undefined in 1818 and the Company carried on its operations as far south as the Columbia river flowed. Its activity held back the American fur-traders who in the 1820s and 1830s were no more numerous and rather less well supported than the Company, but it left open the question of what would happen if Americans wanted to settle in the region in large numbers.

The Dynamic Empire

While Britain's possessions on the mainland of North America had been transformed between 1760 and 1820 from a thin but relatively densely settled Atlantic coastal strip into a loosely sketched land mass running from east to west right across the north of North America, the old-established colonies in the West Indies had begun in the same years to feel the impact of changing moral views in Britain. In the first half of the eighteenth century slavery had been accepted as an unusual but perfectly legitimate form of property; in 1774 Mansfield had said in Somersett's case that it was so odious that nothing but a positive law could make it legal, which meant slave-owners could not expect to hold on to slaves in Britain without new legislation (which led to the release of up to 10,000 slaves already in the country) but left it perfectly legal in the American and West Indian colonies, where the entire structure of laws supported it. People in Britain approved of the judgement in Somersett's case, and by the 1790s the new ideas of government as an instrument of benevolence were having an effect. A colony for slaves freed in Britain or at liberty after fleeing from the American Revolution had been founded in Sierra Leone by British philanthropists and when, after twenty years of effort, it was clear that they could no longer support it financially, the Colonial Office arranged in 1807 to take it over.

Slave-owners could hardly be deprived of their property, but the slave trade was more open to attack. It was as brutal as slavery, but ending it would not involve a general attack on the rights of property; the trade was an unspectacular part of the national economy which yielded the shipowners a little under 10 per cent a year after allowing for the fact that, as in any ocean-going trade, they had to wait some time for their money. Taking trade goods to West Africa and bringing sugar back from the West Indies were perfectly normal types of commerce; the 'middle passage', the voyage across the Atlantic, with slaves bought from African war leaders who had captured other Africans, was quite another matter. The voyage took about two months; presumably the traders wanted the slaves alive and profitable rather than dead, and yet up to the 1790s over 8 per cent of the slaves loaded on board died at sea. Opponents of the trade naturally pointed to the overcrowding and brutality on board ship, and generalized from disastrous (and financially ruinous) voyages in which a quarter or a third of the slaves died. Defenders of the trade praised it as a school in which seamen learned their trade, and said many slaves simply made up their minds to die after they had left Africa. The first attacks on the trade forced the traders to improve conditions and, partly because this cut the death rate at sea to 3 per cent, and partly because British command of the seas during the long wars opened up markets previously supplied by the French and the Dutch, profits in the 1790s rose to 13 per cent. The wars weakened the political attack on the trade; in the 1780s Pitt as Prime Minister and Fox as his leading opponent in the Commons were not so deeply hostile that they could not work together in attacking the trade, but they were much more sharply divided over the French Revolution than over earlier issues, and in any case many backbenchers accepted the argument that a prudent man would not repair his house during the hurricane season. Sales of slaves went ahead in the captured French and Dutch islands, so British traders did not become very deeply committed to the American market, though the Americans were bringing more slaves to the southern states to meet the growing Lancashire demand for raw cotton.

Most of the captured islands were returned to the French and Dutch by the short-lived Peace of Amiens but were recaptured when the war began again. This step, which looked like the normal course of warfare in the West Indies, turned out to provide the opportunity to end the slave trade. When Pitt died in 1806 the Whigs came to Office, and began putting their anti-slavery principles into effect. First they laid it down that neutrals could not trade with the captured islands, and then they forbade British slave dealers to bring slaves to them, on the grounds that the islands might have to be returned once again after the wars were over. The point was rather flimsy and would probably not have been accepted if the slave trade had not already lost so much support. Nobody seems to have realized that the British trade had become so much a matter of supplying slaves to the colonies of other nations that the 1806 regulations against supplying slaves to non-British colonies eliminated three-quarters of it. Given time the trade might have been able to reorganize itself, but it had been weakened to such an extent that the following year Parliament made dealing in slaves by British merchants illegal, and maintained the wartime regulations against other nations shipping slaves to West Indian destinations. In peace negotiations at the end of the long wars, the British insisted on putting clauses prohibiting slave trading into the treaties; among the victors Prussia, Russia, and Austria had no interest in the slave trade and had no objection to pleasing an ally on this point. The French got their sugar islands back – partly because the British sugar interest had no desire to see competitors brought within the system of tariff preferences – but were in no position to resist the British desire to end the trade.

Making the slave trade illegal was not quite the same as ending it, and the British had to take steps to enforce the provisions of the treaty. Several hundred thousand pounds were paid to Spain and Portugal to induce them to give up the trade. A 'slave squadron' was set up to patrol the Atlantic, rescue slaves, and take them to Sierra Leone. The activities of the slave squadron led to a number of clashes with the United States: the American South was where demand for slaves was rising fastest, and British zeal about intercept-ing ships trying to meet that demand led to complaints that innocent American ships were being interfered with. No doubt there were harsh and evangelically-inclined captains who intercepted American ships without adequate reasons, but then there were also American ships which were free of carrying slaves only in the technical sense that they had been tipped overboard when a British warship came in sight. The slave squadron cost £750,000 a year, or about 2 per cent of peacetime government spending in the early nineteenth century, though it is unlikely that the naval budget would have been cut by the full amount if the slave squadron had been abolished. The British would still have wanted to maintain their superiority, even if there had been no slave trade to intercept; the operation of the slave squadron was a beneficent by-product of naval policy, much as the capacity to capture colonies from other European powers from 1650 onwards was for the British a satisfactory by-product of naval policy.

Slave trading was just a part of the whole shipping business, and presumably the slave traders simply converted their ships to take part in legitimate trade. The West Indian sugar-growers could not change their occupation so easily, but in 1807 their position still seemed unthreatened; sugar imports were rising steadily and the plantations were prosperous, though they were not expanding at a rate that called for many new slaves and they were not able to sell sugar cheaply enough to do without their tariff preference in the British market. They could survive legislation making the slave trade illegal and hope that the rising tide of hostility to slavery would not mount so high that people in England would be ready to contemplate the general blow to property – or else the heavy bill for compensation – that would be involved in setting the West Indian slaves free.

But if the sugar-growers had looked at developments in India they would have seen changes that might have worried them. British policy was becoming less willing to accept the domination of monopolies in commerce, and less willing to allow commerce to dominate the government's economic policy. Neither of these changes was a good omen for the West Indies, and the West Indies were bound to lose in influence in London as India became a more important part of the empire. The prudent approach taken by Cornwallis and Shore was abruptly ended; a judicious policy that concentrated on keeping the books balanced was suddenly replaced by a bold policy that showed no interest in the books and the balances. The architect of this abrupt change, Richard Wellesley, Lord Mornington, became Governor-General in 1798. He was on good terms with the ministers who were his political superiors, and was prepared to obey most of their instructions, but his attitude to his commercial employers in the East India Company was one of aristocratic contempt for men who were all too obviously in trade. While he was far from overwhelmed by the greatness of his position, he felt that, because he needed subordinates he could rely on, he had to fit two of his younger brothers into jobs. His family feeling did not go far enough to lead him to bring out his wife, whose social position was uneasy because she had borne him five children before they got married.

His predecessors had not been interested in territorial expansion. They had taken over Bengal, partly because of the plunder to be seized by Company employees and partly because of the problems of the Bengal succession, but this was the only large acquisition they had made. Their diplomacy aimed at making sure that everybody in India respected the Company, but as long as Indian political society held together there was no reason why the Company should want anything more. The collapse of political stability, and the impossibility of being sure that peaceful trading would be practicable, called into question the non-expansionist policy of the previous thirty years. Wellesley was not the man to give the peaceful policy a chance, and he arrived at a time when Indians who wanted peace and quiet would be ready to welcome any ruler who could end the fighting by crushing all the others. The Moghul Empire had disintegrated, and the Emperor's power to maintain his authority even in a small area round Delhi had been impaired by an Afghan invasion; the power of the Marathas to destroy opposition was not matched by any capacity to build anything new, and the British looked like the least bad choice to many Indians.

The war against France encouraged a bellicose mood in Britain, which Wellesley entered into very fully. He was sailing to India when the French were launching the Egyptian campaign, and landed three months before Napoleon captured Alexandria . . . if Alexander the Great could march from Egypt to India, there was nothing to suggest that Napoleon could not do the same thing. When Wellesley heard that Tipu Tib, the son and successor of Haidar Ali who had been such a danger to the East India Company as Sultan of Mysore in the 1770s, was negotiating with the French, he took it very seriously. Possibly there was nothing in it, but the French were reckoning they could sail down the Red Sea to India in six weeks, so their involvement seemed more conceivable in 1798 than at any other time after 1763. Wellesley marched against Mysore at once, Tipu Tib was killed in battle, and the new Sultan of Mysore had to give up some territory, including his only link with the sea, and also had to make a treaty with the Company in which he was clearly a subordinate rather than an equal.

The Company had been making treaties in India for some time and, while it had treated the lesser princes as vassals or subordinates, it had been willing to accept the more important Indian princes as equals in negotiation. Wellesley was not. Quite apart from taking territory from princes when they were defeated in battle, he tried to make sure that all of them had to enter into 'subsidiary treaties', which usually meant that they could run their own affairs within the territory they retained but had to leave questions of external policy to the British. This was Wellesley's way of dealing with the collapse of central authority in India: if the Emperor could no longer make his rule effective so that the princes were turning into independent sovereigns, the Company would take the Emperor's place by making the princes accept its external authority instead, though it would leave co-operative rulers with the local power which they had held under the Moghul Empire in the days of its greatness. As soon as Mysore had been pushed into this new form of dependency, Wellesley turned his attention to the other great ruler in the south, the Nizam of Hyderabad, and forced him into a subsidiary alliance. In one way it was a model for this diplomatic approach; the Nizam was the most powerful prince to accept this relationship with the Company, and his family's position remained secure under it for over 150 years.

In the north things could not be handled so amicably, partly because – at least after the death of Nana Farnavis in 1800 – the Maratha confederacy had no single head with whom Wellesley could negotiate, and partly because the confederacy had no intention of accepting British supremacy, but the British advance up the Ganges from Bengal towards Delhi went ahead. The Peshwa, who had some hereditary claim to be the leader of the Marathas, made an alliance with Wellesley – although it left him with a position that was not much better than that of the rulers of Mysore and Hyderabad – and Scindia, one of the Peshwa's rivals, was defeated. Holkar, the third powerful leader among the Marathas, was pushed back but not crushed, and he survived to oppose Wellesley's successors. By 1805 the British had occupied Delhi and in practice controlled the Moghul Emperor, though they still went through the forms of acknowledging his position as the heir to what had been the dominant source of legitimate authority in India.

When Wellesley became Governor-General in 1798 the British were one among half a dozen important powers in India. Seven years later Wellesley had transformed the situation; the East India Company, or behind it the British government's Board of Control, was clearly the leading power in India, and the only question was the way in which it would exercise its supremacy. If Wellesley and his relations had remained in charge British policy would undoubtedly have pressed forward, though his brothers would not have been as unrestrained in their policy as Lord Wellesley: Henry was a very competent diplomat and Arthur, later Duke of Wellington, was the greatest soldier ever to organize and lead British troops in India. It could be said that in these years in India he was only learning his profession, but while the armies were less powerful than in Europe the distances were greater and the supply problems more difficult than any that he later handled in his European campaigns. But, although he was one of the most economical of generals, these successes could not be gained without a cost, and by 1805 the cost was becoming too high.

Wellesley felt, and expressed, a most profound contempt for the 'cheese-mongers', as he called the directors of the Company, and he showed no willingness to listen to their complaints about the rising Company debt. By the standard of a politician, looking at the immense debt of about £800m. that Britain was incurring in the war against Napoleon, the increase in the Company debt from £18m. to £31m. during his period of conquest was a matter of no importance. The directors found it more worrying. Eventually it would have to be met, and possibly be paid off by the Indian rather than the British taxpayer, but in the short run the debt reduced the Company's chances of recovering control of its dividend policy. At the same time the British government was afraid that if the Company army suffered a serious defeat, it would have to be helped at a time when Britain was fully committed in the Napoleonic Wars. So, when the directors took the opportunity given by a very slight check to their army to dismiss Wellesley, the government did not try to save him. Wellesley got his blow in first and resigned, came back to English politics, and spent the rest of his life wondering why he never became Prime Minister.

He had disturbed the balance of power in India so much that it could never be restored; the other rulers had lost so much ground that, unless they could achieve a degree of unity unknown for decades, they stood no chance of resisting the British. As things turned out, they were not able to unite but they did try to resist, which meant that Wellesley's successors found themselves involved in a series of wars which usually seemed to be caused by unprovoked Indian lawlessness, but were in another sense the logical result of Wellesley's expansionist policy. This transformation in Britain's political position in India might have been expected to lead to a change in the position of the Company, but the formal structure of power was left unchanged when the Company's charter came up for renewal in 1813. Instead the commercial position of the Company was undermined by the ending of its monopoly of Indian trade. It continued to have a monopoly of the China trade, which meant that it was still the major trader in tea (and a large scale exporter of opium), because very little tea came from India before the 1850s. The Company had always been an importing firm which brought the rare commodities of the east to Britain, and by remaining in the tea trade it earned profits which covered the Company's dividends and contributed about £150,000 a year to the costs of administration and of past debts.

British trade with India was beginning to run in a new direction. As Lancashire cotton spinning became more efficient in the 1780s it captured the markets to which the Company had been exporting the textiles it bought in India. By the last years of the Napoleonic Wars costs had been brought down to a point where manufacturers could even meet the expenses of taking their goods out to India and compete there against local producers. Compared with other textile producers Lancashire manufacturers had a good deal of capital invested in machinery, and were eager to get as much use out of it as possible by lengthening their production runs and selling all over the world. The East India Company was not prepared to turn itself into an exporting firm selling Lancashire textiles to India; the manufacturers pressed for a change in the charter to allow them to trade with India on their own account and in the 1813 revision of the charter they got their way. In the course of the nineteenth-century India became the largest single importer of British textiles, and the Company moved further away from trade and towards becoming an instrument of the British government for civil service appointments, diplomacy, and war.

In the same year that the Company lost its monopoly of Indian trade, settlers in Australia got through the Blue Mountains to the great plains beyond. The two events indicated the future for the British Empire as the

Napoleonic Wars came to an end, and showed how much it had changed in the previous fifty years. At the end of the Seven Years' War the empire was limited and restrained in its nature; it depended on the Navigation Acts for its cohesion, it tried to stop expansion inland in America, and it showed no desire to go beyond its recent gains in Bengal. By the end of the Napoleonic Wars the national debt was a larger fraction of the national income than the debt which had frightened George Grenville in the 1760s, but this did not hold expansion back. In the thirty or forty years after Waterloo the empire grew so rapidly and yet with so little sense of strain or effort that it looked as if there was some dynamic force which, once set in motion, carried its boundaries forward until they were stopped by mountains or oceans.

This was not a completely new departure. Though the advances in the 1750s were slow and hesitant compared with what happened fifty years later, people were already beginning to move inland. Between 1600 and 1750 the British overseas had confined themselves exclusively to coastal settlement, and it took the Americans 150 years to cover 200 miles and penetrate the Appalachians. The Blue Mountains were 60 miles inland and the Australians took only 25 years to cross them, and this expansion had begun before changes in methods of transport had made much difference to the difficulty of the task. Better canals were being built by the end of the eighteenth century and they could sometimes be used to link newly-settled areas with the coastal settlements, and by the middle of the nineteenth century many problems could be solved by building railways, but the first generation of people moving inland could not make use either of railways or of canals.

New Institutions in Britain

Several institutional changes helped imperial development in the early decades of the nineteenth century. After 1815 the new Secretary of State was able to concentrate on the colonial side of his duties. Lord Bathurst held the position for fifteen years from 1812 to 1827, a far longer tenure of office than anyone enjoyed before or since, and this long period of continuity (apart from meaning that Bathurst's name was given to more places in the English-speaking world than he could ever have expected) allowed the government to get used to the complexities of ruling an empire with a much greater range of different types of constitution than had ever been known before: Upper and Lower Canada looked quite like the old American colonies, the ruling class in the West Indies was under pressure about slavery, New South Wales was run like a prison, Gibraltar like a fort, British Guiana like a conquered territory where the new rulers wanted to adopt some of the institutions of the old rulers, and Sierra Leone like a missionary settlement with a tendency to go bankrupt.

This diversity probably helped keep political problems under control in a way that a uniform system could never have done, but anyone who wanted to reduce it to a coherent pattern would have found it an alarming legacy from the past. Perhaps the Colonial Office never quite caught up with it, but at least the new organization in London had more chance of making sense of it than any of the old administrative contrivances set up in the days when all colonies were run by a governor and assembly could ever have done. Continuity in office and concentration on colonial problems without other responsibilities was a great help, and so was the long period of peace after 1815. The British had gained from a series of wars at a time when expansion was a matter of taking coastal colonies away from other European countries, but expansion inland would have been very expensive if it had involved renewed fighting. Moving inland involved more risk-taking by individuals than most of the expansion since 1650 had done, so there was something like a return to the individual efforts of the first half of the seventeenth century, which was almost the only previous period of their history in which the British had enjoyed anything like the freedom from involvement in European wars which they had in the nineteenth century. The British government in the nineteenth century did not show much willingness to concern itself with the efforts of Englishmen – whether living in the British Isles or already based overseas – to extend territory inland, and consistently assumed that it should be organized and paid for by private individuals or by the governments of colonies already settled overseas. But while the British government took this thrifty and pacific approach, its unchallenged command of the seas and the long peace in Europe provided conditions in which expansion overseas by private citizens was much easier than it would have been in the eighteenth century.

New developments in Britain during the long wars made it all the more likely that the British would move forward. The preaching of Wesley, and perhaps fear of the French Revolution, had changed the British attitude to religion very noticeably around the turn of the century. In the eighteenth century a decent and composed belief in religion had always been acceptable, and enthusiasm, dedication, and the spirit of martyrdom had been ill received. In the nineteenth century there was much more zeal about religion among Englishmen (including opponents of religion like the secularists), so religious activity overseas was no longer to be seen just as a matter of bringing the comforts of religion to Englishmen overseas, though they were not neglected and, with the consecration of bishops for North American dioceses in the 1780s, a process of expanding the Church of England and making it less confined to England was begun. But nineteenth-century British Christianity went much further in its desire to preach the Word of the Lord to all nations and in its most ambitious late nineteenth-century form it looked forward to 'the Evangelisation of the world in this generation'. The East India Company had employed chaplains for its own staff, but had tried to make sure that no missionaries would raise the religious temperature by coming to India and trying to convert the inhabitants; in the 1813 revision of the charter the barrier against missionaries was struck down. The Baptists, the Congregationalists, and the Church of England had all launched Missionary Societies in the 1790s; the British and Foreign Bible Society, in which it was hoped all Protestants would work together, was launched in 1804. So evangelists poured out from Britain to the colonies and into the less settled lands that lay beyond the frontiers of colonies. The East India Company was quite right to think that missionaries would have an unsettling effect: opposition to slavery and devotion to the idea that the souls of all men were equal in the sight of God could drive a West Indian slave-owner or a strict Brahmin to feel rage and contempt for anyone who so obviously flew in the face of good sense and true religion. The East India Company might have tried to turn itself into just another Indian ruler like the Emperors it had overthrown; when missionaries came on the scene they were going to be committed to the values of the culture from which they came and, even if their religion sometimes made fewer converts than their devotion seemed to deserve, the general message of westernization which they brought with them was harder to resist.

The missionaries fully intended to have an imperial effect, though they preached a kingdom which was not of this world. Another institution spread British influence with rather less intention of doing anything of the sort: during the long wars the City of London had risen to new heights of financial eminence, with a very large volume of domestic business because so much money had to be raised to pay for the long wars that there was a great deal of trading in the massive and liquid National Debt, and a large amount of international business because the British government was eager to finance continental powers which could recruit armies to face France. London had been a great commercial centre for importing and re-exporting for over a century, and the British National Debt had been an attractive security for foreign investors, but the City had not really displaced Amsterdam as the financial centre for everybody connected with the European financial system until the end of the eighteenth century.

After 1815 the London money market devoted a good deal of its energy to overseas financing, at first almost entirely in the form of floating and managing issues of government bonds. In the years immediately after the Napoleonic Wars clients came mainly from the continent of Europe. By the 1820s governments in the Americas were raising loans in London. A certain amount of the Indian long-term debt had moved from India to London, though the Company preferred it to be held in India. Other colonies were not yet fully established enough to be able to raise loans, but as the nineteenth century wore on, one of the links in the imperial connection was that colonies could borrow in London on better terms than other governments of comparable strength could expect, and British lenders could feel confident that colonial bonds, while never as easy to sell at short notice as British government bonds, were a solid type of security. The governments of colonies never went bankrupt, unlike South American countries or states in the United States, which sometimes looked as if they were making no real attempt to meet their obligations. What colonies found really valuable was a British government guarantee for their bonds, which would make them easier to sell, but guarantees were rarely given and normally colonies managed very well without them. Their position in the market was improved in 1900, when their bonds were declared to be safe and suitable investments for British trustees to include in their funds, though this did not mean that the British government vouched for their solvency.

While missionary societies and bankers could be seen as new forces promoting expansion, the most obvious force opening up new territory was the growth of population, proceeding faster than ever before or since in Britain. In the mid-eighteenth century population had not been growing so quickly, and nobody who wanted to settle overseas was likely to think of going anywhere except the colonies on the American coast. By the last decades of the century growth was rapid: the population rose from under 14m. in 1780 to almost 16m. in 1801, to 18m. in 1811, and to 21m. in 1821. The government was worried about the increasing population of the British Isles and encouraged emigration by grants of money and land from time to time, and later by the establishment of a permanent committee to assist it. With changes of direction and fluctuations in numbers, about 20m. people left the British isles in the century between 1815 and 1914. While the United States drew the largest numbers of emigrants, the rates of growth in the new colonies were sometimes even more spectacular. Both Australia and Canada doubled their numbers between 1820 and 1840, to some extent by natural increase but very largely by emigration from Britain. It is hard to see how the British nineteenth-century economy could have grown fast enough to accommodate all these people if they had stayed at home, and one of the major advantages of empire for people in Britain was that it provided a wider range of opportunities for them if they chose to leave the country. Those who stayed at home may possibly have gained by improved prospects for trade and later for investment; most of those who emigrated permanently were likely (as had been the case for those who went to seventeenth-century America) to become better off as a result of their decision. Seen in a wider perspective, one great feature of the history of the world in the last 500 years has been the opening up of empty or thinly populated areas of the globe by people of European descent; the nineteenth-century expansion of the British Empire was a major part of that opening up of the world, and by 1815 the foundations for expansion had been firmly laid.

6. *Expansion Without Effort 1815–1854*

At the end of the long wars with France the British thought – as at the end of every war – of cutting government spending and of enjoying their expanded territories. They still saw their empire as a collection of ports, islands, and coastal regions, held together by the navy and dependent on it for prosperity and even survival. The navy dominated the seas of the whole world to an extent that had no parallel. No other country had a comparable force, and no country was likely to throw away its money in a competition with the formidable fleet already in existence and the immense industrial power behind it. The navy retained its three historical roles of making the country safe from invasion, of protecting trade, and of defending the colonies. When Britain's population expanded to the point where it could be fed only by importing food in exchange for industrial products, the navy took on the new role of making sure that imports of food were perfectly secure. Its role in diplomacy became more explicit during the first half of the century: it could be sent all over the world, and could be used to make Britain's power supreme at any point which lay within a cannon-shot of the sea.

The British government very rarely wanted to push its power any further than this and made no particular effort to advance inland. The inhabitants of the colonies, reinforced by the flood of emigrants after the end of the Napoleonic Wars, moved into the interior without referring the matter to London or paying much attention to the views of their governors. The launching of new colonies in Australia and expansion to New Zealand owed a good deal to the desire of Australians for new land, a considerable amount to the desire of people in Britain for new opportunities, and very little to the policy of the British government. The largest piece of land acquisition in southern Africa, the trek of the Afrikaners into the interior, was an attempt to escape from the British government, and after a few years the British government acquiesced in this attempt. In India the government in Calcutta was settling down as a permanent authority with a mind of its own, though one which would always accept British instructions in the final analysis.

The movement inland was only one sign of the greater wealth and increased population of the colonies. By the middle of the century these changes led naturally enough to a great increase in the colonies' freedom of action. But while the establishment of 'responsible government' and greater colonial autonomy owed something to a general awareness that the colonies in which Englishmen settled had become much better able to look after themselves, it was also affected by the changes in relations between rulers and elected assemblies in Britain, and by a change in British views about the right economic structure for the empire. By 1850 the maritime empire dependent on the navy had started to dissolve into something altogether more complicated which still needed the navy for defence against European powers but now contained colonies which ran their own local affairs and held no special place in Britain's tariff arrangements. The change might possibly have satisfied Washington and Jefferson that all the things they wanted in the 1770s were being achieved by Britain's colonies, and yet nobody in Britain showed much sign of worrying about the change as long as the arrangements for conducting defence and foreign policy remained unchanged.

Emigration and Settlement

For the British who stayed at home, this was all that was needed. Emigrants might have liked something more, and would probably have welcomed support for their advance inland, but the government's response was indifference, qualified by a strong desire not to spend money on colonial entanglements and a grudging recognition that it would not be politically possible to abandon them if they ran into difficulty. The strength of the navy, and the almost complete loss of interest of all the other European powers in any sort of overseas expansion, meant that settlers in colonies were unlikely to meet any enemy equal to them in military strength. But even this did not mean that the British taxpayer could be quite sure that settlers overseas would meet all the expenses of their enthusiasm for expansion.

These conflicting pressures shaped developments in southern Africa in the quarter-century after Waterloo. The British had already held the Cape for most of the twenty years since 1795, but had thought of it as a possession that might be handed back at the end of the war. The wartime regime accepted many of the Dutch ways of doing things, and impinged very little on those of the Dutch who had moved inland as farmers and could be called Afrikaners rather than Hollanders. In 1815 the British kept the Cape as a port that could be useful to the India trade, but had to face the fact that the Afrikaners had made the colony into something more than the simple base for re-provisioning that the Dutch East India Company had originally intended. Domestically they had established slavery; further afield they had moved east along the coast and had already reached the densely-populated areas of Xhosa settlement beyond the Fish River. They were becoming involved in the steady alternation of struggle and peace which went on from 1779 to 1853 in the narrow area between the Fish and the Kei rivers, following a pattern changed very little by the British annexation, that is usually known as the Kaffir Wars. (The Muslims who had been imported as slaves, from the Dutch East Indies, called the pagan Africans 'kafirs'.)

The British government seems to have been quite unworried by the first stages of these wars when it decided, just after the peace with France, to encourage British settlement in the Cape. In 1820 about 5,000 settlers were sent out in an undertaking which came as close as anything the government ever did to paying people to go abroad, and they were fairly consciously planted close to the existing border about 400 miles east of Cape Town. The Afrikaners had moved such a long way east in order to concentrate on cattle-raising, which demanded very large areas of grazing-land because the pasture was so poor. The government seems to have reckoned that this nomadic approach encouraged friction with the Africans, and thought the British settlers would farm on much smaller areas. The settlers tried at first to grow grain, but the soil was certainly not good enough for this. When they switched to sheep-rearing, just a few years after the Australians had taken to it, they did relatively well. The steady development of new machinery was causing a great expansion in the British textile industry and, even though woollen goods were now less important than cotton, the demand for raw wool was growing fast enough for both colonies to be able to sell their clip quite easily. Wool could be exported profitably even when it had to be carried thousands of miles by sea; its value was so high in proportion to its weight – about ten times as high as that of wheat – that it could be moved long distances when the cost of moving grain still protected English farmers from the competition of farmers outside Europe.

While the 1820 settlers were able to establish themselves as a successful farming community, a fairly large number of them were skilled craftsmen who naturally moved into towns to carry on their trades; the division between urban British and rural Afrikaners very soon became visible. The new settlers strengthened the position of the governor, and in the course of the 1820s English became the language of government for all official purposes. This was a natural step to take in the commercial and administrative centre in Cape Town, and the Afrikaner farmers were separated enough from all authority not to notice this change. The Cape was becoming defined as three regions: in the west there was a prosperous and settled section which flourished with the port, the administration, and farming on fertile if rather dry soil; in the east, and along much of the seacoast, the British settlers and an Afrikaner minority had adopted a reasonably static form of agriculture, though they still quarrelled with the Africans further east; and some way inland the more adventurous Afrikaners continued to take on more land, just as they had done in the decades before the British came. They did not like the British government, but as they had not liked the Dutch government previously this did not involve any great change.

Their dislike was intensified by the attitude the new government took to the position of the Africans. The Afrikaners were the descendants of people who had left the Netherlands in an age of religious faith, and their faith was one that drew a sharp line between the saved and the damned. They transferred this attitude to the problem of relations with the Africans and proclaimed that an unpassable gulf lay between black and white, an attitude encouraged by the institution of slavery at the Cape; the difference between slave and free was as clear-cut as the difference between the saved and the damned. The British did not see things in this polarized way. No doubt a white man was normally better than a black man, but they could see a vast range of gradations: a Dutchman was not as good as an Englishman, the Afrikaner farmers were less civilized than the Cape Town Dutch, the racially mixed descendants of Africans and Afrikaners who had not completely accepted the idea of an unbridgeable gulf between the races were naturally going to be even further down the scale, and yet in some sense religion could declare the African population at the bottom of the system the equals of the Europeans who had become their political masters. Before British control had finally been given authority by the postwar settlement, justice was already being administered according to British principles, which meant that British, Afrikaners, and Africans were to be treated as equal for legal purposes.

This seemed to the Afrikaners neither fair nor sensible; they had read their Bibles, they knew God meant the children of Ham (always taken to refer to a black-skinned race, though there is little scriptural authority for this) to be slaves, and they felt convinced that the English were clearly flying in the face of God's commands. But the process of British justice went on: Afrikaners were brought to court for treating Africans in the way that they had been doing for a hundred years, and in 1815 five Afrikaners were hanged at Slaghter's Nek for defying the courts. British administrators in Africa were willing to help Afrikaners run things in the traditional way when this was possible, such as obliging Africans to carry passes which were intended to define their position in the labour market, but the general principle of legal equality still caused irritation. In 1828 the 50th ordinance made the position explicit: Africans (except for those who were still slaves) were to have the same legal status as everyone else in the colony. This seemed so absurd to the Afrikaners that they felt it could be explained only as the result of faulty theology, and this encouraged them to attribute more control over British policy to missionaries than was either accurate or sensible. Dr Philip of the London Missionary Society came to be seen as the villain, in the way that later settlers saw other groups as agitators who were misleading opinion in Europe and trying to impose the new ideas of Europe upon a continent that changed very little.

In reality it was extremely difficult for Dr Philip or any other missionary to get the support of the British government for any policy that required much financial support. The government probably felt relieved that no other part of the empire held out any prospect of comparable missionary activity in defence of the rights of the native population and that there did not seem to be much risk of demands for spending. Canada appeared to be a quietly satisfactory colony that cost very little; after a quick recovery from the losses caused by the American invasion it had settled down to a period of immigration and development. Troops demobilized after the Napoleonic Wars were rewarded with grants of Canadian land, and the fertile land north and west of the Niagara peninsula a little west of Lake Ontario was divided up and sold commercially. It was the colony with open land closest to Britain and most emigrants saw no need to go further afield; for about thirty-five years it attracted more immigrants than any other part of the empire, and in several years drew more than the United States.

One of the attractions of the United States was that – allowing for the unpredictability as well as the discomfort of voyages by sailing ship – it took something like four weeks to cross to New York and about six weeks to reach Montreal, a matter of considerable importance when a ticket cost a couple of weeks' wages and the main costs of crossing the Atlantic were those of buying food to bring on the voyage and of not being able to earn wages during the weeks of travelling. On the other hand it was easier to go up the St. Lawrence to reach open land than to go from New York out to Michigan, and land in southern Ontario cost less than land in upstate New York. Apart from this, Americans had a reputation in nineteenth-century Britain for being slippery and pushy, and many emigrants wanted to remain under the Union Jack, with its assurance that the shock of change would be slightly cushioned; and Scotsmen in particular found support and comfort from those of their connections who had crossed to Canada earlier. Among the men who reached eminence in nineteenth-century Canada, Macdonald, William Lyon Mackenzie, George Brown, Alexander Mackenzie, Donald Smith, and Sir Sandford Fleming had all been born in Scotland and crossed the Atlantic during the large-scale immigration of the first half of the nineteenth century.

In the opening decades of the nineteenth century the British were very conscious of the expansion of the population, and after 1815 unemployment was for several years a drag on the economy. The policy of encouraging emigration was denounced as one of 'shovelling out paupers', but however much the British government wanted to do this there was never enough money to send out many assisted immigrants in the period after 1815. In the years when this policy was most in favour, between 1823 and 1827, only about £65,000 was spent on it. Only a relatively prosperous family could pay for its own passage; and a number of the immigrants were farmers of some substance. Land companies set about selling the land west of Toronto and south-east of Montreal and offered it in freehold lots at relatively low prices, while it was very difficult to become anything more than a tenant farmer in Britain. When immigrants entered a fairly undeveloped area questions of local improvement naturally arose and the problem grew more intense when the population of Upper Canada doubled between 1827 and 1834. The new settlers were ready to clear their own land (and could either sell the wood or make it into potash to increase the fertility of the soil), but they wanted roads and schools, which the government of the colony was not prompt to provide. The advocate of the farmers of Upper Canada, William Lyon Mackenzie, devoted as much space in his newspaper to the question of roads as to anything else, though he explained the government's failure to provide them as part of a whole system of political oppression. The Lieutenant-Governor had to listen to his legislative council, in which the demand for roads and for development of the interior was made, but he paid quite as much attention to his executive council, in which the interest of the richer businessmen concerned with transatlantic trade with Britain could command more support. Mackenzie condemned these men as 'the family compact', and they responded by saying that Mackenzie was pro-American and a republican.

In Lower Canada a problem had developed which could become more dangerous. The elective system set up in 1791 had led naturally to a French-speaking majority in the assembly, and a majority made up mainly of doctors, lawyers, and journalists, under the leadership of Louis Joseph Papineau, who held opinions liberal enough to oppose the power of the church and old-fashioned enough to oppose the Montreal group who wanted commercial and industrial development. Papineau's followers expressed their opinion by resisting the Governor and his executive council in just the way that American assemblies had resisted their governors in the eighteenth century: they refused to vote taxes. Partly because the original 1774 Act had retained some of the old French royal revenues for the government, and partly because Lower Canada did not respond to the stress of its expanding population by trying to find money for roads or for canals, the administration could survive the friction between the Governor and the assembly.

Friction could not run along these lines in Australia, because British institutions like an assembly or trial by jury could hardly be established for a population consisting mainly of convicts or ex-convicts. Acquittal by a jury of ex-convicts would never be totally convincing, and prisoners sentenced to transportation had often been convicted of crimes that deprived them of their political rights. Until 1823 the Governor of New South Wales had unlimited powers checked only by the right of the courts to restrain him from breaking the English law. A legislative council was then set up, but, as the members were nominated and a majority of them were always officials, the Governor's power was still as great as that of governors in Canada before 1791. Socially the colony was divided into three groups: the convicts, the emancipists or freed convicts, and the exclusives or people who had come of their own free will as guards or garrison troops or civilian emigrants. The economic divisions expressed in the phrase 'Sydney or the bush' did not entirely cut across this; there were emancipists in Sydney and the other government-created cities like Hobart, but it was easy for the exclusives to press their claims to superiority in these places, which were the centre of such law and culture as could be found in Australia. The bush was steadily becoming more important to the Australian economy as people built up vast flocks of sheep in the land beyond the Blue Mountains that was sparsely but adequately watered by the rivers of the Murray–Darling system. In an allusion to the very best breed of sheep the nickname 'pure merinos' came to be applied to the exclusives, but not many of them flourished in the bush. It was a rough and lonely life which offered people who would put up with the conditions a chance to make a lot of money, particularly because the land beyond the Blue Mountains could be used as grazing-ground without paying for it. The wealth of these 'squatter' sheep farmers was often attacked by people in Sydney and by governors who thought expansion into the interior should be restrained and that land should be paid for, but the 'squatters' survived, partly because so much of Sydney was involved in the wool business. By the 1830s wool was the leading Australian export and, easily holding off the challenge from the Cape, it came by mid-century to provide half of all British imports of wool.

Uncontrolled westward expansion into areas beyond land surveys and land sales was matched by a movement in the opposite direction by people who crossed the 1,500 miles (2,400 km.) of sea to New Zealand. Some of the newcomers simply wanted whaling bases, but others began trading and buying up land in a way that the government was even less able to control than the expansion inland from Sydney. Australians had been selected in a way that meant they were more brutal than the average man, and those who made the further journey on to New Zealand were not going to be among the gentlest of the Australians. By the 1830s there were 1,000 to 2,000 British settlers in New Zealand and they were causing enough trouble to make the government think it ought to restrain disorder, but its attempts to do this by sending out a few officials with instructions to keep the peace were meaningless. While there were some frontier areas in which a solitary official with no formal basis for his authority was able to establish some measure of peace and quiet, this certainly could not be done in New Zealand.

Within Australia a less spectacular expansion over sea was taking place. Once it had been established that the southernmost land was an island separate from Australia, a subsidiary establishment was launched on it in 1804, called Van Diemen's Land, though it remained part of the New South Wales system of administration. It was given more of a distinct system of administration in 1825 after the government of New South Wales was reorganized, but it remained primarily a convict settlement, and a rather harsher settlement than even New South Wales itself. When convicts were released there, or when free settlers on the island wanted new land, they found expansion into the interior was not satisfactory. They crossed the Bass Strait to the southern shore of the Australia mainland and settled in the relatively open country around Port Phillip (later named Melbourne after the Prime Minister). This new settlement was legally part of New South Wales, though for some years its inhabitants complained that they were neglected by the government in Sydney and deserved to be allowed a separate administration like the nearby colony of South Australia.

In London a theorizer and pamphleteer of insight and imagination, E. G. Wakefield, had worked out to his own satisfaction that the Australian pattern of development by allowing people to press forward into un-inhabited areas was bound to lead to inefficient farming, but that settlers could hardly avoid taking this approach if landowners could not find any workers for their land at wages that would leave them a profit. He deduced from this that the government should refuse to sell any land except for a reasonably high minimum price and that it should use the revenue from land sales to pay the cost of bringing out immigrants who could not afford to pay their passage and would work for wages when they arrived. As they would not travel at all unless they were going to earn more than they could earn in Britain, the capacity of the Australian economy to provide decently-paid jobs and the capacity of farmers to find money to buy land at the minimum price would provide the upper and lower limits to expansion. This elegantly argued *Letter from Sydney* was based not on personal experience of Australia but on perhaps the next best thing; it was written while Wakefield was in Newgate Prison, where he could meet several people who had colleagues who had gone to Australia or who had tried to find out about it because they might be travelling there in the future.

Wakefield's arguments made a considerable impression; they offered a prospect of checking the expansion into empty space, and of enabling the British government to finance the departure of potential workers who added to the problems of poverty and unemployment but had no prospect of paying their own way overseas. The British government set up the Colonial Emigration Committee which between 1840 and 1873 helped about 6.5 million people to go overseas. About two-thirds of them went to the United States, and the Committee's assistance for some emigrants simply took the form of providing regulations to improve conditions on ships, but it provided some financial help as well. The policy for disposing of land in Australia was also changed. Lord Ripon's regulations in 1831 ran on lines that Wakefield could welcome. A land company was set up in 1833 to develop South Australia on Wakefield's principles, though with a larger infusion of God-fearing Church of England principles than was logically essential. As a private land company it was not successful; the effect of limiting land-holding was that once a piece of land was registered as sold it could be bought and resold as a purchasable commodity in a way that the empty space of New South Wales could never be traded, so that South Australia was soon absorbed in a land boom that had very little substance to it. By the later 1830s the government found that the collapse of the land company had left on its hands a new colony which, however respectable its private morals, owed its existence to land speculation.

The speculation had been mainly concerned with land near the tidily laid-out capital of Adelaide, and further inland wheat farming developed and some traces of minerals were found. It was much easier to see how the colony could expand and prosper than to see any similar prospects at the western end of Australia, where a small colony had been established on the Swan River but had shown no sign of being able to advance into the interior. This was an extreme case of a whole colony consisting simply of its capital and seaport, but something of the same concentration of population occurred in all the Australian colonies. Life inland was so much harder than in most of the other areas in which people from Britain settled that it provided material for the Australian legend of the hard-bitten, warm-hearted, pretension-hating man of the interior. The Australian fact, which was developing at just the same time as the legend, was that a very large proportion of the population lived on the coast, mainly in the seaport capitals of the colonies. By the early nineteenth century development had reached a point rather like that of the American colonies a hundred years earlier: overland contact between the colonies was difficult and, while they had some seaborne contacts with each other, their main export market was in Britain rather than in the other colonies. This connection was all the stronger because the links of finance and investment between Britain and these colonies in the nineteenth century were much closer than the financial links between Britain and the eighteenth-century colonies on the mainland of North America.

Policies based on Wakefield's approach and the desire of Australian employers for more workers led to a perceptible increase in the number of immigrants in the 1830s and 1840s. Governments in the Australian colonies encouraged immigration, paying bounties to those who sailed under their schemes – though this was temporarily brought to an end in the mid-1850s, when the Australian working class had enough political power to resist all attempts to flood the labour market. The failure of the South Australia land company did not deter Wakefield or his investors; probably helped by the influence of Lord Durham, who was one of the directors, Wakefield's New Zealand land company was in 1837 promised a charter to develop land in an area that was outside the range of British authority. The idea of a Wakefieldian company arriving and dealing directly with the Maoris concentrated the mind of the Colonial Office wonderfully. The aggressive unofficial settlers from Sydney had created the problem; the land company pushed the Colonial Office into providing a response, which may possibly have been encouraged by the never very firmly based idea that the French were thinking about landing in New Zealand.

In 1839 Captain Hobson of the Royal Navy was appointed consul and instructed to arrange for the cession of areas that could become a colony; in 1840 he came to the north end of North Island and negotiated the Treaty of Waitangi with the local chiefs. It was far from clear that they had the authority to commit very much of the population of the two islands, but the Treaty itself was sensible enough for its policy to endure and be applied throughout the country. Queen Victoria was accepted as sovereign over the native chiefs, who retained their position as local leaders, and as the direct ruler of her British subjects who came to settle in the islands; if Maoris wanted to sell their land to the newcomers, they had to sell it to the government, which would then sell it to purchasers moving into the country. Inevitably a flood of land claims came in from the company and from other people who had bought land, or claimed to have done so, in the years before the treaty had been applied to the entire territory of the two islands; at first sight the titles made it look as if both islands had been bought several times over, but in the course of the 1840s some sort of sense was made out of them. In at least one way the settlement of New Zealand resembled that of Australia; half a dozen ports were established, each with its own colony spreading out into the hinterland, though the ports did not absorb as large a proportion of the total population as in Australia and the separate settlements did not remain politically distinct for nearly so long. The new colony at Christchurch was very deliberately Church of England in attitude and background; and it was here that the publicizer of settlement, Wakefield, retired to live the peaceful closing years of his life.

Westminster in India

The 1840s were a period of expansion in India and in South Africa as well as in New Zealand. Expansion in India was no trouble to the British taxpayer, but in South Africa as well as in New Zealand there was a distinct risk of unwelcome expense. The operations in India can be seen as the fourth and perhaps the last of the waves of expansion that swept the British forward to rule the subcontinent. Both Clive's expansion in Bengal and Wellesley's half-dozen years of treaty-making and annexation were followed by years of tranquillity in which the British position seemed to have stabilized. The East India Company shareholders hoped to use the peace after Wellesley's recall to fight off the dangers of competition from traders who wanted to sell cotton goods made in England, but towards the end of the Napoleonic Wars the Governor-General Lord Hastings (previously Lord Moira, a politician in Britain, and no relation to Warren Hastings) felt that the problems caused by the Marathas, the Pindaris, and the Nepalese ought to be ended. Cavalry raids to plunder nearby regions had been normal enough during the disorder of the breakdown of the Moghul Empire in the eighteenth century, but the British did not find this compatible with trade or with their ideas of civilization, and set about the work of pacifying India and holding a monopoly of the use of force in their own hands. In the third wave of expansion, 1814–20, the British brought all India up to the River Sutlej, the frontier of the Punjab, under their control. On the east side of the Bay of Bengal they took over most of the seacoast of Burma in 1826, and further to the south-east Sir Stamford Raffles in 1819 set up a colony on the island of Singapore whose position on the shortest route between India and China gave it good commercial prospects. Raffles spent most of his time trying to make Bencoolen profitable, but in the event the site he had chosen for his new colony turned out to be much more successful.

'The people of India submitted to British rule because it was infinitely better than that which obtained in India at the end of the last century.'[1] The British could bring peace when nobody else could, and if they had not been accepted by the Indians, the East India Company – heroic though many of its employees showed themselves to be – could hardly have conquered so large a territory with such limited resources. The British found the process of conquest and expansion a little surprising, and for some years after the completion of Lord Hastings's wave of conquests they remained uncertain whether they could keep the political power they had gained, or would find it convenient to do so. Officials like Metcalfe and Elphinstone who had played important roles in the establishment of the British position saw that their government held power because the disorder of the eighteenth century had created a situation in which no other authority could resist the British. From this they argued that after a period of peace and recovery Indians would be able to look after their own affairs again. From a different perspective Macaulay, who had come to India to help carry out a very specific policy of westernization by drafting a uniform code of law for the whole country, could say that the day Britain left India would be the proudest day in her history: the difference was that Macaulay made it clear that this departure was to come when India had been westernized – partly by making English the language for ruling the country – while the men of Lord Hastings's day were still thinking of the revival of an earlier India. The change of approach took place while the British were making arrangements, during Lord William Bentinck's period as Governor-General from 1828 to 1835, for administering the territories gained and paying off the debts incurred in Lord Hastings's wars; by the end of Bentinck's tenure of office it was clear that the British were unlikely to leave India before they had carried out a

---

[1] R. C. Dutt, *England and India 1785–1885* (1897), 45. Dutt, one of the first Indians to enter the ICS, added the generous but not limitless approval that it was better 'than any other rule which it is possible to have at the present day'.

policy of fairly complete westernization. They had deposed the last Moghul Emperor, proclaimed William IV as ruler of India, and issued a standard rupee (showing the king's head) to replace the great diversity of coins that had circulated previously.

The East India Company had been extremely reluctant to inferefere with anything more than the bare essentials of political life in India. It did its best to keep missionaries out, because it thought there was no need to convert Hindus or Muslims and the attempt to do so might easily cause trouble. It tried to make sure that the few newspapers that could not be prevented from appearing were regulated to make sure they did not spread scandal or discontent. It had retained the laws of the Moghul Empire for the vast majority of its Indian subjects. Sometimes, as under Warren Hastings, the policy of avoiding change was followed because the Governor-General had considerable sympathy for the Indian way of life and saw some loss in disturbing it; sometimes, as under Cornwallis, the Governor-General had no very high opinion of Indians but thought that change would lead to conflict, unhappiness, and expense.

Change could not be avoided entirely; in the last decades of the eighteenth century the expansion of the British cotton industry was destroying the export trade in Indian textiles which the East India Company had built up in the previous hundred years and, after India was opened to British textiles in 1813, great inroads were made in Indian domestic markets as well. Lord William Bentinck could see that the collapse of the industry was a serious problem for parts of Indian society but, quite apart from the pressure from Lancashire which had led to the decision to open trade with India to British merchants, the Indian Civil Service contained many convinced free traders. They put their case in a way that in later decades, when Indian manufacturers began asking for tariffs, combined humane feelings with the pleasure of criticizing their political opponents: granted the obvious fact that Indian peasants were poor, and that reducing their living expenses by allowing them the chance to buy economical Lancashire textiles would help keep them a little further from starvation, was it really fair to deny them the opportunity to take advantage of the fall in British export prices and push them back to the edge of subsistence so that a small minority of weavers and factory owners in Ahmedabad would have a captive market of people who had to buy expensive Indian products instead of cheap British products? Reasoning of this sort encouraged the Civil Service in later years to see itself as the friend of the Indian masses against the special interests who wanted to do well out of the enthusiasm for independence. In the early nineteenth century the question was put in simpler terms, but the Civil Service already saw itself as the wise protector of the people, saving them from their vices and follies. As it became impossible to maintain the ban against missionaries and as British opinion became more informed about India and more shocked by what it learnt, intervention by the new rulers became unavoidable and was naturally supported and even pushed forward by enthusiasts in Britain.

Hindu widows were expected to perform the rite of suttee by throwing themselves into the flames when their husband's body was being burnt; this might have been tolerated (for only a small minority of widows did it) if they had always done it voluntarily, but in fact it was clear that they were often killed by their relations, who forced them into the flames. In 1829 this practice was made illegal; the struggle to suppress it lasted some years, and provided one of the more instructive anecdotes of imperial improvement. Some Indians appealed to Sir Charles Napier not to enforce the new policy, because suttee was an old and venerated custom; Napier replied that his country had an old and venerated custom of hanging people who burnt widows alive, and he went on to say that he was entirely committed to enforcing national custom. No Indian was bold enough to ask him why his country was exporting its customs to India, and yet the issue raised a problem about good government and self-government that might have puzzled any political philosopher who approved of national independence and disapproved of pushing widows into the fire. The British in India could see no signs of national feeling, and had no qualms about changing customs they disapproved of. Female babies were not much wanted in India, and were likely to be killed without too much thought or regret; the government forbade infanticide and, after a struggle that ran for about fifty years, was able by the 1860s to say that the practice had been more or less ended. The government also conducted, during the 1830s, a brief and successful campaign against thuggee, which was practised by a subcaste whose religious beliefs committed them to joining groups of passing travellers and then murdering them. Politically this was one of the easier reforms to carry out; once the existence of the subcaste became known and police activity was launched against it in 1836, nobody argued that this religious practice was worthwhile. All three campaigns were naturally welcomed in Britain, and probably all three of them helped make the new rulers of India even more certain that they were the messengers of civilization and that the Indians were benighted.

Some Indians accepted this view; a few were converted to Christianity, but as most converts came from the lower castes, responding to the pressures of Hinduism in much the same way as the people in the lower castes who had become Muslims in earlier centuries, this did not represent a great shift in the sentiments of Indians in a position of importance. A more significant change was the effort made by influential Hindus, of whom Ram Mohun Roy is accepted as the most thoughtful and the most imaginative, to adapt Hindu beliefs to the modern world which was pressing upon them. Bengal was the centre from which British power and influence had spread over the rest of India, and it had become the seat of government in 1833 when

Calcutta replaced Delhi as the official capital and the Moghuls were formally deposed. It now also became the centre of the Indian response to the great transformation. This response underlined the way that change in India was always likely to be linked to religious changes: Young Bengal – a westernizers' name, with obvious parallels in England, in Ireland, and in Italy – enrolled members who were ready to go a long way in laying aside restrictions on eating beef, on travelling overseas, and on educating women in order to deal with the new world that had burst in upon them.

The religious practices that were attacked as criminal by the British were almost entirely Hindu – purdah for Muslim women was no crime and was not attacked – but as the British became more certain that they would stay and that India should be westernized they changed the administration in a way that transferred power from Muslims to Hindus. The revenue arrangements were left unchanged in principle, and the taxes on salt, on opium, and on land were retained. The British lowered the nominal rate of land tax from the level charged by the Moghuls, but they may have been more successful in collecting what they demanded. The Muslims' loss of power was not deliberate policy, but it was inevitable when the British decided there was no need to continue to treat India as part of the Muslim world, and this was all the more natural because the establishment of the boundary on the Sutlej meant that many of the Muslims of the Moghul Empire were not at this point within the British Empire in India. Until 1828 Persian had been the language of formal diplomacy; when English was made the language of diplomacy it merely recognized a change that had already taken place.

A larger change came when the new British code of laws was introduced. Under the old system the Hindu peasants who made up the vast majority of the population were able to run their own affairs under their own laws but people in the ruling classes were normally governed in their relations with each other by an essentially Islamic law. The new code ended the influence of Islamic teaching and the preference for Muslim witnesses of the old system. A large staff of Indian subordinates was still needed to help run the judicial system, but Hindus were employed rather more readily than Muslims, because the Hindus of Bengal took to British education very quickly. Most of the Muslims who had held power lived further up the Ganges valley, close to the old centres of Moghul rule at Delhi and Agra, and did not have the same opportunities for obtaining British education or the same enthusiasm for it. The change from the old code to the new took twenty years to carry out, and was quite visibly accompanied by a loss of authority by the Muslims, which was more a result of replacing a land-based empire by a sea-based empire than any British preference for the Hindus.

As the British position in India became more land-based, they paid more attention to what was happening beyond the geographical boundaries of the subcontinent. The development of the steamship for ocean travel in the

1820s made it much easier to use the Red Sea, which had never been convenient for sailing-ships, to go from India to Suez and then travel overland to Alexandria. This was too expensive a route for goods, which would have had to be unloaded and reloaded, but it enabled passengers to reach India in six weeks or less, rather than spending six months going round the Cape. To make this easier the government of India established a coaling station to refuel its ships at Aden in 1839. Further north, it had been taken for granted that the Iranian empire would hold back the Russians; after the Russo-Iranian treaty of Turkomanchai in 1828 showed this was not the case, the British government in India began to consider whether to take over the very ill-organized kingdom of Afghanistan beyond the range of mountains taken to define the frontier of India and turn it into a fortified outpost against the Russians. British India had no common frontier with Afghanistan; Ranjit Singh, the subtle, disreputable, and powerful ruler of the Punjab was perfectly willing to see Afghanistan conquered and reduced to peace and quiet but he did not want British troops marching through his territory so they had to take a roundabout approach, marching west and north through Sind. It was easy to find a rival claimant to the Afghan throne, Shah Sujah, and in 1839 it seemed almost as easy to depose the reigning monarch Dost Mohammed and establish the British nominee on the throne. The problem was to keep him there: late in 1841 the Afghans rose in revolt, the British retreated, and in the course of their winter flight almost every one of them was killed and so, of course, was Shah Sujah.

The British were not as upset by this disaster as might have been expected. A punitive expedition was launched against Kabul which captured and devastated the town and then withdrew. The next year Sind was offered a treaty which would have reduced it to much the same position as the Indian princely states; when this offer was refused the British under Napier marched forward and annexed it. The Sikh rulers of the Punjab were alarmed by this. If Ranjit Singh had still been alive he might have been able to hold them back, but his successors thought it would be safer to drive the British out of India, and in 1845 they crossed the River Sutlej and began plundering the regions north-west of Delhi. The battles that followed were among the hardest-fought in the entire military history of the British in India, though the British could have won with rather less bloodshed under a more competent general, but in a few months the Sikh kingdoms had been conquered and a network of British officials installed to supervise the activities of the Sikh government. This device proved too subtle to work. The Sikhs rose in rebellion a couple of years later, were defeated in another set of exhausting battles, and eventually in 1849 the Punjab was annexed. The British had virtually completed their conquest of India, though a few fragments remained to be absorbed later. Even the Russian problem had grown less serious because Russian moves towards the western end of

Afghanistan had failed as completely as the British in the south-western side of the country.

Africa and the End of Slavery

The advance in India had become a matter of conquest and formal annexation. British involvement in West Africa in the 1830s and 1840s was much less impressive, but turned out to be the foundation for later expansion. The abrupt end of legal slave-trading in 1807 did not end the practice, but it dislocated African society as much as the gradual building up of the slave trade had done in earlier centuries. British interest at the official level was concentrated on the colony of Sierra Leone. For fifty years or more it was the administrative centre for British possessions in West Africa, and also was the centre for educating Africans and for training them as Christian missionaries who created a church with solid local foundations in most of the areas that came to speak English.

Sierra Leone was not the most prosperous part of West Africa. Its revenue did not cover the cost of government, and even after the Colonial Office took it over the Church Missionary Society provided a subsidy of about £2,000 a year. Traders who wanted to make money went, as they had been going for a century and a half, to the Gold Coast. Here they knew that the coastal traders with whom they dealt, the Fanti, were not the major power in the region, but it was not clear how they could respond to the growing power of the Asanti confederacy inland, or to the disturbance caused by the check to the Atlantic slave trade. In 1821 the British government abolished the Council of Merchants which had been running the administration of the coast, and installed a governor instead. In 1824 a war with Asanti broke out in which the governor was killed and his army was defeated; the government decided the old policy had been sensible, and returned authority to the merchants, offering a subsidy of £4,000 a year to help pay for the coastal forts.

The merchants were fortunate enough to find the ideal man for the situation among the British officers posted on the Gold Coast at the time the government withdrew. George Maclean was made President of the Council of Merchants in 1829 and turned out to be able to get on very well with the Africans, establishing treaty relations that led to peace and quiet on the coast. His legal authority was very slight, and he certainly exceeded it, but in 1831 he made a treaty with Asanti which served as the foundation of a diplomatic structure of trust which persuaded the Asanti not to make any attacks on the Fanti which might force the British to choose between going inland to fight or abandoning the Africans who had relied on them to keep the peace. In the 1830s Maclean established himself as a judge whose decisions the Fanti accepted, and to this limited extent he became the ruler of the region. In 1842 the government, perhaps encouraged by seeing that it was possible to rule the coast peacefully, returned to control the region directly, and Maclean as a judicial assessor continued to exercise real but restricted power among the Fanti. Trade developed a little further east on the coast, based on the palm-oil which African traders brought down the mouths of the Niger (which were, as a result, called the Oil Rivers). This was a region without any central authority to organize the Africans for war, so it was easier for merchants to go about their business without even the minimal authority that Maclean represented further west.

Ending the slave trade had a considerable effect on West Africa, but ending slavery itself had a much greater effect on the West Indies. The abolition of the British trade, and even the steps taken to persuade the other European powers to make it illegal at the end of the Napoleonic Wars, had still left the institution itself apparently invulnerable. Though it might not be as socially acceptable as in the past, its defenders could feel confident that nobody would undertake the immense interference with the rights of property that would be involved in setting the slaves free, but the government showed some readiness to regulate the owners by steps like setting up a register of slaves to reduce the risk of concealed sales. After the establishment in 1823 of the Anti-Slavery Society, which was committed to full emancipation, the government went on to prohibit the flogging of female slaves and the breaking-up of slave families. The sugar industry continued to flourish, but some revolts in the 1820s made it clear that British taxpayers might find themselves being asked to pay to suppress a slave rebellion. When the long period of Tory rule, which seemed to have stretched in an almost unbroken line from the emergence of Pitt in 1783, was brought to an end in 1830, a Whig government came to office in an atmosphere of public enthusiasm for reform. The ending of slavery, instead of being just one out of a number of worthy causes, became an issue on which the government had to try to find a policy. A slave revolt in Jamaica in 1831, encouraged by hopes of what the government was doing, underlined the possibility that British taxpayers might have to pay the military costs of maintaining slavery, and this made the government all the more eager to find a policy to end it. ·

According to long-established practice, questions of this sort should have been handled by the assemblies of the islands concerned. But slavery was one of the very few colonial issues about which the British Parliament cared so much that it was ready to assert the fullness of its power if necessary. When the first Parliament elected after the expansion of the right to vote in the great reform bill met in 1833, it was clearly time for the West Indian assemblies to make the best terms for compensation for emancipation that they could get. Eventually the government agreed to pay £20m. in compensation – not the full cash value of the 78,000 slaves to be freed, who were valued at about £45m., but still about half a year's normal government expenditure. In addition the government accepted the argument that a period of transition was needed for the sugar plantations to turn into economic units run on wage labour, and so the slaves to be freed on 31 July 1834 were to remain as apprentices for four to six years, which meant they had to work a 40-hour week for food and clothing, so that they would be in very much the position of the white indentured servants who had been tied to a master for a fixed period of years. This system did not work well; the masters were too inclined to look back to slavery and the apprentices were too inclined to look forward to freedom for the transition to do as much good as had been hoped, and in 1838 it was ended by general consent.

The West Indies adapted to this great change fairly successfully. They still had their assured position in the British sugar market in the old colonial system, and imports of sugar were rising. In Jamaica there was enough idle land away from the plantations for a large number of the freed slaves to squat there and set up smallholdings of their own, so that the plantation owners never felt that they had a really adequate supply of wage labour. In the smaller islands there was much less surplus land and the freed slaves turned to wage labour for want of any other way to earn a living, and these islands settled down to the new system more easily than Jamaica did. Employers all over the British West Indies complained of the unwillingness of the slaves to work for wages and set about importing a supply of more tractable wage labour from India or China, but their political power in the islands remained unchallenged, though fragile. The right to vote depended on a fairly low property qualification and, while very few former slaves could meet that qualification in the 1830s, the question was bound to arise in a generation or two.

The ending of slavery helped cause one piece of imperial expansion that none of the supporters of emancipation could possibly have expected. Slavery was seen as a West Indian problem, but the government did realize that it also had to deal with the slavery in South Africa bequeathed by the Dutch. It tried to make arrangements to pay compensation for freed slaves there as well, but owners of slaves in the more distant parts of the colony would have had great difficulty in going to collect the compensation, and in any case emancipation was seen even by Afrikaners who owned no slaves as just another sign of a general pro-black bias among the British. Apart from this, Afrikaners suffered from an almost insatiable land-hunger; in 1834 the Governor, Sir Bejamin D'Urban, did undertake a small advance from the existing boundary on the Fish River to the River Kei which was accepted by the local missionary interest as a necessary step towards establishing a manageable frontier, but the new territory did not have much to offer the Afrikaners.

In 1834 they began discussing moving forward north of the Orange River and, after a few scouting parties had gone ahead, the main body began moving north in February 1836. They felt encouraged in their decision when the Governor received instructions the following month that he was to withdraw from the new land between the Fish and the Kei; the Secretary for the Colonies, Lord Glenelg, stuck to the old policy that taking land from the Africans was not morally justified and would only stir them up to make the frontier less stable than before. Opinion in the Cape was dismayed by this; British and Afrikaner settlers were agreed that the new frontier and the new land to the east of the colony were the sort of policy they wanted, and they blamed Glenelg for having listened to too much uniformed pro-black sentiment. Glenelg was undoubtedly an evangelical who felt that the Africans were not being treated fairly, but he must also have been affected by the fact that D'Urban was remarkably inefficient about explaining his policy. The step forward led to another Kaffir War, with the usual financial disadvantages: Cape revenues covered the civil costs of government but the British taxpayer had to contribute at least £100,000 a year to maintain troops at the Cape and was now being asked to provide £500,000 to pay for what in London looked like an operation to acquire new land for the settlers. Compared with this, the Great Trek of the Boers seemed fairly harmless even though it was undertaken by men who felt a deep hostility to the British government. The Afrikaners were taking a risky step but they were not asking the British government to support them, and it could hardly send battalions of troops to stop them crossing the Orange River.

About 6,000 Boers (farmers) went north from the eastern Cape Province. A farmer liked to have 6,000 acres for raising cattle, and it is an indicator of the scale of land-hunger that if each of the 6,000 trekkers had needed an individual farm they would have settled a long strip of land 30 miles wide from the Orange to the Limpopo. Obviously the original trekkers went forward in families, and would not need new farms on this scale in the first generation, but some land north of the Orange could not be used even for cattle-raising, and the region was not empty; there were fewer Africans than around the Fish River, but this was in part because the soil was less fertile. A fair amount of the land was relatively thinly populated; at the same time as the Cape was being transferred from Dutch to British rule with all its effects on the position of the Afrikaners, political changes in Zululand were affecting the inhabitants of the whole eastern side of Southern Africa. Little of this was visible to Europeans; what they saw was the increasing pressure around the Fish River as Africans fled westwards to get away from the efficient and bloodthirsty military organization which had been unleashed by Chaka in Zululand in 1818 and in the course of the next dozen years had driven all other Africans into flight. As a result the area north of the eastern Cape through which the trekkers moved was unusually empty. The trekkers who kept to the northern axis of march did encounter the Matabele, but after an initial check were able to drive them further on to the north and west. The trouble was that this route, however satisfactorily empty, was not very good

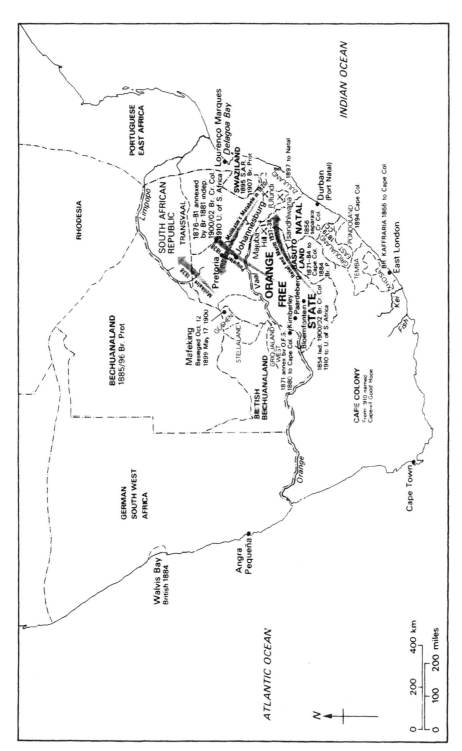

Map 7 South Africa 1337–1902

INDIAN OCEAN

ATLANTIC OCEAN

RHODESIA

PORTUGUESE
EAST AFRICA

Limpopo

SOUTH AFRICAN
REPUBLIC

TRANSVAAL
1876–81 annexed
by Br 1881 indep.
1900/02 Br. Cr. Col.
1910 U. of S. Africa

Lourenço Marques
Delagoa Bay

SWAZILAND
1895 S.A.R.
1907 Br. Prot

Pretoria

Johannesburg

Majuba
Hill X
1897 to Natal

Durban
(Port Natal)

ZULULAND
Isandhiwana
IUlundi

1894 Cape Col

1856
separate
Cr. Col.

BR. KAFFRARIA 1866 to Cape Col

East London

NATAL

ORANGE
FREE
STATE

Vaal

LESUTO
LAND
1871–84 to
Cape Col.
1884
Br. P.

Kei

Fish

Paardeberg

Kimberley

Bloemfontein
1854 ind. 1900/02 Br. Cr. Col
1910 to U. of S. Africa

GRIQUALAND
WEST
1871 annex by O.F.S.
1880 to Cape Col.

GOSHEN

STELLALAND

BRITISH
BECHUANALAND

BECHUANALAND
1885/96 Br. Prot

GERMAN
SOUTH WEST
AFRICA

Orange

CAPE COLONY
From 1910 named
Cape of Good Hope

Cape Town

Angra
Pequeña

Walvis Bay
British 1884

N

0   200
0   100   200 miles
400 km

land; a more attractive prospect opened up to the east, and many of the trekkers made their way up the Drakensberg and then down towards the sea.

This took them towards the centre of Zulu power: the most dramatic moments of the Afrikaner epic of the Trek are the murder of the Boer leader Piet Retief in a treacherous attack by the Zulu king Dingaan, and then the successful defence later in 1838 of a laager on Blood River in which the Zulu army lost so many men that it was unlikely to attack the Afrikaners for a generation. Another part of the Afrikaner epic deals with the reappearance of the British, who thought it was one thing to see the Afrikaners go off into the distant interior, but another matter to see them turn east towards the sea where they might establish a port and become an international factor to be reckoned with. The best harbour had already been settled in 1835 by Englishmen who named it after D'Urban, but the British government could not decide whether to take responsibility for the region or not. It moved in, it moved out, and finally it committed itself to holding the seacoast. The trekkers found this irritating; the government clearly felt a distrust of the Afrikaners balanced by an acute desire not to spend any money, so the trekkers would not want to be under British rule if Natal was taken over. After the eventual British annexation in 1844 the Afrikaners resumed their original march to the north and, over the next twenty years, the new colony of Natal was settled by a white population that was much more uniformly British by descent than the population of any other part of southern Africa. A rather larger number of immigrants came into the colony from India, though Africans naturally still made up the majority of the population and the newcomers were well aware that Zululand remained a formidable military state to the north, even after the new king Panda and his trusted son and heir Cetewayo had established a fairly settled form of government there in the 1850s.

Responsible Government and Free Trade

The disturbances of the Great Trek were not at the time seen as a problem that directly concerned the British government. Rebellions that broke out in the two provinces of Canada in 1837 were seen as a much more important political issue, and were handled in a way that led to a great change in the way that the British ruled colonies with a population of British and European descent. The problems in Lower Canada had become more acute when the Whig government of Britain in 1831 gave up the non-parliamentary revenues that had first been established by the French regime. This was meant as a conciliatory gesture, but it was received as an admission that the British had been wrong not to give the Lower Canadian Assembly the full power of the purse previously. The colony was subject to some pressure from immigration from the British Isles, which was turning Montreal into a city with a British majority and was taking up empty land at a rate that threatened the future prospects of French-Canadians. In Upper Canada the farmers' discontent at the way public services were provided had increased, and they discussed their problems with some of the more radical opponents of the government in Lower Canada; Mackenzie had hoped that the Whig government would introduce reforms but, when nothing was done, he moved towards advocating such American institutions as an elected governor. As the economy slowed down when the North Atlantic world entered the trade depression of the late 1830s, the discontented in Upper and Lower Canada moved towards revolt. From a military point of view this was not serious: in Lower Canada the followers of Papineau, particularly strong just south of Montreal, were conducting a rebellion by the later months of 1837 which was handled by moving troops from Upper Canada to Lower Canada. The first revolt was quickly defeated and while another revolt, with more radical aims, broke out in 1838 it was defeated even more easily. In Upper Canada Mackenzie's men marched to the outskirts of Toronto but the local militia, on which the Lieutenant-Governor had to rely because his troops had gone to Montreal, rallied quickly enough and in large enough numbers to show that public opinion was actively hostile to the rebellion. After half an hour's firing Mackenzie's force broke up and he, like Papineau, fled to the United States.

The British government could see that, however satisfactory the result of the rebellions might be from a military point of view, there was political discontent in both Upper and Lower Canada that demanded attention. In 1838 Lord Durham, a nobleman of great wealth, radical views, and excellent Whig connections, took up the post of Governor-General with authority over all of British North America (the term was taken not to include the Hudson's Bay Company regions to the north) and with the additional task of reporting on the situation. His powers were not full enough; when he ordered prisoners from the rebellions to be deported to the West Indies instead of being executed he was exercising power outside British North America, and the government was so half-hearted in supporting his action that his position became untenable. He returned to Britain to write his report after only five months in Canada, of which less than two weeks had been spent in Upper Canada.

Perhaps because of this, he wrote a report which laid a degree of emphasis on disagreements between the English-speaking and the French-speaking sections of the community which seems overstated, and which did not turn out to be the most formative part of what he wrote. His phrase 'I found two nations struggling within the bosom of a single state'[2] referred specifically to Lower Canada, but more study of Upper Canada might have convinced him that the line of division did not run along linguistic boundaries. But in any

[2] *Lord Durham's Report*, ed. C. P. Lucas (1912), ii. 16.

case this made very little difference to his recommendations; he felt quite confident enough of the superiority of British institutions and of the dominance of British ideas in the modern world to believe that nothing more drastic than exposing the French-Canadians to the system of government that was evolving in Britain was needed to turn them into loyal and devoted subjects. He would have preferred to fuse all of British North America into a single political unit with an English-speaking majority, but he could see that problems of distance might make this hard to arrange and he said it would probably be enough to unite Upper and Lower Canada with a single Assembly.

The Act of Union passed at Westminster in 1840 carried the policy into effect; since the Act gave Canada West and Canada East, as they were to be called for the next quarter-century, equal numbers of seats in a single legislature, the solid English-speaking western section, added to the small group of English-speaking seats in the east, would always have a majority if political divisions ever turned on national or linguistic issues. In the event this turned out not to be an important line of division in the Parliament of the Canadas. There was very little sign of a desire for a separation from the British Crown, and what republican sentiment did exist was certainly not strong among French-Canadians. Complete independence seemed out of the question: the alternatives were to remain under British rule or to pass under American rule, and the example of Louisiana continued to convince French-Canadians that their religion and their language were much safer under British rule. Only the anti-clerical minority could raise the national question in the form in which Durham feared it. No British government wanted to carry out an assimilationist policy, and Durham's other, more fruitful major proposal moved the British government away from the centre of the stage in the colonies.

He argued that the British had not drawn the logical conclusion from their creation of assemblies of elected representatives in 1791. For over a hundred years kings in England had carried on the government 'in unison with a representative body' because the need for co-operation between Crown and Parliament had been recognized since the reign of William III. What he meant was that before 1688 the King could appoint ministers to execute the policy he chose, and could treat the disapproval of the Commons as a minor inconvenience, but after 1688 the Commons could overthrow any minister it really wanted to force out of office. The King still chose the ministers, and in the eighteenth century he was much more than a referee deciding who held a majority in the Commons, but the men he chose had to be able to hold a majority together by oratory, by a tactful distribution of jobs to conciliate the leaders of factions in the House, or in unusual circumstances by an appeal to public opinion. The governors in North America in the 1830s were drifting towards the position of the less successful governors in the thirteen colonies before 1776, because the members of the Executive Council were not ministers who could control the Assembly, and in any case governors were only just acquiring the right to change members of the Executive Council when it seemed politically necessary. Durham said that the Governor had 'to secure the cooperation of the Assembly in his policy', and Lord John Russell, the Secretary for the Colonies, accepted this. In his Instructions to the next governor, Lord Sydenham, Russell wrote that while the Assembly could not be allowed complete autonomy, he saw no real objection to 'the practical views of colonial government recommended by Lord Durham, as I understand them'. He went on to point out that if the sort of constitution that had flourished in England after 1688 was to be set up in Canada, there would be some need for restraint: 'Every political constitution in which different bodies share the supreme power is only enabled to exist by the forbearance of those among whom this power is distributed.'[3]

Russell and Durham had entered politics at a time when the King could still reasonably speak of 'his policy', although Parliament always had a great deal of influence over that policy. Sydenham handled his task exactly as they might have hoped, forming a team of ministers from the Assembly and the Legislative Council who helped in carrying out his business-like policy of balancing the budget for ordinary expenditure and encouraging the building of roads and canals. But Sydenham died in 1841 before his system of government could be fully tested, and his successor Sir Charles Bagot was so conciliatory that he brought into his administration representatives of the Reformers, led by Baldwin and LaFontaine, who argued that the Governor ought to be simply a referee who decided which party had a majority in the Assembly and then made its members his ministers. This step went beyond what Durham had suggested, but the Reformers claimed it was entirely in keeping with the way that William IV in 1835 and Victoria in 1841 had accepted the fact that governments they liked had been defeated by strong and unified parties which would have to be allowed to choose the new government with only a minimum of royal participation. Bagot had invited the Reformers into the government before they had shown their indispensability by winning a general election; shortly after, his health broke down and he was succeeded by Sir Charles Metcalfe who had a reputation as a liberal administrator because of his concern to end official control of the press in India. This did not mean that he accepted the idea that the Canadian ministers bequeathed him by Bagot were entitled to the powers recently gained by ministers in Britain and had the right to interfere with his administration of the government by awarding jobs on the basis of party patronage. His ministers complained, and resigned. Metcalfe responded, like George III

---

[3] Lord John Russell to Lord Sydenham, 14 October 1839, taken from *British Attitudes towards Canada 1822–1849* (1971), ed. P. Burroughs. Russell made it clear that power should not be allowed to fall into the hands of people like Papineau.

in 1783, by setting up a ministry of his own which had no majority in the current assembly and, after a general election in 1844 in which the Governor was quite clearly on its side, the new ministry gained enough seats to stay in office quite comfortably.

George III and the younger Pitt, and quite possibly Lord Durham, would have found this entirely natural, but it was not the way that British politics were being conducted by the 1840s. On the other hand, governors had sometimes to do work done by neither sovereigns nor prime ministers; when Metcalfe had to retire from ill-health in 1845, his place was filled for a few months by Lord Cathcart, the Commander-in-Chief in Canada, the best man to face the American problem. In 1844 Polk had been elected President of the United States with the slogan 'Fifty-four forty or fight', which made everyone think that he would declare war unless American settlers moving into the Oregon country on the Pacific coast were allowed to expand northwards up to the southern end of the Russian settlement of Alaska. The British government was quite ready to see the Hudson's Bay Company give up some of the territory around the Columbia River in which it was operating, but it believed the 49th parallel of latitude, which in 1818 had been accepted as the frontier up to the Rockies, should be the frontier all the way to the Pacific. The Americans accepted this: President Polk, a man of his word, decided to fight, but to fight against the Spanish successor state of Mexico rather than the British Empire, and so in the late 1840s the United States pushed its southwest frontier forward to the Rio Grande and the Pacific. After this, what was really a settlement of Caribbean affairs between Britain and the United States confirmed Britain's possession of British Honduras and her withdrawal from the Moskito coast.

By that time the whole structure of the empire had been transformed in a way that made the British much less concerned about what happened in their colonies. British politicians in both parties who paid attention to the arguments of economists became convinced in the 1840s that reducing tariffs and moving towards free trade opened up the best prospects for Britain's prosperity as a country committed to manufacturing and trading. Peel's Conservative government produced a budget in 1842 which lowered a very wide range of customs duties, reducing the advantage given to colonial products in a good many cases though maintaining the principle of preference. In 1843 Canadian wheat was allowed to come in virtually free of duty, after the Canadian Assembly had placed taxes on United States wheat coming into Canada which would prevent it from being sent on to Britain as though it was low-duty Canadian wheat. The Conservatives still seemed to be committed to the idea of an imperial trading unit: their Possessions Act laid it down that colonial assemblies could go on imposing their own tariffs to obtain revenue, in addition to the common imperial tariff which was to be made into a uniform duty throughout the empire in a way it had never been before, but they were not to be allowed to offer preferences which might disturb the harmony of the system.

But the triumph of free trade was at hand. In 1846 Peel accepted the opportunity provided by famine in Ireland and passed legislation to repeal the Corn Laws and allow grain to enter Britain duty-free from all over the world. This broke up his government; the Liberals while in office from 1846 to 1852 removed most of the remaining duties, eliminated almost all the preferences in favour of colonial products, and repealed the Navigation Acts, thus removing taxes that were estimated to cost British consumers about £5m. a year. The colonies complained about the removal of the preferences but welcomed the repeal of the Navigation Acts which reduced their transport costs. As the imperial tariffs for regulation of trade were being removed, colonial governments were left with a freer hand to work out tariffs of their own. Perhaps the loudest protests were those raised in opposition to the ending of the sugar preference. It was pointed out that, if British colonies had no preference, sugar grown by slaves would be able to drive British sugar grown by free men out of the market, but the government paid little attention and pressed on with its policy of free trade to reduce the cost of living. The implications for colonial policy were not much discussed. The free traders were sure that both Britain and the colonies would be better off when they could buy and sell without any limits on their commercial activity, and so the ending of the old colonial system was seen as a blessing for all concerned. The remaining preferences were removed between 1853 and 1860, by which point Britain had no tariffs except for revenue and the colonies were being treated for economic purposes as if they were foreign countries.

The changes in the British political system that allowed the parties in the House of Commons the power to choose the Prime Minister without any of the previous delicate manoeuvering between Crown and Commons pointed in the direction that the Reformers in Canada had wanted to move, and the relaxation of commercial links made the British all the more willing to move in this direction. Lord Grey, the Secretary for the Colonies in the Liberal government, was a devoted free trader and a strong supporter of greater autonomy or the colonies. He accepted the view that the monarch and the governors of well-developed colonies ought not to be more than referees to decide which party had won an election.

The issue first arose in Nova Scotia, where in 1846 Grey advised the Governor to accept the election results and choose a new ministry, but the events in Canada in the next two years are usually taken as the moment at which 'responsible government' (that is, government by ministers responsible to their local assembly) became established. In 1847 Grey gave the new Governor-General of Canada, Lord Elgin, the same instructions as he had given in Nova Scotia. The ministers who had won the 1844 election with

Metcalfe's support dissolved the Assembly early in 1848 and in the subsequent election, in which Elgin took no part, they were defeated. In March Elgin asked Baldwin and LaFontaine, the veteran leaders of the Reformers, to form a government and they did so. The following year the new government introduced legislation to compensate people who had lost property in the 1837 rebellions, and the Rebellion Losses Bill was drawn up in terms which made it clear that some of the money would go to people who had been sympathetic to the rebellion. When this Act had passed the Canadian Parliament, the British Parliament had to consider the position. Legally nothing had changed; Grey had given Instructions to the governors of certain colonies telling them to leave their assemblies a free hand, and this change had been discussed and accepted by the British Cabinet. The powers of the British Parliament remained unchanged: it had set up the Canadian Parliament by the Act of 1840 and could end its existence or repeal any of its laws by similar legislation. The Rebellion Losses Act was offensive to British sentiment and the British government had a little difficulty in persuading its Parliament that this was not relevant, but in the end the Lords and Commons accepted the idea that certain colonies were to be 'self-governing' so far as their internal affairs went. Grey was willing to see responsible government brought into effect in New Brunswick, though he was afraid the local politicians might be too willing to enter an auction for public favour, and it was established there by 1854. He thought Prince Edward Island and Newfoundland probably did not have large enough resources of talented men to run the new system properly, but decided there was no real point in quarrelling about it once their assemblies had shown they were determined to have it, so by 1854 all five colonies in British North America had governments responsible to their assemblies.

Very few serious political questions had been debated in British North America in the years in which the change took place, which probably reassured the British government that the issue of loyalty did not need to be considered. In Canada the question did not mean much more than a dispute about who was to hold office, but in Australia the momentum for change was provided by disputes over substantial issues like the transportation of convicts and the control of the sale of land. Sentencing convicts to transportation to New South Wales had been ended in principle in 1840, and transportation to Van Diemen's Land was suspended in 1846. By this time the British government had got about 150,000 convicts off its hands and out to Australia, and it was ready to send more if this could be done. This attitude was encouraged by the squatters and most of the other people who were prospering from the wool trade and welcomed fresh supplies of labour, so the British government tried to oblige them by sending out convicts who had served part of their sentences and showed signs of wanting to make a new start in life. These men transferred from Pentonville prison (inevitably known as the Pentonvillains) were very unwelcome to the majority of Australians, who saw convicts as a flow of cheap labour to keep down wages, and thought the policy showed Grey's hostility to them.

Grey might not have been well informed about the views of the majority, but he did want to remedy grievances in Australia. He separated the Port Phillip settlement from the rest of New South Wales and made it into a colony called Victoria in 1850. The new colony and South Australia were given the sort of assembly with a mixture of elected and nominated members that New South Wales and Van Diemen's Land had possessed since 1842. Grey wanted a closer union among the colonies in both British North America and Australia; he accepted Elgin's advice that no progress could be made in this direction in British North America, but he pressed upon the Australians the idea of a federal council to discuss matters of common interest. They were concerned above everything else with ending transportation, and suspected that the federal council was a measure to restore the original dominant position of New South Wales and perhaps strengthen the squatter forces in politics. In addition, they felt confident that they knew much better than Grey what institutions were needed in Australia, a conviction which turned out to be unexpectedly expensive. It was much harder for the Australian colonies to carry out their eventual federation at the end of the century than it would have been in the middle of the century, because so many divergent interests had grown up. At the most practical level, long-distance travel inside Australia was made unnecessarily difficult because the colonies adopted different gauges when they laid their railways: New South Wales preferred 4' 8½'', Victoria 5' 3'', and Queensland 3' 6''. But in the early 1850s the transportation of convicts was the immediate question, and the new assemblies were welcomed because they would provide the various colonies with excellent platforms from which to attack the policy.

Grey's escape from humiliation over transportation was a side-effect of the discovery of gold in 1851, first in New South Wales and then, a few months later and in much larger quantities, in Victoria. People emigrated eagerly enough throughout the nineteenth century, but nothing equalled the power of a gold rush to draw them in immense numbers. The inflow of the early 1850s was comparable to the rush in California a couple of years earlier, and attracted more people than at any other time in the century. The population of Australia rose in the 1850s from 400,000 to 1.1 million. In 1851 only a small majority of the population had been born in Britain; after the gold rush it was clear that Australia would be inhabited mainly by people born in Britain for most of the rest of the century. Victoria became in a few years the most heavily populated and the richest colony on the island. Transportation lost all its power to frighten people: who, it was asked, would be afraid of being sentenced to live next door to a gold mine?

So Grey was able to announce the end of transportation just before the weight of Australian public opinion made it clear that he had no real choice in the matter. He was enough of a Wakefieldian to keep control of public lands for the British government in his 1850 Act, partly because he thought Australian assemblies would be so responsive to working class pressure that they would oppose assisted emigration for fear it would hold wage rates down. But the gold rush reduced the need for subsidized immigrants just at the time when representative institutions were strengthening the working class opposition to it, and resisting the Australian desire to control the land seemed less important. Pakington, the Conservative Secretary for the Colonies who succeeded Grey, conceded control over land in 1852, Australian subsidies for emigration ended a few years later (though they were revived in varying forms several times in the next hundred years), and very few points remained on which the new governments in Australia could disagree with the British.

In New Zealand responsible government came almost without discussion. Sir George Grey had resisted it as Governor because it might lead to trouble between the Maoris and the colonists, but when he left in 1853 the acting Governor accepted the claim of the majority in the Assembly to choose ministers almost as a matter of course. In the Australian colonies there was a little more discussion, partly because politicians tried to express the arrangement more precisely by drawing up lists of issues on which the assemblies had unrestrained power and other imperial questions which they were not to touch at all. Unsuccessful attempts to define this distinction showed that it was much easier to leave the imperial government a general right of veto on the understanding that it would be used only when imperial concerns were involved. And so in 1856 four Australian colonies – though not Western Australia, which was still accepting convicts to meet its shortages of population – established governments responsible to local assemblies in which the Lower Houses were made up entirely of elected members, with Upper Houses to act as restraining influences weighted on the side of stability and property. The power of self-governing colonies to pass laws for everyone living in their territories was confirmed nine years later by the Colonial Laws Validity Act.

In the years just after Lord Grey became Secretary for the Colonies it looked as if British policy in South Africa was based on ideas clean contrary to the principles of withdrawal that underlay his activities in Canada and even in Australia. After some spectacular successes in battles in the Sikh War, Smith had returned to the Cape as Governor with views that had changed very little since the days when he had taken a prominent supporting role in D'Urban's plan to advance to the Kei river. To assert British supremacy he took a rather theatrical approach to the Africans and showed off simple little tricks like blowing up a statue with gunpowder. This suited

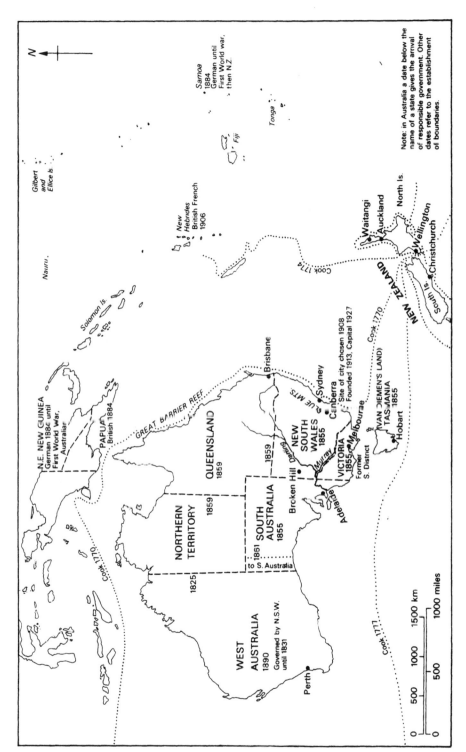

Map 8 Australasia 1825–1914

Note: in Australia a date below the name of a state gives the arrival of responsible government. Other dates refer to the establishment of boundaries.

the British and Afrikaner settlers in the Orange River Sovereignty, most of whom had kept up the idea of a connection with the Cape even though they were outside the legal limits of the colony. In 1848 Smith extended the boundaries of Cape Colony to absorb the Sovereignty and briskly crushed an Afrikaner attempt to rebel against this step.

The British government accepted steps like this contentedly enough until another in the long series of Kaffir Wars broke out. Partly because Smith was overconfident in the beginning, this war was harder fought and, as it cost £2m., was much more expensive than usual; Grey became convinced that Smith's policy was too adventurous to suit the British taxpayer, and he was dismissed. The reversal of policy was taken further. In 1854 the South African Republic, north of the Vaal river, was informed that it could have local autonomy subject to a strict prohibition of slavery. This step was natural enough: the South African Republic (or Transvaal) did not want to be connected with Britain, and it would have been hard to send troops far inland to impose British authority. The decision in 1854 to make a similar arrangement with what now became the Orange River Republic was not so unavoidable. While some of the population had gone north in the Great Trek to escape British rule, many others had simply crossed the river in the unending search for a new piece of land for a farm. On the other hand it was hard to see that the Orange River Republic had any attractions for the British or understand why the British taxpayers should pay its defence costs. The natural way to cut costs was to withdraw, so reducing expenditure implied accepting Grey's policy of extending local autonomy.

While the British government withdrew between 1847 and 1856 from local involvement in five colonies in North America, four in Australia, New Zealand, and the Afrikaner republics, neither withdrawal nor responsible government were thought practicable for Cape Colony and Natal. They were unlikely to be given up because they were on the coast and their ports and their points of entry to the interior had considerable strategic value. But Zululand and the eastern Cape were the boundary areas of the empire in which local wars were most likely to break out on a scale that would make it necessary for Britain to send help to the local population. The two Dutch republics could not expect any such help; and the self-governing colonies were thought unlikely to be involved in expensive local wars. The Kaffir Wars in the Cape were in fact coming to an end. In 1857 the Xhosa became convinced that their gods would take care of them if they slaughtered all their cattle, and after the great slaughter they were left dependent on the benevolence of the Cape government. South Africa remained peaceful for twenty years, but the Cape Assembly was not allowed control of policy in case it provoked the Africans or the Afrikaners in a way that made it necessary for the British garrison to go into action, with all the expense for the British taxpayer and awkward explanations for the British government that that would have involved. In addition, local pressure for responsible government was never strong, perhaps because of the sharp division between the eastern Cape and the western Cape regions, which held out a prospect of continual disagreement if they had to run their own affairs.

The limits of responsible government, and the fact of British predominance in questions of foreign policy, were clear enough. It was also clear that the empire, which had set off in a new direction in the mid-eighteenth century when it began advancing inland and started governing large numbers of subjects brought under British rule by conquest rather than by their British descent, had changed direction again when it gave up the old economic framework and allowed colonies to control their governments in local questions. The reasons for the limits on responsible government could be seen in the later years of Elgin's term of office in Canada. The Tory merchants of the English-speaking section of Montreal were angered by the ending of the system of imperial tariff preferences and were infuriated by the acceptance of the Rebellion Losses Bill; they rioted and they petitioned for the annexation of Canada to the United States, which convinced people that Montreal could not be the capital of the colony, so for some years Quebec City and Kingston took turns at being the seat of government. The ending of the preferential system and the closeness of the United States caused some more serious problems. In 1851 disputes between Nova Scotians and Americans about fishing rights on the Atlantic coast led Disraeli to complain that 'these colonies are a millstone round our necks',[4] an odd thing for one of the great figures of late Victorian imperial enthusiasm to have said, and yet it was natural for him to feel irritated that Britain might have to fight a formidable foreign power in support of colonies who ran their own domestic affairs and were no longer connected to Britain by the old tariff system. Years later he said in his Crystal Palace speech of June 1872 that a unified tariff system ought to have been set up at the same time as responsible government, but this only showed that he had forgotten that responsible government was established just after Britain had decided free trade was the system that suited her interests best.

But if Canada was not a millstone she could be a threat to Britain's desire for peaceful relations with the United States. Everybody believed that the grant of responsible government made no difference to Britain's obligation to defend her colonies against attacks by foreign – as opposed to local and native – enemies. The British government sent a naval squadron across the Atlantic to help persuade the United States to negotiate in a reasonable spirit, and Lord Elgin went to Washington and gave Canadian arguments a weight that Canadian representatives would not have commanded at the time. Even so, the Maritimes fishermen were not really satisfied by the results of the 1854 negotiations. The rest of British North America felt that

[4] W. F. Monypenny and G. E. Buckle, *The Life of Benjamin Disraeli* (1910–20), iii. 385.

the need for a market to replace its preferential position in the British market had been met by Elgin's negotiation of the Reciprocity Treaty, which allowed free trade across the American border for a great many raw materials and foodstuffs. At just about the same time the Canadian Parliament ended the special position of church and public land which appeared to be so important a part of Durham's recommendations, but control of public lands and immigration were vital issues only for people who took Wakefield's ideas very seriously. Control of foreign policy and the defence policy that made it effective remained in Britain's hands as Durham had wanted, and the colonies could see that they were much safer as a result.

Appendix to Chapter VI

Six men called Grey held important posts in British and colonial affairs in the nineteenth century. Charles, 2nd Earl Grey, was Prime Minister 1830–4 (and had a blend of tea named in his honour). His son Henry George was – when known by the courtesy title of Lord Howick – the Under-Secretary for the Colonies 1830–3 and, after succeeding as the 3rd Earl, was Secretary for the Colonies 1846–52; he had a nephew Albert, who was a director of the British South Africa Company, became the 4th Earl, and was Governor-General of Canada 1904–11. Sir George, first cousin of the 3rd Earl, was Secretary for the Colonies 1854–5 and Home Secretary in several mid-nineteenth-century governments; and his grandson, Sir Edward, as Under-Secretary for Foreign Affairs, laid down British policy for the Nile valley in 1895, and was Foreign Secretary 1905–16. Another Sir George, not related to this family, held colonial governorships in South Australia, New Zealand, and Cape Colony between 1841 and 1867, and was Prime Minister of New Zealand 1877–9.

7. Victorian Stability 1848–1871

Britain's interest in her colonies was unusually low in the mid-nineteenth century. Occasionally it was suggested that it might be a prudent, or at least a thrifty, step to give them up and, while there was no real likelihood that this would happen, it was a period in which imperial expansion was certainly not going to be encouraged in London and was not much in favour in the colonies either. The impulse to expand had taken colonial frontiers far into the interior by 1850; at first sight it may look like a constant factor from 1750 to 1920, but it had come to a temporary stop and for the next twenty years the frontiers remained as close to unchanged as at any time in the whole history of the empire. This did not mean that Englishmen were following a non-interventionist policy; it has been suggested that the reason Britain did not acquire more territory in these decades was simply that she was so powerful that she could assert herself on a world-wide basis without any need to acquire territory and, even if this seems to go a little too far in search of the paradoxical, it was certainly a time at which Britain and almost all of her colonies were so free from external danger that there was no need to expand for such defensive purposes as acquiring a safer frontier line. But expansion in the decades before 1850 was certainly not just a matter of people in Britain wanting frontiers that were easy to defend. It had mainly been caused by the desire of people in the colonies to have more land, and by 1850 they had reached a limit to the land they could absorb with the methods at their disposal. No new land could be opened up easily, emigration from Britain went to the United States rather than the colonies, and the empire ceased to expand.

In at least one way this was not a period of inactivity: it was the point at which British rulers in India were throwing themselves most vigorously into the physical process of modernization, and they went on with this even after they saw that it had helped produce the Indian Mutiny. For about seventy years the British in India stood for change and were allied with groups in the country that would benefit from change, but by the 1870s they were beginning to turn into defenders of the powerful and well-constructed structure of government that their predecessors had built. In the 1830s the policy of leaving India after carrying out a series of reforms that would enable it to look after itself still had some supporters; by 1870 very few Englishmen thought the idea of leaving India was worth any consideration. The self-governing colonies were in a quite different position; they were welcome to look after themselves if they could, and in the 1860s they found a new way of doing so. When the colonies of British North America federated themselves to form the much more powerful colony of Canada, they made no formal change in their relations with Britain, but they were in practice preparing for an advance to a position where equality with Britain or indepedence were possible, even though certainly not intended by any mid-nineteenth century colonial politician.

The India of the Mutiny

While the colonies of white settlement were moving to a new and more detached relationship with Britain, under responsible government, India at the end of the 1840s was entering a new and dramatic cycle of modernization and reaction. After the Sikh Wars, the pendulum swung back to peace and westernization: the Punjab had to be pacified and put under British administration, a task carried out by Nicholson and the two Lawrence brothers faster and more successfully than anyone could have expected, and the new Governor-General, Lord Dalhousie, threw himself into the work of developing India with fewer doubts and afterthoughts than any of his predecessors or successors. It was in the year Dalhousie went to India that Marx said that capitalism had achieved more in a hundred years than mankind had achieved for centuries before, and Dalhousie thought it his duty to bring the advantage of this new way of life to India. It was the moment at which the west had most to offer the east, and large sections of Indian society responded as Dalhousie wished, by accepting his innovations and believing that the path of the new rulers was one they should tread without too many questions.

The most visible effect of Dalhousie's activity was the creation of a system of communication that united all India. Previously it had been very hard for anyone except the few men at the top who ruled the whole country to see India – whatever its political boundaries – as a unity. The building of the great road from Calcutta to Peshawar, with a branch to Bombay forking off just south of Delhi, opened up a route that united northern India in a way quite unlike anything before it. In the 1890s Kipling wrote 'truly the Grand Trunk Road is a wonderful spectacle. It runs straight, bearing without crowding India's traffic for fifteen hundred miles – such a river of life as exists nowhere else in the world',[1] and while people had probably grown used to it by Kipling's time, there is no need to doubt that it seemed like a river of life when it was being built in the 1840s.

While roads on this scale were a great improvement, roads of a sort had

[1] R. Kipling, *Kim* (1925 edn.), 55.

been seen before. Electric telegraph wires for carrying messages in Morse or other codes were entirely new; they had first appeared in the United States in the 1820s, so that lines put up in the 1850s were equipping India with modern technology fairly soon after it was developed. In the eighteenth century several countries had postal services but all of them, including those in Britain and in the Moghul Empire, were expensive and were designed more for the convenience of the government users than of private citizens. In 1840 the system in Britain was transformed to allow a letter to be delivered anywhere in the country for a uniform rate of a penny (the sterling penny, worth 1/240th of a pound), a step that could be justified only if there turned out to be an immense load of correspondence that would be sent if the rates were low enough. Dalhousie had seen the change and had seen that it had been completely successful, and he set up a universal system for India. As wages in India were lower than in Britain he decided that delivery anywhere from Ceylon to the Himalayas could be provided for a halfpenny, which reduced the cost of writing from Bombay to Calcutta to about 3 per cent of what it was before. The reduction attracted a vast increase in postal activity, and covered its costs. Probably not many people in Srinagar wrote to Trincomalee, but it did mean that ordinary Indians (including the illiterate, who hired letter-writers) could write to their families when away from home and that politically-minded Indians could keep in touch with their colleagues in other parts of the country; and there were collections of mail for Britain once a fortnight.

Dalhousie had been closely connected with railway building in Britain, because he had been the minister who supervised plans submitted to the government in the railway boom of the 1840s, so it was natural that he wanted to see railways built in India. Only a few dozen miles of track were laid while he was Governor-General, and they only went a little way into the countryside from Bombay and from Calcutta, but they showed what was to come. There had been fears that the cost and the problems of caste difference and timidity about novelty would keep Indians from the trains. None of these factors had any visible effect; Indian trains were at once overcrowded and remained overcrowded as the track spread across India in the next generation. As Marx might have said, all the boundaries of family and tradition are swept away by cheap tickets. Dalhousie's education policy showed the same belief that India should be brought towards the values of nineteenth-century Britain; he was willing to see some help given to schools which taught Indians in their mother-tongues, but his real concern was for a system which would enable the most talented of those who could afford it to acquire a knowledge of English, which could serve as a language for the rulers and their assistants throughout India in the way that Latin and Greek had served in the Roman Empire.

Dalhousie naturally believed that British rule would do more for the people of India than the continued rule of the Indian princes who had been supple enough to ally themselves with the British during the great period of expansion. He was not so bold as to end the whole system of subsidiary treaties, but he did take steps to undermine it. Partly for religious reasons Indians believed that they needed a male heir, so a man without a son was very likely to adopt a boy who would succeed him. The practice was recognized for all property, including succession to a throne, and childless princes were often succeeded by adopted sons. Dalhousie decided that this was not a proper principle of succession and that, while adopted sons could inherit other property, a state whose ruler had no son of his own would 'lapse' into the hands of the East India Company and be placed under the Governor-General. This novel doctrine was applied to rulers in a few cases concerned with succession or pension rights, and other princes saw it as a threat.

Dalhousie's eagerness for reform led him to disturb the princely position in another way: the King of Oudh was exactly the sort of old-fashioned and pleasure-loving monarch that he disapproved of, and so the King was deposed and Oudh was placed under direct British rule. By 1856 Dalhousie had taken India through some decisive stages on the road to modernization, and could look back on a range of lesser steps in the same direction: an additional area of Burma had been annexed in 1852, and arrangements were being made to re-equip the Indian army with the new Enfield rifle, which would fire a bullet much further and more accurately than a musket.

The Indian army of about a quarter of a million men had developed over the years as the East India Company had responded to a succession of challenges, and had emerged as an instrument to inspire pride and wonder. It was organized with far less concern about differences between Hindus and Muslims than could be seen elsewhere in India, its members were respected as men doing their duty under the new rulers and doing it better than ever before, and its officers in the period of expansion had won the affection and loyalty of their men. There were suggestions that the officers of the 1850s might not have been quite as good as their predecessors at holding this respect, but this may simply have meant that in the early 1850s the out-standing personalities were concentrated in the Punjab, where they un-doubtedly gained the loyalty of the Sikhs. The nineteenth-century officers were more earnest than their eighteenth-century predecessors; sometimes they felt it was their duty to preach Christianity to the soliders, who had been satisfied about their position in the army but began to be afraid there was a deep-laid plot to undermine their religious position to make them become Christians by default. When plans were made for Hindu soldiers to go to Burma by sea, this looked like an attempt to undermine their caste status; when the new rifle turned out to have cartridges of which the paper had to be bitten off, Hindus and Muslims were united in common outrage because it appeared that the cartridge paper was waxed with a mixture of pig and cow fat.

In May 1857 the Indian soldiers at Meerut near Delhi mutinied and killed their officers and all the other British they could find, and then marched to Delhi, brought the former Emperor Bahadur Shah out of retirement, and proclaimed him as ruler. Most of the Indian soldiers in the Hindi-speaking region joined the rising and nominally accepted the restored Emperor as their ruler. By June they controlled an area about the size of Britain. While this was a large area to recapture (as can be seen from Map 15),* and was one of the more densely populated parts of the country, much the larger part of India remained more or less unaffected; the British were able to move troops from other regions to attack the mutineers, even bringing the recently-conquered Sikhs from the Punjab to take part in the siege of Delhi which was the military key to the campaign. The more spectacular events of the struggle, which the British in India remembered for generations, took place hundreds of miles to the east: the defence of the residency at Lucknow was treasured as a feat of heroism, the deaths of the captives at Cawnpore, in what seemed to be an outrageous blend of cruelty and treachery, left the British thirsting for revenge. And this they took: as they advanced against the mutineers they proceeded on the principle that any mutineers, or anyone who had helped the mutineers, or anyone who was thought to have helped the mutineers, should be executed.

A large number of people had thrown off British rule, even if they had not worked with the mutineers. It is hard to say whether this was a matter of Hindi-speaking nationalism, or of a return by local chiefs to the local anarchy of the period between Moghul rule and British rule. Undoubtedly they could see the British as foreigners and resist them accordingly, and undoubtedly the area around the ancient capital of Delhi had suffered from the transfer of power to Calcutta and the shift of wealth to coastal regions like those round Calcutta, Bombay, and Madras, but the lack of unity in the resistance, and the readiness of the rebel leaders to disagree with one another, shows how little of a common cause they had. If this had not been the case, resistance might have been more successful, for the British were outnumbered in most of the battles they fought. But none of the Indian troops had held any military rank high enough to give them experience in command, and the Indian princes whom they brought in to lead them were not much better. By May 1858 the sepoys had been defeated, and what remained was a matter of ending local rebellions that had broken out with the ending of British authority. The Governor-General, Lord Canning, was given the nickname of 'Clemency' (which was intended as a term of disapproval) because he did his best to stop the rush for revenge,† though his proclamations declaring forfeit the estates of the semi-independent chiefs in

*For Map 15: India 1850–1947, see p. 326 below.
†M. Maclagan, *'Clemency' Canning* (1962), 137–8, 315.

Oudh probably stiffened their resistance, but by the summer of 1859 the rebellion was over, and only a few of the leaders had managed to disappear from sight.

The British always called the rising a mutiny, which was reasonable enough because none of the chiefs and princes could have done anything or rallied their subjects if the soldiers had not mutinied first, and Englishmen eager for revenge probably felt more at ease about their acts of vengeance if they could say that it served the mutinous soldiers right. But the wide-ranging changes made between 1858 and 1861 show that purely military precautions (such as increasing the proportion of British to Indian troops in the Indian army, and making sure that the artillery was made up entirely of British troops) were not thought to be a complete guarantee that nothing like this could happen again. At the level of symbols British India became a territory directly under the Crown and Parliament. The East India Company's vestigial involvement in government and in civil service appointments was brought to an end, and it became simply an accounting department for paying interest on Indian bonds. When John Stuart Mill, the most talented of the Company's employees of the day, presented its petition against being displaced, he stressed the Company's services in adding all of India to the British Empire without costing the taxpayers anything, which really meant that, like all conquerors before them, the British made their newly-won Indian subjects pay the expenses of conquest. The British made one innovation: instead of taking enough loot to cover the cost of war like Babur or Aurangzeb, they entered the costs of war as part of the Indian debt to be paid by the Indian taxpayer. When the Company lost its last functions, the debt remained as part of the obligations of the Indian government.

When India came directly under the British government, the Governor-General became the Viceroy, and the President of the Board of Control became the Secretary of State for India, with a Council of India that looked like an attempt to create a body of advisers with the power to inform and persuade the minister, which was all that the Company could do in its last decades. The Queen's Proclamation of 1858 laid it down that Indians were to have an equal chance of joining the Indian Civil Service, but this had little effect on recruiting in the next generation, and it was not the sort of change in which the rulers in India were most interested. The Mutiny seems to have convinced the British that the old ruling classes of India were the serious danger, but a danger which could be disarmed. The princes were assured that the doctrine of 'lapse' would not be employed in the future, and viceroys tried to bring men from the old ruling classes into the British administration. The creation of the new title of Empress of India for Queen Victoria in 1876 and the great ceremonial occasions like the durbar of 1911 are sometimes interpreted as attempts to enlist the old ruling classes as allies against the new potential ruling class that was rising through the process of western education. Undoubtedly the British could not rule India by themselves. The mutineers had shown they understood how the system worked because they turned on the English-speaking Indian assistants to the administration almost as fiercely as on the British themselves, but in the 1860s the British, while worried about all Indians, were particularly concerned about those who had not been pacified and westernized. Indians with a western education were not seen at this stage as a threat.

The main instrument of modernization in the years after the Mutiny was the railway. About 5,000 miles of track were laid in the 1860s, and by the end of the decade railway bonds made up about half of the total Indian debt of £200m. Edwin Arnold wrote that 'Railways may do for India . . . what the genius of Akbar the Magnificent could not effect by government . . . they may make India a nation',[2] and he added that if India became a nation the British would have to leave. The government sponsored the system which meant that the money for the railway could be borrowed at only 5 per cent, and also said where it should run, so it was to some extent laid out to serve military purposes like the European government-designed systems, which was not normal in English-speaking countries. The railways made it physically possible to do much more to relieve famines than had been feasible in the past, when grain had to be carried by bullock-cart to districts suffering from famine. The bullocks travelled only a very few miles a day and had to carry their own fodder as well, so that a bullock team could not bring food very far into the district – its capacity would all be taken up by its own needs. The railway ended this; governments which had previously treated famines as unavoidable disasters could now bring food where it was needed.

Perhaps because the wars of the eighteenth century, which interfered with harvests and were often accompanied by famines, had prevented any noticeable increase in population, the growing population of the first half of the nineteenth century was not pressing on the limits of resources and food was more readily available than in the seventeenth and eighteenth centuries, with only one major famine between 1801 and 1866. By the second half of the nineteenth century the return of peace to the subcontinent, ambitious irrigation schemes, and public health measures which reduced deaths from diseases like cholera had produced a striking increase in the population; there was general surprise when the first Indian census, held in 1872, showed that the population had reached at least 206 million. But this was stretching the capacity of Indian agriculture, and famines became as frequent as in earlier centuries, though the government could do more about them than any of its predecessors by transporting food by railway and by organizing public works at dam sites for irrigation schemes, which served the two purposes of producing more food for the future, and of giving people made

[2] This quotation from Edwin Arnold is taken from S. C. Ghosh, *Dalhousie in India* (1975), 92.

destitute by famine a chance to earn a bare subsistence. In the 1874 famine there was hardly any direct loss of life from starvation, though there was still severe malnutrition. The government of India was much more interventionist than the British government, as was shown by its support for railway building, but it was sufficiently afraid of leading peasants to become permanently dependent on government support, to take care not to let provision for famine relief spill over into wide-ranging generosity.

Willingness to spend money was held in check by the belief that the best thing the government could do for the peasant masses of India was to keep the burden of taxes as low as possible and reduce it when this could be done. The internal customs duties on goods moving inside India had been abolished by the time of the Mutiny. The tax on salt, which had also been inherited from the Moghuls and was an important part of the revenue, was criticized on the grounds that, because everyone eats roughly the same amount of salt, it took a higher proportion of the incomes of the poor than of the rich; it was simplified and reduced, but was retained to underline the principle that all Indians should pay taxes. The same rather cool benevolence could be seen in questions of frontiers and foreign policy: conquering Afghanistan might possibly guard the frontiers of India against Russian expansion to Bokhara and Samarkand, but it would undoubtedly be expensive, and in the 1860s the government of India thought the Afghans should be left alone.

The British in India became more withdrawn in their attitude to Indians. The Mutiny was not forgotten, and was forgiven only in a fairly technical sense. Despite the regulation which said that Indians were to be treated as equals and were to be admitted to the covenanted Indian Civil Service of about 1,000 men which was the effective ruling class in India, very few Indians were able to succeed in the examination in the generation after the Mutiny. They had to learn English to compete with people who spoke it as their native tongue and they had to sail to London, which was impossible for devout Hindus. A large number of Indians joined the less powerful but still rather well-paid uncovenanted civil service, as an essential part of the administrative system, but this did not counteract the readiness of the British to see themselves as a garrison in a country which could still explode into disorder and revert to the civil war of the eighteenth century if their central power was removed. It has been suggested that part of the reason why British attitudes to Indians became more hostile after the Mutiny was that British women came to India in larger numbers as the Suez route became less troublesome and were more concerned about keeping a due and proper distance between Indians and themselves than men had ever been. In the eighteenth century Englishmen had enjoyed close and widely accepted relationships with Indian women that sometimes led to marriage, and certainly led to a better understanding of Indian attitudes, and this was sometimes contrasted with the more repressed Victorian Englishmen and the stricter attitudes that prevailed as more women made the journey in the later nineteenth century. But the change had come earlier: relationships with Indian women had come under criticism in the first half of the century, as missionary zeal appeared in India, and obviously English women and children had been in India at the time of the Mutiny. The opening of the overland Suez route – which enabled troops in late 1857 to travel from Britain to India in 37 days – may have had some effect; but it seems safe to say that all this was secondary to the Mutiny itself in changing British attitudes.

By the 1860s a steadily increasing number of educated Indians had hoped to be accepted by the British as some sort of equals, and were disappointed to find that this was not the case. The British could accept the old ruling families of India and try to turn them into an exotic variety of the British nobility once they had signed treaties with the government, but education was not so likely to command respect. The young men from Britain in the first generation of those entering the Indian Civil Service by competitive examination (who were called 'competition-wallahs' for their pains) did not win the respect of the old generation at all easily, so Englishmen in India were not likely to think much better of Indians just because they were well educated. More fundamentally, after the Mutiny the British felt they had fought for India and had won. The earlier idea that Britain's position in India might pass away once peace and tranquillity had been fully restored had been dying even before 1857, but the defence of Lucknow and the siege of Delhi killed the idea that the British could ever leave. India seemed a very long way from being peaceful enough to rule herself and the British saw no reason to think that this would change in the future.

Crown Colonies

Another revolt, a few years later and on a much smaller scale, helped to change the way the British thought about their empire. The West Indies had suffered no immediate setback from the emancipation of slaves. In the smaller and more densely populated islands the change from a slave labour force to a wage-earning labour force was carried out fairly smoothly, and in Jamaica ex-slaves who did not want to work for wages could set up as squatter farmers on land that was not suitable for growing sugar. The sugar-growing economy ran well enough until the removal in 1849 of the tariff preferences for British sugar that kept out slave-grown sugar, which cost about half the price of sugar from the British islands. While the end of slavery had transferred a certain amount of the wealth of the British West Indies from the planters to the ex-slaves it does not seem to have changed the total wealth of the islands much, but opening the market in Britian to sugar from the rest of the world damaged the British islands quite severely and contributed to an increase in political tension. In the first decades after emancipation political power remained in the hands of the wealthy, which meant the richer members of the white community. By the 1850s men of mixed black and white descent were beginning to make their way forward in politics in Jamaica, and at the same time the black working class was finding its position was deteriorating as foreign sugar captured the British market. When they protested they were given, in what came to be known as the Queen's Letter, the rather bleak assurance that thrift and hard work would enable them to prosper.

In 1865 there were extensive riots which looked like an attempt to revolt by the black population. Governor Eyre responded briskly and suppressed the rioting by applying martial law, which was a normal enough step under the circumstances. In one instance he went further than usual. A preacher and politician of mixed descent, William Gordon, who had been putting the case for reform was arrested in Kingston, where martial law was not in force, taken to an area where it was in force, and executed on the grounds that his speeches had done a lot to raise the political temperature. Eyre's conduct was debated fiercely and most of the prominent intellectuals of the day argued either that the black population was dangerous and Eyre had taken prompt and appropriate steps to check rebellion or on the other hand that the execution of Gordon was an act of judicial murder. British opinion was no longer so much moved by the eighteenth-century ideal of the noble savage or by the early nineteenth-century humanitarian ideal that had done so much to help end slavery, and some people were coming to regard the empire's black and brown subjects as natural inferiors – the mere fact that they had been conquered showed that they were inferior at least in terms of efficient government and military organization.

The government was clearly not pleased with Eyre, who was given no further appointments, but when it thought about how the West Indies were to be governed it could see that the people whom Gordon represented were going to dominate the assemblies in a good many West Indian colonies as soon as they realized the power that the vote, given on quite a low property qualification, could provide. The government would not welcome black-dominated assemblies legislating in colonies with a rich white minority, but it would not want to spend its time overruling legislatures of this sort if they came into existence. The white minorities in the islands could see the point as well, so later in 1865 the Assembly of Jamaica voted to ask the Westminster Parliament to annul the island's Constitution; and the assemblies of the less harmonious of the other islands followed the same policy in the next few years. In a few islands like Barbados, Bermuda, and the Bahamas, where the white population was not so obviously exposed and felt confident about its position, the assemblies survived as a reminder of the days when the whole empire had consisted of colonies like Barbados ruled by a governor with executive authority and an assembly which could pursue an independent line on taxation and legislation. The changes of the late 1860s made a rather sharper distinction between the self-governing colonies, in which the assemblies found that the governors were useful advisers for the first few administrations under self-government but then came to think of them as imperial icing on the local cake, and the Crown colonies, in which governors exercised a great deal of personal power and were not much restrained by their legislative councils which usually consisted of officials and perhaps a few men of importance nominated from the 'non-official' local community.

Although the changes in the West Indies increased the number of Crown colonies, the British were not acquiring new territory to place under Crown colony government. Some small advances were carried out by the self-governing colonies but the spirit of retrenchment, combined with a feeling that new territory would not provide any particular advantages, led British politicians – including even the boldest exponents of a forceful foreign policy – to try with considerable success to avoid acquiring any new possessions in the 1850s and 1860s. On the west coast of Africa Maclean's success in building a British sphere of influence, with a reasonably high level of peace and quiet, had not led to expansion inland from the old forts on the shore of the Gold Coast. When the slave squadron rescued Africans from ships which, at least until the 1860s, went on taking them to the Americas, they were brought back to Sierra Leone, still the main British colony in West Africa and the only one to which the British felt a political and humanitarian commitment. The few trading posts dotted along the coast line a little north of the equator were not particularly welcomed by the British government, and were certainly not expected either to expand inland or to acquire any considerable area of territory along the coastline to link up with one another and form a continuous coastal belt.

Africans as well as Englishmen realized the importance of opposition to the slave trade as a basis for policy. In 1851 Arikoye, a deposed king of Lagos, asked for British support on the grounds of his opposition to slave-trading, received it from the interventionist local consul, and regained his throne. But he was not on other grounds a strong candidate, and his opposition to slave-trading weakened his hold on his African subjects. His successor found himself in the same weak position and in 1861 Britain formally took over Lagos, and the authorities were displeased to find that once they were in Lagos all sorts of local pressures to end slavery or to keep the peace led to expansion along the coast.

A much more serious problem developed on the Gold Coast, where disputes between British-protected Fanti and the Asanti kingdom to the north broke out once more. In 1863 and 1864 the British fought an inconclusive little war with Asanti; it led to none of the disasters of the 1824 campaign, but it was expensive enough to lead a House of Commons committee to look at West African policy and to issue in 1865 a report that criticized it strongly. The report did not recommend immediate withdrawal but it did say that there should be no further expansion, that the government should prepare to hand all colonies in the region except Sierra Leone to African rulers, and that costs should be kept down. And at just about the same time the victory of the North in the American Civil War did offer some hope of reducing costs; if the United States ended slavery and was committed to opposing the slave trade more whole-heartedly than before, the slave squadron could probably be cut without doing much harm, a step that attracted Disraeli when he was Chancellor of the Exchequer in 1866.

When the Liberals came back to office a couple of years later they considered simplifying relations with France in 1869 by exchanging Gambia, the British settlement that lay furthest to the north and west and so was in an area of French activity, for the French territories and claims further south, in the line of coast that stretched from Sierra Leone to Lagos. This exchange might tidy up the map but there was no compelling reason to carry it out, because nobody thought that possessing a continuous coastline was an objective worth much trouble. As a result British opinion was quite ready to listen to the objections to the transfer raised by the British and the African inhabitants of the Gambia. If anything, the Africans were more committed in their opposition; British traders would be sorry to have to move elsewhere and lose the connections that they had built up in the local community, but the Africans could hardly move away and those who had invested time and prestige in learning English and fitting themselves into the British system in the colony would find their position much more disturbed by the need to learn a new European language. Because of this united opposition the idea was laid aside in 1871 and revived only briefly in the 1870s

Interest in the eastern coast of Africa and its hinterland had been growing in the 1850s. David Livingstone had caught the public attention with his accounts of his explorations and his reminder that a slave trade on the east coast was still taking a great many slaves across the Indian Ocean to the Arab world. When he said that he was going back to Africa to make an open road for commerce and for Christianity he meant that unless a natural alternative was provided the slave trade was bound to go on. Other explorers were putting together pieces of the map of East Africa, though at the time of Livingstone's death in 1873 the intricacies of the system of lakes and rivers had still not been worked out, and any politicians rash enough to think of taking an interest in the African interior would have found it hard to know where they were going. Advances inland were becoming a little more practicable because of advances in technology; people had known for centuries that quinine was a useful drug for tropical diseases, but it was really not until an expedition up the river Niger in 1854 succeeded in keeping its death rate very low by laying down that everybody must take a regular dose of quinine that the drug's comprehensive value for preventive purposes was accepted. The use of steamships which could make their way up the rivers, or even be carried overland to the larger lakes and be assembled on the spot, made water transport much easier. The spread of breech-loading rifles in the 1850s and 1860s meant that European soldiers had weapons that were greatly superior to anything the African population could obtain or could make for themselves.

The Empire in Equilibrium

But even if expansion in Africa was now possible, British politicians were not interested. This was shown most conclusively by the Abyssinian expedition: King Theodore, in a mood a little like that of a boy who is naughty in order to be noticed, had imprisoned the Europeans in his country, and in 1868 General Robert Napier led forces forward to rescue them. Everything went as the British hoped: Theodore's forts were stormed and he committed suicide, the prisoners were released, and Napier and his army then marched home again. The total cost of over £8m. was large enough by the standards of the time to deserve attention, but there were no complaints about the cost and also no suggestions that the conquered territory should be kept. On the whole it seemed to be accepted that, although it was sometimes necessary to go out and defeat some of the less orderly rulers in the world that lay beyond British control, the expense of a punitive expedition was quite enough of a burden, so that it would be foolish to think of spending more money to retain the territory afterwards.

The same willingness to go to war, combined with a lack of interest in taking tracts of new land, was shown in China. In the eighteenth century the East India Company had been able to trade at Canton under tightly controlled conditions and exported increasing amounts of tea, which could then be obtained only in China. The Chinese government had no high opinion of this trade; when Lord Macartney went to Peking in 1793 to try to ease relations he was received contemptuously and nothing came of his mission. In the 1830s the Chinese government became worried about the immense increase in imports of opium, which had quadrupled in the previous twenty years because it was brought from India by the Company to pay for tea, and it decided to ban the drug and its import. Opium was at the time sold in Britain with no restrictions; the British thought the Chinese ban was about as sensible as if they had tried to outlaw alcohol and that it was just a trick to increase the commissions that had to be paid to supplement the salaries of Chinese officials. So when, in 1839, the Chinese tried to make the ban effective and to punish the British traders, the British government was quite willing to respond by going to war, and after it had won the war, it acquired Hong Kong in 1842 and also obtained a much more limited right to trade in five other Chinese ports. British trade with China went on, but in the late 1850s it was interrupted by disputes which led a joint Anglo-French force to march on Peking in 1860, though the Chinese agreed to a treaty before the city was attacked. The victors were not interested in territorial expansion: after plundering the Summer Palace of the emperors in revenge for the killing of prisoners by the Chinese they went home again, having shown that they could seize part of China and that they were not interested in the expense of holding on to it.

Lord Palmerston, who was a dominant force in British foreign policy in the 1830s and from the time he became Foreign Secretary in 1847 until his death in 1865, represented a number of political attitudes that appear hard to reconcile. He was willing to use force when Englishmen had been attacked and robbed of their money by force, and this entitled him to the gratitude of British merchants overseas. On the other hand he had rather less comfort to offer British investors overseas who had lost their money because the borrowers had defaulted; he laid down the general principle that it was entirely a matter for the government to decide whether to make diplomatic representations on their behalf, and in practice he argued that they knew from the high rate of return that they were getting into a risky business, and there was no need for the government to help them. The Palmerstonian attitude has been described as 'the imperialism of free trade' involving a policy of 'trade with informal control if possible, trade with rule where necessary'.[3] This obviously could be an attractive and economical approach, though it does not explain why people turned away from the expansionism of previous decades or why they came to so few places where 'rule' seemed to be necessary for trade in the 1850s and 1860s.

Palmerston saw no reason to think that Britain would be any better off for owning more land overseas and did not insist on retaining territory for sentimental reasons. In 1864 he arranged the transfer of the Ionian Islands, which had been given to Britain in the 1815 settlement, to Greece, which had become strong enough to keep them out of the hands of the Turks. Palmerston would not have objected if any of the self-governing colonies pushed ahead into lands in the interior, as long as it was not done at the expense of the British taxpayer, and he was assertive enough to have a considerable impact on events in Greece, in Turkey, and in Italy, but spending on defence was kept low; he worked for several years in an uneasy partnership with Gladstone, and Gladstone's main concern as Chancellor of the Exchequer was to keep the cost of government down, partly out of a belief that this was the prudent way to run the economy, partly out of a belief that small armaments would encourage peace, and partly out of a realization that taxpayers would welcome a frugal government that showed it could control official expenditure. So Palmerston's moments of asserting Britain's position in the world did not lead to a policy of expansion or of militarism. He

---

[3] R. Robinson and J. Gallagher, 'The Imperialism of Free Trade', *Economic History Review 1953–54*, especially p. 13.

was alarmed when Napoleon III's Second Empire adopted a policy of self-assertion – a policy which led (more particularly on the continent of Europe) to the term 'imperialism' being applied to any aggressive approach to questions in foreign affairs – but his response was to build a defensive line of coastal fortifications to fend off invasion. The Royal Navy remained strong, and it was during the Palmerstonian period that it was converted from a fleet of wooden sailing-ships into a fleet of iron coal-fuelled steamships, but it was still a force that could protect Britain against invasion and safeguard food supplies as Britain became established as a food-importing country, rather than take a decisive part in attacking another country.

Palmerston wanted to avoid having to choose between advancing or letting other nations advance. This led him to try to stop the Egyptian government from deciding to let de Lessep's French company build a canal through the isthmus from the Mediterranean to Suez because he was afraid it might lead to increased British involvement there. He could see that, if the Canal was built, steamships would use the Red Sea route for goods as well as for passengers and letters, so that all communication with India and most communication with Australia and New Zealand would go through Egypt. If the Suez route increased its importance in this way it might become hard for Britain to continue to accept the fact that it did not have as much influence in Egypt as France. But de Lesseps got his canal concession, and work started in 1859. At times it looked as if there might not be enough money to complete it, but de Lesseps was saved by the American Civil War and by the accession of the Khedive Ismail in 1863. The Civil War in the early 1860s and the blockade of exports of cotton from the American South meant that there was a great demand for Egyptian cotton, and the country's prosperity rose rapidly. Ismail was eager to modernize his country, and very ready to borrow money to do so. The Canal went ahead, and Ismail borrowed against the cotton revenues. This prosperity faded with the end of the Civil War but by then the Canal was safe. When it was opened in 1869 the Khedive celebrated it with pomp and circumstance and encouraged Verdi to compose an opera – *Aida* – as part of the festivities. By this time he was far enough in debt to French and British bankers for them to suggest that it might be sensible for him to start reducing his spending, but he took no notice.

At the time it looked as if the completion of the Canal would weaken the financial position of South Africa still further. Earlier in the century South African wines had been taxed at a lower rate than foreign wines coming into Britain, but Gladstone's 1860 budget gave effect to the trade treaty Cobden had negotiated with France and ended the preference, after which South African wines had great difficulty holding on to any position in the British market. There was a satisfactory trade in wool which accounted for about three-quarters of all exports, and South Africa had a monopoly of the ostrich feathers which were fashionable for most of the century, but the South

African economy still depended to a considerable extent on selling supplies to ships passing the Cape of Good Hope. The Suez overland route had cut into this trade; the opening of the Canal, which reduced the length of a voyage to India by two months, was bound to affect it much more, so there was unlikely to be any British pressure for expansion. The map of South Africa was a black and white checkerboard. The black squares – Griqualand East and Pondoland between Cape Colony and Natal, Zululand north of Natal, Basutoland between the Orange Free State and Natal, Griqualand West down the river from the Orange Free State, and Swaziland east of the Transvaal – were peaceful, and the British goverment showed no sign of wanting to change the situation or of allowing the British colonies enough local authority for them to be able to change it. The constitutional position of Cape Colony and of Natal was rather like that of the West Indian colonies; they had assemblies but the governors could decide day-to-day policy for themselves, though they could not make the assemblies pass laws or vote taxes.

As they did not have governments responsible to their assemblies and were divided among British, Afrikaners, and Africans, the South African colonies were often not considered when the position of the self-governing colonies was being discussed in mid-Victorian Britain. A small minority of politicians could be described as followers of Cobden in the sense that they wanted the colonies to make themselves independent as soon as possible – it would save Britain money and it would increase the colonies' self-respect as well as their ability to run their own affairs. Few ministers said this, though Molesworth, who argued that colonies cost about £4m. a year (mainly in military and naval expenses) and should be abandoned as an economy measure, went on to become Secretary for the Colonies in 1855 and might have gone further if he had not died young. Many more politicians thought separation was inevitable: Lord Grey had himself felt sure that self-governing colonies would want to stay in the empire, but he noted with surprise and regret that Gladstone, Graham, and Peel seemed to take separation for granted. Politicians in this group believed that once colonies had gained self-government they should not expect Britain to spend any money on them except to defend them from attack by a powerful foreign state, and they also believed that Britain should adjust her policy so as to reduce the cost of the colonies. Probably several ministers and most of the ordinary backbench politicians of the period wanted the self-governing colonies to stay in the position they had reached, and would not mind if it cost a little money to protect them from danger, while reckoning that Britain's best contribution to their security lay in providing a navy which, as well as ensuring Britain's own safety, made is most unlikely that a European power would attack any colony.

When the *Edinburgh Review* analysed Molesworth's estimate of the cost of the colonies it argued that the actual expense was under £2m. a year and that that money protected them, kept them at peace, stopped the white populations of South Africa and the West Indies from ill-treating the black, and restrained colonial attempts to impose protective tariffs on British goods.[4] Even so, it would have been hard to find anyone in British politics who would have wanted to resist by force if any of the colonies of white settlement had proclaimed their indepedence. Such a step was hardly within the bounds of possibility; although the flood of emigration from Britain flowed more to the United States than to the colonies, for most of the century the majority of Australians and New Zealanders, and of the English-speaking part of the Canadian and white South African population, had been born in Britain. Irritation with British governors might have led to trouble in Canada and in various parts of Australia around 1850, but responsible government, although it turned out to mean something slightly different from what Durham had intended, was quite as effective in curing the irritation as he had hoped.

Responsible Government at Work

This did not necessarily mean that the new system provided upright and stable government. The Australian colonies had had very little time to grow used to representative institutions before responsible government was set up and they had to run their own administrative systems as well. Partly because of this and partly because there were at the time no deep divisions in Australian society after the domination of the squatter wool magnates had been reduced and before the tension between employers and employees had taken an organized form, no firmly defined political parties emerged. As a result governments in the Australian colonies stood on insecure foundations; between 1850 and 1890 governments lasted on average for about eighteen months in New South Wales and Victoria, and for even shorter periods in South Australia. The results were not as anarchic as this might suggest. At the level of national politics, governments in Britain in the 1850s lasted only about two years each, and later in the century governments in the French Third Republic were very short-lived; and the governments in the colonies were in some ways more like municipal than national governments. Even so, these governments carried out substantial programmes of railway building, and large changes of policy could be made if it seemed necessary.

As the urgency of the gold rush died down, difficulties were caused by the enormous increase in the population of Australia and in particular of Victoria, which from the 1850s until the end of the century had more people than New South Wales, which in turn had far more people than all the other Australian colonies put together. Mechanized working of gold below ground by a relatively small number of wage-earners replaced the surface opera-

[4] 'Shall we Retain our Colonies', *Edinburgh Review*, April 1851.

tions of a great crowd of individuals working on their own account, and
Victoria faced a problem of over-population. This was met in the 1860s by a
switch from the free trade policy appropriate for a mining community to a
protectionist policy intended to create small farms and provide jobs for
workers who could no longer make a living by mining. In different circumstances this change would have been carried out by a great party leader; in
Victoria it was inspired by David Syme, the editor of *The Age*, who was one
of the first men to see what use could be made of the scientific protectionism
which flourished in the later decades of the century.

Protectionism came to Victoria as a policy intended to do something for
the working man, while free trade was seen as the policy to help the working
man in Britain or the food-exporting farmer in Canada because it would
keep down the cost of living. Protectionism spread fairly quickly to most of
the other Australian colonies. New South Wales stood aloof from this
because it remained sufficiently committed to exporting its products – which
were still dominated by wool although it also exported minerals – to retain its
free trade policy for the rest of the century. The British were not pleased by
the shift to protectionism, but they felt it caused them little direct harm, and
in any case the theory of free trade said that high tariffs hurt the people who
adopted them more than anyone else, so that protectionism was its own
punishment.

Much more annoyance to British politicians – who had to listen to missionary protests about it – was caused by the New Zealanders' application of
responsible government and the way they brought on wars with the Maoris.
The settlers in New Zealand never treated the Maoris very badly by comparison with what went on elsewhere. In some colonies the native population was exterminated (in the old sense of being driven out of their land),
and in small islands like Newfoundland and Tasmania, where there was
nowhere for them to retreat to, they died out. In Australia, as in South
Africa, settlers had begun by feeling that killing the native population was
no more of a crime than killing wild animals, until Governor Gipps made it
clear in 1838 that this was not so and that murderers should be executed. The
decision was received with a better grace by all concerned, including the
murderers, than had been the case in South Africa at Slaghter's Nek, but this
doctrine of common humanity was still received with a certain amount of
surprise.

Governors in New Zealand did not have to dwell upon this point, but the
land dealings of the 1840s left a difficult situation. The Maoris who sold their
land may not have realized that they were taken to be selling a freehold
which gave the purchaser unlimited rights over the land. They were accustomed to leaving land vacant while they wandered elsewhere and in the early
stages of development the land investment companies, buying land to be
divided up and sold, were bound to look very like nomadic pastoralists

leaving vast tracts of land empty. As the land was sold off and more immigrants were brought out, the British population of New Zealand increased steadily so that by 1860 they probably outnumbered the Maoris and were pressing forward to take up all the land that they could claim to have purchased. This inevitably led to frontier wars; the Maoris tried to set up a king who would be able to unite them for purposes of self-defence, and in the 1860s the 'Maori king' wars were a burden on the British exchequer.

From the settlers' point of view the position was ideal; they had a well-trained force at their disposal, the local economy benefited from the money brought in by British troops, and the British taxpayer met the costs. The amounts involved were substantial enough by the standards of the day to attract attention; the 1865–6 Vote of Credit of £¾m. for operations in New Zealand was smaller than expenditure on the Kaffir Wars, and the struggle in New Zealand did not go on so long, but the British government was very conscious that its money was being spent by a government whose domestic policy it could control only by carrying out an invasion – which was un-thinkable – or by withdrawing the troops and telling the New Zealanders that they should run their own affairs on a basis of complete independence. The wars were conducted without any cause for deep or lasting animosity and the more sport-loving of the British convinced themselves that the Maoris enjoyed the struggle and regarded warfare as the natural way for a man to express himself. Certainly Maoris accepted warfare as part of the natural order of things, though it is not so certain that they regarded loss of land as a natural consequence of defeat in war. But there was no suggestion that they were being reduced to slavery, and it was true that the Maoris retained as good a position and survived the problems of the sudden onrush of western industrial civilization as well as any of the other native peoples outside Asia whom the British had overrun.

While New Zealand and the Maori wars raised the question of British financial involvement under responsible government in an acute form, none of those who expected responsible government to lead to independence would have thought New Zealand would be the first colony to end its formal political connection with Britain, if only because of the high proportion of recent British immigrants in the population and the close commercial links with Britain. Believers in independence for the colonies expected to see it come first in Canada, perhaps because most of them had a high opinion of the benevolence of the United States and of the readiness of Canadians to trust the Americans. British North America had at first flourished under Elgin's Reciprocity Treaty, and the anxieties of the next dozen years were not always easy to understand. In the two united Canadas politicians worried about the problems of making sure that neither section got more than its fair share of cabinet posts, and they worried about the instability of governments. As the disadvantages of a peripatetic capital became obvious they asked the Queen to choose a site, and when she put forward a sensible compromise and selected a small town on the Ottawa River that flowed between Canada East and Canada West they first defeated the government that brought her decision forward, and then reinstated it for want of anything better. Ottawa duly became the capital, and Canadians brought the idea of a federation into serious political discussion for the first time during the crisis. But it was not a period in which parliamentary government was expected to bring stable government, and by the standards of Australia in the 1850s party discipline and loyalty in Canada were fairly high.

Most of the time power lay in the hands of the Conservatives led, or at least held together, by John A. Macdonald. As the party rested on an alliance of French-speaking Roman Catholics with the Orange Order who opposed the Irish Catholics in Ontario, there were obvious dangers that one section or the other would find its religious loyalties made it impossible to continue the partnership; what kept them united was a fear that the godless English-speaking republic to the south would swallow them all up if they began quarrelling. The groups in opposition looked as if they ought to have found it easier to work together. The anti-clerical *rouges* of Lower Canada (victims of sermons in which politically-minded *curés* reminded their flocks that 'le ciel est bleu, l'enfer est rouge') ought to have had no difficulty working with the more open-minded of the inhabitants of Canada West. But in the 1840s Canada West was one of the great magnets for British migration, and when the flow slackened in the 1850s, the Canadian government began a policy of advertising for immigrants. As Canada West came to outnumber Canada East, English-speaking Liberals began to be attracted by 'rep by pop', or representation by population, which would have meant that the equality of seats between Canada East and Canada West would be ended by giving Canada West a majority based on numbers.

Although it was hard to form a political party which would not be split either by questions of religion or of regional advantage, the system worked well enough in the 1850s. The Canadian government was able to defend the general claim of the colonies to freedom in tariff questions: colonies always said that their increases in tariffs were imposed to obtain revenue, and it was accepted that they needed this source of revenue because they did not follow the uniquely British practice of imposing an income tax. Galt's 1859 budget raised Canadian tariffs to a level at which it was impossible to believe that they were intended to produce revenue, and the Colonial Office pointed out that the new tariff was clearly protectionist; the Canadian government replied that it was in charge of the matter and would take the responsibility. The Colonial Office accepted this reply calmly enough and for years to come watched colony after colony rushing into adopting protectionist policies as one of the stages of growing self-reliance.

Holding a Canadian government together became even harder in the

1860s, and at the same time an external danger became steadily more visible. The United States was not a comfortable neighbour. In the 1850s there had been signs of tension across the border at the two points where the Hudson's Bay Company had supported settlement, on the Red River and near Vancouver Island. Some Canadians had thought about westward expansion; no Canadians would feel happy about American northward expansion. The immediate danger was removed in 1861 by the outbreak of the American Civil War, but this was a cause for relief only in the shortest of short terms. Britain and British North America sympathized with the southern states, and would not have been sorry to see some misfortune overtake the North. This attitude may have been understandable, but if it was followed by failure to observe strict neutrality–such as the British failure to stop the *Alabama* escaping from a British port or the Canadian failure to prevent Southerners from using Canada as a base for attacking Vermont in 1864 – it might lead to war with the North. Looking slightly further ahead it could be seen that the North would either emerge from the Civil War angry because she had been bereft of the southern states and eager for compensation elsewhere, or else triumphant, endowed with a victorious army, and ready to go on with the work of taking over North America that absorbed so much of her energy in the nineteenth century. Even if peace could be kept, it was fairly clear that Elgin's Reciprocity Treaty would not be renewed when its initial 12-year term expired in 1866.

In the summer of 1864 the governments of Nova Scotia, New Brunswick, and Prince Edward Island met to discuss the possibility of a closer union to protect their interests in the harsher times that clearly lay ahead. Just after the news that they were to meet had reached Canada, yet another Canadian government was defeated and Parliament faced the prospect of a third election in three years. It was reprieved by the suggestion of a coalition government to create a British North American federation, put forward by George Brown, the political heir of the Reformers. A federal system with two levels of government, each sovereign in the spheres of activity allotted to it, looked like the best way to create a central government in which claims on grounds of population to political influence would not be frustrated by the over-representation of Canada East, and at the same time create provincial governments that would enable the French-speaking Roman Catholics of Canada East to retain full control over those issues of religion (and, to a lesser extent, language) in their own region that really mattered to them. Macdonald, probably the most far-sighted as well as the most dextrous of Canadian politicians, did not care for federalism and thought it was the cause of a good many of the troubles of the United States, but he could also see its advantages, of which the main one was simply that no other system would work. So he devoted himself to creating a federal system in which as much power was put in the hands of the central government as possible.

Brown's suggestion of a coalition led quickly to the creation of a government committed to a policy of federation, and the new government soon proposed itself as a visitor to the conference of Charlottetown. The arrival of the Canadian ministers transformed the situation; unification might have been the rational way for the small Maritime colonies to deal with the problem of survival in a harsh world, but it was not clear that politicians or their constituents would put up with losing all trace of their local and traditional governments. Federation (or Confederation, as it has always been known in Canada, though a political scientist would use this word for a much looser type of union than the Canadians had in mind and eventually achieved) meant that the smaller colonies would not vanish from the political map, and by February 1865 proposals for a federal union had been agreed. The constitutional relationship with Britain would not change, though the legal authority of the Westminster Parliament would be needed to carry out the rearrangement of power: the new government of the Confederation and the governments of its provinces would between them have just the same powers as the old colonies and just the same relationship with the Crown, in the sense that both of the new levels of government would be responsible to the Canadian or to a provincial parliament. Between them they would control the militia, and the new government of Canada could perfectly well create a navy or a regular army if it wanted to, just as the existing government of Canada East and Canada West could have done.

Confederation did change imperial relations, but it did this by creating a much larger state with a greater capacity to take on new functions rather than by altering the legal framework. Everybody knew that the change would be considerable; the British government welcomed the proposal and supported it because the new constitution looked like creating a political unit that could convince the United States that it was running its own affairs, which would reduce the need for British military support. American annexationist spirit stayed alive for at least another half-century, but that spirit depended largely on a belief that the people in British North America were in some way not free to choose what to do, which led on to the assumption that, if they were free, they would choose to join the United States. The creation of a larger unit which would organize more of its own defence would clear away this misunderstanding and relieve the British government of much of the military and diplomatic work of helping defend Canada. So, while the British sent reinforcements to help guard Canada in the period of tension caused by the American Civil War, they hoped that this involvement in North America would not be needed in the future. As a result New Brunswick's reversal of its pro-confederation policy in the general election of 1865 caused almost as much alarm in London as in the Canadian Parliament.

The United States continued to be Confederation's best friend. The

American government made it clear that there would be no new treaty to replace the 1854 Reciprocity Treaty, so opponents of Confederation in New Brunswick and Nova Scotia found it hard to present any alternative policy. When another election was to be held in New Brunswick in the summer of 1866, Fenian supporters of independence for Ireland were able to invade Canada from New York and Vermont with very little attempt at restraint by the American authorities. British North Americans might not really have faced a choice between Fenianism and Confederation, but this was what many of them thought their position was in 1866 and in this case they would certainly choose Confederation. By the end of 1866 the 1865 proposals had been accepted by New Brunswick, Nova Scotia, and the two Canadas. Early in 1867 the British Parliament passed the British North America Act with an absence of interest that later generations of Canadians resented almost as much as they would have resented any attempt by the British Parliament to rewrite the legislation that had been so delicately worked out by the politicians of British North America. Only the imperial parliament could change legislation like the 1840 Act that had united the two Canadas, but British politicians were no longer expected to undertake the roles in drafting legislation and deciding policy that they had played a quarter of a century earlier, and so they simply accepted the legislation on which the Canadians had agreed.

On 1 July 1867 the Dominion of Canada came into existence. Macdonald would have liked it to have been the Kingdom of Canada, but Dominion was a word with its own programme for the future – the word had been taken from the text 'He shall have dominion from sea to sea', and the question of 'sea to sea' was to exercise the minds of Canadians for twenty years to come. In the east Prince Edward Island was brought into the federation in 1873. In the west there were two sets of negotiations to be carried out and in both cases the negotiations affected Canada more deeply than could have been expected.

The small settlements around Vancouver Island which had been the main target of President Polk's slogan '54°40' or fight' had been separated from the Hudson's Bay Company territories and made into a colony in 1858. The old-established Hudson's Bay Company, which ruled over an area of 3 million square miles in which it did little to disturb the balance of nature and population, had in 1863 sold its rights and authority to a new group for £1.5m. The new owners thought of building a transcontinental telegraph line, which would very probably be followed by a transcontinental railway. If the government of Canada was to extend the area it ruled west to the Pacific, it had to have the political authority of the Hudson's Bay Company extinguished and it had to persuade the government of British Columbia to join the Confederation.

Negotations with the Company were made more difficult by the readiness

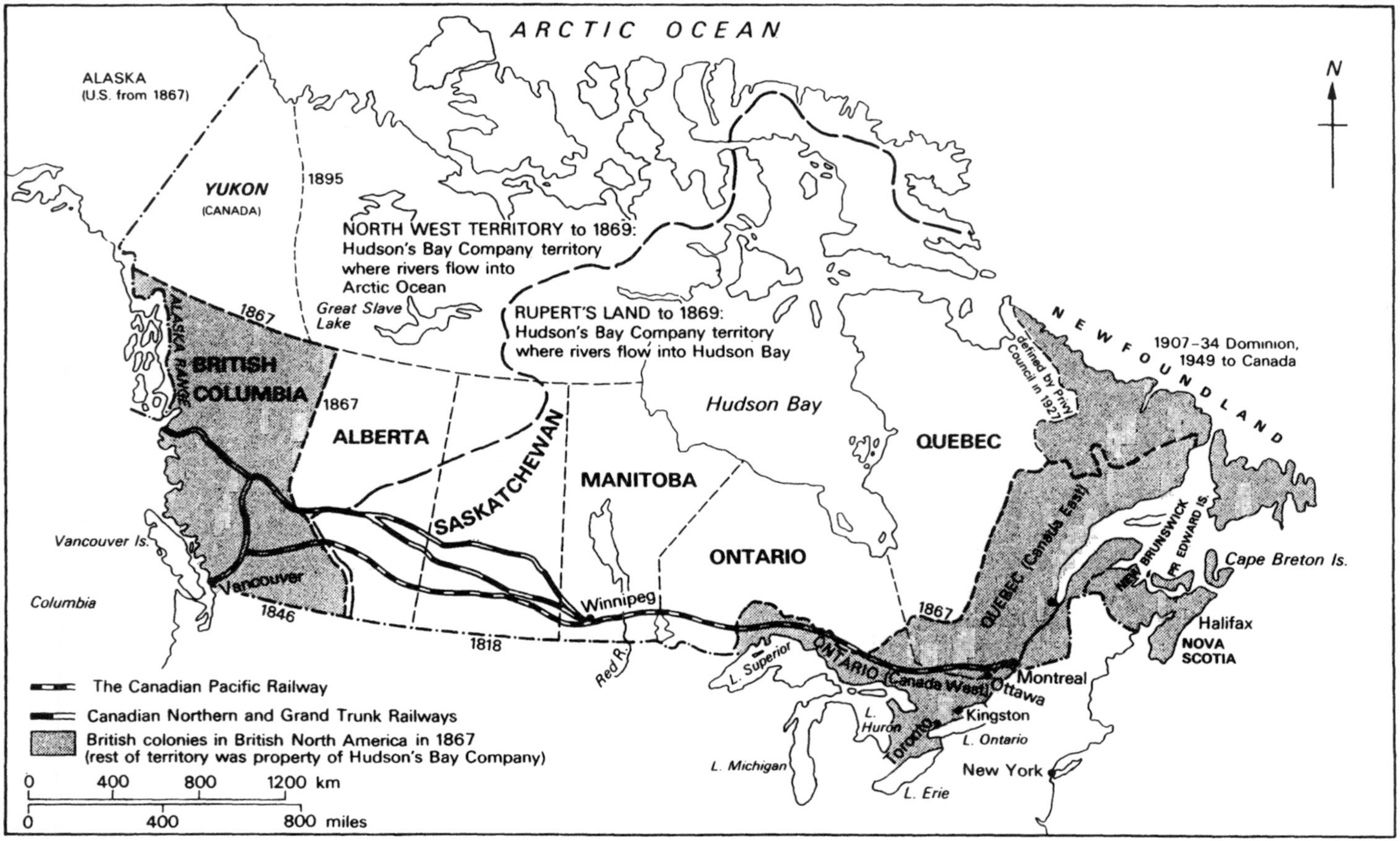

Map 9 Canada 1867–1949

ARCTIC OCEAN

ALASKA
(U.S. from 1867)

YUKON
(CANADA)

1895

NORTH WEST TERRITORY to 1869:
Hudson's Bay Company territory
where rivers flow into
Arctic Ocean

RUPERT'S LAND to 1869:
Hudson's Bay Company territory
where rivers flow into Hudson Bay

Great Slave
Lake

Hudson Bay

N E W F O U N D L A N D

1907–34 Dominion,
1949 to Canada

defined by Privy
Council in 1927

QUEBEC

QUEBEC (Canada East)

Cape Breton Is.

Halifax

NOVA
SCOTIA

P. EDWARD IS.

NEW BRUNSWICK

Montreal

Ottawa

Kingston

L. Ontario

New York

L. Erie

1867

ONTARIO (Canada West)

Toronto

L.
Huron

L. Michigan

ONTARIO

L. Superior

MANITOBA

Winnipeg

Red R.

SASKATCHEWAN

1818

ALBERTA

1867

BRITISH
COLUMBIA

1867

ALASKA RANGE

Vancouver

1846

Vancouver Is.

Columbia

The Canadian Pacific Railway

Canadian Northern and Grand Trunk Railways

British colonies in British North America in 1867
(rest of territory was property of Hudson's Bay Company)

0   400   800   1200 km

0   400   800 miles

of the Canadians to argue that the original grant of 1670 which gave the Company its rights over its initial 1.4 million square miles in Rupert's Land was not legitimate, and that its extension north-west into the basin of the Mackenzie had even less foundation. The British government was ready enough to encourage the ending of the Company's political power, partly because it could see a danger that the settlement, on the Red River where the descendants of Lord Selkirk's settlers had formed a reasonably stable community, might object to continued Company rule, but it was not going to allow the charter to be treated as a nullity. After a year of negotiation the government of Canada bought out the political and the general territorial rights of the Company for £300,000 in 1869 and acknowledged its claim to keep its trading posts and to be endowed with a very large grant of open land as well. The government of Canada was then certain that this problem had been solved; the Red River settlers had grumbled often enough at Company rule for the Canadians of the Great Lakes to feel sure that they would be greeted as harbingers of freedom and civilization when they arrived.

Things did not work out in quite this way. The Red River's long-distance trading links were in London, and the shorter links ran up the river to the United States; Canada was separated from the settlement by the vast expanse of empty land north of Lake Superior. Probably the larger and certainly the more violent part of the population wanted some guarantees of their position before they were absorbed into Canada, and under the leadership of Louis Riel they set up a provisional government. It was able to resist the official representative of Canada for a few months and, even when it was pushed aside by a British and Canadian force under General Wolseley, Riel retained his reputation as a man who understood the needs of the people of mixed Indian and European descent who lived on the edge of settlement. But it seemed unlikely that this fairly small group of Metis would trouble the situation further, and Canada took its next step to the west. In the summer of 1870, just as Riel's government was disappearing, representatives from British Columbia were negotiating their colony's entry into the Canadian Confederation and this was confirmed by their legislature in January 1871. The most important feature of the agreement and far the hardest to fulfil was that the Canadian government promised to build a railway line from sea to sea within the next ten years.

So by 1871 the creation of a new political unit was complete. The British withdrew their military garrisons, leaving behind only the naval bases at Esquimault in British Columbia and at Halifax. Canada would still be entitled to expect support if danger from the United States appeared again, but the new self-governing colony was strong enough to reduce the risk that this would happen. The example of Canada was taken up and applied in several other colonies over the next hundred years. Because of the haphazard pattern of English expansion in the seventeenth and eighteenth centuries, when a collection of ports and forts was all that was wanted, nobody had thought of the advantages of having colonies that could make a real contribution towards defending themselves. But whenever colonies at all close together showed any interest in looking after their own affairs, unification seemed the natural next step; and no contiguous colonies escaped having its advantages pressed upon them. Federation – in the sense of creating a central government, but not submerging the original colonies in it totally – often seemed the most practical policy, with the result that, while Britain had one of the most unitary of governments, Britain's colonies habitually turned themselves into federations in the course of their political development. Sometimes these federations had federal constitutions in the strict sense that the central government had authority in some areas of activity while other areas were reserved for the state or provincial governments. In any case it was rare for so thoroughgoing an amalgamation to be arranged that an existing colony passed out of existence. Encouragement of federation was a sign of Britain's willingness to reduce the burden of empire, and in the case of Canada there was still something left of a mood of willingness to give the burden up altogether when the new country was launched on a wider existence. But moods of weariness with empire come and go, and a student of imperial organization who looked at the course of events, and noted the withdrawal of political authority from the Hudson's Bay Company and the final winding-up of the East India Company in 1874, might have confined himself to the rather safer prophecy that the chartered companies which had done so much for the expansion of the British empire had vanished from the scene.

8. Victorian Activity 1869–1890

Cutting military spending by withdrawing troops from Canada after the scattered colonies had been strengthened by Confederation was such a satisfactory piece of retrenchment that British ministers looked round for similar opportunities to save money. But somehow they never occurred; the detachment from imperial expansion which had been so general a feature of policy since 1850 was replaced by the re-emergence of the century-old tendency to move forward all over the world. It could not be said to be inspired by an outburst of direct imperial enthusiasm in the opening stages; at least until Queen Victoria's Golden Jubilee in 1887 the process of imperial expansion was something that took place with very little discussion, no continuous public pressure – if imperial sentiment helped Disraeli win an election in 1874, it did nothing to save him from defeat in 1880 – and every sign of being a response to particular challenges rather than formed policy. The only surprising thing was that the response to challenges so often took the form of a decision to move forward or, at least so far as the London government was concerned, a decision to accept the desire for forward movement of people on the frontiers or of merchants in Britain. The government did sometimes impose a policy of restraint, for the sake of economy or of good relations with other European powers. If there had been comparable pressure for expansion from the frontiers in the 1850s and 1860s, the government might have resisted it, but this was never put to the test; the change from a policy of standing still to a policy of advancing was not one that was decided by sentiment inside Britain.

It was undoubtedly affected by changes in technology which made it easier for active and energetic men to think of moving forward, and it may have been encouraged by a shift towards a version of Darwinian thinking which encouraged the strong to think that their strength was in itself a proof that they were morally entitled to take over the territory of the weak. This change did not have its effect only in Britain; part of the pressure from the frontiers came from people who could see other European nations moving forward in a way they had not done earlier in the century, and felt that only a British advance could neutralize the effect of French or German policy. But the tendency to advance on the frontiers became visible in British policy at least as early as anywhere else, and perhaps can be seen first of all as a reaction against the attempt to cut down on imperial spending at the beginning of the 1870s.

Expansion Resumed

In 1869 troops were withdrawn from New Zealand despite pleas that they should be allowed to remain or that the British government should at least provide a substantial loan for purposes of defence against the danger from the Maoris. The Colonial Office replied very curtly that the New Zealanders were supposed to be able to look after themselves and that self-government involved taking care of local problems out of local resources. The tone of the correspondence made it seem quite possible that the Colonial Office wanted to provoke the New Zealanders into proclaiming their independence, which would have made them responsible for all levels of spending. The New Zealanders had no wish to have so much freedom thrust upon them, and an argument broke out in Britain about the government's policy. As ministers began by saying that it was not British policy to hold on to colonies against their will, which was not what the New Zealanders were talking about at all, it did look as if the government was thinking actively about separation.

British interest in the empire had been declining for some years but the New Zealand issue aroused concern and support for imperial activity, shown by steps like the establishment of the Royal Colonial Institution (now the Royal Commonwealth Trust). The British public clearly did not want the colonies to separate; by degress the government drew back from its opposition to colonial commitments, the New Zealanders got their loan for defence, and when Lord Granville was promoted to Foreign Secretary in 1870 his successor at the Colonial Office, Lord Kimberley, was ready to take a more sympathetic attitude to the problems of Englishmen overseas. He was very soon able to put his name on the map in the literal sense. Diamonds had been found in South Africa in 1867 and this opened up a brighter future than had seemed possible for the past ten or twenty years. Prospectors who were busy digging and shifting the earth were not really concerned about which government owned the land in which they were working. The 'big hole' that they dug was north of the Orange River, the boundary between British and Afrikaner territory, though it was well to the west of the area of Afrikaner interest and settlement. Kimberley did not want the Afrikaners to expand, and in 1871 he declared that because the region had always remained in the hands of its Griqua inhabitants the British government could annex it when the diamond miners moved in.

Although the Afrikaners naturally saw this as a piece of British interference, Kimberley saw the step as a way to reduce British involvement in South Africa: in 1872 he succeeded where earlier Secretaries for the Colonies had failed, and persuaded the Cape Parliament to undertake responsible government. In the past the financial and military burdens of self-government had held the Cape politicians back, but the wealth from supplying the new diamond city, named after Lord Kimberley, made these expenses much easier to bear. Most of the skilled miners who came to the diggings were British, most of the unskilled work was done by Africans attracted by relatively high wages, and most of the men who gained financial control over the mines came from the continent of Europe and had connections with the Dutch and German diamond markets. The great exception among the financial magnates, Cecil Rhodes, came from a sufficiently upper-middle-class background in England – he had originally gone to farm in South Africa for the sake of his health – to think that the natural thing for him to do was to make a fortune, get an Oxford education, and then go into politics.

Lord Kimberley could have avoided moving forward, but it was clear that Englishmen were going to the diamond mines and that there would be a vacuum of authority or a clash with the Afrikaners if he did nothing; moving forward turned out to be less trouble than standing still. The same thing happened elsewhere. Unofficial expansion from Australia to New Zealand in the 1830s had pulled the British government along behind it, to avoid the problems of disorder, and in the 1860s traders and settlers had taken another step forward and moved on to Fiji. By 1872 the King of Fiji could see that his authority was not going to survive the influx for long. He already had a government with an Englishman as his chief minister, and he decided that it would be safer to hand the island over to the British government, in the hope that it would be a conservative force, rather than have irresponsible outsiders destroy it bit by bit. The British government would have found it very hard to keep Englishmen off the islands: the government had no legal means to stop its subjects going wherever they pleased; any attempt to acquire that sort of legal power would have been extraordinarily unpopular, and, if obtained, it could hardly have been enforced outside British possessions. The determination to keep down costs might have led the government to decline the King's offer and leave the islands to look after themselves, but Kimberley decided to investigate the problem. By the time his commission had reported, urging the government to take over the islands in order to maintain the peace, the Conservatives had come to office and, after noting with distaste that the islands were certainly not going to cover their costs, the new government accepted the report in 1874. Fiji was a good small-scale example of the way British possessions grew because the British government was not strong enough to stop the activities of its expansion-minded subjects nor insular-minded enough to refuse to have anything to do with them.

The policy of punitive expeditions followed by withdrawal still went on. Asanti had again been attacking Africans who lived in the Gold Coast, and late in 1873 Sir Garnet Wolseley was sent inland to stop this. His neat and tidy campaign, ending with the destruction of the place of human sacrifice at

Kumasi, was not followed by occupation and closely resembled the expeditions to Peking and to Abyssinia in the 1860s; but is also showed how easy it was to defeat an African Kingdom now that troops had breech-loaded rifles and knew that a steady consumption of quinine would protect their health. Kimberley also allowed a move forward in Malaya. The sultans of the little kingdoms of the peninsula maintained a much lower level of law and order that the British in Penang and the Straits Settlements found comfortable. Kimberley authorized the Governor to send Residents to the sultans' courts, and probably expected that they would exercise moral suasion like the Residents at the courts of Indian princes. But the Residents in India were effective because they had great strength close at hand, and the Residents in Malaya had to assert themselves much more obviously than Kimberley had intended, which began the process of undermining the sultans' authority.

While the Liberals had in fact shifted during their term of office to a position of greater activity in imperial affairs, they suffered in the election of 1874 because the electorate felt they had done too much at home and too little for the empire. Disraeli, who had not shown any particular enthusiasm for the empire in earlier decades, moved to a pro-imperial position in June 1872, and made the suggestion that responsible government ought to have been accompanied by arrangements for a customs union. However out of touch with the realities of the 1840s this might have been, Disraeli was expressing an imperial sentiment that people were ready to welcome in the 1870s.

Despite this he concentrated for most of his premiership on the problems of the eastern Mediterranean and relations with Russia. By the end of the eighteenth century Russia was powerful enough on the Black Sea to threaten Turkey, and for most of the nineteenth century Britain followed a pro-Turkish policy to hold Russia back. When a revolt against Turkish rule broke out in the Balkans in the 1870s Gladstone argued, as an active supporter of Christianity and of nationalism, that the best policy was to make the Christian areas of the Balkans into independent states which could defend themselves against Russia's advance and serve as a buffer to keep her confined to the Black Sea. Disraeli argued that the traditional policy of supporting Turkey would hold Russia back much better. Russian victories over Turkey in 1877 and the arguments of his Foreign Secretary Lord Salisbury forced Disraeli to accept the fact that Turkey was going to have to give up territory. His response, which was designed to demonstrate an active interest in the eastern Mediterranean, was to insist that if Russia and Austria were going to acquire parts of the Turkish empire, than Britain must also have some Turkish territory, and thus the British gained Cyprus, where the mainly Greek population was glad to emerge from Turkish rule.

Concern about Russia affected Britain's policy further east. In the 1860s the Indian government had stuck to a policy of leaving Afghanistan alone and trusting to the effects of great distances and difficult country to keep her safe from Russia. Because the main Afghan cities, Kabul and Kandahar, and the rather rudimentary organs of government were close to the border with India, a British advance on the north-west frontier meant an immediate conflict with the Emir, while a Russian advance might capture parts of the less settled western areas of the country almost without anyone noticing. Disraeli tried to encourage the Viceroy to adopt a more active policy; when Northbrook resigned rather than do so, Lytton was appointed to replace him.

This was not a good choice, for the new Viceroy had too much imagination and too little sense of what was practical to suit the post. In domestic policy he strengthened the post-Mutiny approach of conciliating the princely class, which his predecessors had undertaken mainly to avoid provoking any fresh revolts. Lytton thought westernized Indians would be dangerous if they entered the Civil Service or any other route to political power, so he believed it was important to bring the Indian nobility into the administration even if it means using methods of entry that sidestepped the examination for the ICS. The policy was unsuccessful because the princes were not attracted by the thought of becoming bureaucrats. Lytton was more successful in appealing to the princes when he and Disraeli decided to proclaim Queen Victoria Empress of India in 1876; the appeal to the past of making her the heir to the Moghuls probably did reassure the princes that the British would not return to Dalhousie's policy of drastic modernization, even if at the same time the new title disturbed Liberals in England. Lytton soon acted upon the policy of moving forward and in 1876 Baluchistan, the very unsettled tribal area south of Afghanistan, was made into a British protectorate. Lytton's concern about the Russian advance in central Asia became more acute when in 1878 the Emir felt obliged to accept a Russian envoy at his court, and the Viceroy responded by insisting that he should accept a British envoy. In 1879 the people of Kabul rebelled against this and the envoy who had been installed more or less at the point of the bayonet was killed. The government of India carried out a well-planned punitive expedition to Kandahar, but the forward policy was obviously not a complete success.

The Confederation of Canada had been successful enough to mean that federation was very soon seen as an effective device that could usefully be applied elsewhere. South Africa, with its divisions between British and Afrikaner and the possibility of attack by the Africans, looked like an obvious place to encourage the same policy. In a struggle for the Zulu succession the crown had in 1873 passed to Cetewayo, who had attracted to his side the factions who wanted a return to the days of military glory. Cetewayo was probably too shrewd to want to disturb the peace he had helped maintain for the previous twenty years, but he sounded dangerous and the South African Republic north of the Vaal was weak enough to look like a possible victim. Self-reliance and the desire for independence had led the Afrikaners to keep taxes too low for their own safety; when Carnarvon, the Colonial Secretary, began to push forward with his policy of federating the four colonies and republics he found the South African Republic in no condition to do anything other than accept. His representative Shepstone came to Pretoria as something more like a trustee in bankruptcy than the creator of a new south African nation, but his mission was accepted with resignation and in 1877 the Republic was brought under British rule.

The next step was to disarm the Zulus, and in 1878 Cetewayo was presented with an ultimatum which required him to disband his army. No Zulu king would have survived an attempt to comply with such a demand; warlike or peace-loving, Cetewayo was bound to lead his troops forward and, after a brief initial success, his army suffered the destruction that inevitably overtook spearmen charging lines of well-disciplined riflemen. Until July 1879 the Zulus had been a part of the political scene in Africa that could not be ignored; after the battle of Ulundi and a number of smaller wars at about the same time, the British and the Afrikaners could go ahead with their plans without needing to think about the Africans. Because they had been freed from the danger of African attack, or because they disliked British rule when they experienced it, the Afrikaners of the South African Republic began to want to be independent again. The annexation had been attacked by the Liberal leader Gladstone, and the Afrikaners probably though he would reverse it when he became Prime Minister in 1880. He decided that the advantages of federation were too great to be thrown away, and in December 1880 the Afrikaners rose in revolt. At this point the British government decided that it ought to yield to the Afrikaners' desire for independence but, before instructions to withdraw and negotiate could reach the British forces, they had attacked an Afrikaner position at Majuba and had been badly beaten. The government stuck to its policy of withdrawal and in 1881 made an agreement which gave the Republic self-government subject to British suzerainty, but what would at first have looked like an acknowledgement that there had been a misunderstanding in 1877 now seemed to be an admission of powerlessness in the face of defeat. The unification of southern Africa, which had been the objection of Disraeli's original advance, now appeared to be further away than ever, though it was hard to see that what went on in the interior of Africa was likely to be very important to anyone.

The Impact of Bismarck

The chequered course of the Afghan and Zulu wars probably contributed to the Conservative election defeat in 1880. Certainly Gladstone came to office committed to the idea that imperial adventures were wrong and extravagant – 'in these guilty wars,' he commented, 'it is the matter of paying which appears to be the most effective way of awakening the conscience."[1] But despite his anti-expansionist feelings his 1880–5 government found itself involved in so many entanglements all over the world that it must have seemed as if imperial activity had become the normal though inconvenient background to political existence. The Conservatives had left a directly identifiable legacy in Egypt; once the Suez Canal was open, Disraeli accepted the argument that Britain was involved in Egyptian affairs because three-quarters of the shipping using the Canal was British, and he found an excellent opportunity to make his position clear. The Khedive had spent too lavishly, partly because he had expected his cotton revenue to remain at the very high level it had reached during the American Civil War, and by the 1870s he was raising money on every asset in sight. He owned almost half the shares in the Suez Canal Company, and in 1875 the British government bought this holding for £4m. In the long run this turned out to be a profitable investment, and at the time, though it did not give the British anything like voting control over the Company, it enabled Disraeli to assert his interest in Egypt unmistakably and without any need to make speeches which might give offence.

The sale of the shares provided only a short respite for Egypt's finances, and the governments of Britain and France found themselves drawn towards taking a close interest in the Khedive's affairs because so much of the debt was owed to French investors and so much of the Canal shipping was British. By the time the Liberals came to office the British were already beginning to dominate the commissions that had been set up to supervise Egypt's finances. The French always had to look over their shoulders to see what Germany was doing, and they were not so directly concerned with their investors as the British were with the trading interests that used the Canal.

The brilliant and over-ambitious Khedive Ismail had been forced to abdicate in 1879. His nominal sovereign the Sultan of Turkey, had given him his title and also had laid down that his throne descended by hereditary right, but still his son and heir, Tewfik, saw the debt mount at a rate which made bankruptcy, or at least a drastic scaling-down of the debts, seem almost unavoidable. The only alternative was to cut spending very sharply, which meant reducing the size of the army. The army officers did not like the steps taken in this direction and took the lead in organizing the popular resentment at the extent of French and British involvement in Egypt's affairs. Gladstone's government hung back and the French took the lead in saying that the authority of the debt commissioners must be recognized and the army must be brought under control, but when the situation became really inflamed in the summer of 1882 the French realized that they did not intend to become still further involved in Egypt when Germany was their main concern.

[1] F. W. Hirst, *Gladstone as Financier and Economist* (1931), 312.

The British had no such restraint on their actions: the Navy bombarded Alexandria and in September an army led by Sir Garnet Wolseley (who by this time was becoming known as 'England's only general') landed, defeated the Egyptians at Tel-el-Kebir, and occupied Cairo. It was announced that this was to be a temporary measure, and temporary it remained at least for the next thirty-two years. The Khedive stayed on his throne and the British confined themselves to giving him advice through a Consul-General who legally was simply the equal of the diplomatic representative of any other nation. But, as none of the other diplomats had an army on the spot, advice from the British Consul-General came by degrees to seem very like a command which would in the last resort be made effective by forcing the Khedive to abdicate. The initial military intervention intended to preserve law and order and take care of the Canal's safety changed in the course of about three years to the assumption of ultimate control over Egypt.

Most of the changes of policy which led to this result were concerned with the question of the Sudan, which had been claimed as Egyptian territory for half a century. The rulers of Egypt had tried to bring it into the modern world but steps like the abolition of slavery, which were practicable enough in Egypt, were attacks on the social structure of the Sudan that only a very strong government could carry out. At the end of the 1870s a religious leader, the Mahdi, had risen in the Sudan and called for a return to the pure and original teachings of Mohammed. The Mahdi was a leader of great and compelling power, but his message gained some of its support because it meant the restoration of slavery and of a social system that made sense to the Sudanese, however offensive it might be found in Cairo or in London. As his forces gained ground, the Egyptians became concerned. The British occupation in 1882 made no difference to this because, as long as there was an Egyptian government with any freedom of action, it was going to try to reconquer the Sudan. The trouble, it became clear after an Egyptian force had been annihilated in 1883, was that Egypt could not reconquer the Sudan and would only make her financial troubles worse if she tried. On the other hand, when the British forced this on the Khedive and insisted at the beginning of 1884 that he should appoint a government under Nubar Pasha that was willing to abandon the Sudan, the new government (sensible though its policy might be) owed its position to the presence of the British army and not to any support it could gain inside Egypt.

Even after the new government had been installed it was bound to have difficulty in withdrawing the Egyptian garrisons which still held a number of cities in the Sudan and in particular the administrative capital at Khartoum. The British government took the responsibility of finding a man to do the job, and selected General Gordon, whose magnetic personality and previous experience of the country made him look like the obvious choice. But asking a man like this to conduct a withdrawal was dangerous: he reached

Khartoum in February 1884 and very soon convinced himself that it was neither humane nor necessary to abandon the Sudan to the Mahdi. So he stayed in Khartoum and when the Mahdi's forces arrived and besieged the town he organized the defence with great skill and a courage that struck the other defenders as superhuman. Gordon's disregard for his instructions, which he ignored in a way that seemed intended to compel Britain to intervene, infuriated the government but after some months it did have to organize a relief expedition to march up the Nile. The expedition arrived too late; in January 1885 Khartoum was stormed and Gordon was killed. There was naturally an outburst of popular horror and outrage in Britain, but the government stuck to its policy of keeping out of the Sudan. It was lucky enough to be helped by a Russian move forward in central Asia which seemed to make it necessary to send reinforcements to India. Its determination to withdraw from the Sudan and press on with the stabilization of Egypt's finances showed that restraint about spending money on imperial activity could survive even the deepest shock to popular sentiment.

Imposing this policy had led the British to become increasingly dominant in Egypt. The French, whose holders of Egyptian government bonds might have been expected to welcome a policy of thrift in Egypt, were annoyed that British influence had replaced French in a country that had been linked to France since the days of the first Napoleon. For the next twenty years Anglo-French relations were blighted by the occupation of Egypt. Lord Cromer, the British Consul-General for twenty-five years, laid down priorities which placed retrenchment first, reform of the civil service next, improvement of the position of the peasant lower classes next, and recognition of the feelings of the politically active so low that it hardly needed to be considered. He enjoyed a good deal of success in the things he thought important. The debt was reduced from about £97m. in 1883 to about £87m. in 1900 and the rate of interest was brought down to a straight-forward 3½ per cent. The civil service was made sufficiently less corrupt for Cromer to be able to use it to carry out his policy. Forced labour on public works was abolished, and so was the use of the lash, which had been the main instrument of civil government under the previous rulers. Hydraulic engineers were brought from India to restore and then to improve the system of irrigation and improve the productivity of the land. Rates of taxation were reduced, though expansion of the economy increased the total yield. A good deal of the improvement simply led to the increase in population a disciple of Malthus would expect, but some small rise in the peasant standard of living could also be seen.

These benefits and the hostility of the Egyptian nationalists lay in the future. Gladstone and his government were left with the problems of an acquisition that they had never intended to make, a difficulty that occurred in several other places. One acquisition came with so little discussion that no minister could remember quite what had happened. The more settled southern parts of the large island of Borneo had been a Dutch colony for a long time. On the north-west coast was a territory that in any well-regulated empire would have been considered an anomaly: an English family from Kent, the Brookes, had established themselves as rajahs, organized their own little kingdom with its army and a fairly primitive civil service, and maintained as much in the way of law and order as the local population, who were slowly persuaded to give up the practice of headhunting, would accept. The Brookes continued to be British subjects, but their territory had no definable connection with the British Empire. When British business men wanted to develop the timber at the north end of the island, they did not feel that an extension of Brooke rule would quite meet their needs. So they looked back to the past and asked for a charter to run their chosen territory with the sort of power to maintain law and order that the East India Company had possessed in the eighteenth century. Gladstone's government granted the charter in 1881. It left no record of what it had done but the precedent had decisive effects for the rest of the decade. The British Borneo Company limped along for over sixty years and never did very well, but government under the charter was successful enough and the Colonial Office had many territories more troublesome than Borneo to worry about.

In almost all of his long tenure of office, Bismarck showed no sign of thinking that colonies would benefit Germany, but from 1883 to 1885 a sudden burst of German activity, in which she gained 95 per cent of all the overseas territory she ever held, affected all imperial policy very deeply. This sudden and unsustained expansion seems so out of character that historians have been puzzled by it. Although domestic pressures for colonial expansion were strong in the 1880s, some writers have suggested, because Bismarck is known to have been pleased that Britain and France were divided by the question of Egypt, that the hope of similar diplomatic benefits rather than any direct desire for colonies is the best explanation for his sudden interest in them in the early 1880s. But if his interest in colonies was meant either to alarm the British or to convince them that Germany was an essential ally, it was not successful. The British felt that Germany's desire for colonies was very natural and that there was no adequate reason for opposing it.

The response in the British colonies was rather different. The Australians were legally as far from being united in 1880 as in 1850, but in ways that went beyond legal form they thought of themselves as one people. Perhaps because it was so male-dominated, the country was devoted to sport. By 1880 a cricket team representing all of Australia could go to England and do well enough to be treated with respect, and in 1882 another team inflicted on the England eleven a defeat which was understood to have been followed by the death and cremation of English cricket (all subsequent series of games between England and Australia have been played for the Ashes), which probably helped Australians to see themselves as a nation well before political union in 1900. When there were signs in 1883 of German interest in New Guinea the Queensland government proposed to annex the half of the island that the Dutch had not colonized, and the other Australian governments which had already been pressing Britain to expand, joined Queensland in insisting that Britain should do something – preferably that it should annex all islands in the Pacific south of the equator that had not previously been occupied by a European power.

The British government received this with a noticeable lack of enthusiasm: it saw no reason to think that these islands could pay for themselves, no reason why the British taxpayer should pay for the occupation, and no reason why Britain should quarrel with Germany – and, in all probability, with a number of other countries – over such a policy of universal annexation. In 1884 Britain set up a protectorate on the south-east coast of New Guinea but made it clear that the Germans were welcome to the north-east quarter of the island. The Australians were bitterly disappointed by this British policy of offering no opposition to expansion, and became determined to gain a position where they could press more effectively for their own interests. They obtained legislation setting up a Federal Council of the governments of the Australian colonies to discuss external policy, and Queensland offered to pay most of the costs incurred in New Guinea.

A problem of the same sort disturbed the north-west border of Cape Colony. In 1883 the German government asked if the British government would protect a small German coastal settlement at Angra Pequena or would be willing to see Germany protect it. After waiting a year and receiving no reply Bismarck in a mood of understandable irritation proclaimed German authority over Angra Pequena and a large expanse of its hinterland in the Kalahari desert; the British government seemed not to have taken his enquiry seriously, though in fact most of the delay had been caused by the inability of successive governments in Cape Colony to make up their minds what to say. Once the Germans had arrived the Cape could agree that it did not like the new development and that the British government was to blame, though by this stage Gladstone was under presssure in so many places that one more complaint made little difference.

For years merchants had traded on the west coast of Africa, taken their chances, and not expected their governments to do anything for them, but by the 1880s the French were moving eastwards from Senegal, the King of Belgium was setting up a private estate of a few hundred thousand square miles on the Congo, and the German government was securing smaller territories in Togoland and the Cameroons. The British government could not afford to look entirely passive. Almost all the British companies trading in palm oil in the Niger delta had been brought together in 1879 in

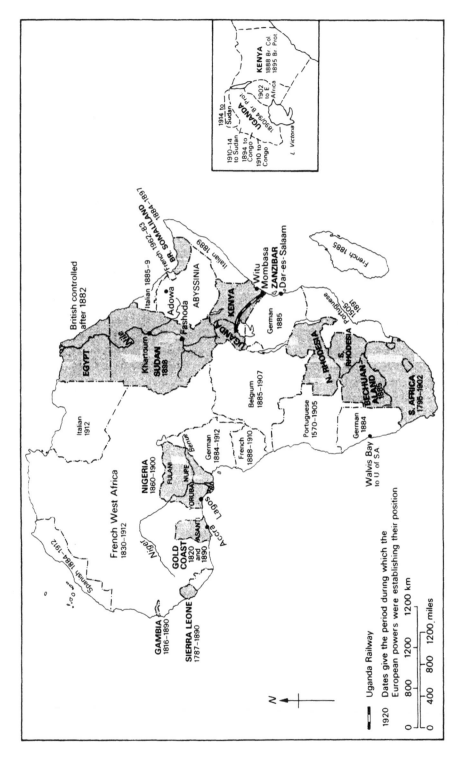

Map 10 The Partition of Africa

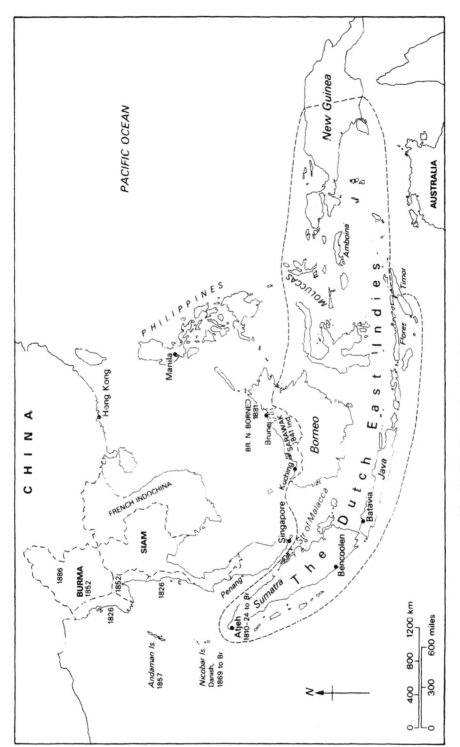

Map 11 The East Indies of the Nineteenth Century

an amalgamation organized by George Goldie, and by 1881 Goldie felt threatened enough by the French advance to ask if he could have a charter to give his company powers of government, but the request was turned down. By 1884 the government was becoming willing to listen to Goldie and gave effective diplomatic support to his case at the Berlin conference held in 1885 primarily to regulate the affairs of the Congo. The government was encouraged by the thought that Goldie said he would not cost it anything, while other British merchants might expect the government to pay the normal costs of administration, and in 1886 he was given a charter with powers of government in the Niger basin north of the coastal region.

In the event Goldie turned out to be an excellent horse to back. His administrators were able to compete successfully with other European countries in inducing African chiefs to sign the treaties upon which expansion in Africa depended for its legal validity. The treaties usually committed the chiefs to refrain from negotiating with other European powers and thus to recognize as their overlord the power with which they made the treaty. This was a normal enough provision under the international law of the time, which had no difficulty in accepting the existence of subordinate states with some autonomy of their own: the South African Republic and states in the Gulf such as Kuwait entered into this sort of agreement with Britain, and the colonies with responsible government were probably seen as informal examples of the same relationship. For African chiefs, signing the treaty (usually with a mark) was natural enough; explorers and negotiators did not travel alone in Africa and were supported by armies of African bearers large enough to show that they or their superiors must be very powerful by comparison with the hundreds, if not thousands, of chiefs in Africa. Whether Queen Victoria (or any ruler named in a treaty) really existed or was simply a devoutly respected deity was not much to the point. She, or her representatives, paid lavishly in trade goods for signatures and the Africans took the treaties at least as seriously as they took treaties they made acknowledging African overlords, though they probably did not realize that these treaties would be enforced more strictly than their ordinary expressions of respect, and they certainly had no idea how much force was available to enforce a treaty.

The political base might be secure but in most of Africa there was no economic base to support a European administration. It had to depend either on subsidies from Europe or on successful local trade. The British government was rather less willing to give subsidies than most of the other European governments involved in Africa, and so it relied on trading companies being able to absorb their own police and transport costs as part of the overhead to be met out of trading profits. None of the charters granted in the 1880s gave the companies the monopoly of the British market which had been the major economic advantage provided by the seventeenth-century charters, so profits were in most cases not large enough to maintain an administration and an army. The Niger basin was so rich and so densely populated that by using his charter and stretching its powers in a way that enabled him to set up a monopoly of trade on the river, Goldie was able to pay the costs of government and show a profit, a level of commercial success equalled only by King Leopold, using much more brutal methods, in the Congo. But all that the British had done was to establish themselves in the hinterland of a coast in which they had taken an interest for a long time. After seventy years in which Britain had clearly been the leading trading force on the west coast of Africa the region had returned to the eighteenth-century pattern of politics, in which several European countries were involved in the area and none of them was unmistakably dominant.

Gladstone's troubles in Africa were not over. The South African Republic was not content with the amount of autonomy it had gained in 1881, and some of its citizens wanted more land and greater freedom from the Pretoria government. They moved west from the high veld, setting up two new republics of their own, Stellaland and Goshen, that would have occupied the fertile and easily traversible land in what came to be known as Bechuanaland up to the edge of the Kalahari desert. This was not welcome in Britain because the new republics lay across the route used by missionaries on their way to the north, and it was not popular in the Cape because people there hoped to be able to use that route in order to occupy the territory north of the South African Republic if they ever ran short of land. Cecil Rhodes the diamond magnate had gone to Oxford in the intervals of building up his de Beers diamond firm, and there he had heard John Ruskin preaching a gospel of empire: 'England must found colonies formed of her most energetic and worthiest men seizing every piece of fruitful waste ground she can.' Many people made general statements to suggest that Britain ought to prepare for difficulties to come by 'pegging out claims for the future', but it is hard to see who acted on them except Rhodes, and even he expressed it in a less than obvious way when he spoke in the Cape Parliament. 'We must', he said, 'eliminate the imperial factor', by which he meant that the Bechuanaland problem would be handled best if the British government kept out to avoid irritating the South African Republic, and allowed Cape Colony to annex the territory.

Rhodes was enough of a Ruskinian to want to unite all the colonies and republics of an expanded south Africa under the British flag, but he was enough of a south African to see that this could be managed only if the Afrikaners were conciliated. His attitude helped him build a position as the Englishman who was most acceptable to Afrikaners, but he found the imperial factor unwilling to be eliminated. Gladstone's government was ready to help the Cape and the missionaries keep open the road to the north, but its main reason for annexing Bechuanaland was to block any possibility that the Afrikaners might bring the Germans from Angra Pequena into south African politics, and it did not propose to let the Cape government control this aspect of Anglo-German relations. In 1884 it made a new agreement with the South African Republic which said nothing about suzerainty but laid down that Britain would control the foreign policy of the Republic and would rule Bechuanaland, which had its old eastern frontiers restored.

As if to show there was no end to the problems Bismarck could raise, the Liberals had also to deal with the question of Zanzibar. This island off the shore of East Africa had been conquered by Arabs who in the mid-nineteenth century still found it a very convenient port for sending slaves north to their original base in Muscat and Oman. British opponents of slavery looked for ways to stop this. The anti-slave squadron did its best in the Indian Ocean but, as Livingstone recorded right up to the end of his life, very little was achieved. The British had already gained some influence on the island; in the 1850s and 1860s they had in effect a veto over succession to the throne, and in 1870 they encouraged the succession of Barghash whom they had previously kept out because he was too independent and too committed to slavery. Barghash and the British consul, Dr John Kirk, became quite close friends; Barghash was forced to close down the overseas slave trade from Zanzibar in the early 1870s, but he accepted the change because he reckoned that with British approval he could retain his throne even though he was carrying out such an attack on his island's trade.

As ruler of Zanzibar he commanded great influence as far inland as the immense lakes of the Rift Valley. This may have been weakened by the attack on the slave-exporting business, but he seems still to have had considerable authority on the mainland when the German drive for colonial expansion swept into east Africa. The British government would have liked Barghash to assert his power inland and would have like British business men to take more interest in the area, but none of this had any effect. Barghash's authority could not stop a dozen chiefs on the mainland closest to Zanzibar from signing treaties in November and December 1884 which accepted German control over their policy, and declared, rather improbably, that they had never heard of the Sultan of Zanzibar. After this the British business men grouped around Mackinnon of the British and India Steam Navigation Company said that the east African interior was no longer attractive. In 1885 Barghash saw the mainland pass under German rule; his British alliance had proved useless when another European power came on the scene, and the Sultans of Zanzibar now rapidly sank from being honoured assistants in the struggle against the slave trade to being holders of a purely nominal title.

Salisbury and the 1890 Settlements

When Lord Salisbury, the Foreign Secretary of 1880, returned to the same office in 1885 he was understandably astonished at the way the whole African picture had changed. There were to be no further diplomatic steps as decisive as those of the early 1880s. Britain had taken up her position in Egypt, and Bismarck never again showed as much interest in Africa and in fact realized that such a policy could only make his European problems more complicated. He once said his map of Africa was France on one side, Russia on the other, and Germany in the middle; if so, it made no sense to quarrel with Britain. Because he was now Prime Minister as well as Foreign Secretary Salisbury had to devote most of his energies in 1885 and 1886 to the political crisis caused by Gladstone's move to commit the Liberal Party to Home Rule for Ireland. Although Home Rule was a type of devolution which would give Ireland rather less power within the United Kingdom than the provinces had within the Canadian federation, most Englishmen saw it as a terrible threat to their country. When the crisis ended in mid-1886 the Liberals were out of office, and they stayed out of office for most of the next twenty years while Salisbury enjoyed a stronger position than any Conservative leader in the previous half-century. His own estimate was that by raising the question of Ireland Gladstone had roused the sleeping giant of imperialism, but this may have been foreshortening things a little. Interest in imperial affairs in the later 1880s was rather less than in the early 1880s. The diplomats were tidying up problems from the period of crisis and business men were moving forward to see what could be made of the changed situation, but no new problems caught the public's attention.

The most dramatic of all the economic changes in Africa had just begun. Gold was discovered on the Witwatersrand just south of Pretoria in 1886. This was much the largest magnet for economic activity in Africa: Goldie's company was chartered as the Royal Niger Company in 1886 with a nominal capital of £1m., the Suez Canal had cost over £10m., and perhaps three or four times as much money had been invested in Kimberley diamond-mining, but the Rand was far bigger than any of these, and involved more investment than any single mining area ever before. It gave South Africa commercial prospects that could rival Australia or Argentina, and inside South Africa it raised the South African Republic from bankruptcy to economic dominance within a dozen years. Rhodes was able to unify the mining magnates at Kimberley by convincing them that there were limits to the world demand for diamonds – he thought young men needed £4m. worth every year, for engagement rings – and that competition which produced too many diamonds would be ruinous. Nobody saw any risk that there would be too much gold, and the Rand interests were never united. Johannesburg was at first as unsettled and as unprepared for permanence as any other mining town but, as it became clear how enormous the reef was, some of the miners became attached to their new home. The nature of the operation encouraged this. In other gold-bearing regions most of the recoverable metal was found in nuggets or at least in flakes that could be separated from the soil simply by washing it, but on the Rand the work of separating little flecks of gold from the soil soon became an industrial undertaking, and the shift to a highly organized, highly capitalized business became all the more unavoidable when it became known that the reef went down a very long way. The deep mines completed the process of turning Johannesburg from a mining camp into an industrial city for processing vast quantities of gold-bearing reef, and this meant that it attracted a permanent population of miners and engineers from outside Africa – mainly British but with quite a number of Americans and Germans as well. In addition Africans were drawn to the Rand from a large area of Southern Africa by the attraction of jobs which they could earn considerably more than was possible anywhere else.

None of this looked like an unmixed blessing to the South African Republic. The mining companied paid taxes on a scale that made the Republic rich, but they constantly complained about the government's inefficiency and hostility. Unfortunately the only mining magnate who applied himself to establishing good relations with the Afrikaners never took Johannesburg mining as seriously as he took mining at Kimberley; in the late 1880s Rhodes was moving forward in Cape politics and also was taking an active interest in the territory north of the South African Republic. These activities were closely interconnected. In Cape politics ministerial office was held almost exclusively by the English-speaking politicians, each with his own little group of followers, but a large minority of seats were held by the Afrikaner Bond. Rhodes sat for an Afrikaner farming constituency near Kimberley, and devoted himself to establishing good relations with Hofmeyr, the leader of the Bond. He could understand the farmers' desire for new land in the distant north on the high ground near the river Zambesi; if he could satisfy their desire he could reckon on strong Afrikaner support, but to do this he had to get some sort of agreement for expansion from Lobengula, the Matabele king.

Rhode's interest in the north was not just a matter of gaining land and winning friends in Cape politics; he was a mining leader, with investors anxious to follow him, and the Rand was believed to be the southern edge of a saucer-shaped gold reef whose northern lip lay well to the north, probably in Matabeleland. Lobengula was besieged by British and other mining prospectors and speculators who had come to his kraal for permission to explore. Rhodes's representatives persuaded Lobengula that they would make the largest annual payments for the mining rights and also were in the best position to guarantee political stability for his kindgom. The British government was ready to accept this – the mining investors were going to bear all the expenses and the move to the north would stop the South African Republic from moving in that direction – but the Colonial Office encouraged Rhodes to share the mining rights with the most respectable of his rivals and made it clear that a company which was going to have political powers in the region round the Zambesi should have men of public standing in Britain on the Board of Directors. Rhodes recruited two Dukes and Lord Grey's heir for the Board, was given a charter in 1889 which entitled the company to exercise political functions north of the Limpopo, and launched the British South Africa Company – so much the best known of the companies that carried out the British occupation of Africa on the basis of a charter that it became know as 'the Chartered Company', as if it was unique.

This was not so: Goldie's company was sending its steamships and its tiny army up the Niger in the later 1880s, and a company had been launched in East Africa. Salisbury had been ready to do something in the area when the vigour of German involvement there died down. Mackinnon and his friends, who had got no encouragement in the 1870s when they asked if the government would support a move inland and had been unwilling to step forward in the mid-1880s to compete with the Germans when they were signing treaties to gain control over the territory inland from Zanzibar which had been under the Sultan, at last found the British government in a mood that was neither too cautious nor too enthusiastic. In 1888 the Imperial British East Africa Company received a charter allowing it to hold and rule the section of East Africa that lay between German East Africa and the Italian claims in Somaliland. In practice this meant the port of Mombasa and a piece of territory running north-west towards Lake Victoria, and the company felt uneasy about pressing inland at anything like the pace the British government wanted. Its position became more secure when Bismarck and Salisbury began discussing the various places in Africa where their countries might collide, and these negotiations were only briefly interrupted when Bismarck was dismissed and a new German government installed in the spring of 1890.

Salisbury knew what he wanted out of a general settlement: he had become convinced that Britain was going to stay in Egypt and that holding on to the whole Nile Valley was necessary for the quiet enjoyment of Egypt, so he gave up the North Sea island of Heligoland in exchange for German acceptance of the British takeover of Zanzibar and a free hand for the East Africa Company as it moved towards the kingdom of Buganda on the north side of Lake Victoria. This 1890 agreement made Anglo-German relations so secure that Britain's position in Egypt became much easier: France continued to be very annoyed by the British occupation but this was important only if France could hope for German support in the Egyptian question. Salisbury had persuaded Germany to accept the British position in Egypt and her right to claim the whole valley of the Nile. Two shocks to stability, the occupation of Egypt and the assertion of German interests in

Africa in the mid-1880s, had temporarily dislocated diplomatic relations and perhaps led the British to move further forward than they would otherwise have gone, but Salisbury could now hope to get the expanded empire to settle down. As soon as the German settlement had been made Salisbury turned to France and negotiated from strength over some minor issues. The Royal Niger Company had made its way up the river successfully, and it had also made some vague and dubious treaties with the rulers of Gandu and Sokoto a few hundred miles to the north. Salisbury was able to get the French to accept these documents as the basis for a claim that the Company (and thus the British government) had authority over these powerful Muslim emirates, which had no idea of being subordinate to the British and had not conceded anything like this in the treaties.

Salisbury was so exhilarated at his success in pushing the French claims north into the Sahara desert that in a speech he talked about 'giving away mountains and rivers and lakes to each other, only hindered by the small impediment that we never knew exactly where the mountains and rivers and lakes were', and he went on to sneer at the large stretches of the Sahara conceded to the French by calling it '"light" land'.[2] It was true that the area under discussion had been explored much less than most of the territory divided up in the partition of Africa. The British treaties did not give them any claim to the territory, though they did have some claim to diplomatic standing north of the river Niger and the French had no treaties at all to justify any counter-claim. Treaty-making had run ahead of map-making, and the process of partition had gone well beyond any point at which there was an immediate risk of collision between European powers. It remained to be seen whether the powers could absorb their gains without being troubled by any reaction from the Africans whose territory they had brought into their empires. The European diplomacy which was one aspect of the occupation of Africa turned its attention to other things; the slow process by which Europeans established their control over the Africans assigned to them, which was the other aspect of occupation, went ahead without interruption, even if it was occasionally punctuated by its own local wars and unsuccessful revolts.

Canada and the Canadian Pacific Railway

Just the same distinction between the acquisition of a right to a piece of land by a transaction that was valid in international law and the acceptance of the transfer by the people who actually lived on the land affected the development of western Canada in the 1870s and 1880s. Riel's resistance to the Canadian government's purchase of the rights of the Hudson's Bay Company in 1870 had indicated the problem. The Canadian government still had a great deal to do in the west. Part of the reason why the central government

[2] J. Flint, *Sir George Goldie* (1960), 166–7.

had been given much more power by the constitution than the federal government of the United States was that the Canadian government was expected to be active, and for most of the twenty years after Confederation it was as active as anyone could have hoped. By 1871 it had completed the diplomatic task of uniting the mainland territory of British North America and it then set the immense physical and financial task of building the transcontinental railway which had been the price of British Columbian agreement to join the federation – a price that could be accepted as a nation-building opportunity comparable to the unifying effects of railways in India. But the awarding of the railway contract was also an opportunity to replenish the Conservative party treasury for the 1872 election and, when the story came out, the Conservatives were forced from office and replaced by a Liberal government, which then had the misfortune to be blamed for the economic collapse of the 1870s. In 1878 Macdonald was back in office, with a policy of higher tariffs than ever to build Canadian industry and to provide an economic basis for the railway. In six years, from 1880 to 1885, the rail was brought to Winnipeg and then thrust across half the continent, with all that this involved in finding ways through the Rockies and laying track under conditions of great danger; and also what it involved in raising the capital for a total investment that must have exceeded Canada's gross national product for any single year in the 1880s. When the line was complete the engineer in charge commented accurately, and with some restraint, 'All I can say is that the work has been well done in every way.' Sandford Fleming, an earlier engineer for the railway, had become so aware of the difficulties of time-keeping for a railway that ran one-sixth of the way round the world that he began a successful campaign for a universal system of time zones based on the Greenwich meridian. Donald Smith, one of the more picturesque railway financiers, who had survived from the days when the Hudson's Bay Company ruled the west, went off to an active retirement, becoming Canada's High Commissioner in London and, as Lord Strathcona, raising his own regiment – Strathcona's Light Horse – for the Boer War.

The railway was an essential part of the policy of absorbing the western prairie into Canada, and the western prairie soon showed it did not want to be absorbed. In 1884 Riel came back from exile and around him crystallized the uneasiness of everybody who felt threatened by the railway, by the government system of registering land grants, and by the prospect of settlers from the east. For the rest of the year the discontent gained ground. By the winter the government had lost control of a large part of the area between Winnipeg and the Rockies, and could not bring troops there before the spring. The crisis did wonders for the railway by showing everyone in the east that the country needed effective lines of communication. In March 1885 the discontent became a rebellion, in April troops were brought to the edge of the affected area by train, and in May the rebellion was crushed. The government managed to deal not too unsympathetically with the anxieties of the westerners. But in his brief period of authority in 1870 Riel had had an Ontario man executed: Ontario insisted that Thomas Scott must be avenged, Quebec insisted that Riel should be spared as a Catholic and a French Canadian; and Ontario's view prevailed. The execution of Riel divided central Canada, gravely weakening the alliance that supported the Conservative party, and turned him into a martyr for French Canada, which obscured the way that his career had been the product of the uneasiness of the Canadian west at the expansion of the east.

The Conservative dominance in Canadian politics might have survived even the quarrel over Riel if the Liberals had still been a party based on Ontario protestants supported by a few Quebec anti-clericals. But when its leadership went in 1887 to Laurier, a French Canadian and a liberal Catholic, Quebec began a great change from being a Conservative to being a Liberal stronghold. Macdonald was able to win his last general election in 1891 by appointing to the willingness of some Liberals to consider steps towards union with the United States with all that that would mean (including an income-tax), and by a renewed appeal to the sentiment which he had roused on many previous occasions with his statement 'A British subject I was born, a British subject I will die.' This was a statement of a legal fact, but it was something much more: for English Canada it was a reminder of ancestral roots that meant a great deal more, and even for French-Canada it was at least some sort of protection from the expansionist, secular, and anti-Catholic United States. Nor was it confined to men of Macdonald's own generation. His private secretary, who remained a civil servant until the 1920s, expressed the national feeling of a great many people born and bred in the colonies when he wrote of his first visit to London in 1884 that he had 'a feeling of pride and exultation that I belonged to a country of so much glory and greatness'.[3] This was a very natural sentiment for anyone of British descent, and for many others who had been absorbed by the power and prestige of the British Empire in the decades when its position was at its strongest. Anyone in colonial politics had to bear this sentiment in mind; by the 1880s it was clear that this sentiment had prevailed over any ideas of separation and dissolution, but the question could now be asked whether it was going to lead to any substantive changes in policy.

[3] Ed. Maurice Pope, *Public Servant: the Memoirs of Sir Joseph Pope* (1960), 86.

9. *Victorian Imperial Enthusiasm 1883–1899*

The changes that had led to the territorial acquisitions of the 1870s and 1880s were changes in the worlds of commerce and diplomacy. Miners and traders might want to gain land or at least have it made secure for them to go about their business, and diplomats might devote their attention to making sure that disputes and wars did not break out in Africa that might cause unwanted trouble in European affairs, but all this took place against a background of lack of public interest that made politicians uneasy about committing their countries to too much expense. The strength of the resistance in the *chambre des députés* to French expansion in Indochina was the most clear-cut example of parliamentary opposition to spending money on colonial adventures. Political leaders may have kept episodes like this one or Gladstone's anti-expansionist electoral success in 1880 in mind even longer than was necessary. In the Britain of the 1890s there were signs that some ministers were slow to catch up with the way that imperial enthusiasm had by that time made people think that a little extra spending or a little war overseas were enterprises they were ready to support.

Imperial enthusiasm took two distinct forms in the British Empire: enthusiasm for closer relations between Britain and the self-governing colonies most of whose inhabitants were of British descent, and also enthusiasm for expansion by the acquisition of new territory. There was not much logical connection between the two and in theory someone could have supported one development and opposed the other, but in practice people behaved as if the two issues were closely linked. Closer union and territorial expansion were expressions of nationalism. Some constitutional theorists in the self-governing colonies undoubtedly thought that achieving sovereignty was the natural way to express national feeling and did not see the re-creation of closer links with Britain as a nationalist proposal. Most people were not interested in constitutional theories and they chose other ways to express their national feelings. In the 1880s and 1890s many people in the self-governing colonies wanted to play a role on a wider stage, and believed that closer union was the way to do it by allowing them a share in controlling the policy of a united empire instead of trailing along behind a policy made in

England. In India the first stirrings of political involvement expressed themselves in something like the same way; the early politicians were decidedly pro-British and part of their programme was simply to ask for the same opportunities as Englishmen already had in India, so they could not ask for great changes in the constitutional connection between Britain and India. They found to their regret that they were held at arm's length by the British, who regarded themselves as the predestined rulers of India.

The same consciousness of a manifest destiny to rule affected Englishmen when they looked at Africa. The advances inland in the 1890s were more sweeping than anything made in the 1880s, were marked by less awareness of the trouble they could cause if things were not handled carefully, and were more likely to provoke a large-scale war than the earlier developments. The technological superiority of Europeans over Africans, expressed rather briskly in the lines 'Whatever happens, we have got The Maxim gun, and they have not', meant that African rulers were most unlikely to be able to resist the European onrush. But imperial enthusiasm was aflame in several European countries, and it was always possible that if they did not work out their requirements in preliminary negotiations they might drift very near war, as France and Britain did in 1898. The British had the special problem that in South Africa they faced Afrikaners who possessed European technology and a fierce national spirit. Imperial enthusiasm and Afrikaner traditionalism led to war in 1899.

Australian Unity and New Zealand

At just the same time as the British were moving to war with the Afrikaners the Australians were carrying out the last stage in the political unification of their country, a process that brought out some of the connections between colonial nationalism, closer union, and imperial enthusiasm. Moves in this direction had begun over a dozen years earlier. The political disturbance aroused by Germany's brief period of advance in the Pacific from 1883 to 1885 had made Australians more concerned about their position in the world and more willing to look at ways of uniting the colonies, and they were encouraged in this by realizing that they all responded in very much the same way to German expansionism and British lack of interest. But although this discovery of their common interest had led to the creation of the Federal Council, they did very little more about it in the 1880s. Australia was being swept forward by a great surge of prosperity which left no time for long-term plans. Its solid initial base was the development of mineral wealth, mainly in the form of copper and lead, and later of silver from the Broken Hill region in western New South Wales. Most of the metal went south and brought prosperity to Victoria and in particular to the financial and shipping centre of Melbourne. Men and money flowed from Britain to share in the boom; it was in the 1880s that Australia drew ahead of Canada in numbers of inhabitants of British descent. Some of the money went into sound investments, but a fair amount of it was invested in Melbourne – 'Marvellous Melbourne' as the expansive debt-ridden city was glad to be nicknamed – to finance a housing boom that depended on the belief that house prices would go up every year.

In this atmosphere the Federal Council had difficulty in holding people's attention. It pointed to a desire for unity but did little to advance the cause. In 1889 the idea was put firmly into the political arena by Sir Henry Parkes, one of the small group of men who took their turns at displacing one another from the premiership of New South Wales; he argued that, now there were about as many inhabitants in Australia as there had been in America when the United States was formed, it was time for the Australian colonies to unite. Two meetings in 1890 and 1891 laid the formal foundations of Australian constitution upon which all the arguments of the 1890s were based. It was taken for granted that Queen Victoria would be head of state and no delegates at the conferences thought of having an elected president or of doing anything to interfere with the system of making ministers responsible to parliament. On this basis the colonies set out to build a federal and democratic system and – unlike the Canadians, many of whom had thought it was a nasty warning – they regarded the American federal system as a useful example. There would be a lower house, elected on a basis of representation by population, and an upper house in which all the colonies would be represented equally, as in the United States Senate (though with senators chosen by popular vote rather than being elected by state legislatures, as was then the case in the United States) in order to reassure the smaller colonies. This left the problem that the federal parliament would have two Houses, either of which might claim to defeat the government, and if different bases for representation led to different parties having majorities in the two Houses there might be trouble. So it was suggested that simultaneous elections might be called in the case of such deadlock and, while it was presumably intended that the House elected on a basis of representation proportionate to population would be the House that chose the government, as in Britain or in Canada, this was not written down and would probably not have been acceptable to the smaller colonies. The six colonies were to be known as states after the federal system with its new central government had been set up, probably to indicate that they were to have the strong position given in the United States Constitution rather than the legally weaker position of the provinces in the Canadian Constitution.

New Zealand was at first included in the discussions, as she had been included in the Federal Council of the 1880s, but it was soon clear that this would not work. New Zealand might be no further from Sydney than Perth in Western Australia was, but the sense of unity of Australians did not extend to New Zealand. In the 1890s a well-developed New Zealand idea of the role of government in society was put forward and for some years commanded the attention and admiration of some of the most thoughtful people in the outside world and made the sense of division from Australia more complete. Until the 1880s political parties in Australia and New Zealand had been very shadowy organizations; most MPs were independent-minded men who went into politics because of their importance in their own constituency or region, and their usual objective was to negotiate with the government on behalf of their own people. In the 1890s parties in Australia were shaped by the questions of uniting the colonies, of setting tariffs, and of defining the political position of the working class. In New Zealand the 'perpetual ministry' that had held office almost all the time since 1870 was losing its monopoly of power: its policy of borrowing to pay for future development that had been introduced by Sir Julius Vogel had worked well in the 1870s, but by the 1880s the load of debt was too much to be supported even by the new prosperity provided by exports of chilled food. In the late 1880s a coalition of reformers on questions of social reform was put together by Ballance, and in 1891 it came to office.

Its major policy commitment was to 'burst up' the great estates that had been created in the first generation of settlement and to provide adequate holdings for smaller farmers, and it went on from there to a wide range of progressive legislation: votes for women, limitation of working hours, compulsory arbitration to bring about better industrial relations, and temperance legislation laid down a policy which meant that at the turn of the century New Zealand was seen as an example to the world of how state intervention could be used to bring about the objectives of the politicians who wanted to do something positive to benefit people as well as release them from the older forms of political and religious inequality. It would have been hard to combine this fervent activity with full participation in the debate over Australian unity, and attendance at the early discussions never looked like leading to full involvement. Australia and New Zealand had some common interests in foreign policy, but their concerns could be met by active membership of the British Empire, which was taken for granted in New Zealand even more unquestioningly than in Australia. They had very few common interests in economic policy, because their exports were similar enough to mean that they sold relatively little to each other and were more concerned with getting a full share of the British market than with anything else.

By the end of the 1880s the Australian boom reinforced by borrowing from Britain had come to an end, and only the debts remained as a conspicuous memorial of past prosperity. As the years of depression began, industrial relations got worse and a series of strikes, which showed very little respect for the boundaries between one colony and the next, helped underline the fact that Australians had a great many interests in common.

The end of the boom and the strikes of the period up to 1893 did a great deal to arouse Australian nationalism, even if they distracted politicians from the details of federation. The period of unification was a period of a certain amount of anti-British feelings, and some of this was encouraged by the fact that British investors who had lent their money in the period of prosperity now asked for it back in the period of depression.

When the politicians returned to the problems of unity in 1894 and 1895, they still faced serious problems in New South Wales. It was the senior colony but had been dramatically overtaken by Victoria in the middle of the century and, although it was making up lost ground, it had not yet regained its position as the richest and most populous colony. It was suspected of being jealous of Victoria and, at a more practical level, it had stuck to a free trade policy while all the rest of Australia had moved to higher and higher tariffs. New South Wales's position as a large-scale exporter of wool and base metals benefited from keeping down the cost of production which enabled her to compete on world markets. The success of the wool exporters who had regained the lead that they had briefly lost to Victoria was something of a justification of the free trade policy. So New South Wales politicians described the attempt of the five protectionist colonies to lead her into a federation as something roughly equal to an attempt by five drunks to persuade an advocate of temperance to accompany them into a public house, even though these free trade principles were not completely unshakeable.

The attractions of trade with the other colonies and of a unified railway policy to repair some of the damage of the 1850s, and the force of Australian patriotic feeling all helped the policy of unity forward. New South Wales sent her elected delegates to join those of the other colonies at a conference in Adelaide at which the 1891 plan was revived, amended, and then in 1898 presented for the electorates of the colonies to vote on in referendums. The New South Wales legislature laid down that, to be effective, approval would have to win the support of at least 80,000 voters, and while all the other colonies were voting firmly for federation, New South Wales approved it only by 71,596 votes to 66,228. The negotiators resumed work but made it clear that not many concessions were available for New South Wales, and the only real change offered was a promise that when the Commonwealth of Australia was established it would some time in the future build a brand-new capital city, which would be located in the southern part of New South Wales. Because Victoria had been so deeply committed to federation for so long and because Melbourne had just enjoyed its building boom, it had looked like the obvious capital for the Commonwealth, but this choice would have led to unending complaints from Sydney. Establishing a capital at Canberra may not have made anyone positively happy, but it reduced the level of jealousy.

The revised terms were accepted by all the colonies, though parts of

Western Australia were very doubtful about them, and a delegation went to London to persuade the Colonial Office to accept them and put them through Parliament; like the Canadians in 1867 they needed the legal authority of the imperial parliament if existing colonies were to be merged in a new federal system. The Secretary for the Colonies would have preferred the new constitution to contain more symbols of Australia's links with Britain and objected to the denial of a right of appeal to the Judicial Committee of the Privy Council, but eventually he conceded the point subject only to a provision that if both parties in a case wanted to go to the Privy Council to decide it they were to be free to do so, and with this settled he agreed to put the legislation through Parliament. The Commonwealth of Australia emerged as a self-governing colony with a federal constitution on 1 January 1901. Its framework was more democratic than that of Canada, and also was more obviously designed with the possibility in mind that Australia might want to act as an independent nation. The decision to create the Commonwealth of Australia was given popular approval by referendums, the senate was elective, and the constitution – although formally an act of the Westminster Parliament – could be changed if a majority of the states and a majority of the electorate voted for a change in a referendum, whose decision would then be automatically accepted in London. In Canada, on the other hand, the senate was appointed by the central government, and changes to the constitution were made by votes of the Canadian Parliament, approved and turned into law by the British Parliament which was unlikely to object but was not bound to accept proposals in the way it was bound to accept referendum results from Australia.

After the struggle for federation was successfully concluded, Australian feelings for Britain became much warmer. Some of the tension had been due to the debts and the British desire for payment, some to the fact that the people who were most attached to the connection with Britain were the supporters of free trade in Sydney who wanted to trade with Britain and opposed federation because it was going to lead to protective tariffs. The Australian Natives Association – an organization not for 'blackfellows' (politely known as aborigines) but for emigrants' descendants who had been born in Australia – strongly supported federation and some of its members hoped that it might lead on to independence and a republic, which were taken for all practical purposes to be the same thing. But most Australians saw federation as a way of playing a more important part within the British Empire, not as a step away from it. Such a large proportion of the population had been born in Britain that it would have been surprising if they had seen relations with Britain in any other light. Immigrants in the colonies enjoyed a position that has been held by very few other immigrants: being born in Britain gave them a prestige in their new homes that was not given to those who had been born there, an attitude that helped bring about the creation of groups like the Australian Natives Association to uphold the position of the older inhabitants. Perhaps the attitude of respect for the immigrants was rational enough; the reluctance of New Zealanders in the nineteenth century to elect political leaders who had not been born in Britain may have reflected a feeling that their politicians needed to know more about the outside world than they could learn while living on their two remote islands.

Greater Britain

Quite apart from the flow of immigration, there was pride in association with the country which was in so many ways the leader of the English-speaking countries and in some respects of the whole world. It was not necessary to have read Darwin or Spencer or Mill to know that they were Englishmen whose influence ran beyond the area in which English was spoken. That area had itself grown: in the eighteenth century French was a second language for most of the rulers of Europe, but in the nineteenth century English began to advance to a position where it was the second language for the rulers of most of the world. Much the same satisfaction in British financial and naval strength must have gone into the Canadian Post Office's issue of a stamp for Christmas 1898 which showed a map of the world with the empire marked in red and the motto 'We hold a vaster empire than has been.'

Sentiments like this owed some of their impact to the tangible benefits of links with Britain. The growth of trade in food made the British connection a matter of increasing importance and advantage to people in several parts of the empire. In the eighteenth century British colonies had depended for their exports on the flow of consumer luxuries like sugar and tobacco to Britain, and in the early nineteenth century this has been supplemented or even replaced by an emphasis on raw materials for industry such as wool and timber. Until the middle of the nineteenth century Britain had been the world's largest producer of tin and copper, but as these mines had reached their peak of production and new sources of supply were opening up elsewhere, imports of these base metals increased sharply and by the end of the century coal was the only branch of mining that still flourished. In the last third of the century improvements in shipping which reduced the cost of ocean transport to a seventh of what it had been a century earlier, combined with Britain's adherence to free trade, shifted the emphasis of colonial exports. By 1880 Britain had responded very successfully to changes in world shipping arrangements, and had gained a supremacy in commercial shipping she had not enjoyed in the days of sail, with the result that half the world's shipping was British-owned. Steamships could keep to much more precise timetables than sailing ships and make their way through the Suez Canal far more easily, and much larger ships could be built in iron because the dimensions of wooden ships were always limited to the size of the largest complete trees that could be found, which were used for the parts of the

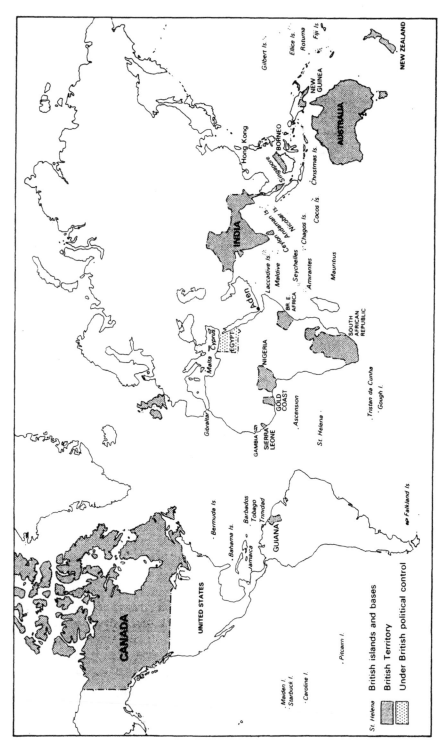

Map 12 Queen Victoria's Empire 1897

ships that bore the heaviest stress. In the 1840s a voyage to Sydney from London might take four or five months; in the 1850s it could be done at great expense in two months; by 1914 it could be done in as little as thirty days.

Engineers had known for some time how to chill or freeze meat but installing the machines (which produced a great deal of heat) on a wooden sailing ship would have been dangerous. Once iron steamships were established business men in Australia started to send meat and butter to Britain and, after successful voyages early in the 1880s showed that it could be done, lamb or mutton from Australia, butter from New Zealand, fruit from the Cape of Good Hope, and cheese, apples, and bacon from Canada flowed into Britain. Economic growth in these years was slow in many parts of the world and unemployment in Britain was rather higher than usual but the new supply of food fairly certainly helped cause an improvement in the British working class standard of living that was as rapid as anything that had happened in the period of easy economic development before the turning point of 1873. While improved transport made it easier to send perishable goods across the sea, this was not the only sort of food that Britain was now buying in larger quantities from the empire. Tea exports from India and Ceylon had suddenly risen to displace the China tea which had held something of a monopoly since the beginning of the tea trade, so that by 1890 most of the tea in the world market – which mainly meant being exported to Britain – came from India and Ceylon. The opening up of the Canadian west and the building of the railway depended on being able to raise enough wheat to cover the cost of development and on finding a market willing to import it. Britain was the obvious market, and the only market large enough to repay the investment.

Many European countries responded to the prospect of increased imports by adopting a more protectionist policy. French farmers, Italian peasants, and German junkers could agree that imports of food from outside Europe could be resisted, and were able to force their political leaders to accept this view, so that farmers who wanted to develop new lands could find very few markets other than Britain. There was of course competition to supply the British market; American wheat growers and Argentinian cattle raisers benefited by improved shipping just as much as farmers in the colonies, and colonial farmers and politicians looked for ways to improve their position against this competition. For them, the obvious step was for Britain to impose tariffs against foreign products. Protective tariffs were not quite as unthinkable in the Britain of the 1880s as they had been in the middle of the century. British exports in 1867 were almost four times as large as in 1842, but after that the impetus to growth slowed down. It was argued that British industry suffered because foreign industrialists with a protected home market could sell to their domestic customers at a high price to pay for their initial invesment and then extend their production run and sell the rest of it at an export price that did not have to cover much more than raw materials and labour. Because of the protective tariffs, British manufacturers could not respond to this 'dumping' by selling at equally reduced prices in their competitors' home markets. British iron and steel exports, which had been rising satisfactorily between 1868 and 1882, were then sharply checked; the United States and Germany quickly emerged as the major industrial powers of the last years of the century. Some people saw in this an argument for overseas expansion; even if a colony did not directly favour British goods (and some, like the Royal Niger Company's trading area, undoubtedly did), it would still be helpful to keep territory out of the hands of countries that would set up tariffs to exclude British traders.

Other people were ready to see a larger change in policy and said the way to survive was to have 'fair trade', by which they meant protective tariffs. The 'fair trade' movement did not get the unequivocal support of any leading British politicians in the late nineteenth century, but a number of Conservatives took it seriously and it could easily be worked into the mood of greater interest in the empire that was developing. Seeley's *Expansion of England* is now most often remembered for the comment 'We have conquered half the world in a fit of absence of mind' (made, in 1883, just before the British took over much of Africa), but at the time the phrase that attracted attention was that 'If Greater Britain really existed, Canada and Australia would be to us as Kent and Cornwall.'[1] Putting forward the cause of Greater Britain in these terms may have slightly underestimated the beginnings of colonial nationalism but it was attractive enough and close enough to practical politics in the 1880s to arouse interest in Britain.

Arguments like this were helped by concern about the rise of larger political units in the world. The 1860s had seen the emergence of Germany, Italy, and Canada, and the United States's survival in the Civil War; if larger units like this were to be the political system of the future, then the British Empire could be the largest of all and in 1884 the Imperial Federation League was created with this in mind. The organization tried very hard to be bi-partisan; Liberal members were in short supply, though the rapidly rising Lord Rosebery was an important and a whole-hearted recruit. Politicians from the self-governing colonies were easier to find, and they encouraged overseas branches of what was initially a British movement. The League was not committed to federation in the technical sense of wanting a structure of government with a central legislature to deal with specified topics, and went no further than asking for the 'closer union' of the empire. At times it did discuss possible constitutions for an empire with a central parliament, but this was not an important part of its programme and its members were not worried by the lack of interest in this side of the problem.

[1] J. E. Seeley, *The Expansion of England* (1906 edn.), 10 and 75.

The League's greatest successes came in the first years of its existence. In 1886 *The Times* said the League had 'compelled men to ask themselves, not whether the federation of the Empire is desirable or feasible but how it can be accomplished'. The following year it persuaded Lord Salisbury that Queen Victoria's Golden Jubilee would be an excellent opportunity for the important people who would be coming to London from the colonies for the celebrations to meet and hold discussions with the government. The 1887 Conference was not an official meeting between men who had been invited because they held specific positions of power, but it was recognized as an important occasion: Salisbury gave the opening address, the Secretary of State for the Colonies took the chair at the other sessions, and policy was discussed by people who were in office or close to it.

Hofmeyr, the leader of the Afrikaner Bond, never took office in Cape Colony but had so much influence there that anything he said had to be taken seriously. At the Conference he proposed that Britain and the self-governing colonies should place a 2 per cent duty on all imports from outside the empire, which he reckoned would yield about £7m. a year, and that this should be spent on improving imperial defence. He had thus brought together the questions around which arguments about imperial unity were to resolve at least until 1914: tariffs, defence policy, and the foreign policy that must accompany defence policy. Free trade was firmly enough established in Britain to mean that he made no immediate progress, though the idea of imperial preference which was involved in the proposed tax had a long life before it. Some changes were made in defence spending; the Australians had realized the weakness of their position in the New Guinea dispute when the British pointed out that a conflict in the Pacific could only be fought by the Royal Navy, for which Britain paid, and as a result Britain would decide if anything was to be done. At the Conference politicians from the Australian colonies offered a contribution of £126,000 a year to be spent on the Navy, with a provision that ships would be kept in Australian waters. The British may not have felt that this was a very large payment but it was obviously the sort of first step that was well worth encouraging and over the next thirty years comparable contributions were made by Cape Colony, Natal, New Zealand, Newfoundland, and Malaya, and were discussed in others.

Bismarck's expansionist moves had made colonies more aware of their involvement in foreign policy, and made them want to have an effective influence on the way Britain conducted her world-wide policy, partly because of their sense of themselves as Englishmen and partly because the power at the disposal of a united empire – and especially the naval power, which was what mainly concerned colonies a very long way from Europe – was so much greater than anything they could create for themselves. Small countries had difficulty staying independent enough to have foreign policies of their own in the nineteenth century, and it would have been rash for the

colonies to expect great powers to treat them any better. Colonial nationalism first emerged because people in the colonies could see ways in which
they differed from Englishmen and wanted administrative arrangements to
express the fact, but it did not mean they wanted to disturb the framework
of imperial unity. Most colonial politicians supported home rule for Ireland;
some of them merely wanted to conciliate any fervent Irishmen they might
have among their voters by advocating a fairly modest change but some of
them, of whom Cecil Rhodes was the outstanding example, believed that a
discontented Ireland was bad for imperial unity and a pacified Ireland with a
certain amount of devolution would serve as an example that would make it
easier to build a united empire that could agree on a common policy.

The self-governing colonies valued the autonomy they had gained in the
middle of the century and would not want to surrender it to a united
parliament of the empire dominated by the numerical preponderance of
English voters. One use they had made of their autonomy in the previous
thirty years was to create industries protected by local tariffs, so proposals
for a 'zollverein' – a system of free trade throughout the empire, like that
among the then-independent states of Germany in the middle of the century
– were bound to run into opposition because such a step would have left the
local industries exposed to competition from Britain which would destroy
some of them. A system of preferences, protecting their industries but giving
British exporters an advantage over foreign producers, suited them much
better. They argued that as Britain was already importing their products
without a tariff she could go on doing so without damaging any existing
British interests. What was asked was that the imports which Britain was
accustomed to buy should be bought from empire suppliers. The British
government hardly thought it necessary to reply to this proposal, which
would inevitably have driven up prices in Britain; if empire producers were
not more expensive than other producers, then people would already have
been buying from empire sources. But imperial consultation was a natural
policy to follow and conferences were a useful way to put it into effect.
Another conference was held in 1894, at Ottawa, to discuss laying a telegraph cable across the Pacific and as this was a well-defined question on
which governments had to take decisions it was natural that attendance was
confined to ministers and experts, and that the imperial conference should
take a step towards being a formal political gathering.

Indian Nationalism Awakes

Conferences of nations were becoming established as a way to carry on
negotiations; conferences at Berlin had dealt with the eastern question in
1878 and with the Congo question in 1885; conferences were held on postal
questions and on currency problems, and meetings on these technical issues
were not confined to the representatives of sovereign states. As India was

one of the most important countries still using a silver currency as its monetary base it was naturally invited to the discussions on the bimetallic problems that arose as countries switched from silver to gold currencies. The government of Britain and its government of India tried to avoid disagreeing, but Britain as the central power within the expanding system of the Gold Standard was bound to see things differently from India, which could not give up the silver rupee but was losing badly in purchasing power as all silver-based currencies fell in value by comparison with all currencies which used gold as their monetary base. When Miss Prism, in *The Importance of being Earnest*, told her pupil Cecily Cardew that she need not read the chapter on the fall of the rupee in her book on political economy – 'even these metallic questions have their melodramatic side' – she was referring to an important issue.

The fall of silver in terms of gold was a devaluation, which helped the sale of Indian exports and acted like a tariff barrier to keep out imports but, while this may have helped her overseas trade, India had also to pay about £17m. a year (or a fifth of total Indian government spending) to cover obligations fixed in sterling which cost more (in terms of Indian resources) as the rupee fell in terms of gold. The obligations included the old East India Company debts run up in the conquest of India, the more recent railway loans, and the pensions of civil servants who had retired to Britain. In 1850 all this might have passed unnoticed; by the 1880s there were British and Indian critics of 'the drain', as these payments became known. Englishmen were bound to wonder if government in India had lived up to the ideal that it ought to exist for the good of its subjects, and educated Indians began to criticize British rule for failing to live up to this ideal. Probably the majority of Indians took it for granted that governments were going to extract whatever they could from their subjects and were unimpressed by these complaints, just as they were unimpressed by the government's carefully documented explanation that it was taking a smaller sphere of peasant income than any previous government in India.

The Indian intellectuals who in 1850 had been committed to Britain and modernization were by 1880 less confident about relations with Britain. They naturally hoped to join the ruling élite by passing the examinations which opened the door to the élite, but they soon discovered that the British were not going to make this easy. Lytton's attempt to recruit a rival élite from the princely classes had not succeeded and was soon abandoned, and when the Liberals sent Lord Ripon to take his place there were some signs that the rulers in Britain understood the problems facing educated Indians as they tried to make their way forward. One of Ripon's proposals had consequences which served to underline the gap between the British and the educated Indians rather than to close it. As Indians advanced in the Civil Service they were likely to be promoted to judicial offices in which they had to judge cases involving Englishmen, and in 1883 a bill was brought into the Viceroy's Legislative Council by Sir Courtenay Ilbert to confirm their authority to do so. The proposal was greeted with a howl of outrage by the British community in India, and business men and journalists, who were not restrained by being employed by the government, went to extraordinary lengths in denouncing it.

Their protest succeeded: Indians would be allowed to judge Englishmen, but only with the aid of a jury half of whom were British. It was made quite clear that the British community did not trust Indians to judge them fairly, and it was also made clear that a really determined agitation could make the government go back on a policy to which it had committed itself. Ripon himself was seen as a supporter of Indian interests; almost as soon as he arrived he had repealed the legislation by which Lytton had set up a system of censorship of the vernacular (Indian language) newspapers, and in 1882 he had set up local boards which gave well-educated and prominent Indians an opportunity to run some of their own affairs at the level of county or municipal councils. The Viceroy still had no reliable way to discover the views of educated Indians on wider issues. He could easily meet Indians of the princely class socially, but there seemed to be a great gulf fixed between the rising class of western-educated Indians and the administration. One possible way to bridge the gulf was explored with great skill and persistence by Dabadhai Naoroji, a Parsee who lived in London and organized pressure groups, such as the London India Society, to try to influence British opinion. His efforts reached their logical conclusion when he was elected to Parliament as a Liberal in 1892; if India's fate was to be settled in London this was undoubtedly the best approach to take.

Another approach had already been found. In the 1880s educated Indians were founding societies in the great coastal cities of Calcutta and Bombay and Madras to discuss their problems with one another, and in December 1885 the first meeting of the Indian National Congress was held in Bombay. The meeting had been encouraged by a few members of the Indian Civil Service, one of whom, A. O. Hume, had done as much as anyone to bring it about. The new Viceroy, Lord Dufferin, had expressed his approval of Hume's activity, though he may later have come to think that Hume was interpreting his encouragement a little too liberally and was giving the Viceroy more advice than was necessary. As far as the Indian members of the Congress were concerned Dufferin was entirely in favour of their organization, and when they met at Calcutta the following year he showed his official approval of them by holding a reception for them at Government House. At this point there was no idea that Congress would act as a political opposition; it was intended by its founders and by the Viceroy to be the recognized pressure group for Indians who were so educated and westernized that they might have attempted to enter the Civil Service and had gone on to careers in teaching, law, and business. Its meetings were held in English, which was a sign of the high level of education of the members, and also of their wide distribution over the country. Using any Indian language would have made the meeting into a particularist occasion; the use of English meant that an 'All-India' movement, of a sort that would have been inconceivable before trains and telegrams, could be launched.

The Viceroy could see that it was his business to know what such people thought and to find how the system could be adjusted to fit their needs without causing any trouble. Dufferin's calm attitude was not shared by many Englishmen in India. They did not see Congress as a body of people who simply wanted to get inside the system of government and join in ruling India, and were convinced that it was bound to develop a spirit of nationalism that would make its members want to be the sole rulers of India. At the time this was not the case: members of Congress asked for home rule rather than the wider range of powers included in Responsible Government, and probably thought their position was better under the British than it could be in an independent India. Under the British, educated Indians might be able to rise in the Indian Civil Service and eventually take it over. If India were independent, power would be likely to fall back into the hands of the princes and soldiers and the scope for an educated civilian élite would be less great.

Congress had another problem, which was an almost unavoidable result of its position as a group of highly educated men; it was made up very largely of Hindus. Bombay and Madras were very largely Hindu cities, and most of the people in Calcutta who were rich enough to acquire the very high level of education of the supporters of Congress were Hindus. The richer Muslims of the area round Delhi or in the Punjab were much less concerned about education and the route to power it offered in a bureaucratic system of government, so that very few of them shared the interests of the average Congress member of Dufferin's day.

Dufferin naturally did not regard relations with Congress as a major activity in his Viceroyalty. In 1885 the Indian government took its third and final step forward to bring the kingdoms of Burma completely under British rule, and when Dufferin was raised a step in the peerage he became Marquess of Dufferin and Ava, because he added the name of the Burmese city to his title. The Burmese king Thibaw ruled his subjects brutally enough for British opinion to feel quite sure that suppressing him and merging Burma into the Indian empire would be a humane policy, but it was most unlikely that the Secretary of State for India would have reckoned that decisive intervention would be popular if Thibaw had not also been making life difficult for a British company trying to carry on business in his kingdom and if the French a little further east had not looked intent on expansion. The British may have been worried unnecessarily about the early stages of

France's interest in Indochina, but their reactions in Burma took them forward to the border of Siam, which survived as an independent state in the period of European expansion largely because Britain and France found it convenient to have a neutral state between them. Burma became part of the Indian administrative structure, but it was never absorbed into India and Burmese national feeling was always entirely separate from that of India. It was more prosperous than India, and Indians emigrated there to share the trading opportunities provided by its exports of teak and rice. Inside the Civil Service it was regarded as an interesting backwater. A post there was not likely to lead on to the highest places in the Viceroy's councils but men who served there did not make the hostile comments on the people they ruled which were to be heard in India.

This was partly because the Burmese were self-reliant, rural, and not educated. In the closing years of the century the British in India were developing an attitude of hostility to educated Indians. The title 'babu', which was one of some prestige among Indians, was picked up by the British and applied to members of the rising educated class with an implication that they were subtle, untrustworthy, and perhaps a little cowardly. Sometimes the efforts of Indians to get an education invited a supercilious smile; it was understood that men who had got into a university but not completed the course would put 'Failed B.A.' on their visiting cards. The less educated people of the Punjab were thought more worthy of respect – more violent, it might be, but certainly more straightforward. The British rulers had grown to see themselves as defenders of the great Indian peasant majority, and now saw themselves as resisting two dangers to their charges. There was still the need to maintain peace and security, expressed satirically by H. G. Wells in his reference to the apochryphal native ruler in the north-west who said that if the British left India 'in six months not a rupee or a virgin would be left in Lower Bengal'.[2]

At the same time there was a fear that simply maintaining the peace would mean that the peasants would fall into the hands of lawyers and money-lenders, and there was some foundation for this fear. During the eighteenth-century anarchy in India loans had not been secure and under Indian customary law land was very hard to mortgage, so the riskiness of lending may have justified interest rates of 48 per cent and more. British law and order made money-lending much safer in the nineteenth century, but interest rates did not drop, and one result of this situation was a notable breach in the barriers of caste: the money-lending caste quadrupled in numbers in the last thirty years of the nineteenth century. The Civil Service saw the danger that peasants would run into financial difficulties and forfeit their land as one of the results of the rise of the educated Indians, and it was

[2] H. G. Wells, *The New Machiavelli* (1911), 356.

clear enough that, of the two threats to the Indian peasants, many of the British felt less hostility to the ferocious men of the frontier than to the educated men of the city.

India gained an entirely new hold on the attention of the English-speaking world that Rudyard Kipling began writing about it in the 1880s. Very little had been written in English previously that could help anyone to understand either India or the British in India. This probably indicated that not many people in Britain were deeply concerned about India, and it certainly made it hard for them to become more involved with the question. Kipling himself had lived in India for the first six years of his life, and for six more years as a young man; he was only 23 when he left India and began publishing the books that have given one view of the country its permanent form. At first he wrote about the civil servants, the army, and the government of India. As it became clear that readers welcomed a view of India that, though it might be harsh and primitive, was written in a manner that could be accepted as truthful, he spread his wings further. He wrote about the Indians as well as the British in India and eventually in *Kim*, which was more or less his farewell to writing about India, he tried to paint a picture that brought together the bold (and Muslim) Indian of the north-west, the subtle and educated (Hindu) Indian of Bengal, the holy man seeking enlightenment, and the British boy who had grown up in India, with the Indian population and landscape as the background. It is a novel of northern India, from Lahore to Benares, but this area had dominated India in the past and was to dominate it in the future. It is a novel that took British rule for granted and paid no attention to ideas of internal change, but Kipling's own experience of India had been in the years up to 1888 when the prospects of political changes were very hard to see. Kipling had two sides to his head and could see some way into the question of what Indians wanted (though never deeply enough to be in the least reconciled to the advance towards Indian independence), but many of his admirers were people who did not see that there were radical as well as conservative implications in his *Ballad of East and West*.

> East is east and west is west
>   and never the twain shall meet
> But there is neither East nor West,
>   Border, nor Breed nor Birth
> When two strong men stand face to face
>   Though they come from the ends of the earth

Admiration of this sort for strong men, even if it did rise above all racial feeling, probably encouraged support for the more aggressive, less educated Muslims in any political struggle.

The educated and westernized Indians in Congress in the first years of its activity were often secularized enough in their views to think of religion in much the same terms as Herbert Spencer did, but they could not entirely cut themselves off from the communities from which they came. Congress leaders realized their movement was likely to attract many more Hindus than Muslims, because of the regions that were involved and because of the way education had spread. They tried to correct this but their freedom of action was limited. The people in Congress were a tiny minority and they had to attract outside support if they were to have any impact. Religion was for the great majority of Indians the organizing principle that governed their lives, and keeping it separate from politics was harder than might be thought. Congress opposed the Age of Consent Bill of 1891, which was intended to prevent child marriage; members of Congress did not like the practice, but they could not cut themselves off from their political base. In the early years of Congress many more people were involved in the work of the Cow Protection Society than of Congress, and this raised another problem. The Society was Hindu in all of its assumptions and objectives, and its desire to make the government pass laws forbidding the killing of cattle and the eating of beef was almost uniquely calculated to drive the British and the Muslims together. Congress had very little sympathy for the Society, but denouncing it would have been a very difficult step to take.

This encouraged Muslims to feel that Congress was not really trying to understand them; despite the best attempts of Congress to conciliate them, including holding some of its annual conferences in Muslim cities like Lahore, Muslim attendance declined. In 1906 the Muslim League was launched, a parallel organization to Congress which would not have emerged if the earlier body had not been founded, but which did underline the fact that the first generation of Congress leaders had not been able to include the Muslims in their approach to politics. There were very few highly-educated Muslims in a position to share the ambition of the early members of Congress to move up into the bureaucracy and rise to high position within the existing order, and as time went on the Muslims became suspicious about the capacity of Congress to stick to the non-religious approach of its original members. Keeping Congress secular-minded was bound to be difficult when it contained a large Hindu majority; the Muslims decided to insure themselves against any possible failure in this direction.

In this they got a certain amount of encouragement from the British. Congress called this 'divide and rule', which may have been a fair comment on what the British were doing but was a dangerous underestimate of Muslim political consciousness. In a way Congress's trivialization of the Muslims' feelings was matched by a trivialization of Indian nationalism indulged in, for the most amiable of motives, by progressive opinion in Britain. The idea grew up in Britain that 'bad manners lost the empire' (or, as E. M. Forster put it rather more subtly, 'one touch of regret would have made the British Empire a different institution'[3]). But as nationalism spread over the whole world, it became harder and harder to imagine that rule by even the politest and least racially conscious of Englishmen would really have been regarded as a satisfactory alternative to independence. Congress supporters who would have been either insulted or amused by the suggestion that their national spirit was simply a reaction to British bad manners had nevertheless great difficulty in understanding the possibility that the Muslim minority might develop a national feeling of its own. Eight centuries of Muslim rule in India, a tradition of military dominance, and a sense of religious unity were quite enough to make the Muslims see themselves as a distinct community in northern India, with numerical majorities in both the north-west and north-east and a historic position as the ruling class along much of the length of the river Ganges. It was most unlikely that the readiness of this community to see itself as a nation would be affected one way or the other by the attitude of the English. Congress supporters who spoke as if British encouragement was at the root of Muslim community feeling were deceiving themselves and losing whatever chance there was of bringing everyone under British rule together as a single Indian nation.

The attitude of the Civil Service showed some sympathy for the attempt of the Muslims to organize themselves. There was a frivolous feeling that it was good fun to see the Indians – more particularly the nationalist-minded Indians – quarrelling among themselves, but the British image of themselves as protectors of the weak also inclined them to approve of the desire of the Muslim minority to make its position known. The Conservative government of Lord Salisbury had expanded the provincial councils further than Ripon had done but still provided that all the Indian members of councils were nominated; when the Liberals came to office in 1892 they amended the legislation so that some Indian members were elected. The Muslim community asked for some restricted seats for which only Muslims could be chosen, and the British agreed to this; a minority was in danger of being swamped by the majority and, because the councils were seen not as embryo parliaments (in which a government might need a clear-cut and homogeneous majority) but as bodies to be consulted about Indian opinion, the administration needed representatives of minority opinion and was not concerned if this restricted the position in the council of the majority party. The Liberals were convinced that the government should listen to Indian public opinion, but they did not believe that Indians ought to be able to control the government or that all Indians ought to express themselves through a single organization.

---

[3] E. M. Forster, *A Passage to India* (Penguin, 1960 edn.), 50. In a letter written in the 1920s Forster came closer to the crude version of the argument when he wrote 'English manners out here have improved wonderfully. . . . But it is too late.' E. M. Forster, *The Hill of Devi* (1953), 155.

Africa in the 1890s

These important developments could not keep public attention away from Africa, which after a brief moment in 1890 in which equilibrium seemed to have been restored, looked more of a danger to peace in Europe than in the 1880s. There had been public anger in Britain at the withdrawal from the South African Republic after Majuba, and at the death of Gordon, but neither outburst of feeling had affected the government's policy. No European politician thought anything in Africa was worth a full-scale war, and difficulties in Africa had been sorted out with little pressure from public opinion.

After the main lines of the partition of Africa had been drawn on the map and accepted in principle by the politicians, the public began to realize that something important was happening in Africa, and its interest then sometimes rose to a level that the politicians found embarrassing. By 1889 Lord Salisbury had become convinced that possession of Uganda was an important part of a strategy of securing control of the whole length of the river Nile, apparently because he was afraid that a hostile power might reach the upper Nile, build a dam across it, and cut off Egypt's water supply.[4] The idea that anyone could get materials to the spot, let alone build such immense (and almost certainly unprofitable) works on the river is so implausible that it is hard to see why Salisbury built his policy round it. But he fairly clearly thought the threat was real, and he was determined to do everything he could to avert it, short of asking the taxpayer for more money. The existence of Mackinnon and his British East Africa Company seemed to solve the problem of establishing a British presence in the area north of German East Africa without involving the British government. Mackinnon and his Company appeared to have higher and more philanthropic ideas than Goldie; they thought in terms of ending the slave trade in East Africa by providing the legitimate commercial competition which was the only way of driving the slave-traders out of the field without running up impossible expenses. The government even formed the impression, which turned out to be incorrect, that the Company could survive without profits.

By 1890 the Company had begun to get involved in the politics of the Buganda kingdom (which had given its name to the wider region called Uganda by Europeans). European involvement had come first in the form of religion: British missionaries had made converts to Protestantism and French missionaries had made converts to Catholicism, while the King remained opposed to Christian influence (possibly because he felt missionaries were likely to bring in challenges to his power), but fluctuated in his own beliefs between paganism and Islam. At the end of 1890 the Company's representative, Captain Lugard, marched inland to Buganda and in a few

[4] R. Robinson and J. Gallagher, *Africa and the Victorians* (1961), 283–4.

weeks imposed himself on the situation so successfully that with virtually no bloodshed the King accepted the Company as his overlord and recognized the fact that power was going to be in the hands of the British and the pro-British protestant section of his people. This was politically satisfactory for the British government, but made very little financial sense for the Company. The Royal Niger Company could afford to run military operations and dominate the political scene in its region because it was a commercially successful firm earning profits from trade on the river, and the British South Africa Company could do the same thing because it had patient investors, some of whom had a great deal of mining money behind them, but the British East Africa Company had a much weaker financial base. It felt that Salisbury had held it back while he waited to reach a settlement with Germany in 1889 and 1890, and that it had then taken on too much by plunging directly into Buganda, over 400 miles from Mombasa. There was not enough trade to justify going so far inland, and the cost of keeping Lugard supplied was eating up the Company's money. In 1891 it hoped to solve the problems by persuading the government to help build a railway inland. Salisbury was anxious enough about the Uganda route to the Nile to respond favourably but he drew back when the Opposition objected.

When his government lost the 1892 general election the Company's prospects looked bleak, but the Liberals chose as their Foreign Secretary Lord Rosebery, who shared Salisbury's views about the importance of Uganda. Because – for quite different reasons – he really did not want to be in the government, his threats of resignation if he did not get his own way on the issue had to be taken seriously. He was able to push the government into taking over Buganda as the Company drew back. By the time the Conservatives came back to office in 1895 the Company was bankrupt, and the new government compensated it for the money it had spent on administrative activity. This was as close as any politicians came to acknowledging that company intervention was sometimes encouraged as an instrument of government policy and that in this case the instrument had been overstrained. Even so, the shareholders got no compensation for the money lost directly in the over-ambitious trading activities they had been persuaded to undertake.

The Conservatives then built the Uganda railway that had been proposed, a considerable engineering achievement as it went up from sea level at Mombasa to a height of land which even at the equator was perfectly comfortable for people from Europe, and then ran down again to the north shore of Lake Victoria. The construction was carried out thriftily, at a cost of £5.5m. for 580 miles of track built under difficult conditions – of which the most spectacular but not the most serious were the lions who occasionally ate workmen from among the railwaymen brought over from India to lay the track – but commercially it was not much sounder than the company which had gone before it. British expansion rested on the assumption that regions would be occupied only if it made economic sense to do so, and that colonies would pay their own local costs. East Africa was too poor and too short of people to fulfil these expectations, and governments were delighted to see any developments which looked like producing more revenue. A few British settlers were atttracted by the very thinly populated high territory through which the railway ran close to the African village of Nairobi, but at the beginning of the twentieth century the two colonies of Kenya and Uganda into which the British East Africa Company's territory had been divided still depended on grants from the British Exchequer and had lost their strategic importance because the government had solved its problems about the Nile before the railway was complete.

The government's willingness to build the railway owed something to a new personality at work. When he formed his 1895 government Salisbury asked Joseph Chamberlain, the leader of the Liberal Unionist allies in the Commons, what posts interested him. Chamberlain replied that he wanted to be Secretary for the Colonies, in order to encourage closer union with the colonies. The post had not been important in the immediate past; major negotiations in Africa had been handled by the Foreign Office, and the Colonial Office was seen simply as the administrative unit for controlling governors and their subordinates in the colonies that were not run by the India Office. As Chamberlain's entire office staff numbered only about a hundred he obviously could not exercise any close supervision, but he could put a new spirit into the system, perhaps best expressed by his remark that the colonies were a 'neglected estate' which he was determined would not be neglected in the future. The Treasury stuck to its principles that colonies ought to be self-supporting and that the British taxpayer should not be out of pocket as a result of having an empire, so Chamberlain's plans never developed as he had wished. More government attention than before was given to fighting tropical disease (the importance of which was shown by Ross's discovery of the transmission of malaria), and the problems of the West Indies sugar plantations were recognized by a successful diplomatic campaign against other sugar-growing countries who were given subsidies to enable them to operate at a loss, but no really decisive steps toward colonial development could be taken.

Chamberlain took office at a time when imperial enthusiasm was distinctly greater than before, but it is possible to overestimate this enthusiasm. There had been no complaints when, a little earlier in 1895, Wilde's Miss Cardew (while not reading about the rupee) heard the colonies put in their place in the lines:

CECILY. Your uncle Jack said you would have to choose between this world, the next world and Australia.

ALGERNON. Oh well the accounts I have received of Australia and the next world
are not particularly encouraging. This world is good enough for me.

Lack of interest in the empire while still common was not as universal as it
had been. In 1893 there had been a campaign among missionary societies
and Chambers of Commerce to strengthen Rosebery's position when he
argued that the government ought to hold on to Uganda, and a little later
there was strong pressure from Lancashire trading interests to march north
from the Gold Coast and take over Asanti. Chamberlain responded to this,
and Asanti was annexed in 1896. But by then he had already become
involved in the much more explosive politics of southern Africa.

In 1890 Rhodes's interlocking policies had worked together very successfully. His pioneers had gone north-east through Bechuanaland into
Lobengula's kingdom and, carefully avoiding the Matabele areas, had set up
a new colony in the Mashona territories. He had just become Prime Minister
of Cape Colony. He could point to the way his policies would provide land in
the north for those who wanted it, and his programme also included the
annexation of Pondoland in the east, which eliminated the last African state
between Cape Colony and Natal; scientific development of agriculture; the
encouragement of railways in the colony and an attempt to work out a
railway policy for the British colonies and the Afrikaner republics, reinforced by a customs union; an attempt to divide Africans into those who
were being drawn into the white economy and those who should remain in
native reserves; and harmonious relations between British and Afrikaner.
His alliance with Hofmeyr and the Bond held firm, even though some
Afrikaner farmers were unenthusiastic about scientific agriculture. The size
of the job must not be overestimated; Cape Colony was the most populous
section of southern Africa, but it had only about 375,000 white and a bit
under two million coloured and African inhabitants. But Rhodes's programme offered something for most voters and, while he fell from office
after five years, this was for reasons that had nothing to do with his policy for
Cape Colony.

Despite this policy of improvements in the Cape, political weight was
moving north to the South African Republic. By 1890 the British government could see that the gold mines had made the Republic rich and
powerful, and that supplying the Johannesburg market was opening up new
prospects for farmers and was likely to attract railway promoters as well.
This change made Salisbury more willing to support Rhodes and his policies
than he had been in the 1880s, because this seemed to be the best way to hold
the South African Republic in check. The British South Africa Company's
territory of Zambesia (officially renamed Rhodesia in 1897, though the
name had been in use for four or five years already) turned out not to contain
any of the gold mines expected by those who thought the Rand would have a

northern counterpart, but the Company was able to take over new land. In 1891 the government gave it authority over Northern Zambesia, mainly because the Company was willing to pay the costs of administration and the government was not. In the same spirit of thrift the government sent its administrator Johnston to take over the Nyasa area in which Livingstone had worked a quarter of a century earlier, but allowed the British South Africa Company to pay a large part of his expenses and thus gain a good deal of control over official policy in the area.

The failure of the prospectors to find substantial gold mines worried the British investors in the Company, but the agricultural settlers in Mashonaland did rather better for themselves. Relations with the Matabele were troubled by the almost inevitable quarrels about cattle that occur along a frontier, and also by Lobengula's attitude to the Mashona. He was prepared to let the Cape settlers establish their farms, even though he had not intended to give anything more than a mining concession; their presence was some sort of guarantee that he would not be invaded from the South African Republic. But the Mashona were his subjects, and he claimed the right to send his men to punish them whenever he pleased. The white settlers, who were sometimes employing the Mashona whom Lobengula wanted to punish, denied that he had any right to interfere with their employees, and in 1893 the dispute led to a brief and decisive war. Lobengula's army was destroyed by the rifle and machine-gun fire of the settlers and their small police force. He fled and was never seen again, and the Company's political authority was now firmly established, even if its financial position was no better. In 1894 Queen Victoria noted that Rhodes had just told her that since they had last met (early in 1891) 'he had added 12,000 miles of territory to my dominions.'[5] Presumably Rhodes was simply referring to the assistance he had given the government in Nyasaland, because everything else he did was on a much larger scale. The various activities of the British South Africa Company north of the Limpopo added about 750,000 square miles to the empire. Because this meant spending money on police and administration, the Company was eating up its original capitalization of a million pounds at the rate of over a hundred thousand pounds a year without its being at all clear how the investors were to get their money back.

The discovery of mineral wealth made it possible to build railways on a large scale. In the 1890s tracks were laid to Johannesburg from Durban, from Cape Town, and from the Portuguese harbour at Delagoa Bay, and the British South African Company prepared to lay a line through Bechuanaland to Rhodesia. This railway building showed that Johannesburg was accepted as an established community and that its population was settling down and becoming permanent. This was not welcome news to the Afrikaners; the

---

[5] J. G. Lockhart and C. M. Woodhouse, *Rhodes*, (1963), 217.

miners and the financiers, British, American, German or whatever else, were an assembly of talent that people much less God-fearing than the Afrikaners might have deplored and wished to see elsewhere. By the 1890s there were about as many white adult males in the mining district as in the whole of the rest of the South African Republic though, as in most mining towns, there were not many women or children. If these uitlanders were allowed to vote in presidential elections they would probably be able to outvote the Afrikaners, so they were not given the right. If this large and unruly community was allowed to choose a Mayor of Johannesburg he would automatically be a rival to the authority of the President, so Johannesburg was not allowed to have municipal institutions.

This sort of political exclusion had happened in other mining centres, at least in their early stages of development, and many of the miners were unconcerned about it all. The turnover of population was rapid enough to show that many of them felt they had made enough money to leave, or that Johannesburg did not suit their tastes. But those who were settling down and making Johannesburg into something more than a mining town were concerned about their exclusion from any sort of political power, and in addition several of the more impetuous mining 'houses' (companies which took up a large block of shares when a new mining area was being financed, and often undertook the work of management) felt that a government which was more responsive to Johannesburg's needs would lower the rates of taxation, give out government contracts in a less corrupt way, and allow higher profits. Naturally many of the miners had guns, and a revolt was never impossible. The mining companies began to smuggle in more rifles, as part of a conspiracy in which Rhodes took a leading part.

This was an understandable activity for him to undertake in his role as a dominant partner in Consolidated Goldfields of South Africa, but nobody in Cape politics – particularly not a man who depended on the trust of the Afrikaners – could plot to invade one of the two Dutch Republics and hope to prosper politically. Rhodes used another of his positions of power, his managing directorship of the British South Africa Company, to prepare another step in the plan to overthrow the South African Republic. The Company had just been given control of a strip of Bechuanaland on the border with the Republic to build its railway north to Rhodesia, and Rhodes moved a detachment of the police force from Rhodesia to Pitsani in Bechuanaland from which it could move quickly to Johannesburg. So far as he was concerned, this was enough. He would wait for the revolt to break out in Johannesburg, and his force on the border could then move forward to help. But his commander on the border, Dr Jameson, was impatient. As it began to become clear that the people in Johannesburg were not really very eager to rise in revolt Jameson decided to push them over the brink, and on 29 December 1895 his force invaded the Republic. Jameson's Raid was briskly suppressed by the Afrikaners, Rhodes had to resign as premier of Cape Colony, the plotters in Johannesburg were arrested and felt they were lucky to have the death sentences for their leaders commuted to terms of imprisonment, with heavy fines for a large number of others and the British government had to think again about its policy in southern Africa. It had been relying on Rhodes to settle things, and this had led to disaster. It remained to be seen if London could do better.

Chamberlain had some difficult moments in the next few months as he tried to persuade people that, while he knew that a rebellion in Johannesburg was being planned (and fairly clearly hoped it would succeed) he had no idea that Rhodes was organizing an invasion. Both then and now, sympathizers with the South African Republic have not been convinced by his defence. Chamberlain had already had, in his first months as Secretary for the Colonies, a clash with the Republic: it had tried preventing goods from the Cape crossing the fords (or drifts) across the Vaal into the Republic, and Chamberlain had made the Republic reopen the drifts. Chamberlain could not continue to make this forceful approach immediately after the Raid, but when he chose Milner as High Commissioner for the Cape Colony in 1897 he showed that he wanted to see pressure applied to the South African Republic. Alfred Milner believed in the empire, and he did not believe that time was on his side. He might possibly be willing to act as a constitutional figurehead when doing his duty in Cape Colony, but it was obvious that his main purpose was to conduct relations with the South African Republic in a way that made it fit in with British policy. If the existing government wanted to avoid this, then it must be compelled to give the vote to the uitlanders, so that they would bring the Republic round to an attitude Britain found more sympathetic.

The President of the Republic, Paul Kruger, was unlikely to be friendly to Britain or to be impressed by Milner. He was already 70; he had been president for fourteen years, from just after the re-emergence of the Republic after Majuba and the 1881 settlement; he once found an opportunity to compare the uitlanders, not entirely favourably, with a baboon he had kept, and he showed no sign of changing his view about them or of letting them have more power in the Republic. Before Jameson's Raid younger and more open-minded men in the Republic might have pressed for a change; after the Raid his prestige was too high for him to need to worry about opposition inside the Republic. Even Chamberlain and Milner could see the need for patience.

Just to the north, Rhodes was salvaging the last fragment of his empire. In Rhodesia, both the Mashona and the Matabele had rebelled against the Company's rule in 1896. The white settlers were able to maintain their position and to defeat the rebels, who retreated to strongholds in the Matopo hills. Rhodes went forward to meet them alone, and brought the Matabele rebellion to a quicker and a less bitter end than had seemed possible before his intervention. No doubt it helped that he did not share the belief of most Afrikaners and many Englishmen in South Africa that the Africans were irredeemably inferior. So far as he was concerned, Kruger and Lobengula presented very much the same sort of problem: they were out-of-date, and he would like to remove them if they did not fit in with his plans for the future. When he tried to return to Cape politics after pacifying the revolt in Rhodesia he said his policy was 'equal rights for all civilised men south of the Zambesi' and, when asked, he confirmed that he had included Africans in his phrase deliberately. Most white people in Africa probably felt that a millionaire who supported some degree of racial equality was overlooking the problems of ordinary white men and women who had little except the colour of their skin to keep them in a position of comfort and superiority. The Cape was the most liberal part of southern Africa, and did have some African voters but, if Rhodes's statement was part of an attempt to return to power by creating an alliance between them and the British, it was not likely to succeed.

The Sentiment of Jubilee

But while the British population in southern Africa was weak, imperial sentiment in Britain and imperial success in other parts of the world were rising to a level that made it hard to stick to a restrained and patient policy. It was one thing for Kipling to say in his Recessional:

> For frantic boast and foolish word
> Thy mercy on Thy people, Lord

but getting the people to listen was another matter. The sixtieth anniversary of Queen Victoria's accession was to be celebrated more lavishly than the fiftieth, and in a way that paid much more attention to the empire. The conference at the Golden Jubilee had been a bit of an afterthought, but the conference of all the Prime Ministers of the self-governing colonies for the Diamond Jubilee was to be a major part of the celebration. The parade through London included troops from a vast range of colonies; the review of the fleet at Spithead made it clear how the empire was held together; the Queen's message of thanks to her subjects was sent round the world on British telegraph cables.

One of the leading personalities of the celebration was the Canadian Prime Minister, Wilfrid Laurier – knighted on the morning of the Jubilee church service – who had just embarked on a new policy that indicated one way to closer union of the empire. The Canadian Liberals had always supported free trade in theory, though in practice they often moved towards a policy of reciprocity with the United States, which had exposed them to criticism for being ready to weaken the connection with Britain. Laurier avoided the issue in the 1896 election, and concentrated on the obvious fact that the Conservatives had been in office too long. After winning the election the Liberals reduced tariffs by 25 per cent on certain products from countries that imposed very low duties on Canadian exports. The low level of tariffs that qualified for this preferential reduction was defined in such a way that only Britain and New South Wales met the requirements, and the policy meant that free traders would see it as a step to bring down prices, and believers in the British connection could be convinced that Laurier and the Liberals were doing more in a practical way for good relations with Britain than the high-tariff Conservatives had ever managed.

While the economic effect of the policy was hard to assess, its political success was undeniable: in Canada the Liberals had done something for their free-trade supporters – mainly food-exporting farmers – in a way that the Conservatives found hard to oppose, and in Britain Laurier was one of the heroes of the Jubilee. The devotedly free trade Cobden Club gave him its gold medal, which suggests that the Club had not realized that one of the longer-term objectives of his policy was to persuade Britain to set up a protective tariff with preferential rates (or no taxes at all) for colonial products. When the Prime Ministers held meetings that can be taken as the first formal gathering in what was to become a long series, Chamberlain pressed for a federal council which would lay down a united foreign policy for the empire. The Prime Ministers drew back from this; when they talked of closer union of the empire they did not want an institution based in London and inevitably dominated by Britain which might limit their freedom of action. Their idea of closer union was along the lines indicated by Canada, which meant that they wanted Britain to harmonize her fiscal policy with that of the self-governing colonies and set up preferential tariffs to turn the empire into a self-sufficient economic unit.

In a sense the policies put forward seemed to be attempts to restore portions of the system that had existed fifty years earlier, when British political control and close economic unity had been accepted as the way to run the empire. Obviously Chamberlain was not trying to return to a situation where the British government controlled petty details of local government, but if his federal council had come into existence and set up a defence policy to which each colony was expected to contribute as much money per head of population as Britain did, it would have meant a financial revolution in the colonies. The unanswerable argument for Britain's control of foreign policy was that the British paid much more money on a population basis (and even more as a proportion of national income, because average incomes were lower there) than any of the self-governing colonies to maintain the forces that made the policy effective.

Pessimists might have thought that, between British attachment to free trade and the colonies' attachment to the autonomy they had won over the previous half-century, nothing could be done. But 1897 was not a year for pessimists; the Prime Ministers felt they had identified some problems and would come back to settle them after further thought. They agreed that another meeting should be held in three years time or so, which meant they had decided that the Conference was a valuable event in its own right and that they should not simply wait for the next royal celebration to provide an opportunity for holding a meeting. Laurier encouraged this mood of confident progress when he said in the course of his Jubilee visit that he would find it a proud moment if a French Canadian could join in debates at Westminster. He always may have meant that Canadians could emigrate to Britain and enter politics – in 1920 three members of the British Cabinet were Canadian-born and another Canadian, Lord Beaverbrook, had considerable influence – but he was naturally taken to be saying that the Westminster Parliament might evolve into a central legislature in which representatives of the self-governing colonies would sit and help form policy on matters of common interest. Laurier was not as committed to this policy as he sounded, but he could see the attractions of closer union with the empire as the way to give Canada some control over the question of external relations that affected her. His approach in 1897 certainly led people to see him as an advocate of closer union, and probably to overestimate the popularity of the policy as a result. Later on he complained that in London the talk had all been of empire, empire, empire; he probably realized that at the time he had said things that fanned the flames, and afterwards he wished they could have been taken differently.

Imperial enthusiasm in Britain was encouraged by the Jubilee, but there was nothing unique about the emotion. The United States, Japan, and most of the countries of western Europe were showing a very similar interest in expansion, and in the 1890s probably more diplomatic attention was concentrated on China than on Africa, though with much less permanent political effect. After Japan had defeated China with impressive speed in 1895, Germany, France, and Russia stepped forward to limit Japan's gains. Britain and, a little later, the United States, were anxious to make sure that they were not left out. These six powerful states expanded in two different ways: they acquired ports from China, usually on long leases rather than by direct annexation, and they began an informal partition of the country into spheres of influences, a process which started by acknowledging Russian military power in the north and British commercial involvement in the Yangtse valley, and then fitted other interests around these two dominant facts. In the end nothing came of it; the imperial powers were able to combine to suppress a revolt against western influence led by the 'fists of righteous harmony' (abbreviated to 'boxers'), but in the early years of the new century it was in Africa and the Balkans that diplomatic conflict took place and the flood tide of imperial expansion receded.

Other major powers spent more money on expansion than the British, but the activities of the chartered companies enabled the British to gain so much more land than anyone else that the intervention of government hardly seemed necessary. The bankruptcy of the British East Africa Company was a setback for this approach, but the steady success of the Royal Niger Company showed what could be achieved. Its operations caused some diplomatic problems because it was working in an area in which British and French ambitions clashed, while the French had not shown any serious interest in protecting their missionaries and converts in Uganda. Competition on the Niger from Liverpool merchants in the early 1890s had kept the profits of the Company down until it bought them out. Once it had become the sole purchaser it tried to use its position to push down the prices paid to the Africans for their palm oil, which led them to rebel at the end of 1894. The Company was strong enough to suppress the rebellion without difficulty, but a commission of inquiry was then launched to find how it was using its charter, and by 1896 it was reasonably clear that Company rule was going to be replaced by some form of colonial rule from London in the fairly near future, because the government would be able to keep some sort of balance between African settlers and Company purchasers. The Company had already had to compete with the French in signing treaties with chiefs in order to define its position on the south-west side of the river Niger, and had fought the African rulers of Nupe and Ilorin on the banks of the river. It had been successful in these struggles, partly because of the determination with which it approached the task, and partly because Africans usually preferred the Company, which meant trade and the presents that preceded trade, to the French military men, and because the pagan or animistic subjects of the rulers of Nupe and Ilorin preferred it to their Muslim rulers.

Early in 1897, as the competition for empire grew fiercer, the French moved east into an area that the Company had been administering since the mid-1880s. The Company asked the government for help and argued that granting a charter set up a contract by which the Company would 'undertake all internal native wars and maintain domestic orders without charge on the Imperial Treasury, while the Imperial Government contracts to defend the Chartered Company against the aggressions of foreign powers'.[6] The government (which received no benefits under this hypothetical contract) accepted the fact that it normally did help Englishmen in trouble and would have to do so this time, but it did not want to perpetuate a situation in which the Company's Board of Directors could plunge the country into a European war. The government decided to buy out the political and administrative

---

[6] J. Flint, *Sir George Goldie* (1960), 273.

side of the Company's activities and by early 1898 the government had agreed to pay about £0.5m. for the Company's rights as a governing power, though it preferred to keep the agreement secret while Company officials acted as the government's agents in defining the western frontier of Nigeria and in holding it against the French.

British and French forces marched up and down disputed areas, signing new treaties with the African chiefs, hoisting their own flags as close to those of the other side as seemed practicable without bringing on a war, and all the time waiting to see what negotiations in Europe would produce. On the British side Salisbury and the relatively pro-French diplomats of the Foreign Office would have been willing to give way to France; Chamberlain stood firmly behind the claims of the Royal Niger Company, and as imperial enthusiasm rose to greater heights power passed to him. By the spring of 1898 it became apparent that France would have to give up some of the new territory claimed the previous year, and that she would not obtain compensation by being allowed unlimited navigation rights on the Niger. The repulse of the French advance had been carried out in a way that recognized (and also stimulated) the forces of imperial pride and commitment that were so much more obvious in the 1890s than ten years earlier. The following year the process of buying out the Company's right to govern was completed, for rather more than the amount originally suggested, and the government prepared to rule its new territory as an ordinary though very densely populated colony.

Something like the same story of steady development, suddenly overtaken by a surge of imperial sentiment, could be seen in Egypt and the Sudan. Cromer had gone on with his programme of reducing government spending and making payments on the debt punctually enough to restore the country's credit. The budget showed a large enough surplus for the administration to be able to think about using the re-equipped and retrained army to march south into the Sudan. The Mahdi had died shortly after the capture of Khartoum but the Khalifa (the successor) had established a reasonably stable state which was completely separate from Egypt. The British controllers of Egypt wanted to do something about it; after the decisive defeat of the Italians by the Abyssinians at Adowa in 1896 they took a few steps south, declaring that this advance was meant to relieve the pressure on the Italian position in Eritrea. It also served to underline Britain's interest in the Nile; Sir Edward Grey had announced that the government would regard an advance by a European power into the area whose rivers and watercourses flowed into the Nile as an 'unfriendly act', which meant that Britain would fight for the Nile basin. The British advance in 1896 was a sign that occupation was to be made effective.

The British government would have liked to charge all the expenses of a march into the Sudan to the Egyptian treasury. The European powers, led by France, did not find this acceptable and declared that the money in the treasury ought to go to paying Egypt's debts, rather than to extending the British Empire. By this stage the British government was so committed to expansion that late in 1896 it asked the Commons to vote money for an advance south along the Nile, and was pleasantly surprised to find how little oppostion it met from the Liberals. By the time of the Jubilee the Egyptian army under Kitchener and his British officers had moved halfway from the Egyptian border to Khartoum. The advance was slow because the British were not just launching an attack on the Khalifa; as they moved south they were laying a railway line, and they clearly intended to hold on to the Sudan if they conquered it. From the British point of view the Khalifa performed the useful negative function of making sure that nobody else tried to occupy the Nile valley and, once his army was defeated, other European powers would be ready to take over the Sudan if the British did not. An advance north from Uganda was considered as an alternative to the march down the Nile. When it became clear that this was impossible because of the great marshes in the southern Sudan the British committed themselves even more fully to the Nile route and sent British forces to strengthen the Egyptian army. In April 1898 Kitchener defeated the last Sudanese force north of Khartoum and began laying more railway track to follow the army south again. On 2 September the Khalifa's army was massed at Omdurman outside Khartoum, and then rode forward to attack the Anglo-Egyptian force. This was a piece of meaningless courage; Kitchener lost 368 men, the Khalifa lost 11,000. The British and Egyptians could now claim the Sudan by right of conquest and they set up a form of joint ownership over it.

Their position was not unchallenged. A small, determined, and efficient French force under Captain Marchand had been moving north-west from the French Congo for about two years and had – after desperate struggles – reached the Nile at Fashoda two months before Omdurman. Kitchener moved south to meet Marchand and explained that the long march did not affect the political position in the Sudan: France had no claim to effective control, while the British could rely on their right of conquest and did have effective control. In Europe Salisbury explained the same thing almost as politely, and added that the British would certainly fight for the Sudan now that they had an army on the spot. He had seen that the crisis might come: in the previous four years the navy had been built up, problems of foreign policy concerning China had been settled in a way that conciliated Russia and meant she would not want to see her ally France go to war with Britain, and British public opinon was at least as committed to war as French. After a few weeks the tension eased and the French withdrew their claims in the Nile Valley. It would not have been rational for European powers to go to war over any of their colonial claims in Africa, but it would have been even less rational for the French to get into a war they could not win, because of their problems of communication across the sea and over the Sahara desert, than it would have been for the British to fight a war under favourable circumstances.

In diplomatic terms the Fashoda crisis did no lasting harm. The countries had defined their positions and Britain had shown it was going to keep Egypt and do anything that might be necessary to retain control. The French government could see that Britain was deeply committed to north-east Africa and that the best thing to do was to find other areas where Britain might support France in return for a formal withdrawal of claims in Egypt. Public opinion was less reasonable: the mood in France was strongly anti-British, while British public opinion – apart from feeling that France had been taught a useful lesson – became convinced that force or the threat of force would solve most problems. The dispute in southern Africa, which had been left on one side while the problems with France on the Niger and the Nile were settled, was now approached in this unconciliatory mood. No doubt little could have been done while the British were feeling humiliated by Jameson's failure and the South African Republic was excited by its success but, by the time Chamberlain returned to the problem, the British were also feeling excited by success, and a compromise about questions like the position of the uitlanders was unlikely. The British government would have liked to cut the South African Republic off from the outside world by expanding all round it, and in 1898 this seemed possible: the British began negotiating to buy the southern part of the Portuguese colony of Mozambique, which would have completed the circle of British territory around the Republic. The Portuguese decided that this would be too much of a confession of the weakness of their empire, the British did not want to press them too hard, and the plan fell through.

While the British government thought the problem was that the Republic might get in touch with other European powers such as Germany, Milner was more worried by the danger that its growing wealth would give it a dominant influence over the rest of southern Africa and draw the colonies away from loyalty to Britain. The only answer to this problem was to change the government of the Republic, peacefully if possibly, though Milner was never very confident of this. By the end of 1898 he was pressing the question of the uitlanders' right to vote, though it was never clear whether he was doing this because he thought an uitlander-dominated Republic would slip naturally into the British Empire or because he thought the issue would enable the British to go to war on the popular slogan of Englishmen's right to vote in a territory under British suzerainty. Although the prospects for agreement on the franchise were not good, a conference between Kruger and Milner was organized in the (South African) winter of 1899. The discussions at Bloemfontein went well enough at first for Chamberlain to encourage Milner to keep negotiating, but Milner lost patience or perhaps felt he had done enough to show that he had been negotiating seriously while Kruger was making concessions as slowly as possible and with as little good faith as he could get away with. By springtime the two sides were thinking in terms of war. The British began bringing in additional troops; the South African Republic sent an ultimatum on 9 October to tell them not to do this, and war followed immediately.

10. *Fighting and Reorganizing 1899–1922*

The Boer War marked the end of a period of territorial expansion of the empire, and led to a time of imperial rethinking and reorganization. The setbacks and defeats of the first stage of the war, and the unexpectedly long-drawn-out closing stage poured cold water over imperial enthusiasm, but they did not lead to any suggestion of imperial withdrawal. In the years after the war economic development and domestic reform received more attention than they had done for some years, but these new steps were sometimes expressed in the language of empire: the rehabilitation of South Africa after the Boer War was directed by ardent exponents of the imperial idea, and Liberals in Britain expressed their ideas for reform in a book entitled *The Heart of the Empire*. So much new land had been acquired, and so greatly had relations with some of the colonies changed that the task of administration was enough by itself to absorb all the energy that people were ready to devote to the empire. The colonies' idea of encouraging closer union by changing the tariff system was defeated so decisively in the British general election of 1906 that the idea could hardly flourish in that form for some years to come; the British idea of advancing to closer union by discussion of foreign policy and colonial contribution to defence spending made a certain amount of progress, but was never at the centre of men's minds.

The steps taken in this direction were helpful for imperial planning when the First World War broke out in 1914, but the general effect of the war was to transform the British Empire and the way that people thought about all empires. The Dominions and India became much more conscious of themselves as nations during the war, partly because the rhetoric of the war, with its references to 'the rights of small nations' and 'self-determination', encouraged them to do so, and partly because they were taking military decisions of the type that had in the past been taken only by sovereign states. As a result they emerged from the war much more like independent nations than they had been in 1914, and a new way to run the empire had to be found to take account of this. Lloyd George, the British Prime Minister, thought the answer lay in the practice of 'continuous consultation', but the problems of dealing with the new territories that Britain was acquiring in the Middle East turned out to be so complicated and so far removed from the Dominions' interests that the practice was not applied for long. By 1922 it had become clear in the Chanak crisis that a new approach would be needed.

Chamberlainism in Decline

The first weeks of the Boer War dealt a sharp check to imperial enthusiasm, and a blow to Britain's confidence in her army. Well-equipped forces moved forward quickly from the two Dutch Republics to beseige Mafeking in Bechuanaland, Kimberley in Cape Colony, and Ladysmith in Natal. The British had to take the offensive sooner than was prudent, in an attempt to relieve the border towns. If they had not had to advance they could have assembled reinforcements from Britain, and could have learnt more about the problems of a new type of warfare. As it was, they pressed forward and were thrown back; nobody had realized how hard it would be to advance against troops dug into trenches and armed with up-to-date rifles. In November and December 1899 the British were defeated in a number of attempts to advance and suffered losses which, by the standards of the little colonial wars for which their army was designed, were unusually heavy.

This did not last long. Early in 1900 Roberts, the successful general of a dozen small-scale campaigns on the frontiers of India, arrived with a large army and marched fairly directly north-east from Cape Town, surrounding and capturing the main body of the army opposing him at Paardeburg in the Orange Free State in February and entering Pretoria in June. At this point the war seemed to have gone just like so many other colonial wars; a few setbacks at first, perhaps attributable to the fact that the British had not been preparing for war as single-mindedly as their enemies, and then a fairly rapid recovery and success. The three beseiged towns were all relieved success-fully; and hysterical enthusiasm over these successes, particularly at the relief of Mafeking, did suggest that people had been badly shaken by the early defeats, but in mid-1900 that hardly seemed to matter. Roberts re-turned to Britain leaving Kitchener of Khartoum to finish the job, and the government dissolved Parliament and held a general election in October to judge its handling of the war. Its majority of about 130 seats showed practically no change from what it had been in the 1895 election; the Liberal opposition could criticize the numerous examples of military inefficiency that had come to light during the war but this was unlikely to make much impression on an electorate which could see that the Liberals were unable to agree among themselves whether the Dutch Republics should be annexed and, if so, on what terms. The government had no doubts about what should be done. It intended to annex the republics and was waiting only for the shattered remnants of the enemy army to ask for peace.

The small groups of Afrikaners still in organized formations had no intention of giving up. At first they hoped to rouse the Afrikaners of Cape Colony to rise in rebellion to support them; then they hoped that the British would get tired of the war; finally they recognized that the best they could do, in the face of Kitchener's steady sweeping of the ground with his immensely superior force, was to struggle for acceptable peace terms. At a time when aerial reconnaissance could not be used to survey wide areas of open land, probably nobody could have done better than Kitchener, but the British expected colonial wars to end quickly and were certainly not accustomed to the idea that small groups could hold out for a long time.

The twenty months of guerilla warfare produced some advantages for the Afrikaners. In 1900 the British government had expected to impose its will without much difficulty and had even thought the colour-blind Cape Colony property qualification for the right to vote could be made universal throughout South Africa. By the time peace was made in the Treaty of Vereeniging in May 1902 the government saw that public opinion in Britain was tired of the war and was alarmed by the cost, which was rising towards £¼bn. Kitchener was eager for peace; at Vereeniging he assured the Afrikaner negotiators that the Liberals would probably win the next general election in Britain and would then allow them to become self-governing colonies like Canada and Australia. So, after insisting on a clause in the peace terms to say that voting qualifications would not be changed before they became self-governing, the Dutch republics made peace and were annexed as colonies, initially under the direct rule of Milner as governor. The new Afrikaner leaders from the Transvaal decided that they must now work in harmony with the British, which was reasonable enough because in their colony the two groups had roughly the same strength in the electorate. The Orange Free State, which was much more purely Afrikaner in population and had been the scene of most of the guerilla warfare in the last phase of the war, was more intransigent. For a generation to come, its leaders were the main opponents of accepting British success in the war as the basis for reconciliation among the white population.

Long before this, imperial attention had moved away from South Africa. One gratifying feature of the war had been the readiness of the self-governing colonies to send troops to help Britain. The Australian and New Zealand governments had sent them eagerly; the Canadian government had tried to limit its involvement to approving of the activities of individual volunteers, but the British government had declined to accept this and Canadian public opinion had pushed the Canadian government into making an official military contribution. This support from the colonies convinced the British that, even though the war had been unusually widely condemned on the continent of Europe, they had a strong body of opinion behind them (though other countries probably did not realize that the self-governing colonies had a perfectly free choice whether to send troops or not). The military assistance from the colonies had been useful and, for obvious political reasons, received the praise that it deserved.

In 1902 the Prime Ministers of the self-governing colonies met in London for another royal occasion, the Coronation of Edward VII. Chamberlain seized on the lessons of the war to argue that Britain needed help with her world-wide commitments and that some co-ordinating machinery should be created to plan a unified policy. During the war Laurier had said 'If you need our help, call us to your councils', and Chamberlain was now eager to show that he would take Laurier at his word. But the premiers were not nearly as interested in consultation about foreign policy as they were in gaining a preferential tariff position in the British market. About 60 per cent of their exports already went to Britain and a small amount went from one self-governing colony to another, so an imperial trading system bringing in Britain suited their needs very well. Chamberlain could not commit the government to anything when replying to this case for an imperial tariff policy, but he was impressed by what was said. Creating a tariff system with preferences would be a striking departure from existing policy for Britain, and one which could not be justified simply by imperial sentiment. Only about 15 per cent of Britain's exports went to the self-governing colonies (and another 15 or 20 per cent went to the rest of the empire), but it could be argued that tariffs would in addition protect the older British industries from competition and at the same time provide new industries with the initial encouragement needed to get them started.

In the later months of 1902 Chamberlain was thinking about the general case for protective tariffs and also about the specific problem of the small tax on corn imports that had been imposed to help pay for the Boer War. If this tax were removed for imperial imports and retained for imports from the rest of the world, the price would presumably be brought down slightly and at the same time a clear example of an imperial preference would have been provided. Ritchie, the Chancellor of the Exchequer, who was strongly encouraged in his free trade views by his Treasury officials, removed the duty from all imports of corn in his 1903 budget and struck Chamberlain's immediate weapon out of his hand. Chamberlain thought about the situation for a few more months, and then committed himself to a policy of imposing protective tariffs and giving an imperial preference which he christened 'tariff reform'. In October he resigned from the Cabinet, the Prime Minister ambiguously expressing hopes that he would be able to convert the Conservative party to his policy. In a way Chamberlain was very successful: most Conservative candidates in the 1906 election were sympathetic to his policy, and the vast majority of those elected were firmly committed to it.

The electorate was not nearly as easy to convert as the Conservative party, and the voters decisively rejected Chamberlain's policy. The Liberals might not be able to agree about South Africa, but they could all agree that protective tariffs would drive up the cost of living for their working-class supporters, damage the export prospects of the textile industries, make it harder for shipbuilders and bankers to go on with their international business, and in every way hamper the thriving and expanding sections of the British economy. Chamberlain spoke for the past and for a hypothetical future; the free traders – of whom Asquith was the most lucid and the most forceful – spoke for the country's present. They also spoke for the view that the Boer War had brought quite enough imperial excitement and expenditure. Domestic reform had its claims, which would be impeded if heavy costs were imposed on everyone to encourage an imperial unity that could be founded more solidly on friendship than on skilfully drawing up a list of customs duties. The Liberals did their best to remind voters how bad things had been under the old colonial system or, to use the language of British politics, before the Corn Laws were repealed. Models of the little loaf of bread that had been all that housewives could afford when corn paid an import duty, set against the big loaf that they could afford when free trade had come, were used to drive home the lesson that Chamberlain was going to reduce people's standard of living. Having an empire was enjoyable and nobody cared much whether it also brought in a profit, but very few people were going to vote for an empire that drove up the price of food.

Liberal resistance to imperial policy in South Africa had already inspired a book which has shaped all subsequent thinking about empire, J. A. Hobson's *Imperialism*, published in 1902. Hobson had been to South Africa, knew a fair amount about the policy that had led to the Boer War, and did not like what he knew. *Imperialism* took his South African experience and made it into the basis for a general theory of imperial expansion that for eighty years has inspired American anti-imperialists, Marxist enemies of the capitalist system, and political leaders in colonies struggling for independence. Historians of imperial activity often write as if overseas enterprises were vital to the British economy, though historians writing about British economic development usually find that they can explain it without paying much attention to the empire. Hobson had seen in South Africa that, while the policy of the British government might have been inspired by other motives, British opinion had been stirred up by questions about the treatment of Englishmen living there, and he argued that this public agitation had been fomented by capitalists who had brought large sums of money from Britain to invest in South Africa and at the same time had used their financial control of the South African press to steer British journalists in the way they wanted, and thus had moulded British feeling. While Hobson did not go into the question whether Englishmen in Johannesburg had genuine grievances, this was still a comprehensive enough argument to convince people for decades that it revealed the truth of what had caused the Boer War.

Imperialism paid surprisingly little attention to the position of British emigrants and really came very close to arguing that, because only a minority of emigrants went to the colonies, they could not have caused much imperial expansion. One basic premiss of the book was that all expansion was rather like expansion in South Africa with the uitlander question left out. It declared that the underlying dynamic force behind the British expansion of the last three decades of the nineteenth century was the vast sums of money that had been invested overseas, which led to huge tracts of territory being taken over. Britain had invested something like £2bn. overseas between 1870 and 1900 and in the same period had acquired 4.75m. square miles of territory with about 88m. new subjects, and the clear implication of the juxtaposition of these facts was that the flow of money and the acquisition of territory were connected. Hobson did not explain where the money had been invested, but this has subsequently been investigated in some detail. Historians have concentrated on tracing the location of British investment in 1914, and they have concluded that by then the British had invested overseas roughly £4bn., which was about twice the annual national income, of which about £¾bn. had gone to the United States, about £½bn. to Canada, about £¾bn. to the rest of the Americas (of which about half had gone to Argentina), a bit over £400m. to Australia and New Zealand, a bit under £400m. to India, a little over £200m. to various European countries, and another £200m. to other foreign countries of which the largest single amount had gone to Japan. None of this money could really have been said to have inspired any territorial expansion or to have led the British to have asserted their power any more aggressively in 1900 than in 1870. British power in Canada and in Australia had probably diminished during the period. A new challenge to Britain's power was developing in India, and the United States was certainly more conscious of her own strength in 1900 than in 1870.

So over three-quarters of British investment clearly had nothing to do with British expansion. About as much money had been invested in South Africa as in India, about £100m. had gone into other colonies, and about £40m. was invested in Egypt, so that a bit over an eighth of the total had gone to places in which Hobson's argument might have applied. It could still be argued that, if only a minor fraction of investment had all this impact, then a minor fraction of emigration might also have had an important effect. Some of his later writing showed that when he was not absorbed by the South African issue Hobson saw rather more to be said in favour of overseas investment; and he once went so far as to say that 'the development of a backward country by foreign capital is always beneficial to the country itself, to the industrial world at large and to the investing country in particular.'[1] Hobson was quite right to see the flow of money out of

[1] J. A. Hobson, *The Economic Interpretation of Investment* (1911), 100.

Britain as something altogether extraordinary, though lending money to Canadians or Australians would not have seemed like foreign investment to the Englishmen of the 1880s or 1890s. It was also true that the flow of investment had accelerated at just about the same time as interest in acquiring territory overseas had been reawakening, but the fact that the flow of money went on at an increasing rate down to 1914, while interest in new territory almost completely evaporated after the Boer War – the extension of the federated Malay states to take in the northern, or 'unfederated', states, was about the only expansion undertaken between 1902 and 1914 – may have suggested to him that the connection between investment and territorial expansion was not as direct as he had thought.

In South Africa trouble had been caused by the flow of a great deal of newly invested British money and a great many recently invested British immigrants to Johannesburg, and investment without immigration or immigration without investment would have caused fewer problems. Very little money was invested in the areas taken over in the scramble for Africa; the distinctive feature of the scramble was simply that it was so much easier than it had been either earlier or later to take over large, fairly densely populated areas of land. This may have been due to European technological superiority or it may have been due to the political structure of Africa, which made it rather easy for Europeans to place themselves at the top of a pyramid of obedient subjects. It was certainly not due to the inflow of a vast mass of money; the three chartered companies which carried out most of British expansion in Africa were founded in the late 1880s when the over-all level of overseas investment was high, and they had a total capitalization of about £5–10m., well over half of which was spent in the Rhodesias by the Chartered Company.

It seems unlikely that much more money could have been invested in the half-dozen colonies the chartered companies took over, unless minerals had been discovered; societies weak enough to be taken over by the limited resources the chartered companies could muster were not likely to be able to absorb investment of the size that Hobson was discussing. A million pounds invested in Africa would have a much greater political impact than a million pounds invested in North America or Australia – it could be used to conquer a kingdom as well as build a railway into Uganda or up the Nile – but this was a comment on African weakness rather than on the flow of investment. Once the British had begun investing heavily overseas it was quite likely that a little of the money would be spent in parts of Africa not touched by Europeans and that this would be fatal to their independence, but this was not what concerned Hobson. He believed that overseas investment was the product of an ill-balanced economy, and that if domestic demand was stimulated foreign investment would decline. In this way he would provide a policy that would make the existing capitalist system work better.

Lenin, who followed a good deal of Hobson's argument in his *Imperialism, the Highest State of Capitalism*, parted company with him at this point and said that if a capitalist system was able to show enough awareness of its problems to stimulate domestic demand, and thus reduce the problems of which foreign investment was the symptom, then it would no longer be capitalism. For Lenin imperialism and the eventual overthrow of imperialism by revolution were inevitable, but Hobson thought these developments were no more than possibilities, and he thought revolution neither necessary nor desirable. The absence of territorial expansion between 1902 and 1914 would have pleased him, but he must have attributed it to unpleasant memories of the high cost of the Boer War rather than to any reorganization of the British economy. The lack of vitality in the economy that Chamberlain had noted during his tariff reform campaign still persisted, and overseas investment rose to the point where in 1913 it was absorbing 7 or 8 per cent of the national income. The great bulk of it continued to go to prosperous countries, and did not produce any extraordinarily high rate of return: the estimate at the time was that investment in Britain yielded 3.1 per cent, investment in the empire 3.5 per cent, and foreign investment 3.7 per cent, which do not seem very high premiums for the slight loss of security and liquidity involved in investment overseas.

The borrowers of course sometimes took a more hostile view when the question of repayment came up. A later historian expresses the mood of resentment when commenting on activity before 1914 by saying 'although British venture money was vital in reviving Australian mining it exacted its price',[2] a phrase that expresses rather well the colonial feeling that only an unlovable combination of Shylock and Scrooge would hope to make money out of helping the Australian mining industry. Even more money had gone to Canada than to Australia, and in the last years of the boom before 1914 over half of all British overseas investment was going there, mainly for an immense extension of railway track intended to provide the wheat-growing prairies with two new lines of rail north of the area served by the Canadian Pacific. This was not a sound investment, and it was taken over by the Canadian government during the First World War on terms which eventually led to arbitration that left the British investors with nothing. This was the end of the century of British investment by buying bonds to finance the business of local entrepreneurs; when large-scale foreign investment resumed in the 1950s it took the form of corporate investment which was much more like the activity of the chartered companies than that of the passive holders of bonds. There were many other reasons for this, but the collapse of the Grand Trunk and the Canadian Northern Railways could not have been without their effect: if Canadian railway bonds were not safe, where could a prudent man put his money overseas?

2 G. Blainey, *The Rush that never Ended* (1969 edn.), 256.

In the years before 1914, hard feelings in Anglo-Canadian relations had been caused by territorial questions, and in particular the issue of the Alaska Panhandle, the land which runs south from the main body of the state. Assertive Canadians felt they had been treated as badly by the British as the Australians had been in the Pacific twenty years earlier. A discovery of gold in the Yukon caused one of the last of the old-fashioned gold rushes in the Klondike in 1898, and until the gold turned out to be a matter of surface working with none of the depth of the Rand it looked as if supplying the miners would be profitable. As a result the old Anglo-Russian treaty of 1826, which had laid down a none-too-well-defined border between the Russian otter-hunters and the Hudson's Bay Company, was examined more closely than before. The Canadian government claimed that south of 60 °N the Russian territory which the Americans had bought in 1867 was only the narrowest fringe of land on the mainland, while the Americans claimed that they had bought a substantial sweep of territory inland. The British government, which was legally the representative of Canada in negotiations with sovereign states, supported the Canadians in a tepid way; it had serious doubts about the validity of their claim, which did not seem to be supported by the maps accepted by the British public of the time, but the Canadians thought they were being sacrificed to Britain's desire for good relations with the United States.

The British government believed that in 1903 it gained a decent compromise which gave half the territory in dispute to Canada. The Canadians felt that British support for their claim ought to have been unqualified and unlimited, but even Chamberlain's exuberance would not have led him to support the Canadians by threatening the United States with war. Whatever the merits of Canada's boundary claims, Britain was moving towards a closer relationship with the United States which became an important feature of international diplomacy in the first half of the twentieth century. This made Canadians feel afraid that they were going to be neglected and convinced them that they ought to organize their own diplomatic arrangements to protect their interests. Canada already had commercial representatives in foreign countries, and after 1903 began to ask what arrangements could be made for direct representation at Washington.

While the 1903 dispute made very little impression in Britain and certainly did not affect the 1906 election there, and some important purely domestic issues faced the voters, other imperial issues came close to dominating the election, which turned out to be an overwhelming defeat for those who advocated a more active imperial policy. Apart from tariff reform's threat to food prices, there was another issue which seemed to show that the empire did ordinary people no good. After peace had been made in South Africa, the Johannesburg gold mines took a little while to return to their pre-war levels of production. The mineowners said that one problem was that

Africans who had got used to working in the mines had had to stay in the countryside while the war was going on, and so had lost touch with mining work. Milner agreed to help get the mines working again by bringing in Chinese workers on long-term contracts a little like those that had taken English indentured labourers to the West Indies in the seventeenth century. Humane Englishmen were shocked at the conditions under which the Chinese were employed, and denounced the whole scheme as slavery; people from the working class were even more angered by the thought that they might find indentured labour being imported into Britain in the same way to compete with them, and this opposition was echoed in the self-governing colonies. For electoral purposes the Chinese were shown as villains stealing men's jobs more often than they were shown as helpless victims of Milner's tyranny, but in either role they were bound to harm Chamberlain and his imperial policy. The Liberals and their free trade allies won three times as many seats as the Conservatives, though the protectionists inside the Conservative party gained a position that they never entirely lost afterwards.

The Liberals' Empire

The Prime Ministers of the self-governing colonies came to London the following year for the first conference to be held with no royal occasion to promote it, as the 1897 agreement to hold a conference independent of royal activity had come to nothing because of the Boer War. The Liberal government received them politely and did its best to soften the blow of a complete rejection of all proposals for imperial preference by suggesting that the self-governing colonies should in future be called Dominions and should have a separate section of the colonial office devoted to Dominion affairs. But the real atmosphere of the occasion was expressed fairly bluntly by the Under-Secretary for the Colonies, Winston Churchill, when he said 'We have banged, barred and bolted the door against protectionism.' The Australian Prime Minister, Alfred Deakin, put the case for closer unity and for the sort of imperial council that Chamberlain had advocated but the proposal fell on fairly deaf ears, though some British Conservatives suggested he should move from Australia to take over the leadership of their party.

After 1906 the Liberal government in Britain took little interest in either aspect of the imperial enthusiasm of the last decades of the nineteenth century. It was not interested in closer unity, and it was very sceptical about the advantages of acquiring new territory. The Secretary for the Colonies was concerned mainly with organizing the administration of the new colonies gained in the previous twenty years, and the government in general had to face the much more urgent problems of domestic reform, Ireland, and foreign policy in Europe. Even so, some steps towards imperial co-operation were taken that showed the drive for closer union had some force behind it. The General Staff that the British had set up to enable them to deal with modern development in warfare became the Imperial General Staff and brought some uniformity if not unity into military arrangements with the colonies. Most Dominions made cash contributions for the Royal Navy or built ships to work with it. The Malayan sultans, who were prospering because of the expansion of tin and rubber production, gave a battleship. At the conference of Prime Ministers in 1911 the British Prime Minister and Foreign Secretary told the Dominion representatives at least as much as they told their cabinet colleagues in London about European diplomatic problems. The New Zealand Prime Minister, Sir Joseph Ward, proposed the sort of machinery for united action by the empire which Chamberlain had suggested earlier, which seemed to be implied by Laurier's assertion that if Britain wanted co-operation from the Dominions she should call them to her councils, and which Deakin had advocated in 1907. Nothing came of it. These calls for unity were the natural step for Dominion leaders to take when they were first confronted with the problems of foreign policy. All of them started by thinking that they could achieve much more if they could help direct the policy of a united empire than if they had to devise a policy for their own country by itself, and it took them a little while to see that a united policy for the empire was bound to be controlled by Britain because of her wide diplomatic commitments and because of her immensely powerful fleet.

Chamberlain had made an effort to work with the Dominions and, on imperial preference, was won over to their point of view. His Liberal successors made it very clear that they would make their own foreign and commercial policy, but their opposition to tariffs and formal commercial relations within the empire was thorough-going enough for them to be willing to see the Dominions work out commercial policies on their own. When Laurier in the last stages of his premiership wanted to return to the Liberal policy of the 1880s and negotiate some sort of tariff reduction treaty with the United States, the British government offered no objection. The Canadian electorate did object; the political parties were still fairly equally balanced in federal politics, and the Conservatives returned to office in 1911. They tried to deal with the issue of a Canadian naval contribution by suggesting a payment to Britain for battleships as a first step, to be followed by building a navy entirely under Canadian control in the more distant future. The Liberals still had a majority in the Senate and were able to defeat the proposals there, a step which reflected the increasing importance of Quebec opinion within the Liberal party and Quebec's desire to avoid involvement in European affairs, especially if it meant reinforcing British military power.

In South Africa it was very clear that, even if occasional notes of disharmony could be heard, the issues of the Boer War had been buried and were not to be allowed to interfere with practical politics. Milner and the Conservatives had hoped to consolidate Britain's position after the war by encouraging large-scale immigration to increase the English-speaking population until it matched the Afrikaner in numbers. This plan never stood much chance of success; the numerical superiority of the Afrikaners was already too great, their dominance of the countryside could never be challenged because of the very restricted attraction of life there, and their birth-rate was too high for an attempt to swamp them to be at all likely to succeed even if it was financed lavishly and pressed forward enthusiastically for a period of many years. This approach was naturally laid aside after the Liberal victory of 1906. Campbell-Bannerman (who, when Leader of the Opposition, had won Afrikaner approval by denouncing the British approach to the Boer War as 'methods of barbarism') decided that, as an Afrikaner government would certainly be elected eventually in the Orange Free State and probably in the Transvaal as well, the difficulties had better be faced sooner rather than later. The restoration of self-government in 1907 to what had been the Dutch republics, followed almost at once by elections for which constituency boundaries were drawn in a way that gave Afrikaner farming votes considerably more weight than English-speaking urban and mining votes, opened the way for the reversal of at least some of the results of the Boer War. Botha and Smuts, who came to power in the Transvaal, had no intention of reviving the struggle and were quite ready to accept the Johannesburg mining interests as an important part of South African society which should not be alienated. In this way they laid the foundations for a political party which could unite the less intransigent sections of the British and the Afrikaner communities.

This approach may have glossed over some problems but it was ideal for the next stage in southern African development, the unification of the four self-governing colonies. The gold industry of the Rand had recovered from the war, and the immigration of the Chinese indentured labourers had been put into reverse gradually enough to give the mineowners time to replace them with Africans. As a result the Transvaal returned to the position of financial dominance it had held before the war, and in particular it regained its commanding position in the development of the railway system. The Transvaal leaders wanted a united South Africa, but if the worst came to the worst they could always threaten to adopt a transport policy that would impoverish Cape Town or Durban, or even penalize both of them by falling back on the eastern route through Delagoa Bay. Because of its strong position and the dexterity of its negotiators, the Transvaal was able to get most of what it wanted in the 1908 discussions that led up to the creation of the Union of South Africa in 1909.

The state was to be a unitary, not a federal system of the Canadian or Australian type; the South African politicians wanted a powerful central government that could deal effectively with African rebellions like the one that the Natal government had handled with every sign of panic in 1906. It was true that in Canada federal arrangements had reduced tensions between English and French, but they had this effect because the great majority of the French-speaking population lived in communities almost completely separate from the English-speaking section and were concentrated in a single large province which could control its own cultural policy. In South Africa Natal and the Orange Free State were homogeneously British and Afrikaner respectively, but the two large provinces of the Transvaal and Cape Colony were inhabited by fairly inseparable mixtures of the two groups. Federalism would do nothing to reduce their problems. So the new state emerged as a union, recognizing the claims of the former colonies by establishing the administration at Pretoria, the parliament at Cape Town, and the central law courts at Bloemfontein. As in the past, the distribution of parliamentary seats favoured the countryside at the expense of the towns, and it also favoured all the other provinces at the expense of the Cape. The divisive question of giving Africans the vote was handled by confirming the existing practices of the four colonies: the Cape gave the vote to any man who met a property qualification low enough not to be much of an obstacle to an African who had left his tribal organization with its system of communal property, while the other provinces confined the right to vote strictly to white men.

In South African terms this was a sound and natural compromise but in London the left-wing Liberal and the Labour MPs who took an interest in imperial affairs opposed it as an attack on the position of the Africans and called on the government to refuse to pass the British legislation needed to give legal effect to the union of South Africa if it contained any such provision. These Liberals were in a paradoxical position: they had opposed the war in which the British government had established partial control over South Africa, and now they wanted the government to impose on South Africa one of the points against which the Afrikaners had most explicitly and successfully fought in the later stages of the war. But this was in a good nineteenth-century Liberal tradition; Palmerston had asserted a good many Liberal principles which he knew he could not support with anything but words. In Britain the government and its Conservative opponents were in favour of the union, which had first been suggested by Milner-appointed civil servants in 1906, and they were not going to try to impose Liberal ideas about voting qualifications on people 6,000 miles away. The British Conservatives were agreeably surprised to find how well Botha and Smuts got on with the mining interests of the Rand and how ready they were to help the mineowners resist a strike of their white workers in 1913.

The Dominions would have given Britain much less support in a quarrel about the franchise than they had done in the Boer War. They did not want to see any precedent set for British Liberals to try interfering with the way they treated their non-white populations, and were particularly concerned that they might be pressed to treat all British subjects as equal. The most immediate practical implication of this principle would have been that Indians would be allowed to come into Canada or Australia as freely as Englishmen did. Supporters of the 'White Australia' protested loudly against any such attempt to undermine the workingman's standard of living and resisted it in the way that their forefathers had resisted the influx of convicts around 1850. Objections to non-Europen immigrants were not yet so firmly established in Canada, and the Canadian Pacific Railway had been able to bring in Chinese indentured labour for a good deal of the building work in the 1880s. But opposition to Asian immigration was growing in strength, especially on the Pacific coast, and the Canadian government was moving towards a policy of allowing white immigration only. Laurier was fortunate enough to have a young politician of great charm, Mackenzie King, to smooth unpleasant things over, and in the early years of the century he negotiated agreements to keep out Chinese, Japanese, and Indian workers.

Non-European governments disliked the attitude of the Dominions, but accepted the fact that the most they could gain in negotiations was to put exclusion upon some nominally non-racial basis such as a literacy test which could be used to let middle-class visitors travel freely and to leave open the possibility that the government might change its policy by administrative decision in future. The government of India found itself in a difficult position, because it had to contend for the principle of the equality of all British subjects at a time when the dominion governments were making it clear that they did not accept the principle, and it had to look after the interests of Indians who had already settled in the Dominions, without presenting its case on either issue in a way that would damage imperial unity.

The Indian community in Natal, which was spreading out into the rest of South Africa, was one of the emigrant groups under severe pressure. The newly-created Union of South Africa set out to impose limits on the ways Indians could earn a living, and tried to drive them back from shop-keeping and small-scale business enterprises into serving as wage labour in the way they had done when they first came to the country. The Indians resisted this with a certain amount of success; it was clear that no more Indians were going to come in and that those already in the country would remain in a subordinate position, but they were at least able to gain assurances that their status would not be made any worse. Smuts handled the negotiations for the South African government in the years before 1914, and was impressed by the character of the Indian leader, Mohandas Gandhi, a lawyer who had been practising in South Africa for some years and working out a technique of non-violent resistance that compelled a civilized government to take him seriously. He was helped by the unity of the Indian community, which did not become divided into Hindu and Muslim groups as had happened in India. He was also helped by the fact that this was a defensive campaign. The Indians were only trying to keep what they already had and had no hope of getting political representation, which they enjoyed to only a limited extent in their native land.

The situation in India had been changing a little just when Gandhi's campaign of non-violent resistance was going on in South Africa. In 1898, when Lord Curzon became Viceroy, political activity in India had died down to a very low level, and he was bold enough to say that one of his objectives was to preside over the peaceful demise of the Indian National Congress. But everything he did in India involved raising the level of political activity by stirring the administration to intervene in more and more aspects of Indian life. Curzon need not be taken to have revived Congress single-handed, but he forced the political temperature up, and in practically every way that he did this the effect was to encourage Congress. When some British troops raped Indian women and their regiment tried to cover it up, Curzon stepped forward to condemn the regiment; the British in India complained so loudly at his intervention that they showed the Indians that the Viceroy was not an autocrat at the head of an undivided structure of power, even though his opponents in this case certainly had no intention of encouraging Indians to criticize the government. Curzon was also fluent about the deficiencies of character of the Indians, and this naturally led them to resent his imperial condescension.

At a more substantive level, Curzon did most to provoke political activity by his partition of the densely populated province of Bengal into a mainly Hindu western half and a mainly Muslim eastern half. There was a lot to be said for this on administrative grounds; the province was far too large and rather too diverse in economic and in religious terms (as its subsequent history was to show) to be at all easy to handle as a unit. But partition was a blow to the regional feeling of educated Congress-minded Bengalis, and was fairly clearly inspired by a belief that the opposition to the government would be easier to control if it was divided. Partition provided Indian leaders with an obvious grievance which strengthened the hands of the more extreme members of the revived Congress. The leader of the extremists, Tilak, was in a number of ways a voice from the past, and more particularly from the Hindu past. The Society for the Removal of Obstacles to the Hindu Religion responded to his arguments and concluded that the logical next step was to embark on a programme of assassination. The Congress moderates, organized by Gokhale, tried to hold Tilak back and stop him from committing the organization to armed rebellion, and eventually decided in 1906 that the only way to keep the extremists out was to bring Dadabhai Naoroji, the most distinguished Indian politician of an earlier generation, back from London to take over the presidency of Congress. Even with this powerful reinforcement for the moderates Congress had by 1908 moved on to asking for the same system of government as the Dominions, though making it clear that this was to be achieved by peaceful means.

Curzon's activity caused trouble but it also brought some advantages. His readiness to follow an independent Indian foreign policy and his desire to provide safe passage for Indians who wanted to go on pilgrimage to Mecca led him to start asserting the authority of the government of India over the pirates of the Gulf with whom it had had ill-defined relations ever since a treaty made in 1820 acknowledged the position of some of them, known as the Trucial States. He improved education, especially for agriculture, and continued the great irrigation works. He reduced the age-old salt tax. And he made both Indians and Englishmen aware of the artistic and architectural beauty of past centuries that was rotting in neglect. He also did several things that infuriated his ministerial superiors in London. At a time when Balfour's government wanted a period of calm in foreign policy he advanced into Tibet. He quarrelled with Kitchener, who had moved from Africa to the post of Commander-in-Chief in India, and eventually in 1905 chose to resign as Viceroy rather than give way.

The government had had enough of this attempt to have a policy made in Calcutta that was quite distinct from London's policy and appointed a successor, Lord Minto, who would have been an ideal man to maintain the status quo without causing trouble. But when the Liberals came to office later in the year, Minto was faced by John Morley, a prudent reformer, as Secretary of State. In the nineteenth century Viceroys had laid down policy, and even the completion of the cable for sending telegrams to India in 1865 had not really enabled the Secretary of State to assert the authority of London. But in the twentieth century, possibly because of the alarming example of Curzon, Viceroys lost a good deal of their power and the Secretary of State took the lead in deciding most important changes of policy, though power returned to the Viceroy when attacks on the structure of British authority made it possible for him to claim that only a man directly in touch with the situation could see what had to be done to maintain stable government.

Morley had gained his position in politics mainly because of his commitment to Home Rule for Ireland. Just as in Ireland, he did not want to see people put in prison in India for political offences, which usually simply meant expressing opinions that anyone in Britain was free to utter, so he began by pressing the Viceroy to release as many of these prisoners as possible. He wanted Indians to have more scope for political activity, though he did not mean to play the final role in deciding policy or to give India the same position as the Dominions, much as Home Rule would not have given Ireland the same degree of autonomy as the Dominions. The argument between Morley and Minto came mainly over the government's readiness to see Indians entrusted with more power at the legislative and at the executive level than the 1892 legislation had allowed. The admission in 1909 of Sinha, a very successful Calcutta lawyer, to the Viceroy's Executive Council as legal member (the post held by Macaulay seventy years earlier) was seen as a considerable step, but in the long run it was of much greater significance that Morley and the Liberals passed legislation to expand the councils set up in 1892 and to provide that at the provincial level civil servants were no longer to hold an automatic government majority in the assembly. This sort of step in Australia in the 1840s had been the immediate forerunner of responsible government, though the British system in India looked far more immovable than the rather fragile government in Australia had done.

In the new councils the non-official majority was to be made up of elected members, some of them chosen to represent special interests; some members, as in the 1892 system, were to be elected as representatives of the Muslims, and early in his Viceroyalty the argument was put to Minto that, in a system which the whole electorate voted for the Muslim representative, it was in effect the Hindu majority who chose who was to represent the Muslims. The only way to find people who would say what Muslims were really thinking was to have the Muslims elected by a separate electorate of voters listed by religion. The British acceptance of this argument in the 1909 Act was afterwards seen by Congress as an important step that made the Muslims more likely than before to think of themselves as a separate community. The Muslims replied that until the discussions leading up to Morley's 1909 Act the idea of power passing into Indian hands had been so distant that it did not seem to matter how their representatives were chosen, but that the Morley–Minto reforms had made it necessary to think about the way that things might change in future. The Muslims at this stage showed no sign of wanting a separate state of their own. Religious divisions obviously were important in India, just as lines between one religion and another were given more prominence than linguistic and ethnic differences by political leaders in Canada when they drafted the British North American Act as their constitution, and, while they were not the only problem, religious disagreements were clearly the division that made it hardest to evolve a unified Indian nationalism.

In 1885 it was perfectly possible to see Congress as the expression of the desire of western-educated Indians to be treated just like Englishmen without any prejudice being allowed to hold them back. By 1909 Congress was less concerned with individual opportunities and more interested in nationalist claims than it had been at first. The power of Indian opinion was given some recognition in 1911 when, as part of the celebrations of the Coronation of George V, it was announced that the divided parts of Bengal would be reunited (though non-Bengali-speaking areas in the west and north-east were excluded from the new Bengal). At the same time it was announced that the capital was to be moved from Calcutta to Delhi. As a measure in urban planning, it was a merciful relief to remove one of the attractions that drew people magnetically to the expanding and chaotic city; other changes might be needed, but the transfer held out some hope of controlling Calcutta's headlong growth. At the time everyone saw the move to Delhi in much more political terms: the British saw it as the final statement that they sat on the throne of the Moghuls and held an unshakeable position in India, and the Indian nationalists saw it as a sign that the British were alarmed by Calcutta's increasing political activism and wanted to retreat to a city that could be policed more easily. The move to the great new capital city designed by Baker and Lutyens, in a fairly successful blend of eastern and western styles, coincided with a shift of emphasis in Congress. At first the movement had drawn most of its support from the educated men of the great seaports which had been created by British trade. By 1914 Congress was winning support in the cities inland which could provide a much wider base for the movement. The effect of this was not obvious while power remained in the hands of constitution-minded leaders, but the nationalist upsurge of the First World War shook their position and greatly reduced the influence of the men from the seaports over the movement.

While the Secretary for India was gaining in authority because he had more control over the Viceroy, the Secretary for the Colonies was losing some of his importance, mainly because direct relations with the Dominions were becoming a matter for Prime Ministers and technical questions like the co-ordination of arrangements for defence were being handled by the British and Dominion government departments concerned with them. In the nineteenth century the Colonial Office had devoted a lot of its time to the affairs of the self-governing colonies, but after 1900 it turned to the creation of an administrative system for the new empire that had been acquired in the last decades of the nineteenth century. If people had ever intended to 'peg out claims for the future', in the mining prospector's language, they were now faced with the problem of raising funds to develop their claims. British East Africa, which had been taken over from the chartered company because the revenue would not cover even the rather sketchy administration provided by the company, was obviously not going to be able to cover its own expenses and it had to be supported by grants-in-aid for some years. The administrative frontiers were redrawn; at first Uganda had been based upon the area under the authority of the Kabaka of Buganda, and it was very soon extended to take in the whole area around the British half of Lake Victoria, while the land between the lake and the sea was left as British East Africa. But as the idea of settlement in the empty areas of high land along the equator began to attract rich Englishmen who felt restricted and short of space at home (of whom Lord Delamere, who after earlier visits settled permanently in January 1903, was the leader and perhaps the archetype), the slogan that Kenya was to be a 'white man's country' began to be heard. In 1902 the frontier was redrawn to give it more territory, including most of the area through which the railway ran and most of the high ground up to the Ugandan lakes.

One source of trouble for the future was that the nomadic Kikuyu had not intended to give up the highland area for ever. The small group of British settlers who moved into what became known as the 'white highlands' were arriving at a time when the area was empty but was not regarded by Africans as unclaimed. Partly because of this, East Africa was not quiet and peaceful enough for prosperous farming and frugal administration in the dozen years after the British moved in. So far as the British were concerned, the question of their claim to the land had been settled when they made treaties with the local rulers and when their position based on those treaties had been accepted by the Germans and Italians who owned the adjacent colonies. When trouble broke out, punitive expeditions were organized to bring the situation under control; at the same time the British saw these revolts as a form of disobedience and backsliding on the part of their new subjects, and later on African nationalists saw them as an early stage of African resistance to imperial rule.

Both of these views rested on the assumption that there was something unusual about fighting breaking out in Africa, but this was hardly the case. Only a very successful African ruler could bring about the level of peace and quiet that the British found necessary, and he would probably have had to fight to establish his position at first. What the British took for disobedience was often the normal activity of African society, and what later spokesmen for African independence took for an assertion of nationalism was simply a failure to realize how large a change European governments, strengthened by their system of officials and their sense of permanence, were going to bring. In Africa, local wars had been as normal as in medieval Europe; Africa was in two decades pushed through a process which in countries like England and France had taken two centuries, from 1450 to 1650. By about 1910 most of Africa had reached the stage where it was accepted that the colonial governments had a monopoly of the right to use force.

This pacification benefited the revenue. The Kenya government ran for some years at a loss which cost the British taxpayer about £100,000 a year, but by 1912 it was covering its costs and could raise loans on the commercial market in London. The growing number of rather wealthy British settlers made this easier, and helped provide the cash crops such as coffee and pyrethrum which travelled as freight on the railway line and made it much less of a money-loser than the government had feared. British settlers were not essential for getting cash crops grown for export; there was no great influx into Uganda, because it was rather low-lying and also had no stretches of empty territory to tempt them, but its economy managed well enough by growing cotton and the structure of African society remained relatively untouched.

Because of the climate British farmers were never likely to establish family estates and settle in west Africa, but around 1910 there was a debate whether British investors should be allowed to develop the area by cultivating large plantations. The colonial governments were never enthusiastic about it, and cocoa-growing in the Gold Coast developed in a way that showed it was not necessary. The world was consuming more and more cocoa, mainly because the demand for it as a beverage or a flavouring was now supplemented by the growing market for chocolate to eat. The Gold Coast made the most rapid and the most efficient response to this new opportunity and for the first half of the century cocoa cultivation, developed almost entirely by Africans, made the Gold Coast into one of the richest countries in Africa. Government agricultural advisers believed that yields would improve if they could get the growers to root out diseased trees sooner, but the success of the crop was quite adequate enough to show that there was no need for a plantation system run by British firms. In Nigeria the palm-oil trade continued to do well and the trading firms went on buying from Africans rather than starting plantations. The interior of the Gold Coast (formally referred to as the Gold Coast protectorate, as distinct from the colony, which was the partially westernized coastal area) was so much dominated by Asanti that once the Asantahene accepted Britain's rule the whole area could be ruled with little disturbance. In Nigeria there were revolts and local wars until about 1914, though they caused the British rulers no more inconvenience than the wars in East Africa and were probably of much the same significance.

For twenty-five years Nigeria's development was moulded by Lugard, who had served as the Royal Niger Company's military leader and then became Governor of Northern Nigeria and eventually was the governor under whose leadership North and South Nigeria had been united for administrative purposes by 1914. In the north he had defeated but not deposed the ruling emirs in a series of wars from 1901 to 1903, and had then tried to place them in much the same position as the Indian princes occupied under the British raj. This reduced the dislocation that British expansion was bound to cause in African society, and enabled the British to rule the north with a minimum of friction through District Commissioners who gave their views to African rulers tactfully and accepted the fact that sometimes, on matters not of vital importance, the Africans had to be allowed to ignore the advice they had been given. Maintaining the prestige and the self-respect of the African rulers was worth a little inconvenience, if only because this approach kept down the level of government spending. This technique had been used with many rulers from the sophisticated Indian princes to the more vulnerable headmen of Northern Borneo, but Lugard made people more conscious of what they were doing. Under the name of Indirect Rule the system was applied in several African colonies; there were rulers in Uganda and Asanti and Basutoland who could take on just the same role as the emirs in Northern Nigeria.

Leaving power in the hands of the traditional rulers held back the process of modernization, and Lugard was not so convinced of the virtues of the modern world that he wanted to draw Africans into it at all quickly. Indirect Rule raised a more immediate problem: the local administrators adopted the principle 'First find your chief', and then gave him the government support implied by the policy. This was perfectly reasonable in Northern Nigeria but in other areas the ruler's position under African custom was much less secure and by protecting him from being deposed the British were changing the local political structure. Rulers in eastern Nigeria were so weak that anthropologists concluded there were no chiefs, and Indirect Rule was hard to establish. In most places the system worked satisfactorily; it enabled the British to run their new territories without large grants in aid from Westminster and still carry out in Nigeria some of the liberal changes on which British public opinion insisted. Slavery was ended by stages, in the same way as in most African colonies: first trading was forbidden, then the status of slavery was abolished, placing slaves in the same position as slaves in Britain after Somersett's case in 1774 allowed a slave to leave his owner if he wished and look after himself without any fear of punishment, and finally slave-owning was declared illegal. By 1914 the process had been brought almost to completion with none of the conflict that might have been caused by ending a traditional form of property that had been almost the only way of employing labour in non-money economies.

Lugard and his disciples in colonial administration (who often had started their careers in Northern Nigeria and then went on to hold enough colonial governorships to cause some jealousy) approved of this sort of change but both their devotion to the traditional system of authority and their dislike of trade and capitalism led them to oppose the advancement of the 'educated African'. Indirect Rule by the existing rulers was a policy for the interior; on the coast which had been affected by centuries of British trade many Africans, like those in the Gambia in the 1870s, depended on the British connection and expected to be a part of it. Their position was deteriorating in the opening decades of the new century; as progress in fighting malaria made it easier for Englishmen to survive in jobs in West Africa, the Africans were no longer given the responsible jobs as civil servants, churchmen, and officers which they had held in the nineteenth century. Their reaction to this was not expressed in nationalist terms, and it would have been hard for them to use such terms because the local political units were not yet clearly fixed in men's minds. Educated Africans of the coast had been taught in Christian missionary schools and read newspapers written for the small group in the West African colonies who wanted to be black Englishmen treated as equals by white men. They had very few links with the rural hinterland, and had much more in common with other educated Africans in other colonies a short sea-voyage away than with the rest of the Africans in the same colony. In India there was a common historical heritage to look back on, and a single administration to deal with; the four colonies of West Africa had all been created by British desire for expansion and by European diplomacy, so none of them had a unifying basis of a common culture and in all four of them there were sharp differences of education and religion between the Africans of the coast and those of the interior.

As time passed, politically active Africans recognized that the best prospects for effective action lay in trying to influence the policy of the governor of their own colony, and that they stood a better chance of doing this when they could show that his policy affected a large number of people in the colony. It was natural that the first political response of those who had hoped to become black Englishmen (or black Frenchmen) was to turn to pan-Africanism – the idea that all Africans had a cause to unite them against all Europeans – when it was clear that assimilation on a basis of equality was not a practical programme. Pan-Africanism appealed to most of the tiny handful of Africans who had received a higher education, but it meant very little to ordinary traders and farmers, even though they might be well informed and have a clear idea of what they wanted the government of their colony to do. Most Africans, when they were drawn into politics, saw it as a matter of reacting to the government they had to deal with, and in this way African nations were created initially as a reaction to the colonial governments imposed on them. The leaders of the colonial administration had to treat the newly established colony as a political entity in its own right: Lugard was not a Nigerian nationalist, but when Northern and Southern Nigeria were united in 1914 he was the first person to be able to see Nigeria as a country which could enjoy some degree of control over its own affairs, and a certain amount of his time as Governor-General was spent arguing with the Colonial Office to get more grant-in-aid support.

Some critics of the partition of Africa talked about the European boundaries that ignored tribal divisions, and at times argued as though they wanted time and trouble to be spent on enabling better tribal-based boundaries to be established. The organizers of imperial expansion thought that they had recognized existing divisions by drawing frontiers which accepted the boundary between the authority of one treaty-signing chief and the next, but it was certainly true that imperial boundaries cut through some linguistic groups. The problem for the future was whether people in the divided linguistic groups would organize themselves politically by asserting that they felt a unity which transcended the imperial frontiers and would sweep them away, or by accepting the imperial frontiers and reacting to the governments of the colonies in which they lived.

While the colonial administrators settled down to ruling the new colonies, British interest in the outside world turned from the empire to its more usual concern with Europe. Germany was beginning to be seen as the potential enemy in any future war, in much the way that France had been for most of the previous 200 years. British foreign policy and defence policy became more and more dominated by the fact that Germany was building a navy which seemed designed to win control of the North Sea, which would expose Britain to invasion or starvation. The nineteenth-century ideal of 'splendid isolation' was abandoned and the British first entered an alliance with Japan to strengthen their position in China and the Pacific; then reached an understanding with France to make sure that the alliance with Japan did not drag them into a war with France because Japan was at war with France's ally Russia; and finally made an agreement with Russia in order to work out problems that might have caused difficulties with France. So in the brief period from 1902 to 1907 Britain had been drawn into the complexities of European diplomacy by stages which the majority of cabinet ministers were not told about in the way that Asquith explained it to the Dominion Prime Ministers in 1911.

These European agreements affected Britain's position in Egypt and in the area between Egypt and India. As part of the settlement of disputes all over the world which was concluded in 1904 the French gave up their opposition to Britain's dominance in Egypt, and in return the British promised to support France's claims to a similar position in Morocco. The British administrators in Egypt did not notice that their lives had become any easier after this, because the growth of Egyptian nationalism caused them more difficulties in the years between 1904 and 1914 than French complaints had ever done between 1882 and 1904. The British administrators saw their duty in much the same light as the Indian Civil Service: they wanted to raise the standard of living of the peasant majority and defend it against the middle class which was eager to gain positions of power and profit. In some ways the British position in Egypt was distinctly less comfortable: the Indian middle class had become anglicized and the opponents of British rule were for the most part highly anglicized, while the Egyptian middle class was at least as inclined to France as to Britain. On the other hand the nationalists – like their Indian counterparts – had not established any mass political movement which could bring the peasants into politics, so that the British position in Egypt before 1914 was not under serious challenge.

Further east the British interest in the Gulf had expanded beyond the Indian government's attempt to establish some control over the small pirate states there. One of the few exports from the Gulf – sea-shells to paste on papier mâché boxes – had been the original line of business of a London firm run by Marcus Samuel. When he found the demand for oil and paraffin was expanding in the east he set up a marketing organization to meet it. The new line of business, which at first concentrated on customers in the Indian Ocean, did so well that the company became almost entirely committed to the new product, though its name and corporate symbol continue to indicate its original business to the present day. The Anglo-Persian Oil Company, which had a more wide-ranging imperial flavour than Shell – the man who drove it forward, Knox D'Arcy, had done well in mining in Australia and Donald Smith, Lord Strathcona, was chairman of the board – had begun searching for oil in Iran and its eventual success there led Churchill, as First Lord of the Admiralty, to invest government money in the firm because he believed that the change from coal-fired to oil-fired boilers in warships made it necessary to have a supply of oil that the Royal Navy could control.

British interest in Iran was not confined to oil. It was less and less possible to imagine that the country could serve as part of the outer defences of India, and this was underlined when Russia moved forward to assert her authority in northern Iran in 1906 when the Qajar monarchy was faced with a revolution. Twenty years earlier Britain might have tried to oppose the Russian advance and to support the alliance of religious and political groups who were trying to set up a new constitution; in the new conditions indicated by the agreement with France the British government handled the situation by coming to an agreement with Russia, Iran was nominally left independent but for practical purposes was cut up into three sections. The politically dominant north became a Russian sphere of influence; Britain gained a substantial area in the sandy south-east to keep the Russians away from India; and the remaining third was left as a neutral zone between the two. The division was shaped by the old politics of the balance of power and was uninfluenced by the new politics of oil. The oil fields were in the neutral zone, and the British showed no desire to extend their zone west along the Gulf to include them.

The First World War

Agreements like this helped to bring Britain into the system of alliances which decided how countries would respond when the First World War broke out in 1914 over problems in the Balkans which meant little to Britain and had even less to do with the imperial expansion of the preceding decades. But while the reasons for going to war over Serbian or Belgian problems really could not have meant much to them, people all over Europe and throughout the British Empire were swept forward by enthusiasm for the struggle. The main effect on the British Empire was to encourage national feelings that were expressed, entirely sincerely, in terms of great attachment to Britain and yet turned out to have the effect of helping to dissolve the empire. Soldiers went out to fight because Britain was at war, but they found that they fought as Canadians or as Australians.

The landing of the Australian and New Zealand Army Corps at what became known as Anzac Bay did not lead to military success in the attempt to force open the Dardanelles Straits, capture Constantinople, and open a supply route to Russia, but it did mark a moment at which the two Dominions found themselves acting as nations in a way they had not done before, and Anzac Day became a national holiday. Vimy Ridge in 1917 came to have much the same meaning for a generation of Canadians. Men on the continent of Europe had little chance to show individual commitment to the war because their armies were made of conscripts summoned from peace-time life by carefully prepared plans; military service throughout the British Empire had been voluntary, except for militia training in Australia, so the war began with immense efforts to raise armies of volunteers and this effort went on as part of the background to the struggle. Appeals had to be made to patriotic feeling not just to raise volunteers but also to keep people devoted to what became more and more a struggle that involved the whole population of each country taking part. The patriotism to which these appeals were made was that of Britain and of the individual Dominions, not that of the British Empire as a whole, which reflected people's feelings and the way that the individual dominion governments were entirely responsible for their national war efforts.

There were divisions in some of the countries of the empire. In 1914 a few Afrikaners thought the outbreak of war might be an opportunity to reverse the defeat suffered in the Boer War, but Botha and Smuts quickly subdued them, carefully using only Afrikaner troops for the purpose. When Britain decided in 1916 that voluntary recruitment could not keep up the strength of her army, conscription was not applied in Ireland out of a feeling that, although many Irishmen had volunteered, there was enough opposition to mean that conscription would be more trouble than it was worth. The outbreak of war had held up the implementation of legislation giving Ireland Home Rule; at Easter 1916 a group of determined Irishmen seized the Dublin Post Office and proclaimed the Irish Republic. The rising was crushed, and at the time was not popular; however, when the leaders were shot after trial by court-martial a feeling of sympathy for them and their cause began to grow into a force that would clearly make for great changes after the war. In Canada the province of Quebec had been perfectly willing to accept the war but saw no need for total commitment. The rest of Canada responded to this with extreme disapproval, and pointed out how much better the recruiting figures were for the rest of the country. This was not entirely fair, because one striking feature of Canadian recruitment was the number of recent British immigrants who volunteered when the war broke out, and Quebec did not provide so much smaller a contingent than other provinces when comparisons were made only from among those born in Canada. But the view became firmly established in English-speaking Canada that a greater effort was needed and that it was French-speaking Canada's fault that things were not going better. In 1917 a coalition was formed in which almost all the English-speaking Liberal leaders joined the Conservative government, conscription was imposed, and an election was held in which the government won almost every single seat in English-speaking Canada and the Liberals won every French-speaking seat in Quebec.

Britain and all the Dominions showed the same desire to find governments completely committed to conducting the war energetically. At first the Dominion governments accepted Britain's leadership with little question, partly because of the immense efforts Britain was making but also because they thought the British leaders would know more about organizing for war than anyone else did. They found, to their surprise, that Britain's efficiency in war came nowhere close to equalling her determination. Perhaps the surprise was unjustified; nobody had any real idea of what a long-drawn-out war involving the whole population would be like, and Dominion governments which had carried out large-scale projects for public development building railways had had a type of experience that no British politician possessed. As the war went on, it became clear that British leadership would not be taken for granted, and the British responded to this reasonably well. Coalition governments were formed in Britain and Australia as well as in Canada; allowing for some local differences it could be said that each of these governments was an alliance of the Conservatives with those of the Left who felt most committed to fighting the war; and, more generally still, it could be said that the shape of party politics for a generation to come was laid down by wartime changes in most of the countries of the empire.

Lloyd George, the Liberal who emerged as the British Prime Minister at the head of a coalition government at the end of 1916, was much more energetic than Asquith, and realized the importance of discussing policy with the Dominion Prime Ministers. In 1917 he called together a conference of the Prime Ministers and took advantage of the occasion to set up what he called an Imperial War Cabinet; it was in fact simply the British War Cabinet discussing problems with the visiting Prime Ministers. Nobody could insist on its showing full cabinet solidarity, because no Prime Minister would resign the position to which his own people had elected him simply because he disagreed with the policy undertaken by the others in London. But while there was no formal cabinet solidarity there was the pressure of the common purpose of winning the war, an objective which in 1917 did not seem at all certain to be achieved. This encouraged a degree of unity so complete that it seemed sure to survive after the war; none of the wartime leaders were weakened by doubts about their own capacity to look after their countries' interests, so they could meet on a comfortable basis of equality.

Imperial relations changed a great deal from the position of the years before 1914: at the 1911 conference Asquith and Grey had explained the problems of diplomacy to men who knew so little about them that they had no real basis for criticizing British policy, but by 1917 the trust that the Dominion Prime Ministers placed in Lloyd George was based on their recognition that he claimed no superiority for himself apart from what he could win by his own dexterity and eloquence. The Imperial War Cabinet expressed its attitude to the problems of the post-war world in a series of resolutions, one of which accepted a tariff policy of imperial preference as a desirable objective, and it was agreed that in future the Prime Ministers would work out an imperial foreign policy towards the rest of the world by a process of 'continuous consultation'.

The Commonwealth after the War

This approach was applied very satisfactorily at the Peace Conference. When other nations at Versailles refused to accept the Dominions' claims to be represented there, the British Empire delegation replied that the Dominions had put much larger armies into the field than most of the smaller sovereign states at the Conference. The legislation to raise the armies, the taxation to pay for them, and the administration to run them had all been provided by the governments of the Dominions, which had acted as independent governments running their own policies. This argument was accepted, and the Dominions gained the advantage of being represented as part of the British delegation for some issues, which meant they could enlist the support of a major participant, while on other issues they were represented individually. Smut's ingenuity affected the whole financial shape of the Treaty: by persuading several leaders that the costs of war pensions ought to be included in the bill for reparations presented to Germany, he greatly increased the total size of the bill and also substantially increased the proportion of the total that was assigned to be paid to Britain.

Smuts also helped clarify the section of the Treaty devoted to mandates: the victorious allies were determined that Germany should lose all her colonies, but it did not seem quite consistent for the victors simply to seize the territories and make them into colonies of their own. So the doctrine emerged that former German colonies were to be held under mandates from the League of Nations, and that countries administering them should be responsible to the League. With this proviso, most of the German colonies were taken over by countries of the British Empire (or, as it was just beginning to be called, the British Commonwealth): Australia was given responsibility for the portion of New Guinea she had wanted Britain to secure in 1884, New Zealand was given Samoa, and South Africa was given

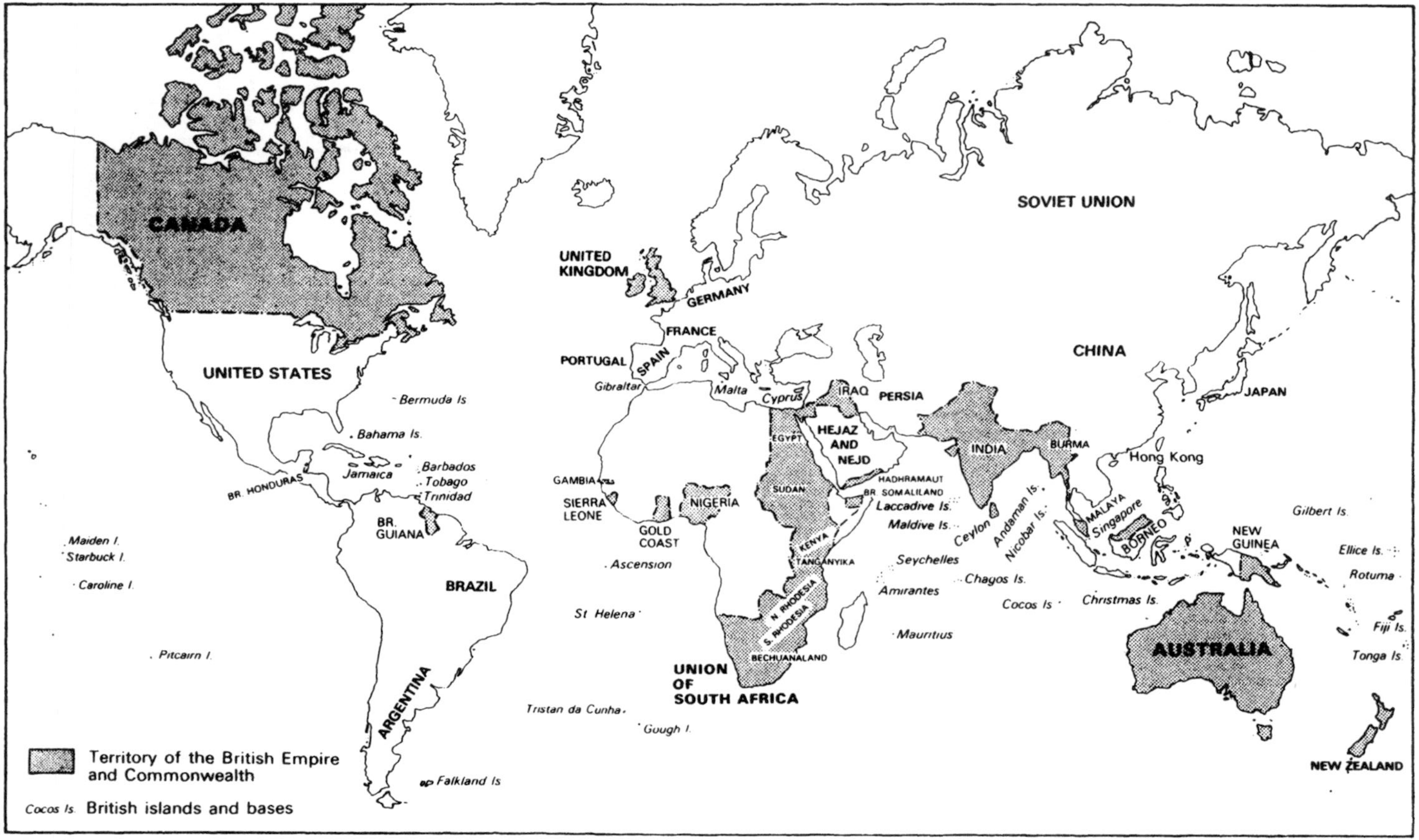

Map 13 The Empire in 1920

Territory of the British Empire and Commonwealth

British islands and bases

Cocos Is

SOVIET UNION

CHINA

JAPAN

NEW GUINEA

AUSTRALIA

NEW ZEALAND

UNITED KINGDOM

GERMANY

FRANCE

SPAIN

PORTUGAL

Gibraltar

Malta

Cyprus

IRAQ

PERSIA

HEJAZ AND NEJD

INDIA

BURMA

Hong Kong

Singapore

Ceylon

Andaman Is

Nicobar Is

Gilbert Is

Ellice Is

Rotuma

Fiji Is

Tonga Is

Christmas Is

Cocos Is

Chagos Is

Maldive Is

Laccadive Is

Seychelles

Amirantes

Mauritius

HADHRAMAUT

BR. SOMALILAND

SUDAN

NIGERIA

GOLD COAST

GAMBIA

SIERRA LEONE

Ascension

St Helena

KENYA

TANGANYIKA

N. RHODESIA

S. RHODESIA

BECHUANALAND

UNION OF SOUTH AFRICA

Gough I.

Tristan da Cunha

UNITED STATES

CANADA

Bermuda Is

Bahama Is

Jamaica

BR. HONDURAS

Barbados

Tobago

Trinidad

BR. GUIANA

BRAZIL

ARGENTINA

Falkland Is

Maiden I.

Starbuck I.

Caroline I.

Pitcairn I.

German South-West Africa. Britain was given Tanganyika (previously Germany East Africa), and also gained other mandate territories from the Arab portion of the Turkish Empire, which were held under terms that made it clear that the inhabitants would have some control over their own future and were organized in the following three or four years into the states of Iraq, Transjordan, and Palestine.

All of this made it look as if what might be called the 'Land of Hope and Glory' programme for Britain – 'Wider and wider yet, Shall thy bounds be set' – had been given a more speedy and a more literal fulfilment than anyone would have expected before 1914. But this was something of an illusion; the upsurge of national feeling in the Dominions meant that they would expect to be placed on much more of an equal footing with Britain in the British Commonwealth than they had enjoyed in the pre-1914 Empire. In addition, they had developed their own industries during the war, and so had become less dependent on a large British market to take a steady flow of exports.

A much larger change – probably the largest change in the political ordering of the world caused by the war, and one which was bound to affect the British Empire – was the break-up of empires. Austria-Hungary and Turkey were empires in the sense that a variety of national groups were gathered in a single political unit held together more by loyalty to an emperor (or sultan) and his government than by any sense of common nationality. Both of these states were shattered by the war. The division of the Austro-Hungarian Empire and the rearrangement of its territory within half a dozen states based on national principles had economic disadvantages forecast by J. M. Keynes in his *Economic Consequences of the Peace*, but nobody wanted to listen to such a doctrine and this part of the book passed unnoticed. In much the way that Austria looked like the heir to the Austro-Hungarian or Habsburg Empire because it contained the capital and was the home of the old German rulers, the Anatolian lands that kept the name of Turkey looked like the heir to the Turkish or Ottoman Empire while its Arab subjects, who had been prepared to put up with the rule of the Sultan, were certainly not going to accept the modernizing state that his successors tried to create.

Two other, more securely established land empires suffered much less change. The Emperor of Germany fell, and a good deal of the non-German periphery of his state like Alsace-Lorraine was transferred to nearby nation-states, but the Germans at the core of the old empire still made up a formidable nation. After the fall of the Tsar the Bolshevik successor state committed itself to hostility to all imperial rule, but it also devoted itself to a desperate struggle to hold on to as much as possible of the Tsar's territories and, despite some losses of land in eastern Europe, the Soviet Union was generally successful in maintaining the old boundaries of Russia. Its readiness to support the opposition to all other empires provided a base, ideological and sometimes financial, for a wide range of nationalist movements.

On the face of it, the weakening or break-up of these empires was a matter of European politics. The overseas empires of France, Portugal, Belgium, and the Netherlands stood unshaken by the war, and the change that the development of the Dominions might cause to the British Empire was far from obvious. Experience in Europe turned out to show how things would go in the future: if new nations could emerge, and old empires be swept away in Europe, perhaps the same thing could happen in Asia and Africa. If nationalism asserted itself, it might be able to destroy any empire undergoing difficulties like the defeats in war that had undermined the empires which lost control of their subject nationalities in 1918. A successful and powerful empire might reasonably expect to continue to have a magnetic power over its subjects that would make them continue to think that it was better to live in a great empire than to be a citizen of a small nation which was likely to be the prey of its powerful neighbours. The terms of the equation might change in the future: empires might lose their magnetic power, nationalism might come more and more to be seen as the only acceptable way to hold a state together, and the world might be made safer for small nations. In 1919 none of these changes could be called inevitable, and the overseas empires seemed to have generations of life in them.

A change in Britain that was almost as large as any change in the rest of the empire was the establishment of democracy, with the arrival of almost complete adult suffrage. There had been parliaments and elections in Britain for several centuries, but they had been elections to show which members of the ruling class commanded most support among the men who were high enough up the social scale to be entrusted with the right to vote. This was an electoral, and a representative, system that expressed very well the sense of graduated power stretching from the monarch down to the humblest subject: if many men and all women in Britain had no right to vote, then it was relatively easy to say that at least for the time being men and women in the empire could not expect to have any greater control over their own destiny. In the nineteenth century it had become possible to think that the right to vote might become more and more widely spread through British society, and might even lead on to universal suffrage. If that happened, it would be rather harder for the British to talk as though the whole empire was an elegantly sloping pyramid in which most of the upper ranks were held by Englishmen but in which there was no doubt that an Indian maharajah or a French-Canadian lawyer was more important than a member of the English lower classes. If there was to be universal suffrage in Britain, and effective rule of the empire from Britain, then the problems of the 1760s were likely to recur; people in the colonies might accept the rule of a noble government in Britain but they were not very likely to accept the rule of the whole British people; and, while a British aristocracy could assert its rule over the whole empire simply on the grounds that it always did rule as natural superiors ought to, the British people could assert its rule over the whole empire only on the basis of some very explicit theory of racial superiority, to which it had made no claim. The incompatibility of democracy and empire had been asserted in the past, though nobody had seen how a racial theory could be used to claim authority for one group over another group. In the Britain of 1919 there were many more important questions to be handled immediately, and the problems of reconciling British and imperial constitutional develop-ments were ignored completely.

At the end of the war British politicians were much more worried about the ambitions and prospects of the United States. The German Navy had scuttled itself in 1919; the only possible challenge to British seapower was that of the United States, but it was quite clear that the United States could build a navy bigger than Britain's if she wanted to. A more general threat to Britain's position in the world was also associated with the United States. Britain's powerful position in the nineteenth century depended to a great extent on the communications systems provided by railways, steamships, and underwater cables, in each of which British development had been very important. By 1918 the revival of road transport after the century of the railway was already visible, and it seemed quite likely that aeroplanes, telephones, and broadcasting would be the important forces of the future. These new forms of communication offered opportunities which the Americans seized and which the British approached with the restraint of men who thought that the old ways might well be the best ways. The shift from coal to oil was another change that could only weaken Britain's imperial position. These changes did not so much mean that Britain was in danger as that she could no longer be so sure of playing her nineteenth-century role as the country which the world – and in particular the English-speaking world – believed was able to chart the course that other countries would follow in the future.

Until the war the view east across the Atlantic from the United States was dominated by Britain; after the war American writers became much more willing to think about the United States as a cultural centre in its own right (and to believe that the proper place from which to observe it was Paris). American writers no longer became Englishmen as James and Eliot did; perhaps the change is most precisely indicated in Fitzgerald's *This Side of Paradise* with its shift from an England-dominated view of life and literature in the first, pre-war half of the book to a self-contained American view in the second half. No change of this sort could readily be seen in any of the Dominions, though there was a change of some importance in Canadian-American relations. Until the First World War many Americans thought it was Canada's manifest destiny to join the United States when she completed the process of becoming independent of Britain, with the inevitable result that any Canadian who expressed feelings of close friendship was assumed, both north and south of the border, to be working for a united North America. The war convinced the United States that this was not going to happen, and relations became more amicable. By the 1930s it was possible to speak of the Canadian-American frontier as the 'undefended border', a phrase that would not have made much sense in earlier decades. To the extent that Canadian attachment to Britain was based on a desire for a strong ally against the United States the reduction of tension in North America lessened the need for a close relationship with Britain. In 1900 hostile comments on Britain and her empire were to be heard more often in Australia than in Canada; by 1930 feelings in Canada had changed perceptibly, and Australia's friendly feelings to Britain – which owed something to fear of Japan – survived even the appearance of an English cricket team which showed a positively Australian determination to win the Ashes in the 1932–3 series.

Britain had been alarmed by the difficulties of the war and impressed by the performance of the Dominions; in many ways the 1920s and 1930s were the period in which the British were most aware of their empire, rebuilt parts of London (especially around the Aldwych) in a way that stressed Commonwealth connections, and tried to include some explanation of the empire in their schools. It had of course become more diverse than ever, and harder than ever to explain. The Versailles Conference increased the complexities: Canada, Australia, South Africa, and New Zealand were self-governing and became members of the League of Nations; India was not self-governing, but also became a member of the League; Newfoundland was self-governing, and did not become a member of the League. No doubt this simply meant that the League decided that India was important and Newfoundland was not, but it showed what a complicated system the British were running. There was of course no logical reason why any colony should have the same constitution as any other, but the numbers of differences – granted the broad outline that a colony needed a governor, and a governor needed a small council to advise him on day-by-day policy and a larger council or assembly to give legal validity to laws and taxes – was so striking that any attempt to explain it in terms of a general plan would only have added to the confusion.

Theorists who generalized about the pattern of development would say that new Dominions emerged by making the ministers in the governor's small council responsible to the majority in the assembly, rather than to the governor as the representative of the Secretary of the Colonies. That was a reasonable enough statement in principle, but in fact the only new Dominion to emerge in the years between the world wars came into existence in a different way. In the United Kingdom general election of 1918 almost all the seats in the island of Ireland outside the six north-eastern counties were won by representatives of Sinn Fein, who had taken up the struggle of the men of 1916 and were pledged to set up their own parliament in Dublin rather than go to Westminster. Lloyd George had promised in his election programme that he would put Home Rule into effect, and that he would provide special treatment for the protestant north-east. In 1920 he tried to meet these commitments by creating two parliaments, each with the powers promised in the pre-war Home Rule bills, one for the six north-eastern counties and one for the remaining twenty-six counties. This was probably more than the north-east wanted, and it was certainly less than the rest of the island wanted. The Sinn Fein Parliament had already been making good progress in setting up a parallel government, and by 1920 was engaged in a wide-ranging civil war with the British army.

It was a time of irregular armies: the Irish Republican Army could have no legal existence, private armies were fighting across all the eastern European frontiers created by the Versailles treaty, and the British government created its own irregular armies – the black and tans, and the auxiliaries – to fight the IRA. As a military device for a civil war this was successful enough, but it weakened Englishmen's confidence in the justice of their cause to see the rough instruments that had to be used to make it effective. By 1921 it was clear to Lloyd George that he could not have the complete victory – in the sense of forcing Sinn Fein to accept the 1920 Act – for which he had hoped, and he settled down to negotiate with the Irish leaders. They wanted a republic completely independent of Britain; Lloyd George knew that his political followers would see this as a humiliation, and he wanted some check on Irish foreign policy. He was prepared to accept Sinn Fein's twenty-six counties as a Dominion, in the new sense of a state as close to independence as could be imagined; and at the end of 1921 he forced the Irish representatives to accept the status of a Dominion, called the Irish Free State and defined as having the same rights and powers as Canada. Whether the Irish negotiators really had got the best settlement they could, or had allowed themselves to be frightened more than was necessary by Lloyd George's threats to resume fighting, is a question that will never be decided. Undoubtedly the Free State was set up in a way that was bound to divide Irishmen who wanted independence, though Lloyd George warned them that, if he tried to give them more, he would be replaced by a British Prime Minister determined to give them less.

The development of national aspirations in India followed a less violent and a less embittered course. Indian sentiment responded immediately and on a vast scale to Britain's danger in war but, much as the war encouraged national consciousness in the Dominions, it helped Congress to assert India's claims to nationhood. What had been a minority pressure group for a specialized group of intellectuals turned into a large organization with some claims to be a national movement. In 1916 Congress reached an agreement with the Muslim League in the Lucknow Pact which accepted the League's desire for seats chosen by a Muslim electoral roll as provided in the 1909 Act, and this put Congress at the head of a united nationalist wave of opinion.

One of the leading roles in holding together the alliance of Congress and the League was played by Gandhi, who had come back to his native country in 1915 after his years in South Africa and was able – like a number of other nationalist leaders in later decades – to make good use of his detachment from previous disputes. South African Hindus and Muslims had worked together to resist specific attacks on their position and, once back in India, Gandhi looked for specific issues on which he could rally people in one region or another. He intervened in some conflicts which seemed at first sight to have little to do with the nationalist struggle and to be concerned with the ill-treatment or poor working conditions of peasants or factory workers. His techniques of non-violent involvement and of mass commitment helped indicate the advantages of independence to many groups and regions who would otherwise have seen it just as a step that would put the power held by the educated British into the hands of the educated Indians, without doing anything at all for ordinary people. As part of this process of building a nationalist alliance on a large number of concrete issues, Gandhi decided that the way to mobilize the Muslims against the British was to concentrate on the status of the Caliph: the Sultan of Turkey was also a religious leader, accepted by most Muslims as the successor (Khalifa) of the messenger of Allah, and because the British were attacking his position as Sultan a campaign to defend his position as Caliph might turn the Muslims in India against the British. Some Indians thought this approach artificial, but it was successful; Hindus and Muslims were able to co-operate against British rule better than at any other time.

The British had already seen the change in Indian national feeling and in 1917 moved to meet it. Lloyd George's Secretary for India, E. S. Montagu, announced very soon after taking office that the government looked forward to the 'progressive realisation of responsible government' in India. It was not clear if this meant India would reach the same position as the Dominions, just as it was not clear in the middle of the war how the position of the Dominions would change. Indian nationalists hoped for a dramatic alteration of the constitution to acknowledge the fact that India was a nation and was entitled to self-determination. Montagu's 1919 Government of India Act did not go as far as that, though it certainly showed the immense change caused by the war. At 'the centre', as the government in Delhi was always called in such discussions, there would be representative government with an assembly to pass legislation and vote taxes and in other ways take on much the same role as assemblies of British colonists had played in the decades before the Durham Report. The Viceroy still had his Council for executive purposes, with three Indian members, and could still in the last resort control the whole system through his emergency powers. At the provincial level some departments (such as the police) remained in the hands of officials responsible to the British administration but other departments were placed in the hands of elected political leaders responsible to the provincial assembly. This was complicated, but it looked transitional enough to mean that in calmer circumstances it might have been accepted as a substantial step towards responsible govenment.

At the end of the war India – like much of the rest of the world – was not in a calm mood. The world-wide influenza epidemic was killing millions of Indians, wartime prosperity was driving the rupee up in terms of the pound, and at the same time it was encouraging increases in prices that dislocated the traditional structure of commerce. The government of India was very nervous about the situation and wanted powers to control agitation, Bolshevik plots, and Congress rebellion. This led it to pass early in 1919 the extraordinarily severe Rowlatt Acts, allowing trials without juries and imprisonment on the order of a provincial governor, which provided Congress with a very easy target. Large protest meetings were held to oppose this return to the nineteenth-century limits on political activity. Most of the authorities responded to these protests in April reasonably and sensibly, but at Amritsar General Dyer was so alarmed at the thought of a new Indian Mutiny that he ordered his troops to break up a meeting by firing at it, and about 400 people were killed. The British government thought Dyer's actions indefensible, but enough Englishmen supported him to mean that the British got the worst of both worlds: they did not follow a policy of repression but they got no credit for admitting that something had gone wrong.

Congress took some time to build up its campaign but in 1920 it made very effective use of Gandhi's methods of peaceful resistance to the government by refusing to have anything to do with its orders and by boycotting British goods. Some of its members went peacefully to prison when civil disobedience led them to break the law. This approach left the British very embarrassed; a violent attack on their government could have been resisted confidently enough, probably by the methods Dyer had used, but the Gandhian approach showed that the masses of Indians who took part in this type of protest were deeply sincere and gave the British no chance to claim that their rule was being challenged by anything except the force of Indian public opinion. The immense moral strain of non-violence was in the end too much for some supporters of Congress. When the movement slipped over into violence and a group of policemen was killed by a mob, Gandhi took it as a warning that his followers were not disciplined enough to operate his system much longer. Well before his followers could see the danger that the government would be able to justify the use of repressive measures he called the campaign off. Their response was puzzled obedience rather than a full understanding of what he was doing. The government of India breathed a deep sigh of relief and charged Gandhi with encouraging rebellion, for which he was sentenced to six years' imprisonment in 1922. The government turned to ruling in the way laid down in the 1919 Act, which became accepted as the new constitution by the mid-1920s.

This meant allowing Indians some control over their own affairs. For decades they had been arguing that Indian industry needed protective tariffs, while the Civil Service insisted that this would drive up the cost of living for the poor. Under the new system the Indian government was given fiscal autonomy in 1921 and became more responsive to educated Indian opinion and less responsive to British economic theory, so it began creating a system of protective tariffs to encourage its cotton spinning and its iron and steel industry. The Indian government was becoming recognized as an international power in a way that should have pleased Curzon. Its membership of the League of Nations was a reasonable recognition of India's substantial military efforts in the World War, and yet it seemed odd to give this position to a government whose head, the Viceroy, was clearly subordinate to the Secretary of State in London. No doubt the Viceroy would take a Curzonian view of the depth of his commitment to the people of India, but no Indian nationalist could see it in that light. On the other hand, while Congress members did not agree among themselves whether they should make use of the institutions provided by the 1919 Act to put forward their objectives, they could all see how the field of action had been widened for them. Before 1914 their policy looked rather like that of the supporters of Home Rule in Ireland because, even if they could take the places of the Englishmen who held official positions in India, those positions were still subordinate to London. After 1918 the Englishmen who ruled India were doing so in a way that was less dependent on London, and in this way preparing the ground for a transfer of power that would not come as a complete shock to established British interests.

At the same time as this partial and ill-understood retreat was taking place, British rule was extending its authority in the Arab region to the west of India as a result of the dissolution of the Turkish Empire. Twenty years earlier Turkey would almost certainly have been on the same side as Britain in any European war in which the two countries were involved, but Britain's activities in Egypt and German support for the modernizing groups who were gaining power in Turkey had between them led to Turkey's entering the war on Germany's side in 1914. This led to the unsuccessful attack on the Dardanelles and it also led to British support for attacks on Turkish rule in the areas inhabited by Arabs. The British made agreements with Arab leaders, particularly with Feisal and Abdullah of the Hashemite family, they made agreements with the French, and (for reasons which lay outside the politics of the Turkish Empire) they made agreements with the Zionist section of the Jewish community. By the end of 1918 the Turks had lost control of all their Arab territories, Britain and France had moved forces into the Dardanelles and the Bosphorus, and all that remained was to apply the various agreements. France was given a mandate over Syria (though not over the whole Turkish province of that name) and Britain was given a mandate over Iraq, made up of Mesopotamia and a good deal of Kurdistan, and of Palestine, an area taken out of the old province of Syria and stretching east to Arabia and the south-western edge of Iraq.

In 1917 Britain had committed herself to establishing in Palestine a national home for the Jewish people in which the rights of the existing Arab population were to be recognized. On the spot things were less simple: Britain's leading Arab ally, Feisal, had taken control of most of the old province of Syria, and Iraq was in revolt at what looked like a simple transfer from Turkish imperial rule to British. When the French forced Feisal out of Syria, Britain compensated him by making him king of Iraq under the mandate in 1921, and also by partitioning Palestine and giving his brother Abdullah the larger and sandier portion of it under the name of Transjordan. Iraq became independent in 1932 and Transjordan remained relatively tranquil under the mandate. Palestine – the western section of the original mandate – gave everybody more trouble. Most Arabs showed no readiness to accept the small stream of Jewish immigrants in the 1920s, though local landowners sold the newcomers land at prices that were higher than anything seen before. Politicians in Britain were on the whole sympathetic to the desire of the Jews to have a country of their own and could see that they were increasing the prosperity of the mandate area; British officials in the Middle East were on the whole sympathetic to the position of the Arabs. This sympathy had its blind spots: what they admired were the splendid Arabs of the desert, unmarked by civilization, whom Lawrence of Arabia led to battle against the Turks in the last years of the war. This vivid picture underestimated the role of the gold sovereign in persuading the Arabs to come out and fight, and it helped encourage an attitude among mandate officials that was pro-Arab and anti-Zionist.

In Egypt the officials did not see the Arabs through a shimmering haze of desert sand and certainly did not like the idea of Egyptian nationalism. They were dismayed when Lord Milner and General Allenby, who were seen as the fine flower of imperial policy, became convinced that the 1914 annexation of Egypt – taken on the grounds that the country was nominally a part of the Turkish Empire – could not be made permanent and that it would be sensible to accept the Egyptian desire for independence and then retain as strong a position in Egypt as possible. This approach was followed with considerable success; Egypt became independent in 1922 but it was an independence which did not depart too far from Cromer's pre-annexation

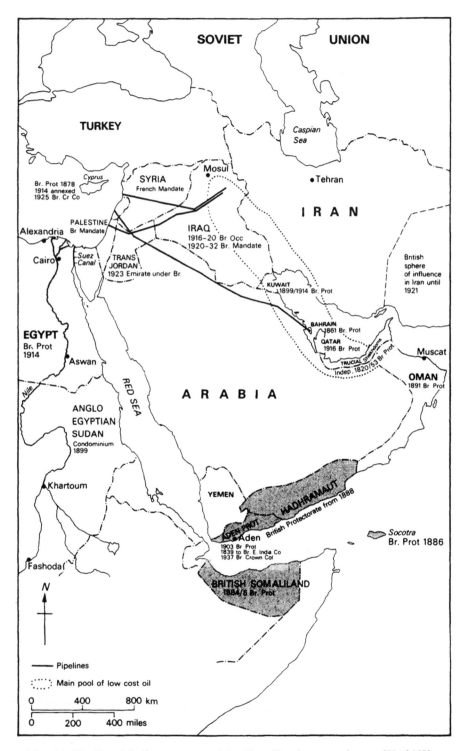

SOVIET UNION

TURKEY

Caspian
Sea

Cyprus
Br. Prot 1878
1914 annexed
1925 Br. Cr Co

SYRIA
French Mandate

Mosul

●Tehran

I R A N

PALESTINE
Br Mandate

Alexandria●

IRAQ
1916–20 Br Occ
1920–32 Br. Mandate

Cairo●

Suez
Canal

**TRANS
JORDAN**
1923 Emirate under Br.

British
sphere
of influence
in Iran until
1921

KUWAIT
1899/1914 Br. Prot

EGYPT
Br. Prot
1914

Aswan●

BAHRAIN
1861 Br Prot
QATAR
1916 Br Prot

TRUCIAL Sheikdoms
Indep. 1820/53 Br. Prot

Muscat

OMAN
1891 Br Prot

Nile

RED SEA

A R A B I A

**ANGLO
EGYPTIAN
SUDAN**
Condominium
1899

▲Khartoum

YEMEN

HADHRAMAUT

British Protectorate from 1888

Socotra
Br. Prot 1886

ADEN PROT

●Aden
1903 Br Prot
1839 to Br. E. India Co
1937 Br Crown Col

●Fashoda

BRITISH SOMALILAND
1884/6 Br. Prot

N

—— Pipelines

⋯⋯ Main pool of low cost oil

0   400   800 km

0   200   400 miles

Map 14 The East Mediterranean and the Near East between the two World Wars

system of controlling the country through a British official (after 1922, a High Commissioner) whose advice on a number of military and diplomatic subjects had to be taken very seriously. The King probably wished that the British would go away and leave him in peace. On the other hand, he could see that if he did he might be unable to resist the pressure of the Wafd, the only effective political party in the country, which had gained a great deal of support by its resistance to formal British rule in 1919 and 1920; and the Wafd recognized that the British were more of a modernizing force than the King would be if left to himself. In practice the modernizing benefits of British influence were less noticeable after 1918 than earlier, but this did not overturn the uneasy triangle of forces that had been set up.

While the British were eager to take over the Arab sections of the Turkish Empire, they were not agreed in their attitude to the Anatolian peninsula, in which the Turks made up the great majority of the population. Lloyd George, as a Gladstonian Liberal, wanted to see the influence of Greece expanded as much as possible and to see Turkey reduced in importance still further. He encouraged the Greeks to seize the western coastline of Asia Minor, where there were several seaports with Greek populations, and to march further inland to compel the Turks to accept the fact that they had lost this territory. This was an adventurous policy to follow, but British governments had done comparable things previously and saw no reason why they should consult the Dominions about activity of this sort. When Lloyd George thought of continuous consultation within the Commonwealth, he had in mind such things as the organization of the British Empire delegation to the Washington conference on the limitations of naval armaments, and the discussion of the proposal to renew the Anglo-Japanese Treaty, in which Australia and New Zealand argued in favour of renewal and Canada opposed it. It was not possible to please everyone, and the eventual decision not to renew the treaty owed a lot to pressure from the United States, but the process of consultation was taken seriously in these questions that obviously mattered to the Dominions.

Consulting the Dominions about the Turkish question seemed a much less appropriate idea, and there is no sign that they would have welcomed it. But in August 1922 the conduct of Commonwealth policy was abruptly altered by events in Asia Minor. The Turks had no intention of being forced to accept Lloyd George's neo-Gladstonianism. When the Greeks marched inland to force them to recognize Greek control of the Ionian cities the Turks rallied their forces and in the summer of 1922 defeated and routed the Greek army. The Greeks fled to the coastal cities and then had to evacuate them; those who could get into boats sailed to the nearby islands, which remained Greek; those who could not get away were massacred. Up to this point neither British nor Commonwealth interests were involved; but there were British troops on the Asian side of the Dardanelles, still maintaining the occupation begun in 1918. By mid-September the Turkish army was closing in on these forces at Chanak. Britain had discussed Turkish policy with France but not with the Dominions; one of the problems about continuous consultation was that Britain was involved in so many issues, many of them in parts of the world that meant little or nothing to the Dominions, that consultation on every aspect of them would have turned cabinet meetings throughout the Commonwealth into a perpetual seminar on British foreign policy. This could be avoided easily enough; the Dominions showed no sign of being worried if Britain pursued her own policy in some areas without troubling the Dominions.

But the British wanted the best of both worlds; after allowing a fairly difficult situation to develop without consultation, the British cabinet sent a very direct request to Dominion governments on 16 September, asking them to send military assistance to help deal with the problem. This support could only have been of moral value, because the crisis would be settled before any Dominion forces could arrive, and in the event Britain and Turkey arranged a calm and honourable withdrawal for the British forces. But the request for help had come as a great shock to Dominion ministers, and it was made no more soothing by the fact that it appeared in the newspapers before some of them had been told about it. Before 1914 Britain had passed through many crises, but had never summoned the Dominions to give help. The new policy had assumed that help might be forthcoming but that it would be assistance for a policy which the Dominions had discussed and helped to form. Either Dominion detachment or continuous consultation were policies that might be successful, but commitment without consultation could not be acceptable. The British request for assistance was accepted by New Zealand and by Newfoundland willingly, and by Australia less enthusiastically; the Canadian Prime Minister said that this was something that must be decided by the Ottawa Parliament; and the South African government prudently refrained from saying anything. Continuous consultation had been struck a mortal blow because the British government wanted the benefits that the policy might have brought, but was not prepared to accept the limits on its freedom of action that consultation would have involved.

11. *The Defeat of the Imperial Idea 1922–1945*

The failure of the policy of continuous consultation meant that the Common-wealth had to work out a new way to run external policy. Inside Britain the threat to peace revealed at Chanak helped weaken Lloyd George and played some part in his being replaced as Prime Minister by Bonar Law. The exertions and dangers of continuous consultation had no attractions for Law, and the sharing of power implied by it irritated his Foreign Secretary, Curzon. The policy was allowed to drop; when Commonwealth Prime Ministers came to London for the 1923 conference they found the British government was not very interested in working out an agreed policy, and this settled the way things were run in the decades ahead. The British drew back from Lloyd George's system of relations to something like the pre war position, where Britain pursued her own policy and expected to fight her own wars but hoped that the Dominions would come and help if there were any really serious problem. This was not enough for the Dominions; they wanted their position defined in constitutional terms which recognized the immense change in their status in the international community since 1914. In 1926 an attempt was made to define Commonwealth relations in the Balfour declaration which established the equality of the members of the Common-wealth and the great importance which they attached to membership. This settled the really pressing questions of status but there was still a problem about legal powers to be worked out and, proceeding at a more leisurely pace, the lawyers had by 1931 devised the Statute of Westminster which clarified the legal position of the Dominion parliaments and gave them as much control over their own constitutions as they wanted to take. Those who were accustomed to the idea of an empire held together by a compelling central force in London no doubt saw this as a step towards disintegration of the sort foretold by H. G. Wells: 'For the British Empire there was to be no such decline and fall as happened to Rome [or, he might have said, Spain]. Instead it relaxed . . . to nothing. Unhappily before it relaxed in India it had, as in Ireland, a brief convulsive phase of "firmness"'.[1] This was not at all a bad prophecy to make in 1933, but at the time imperial opinion saw things

[1] H. G. Wells, *The Shape of Things to Come* (1933), 144.

distinctly differently. So much energy had been invested in the idea of closer commercial relationships by those who were concerned about imperial unity that they were certainly convinced that the Ottawa trade agreements which set up a system of imperial tariff preferences in 1932 did more to strengthen imperial cohesion that the centrifugal effect of the Statute of Westminster could have done to weaken it.

These processes of change were almost always amicable. Such imperial struggle as took place in the 1920s and 1930s was in India, where the 1919 constitution came under great pressure at the end of the 1920s. Congress had spent the years after 1922 in building up its support. By 1929 it was poised for a determined, though non-violent, attack on the British position, and this attack had passed its peak by the time Wells was writing. The onslaught had been restrained by cause of the ambivalent feelings about the existing system of both its attackers and its defenders. The Congress leaders wanted to maintain parts of the old system, and many of the British leaders wanted to change it, as they showed in their 1935 Government of India Act. The Act gave India what Lord Durham would have seen as 'responsible government', though not Dominion status in the sense that the term had acquired by the 1930s. Final power of peace and war for India still remained in British hands in 1939.

In a number of other places British diplomacy and concessions preserved enough of a legacy of empire to allow her to mobilize almost the maximum possible support for the Second World War, in which she acted as a great imperial power for the last time. The Dominions behaved in the war as full members of the international community, and for the first time were recognized as such by everyone else. British strength was exerted all over the world, but clearly was overstrained. Some specific defeats – the fall of Singapore is always taken as the one with the greatest symbolic significance – showed that imperial power could no longer be exercised on a world-wide basis. The rhetoric of triumphant allied power in the war was hostile to imperial rule in any form, and went further than ever before towards saying that the right of self-determination was universal. By the end of the war it was becoming clear that everyone in the world was expected to be a citizen of an independent sovereign state that would – unless it was too evil to be admitted – be a member of the newly created United Nations. The organization had an assembly which, though not a world parliament, would be a little like the colonial assemblies of the seventeenth century, giving advice to the real holders of power.

The Dominions, which took a particularly important part in the war because many of the opponents of Germany had been conquered and their governments forced into exile, wanted to show that they had a position more important than that of the general run of small states in earlier decades, which had been ignored and neglected by the great powers on almost all diplomatic occasions. Dominion leaders in 1945 introduced the idea of a 'middle power'; they did not expect their countries to be as important as the United States, the Soviet Union, or Britain (whose decline to a position of less importance than the other two they were still a long way from understanding), but they did feel that if they were to be members of a world full of sovereign states, they would like it to be known that they were more important than most of the others.

Dominion Status

This 1945 situation was a long step away from the position in 1923. It might be a relief to be free from continuous consultation, and it was certainly a relief to know that there would be no more summonses to help get the British out of their imperial problems in places like Chanak, but that did not really make it clear how the Dominions ought to work out their own foreign policies. The years immediately after the end of the First World War saw transformations in the balance of political parties of the Dominions which fixed the pattern of politics for at least sixty years. At first it looked as if politics in Britain might have changed in just the same way, but the British quickly returned to the alternation of parties in office. Two decades of Conservative dominance ended in 1945 and after that Labour and Conservative governments held power for very nearly equal periods of time in the following thirty-five years. In the Dominions it could reasonably be said that the party which was dominant in the 1920s remained dominant in subsequent decades (except in Ireland where the Fianna Fáil opponents of the 1921 settlement with Britain did not come to power until 1932, but then remained a dominant party in just the same pattern as in the other Dominions). In Canada Mackenzie King was able to retain the support of the French-Canadians and ally them with the free-trade farmers against the high-tariff anglophilia of Ontario, in a pattern that kept the Liberals in office almost continuously until the late 1950s when the Quebec Liberals found they needed new allies and united with urban Ontario to form an equally durable and equally successful alliance, with the result that the Liberals were in office for 50 of the 60 years after King became Prime Minister in 1921. In Australia the Hughes wartime coalition reorganized itself after the war and got rid of Hughes, but the dominant group from the wartime coalition, helped by an alliance with a Country party of farmers, survived to hold office for about 45 out of the 60 years from the end of the First World War. At first the farmers wondered whether they could not work with the Labour party; the decisive issue, which placed farmers on the left in Canada and on the right in Australia, was that farmers in both countries needed export markets and naturally supported free trade, which was the policy of the right in Australia and of the left in Canada.

Both countries had federal systems but in both of them the lower level of government (provinces in Canada, states in Australia) seemed to be losing power, though they acted as a balancing force both in providing a check to the federal government and in giving unsuccessful political parties a regional base. Until the 1930s the Canadian provinces seemed particularly weak, with nothing but a few judgements of the Privy Council (regarded as eccentric by enlightened opinion in Canada) to save them from the onward march of the central government; and provincial elections normally went the way that a glance at federal election returns would lead anyone to expect. In later deades Canadian federalism took two unexpected turns: the provincial governments themselves became much more powerful, partly because they were responsible for social welfare, which had been left to them as an unimportant function in 1867, and partly because nationalist sentiment in Quebec made independence a possible alternative to centralization; and at the same time, voters behaved as if they thought the cure for a federal government they disliked was to vote for a provincial government of an opposing party. In the early 1980s Canadians were ready in provincial elections to elect Conservative or Social Credit or Parti Quebecois or New Democrat provincial governments, but were nowhere willing to elect a Liberal provincial government. The Australian states continued to lose power to the central government, and were not used as an electoral balancing force to nearly the same extent as in Canada.

In the 1920s the Irish Free State was ruled by a Fine Gael government which wanted a policy of good relations with Britain. It lost office in 1932 and its Fianna Fáil successor followed a policy of keeping as separate from Britain as was practicable. In New Zealand the reforming alliance of the 1890s had broken up; by the end of the First World War the right-wing Liberals – later, the National Party – were established as the dominant force, and held office more often than their Labour opponents, though of all the Dominions it was the one that came closest to having two strong parties that alternated in office as a result of general elections. In South Africa electoral politics were shaped by ethnic and linguistic divisions among the white voters even more than Canadian politics were affected by the divisions between the French-speaking and the English-speaking sections, but parties did not settle down on a stable basis until after the Second World War, when a pattern of one-party dominance emerged.

Until then the country was led by three Boer War generals, whose positions changed as they put together different alliances. The changing names of the political parties may have given an impression that the voters' commitment was unstable, but this was not really the case. Up to his death in 1919 Botha was drawing together around himself a party of the prosperous, the successful, and the supporters of close links with Britain, Smuts succeeded him as Prime Minister and followed the same approach, with perhaps slightly less awareness of the dangers to avoid. The party which

Hertzog built up, and which he led to victory in alliance with the Labour Party in 1924, was less confident, and more inclined to draw up the ox-wagons into the traditional laager for self-defence. Smuts's South Africa Party allowed its nineteenth-century liberalism to modify its commitment to white supremacy slightly. As it believed that capitalist development would help South Africa forward, it was ready to let the African majority do as much for the economy as it could without endangering the white grasp of political power. Hertzog's Nationalists were more frightened of the Africans and more inclined to repress them. In electoral terms they would have got on quite well with Hobson and his followers: he sneered at 'cosmopolitan' capitalists and they denounced the business man caricatured in the Afrikaner press as 'Hoggenheimer'; he was opposed to imperial expansion, and the Nationalists wanted to establish that they had the right to leave the empire if they wanted to.

Their alliance with the Labour Party rested on a common fear of both the capitalists and the black workers. In practical terms the bargain was sealed by the colour bar legislation which kept black men out of jobs reserved for whites, and prevented the employers from cutting their wage bills by opening up jobs held by white men to Africans at wages far below white wage levels, even if well above anything paid to Africans. The possibility of cutting the wage bill reinforced business calculations about the advantages of expanding the South African market to include a reasonably prosperous African working class, and thus made the richest men in South Africa the most racially tolerant. The Oppenheimers, who eventually reassembled all of Rhodes's financial empire within their own Anglo-American Company, were also heirs to his idea of equal rights for all civilized men south of the Zambesi; and the Afrikaner case against 'Hoggenheimer' was that, as well as being an enemy on the race question (which in the 1920s meant the conflict of English-speaking and Afrikaans-speaking) he was also unsound on the native problem.

Dominion relations in the 1920s had to take account of the desire of the governments of Australia and New Zealand (and also of Newfoundland, which continued to count as a Dominion) for close links with Britain, and the concern of King and Hertzog and Cosgrave of the Irish Free State to preserve a prudent distance from Britain. This assessment must be seen against the background of their times: King was constantly alarmed by the idea that the British government would 'appeal over his head' to the Canadian people, a concern which seemed to assume that a large proportion of the Canadian people would respond to such an appeal. King must be left to be the best judge whether this was true; however it is fairly clear that the British government never had any intention of doing so, and would not have known how to do such a thing if it had wanted to. On the other hand, the pro-British governments of Australia and New Zealand were much more willing to undertake policies of their own and much more ready to criticize the London government than would have been the case before 1914. All the Dominion governments were mildly surprised when the British government signed the Locarno Treaty of 1925, settling frontiers in western Europe, with a specific note that it was not to be regarded as binding on the Dominions.

This was a sensible acceptance of the post-1922 situation, but it left several question unanswered. One of the problems took practical shape in 1926: King and his Liberal government lost seats in the 1925 election, and needed the votes of the independent farming MPs of the west for a majority. When King looked like losing their support during a debate on a scandal in the customs administration, he asked for a general election. The Governor-General replied that there ought not to be a dissolution in the middle of a debate, and that the Conservatives should put together a majority. King resigned, but the Conservatives were not able to maintain a majority and in the election which was then inevitable the Liberals gained an adequate majority. King treated the power of dissolution as a matter of imperial relations. During the crisis he had suggested that the Governor-General should ask the Secretary for the Dominions for instructions, though the Governor-General had then replied that the problem was a matter to be settled inside Canada. This sounded reasonable, but it was still true that he was appointed by the British government and for some purposes was responsible to it. Because his post was the direct descendant of the original governors who had had executive authority, he was the nominal director of any foreign relations that the Dominion might have and at the same time he was the only diplomatic representative the British government maintained in the Dominion. When domestic affairs were being discussed he would naturally take the advice of his Dominion government because it had a parliamentary majority, but if the British government wanted to discuss an issue of foreign policy with the Dominion government, it was the Governor-General who had to act as the advocate of the British point of view.

Whatever the merits of the 1926 dissolution, it was inconvenient that the power to dissolve Parliament was in the hands of a man who was sometimes required to consider British rather than Dominion interests. In 1927 the post was divided: Britain appointed High Commissioners to all the Dominions to express its point of view in diplomatic issues, and left the Governors-General as formal representatives of the King as head of each state. After this change the Dominions could consider appointing people who lived in the country rather than bringing Englishmen of distinction or noble birth to undertake this mainly ceremonial role. The first native-born Governor-General, Chief Justice Isaacs, was appointed in Australia – after some expressions of disapproval in London – in 1931, but this was not taken as a guiding precedent, and it took about a generation to establish the rule that members of the Commonwealth which continued to be monarchies, recognizing the British sovereign as the head of state, would appoint a local man as Governor-General.

These ceremonial changes followed from the determined efforts that were made to define the Commonwealth to its own satisfaction in 1926. At the conference in October Hertzog brought forward a draft declaration that he wanted accepted as a sign that membership of the Commonwealth was really no restriction on South Africa's freedom of action and, after amendments to provide phrases to fit the susceptibilities of all the members, the conference agreed on a declaration drafted by Balfour that the United Kingdom and the Dominions were 'autonomous communities within the British Empire, equal in status, in no way subordinate one to another in any aspect of their domestic or external affairs, though united by a common allegiance to the Crown, and freely associated as members of the British Commonwealth of Nations'. This statement might leave questions about what would be the practical results of being 'freely associated', but in fact the immediate consequences were more a matter for lawyers, as the members of the Commonwealth tried to work out how to give legal effect to what they had said.

The Colonial Laws Validity Act of 1865 would have to go. In its day it had clarified the powers of self-governing colonies by assuring them that they could pass laws for anyone resident in the colony (or a little way out to sea); by implication the British government would not try to legislate on issues that concerned the colonies' internal affairs. But one of the attributes of a sovereign state is that it can legislate for its citizens anywhere in the world, and the British in the nineteenth century would not allow colonies to exercise that power, just as a federal government at the present day would be taken aback if a state or provincial government tried to legislate as to what its residents should do when they had gone to another part of the federation. By 1931 the constitutional lawyers had agreed on the repeal of the Colonial Laws Validity Act, so that each Commonwealth country possessed this power to legislate for its citizens all over the world.

While everybody could agree to this, expressing the legal nature of the Commonwealth in the Statute of Westminster of 1931 also raised the much more complicated problem of enabling Dominions to amend their own constitutions. The Irish constitution depended on the 1921 treaty; the constitutions of Australia, Canada, New Zealand, and South Africa depended fairly directly on British legislation, and that of Newfoundland depended mainly on Colonial Office instructions to governors. All of them except Canada had well-defined ways of deciding when a change in the constitution was desirable, but the idea of going to London for formal ratification of the change was unwelcome in Ireland and South Africa, and in the Statute they gained the right to change their own constitutions; initial changes would have to start from the original constitution authenticated in Britain and would have to follow the methods of change laid down in it, but these two Dominions wanted to feel that, after taking a few preliminary steps, they could have complete freedom of action in subsequent constitutional questions. In Australia, New Zealand, and Newfoundland there was no such desire to be able to change the constitution locally. People rather liked the idea that a constitutional change was a serious matter that went through the formal process of approval by the Mother of Parliaments at Westminster. In Newfoundland and New Zealand there was also the thought that as they had unitary systems of government, with none of the Australian rules for referendums with qualified majorities before making a change, it could do no harm to have the British Parliament as a force in reserve to deal with aberrations. So these three countries left the power of amendment in London, with the knowledge that they could ask for it to be transferred to them at any time. Australia and New Zealand did ask for it in the 1940s, as war strengthened their feelings of national self-reliance; Newfoundland was unable to survive the depression financially, and in 1933 returned to being a colony ruled from London until, in 1949, it voted to become the tenth province of Canada.

The legislation that defined Canada's position, the British North America Act, contained many clauses of no constitutional significance, and only a small part of it was concerned with the vital question of the powers of the provincial governments. It contained no provisions for amendment; fairly certainly the negotiators of 1867 expected that future Canadian governments would recommend changes to the British government, and the British government would use its discretion and enact the changes it thought appropriate. By 1931 the British government's power to reject legislation it disliked had atrophied, but if this simply meant that it had to pass anything Ottawa asked for, the central government had much more power over provincial governments (including theoretically the power to eliminate them) than was consistent with any normal idea of a federal constitution. If all the Dominions had taken the same approach as Ireland and South Africa, no doubt the Canadians would have had to work out a way of amending their constitution that preserved the federal system; because Australia, New Zealand, and Newfoundland kept the practice of amendment in London for reasons of sentiment, Canada could arrange for the Statute of Westminster to allow the Ottawa Parliament to alter the sections of the British North America Act which had no constitutional significance, while sending constitutional changes to London as before. This pleased Canadians who liked the link of sentiment with Britain, and it also reassured people in Quebec who thought London was rather less likely than Ottawa to be swept away by anti-Quebec or centralizing enthusiasm.

Nobody in Canada felt the least desire for prolonged constitutional discussion to decide on a method of amendment. The Statute of Westminster was a welcome piece of Commonwealth house-cleaning, but it was passed at a time when constitution-making was a long way from being uppermost in the minds of Dominion politicians. The world was entering the great depression of the 1930s and the Dominions were particularly exposed to its pressures. The prices of their exports, which consisted mainly of food and raw materials, were much more volatile than those of their imports, mainly because production of the manufactured goods which they imported could be cut much more quickly than farmers could reduce the amount they grew. During the 1920s they had been prosperous and they had borrowed money: Australia and New Zealand went to London, Canada turned to the New York market, but all of them had large debts which had looked much more productively invested in 1928 than in 1931. The bankers were denounced for their rapacity in wanting their loans repaid, but in most cases they did receive prompt payment.

Britain was in no better state – her exports were being cut in volume at the same time as the Dominions' exports were being cut in value. Ever since Joseph Chamberlain's campaign for tariff reform leading up to the 1906 defeat, some Conservatives had wanted tariffs and imperial preference; in the financial collapse of 1931 their time had come. Just as the Statute of Westminster was going through Parliament the last free trade government in Britain was breaking up, and was quickly replaced by a coalition dominated by Conservative supporters of imperial preference. Tariffs were imposed by the end of the year; the British looked forward to a conference the following year at which the countries of the Commonwealth could work out a system of preferences. The 1932 Ottawa conference disappointed a number of the participants; negotiators in the 1930s were all too ready to expect a great deal from a conference once one had been held, and the Ottawa agreements lost some popularity because of this. All the other members of the Commonwealth were delighted to see that Britain had become converted to protectionism, and both they and the British tended to assume that once this point of principle had been settled the rest would be easy.

The particular problem for the Dominions was that the British were trying to negotiate preferences from them at a time when any reduction in tariffs was likely to mean that British imports were likely to take away jobs in already suffering industrial sectors of their economies. Imperial preference had been expected to be at the expense of the foreigner: Britain would cease to buy cheap raw materials and food from foreign suppliers and would pay somewhat more to buy Commonwealth goods, and the Dominions would replace some of the industrial goods they bought from foreigners with British products. There were of course marginal cases in which that could be done; the Canadian Conservative government of the early 1930s was acting entirely in accordance with the unspoken assumptions of Imperial preference when it increased its general tariff, to give its own manufacturers even more protection against imports than before, and then gave Britain a preference to reduce the damage to her interests.

But, however rational this might have been, it was not quite what the British had expected; they had really behaved as though what was involved would be a step towards empire free trade, by which all tariffs against the goods of other members of the Commonwealth would be reduced. Furthermore, they had no experience of the fairly stiff bargaining involved in any tariff meeting and found that the fault of the others was giving too little and asking too much. The Dominions argued as if they did not understand why Britain, which had had no tariff at all against their products, now found it necessary to set one up: they thought disturbance for the British economy would have been minimized and advantage for Dominion producers maximized if Commonwealth products had continued to enjoy free access while foreign products faced prohibitive duties. The British government realized that free entry for Commonwealth products kept down the price of food, but on the other hand it had to give its farmers some advantage from the switch to protection, which could be expected to increase the price of everything that farmers imported. So it settled on a system of quotas, letting stated amounts of Commonwealth production in free of duty, and protecting the British farmer against all other imports, foreign or Commonwealth.

The Ottawa system never had the clarity of empire free trade, a policy which had been dismissed almost as soon as it was considered, and more and more modifications to the agreements were made as the members of the system found they wanted to negotiate exemptions for non-Commonwealth trading partners. It was hard for Canada to maintain for long a tariff arrangement that seemed aimed at the United States, and Britain could not yet reduce her trading links with Argentina to a level that paid no attention to the commercial habits of the nineteenth century, but all this meant only that imperial preference did not fulfil the hopes of those who had been evangelizing for it for the previous quarter-century. Perhaps world-wide reflation and free trade would have been better, but this alternative was not in the realm of practical politics in the 1930s. The Ottawa agreements probably had a mildly encouraging effect on the trading prospects of the participants and it is quite likely that, in the gloom of 1932, the alternative to Commonwealth trade would have been more deflation, a greater degree of national autarchy, and more steps towards bilateral or barter trade.

Much the same thing could be said about the creation of the Sterling Area when the British government gave up the gold standard by ceasing to keep the value of the pound equal to a fixed weight of gold regulated by the fact that the gold sovereign contained about 0.243 oz. (about 6.9 grams) of gold. The pound could float up or down in a way that was alarming for countries whose economic activity was closely linked to Britain. All Commonwealth countries except Canada, which was more closely linked to the United

States, and a number of small non-Commonwealth countries formed an economic unit whose currencies remained fixed in value against one another though they floated against non-sterling currencies. The British government acted as a banker to the Sterling Area, holding the free reserves of the other members, trying to smooth the fluctuations of sterling in a world of abrupt changes of value, and allowing members of the group opportunities to raise loans in London that were denied to non-members. These arrangements had their disadvantages, but they were certainly better than being exposed unsheltered to the economic blizzards of the 1930s.

The trade agreements were seen as a satisfactory conclusion to a decade of rearranging political relationships within the Commonwealth, with the result that there was rather less discussion than there had been in the recent past. After the event this has been regretted: writers who condemn the British government's policy of appeasement in the 1930s have sometimes gone on to comment unfavourably on the foreign policy of the Dominions. In the 1935 crisis over Abyssinia, Canada and New Zealand at first took a fairly firm position against Italian expansion, though Canada reversed her position when King returned to office towards the end of the year. In the four remaining years until the outbreak of war the influence that the Dominions possessed was exerted in favour of a pacific policy, which meant encouraging Britain to go ahead with appeasement. In Canada King had to reckon with the fact that some of his supporters in Quebec regarded Mussolini as a praiseworthy Christian leader and felt that there was something to be said for Hitler's view about the Jews, and in South Africa Hertzog could see that some of his supporters believed that Hitler's attitude to the lower races was more sensible than the approach favoured by the British.

Both men knew that if Britain was involved in war, their countries would be divided: a large part of the population of British descent would want to support Britain and a large part of the French-speaking or of the Afrikaner population would want to remain neutral, so they had powerful reasons of internal policy for wanting Britain to stay out of war. Sections of left-wing opinion in all English-speaking countries wanted to stay at peace because they believed that the last war had been so terrible that the shape of things to come pointed to an even vaster slaughter in any future war. Australia and New Zealand were likely to support Britain in almost any policy she followed; Ireland was unlikely to support her in any circumstances; Canada and South Africa were distinctly pacific influences.

The Prime Ministers were so conscious of having settled most of the economic and constitutional questions facing the Commonwealth in the early 1930s that they met only once more before the outbreak of war in 1939. The British government tried to keep the Dominions informed by advising their High Commissioners in London of the progress of diplomacy, although King made it clear that he would prefer his High Commissioners not be told much. He could see that after a certain point he would become committed to British policy if he knew very much about it, and he disliked the fact that the High Commissioner, Massey, was a devoted anglophile, who believed that Canada ought to have a foreign policy and that it ought to be firmly aligned with Britain's. King felt that his country would be happiest if it could act on the principle laid down by Ernest Lapointe that Canada was 'a fireproof house', though King knew enough about the situation to realize that this was not an adequate policy. What Chamberlain pursued under the name of appeasement was an active policy of putting things right in Europe, while the Commonwealth Prime Ministers who approved of his policy did so for totally different motives. There is not much sign that Chamberlain paid attention to the views of the Dominion Prime Ministers in forming his original policy; it is quite clear that, when he changed his approach in March 1939 and Britain guaranteed the position of Poland, he did not consult them. This was the logical result of the failure of continuous consultation and of the attitude the British had taken to European affairs after Locarno; it was also the result of the fact that, while the Dominions had been eager to get the right to have foreign policies of their own, the actual use they made of the right was to try to avoid having foreign policies at all.

The lack of concern about Commonwealth foreign policy reflected the fact that Commonwealth relations, while always close and usually friendly, were not a matter of serious debate inside the member-countries. King ran against the Governor-General in the 1926 election; Lord Beaverbrook attacked Baldwin's leadership of the Conservative party in Britain by encouraging candidates pledged to 'Empire Free Trade', a policy which Beaverbrook knew none of the Dominions would support; de Valera came to power in Ireland in 1932 as the exponent of a policy of keeping as far away from Britain as the geographical facts allowed (and the tariff war between the two countries in the 1930s was something of an attempt to widen St. George's Channel).

At a slightly more substantial level, there were attempts in the 1920s to encourage emigration from Britain to the Dominions and the British government spent about £6m. on it. To some extent the two sides in the discussion were at cross-purposes; the immediate hope of the British was that a number of the unemployed would go overseas, while the Dominions were concerned to avoid becoming a dumping ground for failures. The British sounded as if they had always been sending out people who needed a second chance; the Dominions seemed to think that all previous immigrants had been a choice blend of skilled tradesmen with the healthiest agricultural labourers. British emigration in fact slowed down in the 1920s, perhaps because none of the Dominions any longer had an open frontier on which a man could rise to prosperity by his own efforts, and perhaps because the unemployed were rather better treated in Britain than before 1914. The small-scale scheme of assisted emigration in the 1920s failed to change this, and the general increase in unemployment of the 1930s brought the schemes to an end. For a short time the whole pattern of the previous three centuries was reversed. The flow of population of the English-speaking world was into Britain rather than away from it, and Britain's population increased by 0.5m. from migration in the 1930s. Presumably this mainly meant that recent emigrants felt that, at a time of distress and depression, they stood as good a chance of earning a decent living in south-east England as in Canada or Australia, and that if the worst came to the worst they might as well be miserable with their families in Scotland, Wales, and the north of England, but it did suggest that one type of connection that had constantly nourished the empire might be coming to an end.

Aspirants to Dominion Status

While the Commonwealth was not part of normal political discussion in Britain, which could be taken to be a natural result of the Dominions' virtual independence, problems of the empire – using the word, as was now common, to refer to colonies ruled from Britain – took up a certain amount of political attention. The position of the African colonies was still being defined in the 1920s. In 1919 Kenya received representative government in the form of an assembly for a white electorate, and the Governor, Sir Edward Northey, went a step further by saying that the interests of Europeans must be 'paramount' throughout the country. He showed what he meant by approving a regulation which would have imposed forced labour on the African population. British opinion was prepared to accept hut or poll taxes which forced Africans to find paid work to pay their taxes, but legislation for forced labour was quite different – people in Britain were resigned to paying taxes themselves but would have resisted forced labour, so the ordinance establishing forced labour was fiercely attacked and never came into law. After this the basis on which Kenya was being governed was examined a little more closely, and in 1923 the Secretary for the Colonies, choosing his word carefully to emphasize his repudiation of Northey, said that the interest of the Africans must be 'paramount'. It was easier to state this view in Britain than to enforce it in Africa; on the spot there was no doubt about white supremacy, and chiefs at times provided forced labour for public works.

In 1922 the British South Africa Company gave up the charter which had made it into a political power in Rhodesia, partly because the white settlers opposed its authority and partly because the costs of administration were eating up all its profits. Northern Rhodesia became a colony under the Colonial Office; the white settlers of Southern Rhodesia, farming the land south of the Zambesi, were consulted in a referendum to find out if they wanted to join South Africa, with the likelihood that they would be given responsible government if they voted aginst the union. Although both Smuts's government in South Africa and the Colonial Office would clearly have preferred them to join South Africa, they voted 8,774 to 5,989 against it in November 1922, probably because they felt South Africa had too strong a central government, which was likely to fall into the hands of Hertzog and his Afrikaner republicans at some point. The British government could see the difficulties about giving responsible government to 30,000 whites ruling more than a million black Africans, but it had no intention of trying to rule the colony from London and in 1923 Southern Rhodesia received responsible government in Lord Durham's original sense, with the British government retaining some control over legislation affecting African interests. If Southern Rhodesia had joined South Africa, the British government would probably have transferred Bechuanaland to the Union and might even have handed Basutoland and Swaziland over as well; the result of the referendum put this in doubt, and made the British a little more resigned to holding on to these three territories which the British High Commissioner for South Africa ruled on behalf of the Colonial Office.

Between 1924 and 1929 the Colonial Office was in the hands of Leopold Amery, the most enthusiastic advocate of empire since Joseph Chamberlain. It was appropriate that Amery was almost the only man ever to combine the Secretaryship for the Colonies with the newly created Secretaryship for the Dominions which emerged from the Dominions section of the Colonial Office set up in 1907 (strictly, Lord Passfield combined the two for just under a year in 1929–30); most of the important work of relations with the Dominions was carried on at the level of the Prime Ministers, but Amery could devote himself to encouraging emigration and to supporting empire marketing schemes which he clearly saw as a prelude to imperial preference, so that he had solid work to do. But most of his time was spent on the colonies, and more particularly on the African colonies.

Proposals for Closer Union in East Africa aroused most concern in Britain. A commission had suggested that the Governors of Kenya, Uganda, and Tanganyika could usefully meet to discuss the problems of their region, and they began doing so in 1926. Amery clearly felt that the region would benefit from some form of federation, though this was hard to apply because of the status of the colonies involved: Kenya had representative government for a white minority whose support for Closer Union was inspired by a desire for a larger supply of African labour and a hope that they could move further away from Colonial Office control; Tanganyika was a League of Nations mandate although held on terms which did not rule out Closer Union, and was run by a Lugard-trained governor, Sir Donald Cameron, who wanted the Africans to develop without too much European influence and shared the Colonial Office suspicions about trade, commerce, and white settlers; and Uganda contained classic cases of Indirect Rule in which Buganda and

Bunyoro were seen as excellent examples of local African government under traditional rulers. A new commission under Hilton Young gave Amery evidence with which to push Closer Union forward, but the campaign proceeded slowly; the missionary influence which in the past had been directed against slavery was now turned against attempts to obtain cheap labour, and regarded Kenya and Southern Rhodesia as the places where this was most likely to happen. Their influence was supported by that of the Labour Party, whose supporters were usually denounced – not always accurately – by the white settlers as 'Fabians'. But it was a Fabian, Sidney Webb, recently made Lord Passfield, who issued the 1930 White Paper confirming the High Commission for the three colonies but reasserting the paramountcy of African interests and making it clear that there would be no responsible government for Kenya and no Closer Union until ways had been developed to consult African opinion.

In East Africa modernization was so linked with the position of the white settlers that resistance to Closer Union almost turned into opposition to economic development. No such side-issues distracted people in West Africa; the governments of the colonies could float loans for development in London, and in the Gold Coast Guggisberg took modernization and Africanization as linked issues while he was Governor in the 1920s: Africans were brought into the higher civil service of the colony, most of the non-official members of his legislative councils were Africans, not selected from the traditional rulers but elected directly or indirectly by provincial councils, and by the end of the 1920s Gold Coast nationalists could declare that they wanted their country to advance until it became a nation within the Commonwealth.

Because it was larger and contained more disparate elements than the Gold Coast, Nigeria was much harder to unite and rather harder to modernize. Lugard had united the general administrations and held the position of Governor-General in 1914, but because the northern colony continued to be under the system of Indirect Rule, it could not work with the south, in which a legislative council for the area developed in a way much more like that of the Gold Coast. The trading companies were slowly drawn together into the United Africa Company, a subsidiary of the Anglo-Dutch firm of Unilever, which understood the Colonial Office's uneasiness about business men, and made itself as inconspicuous as it could. The Colonial Office, perhaps because it had a fairly free hand to direct development, encouraged railways which were the form of transport which it knew and had seen financed in the past, when after 1918 a shift to road transport might have suited the new conditions better. One of the administrative attractions of railways was that they could be expected to pay for themselves if there was credit with which to raise a loan and a rate structure which brought revenue and encouraged trade. Nobody was going to recommend toll-gates on roads, so roads would be charges on general revenue and could be paid for only by higher yields from general taxation.

The British official view was what it had been throughout its imperial experience: colonies could very well float loans if their credit would support the effort, but there was no reason for the British government to provide grants-in-aid. In the nineteenth century a colony which needed a grant-in-aid would have been regarded as a very dubious asset, and in the early twentieth century it would probably have been examined for signs of inefficient administration, but the rule that a colony ought to cover its own costs was changed only when legislation in 1929 allowed £1m. a year for the economic development of the colonies, and this amount was not increased during the next ten years. The attitude was natural enough. Building railways was almost the only aspect of developing what later became known as infrastructure on which nineteenth-century governments spent much, and even that was often left to private companies. Money for development was raised by loans in London, and the degree of ease with which bonds were floated gave some idea of what people outside the government thought of a colony's prospects. In the twentieth century governments spend more lavishly on a wide range of things from roads to education which could not easily be financed on a large scale by private spending, even though they were likely to increase the productive capacity of the economy in the future. In the 1920s and 1930s, the flow of overseas investment by private lenders dried up, and direct investment by large companies was not yet important enough to take their place. British colonies in Asia and Africa were close enough to subsistence for their governments not to be likely to have budget surpluses available for spending on the wide range of activities from preventive medicine to agricultural research which could not easily be financed by private investment but were likely to increase the wealth of the colony in the future. In the nineteenth century perhaps the best that a government could do for its subjects was to refrain from spending money and keep the taxes as low as possible, but in the twentieth century colonies were cut off from some types of productive expenditure by nineteenth-century ideas of thrift and seventeenth-century ideas of colonial self-sufficiency.

The division between the commercialized and partly westernized coastal regions of Nigeria and the Gold Coast and the almost unaltered interior made it hard to impose a development policy, which at first would have benefited the south much more than the north, and this division between coast and interior affected political development in these colonies and also in Sierra Leone and Gambia. Along the coast, or at least in the capitals, there were groups of informed and educated Africans who would have liked greater political power for themselves but were uneasily aware that the great majority of the population who lived further inland were much less sophisticated and would be bound to gain most of the political power to be obtained by any large-scale withdrawal of British authority. The educated men of the coast were in very much the same position as the first generation of supporters of Congress in India: they wanted to be accepted as part of the British ruling group, they did not see how to control the majority of their countrymen politically, and so they felt no great enthusiasm for power to be transferred to them directly.

In India this political pattern had been destroyed by the agitation for national rights from 1916 to 1922. By the time things quietened down and the British began to apply the 1919 Government of India Act, Congress had been turned into a nation-wide movement which involved many more people than before, and the first generation of leaders had passed from the scene. The new leaders were confident enough about their links with the mass of the people to be unworried about problems of power after independence. Jawharlal Nehru, who had been converted to nationalism by Gandhi and in his turn converted his father Motilal from a devoted supporter of the British administration into a leader of Congress, did his first important political work among peasants in the rural hinterland: this was a step that political leaders had to take if Congress was to be a mass movement, but it was a step which the first generation of Congressmen – just like the political leaders of West African coastal cities – would have found very difficult.

Motilal Nehru retained some pre-war attitudes; he had been reserved in his enthusiasm when Gandhi introduced the labour of daily spinning into the way of life expected of a dutiful member of Congress, and he did not want to miss the chance to take part in the political activity of the enlarged legislative assembly at Delhi and put the case for Dominion Status under the name of swaraj. The swarajists in the assembly were at the time a problem for the Viceroy and his officials, though in a wider view of the future they could be seen as a sign that India might turn into a Dominion much like the others. The British rulers sometimes found it hard to realize that in their respect for British example, their desire to run their own affairs, and their willingness to keep strong links with Britain, the Congress leaders were very like the Canadian and Australian politicians of the end of the nineteenth century. Certainly Motilal and Jawaharlal Nehru and Gandhi (referred to, in a not entirely unfriendly way, by the British in India as the father, the son, and the holy ghost) were much more attached to Britain and the British way of doing things than either Hertzog or de Valera. They were quite determined that their country should stand on a footing of equality with Britain for political purposes, but then by the 1920s this was equally true of the most conservative of Australian or Canadian anglophiles.

Gandhi played no immediately central role in politics in the 1920s, after being released from prison when he had served two years of his six year sentence. His work lay in building on the foundations laid in the early 1920s and turning Congress into a mass party. In some ways he was ideally suited for this: the great majority of Indians were still peasants, and recognized only two types of power – that of the ruler, typified by the King-Emperor and his Viceroy, and that of the holy man. For the majority of Indians Gandhi was a saint, and if he told them to follow his political lead they would do so mainly because of his religious position. Englishmen could appreciate this type of power, and appreciate it more fully if they accepted their own Christian heritage. But, apart from the asceticism, it meant very little to Muslims, who had rather different religious commitments and found a quite different set of teachings about force and violence in Islam. As a practical matter, for dealing with the British, non-violence was tactically more effective than anything Islam had to offer, but the adoption of so distinctly Hindu an approach had the effect of driving the Muslims out of Congress. In 1928 Jinnah, the leading Muslim of the new generation who had taken an important part in working out the Lucknow Pact, repeatedly made it clear that he thought there was no longer any room for Muslims in Congress and eventually withdrew to London to see what the future held.

By then Congress had been presented with the first of the issues that brought its capacity for propaganda back to the peak reached in 1920 and 1921. A Royal Commission was required to see how well the 1919 Act was working out, and in 1927 the British government appointed a commission under Sir John Simon which had no Indian members. Indians were annoyed at this sign that they were not trusted and were not to have an effective voice in influencing their own political evolution; the meetings of the commission were boycotted, and Congress moved towards asking for complete national independence, though it was clear that Dominion Status would in fact satisfy almost everyone. In 1929 the Viceroy, Lord Irwin (later Lord Halifax) decided to act on this; after consulting the newly elected Labour government in Britain he announced in October that Dominion Status was the 'natural issue of India's constitutional progress', an approach which made the Simon Report, with its recommendations for complete responsible government at the provincial level, out-of-date before it was published.

Irwin's declaration came too late to stop Congress's organization for non-violent resistance. Gandhi showed his Gladstonian capacity for leadership: without co-ordinating plans with the Congress leader, who would probably have been too concerned about constitutional theory to see the attraction of what he intended to do, he announced that he was going to set off on a march to the sea to make salt. This was illegal; the salt tax had been a burden on the poor that the British had kept as a legacy from their Moghul predecessors, and everyone in India could grasp the message that independence under Congress direction would mean an end to the salt tax. So Gandhi's march to the sea attracted immense attention, and when he had made salt on 5 April 1930 and been arrested, all followers of Congress felt called on to break the salt laws in one way or another. At the peak of the civil disobedience campaign about 60,000 Congress supporters were in prison, but Irwin managed to remain on negotiating terms with Gandhi and to arrange that, while the Simon proposals were clearly dead, the civil disobedience campaign would end and Gandhi would come, eventually acting as Congress's sole representative, to a Round Table conference in London in 1931.

A Round Table conference, which Irwin had suggested before the civil disobedience campaign began, put Indians on equal terms with the British, but this did not by itself decide which Indians were to be represented. Congress claimed to be a national movement that spoke for all Indians; the British replied that the Muslims were not willing to be represented by Congress, that there were political Liberals who had served in the legislative assembly, and that a prudent government must try to draw the Indian princes into a federation, so they would have to be heard as well. The British tried bringing the untouchable Hindus at the bottom of the caste ladder into the calculation as a separate group with interests of their own; Gandhi was able to induce them to return to the Congress grouping by threatening to go on a fast until he died if they did not accept his leadership, but neither the Muslims nor the princes could be brought under a Congress umbrella in the same way. After negotiations with these groups the British government felt it knew enough about their strengths and weaknesses to press forward with its very detailed 1935 Government of India Act. The simple immediate point was that responsible government was to be set up in the provinces; the promise for the future was that the Act's transfer of some ministries at the centre to Indian politicians responsible to the assembly carried the implication that the other departments concerned with foreign affairs and defence would pass into the hands of Indian politicians in the fullness of time.

In the negotiations leading up to the passing of the Act, the British were very concerned about the position of the 500 or so Indian princes, who ruled about a third of the land area and a quarter of the population, and were rather less concerned about the position of the Muslims. The Muslim League appeared to be working out a system of electoral co-operation with Congress. The princes had a well-defined position in the British structure of rule, as subject of the Emperor and his Viceroy but, because their position would not be nearly so well-defined when the authority of the Viceroy in British India passed into the hands of Indian leaders, attempts were made to apply the idea of federation in this new setting. Considerable efforts were made to draft the constitution in a form that made it easy and natural for the princes to join the new nationally-based government in India that was emerging. The imperial government that was fading from the scene and its Indian Civil Service wanted to leave a united India as its legacy but it felt closer social links of friendship with the princes than with the Indian political leaders, so the line of division with which it was most concerned was the division between the area the British had conquered and the area of the princes who had prudently made treaties with the British during the period of expansion.

The operation of the 1935 Act threatened to divide Congress between those who wanted to use it to acquire fuller authority than before at the level of the provincial governments and those who wanted to boycott the system to protest against the continued denial of responsible government on the most important questions of policy at the centre. After deciding to refuse ministerial appointments at the centre, Congress contested the 1937 elections with great success, winning over half the seats and clearly establishing itself as the only nation-wide party. The Muslim League showed that it was still not able to win the support of Muslims on a nation-wide basis. Its attempts to work in co-operation with Congress led to trouble after the election. The League claimed that provincial governments ought to be set up as coalitions between Congress and the League, while Congress said that members of the League would be welcomed into Congress governments provided that they entered as politicians taking part in a united movement led by Congress. The League declined this, but seemed to have little prospect of doing anything else.

The confidence for the future felt by Congress was increased by the role played by Jawaharlal Nehru, who travelled round the country arousing a level of support which suggested that, if Gandhi led his people to the borders of the Promised Land, then Nehru might be the Joshua under whom they entered it. Nehru's own comments were more restrained: in a comment that he published under a pseudonym about the fervour of his reception he ended by saying – with an awareness of the temptations confronting a leader in whom a nation puts its hopes and an indication of his own fears about fascism – 'We want no Caesars.'[2] After the election Congress ministries took over successfully in most of the provinces. The Viceroy was left to run things at the centre in what was clearly a transitional manner, and presumably India could expect to move on steadily to Dominion Status.

The Second World War

All of this, and much else about imperial development was interrupted – or accelerated – when the government of Britain went to war with Germany in 1939 to resist Hitler's march to mastery in Europe. In India the Viceroy announced on his own authority that the country was at war. Congress said that it ought to have been consulted. The British paid little attention to this claim; they were sure that India ought to be brought into the war and would have found Congress reservations on political or pacifist grounds a tiresome irrelevance. It has been commented that 'From the point of view of imperial

[2] J. Nehru, *Towards Freedom* (1958 edn.), unpaginated introduction.

relations, England may have been fortunate that the war came when it did . . . in India Congress had not yet tried to take up the powers of government and the Viceroy could commit the country to war on his own authority', and, as the author points out, the British position in Egypt, in South Africa, and in Canada had reached a point where 'in a few years time the bonds of Empire might have frayed a little more in all these places'. In Egypt a treaty had been negotiated in 1936 which gave the Egyptians control over their own army which they had not had since 1882 and defined the British position more clearly than before; in 1922 the British had announced that Egypt was independent but as they had continued to control Egypt's defence and foreign policy and had kept an army in the country to do so, the reality was that Egypt had something like the powers of Canada in 1867, though of course there was much less goodwill about the situation. The 1936 Treaty gave Britain a right to move freely into the country in time of war, but confined British forces in peacetime to a zone around the Suez Canal. While Egypt did not declare war on Germany until 1945, Britain used Egyptian territory in accordance with the Treaty and exercised fairly full control over the country while the war was on, an arrangement which really could only be seen as the result of memories of the pre-1936 balance of forces.

In South Africa the decision was taken in a more dramatic way. Hertzog wanted to stay neutral but Smuts challenged this in Parliament and by 80 votes to 67 his supporters passed an amendment to say that South Africa should fight. After his defeat in Parliament Hertzog asked for a dissolution but the Governor-General refused to give it to him on the grounds that a government with an adequate majority could be found. Smuts formed a government which held office reasonably comfortably, despite the opposition of some Afrikaners who sympathized with Hitler's beliefs, until he fought and won an election in 1943. In Canada there were some pressures for neutrality but King was perfectly clear in his own mind that neither he nor anyone else could keep the country out of war. Canada waited for a week for Parliament to meet because King had always laid it down that Parliament must decide the question of peace and war. This was not a crucial debate in the way that the vote in Cape Town had been decisive and the Canadian government used its week of peace to import war material from the United States that might later have been held up by American neutrality legislation. King could see problems were likely to be caused in the future by the fact that English Canada was so much more committed to the war than French Canada, and by 1944 this did lead to trouble as English Canada insisted on military conscription, but all that King could do in 1939 was to organize for war in the way that divided his country least.

If war had come a year earlier, as it might easily have done at the time of Munich, Hertzog would probably have been able to keep South Africa neutral; what would have happened in Canada can only be a matter of guesswork. Reasonably certainly Australia and New Zealand would have entered a war in 1938, though the leaders then might have spoken as if a choice had to be made, while in 1939 they announced that they were taking part in a way that made it sound such an obvious step that they did not mention the possibility of choice. Ireland did not join in the war in 1939, and obviously would not have done so in 1938; de Valera declared that as long as the island was divided his country would not take part in Britain's wars. This was a disappointment for Chamberlain who had been taking steps, in accordance with his general principle of appeasement, to reduce tension in Ireland as well as in central Europe, but it was certainly in Ireland's best interests to stay out of the war as long as Britain was not actually defeated. The Irish decision to stay neutral, and at the same time to remain a member of the Commonwealth, tested to the limit de Valera's argument that membership was a matter merely of 'external association', and justified his view about the tenuousness of its legal structure.

The rest of the Commonwealth had no desire to explore this approach. Recruiting went ahead as vigorously as in the First World War, and the countries of the Commonwealth turned their unemployed resources to work making munitions and other supplies, training troops, and trying to make up for what had not been done in the twenty years of peace. If Britain was ill-prepared for war in 1939, the level of preparation in the Dominions was even lower. This was the result partly of a feeling that Britain was in charge of such things and could look after them, partly of a widespread belief that preparing for war would make it more likely to break out, and partly of the difficulty of explaining to the voters why developments in Europe should make it necessary to prepare for war. The Balfourian Commonwealth of the years before the wars turned out to be a compromise which brought its own disadvantages; if the Commonwealth had retained the policy of 'continuous consultation' the Dominions would have been more aware of the danger, or if they had insisted on a fuller degree of independence they would have known that they had to watch what was going on in the world, but their position inside the Commonwealth left them with an impression of security which in 1940, when France was conquered by Germany and Britain stood alone in Europe, turned out to be almost completely unjustified.

The passage in 1940 of the Colonial Warfare and Development Act, which committed the British to spend £5m. a year on development, looked like either a heroic response to the war or else an attempt to secure the loyalty of the colonies by a change of financial course, but in fact it was the result of events before the war. The 1929 Colonial Welfare Act had established the principle of colonial aid. The economy of the West Indies had been suffering badly since the startling drop in the price of sugar to about one-sixth of its previous level in the 1880s and 1890s; other countries were growing sugar from cane and also – a new source of competition – from sugar-beet, and so the West Indies were even more exposed than the other Commonwealth producers of export commodities when the price fell again in the 1920s and 1930s. A series of riots in the islands in the 1930s convinced the British government that the problems were more acute than had been realized. A commission of inquiry went out and reported that the West Indies were becoming 'the slums of the empire', and the government was stirred to reconsider the rule, which had been applied from the very beginning of the empire, that colonies must cover their own costs for civil expenditure. In the twentieth century it became harder and harder simply to say that colonies had to be self-supporting no matter what their problems might be, and grants-in-aid or loans for development purposes had been growing more common in the 1920s and 1930s. The new legislation made the change of policy explicit, though it did not have much immediate effect – Britain was hardly in a position to provide much aid in the 1940s and war provided a much more direct answer to problems of poverty in the West Indies (and also in Newfoundland) when American air bases were established. As a signpost to the future the 1940 Act was of considerable importance: the British had moved from the assumption that colonies were inhabited by people who expected to become well-off to a recognition that, whatever the original intention, some colonies had lost their way and were not likely to prosper unless something was done to help them get on the right road. In 1940 this was not thought to be a very large task; the scale of the problem only slowly became clear in the years after the war.

This was a large change in colonial policy, and almost equally large changes were to be seen in British policy in India. Congress's disapproval of the British decision to commit India to war against Germany led the Working Committee, the executive that ran its affairs, to widen its policy of non-co-operation with the 1935 Act and call on all the Congress provincial governments to resign office. The provincial ministers did not like this. They had devoted their political careers to gaining an opportunity to run the government and were handling the work of administration well enough to convince their voters and the British authorities of their fitness for office. To be told to give up power was unpleasant, but it was of course true that they owed their power to the prestige and effectiveness of the Congress organization. So they submitted their resignations and left the British to patch up non-Congress governments or to run the provinces under the old Civil Service system.

The Muslim League had been trying to organize as a mass party under Jinnah after its failure in the 1937 election. A mass party needed a simple slogan that everybody could understand and read as the solution to his own particular problems, and a simple slogan was easily available: Pakistan. Originally this term meant that the Muslim territories of the north-west (Punjab, Afghan, Kashmir, and Sind) should become an independent state on their own, but the policy was later extended to say that the Muslims in eastern Bengal, who were about as numerous as those of the north-west, should also be citizens of Pakistan which would then have a population of 90,000,000. Such a large minority was hard to ignore; when Jinnah committed the Muslim League to a policy of partition and separation in March 1940 he had found a very effective way to assert the Muslim position. He had now to tread a fine line; he could not compromise on the question of independence without being denounced by Congress as a puppet put forward by the British to help them follow a policy of divide and rule, and at the same time he could not follow the same line as Congress because he needed to make his party as distinct from Congress as possible. He solved this problem by being slightly less un-co-operative with the British authorities than Congress but at the same time standing on his dignity in a way that made negotiations with him neither easy nor pleasant.

After the fall of France Britain needed to establish close diplomatic relations with the United States, and to show that she had done so. In August 1941 Roosevelt, the American President, and Churchill, the British Prime Minister, met on board ship off the coast of Newfoundland, and ended their meeting by signing the 'Atlantic Charter' which included the statement that the two leaders 'respected the rights of all peoples to choose the form of government under which they live'. Fairly certainly they were thinking of European countries which had been invaded by Germany when they said this, but it was a phrase which could have a wider application. The British government was soon alarmed by its implications; the Americans, whose anti-imperialism at the conference went no further than trying to break down the system of imperial preference, later took the phrase as a commitment to oppose imperial rule. Nationalists in European colonies naturally took the phrase in its widest sense in the years to come.

On 7 December 1941 Japan attacked the United States fleet at Pearl Harbor, turning the war into a more completely world-wide struggle than anything seen before and making it certain that Britain would survive the war undefeated. Churchill was confident of this as soon as he heard that Japan and the United States were at war, though Germany's readiness to declare war on the United States in support of Japan, which it did a few days later, was the decisive step that shaped the pattern of victory. The immediate effect of the war with Japan was that the British Empire in Asia suffered blows that speeded up the course of change considerably. Hong Kong was captured almost at once; the Japanese then marched rapidly south through Malaya and, after a week or two of fighting, Singapore surrendered on 15 February 1942. It had been reckoned to be the eastern equivalent of Gibraltar in strategic importance and impregnability, and its loss destroyed the idea of the invincibility of the British Empire. The Japanese advance then went on almost equally quickly through Burma, and their operations to capture the American, British, Dutch, and French islands in the Pacific were also successful. By the middle of 1942 they were pressing on the borders of India, were close enough to Australia to cause alarm there, and appeared to have moved far enough east into the Pacific to deprive the Americans of any bases close enough to launch a counter-attack. This was in fact the high-water mark of Japanese success, and the United States was able to conduct successful campaigns in which battles took the form of attacks by carrier-based aeroplanes on opposing aircraft-carriers, but the westward advance across the Pacific took a long time, and the British had immediate problems to face in India and Australia.

In August 1940 the Viceroy had tried to bring Indian political leaders into his Executive Council but he could not offer them anything more than a promise that after the war the situation would be discussed to see how the 1935 policy could be applied more satisfactorily. The Indian leaders were worried by Britain's defeat in Europe but felt the offer did not go nearly far enough. After the Japanese victories the British felt they had to try a new approach in India, and were strongly encouraged to do so by the United States, which was now in a good position to raise the issue. Churchill appointed as his negotiator in India Sir Stafford Cripps, a political lawyer from the left wing of the Labour party, who knew several of the Congress leaders and was an excellent choice to discuss the problem with them. On the other hand he had few concessions to offer and his closeness to Congress was a handicap in dealing with the Muslim League. London did little more than make the Viceroy's previous proposal of moving to Dominion Status after the war more definite. Congress replied that the way to get a really enthusiastic Indian contribution to the war effort was to give control of the Indian government to Indian leaders; Cripps himself would probably have liked to accept this proposal but it went well beyond his instructions. He had to accept the fact that no progress had been made, and probably the only permanent effect of the discussions was that the Muslim minority was recognized as a force to be considered when working out policy for the future.

The failure of the Cripps mission angered Congress so much that it committed itself to the policy of 'Quit India', and summoned its members to mass civil disobedience if the British did not leave India at once. In the past the government of India had been embarrassed by civil disobedience; in the middle of a war it had no doubts that its cause was just and treated the Congress policy as an attempt to organize a rebellion. The Congress leaders were arrested and, when there were signs of a revolt, a great many other people were arrested as well; by November the government was firmly in command of the situation and about 100,000 Congress supporters were in prison. This way of governing could not go on after the war but the approach of the British to India – as to a great many other problems in the early 1940s –

was that they would get to the end of the war first and then see what had to be done to sort out problems afterwards. By 1942 the British accepted the fact that they were going to have to leave after the war, although they still seem to have been sure that they would leave a united India; when Gandhi and Jinnah met in 1944 to discuss the future, it was clear that the prospects for unity were not bright.

The defeats in south-east Asia also affected Britain's relations with Australia and New Zealand. The Australian Labor Party was not as concerned about close relations with Britain as its Liberal and Country Party opponents; fewer of its supporters were affected by the prospects for exports to Britain, some of them felt that attachment to Britain and the glamour of its aristocracy strengthened the opposition to their ideal of a free and equal society, and some of them resented attempts by the imperial government and the government of India to weaken the 'white Australia' policy which was seen as the defence of the working man. So, while the Labor government which held office in Australia for almost all of the 1940s was completely committed to the war effort, it did not welcome Churchill's tendency to think that its contribution to strategy should take the form of 'compliance with my wishes after full and proper discussion', which was understood to be what he expected of his own Cabinet. Churchill tried to re-create the Imperial War Cabinet of the First World War, but the Dominion Prime Ministers saw themselves as leaders in a much larger allied effort rather than as directors of a specifically Commonwealth policy and, while all of them visited London at one time or another, no conferences were held until 1944.

The quick surrender of Singapore drew an embittered response from the Australian government. The defeat showed that Britain could no longer defend the whole empire, and that if Australia needed an external protector the United States was best qualified for this role; but the Australian use of words like 'betrayal' in a way that suggested Churchill was responsible for the problem revealed something more than dismay at the way the war was going. The world was a harsher place than Australians had expected, and someone else had to be blamed for this. But, however harshly the change of policy was expressed, its compelling logic was indicated when the Liberal-Country government, having returned to office after the war under the devotedly pro-British Robert Menzies, decided to enter the Anzus Pact between Australia, New Zealand, and the United States in 1951. Britain was not included in this, and British protests did not change the situation. The war had interrupted the relationship in a way that could not be repaired without ignoring the facts of geography and economics.

This weakening of the British position was not so visible in other areas. The defence of their Egyptian base for the war in North Africa and the Mediterranean led the British to assert themselves all over the Middle East. The King of Egypt was asked to abdicate because he was not sufficiently enthusiastic in his support of the British, though he successfully pleaded for another chance to prove that he could do more to show his commitment. The Shah of Iran failed to convince the British of his enthusiasm, and was deposed. The Prime Minister of Iraq tried to negotiate with the Germans and to organize a revolt, but was defeated and driven into exile. In Palestine Britain's relations with both the Jews and the Arabs got worse. In the early 1930s Jews emigrated to Palestine in much larger numbers than in the 1920s; the number of Jews from Germany settling there was not large enough to support the obvious explanation that this was the result of Hitler's persecution of the Jews, but in any case the hostility of the Arabs to the Jewish population increased. By 1939 the British had considered partitioning Palestine to create a small solidly Jewish state in Galilee but, after finding that this would please nobody, moved to limit Jewish immigration and to consider independence for the country at a time when this would have meant giving power to the Arab majority. The Jews inside Palestine saw this as a betrayal; they armed themselves for defence against the Arabs, and in a minority of cases turned to attack the British as well. In 1944 Palestine was almost the only country in the Middle East in which there was any challenge to British authority.

British self-assertion in Egypt and Iran, just as in India, depended on the fact that the British felt confident about their own moral position during the war and were exposed to very little outside criticism that they felt any need to take seriously. Once the war was over, the British would again have to face the pressures which had been forcing them to give ground in Egypt and in India before 1939. After June 1940 North Africa was the only important area of fighting on land between British and German forces until 1943, which meant that countries in the Middle East were of considerable strategic importance, but the really serious struggle was bound to be in Europe. Imperial concerns could not be ignored but the war in Europe, dominated by the struggle between Germany and the Soviet Union, was the vital issue and it was for this rather than for anything in the wider world that the British gathered their strength and, by the last stages of the war, had almost exhausted it.

In the last year or two of the war it was clear that the powers allied against Germany were going to organize the post-war world in a way that would reduce the power of empires. The Second World War with Germany did not end with a formal peace conference like Versailles in 1919; the clearest statements of the agreed principles intended to guide the post-war world were made at the founding sessions of the United Nations (in its first years, United Nations Organization) in 1945. Because the war was not yet over, the UN began as a league of the victors, and neutral countries, like the half-dozen countries against which the war was fought, were at first not admitted. But once the memory of the wartime alliance became less immediate, new members were bound to be admitted and the basic assumption that every state in the world ought to be a member and everyone in the world ought to be a citizen of an independent sovereign state became explicit. Versailles had ended the empires – states resting on a principle of loyalty to a ruler which transcended or ignored the national feelings of his subjects – in Europe. The Second World War was fought to stop the creation of an empire more ruthless, and more racially conscious, than anything seen in the nineteenth century, a defensive purpose which could be expressed naturally in the language of self-determination and the right of nations to resist imperial rule. The United Nations was not formally much more committed to the ending of imperial rule than the League of Nations had been, but the belief was growing that it was hard to justify and also that rule over dependent territories separated from the imperial centre by salt water was particularly hard to justify.

This was of course completely different from the position at Versailles, where it had been the land-based empires of eastern Europe that were under attack and were, to a greater or lesser extent, broken up into the nations that could be found inside them. In 1945 people were more concerned with the overseas empires which had first emerged from the sixteenth-century expansion of Europe and had gone on growing during the three succeeding centuries of European power. Versailles had been a European conference, and it had been dominated by European countries; the San Francisco conference in 1945 was dominated by American countries – the United States and the Latin American states who made up a large part of the 1945 membership were likely, because of their origins and their history, to be opponents of imperial rule.

The European imperial powers in any case emerged physically weakened in 1945. France, Belgium, and the Netherlands had been conquered, and Britain had used up much of her strength in the war. Imperial rule would flourish as long as the unshaken prestige of the imperial rulers convinced people that being part of a mighty empire was a noble destiny. If the might of empire was less impressive, then people would turn away to think about their own local concerns, probably expressing them in the language of nationalism by the middle of the twentieth century. By the end of the Second World War it was clear that there was a world opinion outside the range of the European empires which would encourage the peoples of the world to think in national terms and would not regard empires as possessing the same sort of political legitimacy as nations.

12. *Independence by Degrees 1945–1960*

At the end of the Second World War Britain's armed forces were larger than ever and were spread over an immense sweep of territory, and her prestige as one of the three leading victorious countries was very high. On the other hand, her two main allies agreed with each other that the British Empire ought to be reduced in size or ended as soon as possible, the Dominions had become more conscious of their position as independent states, and nationalist feeling in the colonies had become more firmly established during the war. The British had no desire to conduct a last-ditch struggle against the forces of change. It had become fairly clear during the war that arrangements would have to be made for India to become independent once the war was over, and this was done. At the eastern end of the Mediterranean, the only formal abandonment of an imperial possession was the ending of the Palestine mandate, but at much the same time the British were withdrawing from Greece, leaving the defence of Turkey to the United States, and dismantling their informal hold on Egypt.

Independence for India (and also Pakistan, Burma, and Ceylon) was followed by a tidy and controlled expansion of the Commonwealth; in the 1920s there had been seven members, and now there were eight, but the Commonwealth of the 1950s looked more impressive and not obviously much less cohesive than the earlier body. This was an illusion, which owed a good deal to the personalities involved, but at the very least it meant that the British could follow a policy of imperial retreat without having their feelings hurt too much. The emergence of India, after what could be seen as some decades of preparation in which Indian politicians held posts of steadily rising importance, encouraged the British to think in terms of training other colonies for independence by a step by step devolution of power. The West African colonies looked likely to become independent in the foreseeable future, and so it was the business of the Colonial Office to make sure that they were fit to rule themselves.

The length of the time scale was never laid down formally, and in any case formality and rigidity were discouraged. What mattered to the British government was that it should control the stages of progress to independence and avoid submitting to pressure from other countries (including other members of the Commonwealth) or from forces inside the colonies themselves. Revolts in Kenya and Malaya which might have accelerated the process in a direction the British did not want to go were resisted successfully, and the government of British Guiana was briskly pulled back some rungs on the ladder leading to independence when it showed unwelcome signs of Marxist influence.

This rather tightly controlled progress was overtaken by events in the late 1950s. The failure of the Anglo-French Suez expedition to assert control over Egypt, the example set by the first colonies to emerge into independence from the period of controlled constitutional development, and the decision of both France and Belgium to give up their African possessions brought the idea of imperial guardianship to an altogether unexpectedly early end. Sometime around 1960 it became clear that the British Empire was going to be wound up as fast as was convenient, instead of going through a dignified process of expanding the Commonwealth to receive colonies which had passed through the qualifying period in a meritorious way.

Indian Independence

This transformation of the way in which empire ended was in part a recognition of how much weaker Britain was than had been realized in 1945. The economic position of the British at the end of the war showed what an odd empire they ran. Their problems were matched by the increased prosperity of several colonies; a good deal of Britain's military activity had been financed not by cash payment nor by direct requisition but by issuing bonds on the London money market to cover the cost. As a result Britain ended the war owing about £2.5bn. to her colonies (and to other countries like Egypt which also had to accept these bonds); India emerged as a major creditor. As these debts were to countries in the Sterling Area they were denominated in British currency and were called – reasonably enough from the point of view of her colonies – the 'sterling balances'. For Britain they were debts, and debts which could not be paid off in any foreseeable future. Eventually they passed from the colonial governments to other creditors and became merged in the general mass of the National Debt, but in the ten or fifteen years after the war they underlined Britain's financial difficulties and increased the problems of sterling as an international currency. Because they held these assets the colonies appeared to have few financial problems and seemed more ready to run their own affairs than ever before.

In the summer of 1945 the British electorate voted Churchill out of office and chose a Labour government for reasons concerned almost entirely with domestic policy. Imperial issues attracted little attention during the campaign, though it was quite clear that the post-war government would face many of them. The position of India was the most important: in principle the

United States and the Soviet Union objected to all colonies, but in practice they did not think that the other British colonies mattered very much or that colonies in Africa could become independent in the near future, and the Indian struggle for independence was what really concerned them. Britain could not expect much sympathy if she tried to hang on there. The change of government in Britain had its effect; the Labour party was committed to independence and Labour politicians were on good terms with the Congress leaders, while Churchill and many of his supporters in the Conservative party were sympathetic to the Muslim minority, deeply suspicious of Congress, and unwilling to accept change. British power in India had been so eroded by 1945 that a Conservative government would probably have had to do with a bad grace what Labour did willingly, though it might easily have got itself involved in serious fighting in the course of withdrawing unwillingly.

The Labour government had disadvantages of its own when it came to deal with the principal change in Indian affairs that had taken place during the war. The Muslim League had clearly won a great deal of support among Muslims and its commitment to Pakistan had hardened with the passage of time. Wavell, the Viceroy, was a taciturn man who seemed to feel that the Indian leaders with whom he had to negotiate had no business to behave as politicians, and he lacked the diplomatic skill to make them change their positions. On balance he sympathized with the Muslims, though he was not pleased when the League responded to his proposal in the summer of 1945 to turn his Executive Council into a cabinet of Indian political leaders by refusing to join if he chose any non-League Muslims as members. Sympathy for the Muslims was a widely held and understandable enough view among the British in India: apart from any admiration they felt for the Muslims of the north-west as good soldiers, they had found the Muslims rather more willing to co-operate while the war was on. The League argued that even a continuation of British rule would be preferable to a Congress monopoly of power, which it condemned as a step towards religious tyranny. The Congress leaders protested at this; their party contained a number of Muslims and some secularists like Nehru, and even its devout Hindu members like Gandhi were accused by members of strictly Hindu political parties of having betrayed the interests of their religion. Elections at the end of 1945 and the beginning of 1946 confirmed Congress's position as the party that commanded the support of the majority of Indians, but the League won the position as the main representative of the Muslims in nation-wide politics that it had failed to gain in 1937. At the provincial level it won a majority in Bengal, and the non-League government of the Punjab held on to power by only a flimsy majority.

After the elections three British cabinet ministers came to survey the situation, and their report proposed a very loose federal system in which, above the governments of the provinces, the Muslim governments of the north-east and north-west would be grouped to form one government at a second level of authority and the Congress governments in the rest of the country would join together to form another government of equal status, and then these two second-level governments would come together to form a third tier of government to handle defence policy, foreign affairs, and communications. This plan might be fragile, but it conceded so much to the Muslims that they would have had great difficulty in rejecting it, even though it meant abandoning the idea of Pakistan. But Nehru was so infuriated by what he saw as an unnecessarily pro-Muslim proposal that in July he denounced it in terms which made it easy for the League to dismiss the scheme.

By September the Viceroy had begun to assemble a government of Indian politicians. On the basis of the elections at the beginning of the year, Nehru was made Vice-President of the Council (over which the Viceroy presided) which in effect made him Prime Minister, and after another month of negotiations Muslim League politicians joined the ministry, though there was some suspicion that they had only joined in order to sabotage progress. Rather more serious was the administration's loss of its power to keep the peace. Hindus and Muslims were starting to fight local civil wars, sometimes in the name of Congress or the League, sometimes as straightforward religious battles known in the jargon of the time as 'communal rioting'. The most violent struggles took place in Calcutta, but there were very few parts of the north of India that could be at all sure of remaining peaceful. The Viceroy prepared a 'breakdown plan' in case law and order collapsed completely, which shocked the British government and reduced its confidence in him. But the danger that the police and the army would be caught up in these religious struggles was real enough, and this would have ended the role as impartial and responsive instruments in the hands of the British that they had played for so many years. During the war Indians had risen to the highest ranks in the army and the civil service; in 1939 it might still be asked if they could run the system of government, but by 1945 the question was whether the Indians who were already running a great deal of the system could retain their administrative impartiality under the immense strain to which they were being subjected.

In December Wavell, Nehru, Jinnah, and other leaders came to London and argued inconclusively about the proposals that had been made for keeping the country together. The meetings convinced the British government that it could not impose unity on India and on 20 February 1947 Attlee, the British Prime Minister, announced that Britain would leave India in June 1948 whatever the situation might be, and that Mountbatten would replace Wavell as Viceroy. This step forced the Indian politicians to work out practical plans for the future and, less obviously, it gave Jinnah and the Muslim League what they wanted. Unless the new Indian state felt it could start its independent existence by fighting a civil war against the Muslim provinces the League had only to sit immobile until June 1948 to make the creation of Pakistan inevitable. Mountbatten shared the British government's sympathy for the Congress point of view, and he and his wife established firm friendships with Nehru, but all he could really do was to persuade Congress to accept partition was a good grace. The recognition given to the League at the time of the Cripps Mission and later had reached its logical conclusion. The leaders of the League clearly represented Muslim opinion and Mountbatten quickly decided that the way to make the best of a bad job was to bring forward the date of independence.

Early in June 1947 Mountbatten was talking of independence 'somewhere about August'; in July the date of 15 August was fixed. This forced upon everybody the practical task of dividing the army, the civil service, and the government's assets between the two new states, and the more explosive problem of fixing their boundaries. Jinnah had accepted the need to divide Bengal and the Punjab even though they had slender Muslim majorities, but the Radcliffe Report which drew the boundaries through the two provinces was not in fact published until after the transfer of power from Britain. As a result no government had a chance to prepare to handle it.

On 15 August 1947 the greatest of all acts of imperial withdrawal was carried out. Nehru's joy, and his reservations about partition, were finely blended when he said:

Long years ago we made a tryst with destiny and now the time comes when we shall redeem our pledge, not wholly or in full measure but very substantially. At the stroke of the midnight hour, when the world sleeps, India will wake to life and freedom.

The fury unleashed by partition was just about to break over the two new countries. The outbreaks of violence in the previous year or two and the drift towards civil war between Hindu and Muslim show how hard it would have been to transfer power peacefully under the best of conditions, but the hurried arrangements made between April and August 1947 took the policy of trust and goodwill to the limits of good sense. Tens of millions of people found the new boundaries had suddenly turned them into religious minorities, and millions of them set out to cross to the other side, where they would belong to the majority. Members of the religious majorities stirred this up by attacking people who did not leave or by attacking refugees while they were fleeing, and this led to massacre. After violence and slaughter had broken out in Bengal, along the newly created border, and in Calcutta, Gandhi came to the province and by fasting and applying moral pressure to the local politicians forced them to restore some degree of peace in which the unavoidable transfers of population worked themselves out with as little damage as possible.

In the less densely populated west of the subcontinent, with its strong

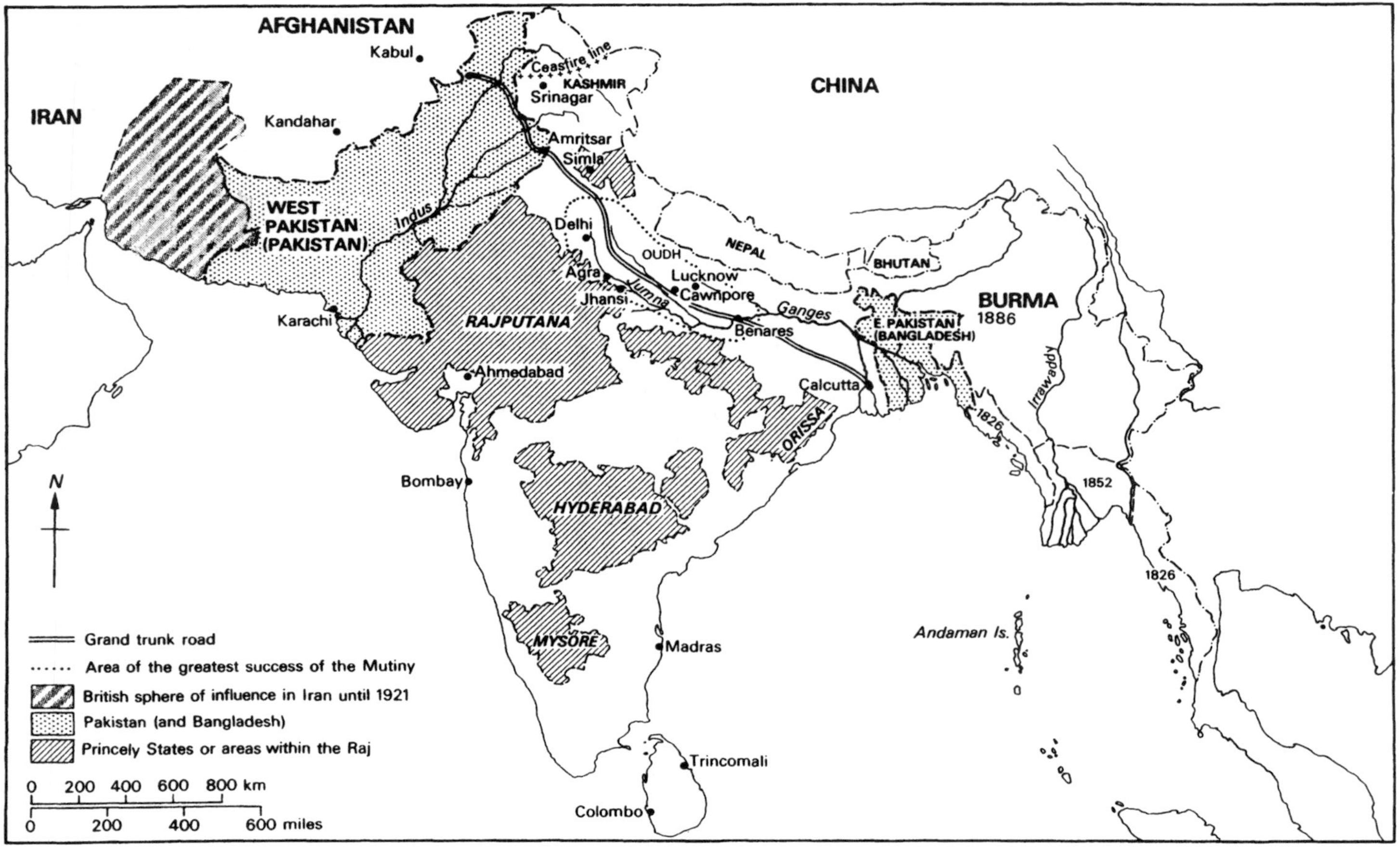

Map 15 India 1850–1947

Grand trunk road
Area of the greatest success of the Mutiny
British sphere of influence in Iran until 1921
Pakistan (and Bangladesh)
Princely States or areas within the Raj

IRAN

AFGHANISTAN

Kabul

Kandahar

WEST PAKISTAN (PAKISTAN)

Karachi

Indus

CHINA

Ceasefire line

KASHMIR

Srinagar

Amritsar

Simla

NEPAL

BHUTAN

Delhi

OUDH

Lucknow

Cawnpore

Agra

Yumna

Jhansi

Benares

Ganges

RAJPUTANA

Ahmedabad

Bombay

HYDERABAD

MYSORE

Madras

ORISSA

Calcutta

E. PAKISTAN (BANGLADESH)

BURMA 1886

1826

Irrawaddy

1852

1826

Andaman Is.

Trincomali

Colombo

N

0   200   400   600   800 km
0   200   400   600 miles

martial traditions, the divided Punjab became the arena for desperate attempts to escape and for hundreds of thousands of deaths. The massacres in the six weeks after independence made it even harder for India and Pakistan to live together as neighbours. India treated Pakistan as a section of the country that had broken away from the legitimate government, and Pakistan's policy was based almost entirely on her fear that India would invade her as soon as this was possible. The atmosphere of suspicion was made worse by the way that India dealt with the princes after independence. Mountbatten had warned them that they would have great difficulty in holding on to their special political status after the British left and that they would be wise to work out terms with the two successor states. Almost all the princely states lay in India or at least were on its borders, and the vast majority of the princes realised that they had to join India or face local revolts. By the end of 1947 almost all of them had given up the feudal semi-independence under the British Crown that they had enjoyed for a century-and-a-half. The Nizam of Hyderabad tried to resist but in September 1948 India invaded his territory 'to restore order' and he relapsed into a position of great wealth inside his new country. The ruler of Kashmir was in a difficult position: he was a Hindu, most of his subjects were Muslims, and his state lay on the borders of both India and Pakistan. He felt threatened by the Muslims, and the struggles just after independence intensified this, so he decided to join India. His Muslim subjects rebelled, and the Indian government swiftly came to help him. A small war, in a very difficult terrain, split Kashmir in two, left India ruling over some dissatisfied Muslims, and made it all the harder for India and Pakistan to live together in peace.

The massacres and the transfers of population might have cast a shadow over the British departure from India, but this was completely submerged by the immense gratification of the Indians at having achieved independence and the relief of the Pakistanis that they had not been treated as part of India. To avoid weakening its future diplomatic position the Pakistan government said little about its belief that the British had leaned to the Indian side. After independence Mountbatten accepted an invitation to stay in India as Governor-General, making it clear that he was sorry not to have had a similar invitation from Pakistan. A little later he may have reflected that, if he had been Governor-General of both countries, he might have had to declare war on himself over the Kashmir question. Other British officials who stayed on after independence sometimes discovered, when they wanted to go on with their pre-independence role that was primarily intended to keep the peace, that the policies of the two new countries did not lay quite such a heavy emphasis upon tranquillity.

Even so, India and Pakistan settled down slightly more happily than the successor states after the ending of the Palestine mandate, though the two problems had looked rather similar. At the end of the war the surviving Jews of Europe were desperate to get into Palestine and were supported by the United States, which asked for 100,000 Jews to be admitted at once. Immigration on this scale would in a few years turn the Jewish minority of 750,000 of the 2 million people in Palestine into a majority. The British government was convinced that this would infuriate the Arab majority and refused to allow substantial immigration. Palestine then became the scene of a three-sided war between Jews, Arabs, and British. In 1947 the British government adopted what looked like the same policy as in India, and announced that the mandate would be given up in May 1948. But Palestine was much more of an international dispute than India had been; the Arabs in Palestine could expect the support of all the neighbouring states, with whom Britain hoped to remain on good terms, and Jews inside Palestine could rely on the support of Jews outside Palestine, and also of the American government: and one great difference between the position in India and that in Palestine was that, while in India the United States simply made it clear that they thought the British should leave, in Palestine they tried in addition to lay down what the British should do to create the conditions after independence that the Americans wanted to see.

As in India, attempts at impartiality led both sides to say that the British were favouring their opponents; such comments by the Arabs made little impression, but the Jews did annoy the British by comparing their policy to that of Hitler. Some American support for the Jewish side was caused by the absence of anyone to put the Arab case in the United States and some by the strength of the Jewish vote in some American states, but a certain amount was probably due to a feeling that the United States had not done enough for the Jews while the war was on. The British felt no such guilt about their wartime efforts, while they did feel regret if not guilt at their failure to keep India together at their departure, though it took place in an elegiac mood which was not much disturbed by the massacres after independence. The retreat from Palestine was much more bitter, with British politicians making it clear that they expected something nasty would happen to both sides after Britain's restraining influence was withdrawn, and inevitably nobody seriously suggested that Israel should become a member of the Commonwealth.

India and Pakistan were clearly interested in the idea of membership of the Commonwealth, but wanted to see what it would mean. After the Second World War the term 'Dominion Status' was still used, though mainly to describe the final stage towards which a colony was evolving, and it was treated as meaning exactly the same as independence, except that 'Dominion Status' involved membership of the Commonwealth. All that was required of members of the Commonwealth was that they should attend Prime Ministers' conferences, which were held more often after 1945 than in the 1930s. During the negotiations about her membership India tested the

Commonwealth relationship in a new way: leaders of Congress had wanted to make their country into a republic as a final proof of independence, and at the 1948 conference they discussed the difficulties of reconciling the position of a republic in the Commonwealth with the phrase in the Balfour Declaration about 'common allegiance to the Crown'. The Indian government may easily have thought that, as Pakistan had become a member of the Commonwealth, leaving would be imprudent. Ceylon joined when she became independent in February 1948, though when Burma became independent in January she declined to become a member, probably out of a belief that this made independence even more complete. Later in the year Ireland proclaimed herself a republic and left the Commonwealth. The British government was angry and contemptuous enough about Ireland's attitude in the Second World War to feel no regret about this, and responded by saying that the position of Northern Ireland would be changed only with the consent of its population.

India was regarded as a much more valuable member of the Commonwealth and was seen as a guide to the future because, if she could change from a colony into a member of the Commonwealth without compromising her independence, then other colonies could do the same. The 1949 Commonwealth conference accepted India's desire to become a republic and altered the phrase about allegiance to the Crown to declare that the King was recognized as 'Head of the Commonwealth', which left it to individual members to decide whether they wanted to continue monarchical rule with a governor-general to represent the sovereign or to become republics with a president as head of state. Later on some republics, though not India, made the president head of the government as well as head of state; the only point of concern to the Commonwealth was to make sure that it was heads of government who attended the conferences. This change of constitutional forms more or less completed the transformation of the Commonwealth machinery from a method of consultation among like-minded countries who hoped to work out a unified policy, into a road to achieve independence in the politest and most amicable way.

In the negotiations which persuaded India to remain a member of the Commonwealth if this was compatible with becoming a republic, the Canadian Prime Minister told Nehru that membership of the Commonwealth meant 'independence plus' – plus, that is, opportunities to meet leaders of other countries with a common language and a fairly similar political and legal background. If India had left the Commonwealth probably a number of other colonies would have seen no advantage in membership, and it might have become frozen as a group of countries with populations of British descent, while the great majority of colonies took some different road to independence. This need not have had any serious long-term consequences, but perhaps the nerves of the British were soothed in the two decades of decolonization which followed by the thought that they were gaining new members of the Commonwealth rather than losing colonies. By the time decolonization had been completed membership of the Commonwealth was obviously not the important factor in any country's policy that it had been in the overseas policy of all the members from 1918 to 1939, but even after 1945 new countries emerging in a sharply polarized world found it useful to belong to a group of nations which could explore the diplomatic situation from a variety of points of view. The British government realized reasonably quickly what a change had taken place; in the years just after the war there were still occasional speculations about a unified defence policy because generals accustomed to the co-operation of the war years thought peacetime policy could be based on agreement among Commonwealth countries, which assumed that they all had roughly the same objectives in foreign policy. So military men in the late 1940s occasionally sounded as if they thought imperial relations had not changed since the days of Joseph Chamberlain, but this was simply because the Second World War had been run so smoothly that they did not realize the spirit of resistance to the common enemy had produced a degree of agreement on foreign policy which could not go on after the war was over. The Labour government was on good terms with the governments of India and of the older-established Dominions in the late 1940s, but this was partly because all these countries were ruled just after the war by governments which, in terms of their own national politics, were left of centre. Opinions shifted towards the end of the decade and by the early 1950s most of them were once more in political agreement, but this time in a position somewhat right of centre. The timing of these changes undoubtedly made Commonwealth relations easier, but there was no doubt that they were relations between independent countries.

African Problems

The Labour government faced a number of problems in Africa in the late 1940s, some of which it had no power to solve. In South Africa the shift to the Right took the form of the defeat in 1948 of Smuts's government, which had looked like a fairly successful attempt to build an electoral majority by bringing together almost all the English-speaking voters and a section of the Afrikaner voters who wanted modernization and good relations with the outside world. The Nationalists who defeated it had a rather strictly Afrikaner view of what the nation should be like, combined with a more popular policy of white unity against the black peril. Even this approach did not give them complete success: they won a majority of seats on a minority of votes because of the over-representation of the Afrikaner countryside. Their hostility to the British ensured them the support of a dedicated minority but would not bring anything close enough to unanimous support among Afrikaners to secure a majority. On the other hand their policy of apartheid, or keeping black and white separate, was something that only intellectuals or large-scale employers would really disagree with. During the war large numbers of Africans had moved into towns and become more fully part of the white economy. Rhodes would probably have been pleased; Smuts was blamed for putting up with it; most white South Africans were rather alarmed and felt there was something to be said for the Nationalist response.

The new government first introduced a variety of small-scale provisions to restore by force of law the divisions between black and white at work and in their daily lives that had been eroded by wartime economic expansion, and went on logically to the establishment of separate states with a limited amount of self-government into which the black population could be driven by use of the laws about passbooks (or internal passports) and out of which they could be drawn by higher wages in the Union of South Africa if their labour was needed. The three High Commission territories could be seen as prototypes of these 'bantustans', and regions inside South Africa like the Transkei which had a densely concentrated African population could be used in the same way. The Nationalists' electoral strategy involved attacking the black Africans some of the time, to unite all white Africans, and denouncing the English and their industrialization some of the time, to keep their Afrikaner supporters enthusiastic. Most people saw its policy of apartheid solely as an attack on the African majority, but some Afrikaners also saw it as a policy to hold back industrialization by making it difficult for the English-speaking section to recruit black labour to push ahead as fast as they wanted. This strategy, helped by a franchise and an electoral system that favoured them, enabled the Nationalists to maintain an attitude on the question of race entirely different from the one that the rest of the world was coming to adopt.

In the British colonies in West Africa hints of change had been growing during the war. Many Africans had served in the armed forces and travelled to other parts of the world. Those who had stayed at home had seen that troops and support forces moving through west Africa regarded the Africans as amiable foreigners rather than servants of empire. As the war drew to an end the Governors of Nigeria and the Gold Coast worked out new constitutions which, while still Lugardian in their concern for the position of the chiefs, opened up the possibility of change. The Colonial Office asked for changes in the proposed constitution, to do more to bring the Africans of the coastal region who had been most affected by the war and by modern ideas into politics. Africans elected directly or by regional assemblies took over from the appointed civil servants as the largest group in the legislatures of both colonies and – so far as such comparisons could be made in a greatly changed world – the constitutional position was rather like that of the British colonists of the eighteenth century, with a governor who held executive power but had to work with public opinion if he was to get his legislative proposals passed into law; and the Colonial Office clearly expected that further development would lead to Dominion Status reasonably quickly.

In the Gold Coast the leading political party, the United Gold Coast Convention, realized that it needed an organization to bring it into closer touch with the mass of the population. Kwame Nkrumah was brought back from London, where he had been trying to develop the pan-African movement, and was asked to set up the new party machinery. He did his work brilliantly; in fact, rather too brilliantly for the taste of his employers in the UGCC. An ex-servicemen's march in Acrra which he organized in February 1948 led to a riot which the UGCC deplored. But the British saw it as a sign that swift action was needed, and quickly set up a system of universal suffrage to elect an assembly which, in a constitution a little like that set up to divide authority in India in 1919, controlled and could dismiss all the ministers in the executive except for those in charge of finance, the police, and the civil service. Nkrumah naturally denounced this as inadequate, and the Convention People's Party which he set up in 1949 quickly swept the UGCC aside. When he was briefly imprisoned as a danger to public order his position was so strong that it only confirmed him as leader of the dominant and politically active coastal section. His party won many more seats than any other in the first election under the new constitution and he was released and made 'Leader of Government Business' (and, in 1951, Chief Minister) in the Executive Council.

By 1952 the Gold Coast was in something like the constitutional position of Canada in the middle of the nineteenth century; Nkrumah spoke of 'Dominion Status' as the object of his policy, clearly using the term to mean independence combined with membership of the Commonwealth, and it could be seen that his country was soon going to achieve it. In the next four years all went well. Cocoa prices rose to new heights, and the Gold Coast still dominated the world cocoa markets; British officials in the colony's financial department insisted on a variable export tax on cocoa to build up a reserve invested in the London money market which could cushion the shock of a fall in prices. Even the high tide of cocoa prosperity left the Gold Coast with a much lower gross national product than almost any independent nation at the time, and it could be argued on economic grounds that Nigeria ought to become independent before the Gold Coast, though Nigeria's internal political problems made this unlikely to happen.

The desire of poor countries for economic growth was beginning to be a preceptible force, and the small-scale efforts of the 1940 Act were put into a new perspective by the immense scale of American generosity in the Marshall Plan. Its success in reviving the economies of western Europe encouraged everyone to believe that a few years of intense commitment to foreign aid would enable the less prosperous parts of the world to do equally well. This was over-optimistic, because Marshall Aid went to a region which already possessed all the requirements for industrial success except capital, but the misunderstanding may have had a good effect. If people had known in the late 1940s how hard it would be to encourage economic growth in most poor countries, they might have decided it was not worth trying to do anything. When the Commonwealth Foreign Ministers met at Colombo in 1950 they launched a plan for economic development in south-east Asia, though its proposals for spending £1.8bn. in six years showed how little they understood the size of the task. The plan was initially expressed within the framework of the Commonwealth but, as was soon obvious, it depended on a large supply of American money for a scheme that was about a quarter the size of the Marshall programme.

The difficulties of encouraging economic growth, the scale on which money could be spent, and the ease with which it could be lost were all illustrated by the British government's attempt to meet its country's need for oils and fat and the East African need for economic development by launching a large-scale scheme for growing groundnuts in Tanganyika in 1948. Very little preliminary work had been done to find out how feasible this was and by 1950 the scheme was virtually bankrupt after spending £30m. and achieving very little. This could be taken to support the traditional argument that governments ought to stick to political and military affairs and should not intervene in economic questions.

In the past federation had been seen as a device for creating territories large enough to manage their own political affairs, but it could also be seen as the way to create successful economic units. After the Nationalist electoral victory in South Africa, the Prime Ministers of Northern Rhodesia and Southern Rhodesia put a strong economic case for a federation of the two Rhodesias and Nyasaland: the copperbelt in Northern Rhodesia would be a good base for development, the relatively large white population of Southern Rhodesia would provide educated administrators and managers, and the overcrowded African population of Nyasaland could find work fairly close to home instead of having to go to the gold mines of Johannesburg for jobs. The three colonies would be able to borrow money at better rates as a federation than as separate political units, which would reduce the cost of large undertakings such as building a dam at Kariba to exploit the hydroelectric potential of the waters of the Zambezi. It seemed quite possible that the federation would be more open to African advancement and friendly to Britain than the new government in South Africa.

In 1951 the Labour government held a conference to discuss the creation of a central African federation, but the idea was received unfavourably enough by African leaders to make the Secretary for the Colonies uneasy about it. Africans thought federation would lead to the extension of Southern Rhodesia's policy of white superiority and strengthen the political and economic position of the white minority, so that it would become more independent of the distant and more equitable rule of London. This sounded very like the objections to the Closer Union scheme for East Africa in the 1920s, and might have been expected to lead to a similar rejection. But the economic logic was so strong and the pressure from the white community so great that the Conservatives took up the proposals when they came to office in Britain late in 1951. The Federation of Rhodesia and Nyasaland was launched in 1953 with almost complete powers of self-government, and its Prime Minister attended Commonwealth conferences as an observer in the way the Southern Rhodesian Prime Minister had done previously. The British government tried to maintain a real veto (apart from the Queen's theoretical veto) over any legislation that might change the position of Africans for the worse, and stated that there would have to be a Royal Commission, rather like the Simon Commission on the 1919 Government of India Act, to report on progress before the Federation could take any further steps towards Dominion Status.

The creation of the Federation did not attract much attention. Britain was concerned in the early 1950s with direct threats to her imperial position, and other members of the Commonwealth were occupied in working out their own foreign policies. Before 1939 small countries, even if they were sovereign states, had not been expected to have foreign policies or to comment on the policies of great powers. Australia was less interested in foreign policy, and more attached to the British connection under Menzies's Liberal-Country coalition in the 1950s than had been the case in the 1940s. The Canadian government became more interested in foreign affairs after the retirement of King and, while St. Laurent was Prime Minister and Pearson was Secretary for External Affairs, it played an active part in encouraging the creation of the North Atlantic Treaty Organization and in smoothing the operations of the United Nations in the early 1950s. Canada and Australia were prosperous enough not to worry much about the effects of their policies on their economic position; India's success in its first ten years after independence was more impressive, because it was able at the same time to receive foreign aid and to argue for a 'non-aligned' policy whose principles included the right of poor countries to receive aid on terms which did not entitle the donors to any control over their policy. The desire to receive aid, and to avoid being committed to one side or the other in the diplomatic struggle between America and Russia, expressed the needs of so many countries that at the 1955 conference of the non-aligned states at Bandung, Nehru was clearly one of the leaders of this section of the world community.

Weaker nations were at times reminded that the older imperial powers, as well as America and Russia, could still impose their will. In 1951 a nationalist government in Iran took over the local holdings of the Anglo-Iranian Oil Company. The large oil companies of America and Europe united to resist this and by making it impossible for the Iranians to sell the oil on the world market they paralysed this move towards economic independence. The Anglo-Iranian Oil Company had to share its concessions with other oil companies, but the main effect of this was to increase the number of interests that the cartel had in common.

Malaya, whose supplies of rubber and tin made it particularly important at a time of international tension, was internally divided along lines that drew it closer to the centre of the struggle between the United States and the Soviet Union than anyone in the country really wanted. The hereditary rulers of the Malay states had been irritated when the British attempted in 1945, almost immediately after returning at the end of the war, to turn the loose federation into a Malayan Union, and succeeded in obtaining a new constitution in 1948 which set up a Federation of Malaya and left them with a good deal of their power. The industrious and financially successful Chinese minority disliked the 1948 constitution because it gave power back to the old-established aristocracy. Some Chinese, partly because of the example of Communist success in China, rebelled and took to guerrilla warfare to bring a Communist government to power. The government of the colony declared a state of emergency in 1948 to organize resistance to the guerrillas, but the British took a little while to see the advantages of basing their policy on the fact that the Malay majority had no desire to be ruled by the Chinese and, as Muslims, had no sympathy with the Communists. Co-operation in the war, on the understanding that Malay would become independent when the threat of Communism had been removed, enabled the British to subdue the guerrillas. By 1955 Tungku Abdul Rahman's Alliance Party won a general election and held most of the ministerial posts, though the British still kept the ministries concerned with organizing defence against the rebellion and with paying for it.

The British also defeated a guerrilla movement in Kenya, in this case without needing to make any political concessions. In the late 1940s Africans pressed for a position in the legislative assembly that would enable them to defend their interests against the white and Indian communities, but by the early 1950s this political movement had been swept aside by the revolt known as Mau Mau – this term was always used confidently by the British government and the white settlers but it seems to have meant rather less to Africans, and some people involved in the revolt may have been keeping to the truth when they said they had nothing to do with Mau Mau. The revolt was aimed at the British farmers who had settled on the high, open land best suited for growing crops for export. The 'white highlands' had been empty when the British settlers first moved in were regarded by the Kikuyu as part of their ancestral possessions and, as their numbers grew, they became more determined to take the land back. At the same time the settlers, who were just beginning to make really satisfactory profits to recompense them for the low prices their products had brought in the 1920s and 1930s, were determined to hang on. The revolt was mainly supported by the Kikuyu, and other Africans showed little desire to help a movement which would replace British supremacy by Kikuyu supremacy, especially as the rebels concentrated on attacking the Africans who went on working for their white employers. Partly because of this the revolt was crushed by 1955, which strengthened the impression that the British were sufficiently in control of the situation in their colonies to decide for themselves what they would do next.

After the substantial decolonization in Asia in the late 1940s the American government became much more concerned to keep its European allies devoted to the struggle against Communism than to suggest that France, Belgium, Portugal, or Britain should give up any more colonies. The rebellions in Malaya and in French Indo-China were so naturally seen as examples of Communist expansionism that the United States government was bound to oppose them, and some aspects of the ritual used in organizing the Mau Mau revolt were primitive enough to mean that it would not receive support from outside. The Soviet Union had not yet become deeply involved in the world outside Europe. Rather like the United States, it expected its allies to be whole-heartedly on its side, so that both powers drifted towards the principle 'He that is not with us is against us.' Although this allowed the British to maintain their imperial position free from external pressure, the expenses of the campaigns in Kenya and Malaya which together cost about £100m. were uncomfortably high. Almost all of Britain's colonies had been acquired at very little cost, for the British were unwilling to move forward if it involved heavy spending and, once a government had been set up in a colony, the cost of maintaining law and order was always charged to the local budget. The experience of the early 1950s, when the British taxpayer had to meet the bulk of the expense, indicated that a larger proportion of the national income than ever before might have to be spent on colonial defence, or alternatively a policy of withdrawal might be unavoidable. Malaya was not going to remain a source of possible expense for long, and by the end of the rebellion in Kenya the government was trying to establish a new political base by encouraging development and suggesting to British companies that they could set up local operations there and employ urbanized and unionized African workers who could be brought into a cash rather than a tribal economy.

Suez and Its Consequences

In the early 1950s the other old-established European imperial governments took the same approach as the British. Development would go ahead steadily, European standards of education and even of prosperity would become more widespread, and with the passage of time people in the colonies would slowly acquire some degree of political competence. The development of British colonies was expected to lead, after careful preparation, to membership of the Commonwealth; in French colonies the objective was even more ambitious, for it was intended that all French subjects should accept the French way of life and become French citizens, with precisely the same voting rights and claims to representation in Paris as the inhabitants of France enjoyed. In Britain the Colonial Office reckoned it would still be administering colonies at the end of the century, and it became more active than before in its efforts to guide colonies in the right direction. In retrospect this does not seem a very practicable policy, but it looked fairly sensible in the years before the politically disastrous attack on Egypt that Britain and France carried out late in 1956.

As the most populous country in the Arab world, with a great centre of cultural and intellectual life in Cairo, Egypt was bound to be important in the Middle East. By 1954 Britain had completed negotiations which established Sudan as an independent country, and provided for British troops to leave the Canal Zone by the early summer of 1956, although the treaty allowed Britain a right to return to the Canal Zone (much as the 1936 Treaty allowed a right to re-enter Egypt). The plan for Egyptian economic development placed considerable emphasis on a large dam for generating hydroelectricity at Aswan on the Nile. But in July 1956 the United States government decided that the Egyptian government of President Nasser was not a loyal friend, and its promise of financial assistance for the dam was withdrawn. The British government did the same, and the Egyptian government responded by nationalizing the Suez Canal. This caused alarm in Britain, partly because people remembered the Canal as the high road to India, and also in France, partly because most of the shares of the Canal Company were still owned in France. Eden, the British Prime Minister, had a more immediate problem in mind when he spoke of Nasser having his hand on Britain's windpipe: the figures of growth in oil consumption and in particular of imports from the Gulf showed that the Canal was gaining a new importance as a supply route to Europe. The French government believed that the rebellion against its rule in Algeria would have been crushed if Nasser had not supported the rebels; Eden saw Nasser as something like a reincarnation of the dictators against whom he had tried to direct British foreign policy in the 1930s. So Britain and France were ready to consider violent action against Egypt and they prepared an invasion force which was always in people's minds in the negotiations of the next few months.

By the middle of October Nasser seemed ready to assure the users of the Canal that he would spend enough of the proceeds levied on shipping to keep the Canal open and efficient and would fulfil his other obligations under the 1888 treaty, which regulated the operation of the Canal. But the British and French Prime Ministers were not really interested in this; they wanted to crush Nasser. The French were in touch with Israel and worked out a plan by which Israel would attack Egypt, and the invasion force would then seize the Canal under the pretext of separating Israel and Egypt. Once Britain had been brought in, the plan was put into effect at the end of October. Israel attacked with British and French air support, and the invasion force sailed forward to make Egypt withdraw 10 miles west of the Canal, which would give most of the Sinai peninsula to Israel and allow Britain and France a zone of occupation along the Canal.

By themselves the Egyptians could not resist this attack, but world opinion had changed so much that the invasion was bound to bring them almost universal sympathy and support. The new conventions meant that wars between the rich countries (which could be taken to include military operations by the Russians against their European subjects) were acceptable, and wars fought among the poor countries were acceptable, but wars in which rich and powerful countries fought against poor countries were not acceptable. So the United Nations almost unanimously condemned Egypt's three enemies, the Soviet Union threatened to launch nuclear-armed rockets at Britain and France, and the United States refused to help them by supplying oil or by supporting the exchange value of their currencies. The attack placed considerable strain on Commonwealth relationships and showed that there was no substance in the idea that there ought to be consultation before any dramatic action, though some opponents of the invasion argued as if they had never heard of Chanak and did not understand that consultation had then been laid aside. India joined in the almost universal denunciation, Australia and New Zealand showed that they were still willing to stand behind Britain without asking whether she was right or wrong, and the Canadian government set about helping to create a United Nations force that could help keep the peace in the Suez area, a step that at the time was seen in English-speaking Canada as an attack on Britain.

Against a background of so much hostility and so little support, only a ruthless disregard of world opinion could have carried the operation forward. While the pressure of international disapproval had to be taken seriously, what really weighed with the British government was that the United States's refusal to support the value of the pound might lead to a devaluation. So the British insisted that the military operations must end while the French, who were much less worried about the value of the franc, made it clear that they thought the British had turned out to be very unsatisfactory allies. The British government clearly felt guilty about the operation. It insisted on concealing the agreement to co-operate with Israel, which puzzled both France and Israel, who saw nothing wrong with working together against Egypt.

Co-operation with Israel and the failure of the operation combined to undermine Britain's position in the Arab world. Iraq had been her main ally there for a generation; the King had been educated in Britain, the leading politician Nuri es-Said, who had been Prime Minister much of the time since the 1930s, was a devoted anglophile, and the country's oil was managed by British companies. In 1958 a revolution overthrew the government, the King and the Prime Minister were lynched and the country moved decisively away from the British connection. To the south-east of Iraq, Kuwait in 1961 ended the 1899 treaty that had committed her foreign policy to British direction. This was an amicable parting of friends, and when the new government of Iraq tried to take over Kuwait in 1962 British troops went to the Gulf and defeated the threat. Britain's interest in the Middle East had now shrunk to the defence of a small area round the north-east and south-east coastline of the Arabian peninsula, but this area was so rich in oil that in the 1960s it looked as if the British had saved the most important part of their position in the region.

Larger and more indirect changes followed from the Suez failure, mainly in Africa. France's problem in Algeria was one of the most difficult of all colonial questions, and by 1958 it had destroyed the French Fourth Republic. When de Gaulle came to office as the ruler of the Fifth Republic he looked like a guardian of the past, draped in glory and in memories of both World Wars. Macmillan, who had become Prime Minister when Eden's health collapsed after Suez, gave much the same impression in Britain. However, both men knew the world was changing and neither of them thought there were many advantages about maintaining an imperial position if it involved any expensive struggle, even though at first both of them gave their supporters the impression that they intended to stand by the cause of the empire. De Gaulle assured the French settlers in Algeria that he understood them and their attachment to France; Macmillan responded to agitation on the island of Cyprus for union with Greece by exiling Archbishop Makarios (who, as an elected bishop, was a natural leader for the Greek majority on the island) to the Seychelles.

Plans for independence for Malaya and for the Gold Coast that had been made well before Suez were now coming to fruition, and showed what future policy would be. In Malaya the Alliance Party had worked out a division of power between the Malay majority and the non-Communist Chinese, so power could be transferred peacefully, but Malaya's relative prosperity and the conscious effort made to maintain racial balance meant that her situation was not a clear precedent for other colonies. In the Gold Coast the position was different in almost every way. Power was about to pass to the prosperous and educated section on the coast that Nkrumah led, and the more traditionally-minded Asanti inland could see that they would not do well out of this. They asked the British to stay longer and to impose on the country a constitution that would recognize their special position but, although it was pleasant for the imperial rulers to see that the Asanti trusted them to be fairer than their next-door neighbours (an attitude often adopted by groups which expected to do badly at independence), the British could see neither advantage nor real justice in imposing provisions for local rights upon a properly elected government which already had responsibility for internal affairs.

Egypt or Ethiopia or Libya or even Sudan might be considered the first colony in Africa to become independent, but the emergence of Ghana (as the Gold Coast called itself upon becoming independent in 1957) had an impact that none of the other moves to independence had had. Other Africans felt that, if the Ghanaians could rule themselves, arguments based on lack of capacity or experience for governing themselves no longer carried much weight. The Ghanaian government encouraged the general desire for independence. Nkrumah had retained his pan-African ideals, and took a deeper interest in the affairs of the rest of the continent than was always welcomed by his own people. He had come to power by building up a spirit of nationalism which, if not based on decades of struggle like Indian nationalism, did mean that controlling unwilling subjects in the Gold Coast from London would be more trouble than it was worth, but this development of national sentiment meant that Ghanaians were citizens of their own country rather than of a vast hypothetical union of all Africa.

At first Ghana gained considerable prestige because it stood as the leading nation saying that all other African states should be free to move on to independence, but this position of leadership could not survive when the other African nations did attain independence, each endeavouring to develop a national spirit of its own. The shift of feeling from pan-Africanism to nationalism could be seen in the change of attitude to the question of boundaries. The previous criticism that the partition of Africa had ignored linguistic lines of division and cut coherent political units in half died away as African countries became independent. Governments were probably afraid that the arguments about the proper boundaries could be unending, but they also wanted to avoid the suggestion that their countries were loose federations of pre-partition tribes which could easily be merged into a united Africa.

The largest changes in Africa came in 1958, when all French territories south of the Sahara were made into members of the French community, and in 1960, when they were made independent. Their capacity to run their own affairs was limited in practice, because the French treated each administrative unit in their empire as a separate state and thus created a dozen new countries, of which at least half had so poor an endowment of administrators and so low a gross national product that nobody would previously have believed that they could survive as sovereign states. Ghana had a population of 6 million and one of the highest levels of income per head in Africa but people had wondered if it was economically able to manage on its own. The French grants of independence on a wholesale basis transformed people's idea of the size and wealth a state needed in order to be given independence. If Gabon, with a population of between half and three-quarters of a million people, could be independent, what colony could reasonably be denied independence?

So the British found themselves confronting the problems of imperial departure in a world that had just seen its old ideas overturned. The Colonial Office was still preparing for the immediate future by working on the constitutional arrangements for Nigeria, which in some ways looked as good a prospect for satisfactory progress after independence as Ghana. With a much larger population its gross national product was distinctly bigger and its claims to future prominence were more securely founded. But at the time it was not as close to being a completely united nation as Ghana; its federal constitution provided for leaders from the Northern Region, the Western Region (which was really the western half of the coastal section), and the Eastern Region (the eastern half of the coastal section) to be returned to the central assembly by indirect election. The Regions institutionalized existing differences and offered no cure for the division which, as in Ghana, ran between the educated coastal community and the more old-fashioned community inland. Because Nigeria stretched further to the north than Ghana the inland community, which at the beginning of the century had been Lugard's Northern Nigeria, contained the majority of the population. Its position was recognized in 1957 when the post of Prime Minister was created and was filled by Abubakar Tefawa Balewa, one of the leaders of the Northern People's Congress.

The northerners wanted the advance to independence to slow down, so that more of them could gain administrative jobs and stop the educated southerners from holding a monopoly of power. The arguments pointed in the opposite direction from those of the pre-independence debate in the Gold Coast: the elected government was asking for delay and for a looser federation, so the British government had no cause to press for speedy action which would have helped the coastal regions. The durability of pre-partition political forces, which had been greatly helped by Indirect Rule, was shown by the amount of power that remained in the hands of the Sarduana of Sokoto – the successor of the ruler with whom Lugard had made an important treaty at the beginning of the century – when Nigeria became independent in 1960. Hereditary princes in India had survived the period of British rule and retained their wealth, but none of them had emerged with so much political power.

The hereditary rulers were conservative and pro-British in attitude. Independence in Ghana disappointed the British: Nkrumah had at once used his position to demand the end of the rest of the British Empire in Africa, and soon afterwards had moved to turn his country into a one-party state in which he held dictatorial powers. Nigeria was much less ready to disagree with Britain, and the Nigerian constitution seemed firmly based on a federal system to express the realities of Nigerian regional politics. Nigerian independence looked so successful that it might have led people in Britain to think that not much more had to be done in the immediate future. But Macmillan had no intention of being caught up by this belief; in 1960 he went on a tour of Africa, visiting colonies and members of the Commonwealth and ending by giving a speech at Cape Town in which he warned the South African parliament that a 'wind of change' was blowing through Africa. The white South Africans gritted their teeth and prepared to resist the wind, no matter how rough, but Macmillan could see very little sense in Britain behaving in such a way.

If he needed a warning of the troubles that resisting change could cause an imperial power, he had only to look at France. Withdrawal south of the Sahara had not been accompanied by disengagement from Algeria because so much of de Gaulle's claim to power in 1958 rested on his ability to satisfy the French army and settlers in Algeria that he would treat them better than the Fourth Republic had done. This committed France to a war which was as costly in men and money as the war in Indo-China had been in the early 1950s, and could never produce results that would justify the cost to France. De Gaulle was well aware of this, and was getting ready to disengage himself from it as soon as his political position in France was strong enough. Macmillan took great care to avoid any military involvements of this sort, and after the 1959 general election he felt able to undertake a policy of decolonization as sweeping and almost as speedy as France's departure from her colonies south of the Sahara.

Race and the Commonwealth

The 1961 Commonwealth conference showed another way in which involvement in Africa could embarrass the British government. During the 1950s, the Nationalists in South Africa had established apartheid, excluded Africans from the prosperous areas of the economy as far as possible, and reserved economic as well as political power for white people. South Africa was not an autocracy: the press was free to criticize the government and its policies, and the courts were able to hold back legislation that did not meet the requirements of the constitution, which delayed for several years the Nationalists' proposals to deprive the coloured people of Cape Province of the political rights guaranteed for them in the 1930s. By the late 1950s the Nationalists wanted some more specifically Afrikaner policy, to show their more dedicated supporters that the party was not just a vehicle for uniting whites against blacks. To rally the faithful the Nationalists held a referendum on a proposal to make the country into a republic, and in 1960 they gained a narrow majority for the change. Probably a few English-speaking voters supported it out of a feeling that they ought to do something to conciliate the

Afrikaners, but the important aspect of the vote was that it reunited the Afrikaners; the alliance of a section of Afrikaners with the English-speaking voters, which Botha and Smuts had built up, was now greatly weakened, and the Nationalists won a majority of the votes cast, as well as a majority in Parliament, in subsequent elections. Conditions in South Africa were stormy; at Sharpeville in 1960 the police fired into a crowd of Africans and killed sixty or seventy people, which was seen as a sign that revolt was on the way, though in the event it simply led to the creation of a much more efficient and all-pervasive system of police control.

When the Commonwealth Prime Ministers met for their 1961 conference they had to consider South Africa's position as a republic; as a result of the Indian precedent it had become accepted that a formal application for renewed membership should be made when a member became a republic and this gave the Asian and African members of the Commonwealth, supported by Canada, an opportunity to insist that the conference communiqué must include a condemnation of apartheid. South Africa was offended enough by this to withdraw its application and ceased to be a member of the Commonwealth when the Republic was proclaimed in May. Macmillan had worked hard to avoid this, and could of course argue that the attack on apartheid was an attempt to interfere in a member's internal affairs which had always been understood to be outside the scope of the conference, but South Africa would fairly certainly have been pushed out of the Commonwealth at some point in the 1960s.

A great shift of feeling on questions of race had been sweeping over the world in the previous twenty or thirty years. Until then it had been regarded as perfectly reasonable to attribute national success or failure to racial differences, and it was often assumed almost as a matter of course that white people were racially (or genetically) superior to everyone else. In a sense the apartheid legislation had simply codified a view that had been widely held for a long time. But the horrible example of Germany under Hitler had changed all this; a lifelong man of the Left like Hobson could write in the 1930s that 'a situation like the present in which lower stocks and lower races displace higher races and higher stocks would denote a human retrogressions',[1] but he would have felt it much harder to say such a thing a dozen years later. Racial theories had been given a bad name; by the 1950s the idea that Asians or Africans were inherently inferior was no longer acceptable, though it could still be argued that they needed more experience in government before becoming independent. The change had been becoming visible by Smuts's last years; for most of his life he had been seen as an apostle of reason and progress (though some people had always said he was more willing than the average Afrikaner to tolerate African advance only because

[1] J. A. Hobson, *Confessions of an Economic Heretic* (1938), 152.

of his political links with the largest employers), but by his last period in office this role was already hard to reconcile with his need to win South African votes. In 1939 it was argued that black Africans could never rule themselves; by 1960 it was argued that they must be allowed to rule themselves immediately.

Opposition to racial discrimination was sometimes seen as part of an advance in the general level of political morality, but pehaps it ought to be compared with the growth of opposition to slavery 150 years earlier. Opponents of slavery had not necessarily embraced a higher standard of political action, except on this particular issue. This did not mean they were insincere in their support for abolition, just as the fact that some African leaders had no interest in freedom of speech or in their citizens' right to oppose the government did not mean that they were insincere in their opposition to racial discrimination. Political leaders who locked up or executed their own political opponents while complaining about the lack of freedom in South Africa appeared willing to 'Compound for sins they were inclined to, by damning those they had no mind to', but it was no more reasonable to charge them with hypocrisy than it would have been to make similar charges against the opponents of slavery on account of their shortcomings in other fields. Racial discrimination had acquired the same status as a uniquely evil institution as slavery had done in the nineteenth century. In its day slavery had brought the British Parliament to intervene in the internal affairs of West Indian islands and override the local legislatures and, whatever the Commonwealth conventions about non-interference in internal affairs, any revival of slavery in any member state would have led to ferocious opposition. Racial discrimination was beginning to arouse the same passionate hostility; South Africa was naturally attacked most vigorously, but any country which held on to African colonies was likely to meet the same accusation sooner or later.

The unwillingness of the Commonwealth to lay down rules for its members in matters less disturbing than racial discrimination had already been shown. The government of Pakistan had broken down under the strain of ruling the two sections of the country. No country-wide elections had been held since independence, and the western section had monopolized power. The eastern section had at least as large a population, but it was in the west that money was spent on the army, the civil service, and on new development schemes. When the army seized power in 1958 it was to a considerable extent reacting to the corruption of the politicians, but the coup also enabled the western section to retain its privileged position without any of the risks of holding elections. Ayub Khan disturbed very few interests in western Pakistan, and provoked very little opposition by taking power. If anyone had told the Commonwealth leaders, even ten years earlier, that they would accept a general who had overthrown his government as one of their number, they would have found it hard to believe, but by 1958 a military government was easier to accept than a racially discriminatory government.

The problems of racial discrimination and of outside intervention in the affairs of a member of the Commonwealth were about to be seen in Britain. Laws about citizenship had not been the basis of policy in the British Empire. The subjects of the monarch lived under laws that varied from one part of the monarch's realms to another. By the late nineteenth century these realms included some portions that were only protectorates, and their inhabitants certainly did not have the full rights of British subjects, but people in Britain probably imagined that British subjects had a right to travel freely throughout the empire. In the self-governing colonies policies for excluding British subjects who were thought undesirable had already been established. People from the poorer parts of the empire were kept out of the Dominions to make sure that they did not undercut wage rates, and Englishmen and Scotsmen who took part in organizing trade unions were expelled from South Africa in 1911 and from Canada in 1919 for revolutionary activity.

Any British subject or person from the protectorates could come into Britain freely, and until the early decades of the twentieth century there was very little restraint on foreigners either. Large numbers of returning emigrants came back to Britain, a few of them with fortunes they had made, and most of them with memories of a new country but no desire to stay away from home all their lives. For centuries black and brown people had lived in Britain, a few brought in as slaves, some coming as sailors, some simply moving to a country where pay was better than in their native lands. Students like Gandhi and Nehru came to the Inns of Court to get a legal education that would qualify them to practice in the highest courts in their own country or anywhere else in the empire. In the 1920s and the 1930s the younger and flashier members of London society showed their open-mindedness – sometimes noting the contrast with American behaviour – by bringing Africans and West Indians into their circle. In the Second World War people in Britain were shocked when they found that troops in the American army were segregated on racial lines. All of this encouraged the British to think that their country was racially tolerant, when really there had been no test of this tolerance.

The movement of population of which the British were conscious after 1945 was a resumption of emigration from Britain. By 1955 about 1.25m. people had left for the traditional areas of white settlement in the Commonwealth. In the 1950s a large-scale flow of immigration into Britain began. In the first stage working-class West Indians, often brought up to think of Britain as 'home' (an attitude handed down by the white rulers of the islands, who were only at this stage losing political power) came to Britain to look for work. Though they found that the native British did not see them as fellow-countrymen, there were no obvious problems in the early 1950s. Unemployment was so low that nobody had any trouble in finding a job; the West Indians got unattractive jobs or had to work awkward hours, but it was easy to see this as simply the normal fate of almost all immigrants. By the late 1950s immigrants were also coming from India and Pakistan, and by 1960 the flow had risen to over 50,000 a year. There had been riots and other incidents that showed British tolerance for newcomers did not go as deep as had been thought; as immigration for 1961 looked like reaching 100,000 or so, the Commonwealth Immigration Act was introduced to impose limits on entry.

Mainly because of the deep personal convictions of its leader, Hugh Gaitskell, the Labour party opposed the legislation. The government argued that unrestricted immigration was encouraging racial division in Britain, and there was evidence to show that this was the case. Opposition to the Act was based partly on the ideal of freedom of movement, but also on commitment to a concept of the unity of the Commonwealth that was becoming out-of-date. Most of the immigrants came from former colonies that by this stage had reached independence and in some cases had laws of their own to restrict immigration. When the governments of India and of Pakistan and of some countries in the Caribbean objected to the legislation, they placed an emphasis upon the ideal of Commonwealth unity that they would not have been willing to see imposed on their own policies. Three years later (after the death of Gaitskell) it was a Labour government which gave full administrative form to the legislation; and in those three years it had become clear that arguments about the Commonwealth as a single unit had been laid to rest.

13. *Independence at Once 1960–1983*

A decisive change in British policy in Africa and in the general attitude to colonies took place at the end of the 1950s. Until then British statements about colonies stressed the idea of training them for independence, which was at times put explicitly in terms of the success of gradual withdrawal from India, and otherwise tacitly drew on memories of the long period during which the colonies of white settlement turned imperceptibly into independent nations. But in the 1960s and 1970s the idea of gradual preparation was laid aside almost completely and was replaced by the determination of the imperial rulers and their colonial subjects to end the process as fast as possible. The accustomed forms of opening the legislative council to elections on a basis of universal suffrage, handing power to a local leader, and holding an independence ceremony on lines that were almost always inspired by memories of Delhi in August 1947 were still observed, but at a pace which transformed the process in the way that a film is changed by being run more quickly.

At the same time the idea that some colonies were too poor or too small to become independent was tacitly abandoned although, if a colony was endangered by the territorial ambitions of a neighbour, the British would remain in the colony and try to negotiate a safe passage to independence. The obvious pressure for independence was the strength of nationalist feeling, and the political unit around which it developed was always the existing colony, so nationalism made it hard to put federations together and as a result most of the new countries that emerged in this period had very small populations. This expanded the number of member states in a way that changed the Commonwealth almost out of recognition; its members came to make up over a quarter of the United Nations and, as almost all of them used English for international purposes, they were the largest language bloc in the organization. Creation of the Commonwealth had served very well to cloak the passing of the British Empire, but it had developed at a time when Britain was far more important on the world stage than all the other members put together and it could not survive on that basis. Efforts were made to turn it from a branch of the British government through which the Colonial Office or the Commonwealth Relations Office ran its diplomatic arrangements into an administrative system to which all Commonwealth countries could respond without feeling that they were compromising their independence.

Britain's attitude to Commonwealth relationships was changing at the same time as her international relationships were being altered, and altered in a way that people in Britain found hard to accept. When Acheson, who had been the American Secretary of State in the late 1940s, said in 1962 that Britain had lost an empire and had not yet found a role, his comment roused howls of protest in Britain. Acheson (the son of a British emigrant) had only been trying to clarify the situation, but it was too early for such clarity. Britain was in fact trying to find a role by joining the European Economic Community, at first scrutinizing the terms very carefully, then entering on terms that seemed unlikely to be a good economic bargain, and never accepting as wholehearted a commitment to Europe as that of her Continental partners. At the beginning of this period of economic realignment, from the late 1950s to the late 1970s, Commonwealth countries were still heavily committed to trade with Britain, but they reorganized their trade as the inclination of British policy became more visible.

The power of nationalism had triumphed over the spirit of empire, but this still left problems when new nationalisms awakened, or old ones revived, within the boundaries of existing states. A number of Commonwealth countries had to wrestle with the problem, and only in the cases of Malaysia, the Federation of the West Indies, and the Federation of the Rhodesias and Nyasaland were plans for federation as a prelude to independence conclusively shown to be unsatisfactory by secession or the break-up of the proposed territory. To this extent the arrangements for independence were successful, though the strain on a number of other states, old and new, was sometimes severe. The British government probably spent more time worrying about the struggle over Rhodesia (now Zimbabwe) between 1965 and 1980 than over the whole of the rest of the process put together, which was not a true reflection of Rhodesia's importance in the world, but did show how things could go wrong and why it was wise to try to get a quick settlement. The risk of bloodshed may have been overestimated in the 1960s but Britain had little to gain by resisting the independence movements. The risk of Communist advance or of a fatal lapse into disorder gave the British a reason to fight in Malaya and in Kenya in the 1950s, but in the 1960s the leaders of the independence movements were not Communist and fully realized the dangers of disorder. Even if the British could have held the change back for some years, a series of colonial wars would have harmed their diplomatic reputation. Imperial withdrawal was not just a matter of saving money, but as acquiring colonies had not cost the taxpayer very much and retaining them had cost practically nothing in the past, heavy spending on resisting change (even if successful) would have been an unwelcome development.

The Great Acceleration

Macmillan's appointment of Macleod as Secretary for the Colonies in October 1959 can be seen as the turning point at which British policy changed from sedate encouragement of steady progress towards independence to brisk action to get rid of all colonies as fast as possible. Macleod had taken very little interest in colonial affairs before he became Secretary of State, and his biography does not really make it clear whether he worked out his policy for himself after he had been appointed, or accepted and carried out very effectively some principles that had been laid down by Macmillan or inspired by officials in the Colonial Office. In either case, he thought there would be 'terrible bloodshed in Africa' unless the pace of imperial departure were speeded, and Macmillan made it clear that he agreed with this assessment.

The problems of the Federation of Rhodesia and Nyasaland had been worrying the British government before the 1959 election. The government of the Federation had become convinced that a rebellion was being planned in Nyasaland and that it had to impose a state of emergency to deal with the problem, but when a British judge examined the situation he reported that Nyasaland had become a 'police state' as a result. Macmillan held his Cabinet and his party on a firm imperial line to avoid weakening its morale before the election, but he could see that this approach could not be sustained for very long. As the original legislation laid down that a Royal Commission had to investigate the Federation and report on its progress before it could reach Dominion Status, Macmillan decided to appoint the Commission at this stage to clarify the situation. The government of the Federation knew that British sentiment was becoming sympathetic to African nationalism, and felt uneasy about British-appointed men of eminence coming to pass judgement. Macmillan had to reassure Welensky, the Prime Minister of the Federation, by going a long way towards saying that the Commission could not recommend the dissolution of the Federation, even though Africans were now pressing for this with great determination. Once the Commission under Lord Monckton had been set up, Macleod turned his attention to East Africa where African eagerness for independence and the question of closer links among the colonies posed complicated rather than dangerous problems.

Late in the term of office of Lennox-Boyd, the previous Secretary for the Colonies, it had been estimated that the East African colonies would take about a dozen years to become independent. Macleod's timetable was much shorter. His guiding principle was to find a man who he felt could safely be trusted with power, and then make sure that he obtained power.

In Tanganyika there was no difficulty: while the country was a United Nations mandate rather than a colony in the strict sense, the United Nations Trusteeship Council never made as many difficulties as enemies of the United Nations liked to claim. Julius Nyerere was a political leader with Christian principles that meant he would not lean too far towards the Soviet Union even if he found the materialism of the capitalist West unattractive. His political party, the Tanganyika African National Union, brought together a wide range of followers from all over the country, so that it was unlikely to become the instrument of a single region or tribe. Nationalists were often attracted by the example of India and Pakistan; these two nations were largely the creations of the Indian National Congress and the Muslim League, which had built up national feeling while struggling for independence, and subsequent independence movements hoped to use a nation-wide political party to avoid the dangers of regionalism. The risk in this approach to nation-building was that it might make the country into a one-party state and rob the party system of its usual function of providing for peaceful changes of government through contested elections. At the moment of independence power would naturally be concentrated in the hands of one man who seemed to sum up the spirit of resistance to imperial rule and, if he was backed by an all-embracing political party, changes of leadership might be delayed longer than was sensible.

Macleod would have seen this as only a very distant problem, and felt he was making a good start when Tanganyika became independent in 1961. Nyerere explored the possibility of remaining at the stage of internal self-government for some years, to wait for the other British colonies in East Africa to become independent, as he hoped that when power had passed into African hands they could organize a federation before the colonial frontiers and divisions had become institutionalized in the form of new nations. This was a rational response to the problems of relatively small and poor countries emerging into the world of independent nations, and also to the problems of Tanganyika as the poorest of the British colonies in the region, but nobody was prepared to wait for it to work. His followers wanted to move ahead to independence at once, and the other colonies did not show as much enthusiasm for the proposal as was needed. The colonies had worked together for various technical and transport services under the British government, and this co-operation could be maintained after independence, but national feeling was already well established within the states that the British had created.

The other East African colonies, Uganda, Kenya, and Zanzibar, presented more difficulties because of their regional and racial divisions. Kenyan politics was at a standstill in 1959. The Kikuyus were obviously going to play an important part in any political change and the only leader who could enable them to play a politically coherent role, Jomo Kenyatta, was in prison. He had spent most of the 1930s and 1940s in Britain and when he returned to Kenya had rapidly risen to prominence by the force of his personality and his capacity to blend modernization and Kikuyu tradition into a unified political programme. Suspicion had then grown that he was the secret head of Mau Mau; he was convicted, and in 1953 sentenced to prison for seven years. The British officials in Kenya clearly hoped that his influence would fade away, and even after he was released from prison in 1959 he was detained too far from Nairobi to be able to take part in politics.

His hold on the Kikuyu leaders and on most Africans was not much weakened; ambitious African politicians might hope that he would retire but they had to plan on the basis that he would return to the scene. Macleod accepted this and moved him to reasonably open detention close enough to Nairobi for Africans to be able to consult him. The small white community had strong enough connections in Britain to cause Macleod some inconvenience; it was still frightened of Kenyatta, and when the Governor of the colony called him 'a leader of darkness and death' he expressed the settler's feelings fairly accurately.

Non-Kikuyu African politicians also disliked the prospect of Kenyatta's dominance and formed the Kenya African Democratic Union from other African groups, led by Daniel arap Moi, to oppose the mainly Kikuyu Kenya African National Union. Most of the white population hoped that change could be held back in the 1960s as it had been in the 1950s, but some of them worked with KADU. In the 1961 election KANU won more seats than any other party and although the Governor was able to build up a majority for KADU this was clearly only going to give time to bring Kenyatta back into politics officially and to allow the unreconciled white population to think again about its position. The KADU leaders could see that, unless they quickly merged with KANU and recognized Kenyatta's leadership, they would be accused of being enemies of independence, and while some of them might have preferred continued British rule to the triumph of Kenyatta, this alternative was not open to them.

The Colonial Office had recognized rather sooner than most of the non-Kikuyu, black or white, that Kenyatta was only a limited threat to the established order. Obviously he stood for African rule and for the end of racial discrimination in the distribution of the good things of life. Once it was clear that he and other Africans would be able to share in the feast, he saw no need to overturn the table. Kenyatta, whose long lifetime stretched from the very first days of British political involvement in the land that became his country down to the British departure from the whole of Africa, was a man who commanded respect and admiration, and he also fitted the political needs of the situation. He could be accepted by the departing British because he would keep the peace and have nothing to do with

Communism, by the Africans who needed a political leader whom everyone would follow, and by the white farmers who stayed on in Kenya, who because the President had himself become a great landlord, felt safer about their estates than they would have done with any amount of paper guarantees.

The groups in Uganda facing the British who were preparing to leave were very similar to those who had been powerful when imperial rule was first established there, but no Kenyatta figure could be found to bring them together. Macleod became convinced that the Protestant group had little to offer and that an alliance between the Kabaka of Buganda and Obote the Catholic leader was the best foundation for a stable government, and by the time he announced in 1961 that the country would become independent in the following year the alliance had become established. The island of Zanzibar had been put on the road to independence, which it reached in 1963, though this was an unstable arrangement because power remained in the hands of the Arab minority; in 1964 the resuscitated Sultan was overthrown and the new government then formed a federation with Tanganyika under the name of Tanzania. In West Africa Macleod had presided over the peaceful progress of Sierra Leone to independence in 1961, and further south he had begun dismantling the Federation of Rhodesia and Nyasaland.

The disturbance in Nyasaland which had led to the state of emergency had begun when Dr Hastings Banda had come back to his native country after several years in Edinburgh and had been arrested when he took the lead in asking for independence. Macleod realized that Banda was a man of very moderate views whose desire to get Nyasaland out of the Federation was shared by almost everybody in his country, so he was released and discussions about self-government began. Plenty of supporters of the Federation in the two Rhodesias were willing to let Nyasaland separate, to reduce the immense disproportion in numbers between black and white in what remained. Nyasalanders had to find work outside their small and very poor country, whether in the Rhodesias or in the Republic of South Africa, and Banda could see that population pressure had placed his country in much the same position as the High Commission territories next to South Africa. The South African government was trying to set up separate states for its black citizens (with very limited autonomy) within the Republic. None of them was accepted by the world outside South Africa, but there was a gloomy kernel of truth in the comment that Nyasaland was going to be an enclave for Africans dependent on the South African economy just like the regions reserved for Africans set up inside South Africa in the name of the doctrine of apartheid.

Macleod had thus, in his two years as Secretary for the Colonies, taken the main step towards winding up the British Empire in East Africa and beginning the transfer of power to Africans that would either transform or terminate the Federation of Rhodesia and Nyasaland. In 1959 Britain might still have tried to follow an interventionist policy in her African colonies, which would have emphasized training administrators to take over from British civil servants by slow stages rather than picking out political leaders, and also trying to modify frontiers if this would enable larger states with better prospects to be created before independence. It was clear by 1961 that in Africa the British were mainly concerned to withdraw from their colonies with as little trouble to Britain and the British taxpayer as could be managed. The Conservative government was turning to an entirely different aspect of British overseas policy: western Europe and Britain's relations with it.

Britain had watched Continental efforts to bring countries in western Europe closer together after 1945 with a detachment that reflected her belief that the Commonwealth, and good relations with the United States, were far more important than developments on the wrong side of the English Channel. Britain stayed aloof when six west European countries launched a customs union whose members would have no tariffs against one another and would maintain a common tariff against the rest of the world (an arrangement called a 'common market' in the General Agreement on Tariffs and Trade, and accepted by it as a legitimate form of preferential tariff system). After the six countries had worked out the 1957 Treaty of Rome, Macmillan proposed that Britain's interests and those of a number of other west European countries should be recognized by bringing them into the customs unions for industrial products but allowing them unrestricted free trade in agricultural products.

This proposal would give Britain a much larger tariff-free market for industrial products than the Commonwealth could provide, and at the same time would allow her to import the low-cost food which successful Commonwealth farmers produced. But the Treaty of Rome rested in practice on the willingness of France to expose the industrial sector of her economy to competition from Germany in exchange for an opportunity to sell her rather high-priced agricultural products in Germany with the help of tariffs to keep out food from the rest of the world. Letting Britain into the industrial market without any agricultural agreement would have seemed a bad bargain for France. The Fourth Republic might have had to put up with it, but power in France had just passed into the hands of de Gaulle, who was determined that Britain would not enter the European Economic Community on terms that would reduce the Community's usefulness to France. So the British application for partial membership was rejected in 1958, and by 1961 Macmillan and most of the Conservatives were convinced that it would be wise for Britain to apply for full membership.

Because this affected the old-established members of the Commonwealth more than anyone else outside Europe, some deep questions of sentiment came into the argument, but the problems raised by relations with the Community concerned many countries of the Commonwealth in ways that had nothing to do with memories of British descent. For a century Britain had been the largest of all food importers and a very important market for food-exporting members of the Commonwealth, whether in the tropical or the temperate zones. The Ottawa agreements had made this explicit but, even if there had been no agreements, they would have found the loss of the British market a heavy blow. New Zealand exporters of butter seemed likely to suffer more than anyone else, but growers who got preferential entry under the Commonwealth Sugar Agreement would obviously also do badly. Canadian wheat farmers needed time to consolidate new markets opening up in Communist countries, and a whole range of suppliers of other goods from tea to cheese had something to lose. The 1962 Commonwealth conference was devoted to the issue, and the final communiqué kept up a fine tradition of understatement when it recorded that various Prime Ministers and Presidents 'expressed anxieties about the possible effects of British entry'. Two generations of Commonwealth statesmen had insisted that members should not interfere in one another's internal affairs, and the communiqué did admit that 'responsibility for the final decision would rest with the British government'. The rule against interference had been evolved to make sure that Britain left self-governing colonies free to run their own affairs; the other members had not really considered that Britain might want to follow a policy that paid so little attention to the Commonwealth.

When de Gaulle insisted, at the beginning of 1963, that Britain's application must be rejected, the other members of the Commonwealth felt relieved; it had been a distinct shock to find that Britain wanted to join a west European community whose members were linked together more closely than members of the Commonwealth had been for some time, though not a shock that had any unifying effect. The Commonwealth provided a platform for expressing some of the optimism of the 1960s and also some of the bitterness that so readily came to the surface in moments of disappointment, but because the optimism was expressed in terms of national self-determination the idea that the Commonwealth could coordinate the policies of its members became less and less relevant.

The desire for economic growth was a widespread concern of the 1960s, although in practice not many members of the Commonwealth had much success at it. The debate about the problems of the British economy produced a particularly fine collection of explanations and remedies. But while half a dozen different proposals were put forward—entry to the Community still retained a great deal of support, and was seen by some as an almost trouble-free route to growth—the analysts and critics practically never suggested that the transformation of the Commonwealth and the loss of the colonies had caused Britain's problems. Just after the War good socialists in the Labour government had been afraid that colonial independence might sharply reduce the standard of living of the British working class but the argument about membership of the Community showed that by the early 1960s people believed that Britain's economic independence from the Commonwealth might help Britain and would certainly damage a number of the other members.

While the dissolution of the empire affected Britain's economy so little, the former colonies found that it brought them very little economic benefit. Before independence they could see that they were poor, and politicians building up national feeling had naturally argued that when they became independent they would become rich. Colonial status caused some economic inefficiencies but it was rash to suggest that eliminating them (even if it were possible) would make much difference. British civil servants had occasionally used their position to live a little better than they were supposed to, and nationalists generalized rather freely from these cases. They also pointed to the high salaries that civil servants received, but talented men were always in short supply and often it turned out that more civil servants, receiving an even higher multiple of the average income in the country than under colonial rule, were needed after independence. The nationalists pointed out that British colonial officials often followed a 'buy British' policy, losing the advantages of buying from more efficient firms in other countries or of using the threat of doing so to push prices down, though colonial governments had never been such large-scale purchasers that uncompetitive tendering was a serious drain on the revenue. Nationalists asserted that the sterling assets of colonies which ran a favourable balance of payments, of which the Gold Coast with its cocoa marketing system was an obvious example, were used for low interest loans to Britain; the British replied that the money was invested at the normal market rate and was bringing in a fair return. What was really at issue here was the nationalists' belief that their countries ought to be carrying out more domestic investment instead of accumulating a balance of payments surplus.

Neither independence nor any other political change could make people prosperous quickly. Even if the pre-independence rate of investment had been too low, finding profitable areas for investment was bound to take time, hard though it would be for politicians who had promised prosperity after independence to explain this to their voters. The electorate was in roughly the position indicated by Yeats when he wrote

> Parnell came down the road, he said to a cheering man:
> 'Ireland shall get her freedom and you still break stone,'

though their leaders were not usually so blunt about it. Political leaders after independence were naturally attracted by the theory of neo-colonialism and argued that all the problems were a legacy of colonial rule. So they were, in the sense that all countries have problems and obviously the people who had been ruling the country have to bear some responsibility for the problems, just as they are entitled to some credit for things that go right—and British politicians were ready enough to take the credit for the speed and smoothness of decolonization. But the theory of neo-colonialism was more concerned about the prices at which rich countries traded with poor countries than with the immediate after-effects of imperial rule. The argument laid some emphasis on the overall improvements in Britain's terms of trade in the preceding hundred years, though analysts primarily concerned with British economic problems often said that these hundred years had been a period of stagnation and relative decline. Some of the most sophisticated exponents of the theory came from South America: there was something a little incongruous about denunciations of imperialism from countries whose populations of European descent owed their position to the extermination of much of the original population and the subsequent importation of slaves from Africa, but even they were not bold enough to argue that their countries' difficulties were a long-term legacy of Spanish and Portuguese rule a hundred and fifty years earlier.

Britain's own previous imperial experience gave no support to theories that political control damaged colonial economic development. In 1850 Canada or Australia were not visibly more economically advanced than Brazil or Argentina and were subject to some degree of overseas political control for decades to come. This did not hold them back; by 1950 it was quite clear that the economic approach taken by Brazil or by Argentina had been less successful. British imperial history suggested that Canada and Australia provided useful examples for economic development: heavy concentration on one or two staple products in export trade, government activity financed by substantial but well-regulated borrowing on the London market to pay for infrastructure and particularly for transport, and a fairly free hand for private businessmen in the rest of the economy had led to great prosperity.

This approach was hard to apply in other places because it required so much money. The 10 or 20 million emigrants in the nineteenth century could expect a substantial amount of capital to be invested in their new countries, but providing comparable support for the 400 million people in India at independence would have stretched the capital resources of the whole North Atlantic area. India took a bold approach in the 1950s by providing government-directed investment in industry to replace imports. Indian nationalist feeling restricted investment from abroad, but successive Plans went reasonably well and until the early 1960s it was often said that the struggle between freedom and Communism in Asia would be a race between the rates of economic growth of India and of China, with the implication that India had a fair chance of success in this race. The Indian economy was unlikely to be overloaded by having too much investment poured into it; the physical system of communications and the intellectual framework of the civil service at independence could support a great deal of industrial investment, and the main limit on what could be done was that there could not possibly be enough capital for industrialization to be very widespread. In the years immediately after independence some African ex-colonies were able to finance more investment than could be absorbed physically: Ghana was the most striking case of this, because the government had in hand the savings from selling cocoa at favourable prices, but it was not unique.

Britain usually gave a relatively large grant-in-aid to each colony at independence, with smaller grants in later years when other colonies took their turn to receive their going-away present. The result was that politicians who believed in an energetic investment policy were able to initiate it but could not be sure of continuing it. The physical and moral infrastructure was not always strong enough for government involvement in economic activity to be useful. Racial arrogance had occasionally had some compensating advantages: a British colonial officer might feel some inhibitions about taking a bribe from an Indian or an African whom he regarded as obviously his inferior, and his inferiors would feel nervous about making any suggestion of such a thing. Some civil servants in the post-independence government of India may on occasion have found the example of the heaven-born of the ICS helped them resist the temptations put in their way when they tried to run a centrally planned economy when everything was in short supply. Many business men were ready to pay a great deal to secure the licences required in the system that Nehru and his planning boards had set up, and inevitably some civil servants gave way to temptation (or to the attractions of comfort: in 1978 the Indian equivalent of *Time* magazine ended a denunciation of senior civil servants for indulging themselves in extravagant air-conditioning by saying 'Such things would not have been done in the days of the Raj'). But the post-imperial changes in India were never as great as in some Commonwealth countries in Africa where cash payments to supplement official salaries became established in the whole system of government and caused a great deal of discontent by the mid-1960s.

Central Africa

The Federation of Rhodesia and Nyasaland was still the hardest problem the British had to face in Africa. Despite Macmillan's hints that the Monckton Commission would find that the Federation had worked well enough to justify giving it more power, the commissioners realized when they took their evidence that the African majority saw the Federation as a device to place power in the hands of the white minority. In 1960 the Commission recommended that the question of dissolution should be discussed. The future of Nyasaland was already clear enough, but Macleod had devised a constitution for Northern Rhodesia which was designed to push black and white politicians into trying to co-operate with each other for electoral purposes, though power was obviously going to pass in the end to the black majority. Lord Salisbury described Macleod's plans as too clever by half, and came closer to suggesting that the minister was a card-sharper than might have been expected. This was offensive, but it did remind Macmillan that there were limits to how much he could ask the right wing of his party to accept in African affairs. Everybody said that Salisbury's comments were unjustified, but Macleod soon moved to another post and a little later the emollient hand and great political weight of R. A. Butler was brought to bear on the situation.

In the 1962 Northern Rhodesia election under the Macleod Constitution the political parties of the African nationalists gained a majority, with Kenneth Kaunda—a Christian and socialist leader whose position resembled that of Nyerere—and his United National Independence Party likely to emerge as the dominant force. Only a few weeks later Nyasaland became self-governing and the pro-Federation supporters of moderate reform in Southern Rhodesia were defeated by the Rhodesian Front, who were determined to achieve independence under white rule and saw the Federation as an obstacle to this. Dissolution of the Federation now looked like the obvious course, and one which only a resolute man who hoped to hold Southern Rhodesia in check could have rejected. In 1963 Butler presided over the division of the assets and liabilities of the Federation, and in 1964 Nyasaland and Northern Rhodesia became independent, changing their names to Malawi and Zambia respectively. Southern Rhodesia, which responded to the renaming of Zambia by calling itself Rhodesia, was now the only area which could cause serious difficulties in British politics—as distinct from arguments between the Colonial Office and African politicians—in the course of Britain's decolonization in Africa. The political careers of Butler and Macleod suffered because of their involvement in Africa, and for a short time the issue was taken as a test of the competence of party leaders.

The white minority in Rhodesia amounted to 8 or 10 per cent of the total population, a distinctly larger proportion than in any other British colony in Africa. Most of the minority in Rhodesia had immigrated fairly recently from Britain or from South Africa; some of the latter were unbending Afrikaners, but much of the white section was uneasy about the South African approach and was prepared to see the black majority treated better, as long as it was not given power, which would, it was thought, lead to economic and social disaster. The troubles of the Belgian Congo were alarming; the Belgians had transferred power with a minimum of preparation, and the results had been everything that a racialist harbinger of doom would have predicted. The problems and the people involved were very different, but the Belgian Congo was only 150 miles from the closest point in Southern Rhodesia, so the Rhodesians had seen a number of refugees who had told them all about the collapse of the new government.

While they had hoped for independence for many years and had originally seen the Federation as a step towards it, the white Rhodesians might have been content with their extensive self-government if everything had remained suspended in the immobility of the 1950s. As it became clearer and clearer that the Conservative government in Britain was anxious to get out of Africa and was prepared to set up governments with a black majority in countries with some white settlers such as Kenya and Northern Rhodesia, the rulers of Southern Rhodesia become frantic to obtain independence quickly, and when a Labour government came to office with a slender majority in 1964 negotiations became more embittered until in November 1965 the government of Rhodesia made a unilateral declaration of the country's independence. No other country recognized the new government. The legal issue was whether the Rhodesians could become independent without the approval of the government in London, but of course the real question was whether a white minority could assert its power over the black majority, and the practical effect of non-recognition was to make it relatively easy to apply a blockade to Rhodesia.

The British Prime Minister, Harold Wilson, made it clear that his government would not use force to invade Rhodesia. This probably convinced the British electorate that he was behaving reasonably but on the other hand it freed the Rhodesian government from some anxieties about its policies. It was fairly clear that military operations in which British troops got killed for the sake of transferring power from white politicians to black politicians would have been very unpopular in Britain, but the British refusal to use force was bound to lead to accusations that Wilson was held back by covert racialist sympathy for the Rhodesian government led by Ian Smith, and some of the British opponents of sending troops clearly did feel this sort of sympathy for him. The critics of the British government argued from an outdated idea of British strength that Britain could certainly overthrow Smith if she chose, so she must be deliberately choosing not to do so, and the only reason for such a choice was an alignment with Smith on racial grounds. This argument was not logically coherent: if the British government had been both as powerful and as racially prejudiced as its critics said, then it would not have withdrawn from its African colonies at all. Part of the problem of understanding the limits on British power was illustrated by a

Canadian journalist who, to explain British policy sympathetically, wrote that in the imperial past the British would have sent a gunboat to deal with the rebels. But the Zambezi is not an easy river for gunboats to navigate and, even if a gunboat had reached the foot of the Victoria Falls, it could not have done much. British weakness in Rhodesia was a new illustration of the fact that British imperial strength had been a maritime strength.

Evolution of the Commonwealth

It was nevertheless true that Britain had intervened militarily in four or five imperial problems in the dozen years between the emergencies in Kenya and Malaya and the Rhodesian declaration of independence. In the early 1950s the colony of British Guiana had been moving towards self-government and had elected an administration under the Marxist leadership of Dr Cheddi Jagan. In 1953 the British government did send a gunboat (with other forces) to remove him and restore the rule of the Governor and the Colonial Office. A much more prolonged military commitment had been made in Cyprus in the late 1950s. A guerrilla campaign to support the desire for union with Greece had broken out, and the British resisted it, partly on behalf of the Turkish minority on the island and partly to maintain British military bases there. In these terms the British were reasonably successful: Cyprus became independent in 1960 as a member of the Commonwealth with a complicated constitution intended to protect the Turkish minority, the bases were retained, and the idea of union with Greece laid aside. But the constitution did not last long and the island passed from a UN-policed truce between Greeks and Turks in the 1960s to what was in effect a partition imposed by Turkey in 1974. The British managed to retain their bases and could always argue that, however bad things became in the 1970s, a full-scale war between Greece and Turkey—which might easily have been caused by an attempt at union between Greece and Cyprus—would have been worse.

There were mutinies in the armies of the newly independent countries of Kenya, Uganda, and Tanganyika in 1964, and their governments asked Britain to send troops to bring the situation under control. Britain's intervention could be seen as a final friendly service by the departed imperial power, though the Tanganyikan government managed to make the worst of both worlds by asking for help and then apologizing to the Organization for African Unity for doing so. Britain became involved in another sort of problem that arose immediately after colonies that were linked to Malaya became independent. None of the other colonies in the region looked like becoming independent countries when Britain left Malaya in 1957; by the standards of the 1950s Singapore was too small and all three colonies on the north-west coast of the island of Borneo—Sarawak, Sabah or North Borneo, and Brunei—seemed too underdeveloped. But as decolonization went ahead there was obviously no point in holding on to these fragments of empire and Macmillan's government looked for ways to launch them into reasonably independent existence. So many colonies had been federated in order to make them better able to look after their own affairs that it was entirely natural to try to link all four of them to Malaya. Brunei did not choose to join and eventually became an independent state in 1983, the government of Malaya was a little worried by the prospect that the large Chinese population in Singapore might work with the Chinese minority in Malaya, but enough of the inhabitants of Sarawak and Sabah were Muslim and Malay to mean that federation would not destroy the existing balance of religious and racial forces in Malaya, and the new state of Malaysia came into existence in 1963.

Sukarno, the expansionist ruler of Indonesia, which included the larger part of the island of Borneo, looked at all this with disapproval. He believed that Indonesia should take the rest of the island over as soon as the British left but reckoned that Britain's departure would come soon enough for it to be sensible to leave the problem to solve itself. If Malaysia was successfully united his aims would be permanently frustrated, and he added a new term to the jargon of politics by encouraging border raids and calling this a policy of confrontation. The British sent forces to help hold the Borneo frontier and after several months Sukarno's hold on power began to disintegrate under the strain. Activities such as this military action in support of a Commonwealth ally showed that the British government was ready to use force to sort out some problems of decolonization, and some African countries in the Commonwealth assumed that intervention against Rhodesia would be just as easy as the half-dozen earlier operations. But the British government intervened only when it still held administrative power and was not faced by any organized force, or when it had been invited in by the recognized and effective government of the country. The Rhodesian government was not legally independent but it had its own army and air force; attacking it would have been about as difficult as it would have been to attack Canada fifty years earlier if Ottawa had declared its independence.

So the British government fell back on a policy of non-recognition and blockade. Before the declaration of independence, Wilson had warned Smith that his country would be commercially isolated. The Rhodesians treated this threat as a useful piece of advice and took steps to protect themselves. The South African government had been alarmed by the advance to independence of the African nations to the north, and hoped to make Rhodesia and the Portuguese colonies of Angola and Mozambique into a defensive belt for the Republic. It did not want to see the Rhodesian economy strangled and it was ready to undermine the blockade. The African members of the Commonwealth, which made up over a third of the total membership in the 1960s, thought the vindication of the rights of Africans was much the most important task facing the Commonwealth. Their main objective was to press the British government to commit itself to refuse to recognize Rhodesia's independence before majority rule was established and, as Commonwealth conferences were held unusually often in the 1960s, they had several opportunities to press the point.

The Commonwealth was moving away from any special commitment or deference to Britain. Up to 1945 the appointment of a secretariat would have been seen as a centralizing move that would probably increase Britain's influence, and in earlier decades the Dominions had been uneasily balanced between hoping that a centralized system would enable them to influence British policy and increase their effectiveness in the world, and fearing that Britain would be able to use it to control their external and defence policies. Nkrumah had persuaded the leaders attending the 1964 conference that they needed a secretariat of their own to take over some of the work done by the British Commonwealth Relations Office. At the 1965 conference a Secretary-General and a staff was established in London with a fair degree of certainty that the Secretary-General would never be an Englishman. New members of the Commonwealth hoped to use the organization to help influence British policy, particularly on the Rhodesian issue. Early in 1966 the Prime Ministers and Presidents met in a conference that was completely different from any of its predecessors: it was held in Lagos, the Nigerian Prime Minister was in the chair, and the object of the meeting was to apply pressure to Britain. Wilson wanted to have a free hand in negotiating with the Rhodesian government, so he was anxious not to commit himself on the issue of enfranchising the majority, and he avoided the issue by saying that in a matter of 'weeks, not months' the economic blockade would force the Rhodesian government to come to terms. But the Rhodesians survived the blockade with no signs of discomfort, and another conference was held in London later in the year to discuss the problem again. This conference went badly enough to show members that, if they wanted to have any more meetings, they would have to think carefully what the Commonwealth could do.

Commonwealth conferences had begun as confidential meetings of Prime Ministers who behaved much as they would have done in a cabinet, minimizing their disagreements and making considerable efforts to remain on friendly terms with each other. For many of the new members of the Commonwealth this approach had no obvious advantages and had the disadvantage of making them look ready to compromise on matters of principle. So they conducted the 1966 conference in London as if it was a meeting of the United Nations, delivering long prepared statements and— as the proceedings were supposed to be confidential—releasing their speeches to the press unofficially. The United Nations had recently conducted a policy in the Congo that suited African nations, which may have encouraged them to think that the Commonwealth could conduct a similar policy in Rhodesia. In practice neither institution was strong enough to work in this way for long because a united policy would be accepted only if everybody agreed with it or if members felt such loyalty to the institution that they were ready to obey its instructions. If the small group of deeply Anglophile Prime Ministers of the first half of the century was unwilling to have a united empire foreign policy, it was not very likely that the diverse and greatly enlarged membership of the second half of the century could agree for long. So Wilson was able to counter-attack by saying that it was impossible for other countries to run British policy by lecturing him, and in this way he avoided committing himself on the subject of majority rule in Rhodesia.

By the late 1960s a different problem was affecting a wide range of Commonwealth countries. In theory they had all emerged as full-fledged nation-states in which minor regional differences would be submerged in loyalty to the new country. Each country took some trouble to devise national symbols such as an anthem and a flag, and most of them spent a fair amount of money on buildings in the capital that could represent the spirit of the nation. This could not immediately solve all the problems of coun- tries which were sometimes rather obviously federations put together to make independence possible. They had not always had time to develop a national spirit: Americans had had half a dozen years of war to bring the great majority of them together, and Australians had felt themselves to be Australians for decades before federating, but many of the countries which became independent in the 1960s had not had either of these experiences. Nationalism could not always be controlled and told 'Thus far and no further,' so a new national spirit could awaken in the regions of a federation and sometimes tear it apart.

The Federation of the West Indies, which was probably one of the flimsier creations of the period of decolonization, disintegrated after half a dozen years. The British really only thought about the West Indies during the cricket matches that England played against them, which may have made the Colonial Office think that the West Indies was a country in just the same sense as Australia. But, despite the cricket team, the West Indies consisted of a dozen different colonies stretching over several hundred miles, with relatively few links with each other. There was not much trade between the islands, because economic activity had taken the form of competition between them to attract tourists or to sell their sugar and other exports in rather distant markets. In the 1950s it was argued that none of the islands was large enough to contemplate independence alone, which was certainly true by the standards of the period, but that if they joined together they could achieve independence as a federation. The Federation was set up in 1958 and, according to the official timetable, was to become independent in 1962. The Prime Minister of Jamaica was himself a supporter of federation but he decided that so important a step should be ratified by a referendum, and in 1961 the popular vote on the island went against remaining in the Federation. Jamaica had just over half the population of the whole Federation and was given under two-fifths of the seats in the legislature, so it could easily be argued that she was under-represented.

In the few years since 1958, ideas of how large a state had to be in order to survive had altered dramatically; by the early 1960s Cyprus had become independent with a population of about 700,000, and Malta with a population of 300,000 was considering it (and did become independent in 1964). Trinidad and the smaller nearby island of Tobago felt certain that as a united state they could manage their own affairs at least as well as Jamaica; though their population was smaller they were richer and could hope that their oilfield would attract industry. So both Jamaica and Trinidad and Tobago became independent, and smaller islands, most of them the original English settlements of the 1620s, then went on, headed by Barbados, to ask for independence as separate states. Half a dozen of the smaller states in the Windward and Leeward islands were able to agree on a common currency, the Eastern Caribbean dollar, and a few other forms of co-operation were arranged. Relations between the islands and Britain remained friendly despite the obvious strain caused by the steps taken in the 1960s to reduce West Indian immigration to Britain to as low a level as possible; and the removal of the prospect of immigration reduced what had been one of the advantages of being a British colony in earlier decades.

The separation of Singapore from Malaysia in 1965 was only a little less amicable. The Chinese in the city did not like the permanent Malay political control of the country; the Malays felt uneasy about the prospect that the prosperous Chinese of Singapore would eventually dominate the country economically. Riots in Singapore and on the mainland showed what could happen, and the Malaysian government at Kuala Lumpur and the Chinese city government of Singapore agreed that separation would relieve the strain. What nobody foresaw was that Singapore would make a spectacular success of independent existence with a flood of economic prosperity which—combined with an autocratic and puritanical government— made the city-state into a latter-day version of Venice without artistic achievements.

In Nigeria it was hard to know whether the force that threatened to pull the country apart was to be called nationalism or tribalism. Only four days after the Commonwealth conference at Lagos in 1966, the Prime Minister was killed in the course of a military coup in which a group of Ibo officers seized power. A few months later another group of officers, this time from the north, carried out a second coup and began making plans to increase the number of regions into which the country was divided and reduce their size, which would make it harder for the governments of the regions to challenge the central government. The Ibos thought this would weaken their position in the east of the country, so in 1967 their section of eastern Nigeria declared itself independent under the name of Biafra. The Nigerian military government condemned the move as a reversion to tribalism and—clearly seeing itself in the role of the government of the United States in the 1860s—mobilized its country for civil war. Biafran resistance was skillful and determined enough to convince some people that this was more than backward-looking tribalism. France assisted the separatist government, and Zambia and Tanzania gave it diplomatic recognition, but the vast majority of states including Britain and all the other countries of the Commonwealth followed the normal rules of international law and supported the federal government which, in the first weeks of 1970, succeeded in defeating the rebellion. Inside Africa the Nigerian government won a great deal of support from people who were afraid that one successful secession could lead to others. The Biafran side won a good deal of sympathy outside Africa, partly as 'a small nation rightly struggling to be free', partly because of a skilful public relations campaign accusing the federal government of genocide. As civil wars go, the Biafran war was in fact rather restrained and one odd result of the war was that the word 'genocide' was used much less often afterwards.

A year later East Pakistan was the scene of a more bloodthirsty though shorter civil war. Ayub Khan's restrained military rule had been running successfully enough for seven years when his country went to war with India over the Kashmir problem. The Commonwealth's sense of solidarity was shaken when two of its members fought each other, but the war was too indecisive to cause serious diplomatic difficulties. Within Pakistan the effects were more profound; the people of East Pakistan saw that the army, most of whose costs they were paying, had not been able to do anything to protect them when the crisis came. India had not advanced into East Pakistan, but Bengalis there inevitably wondered what they gained by being part of Pakistan. At the same time Ayub Khan was losing the support of the ruling group who had helped to maintain his power, and in 1969 he had to resign in favour of the Commander-in-Chief of the army, Yahya Khan. The new President made a bold attempt to face the problem of East Pakistan and of the submergence of democracy by holding parliamentary elections with full representation for East Pakistan at the end of 1970. The results pointed to the end of Pakistan: the Bengali Awami League won almost every single seat in the east and, although it won no seats in the western half of the country, it gained a clear majority in Parliament. The League reckoned that little could be gained by trying to negotiate with Yahya Khan and its MPs felt a little nervous about coming to the west for a parliamentary session, and by March 1971 it was clearly moving towards secession. The Awami League had not been at all explicit about its secessionist aims during the election, which perhaps justified the President and the army moving into East Pakistan to stop the drift towards separation, but it did not justify the savagery with which they suppressed the revolt and tried to restore the control of the west over the east.

The Indian government naturally felt that it was bound to benefit if Pakistan broke in two, and in December 1971 the Indian army marched into East Pakistan, announcing that it was doing so in order to support the claims of East Bengal to self-determination. West Pakistan did its best to resist, but was unable to supply its troops in Bengal and had to ask for peace. East Pakistan became a separate nation under the name of Bangladesh and applied for membership of the Commonwealth; the remaining section of Pakistan objected and, when Bangladesh was admitted, Pakistan withdrew. India was clearly the winner in the struggle, (West) Pakistan the loser, though not as crippled a loser as people thought, and Bangladesh emerged into a world in which, even though she was no longer making her disproportionate payments to the Pakistan budget, it proved very hard for her to deal with all the problems of independent existence.

Nationalism raised questions of separation in the two oldest members of the Commonwealth, Canada and Britain. When Canada had been federated, none of the colonies that joined together could have survived as independent countries next to the United States, but the French-Canadians had shown in the late 1880s, and in the First and in the Second World Wars, that they thought of themselves as a distinct community even if they had not felt dissatisfied (or self-confident) enough to express this feeling as a desire for independence. In the early 1960s they had spoken of becoming 'maîtres chez nous'. 'Chez nous' of course meant the province of Quebec, but 'maîtres' was a much more ambiguous term which at least hinted at the possibility of independence, and a Quebec Liberation Front came into existence. In 1967 Canada celebrated the centenary of its federation with a world exhibition and other festivities, into which de Gaulle put a drop of bitterness by saying in a speech in Montreal 'Vive la Québec libre,' the slogan of the Liberation Front. This was play-acting, because nobody in Quebec wanted a close connection with France, but everybody in Quebec provincial politics knew that they had to pay some attention to nationalist sentiment.

Next year the federal Liberal party chose as its leader (and Prime Minister) Pierre Trudeau, who argued that discontent could be satisfied by protecting the civil rights of individuals and in particular by guaranteeing the linguistic rights of speakers of French across Canada. In English-speaking Canada politics in the 1970s were an orthodox struggle about which party offered the country the best economic prospects; in the province of Quebec the electorate gave Trudeau large majorities in federal elections but in provincial elections it voted for the Parti Québecois which was committed to independence, though it declined to support the PQ desire for negotiations about independence in a referendum in 1980. In this way the people of Quebec avoided committing themselves irrevocably to either Canadian nationalism or Quebec nationalism. Other regions in Canada which thought they had a grievance felt encouraged to use the threat of secession as a way to assert their interests. Western Canada was infuriated by the federal government's fuel policy and this led to some muttering about independence, though at this stage none of the discontent in Canada rose above the level of concern expressed in the thirteen colonies in the 1760s.

During the 1980 referendum the federal government had promised to devise a new constitution for Canada. When it came to carrying out this promise Trudeau's own main concerns were to provide a Canadian Charter of Rights to protect individuals in the manner of the American 'bill of rights' (the amendments added to the American constitution in 1791), to turn the Canadian Supreme Court into an institution which could supervise the work of legislators in the manner of the US Supreme Court, and also to work out a legal framework to enable the Canadian federal and provincial governments to amend the Canadian constitution without asking the Westminster Parliament to play any part in the process. In the new constitution, some powers of government could be amended by a qualified majority of the federal and provincial governments (in a less plebiscitary version of the Australian system), and others could be changed only with the unanimous consent of every government in Canada; this held out promises of full employment for generations of lawyers yet unborn, but it was not welcomed by the provincial governments. The Canadian Supreme Court ruled that existing constitutional conventions did not require the Government of Canada to obtain unanimous agreement from the provinces before asking the British Parliament to give effect to the legislative changes it wanted. On this basis Ottawa asked for changes to the British North America Act which had not been accepted by Quebec to be made into law, and Britain saw no way to refuse this request without producing a diplomatic crisis. While Westminster removed itself in 1982—not without some relief—from the Canadian constitutional process, Canada had been able to amend its constitution only by excluding Quebec from the negotiations that led to the final settlement. Later in the 1980s a Conservative government tried to amend the 1982 legislation in a way that was acceptable to Quebec and to the rest of Canada but these efforts failed and Quebec separatism revived. By 1994 separatists were in office in the province of Quebec; at Ottawa the Liberal government had to one side a separatist party whose members held most of the Quebec seats, and to the other an equally large number of Reform MPs from Alberta and British Columbia who saw no need for a conciliatory policy towards Quebec. When a referendum on independence, with a question phrased in a way that acknowledged a large number of people in Quebec wanted close ties with Canada after separation, was held in 1995 the separatists did much better than in 1980. In the first referendum the votes of the French-Canadian majority had been fairly evenly divided and the federal side had received 60 per cent of the votes cast, but in 1995 the separatists came within a percentage point of success and could claim that, as they had the support of a decided majority of French-Canadian voters, the 'ethnic' minority who spoke English or other languages had frustrated the wishes of the true Québecois. This suggestion that Quebec had two classes of voters was unlikely to produce harmony in the province, but it did indicate one way in which the separatist cause might develop when the issue next came forward. Canada, like many other states that emerged to independence as the age of empires came to an end, had been created by the action of an imperial power which had swept together a number of political units. In the first half of the century imperial loyalty was a large part of what held the country together, even if it was too British-oriented to be satisfactory for French-Canadians; in the second half of the century governments at Ottawa seemed to think that it would be enough to repudiate the imperial legacy and reject the country's British past without searching for anything to take its place. Canada was clearly too mature a country to adopt the non-democratic methods used in other states to fight against division along linguistic or religious lines. The central government and the English-speaking majority outside Quebec seemed to lack any resources more inspiring than fresh amendments to the constitution with which to resist the growth of nationalism based upon language and references to the past in French-speaking Quebec.

The United Kingdom contained materials for three or four nationalist movements. In the late 1960s Plaid Cymru, which had been the party of the Welsh-speaking minority in Wales, enabled people in South Wales who would never vote Conservative to express dissatisfaction at industrial stagnation under a Labour government and, even if fears that it might impose too great a commitment to the Welsh language on South Wales or that some of its supporters were committed to violence meant that it had difficulty in holding the confidence of the non-Welsh-speaking majority of Welshmen, it remained in existence as a reminder that discontented Welshmen had a political method of protest.

In Scotland nationalism had at least as strong a historical base as in Wales, and the language question was not going to cause any division; Gaelic gave the movement glamour and slogan, but provided nothing more substantial. What made Scottish nationalism into practical politics rather than a call to the memory of Bonnie Prince Charlie was the discovery of oil in areas of the North Sea which an independent Scotland might be able to claim if the assets of the United Kingdom were to be divided. Encouraged by this, voters turned to the old-established Scottish National Party and in the general election of October 1974 gave it the second largest number of votes in Scotland. In both Scotland and Wales in the late 1960s and early 1970s the national movement of the dedicated minority, who were inspired by reasons that had nothing to do with calculations of economic advantage, seemed suddenly to have convinced a great number of people that expressing their discontent in nationalist form would provide tangible benefits. This of course was nothing unique; every successful nationalist leader had to be able to convince people who had not previously felt a distinct national consciousness that a diversity of everyday grievances could be cured if they had greater political power to run their own affairs. Wales and Scotland were offered assemblies with limited powers, which were to be set up only if adequate majorities voted for them in referendums to be held in 1979. As neither country provided the required level of support, politicians decided that people had wanted to show that they were discontented but did not see moves towards independence as a way to satisfy their discontent.

In the six counties of Northern Ireland the conflict of nationalisms was about deciding which existing state ought to rule in Ulster rather than setting up a new independent state. The Catholic minority in the province had been badly enough treated under the 1920 system of devolution to insist on changes. In the late 1960s it looked as if a vigorous struggle for civil rights might meet their needs, but by 1971 most of them were returning to the view that the best way to guarantee their position was to unite the six counties of Northern Ireland with the Republic of Ireland. A referendum in 1973 formally confirmed the fact that, as everybody knew, the majority was opposed to the idea, but a fraction of the minority was devoted to its view of Irish nationalism strongly enough and violently enough to enable the Irish Republican Army to conduct a campaign which at times came very close to civil war. This was an instructive demonstration that a guerrilla force, even in territory where the majority was actively opposed to it, could maintain itself in action for years. The minority in Northern Ireland who wanted to join the Republic felt a straightforward commitment to the idea that everybody on the island of Ireland ought to have a common national consciousness. The feelings of the majority were more complicated; they wanted to stay inside the United Kingdom but their Ulster loyalty had a great deal in common with nationalism. The British government maintained troops in Northern Ireland to keep the peace, which was never a welcome commitment, even though the death rate at no point rose as high as in the really strife-torn cities of the period, such as Detroit and New York. People in the larger island of Britain may have wished that Northern

Ireland would go away and run its own affairs, but they could see that it was very hard to drive away a region in which the majority had no wish to leave.

Fragments of Empire

The Labour government in the mid-1960s had to face its awkward involvement in Rhodesia, but apart from this legacy from the past it completed Macmillan's withdrawal from Africa when the three High Commission territories became free from British rule in 1966, and Botswana (previously Bechuanaland), Lesotho (previously Basutoland), and Swaziland then faced the problem of keeping themselves free from South African domination. Between 1960 and 1966 twenty-three new countries became members of the Commonwealth, several other territories such as Zanzibar, Sarawak, and Sabah became independent as parts of federations within the Commonwealth, and a number of states became independent without joining the Commonwealth. After this immense transfer of power the pace slackened, if only because so little remained to be made independent.

Britain's immediate concern with the world outside Europe and North America in the mid-1960s was summed up in the phrase 'East of Suez', which referred to commitments in two widely separated parts of Asia: in Singapore and Malaysia, and in the Gulf where Britain had substantial oil interests and also had military and diplomatic arrangements with ten rulers round the south-east corner of the Arabian peninsula. At the south-west corner of the peninsula the old coaling station of Aden had become less and less important, and nationalist sentiment was increasing. By 1965 the colony was far more trouble than it was worth, and Britain was eager to leave. The nationalists saw no need to negotiate, and in 1967 the British made one of their least dignified departures from a former colony.

Between 1964 and 1967 the Labour government tried very hard to fulfil its duty under the Bretton Woods agreement to keep the pound stable at the value of $2.80 which had been fixed in 1949. Eventually it failed and after a new value had been fixed at $2.40 the government cut down on a wide range of spending in order to maintain the new rate. Early in 1968 it gave up the 'East of Suez' policy and announced that all British forces would depart from the area by 1971, which would end the agreements with the Gulf rulers and leave them fully independent. In opposition the Conservatives strongly objected to this, but back in office in 1970 they found there was very little they could do about it, and in the same way they explored helping with the defence of Singapore but did not follow it up. The rulers in the Gulf might have accepted a steady policy of protection but they were unlikely to reverse the arrangements they had already made to meet the situation after the British left.

Imperial power in the Gulf had probably transferred wealth to the industrialized countries (including the British, who had wielded the power) on a scale so immense that it dwarfed anything else that could have been called 'economic imperialism'. For a period of thirty years in which almost all other prices had gone up steadily, the cartel of oil companies which regulated purchasing for its members had arranged that the price of oil had hardly risen at all. The cartel's blockade of Iranian oil at the beginning of the 1950s had served as a very convincing demonstration of the oil companies' power. The Organization of Petroleum Exporting Countries had been formed ten years later to try to redress the balance; at first it achieved very little, but within half a dozen years of the British withdrawal the oil-producing countries had increased their export prices something like six-fold. If the British political and military presence had kept the price down by only $1 a barrel it would have transferred over £5bn a year from the oil states to the industrialized states in the 1960s. But the timing of the withdrawal is not enough to prove that Britain imposed low prices; Libya and Iran, which took the lead in pushing prices up, had not been under any discernible influence from Britain, and the rulers of Bahrain, Qatar, and Oman and the seven rulers of the Trucial States, whom the British encouraged to form the last of the post-imperial federations, the United Arab Emirates, showed no sign of regretting their relationship with Britain although, like every other Arab state that had been associated with Britain, they showed no interest in becoming members of the Commonwealth.

After the two bitter conferences about Rhodesia in 1966, no Commonwealth conference was held until 1969, but the meeting then was friendlier than expected. The issue of the civil war in Nigeria was handled very delicately, and the conference said that Britain would be justified in settling with the Rhodesian government as long as the terms were acceptable to the whole population, which meant that Wilson did not have to make Smith provide for an African majority in the electorate before independence was arranged. Changes in the organization of future conferences were made. Until 1969 it had been taken for granted that conferences would normally be held in London; after 1969 they were to be held in whichever Commonwealth city seemed appropriate and, to reduce difficulties about organizing a meeting of the sort that had followed the 1966 disputes, were to be held regularly every other year.

The next meeting was held in Singapore in 1971, and a number of nations saw it as a chance to criticize Britain. The new Conservative government had begun negotiations with South Africa about using the base at Simonstown and about renewing the sale of arms for naval defence. This irritated several Commonwealth leaders and they set about telling Edward Heath, the British Prime Minister, how he ought to conduct his foreign policy. Heath could see the disadvantages of his South African policy and drew back from it, but he was clearly very annoyed by the way the conference had gone. One of the leaders of the attack on him, President Obote, was unlucky enough to be deposed by a military coup while at the conference, and the British government quickly hinted that this served him right and suggested (quite incorrectly) that the leader of the coup, General Amin, would be an improvement.

Health had never felt the links of sentiment with the Commonwealth that had inspired a good many British politicians down to the end of the 1960s, and his rather detached attitude probably reflected a shift in British public opinion fairly accurately: The tide of nationalism and the movement to independence had come at a time when economic forces and the political mood in Britain made them easy to accept. The colonies were reasonably prosperous in their last years under British rule because the prices of the raw materials which most of them exported had gone up in the 1940s and had not fallen much in the 1950s. The ideals of self-determination and opposition to racial discrimination which had been encouraged by the Second World War were becoming universally accepted; and people in the imperial powers were no more prepared to spend money on opposing enthusiasts who were ready to fight for their independence than they would have been prepared to pay large bills for the initial imperial expansion. What had changed was that during the period of expansion people in Asia and Africa were ruled in a way that made it very easy for a European power to remove the kings or chiefs at the top of the system and bring everyone else within their empire, but by the 1960s the spirit of nationalism had developed so far that no imperial power, with the possible exception of the Soviet Union, felt at ease about absorbing different nationalities. People conscious of belonging to nationalities different from that of their rulers were ready to make very great sacrifices to win their national independence. Perhaps because the French had more of a military tradition or perhaps because they had invested rather more national energy than the British had laid out anywhere except India, they fought in Indo-China and Algeria to resist independence movements at a cost the British had never been willing to incur, but their sacrifices brought them no reward.

Heath's annoyance at the Singapore conference was all the greater because he shared the general British belief that the country had behaved rather well in giving up its empire so quickly with so little bloodshed, and deserved to be praised for it. From the point of view of the former colonies, the British departure was a simple matter of accepting the justice of their claim to have their nationhood recognized; some of them saw no need to emphasize this and made the sort of amiable remarks about the British withdrawal that oil the wheels of international diplomacy, but some of them felt uncomfortable about being expected to be grateful for their independence when they thought it should have been given sooner or should never have been taken away. Arguments in the economic sphere were equally at cross-purposes. The British felt their contributions of foreign aid were rather generous, and occasionally wondered whether the need for foreign aid did not mean that the ex-colonies were not really able to run their own affairs. The former colonies felt, reasonably enough, that the British had occupied most of them for economic advantage, and moved on to the rather less well-founded conclusion that this advantage must have been gained at the expense of the colonies. This was an up-to-date version of the mercantilist argument that the total amount of trade and production in the world was so limited that one country's trade was another country's loss, which led on to the view that Britain had impoverished (or 'underdeveloped') the colonies, so that foreign aid was no more than overdue compensation for the economic damage done. People who felt guilty about the former colonial relationship argued that the rich nations needed the poor as much as the poor needed the rich, and that foreign aid ought to be given to keep the world's economy moving. Opponents of foreign aid found some support for the view that there were plenty of other ways to keep the economy moving, that too little aid reached the poor it was meant to help, and that recipient countries did not appreciate the benefits of aid.

So the worsening relations at the Singapore conference reflected reasonably well the views of the public in Britain and the Commonwealth countries concerned about former colonial relationships. Commonwealth relations at the time were still seen as a modern version of the essentially bilateral connection between Britain and each of her colonies. A number of attempts at federation had failed in a way that showed Commonwealth countries who shared a common frontier could have friendly relations but were no longer likely to want any closer association. A wide range of organizations for Commonwealth countries developed and were usually greeted as useful steps towards co-operation, though most of them were in fact substitutes for the rather different kind of unity that had been taken for granted inside the British Empire. For many decades the British government, the Bank of England, and the London money market had provided a financial framework for most of the empire. This became more formalized with the development of the Sterling Area between 1931 and 1940, the wartime system of exchange controls insulated governments in the empire from most of the financial fluctuations of the outside world, and annual meetings of Commonwealth Finance Ministers gave more guidance to the running of the Sterling Area than any other system could have provided. But the best of insulation cannot keep the outside world away for ever. After 1945, the governments in the Sterling Area could see that reserves held in sterling would lose value in terms of other currencies if Britain had to devalue, and the British found the anxieties of governments which held sterling an unwelcome addition to the problems of managing their currency.

By the 1960s the Sterling Area was a nuisance: the London money market wanted to get into the larger business of handling the world's eurodollar transactions and Commonwealth holders of sterling wanted to be free to protect their own interests. The Sterling Area was wound up, though countries and individuals continued to keep some of their money in sterling just as they had done previously, because they thought the interest rates paid in London justified the risk of loss of capital. Meetings of the Commonwealth Finance Ministers no longer affected policy, though of course the Ministers learned about a wider range of views, expressed in the common language of English, than they would otherwise have met. Institutions in areas such as medicine, agriculture, and education tried to carry on the work that had previously been done by a single London-based centre of control. The new institutions were more lavishly staffed than the old, but could do much less because they did not represent the old single legal authority. Supporters of the idea of imperial unity at the beginning of the century who lived to see the organizational development of the 1960s and 1970s might have been impressed, but would have noted that the new organizations did not have much power.

The weakness of the British economy, which helped bring about the end of the Sterling Area, continued to be the major issue in British politics, and forced politicians to go on thinking about the advantages of membership of the European Community. Harold Wilson tried to arrange Britain's entry in 1966–7, but was met by a third veto from de Gaulle. When Heath became Prime Minister in 1970 he moved forward more purposefully on the issue than any of his predecessors. He was more truly a European than any of them had been, in the sense that he believed that a policy that benefited the whole Community ought to be followed, regardless of whether it benefited or harmed Britain. As a result he found it much easier to convince the leaders of the Community and, more specifically, President Pompidou of France, that Britain was really committed to Europe. He may have been less concerned than some of the other negotiators to guard Britain's special interests and by the 1970s he was understandably less committed to protecting the position of other members of the Commonwealth than his predecessors had been.

Much of the discussions in the 1961–3 negotiations, for which Heath had been the British representative in direct contact with the Europeans at Brussels, had been devoted to protecting the remaining rights of members of the Commonwealth under the Ottawa and other agreements, about which they had been so concerned. Commonwealth exporters widened and diversified their markets during the 1960s, partly to make sure they would not be in an exposed position if Britain did eventually join the Community, and in the 1971–2 negotiations little attention was paid to the Commonwealth. New Zealand exports of butter were given some protection and a certain amount was done for Commonwealth sugar producers, but most of the other problems were left to look after themselves. This reflected the steady erosion of the Ottawa agreements and the willingness of governments to see them die away, and it also showed that people thought the African, Pacific, and Caribbean colonies and former colonies of the members of the Community would benefit more from a policy intended to cover all of them, as was eventually arranged in the Lome agreements in 1975, than by particular concessions that individual European countries could arrange for their former colonies.

Commonwealth countries could see that the British market was not going to be as open to their exports as it had been in the past; British politicians repeatedly said that the era of cheap food was over and devoted themselves to making sure that, as far as Britain was concerned, this cliché was translated into fact. Canada found new customers for wheat in Russia and China in the 1960s and subsequently sent more and more of her exports to the United States, agreeing to set up a North American Free Trade Area with her in the 1980s; Australia and New Zealand had been taking a greater interest in trading prospects in the Pacific region, and spoke of themselves as Pacific nations; all over the world nations saw regional trading areas and common markets as the new key to prosperity. So in 1971 the successful conclusion of British negotiations to enter the Community was received calmly enough to show how much the Commonwealth had changed and how much less important its members' commercial relations with Britain had become in the 1960s. Heath's own attitude to the Commonwealth and to Britain's activities outside Europe followed naturally from his deep commitment to western Europe, and this was not unique; a substantial section of British opinion expected life to become easier after joining the Community. In earlier centuries Englishmen of the ruling class had normally paid more attention to the continent of Europe than to the outside world, leaving trade to the middle class and emigration mainly to the prosperous working class. The last decades of the nineteenth century saw a change, and for much of the first half of the twentieth century the rulers of Britain paid more attention to the empire and believed that the importance of Europe had been exaggerated, but by 1964 *The Times* was willing to publish a consciously iconoclastic article which called the Commonwealth 'a gigantic farce'.[1] Europe, on the other hand, was something like a new toy, and one whose problems and possibilities were not always examined seriously. As a practical example, if political attention was to shift from the English-speaking Commonwealth to the multilingual Community, then it would have been sensible for schools to teach more children to speak the languages of the Community, but no change of this sort took place.

---

[1] 'Patriotism Based on Reality', *The Times*, 2 April 1964.

Advocates of British entry to the Community made it clear that 'We are a world power and a world influence or we are nothing' and that membership would enable Britain to remain a great nation by taking the lead in Europe. Up to 1955 or 1958 the Europeans might have welcomed such leadership, at least while the initial problems of association were worked out. By the 1970s Britain so clearly wanted to join the Community because her economy was doing badly that it no longer made sense to think that she would gain some leadership in Europe which would make up for the leadership of empire. It was clear that France and Germany would at the very least be on terms of equality with Britain, and Italy would not want to be regarded as a lesser power. Relations within the Community were not to be unfriendly but they were unlike anything the British politicians were used to. The Commonwealth could be seen as a family; in fact, in the first half of the twentieth century it often was described as a family, though usually by people who talked as if mention of a family was enough to ensure immediate harmony. The members of the Commonwealth reacted to one another very much as members of a family do; they did not want to hurt one another's feelings but they were more easily wounded by comments from within the family than from outside; the senior member of the family was sometimes suspected of trying to use undue influence when it was only trying to give good advice; newly emergent members were accused of being disrespectful when they were only trying to avoid being swamped by the weight of tradition and custom; and yet people found themselves emotionally absorbed by the relationship in a way that was not true of other political connections. The European Economic Community started off as a business partnership; for most people in Britain it never got much further than that and some of them found their partners rather hard to trust.

Involvement in the Community drew British attention away from the succession of small-scale decisions about colonies that had to be taken in the 1970s. The great burst of decolonization between 1960 and 1966 left the Colonial Office with no important territories to run, and it and the Commonwealth Relations Office had by 1968 been absorbed by the Foreign Office, leaving behind only the Overseas Development Ministry, which in turn was closed down very soon after the Conservatives came to office in 1970. The British government was still responsible for some clusters of islands, mainly in the West Indies and in the South Pacific, and in the 1970s it set about making it clear to these tiny countries, as politely as possible, that they ought to become independent. A dozen new members with a total population of about 5 million were admitted to the Commonwealth in the 1970s. Nauru, with a population of 8,000, would have difficulty in ever becoming a nation-state in the same sense as Canada or Kenya or Jamaica; the island aroused the same patriotic feelings in its inhabitants as countries with a population a thousand times larger aroused in their people, but the military, economic, and social functions expected of a modern state would have been hard to carry out even with a distinctly larger population.

The old-established British remedy, federation, no longer satisfied people's emotions. It had worked best when it had been used to gather together people who all thought that they were British subjects and were simply restructuring the government through which they expressed their loyalty, but the attachment to Britain that the inhabitants of Nauru or of many other colonies might still have felt would not make them willing to federate with other ex-colonies. The great distances in the Pacific increased the difficulty of holding territories together after they ceased to be colonies. The British had governed the Gilbert and Ellice Islands as a single unit, but the two groups of islands broke up the administration before they became independent as Kiribati in 1979 and Tuvalu in 1978 respectively. In the Caribbean much the same fissiparous pattern could be seen, though it may have been the memory that in the past they had been separate from all the others and had had a parliament of their own that made small islands such as Antigua insist on remaining free from any close connection with their neighbours. These little islands had been acquired at a time when Europe still contained a number of principalities that would not attain full sovereignty; some of them, such as Andorra and Liechtenstein, survive to this day, and one result of the dissolution of the British Empire was the creation of several more states that had to rely for their continued existence on the forbearance of other countries and the convention that nations ought not to swallow up other nations. The world had not become so much more peaceful in the years after 1945 that this was a totally safe support, but delaying independence in order to safeguard the remaining colonies while they made arrangements for future survival would have aroused international disapproval and in some cases could not have brought much compensating advantage.

In the early 1960s decolonization could be seen by generous-minded people in Britain as a great crusade to launch new nations into the world with the best possible prospects, and by nationalists in the colonies as a heroic struggle against an empire which ruled millions of subjects without knowing or caring very much about them. In the rather harsher world of the 1970s it was hard to believe that parting with Tonga or the Solomon Islands was going to change anything of great importance. An odd coda to a very old tune was played in 1980; during the light-hearted scramble for islands in the Pacific, Britain and France had avoided quarrelling over the New Hebrides by making them into a condominium, controlled by the two countries in a way that allowed either of them a veto over practically anything the government of the group of islands might do. When the process of decolonization brought the islands to the point of independence, the local

English-speaking party prevailed over the French-speaking in a brief struggle just before the transfer of power. The ghosts of three centuries of colonial conflict may have smiled at this; the serious issue at stake was that France had exerted more influence over some of her ex-colonies after independence than Britain had done, and the English-speaking party was afraid that French guidance might limit their freedom to run their own affairs. The country's political parties were based on this linguistic division, with all the dangers of inflexibility that this involved, but the islands showed more capacity to handle this than a number of larger and more prosperous communities. After independence, accompanied by a change of the country's name to Vanuatu, the influence of Australia and New Zealand for them, as for much of this part of the Pacific, was likely to be more important than that of Britain. The two large and prosperous Commonwealth countries in the region devoted some attention to setting up councils for diplomatic consultation and for 'economic co-operation', the term used for planned and reasonably long-term assistance, and tried to maintain the stability of the area.

Even those who thought that the half-dozen Pacific members of the Commonwealth had set up states on an inadequate material base would admit that their history was happier than that of Rhodesia in the 1970s, and that they might even have better prospects for the future. After the 1965 declaration of independence Wilson had hoped to resolve the situation by persuading Smith to accept a constitution which left the whites their majority in the Rhodesian Parliament for the time being but set up a property or an education franchise which would allow Africans eventually to become the majority, and also gave the existing African minority in Parliament a veto over any constitutional change proposed by the white parliamentary majority that would make the transition period even longer. Wilson met Smith twice in the late 1960s and Heath's Foreign Secretary, Douglas-Home, met him in the early 1970s to fill in the details of this framework. Presumably the British pointed out to Smith that they had resisted Commonwealth pressure for majority rule, that the white minority could manage very well with a franchise which did not produce an African majority for several years, and that world recognition of Rhodesia's independence would allow her to borrow freely for development. The British may have doubted that these franchise schemes could hold back the majority for very long, but their real concern was to end their last entanglement in Africa and leave people there to sort out their own problems. In the early 1970s proposals were worked out that the white Rhodesians were ready to accept. A Royal Commission had been proposed as the way to find out if the African inhabitants found the terms acceptable, and they mobilized enough opposition, under considerable difficulty, to persuade the Commission that they did not.

Up to this point no effective resistance to Smith had been organized, and the Rhodesian economy had expanded impressively despite the blockade, but by late 1972 guerrillas were operating in the east of the country even though the government of Zambia could not afford to help them and the Portuguese government tried to keep the Mozambique border closed. In April 1974, the Portuguese army grew tired of resisting independence movements in Angola and Mozambique, so a government that wanted to help the guerrillas in Rhodesia gained power in Mozambique. The South African government was afraid that this might bring an equally committed government to power in Rhodesia and, as it wanted a moderate African government in Rhodesia rather than a government committed to the liberation movement, it became the main source of pressure on Smith to settle with his opponents, and Britain turned into a reasonably well-placed mediator.

Smith tried to create an African government that would oppose the guerrillas. In 1979 Muzorewa, who had led the successful opposition to the Douglas-Home proposals in 1972, emerged as the first African Prime Minister of his country and won a general election with a turn-out high enough to show that the guerrillas were not able to force the African population to boycott it. The newly elected Conservative Prime Minister, Margaret Thatcher, was tempted to accept this as an acceptable government, but it was clear that the best way to achieve peace was to persuade the Muzorewa government and the guerrilla leaders to agree on a constitution which gave certain minority rights to the white inhabitants but confirmed power in the hands of an African government chosen in a fresh election. Britain returned briefly as the imperial power to supervise the election in 1980. The British government was clearly not pleased when the guerrilla leader Mugabe emerged with a clear majority over all the other parties, black and white, but, while it would have preferred a government in Zimbabwe (as the new state immediately became known) that was more friendly to Britain, accepting Mugabe in power was better than being accused of using the Muzorewa government to conceal continued white domination. The white minority was hostile to any black government and particularly hostile to the Mugabe government, but it had talents which could not be replaced in the short run; the problems of Mozabique immediately after independence showed the difficulties of running a country which suddenly lost its skilled workers and farmers, and Zimbabwe was a more complex society and more dependent on its skilled workers than Mozambique. The new country emerged from the 1980 election divided into Matabele and Mashona very much as it had been before Rhodes took it over. This could make politics impossible or lead to a one-party state dominated by the Mashona majority. Zimbabwe might not be harder to govern than any other African country, but its citizens had to ask if it could continue to be more prosperous than the others for long after independence. Pre-independence prosperity had been stratified: few of the white minority could have been so well off if they had stayed in Britain, though they might have done as well if they had emigrated to the United States, Canada, or Australia, and before independence a handful of black people had already reached a similar economic position, being joined promptly by the more successful politicians; most Africans who had been drawn into the modern economy had not gained any equally clear-cut economic benefit, and a large proportion of the population had been only superficially affected by the decades of white rule.

14. *The World after the Empire*

In the decades immediately after the great wave of independence at the beginning of the 1960s problems of nation-building and constitutional government arose in several of the countries that had just emerged from imperial rule. The individual colonies that made up the British Empire were in many cases large enough to contain a diversity of groups that could undermine the unity of the new country if they were not handled with great care. Many of the governments faced with this problem decided that the unrestrained democracy that they had welcomed when challenging British rule was too dangerous to be maintained after independence, and tried one-party rule or military rule. There was no sign that these expedients solved the problem, they had many other disadvantages and sometimes they were clearly exploited by politicians who wanted a monopoly of power. By the 1990s most members of the Commonwealth had had enough experience of other constitutional arrangements to understand the implications of Churchill's statement that democracy is the worst type of government, except for all the others. Similar changes were taking place in many parts of the world, but the Commonwealth did express its own commitment to multi-party democracy by policy statements of its own and by steps towards applying pressure to members who did not meet those standards to do better or to cease to be members.

Resolution in South Africa

Throughout the struggle over Rhodesia the British government had been pressed to take more decisively pro-African action and, once Zimbabwe was established, it hoped that Commonwealth meetings would be less embittered. But the end of the Rhodesian problem seemed to some Commonwealth members to open the way for effective action against the regime of apartheid which had been developing in South Africa since 1948. The British had always accepted that they had some imperial responsibility for Rhodesia; they saw South Africa as a different sort of problem, to be handled by patient world diplomacy. Commonwealth countries, and in particular the African members, wanted more direct action and wanted Britain to take a leading role in it. They were convinced that sanctions on trade with South Africa would have a good effect; unhappy experiences with sanctions throughout the Rhodesian crisis had left the British government convinced that they were not the best solution. This was not a simple disagreement in which both sides accepted that everyone was trying hard to find the way to change the attitude of the rulers of South Africa. Some African governments clearly wanted to oppose white rule somewhere and, if they could not have any effect on it in South Africa, were going to denounce it in Britain; the British government appeared to enjoy standing alone against all the other vocal members of the Commonwealth and even appeared to feel that being denounced by them would do its popularity at home no harm at all. When the British government revealed that such supporters of sanctions as Canada and Nigeria were actually increasing their trade with South Africa, it showed rather too clearly that it believed the adjective derived from 'sanctions' was 'sanctimonious'.

In the event the South African situation was solved by a beneficent transformation from within. The ingenious President Botha, who had taken steps to reduce discrimination against the Indian and Coloured minorities in order to bring them over as subordinate allies to the whites, was forced out in 1989 because of his deteriorating health, and his successor, de Klerk, set off on a much more difficult process of transferring power to the majority of the local population than any that the British had ever faced. The British who carried out successive steps in decolonization had not remained at hand to live with the results; white settler minorities might be left behind but the British rulers themselves went home rather than stay on with the consequences of decolonization. Most of the white minority in South Africa had no idea of any other home, and were in an even more exposed position than white settlers elsewhere if the move to majority rule went wrong. De Klerk was fortunate in the leader of the African National Colngress with whom he had to deal; Nelson Mandela had the great prestige and the freedom from involvement in *émigré* politics that went with the twenty-seven years that he had spent in prison for his opposition to the existing government, and yet when he was released in 1990 he emerged well able to understand the motivation of his followers and his adversaries, and astonishingly unembittered by the loss of almost half a lifetime behind bars. Both De Klerk and Mandela had adversaries in their own camps. The Afrikaners who had more or less monopolized power since the Union of South Africa in 1910 might force out of office any politician who seemed to be throwing their position away, and the Conservatives of the Transvaal won by-elections in late 1991 and early 1992 that forced de Klerk to hold a referendum of the existing electorate in March. Just over two-thirds of the white voters supported the policy of change, an impressive rejection of apartheid by people who decided to give up their racially privileged position 'in the absence' (as a distinguished South African commentator put it) 'of any sense of imminent defeat'. It was arithmetically possible that an Afrikaner majority had opposed the change and that, like Smuts's electoral victories, it had been won by the co-operation of a very solid English-speaking group and a minority of Afrikaners, but nobody imagined after the vote that political resistance could hold de Klerk's changes back; the wilder white opponents of change talked about a third Boer War, and others asked for guarantees against future discrimination or for a separate region where they could practise a form of self-chosen apartheid.

On the African side the Inkatha Freedom Party asked for a special position for KwaZulu-Natal and its Zulu majority; in the area from Durban to Johannesburg its dispute with the African National Congress reached a level of violence that moved towards civil war, and relations between de Klerk's government and Mandela's ANC were embittered as it emerged that the official Security Forces had helped and encouraged Inkatha. But a new constitution, with entrenched civil rights, limits on the powers of the government, and a subdivision of the country into nine states, was worked out in 1992 and 1993. The major political parties arranged how they would share power in a coalition government during the transition to a system of universal suffrage and competing political parties, and in April 1994 a general election was held in which the ANC gained a substantial majority, de Klerk's National Party did well enough to retain a firm position within the new government, and the Inkatha Freedom Party did not do so well in KwaZulu-Natal that it could claim a special position for its region. These developments had been watched eagerly by the outside world, and in particular by the African members of the Commonwealth, who were immensely relieved not to have to keep their guard up against a powerful government with an unacceptable racial policy. When South Africa rejoined the Commonwealth in July 1994 it enjoyed better prospects, economic and also political, than most members: the strength of the ANC and the readiness of the National Party to try to expand its base meant that there was quite a good prospect of maintaining two political parties in self-restrained opposition to each other, and Mandela was an ideal leader to bring the country to universal suffrage and the liberation of the majority without much risk that he would remain in office for such a long time that he would overstay his welcome in the way that leaders of several African countries had done in the years after the end of imperial rule. He had accepted the argument that sudden steps to correct the racial bias in the distribution of wealth by drastic measures might underline financial confidence, and had convinced his party that dislocating the system might undermine South Africa's expectations of widespread prosperity.

Europeanization

These expectations showed the way that the situation in South Africa differed from that in most other African countries. In countries such as Zimbabwe Africans might think an overall decline in prosperity would simply mean that the white rulers were less rich after independence while the majority were no worse off than before. This simple sort of arithmetic might be applied in many countries besides Zimbabwe, and can be borne in mind in estimating what had happened during the process of Europeanizing the world in which the growth of the British Empire had been so important a part. By 1980 western Europeans ruled no more of the world than they had done when they started sailing to lands outside their own continent 500 years earlier, but in the 500 years of expanding (and, much more briefly, contracting) European rule, the outside world had been transformed dramatically. In North America, Australia, and parts of South America European emigrants had developed vast spaces of great economic potential and the relatively small native population had become so far outnumbered that it was of very little importance. These emigrants, who enjoyed greater opportunities than they could have expected at home, were obviously the people who benefited most from the whole process. In countries such as Zimbabwe or Kenya, or the former French colony of Algeria, where the settler groups from Europe were much smaller than the native population, the immigrants were, by the later decades of the twentieth century, in a less and less secure position, but even in the more successful of these countries of settlement by a white minority, such as South Africa, the existing local population had been only partly brought into the modern world. The spread of westernization had brought some unquestioned benefits such as the ending of slavery and an increase in life expectancy, but it had also aroused hopes for the future which were unlikely to be met except by some almost unimaginable increase in investment and in productivity. At the beginning of the age of empire Europeans were not decisively better off than people in other parts of the world; by the end of empire Europeans, at home or in their new homes overseas, were much better off than other people, mainly because the age of empire had coincided with an age of investment and industrialization that had had much less effect outside the Europeanized part of the world.

One legacy of the age of European expansion which was unlikely to disappear was the spread of European languages over the world and, despite the great expansion of Portuguese and the considerable growth of Spanish and French, this primarily meant the diffusion of the English language. This could be seen at three levels. The areas of British settlement overseas naturally spoke English and by degrees absorbed members of other linguistic groups—it was easier to find French-Canadians who no longer spoke French than to find people of British descent who had taken to speaking French or Spanish, though there were some of the former in Quebec and some of the latter in Argentina. In colonies which had been ruled by a British minority of administrators, the government after independence almost always found that English was more or less essential for running the new country and holding it together; the language might be modified by circumstances, but it was not necessarily much more distinct from British-English than American-English had become. Finally, because of the dominance of Britain and then of the United States in the century— roughly the period from 1870 to 1970—in which people became aware of the unity of the world as a political system, English was the language in which most international activity was conducted.

It seemed quite likely that distinct English-based languages would, over the centuries, emerge from the end of the British Empire in something like the way Romance languages emerged from the end of the Roman Empire. Two types of English stood some chance of emerging as world-wide languages: American dominance of the mass market for entertainment opened up the possibility of producing film, video, and music expressed in a simple language freed from complexities of grammar and vocabulary that could be sold universally, and could maintain its position in the markets of any nation because of the glamour of 'made in the USA' and the economies of scale that world-wide operations would produce. At the same time a relatively precise and universally accepted language would be required for a number of tasks, in the way that the Roman Catholic Church needed Latin for its church services, for its theological discussions, and for the administration of a legal system that handled some problems all over western Europe. Bankers and international diplomats were likely to need English because of the advantages of having a universal language which they could use internationally. This universal English would need to be able to add new scientific terms to its vocabulary because English became established as the universal language of science around the middle of the twentieth century. Scholars in the social sciences and in literary criticism clearly felt a deep need for languages of their own which would be impenetrable to ordinary people. But this type of universal English would be unlikely to change very rapidly; its users would have difficulty in keeping in touch with one another enough to agree about new development, a large number of them would have to learn it through formal instruction rather than as their mother tongue and its relatively timeless qualities would be very suitable for the rather serious purposes for which it would be employed. The universal English employed for international affairs might be influenced by the fact that Britain had been first in the field. The universal English of the world of international entertainment would probably be much more purely American; although at the more solemn end of the entertainment market a British tradition of television productions based upon novels, plays and other classics, and the widely reported Booker Prize presented annually for the best novel written in the English-speaking world outside the United States (and endowed with money originally earned in the sugar colony of British Guiana) might have their role in maintaining

London's position as a centre of high culture for the English-speaking world.

Ordinary people in English-speaking countries would want to be able to talk to each other in something rather more subtle than entertainment-English and rather livelier than international-affairs-English. The variations in the use of a common language between one place and another, which could easily be seen even when it was just a matter of Lowland Scots speaking a different sort of English from other English-speaking inhabitants of Britain, had become more obvious when the United States consciously developed points of difference in the early nineteenth century. In the twentieth century people from one part of the English-speaking world would sometimes complain about the way things were done differently elsewhere and make it clear that their own local version of the language made it easier to be witty, or to be forceful, or to be subtle, than did the degenerate versions in other places. This provided entertainment for readers of book reviews, but was more reasonably seen as part of the growing-pains of developing separate languages. Castilian, Catalan, Provençal, and the French of Languedoc emerged as separate languages in the centuries after the end of the Roman Empire, although it would be very hard to give exact dates for this change, and presumably different languages for everyday use would develop after the end of the British Empire in much the same way. This diffusion of the English language was likely to be influenced more by the British and then the American impact on the world at large rather than to be anything to do with the British Empire; but then in a sense the British Empire itself was only a reflection of a British strength which had its origins in other areas. Naval strength, commercial strength, and an early start in industrialization would have made Britain important, during its years of dominance, even if it had followed the pure message of Adam Smith and kept entirely away from owning colonies, and there would have been some diffusion of the English language even if the British had done their best to avoid foreign entanglements.

Whether a policy of non-intervention by the British government, which was what opposition to empire meant in the eighteenth and nineteenth centuries, would have made any difference is another question. Apart from maintaining a powerful navy which it needed to prevent invasion and protect trade, the English government did very little for its colonies in the seventeenth century, partly because it saw no need to subsidize emigrants who had gone overseas with good prospects of becoming richer by doing so, and partly because it had no money to spare. Because they got so little help over and above their own resources the English overseas could establish themselves only when there was no very strong resistance. Once they had established themselves by their own efforts they expected to have at least as much political liberty as they had enjoyed at home. Englishmen at the very beginning of the period of expansion lived under a monarchy as strong, in terms of power over its own subjects, as any medieval monarchy could be. In most of the countries that were then expanding, France, Spain, Portugal, and Russia, the monarchy grew more powerful as expansion went on. England and the Netherlands were unusual in having monarchies that were weaker in 1700 than in 1500, and Englishmen developed an acute consciousness of their rights and an unwillingness to let the King or his government interfere with their liberty or their property. The most spectacular results of this was the American War of Independence, but all colonies launched by British settlement expected to have representative institutions.

Even when the British moved away from settling empty territory to a different type of expansion, and started taking other European countries' colonies away from them, the belief that representative institutions ought to be set up when possible still persisted. Nobody thought non-Europeans had the same claim to representative institutions, so when the British moved on from settlement and from annexation of European colonies to acquiring new territory by conquering non-European rulers and replacing them by British rule, a division between self-governing colonies and Crown colonies was drawn. Everybody came to see the attractiveness of having representative institutions, and the desire for them spread throughout the empire. They were used in a way that changed what had seemed to be a specifically European type of government into a device with world-wide potency.

The desire for representative institutions ran ahead of the desire for national identity, and up to 1914 the latter did not necessarily lead to a desire for independence. Inside the United Kingdom Welshmen could make their own ecclesiastical arrangements, by disestablishing the Church of England in Wales, without wanting to separate from England in a political sense, and Irishmen who voted for Home Rule before 1914 could very well have been thinking about land reform rather than Parnell's dictum that it is not possible to set bounds to the onward march of a nation. In later years the descendants of emigrants might say that their ancestors ought to have realized their separate national identity sooner, the message of Robert Frost's lines:

> The land was ours before we were the land's.
> She was our land more than a hundred years
>
> . . . . .
>
> But we were England's, still colonials.

But settlement began long before nationalism was the dominant political emotion, and the steady flow of emigration from Britain until 1914 provided a counterweight to the growth of separate national feeling. For several generations people went overseas as subjects of the King or Queen of England and thought more in terms of loyalty to the monarch than of the prospect that they had settled in a region that might become a new nation.

In the middle of the nineteenth century people could say that Italy was no more than a geographical expression, but in another way they could have said the same thing about Canada or Australia.

During the First World War self-determination was consciously encouraged and, after it ended, people could see that, at least in Europe, nationalism and empire had become enemies, which changed the prospects of European rule overseas more than anyone realized at the time. By the end of the Second World War it had become accepted that people had the right to be ruled by governments which, if not actually of their own choosing, at least did not treat them as inferior to any of their fellow-subjects. The institutions that Englishmen had taken overseas with them provided a way to meet the desire for self-determination: when national spirit replaced loyalty to a distant monarch voters could express it through their representative institutions and transfer sovereignty to themselves without any direct conflict.

The creation of the Commonwealth disguised changes when they took place. In 1914 a great many men in the Dominions decided to go and fight for the empire: when they got home they felt that they had fought for their own countries, and their countries emerged with as much power as the thirteen colonies had wanted in the early 1770s. In 1918 George V and his ministers in London had no more control over what was done in Canada than Jefferson in 1774 would have allowed George III to keep in the thirteen colonies. The existence of the Commonwealth helped to reassure colonies that they were not making too violent a new departure when they asked for independence and to convince the British that they were not really losing anything when colonies turned into sovereign states, and this was obviously useful in smoothing a transition that might have been much harder, politically and legally, than it was. (After independence, the Commonwealth might give political leaders from most English-speaking countries opportunities to discuss problems that interested them, but this was not so directly connected with its imperial origins.)

It was obvious enough that European ideas had a great impact on the rest of the world, and that imperial rule by European countries had been an important part of the transmission of ideas. Whether there was any specifically British imperial legacy, apart from the language, was harder to say. The type of representative institutions which provided a unique road to national independence in the nineteenth and early twentieth centuries were no longer distinctively British by the second half of the twentieth century, and at the time of independence it was no longer taken for granted in the newer and poorer states that they were the best form of government. New nations were no less liable to suffer military coups because they had been part of the British Empire and politicians did not seem any less ready to brush aside the opposition and settle for the comfort of a one-party state because they had first learnt politics within the framework of the Westminster model. The idea of a one-party state commanded more ideological support in former British and French colonies than in former Spanish colonies, which were more inclined to turn to military rule, but experience suggested that in poor and hard-pressed countries tolerance for free speech and the idea that accepted opposition parties were a useful part of the political system did not gain universal support during the struggle for independence. In some former colonies it took some decades after independence for these ideas to become part of the normal structure of politics.

The Trials of Democracy

Because independence movements began with the assumption that the colony ought to be a nation and expected to unite the whole nation by organizing a single political party, opposition to the party looked like opposition to the nation. When, as often happened, the party was led by a man who could sum up the national cause in his own person, opposition to the leader looked like treason. National feeling in the self-governing colonies of the nineteenth century emerged from a background of loyalty to the monarch; in colonies becoming independent after 1945 it only rarely created anything like a new dynasty, but during the independence struggle loyalty to the leader was of the type given to a military or monarchical rather than the conditional loyalty given to a party leader in a struggle between political parties. Self-governing colonies in the nineteenth century naturally operated the system of responsible government in the framework of the two-party system that was familiar to most of them from British experience. The first years of the Irish Free State provided a better guide to the way new states developed in the twentieth century. In the two or three years just before independence the Irish political stage was dominated by a national leader and a united party which represented the desire for independence, though Ireland then acquired a two-party system. Because almost immediately after independence disagreement about the 1921 Treaty divided Sinn Fein in two over the question of relations with Britain, an issue that dominated Irish politics for decades to come, and because de Valera was on the less popular side during the split, he was in future no more than the head of a party in conflict with other parties. He could not claim a position as a universally accepted leader and his party had no monopoly of power.

India, like Ireland, had been partitioned as part of the process of independence, but there was no comparable post-independence division within the party that had led the way to freedom. Nehru's popularity and that of his family, combined with the prestige of Congress, presented India with a pattern of one-family and one-party electoral dominance that lasted for three generations: power was held by Jawaharlal Nehru, by his daughter

Indira (whose husband, though not related to the great leader, gave her by
marriage the honoured name of Gandhi) and then by his grandson, for 37
out of the first 44 years of India's independent existence until the assassination of Rajiv Gandhi in 1991. The five transient and embarrassed phantoms
who held office for the other seven years of the period rarely looked as if
they could provide an alternative to the attraction of the Nehru dynasty.
Nehru may have allowed the pattern of economic development in India to
move too far in the direction of planning in the Soviet style for his country's
good, but he took no steps towards 'democratic centralism' and the Communist justification for a one-party state. There was a split in Congress
under Indira Gandhi's leadership and, although her power was not weakened at the time, it did encourage the opposition and lay some foundations
for a move away from dominance by a single party. In 1975 she proclaimed
an emergency and ruled by extra-parliamentary decrees for two years, but
this was much more like the pre-independence use of the Viceroy's reserve
powers to deal with a crisis than a move towards turning India into a state
in which only one party was legally entitled to exist. Immediately after the
emergency an election was held in which her Congress party was defeated
by a coalition of its opponents and, although the coalition was fragile and
she was back in office three years later, voters were clearly beginning to feel
liberated from the need to re-elect Congress and by the 1990s were creating
a two party system complicated by a wide range of minor parties.

The size of the Indian electorate, which was about twice as large as the
electorate eligible to vote in national elections for the parliament of the
European Union, was always seen as an immense problem, and it was true
that violence and loss of life occurred in Indian elections in a way that
recalled the more lively elections of nineteenth-century Britain. The Indian
economy continued to be involved in what looked like a never-ending race
to mobilize resources fast enough to keep up with the growing population;
there was some response to the comment by Sanjay Gandhi, Rajiv Gandhi's
more politically aggressive brother, that 'India is not a poor country; it is a
rich country full of poor people,' but it was the response of people who were
afraid the poor were going to be with them for a long time. The heartland
of India, although subdivided by the Indian government into states based
upon language, was relatively free from linguistic nationalism; the hardest
political problems were to be found in the frontier regions where some
Sikhs and some Kashmiris disliked being enrolled as members of the Indian
nation and could always hope that Pakistan, on the other side of the frontier
and constantly uneasy about its relations with India, might help them.

While a commentator with strict principles might say that the dominance
of the Nehru family and the Congress Party were flaws in the theoretical
purity of multi-party democracy, almost all the other Commonwealth countries in Africa and Asia encountered more serious difficulties as a result of

the way they had moved to independence. The Indian pattern of development naturally inspired all other colonial political leaders who wanted to advance towards freedom. The All-India National Congress was the model for national movements which concentrated their effort into a single political party which proclaimed independence as its first objective and indicated that a number of secondary issues that could divide the party would have to wait until after independence. The dominance of the national leader of Congress was in fact modified by the need for lieutenants who could look after problems in the different ethnic and linguistic regions of India, but it did encourage political movements following the Indian model to focus attention on the party leader. This was encouraged by the readiness of the British, in colonies which were clearly moving towards independence, to look for a prominent leader into whose hands they could—usually successfully—try to steer power. Nkrumah, Kenyatta, Nyerere, Kaunda, Banda, and others like them emerged at the beginning of the 1960s in the way that Nehru and Jinnah had emerged as creators of their countries in 1947. In a good many cases the leader at independence remained in power until his death, often several years later. Jinnah's death almost immediately after independence was far from the normal pattern, and Nehru or Kenyatta or Seretse Khama in Botswana ruled for over a dozen years, were sincerely mourned by their people when they died, and left a fund of prestige to their successors. But two related questions remained unanswered: what was to be the role of an opposition, and how were these creators of new countries to be replaced, either upon death or, less comfortably, if their people felt that their talents were more suited to wrestling for independence than for running the country afterwards?

During the struggle for independence any party that opposed the main national movement was liable to be seen as betraying the national cause, or as wanting to partition the country. The Muslim League had worked successfully to partition India; the Kenya African Democratic Union had been launched to protect Africans in Kenya who were not members of the dominant Kikuyu group. If a party in opposition to the national movement could be seen as disloyal, it was natural for people to think of the attractions of a one-party state. There had been complaints from quite early in the movement for independence in Africa that the boundary lines drawn by imperial mapmakers had cut through existing political units. In a few cases, such as that of the Ewe who lived in Ghana and in Togo, this was true, though the process of making treaties with local rulers had not allowed many such cases to develop. More problems, some of them serious, were caused when European colonies were so large that they brought a number of political or linguistic units together under a single administration. Some local rulers involved in this process were welcomed as the agents to operate 'indirect rule', and many of them survived until independence. A few of the pre-colonial states submerged within colonies at the end of the nineteenth century hoped to secede after independence and become sovereign states; many more of them quickly became the power-base of a political party, and a party launched in such a way might turn to thoughts of independence if it was electorally unsuccessful. Governments soon denounced political parties of this sort as tribal organizations, and sometimes went on to make them illegal. A one-party state could be presented to the world as the way to save a new country from breaking up into units that would be too small for survival under modern conditions, and world opinion in the 1970s and 1980s accepted this line of reasoning without very much concern about whether it was being used to eliminate all criticism of the government. The handicaps placed on opposition parties ranged from police interference with their organization to legal limitations on their activities and then to illegal practices in elections, and from declaring that no party except for the official national party could exist to laws making it a criminal offence to belong to a party unless its existence was officially approved.

While the drift towards one-party states could not have begun without some real justification and was not just a matter of saving the leaders of the independence movement from any danger of political competition, that was clearly an additional attraction in the minds of some supporters of the move. Politicians who went too far in this direction were likely to run into trouble. Parties in newly independent Commonwealth countries did not have the ruthless commitment, and perhaps did not have the technological capacity, to set up the apparatus for totalitarian states of the Nazi or Soviet type: opposition would find a way to express itself, occasionally in the form of civil war (which was usually denounced as tribally based), more often in the form of a military *coup d'état*.

Ever since independence from Spain, Latin America had been seen as the home of the *coup d'état*, but there was no sign that its example had any direct influence on what happened in a number of countries in Africa, Asia, and Southern Europe in the second half of the twentieth century, although the same social forces might have underlain military involvement in politics. Nasser's Egypt was better placed to be a model for newly independent countries. It had survived invasion by former imperial rulers, had held corruption in check (at least by comparison with the regime that it had overthrown), and had taken steps towards modernization, so it naturally looked attractive in colonies emerging from imperial rule. People believed that its advance had begun with the 1952 military *coup d'état* against King Farouk, and other newly independent states such as Indonesia and Iraq were reorganized after military coups in the 1960s. Armies were always likely to see themselves as the essence of the patriotic spirit of the nation, and it was also easy to think that their discipline would make them efficient and their use of sophisticated equipment would turn them into leaders in the process of modernization. By the last years of the century, after some decades of experience of military leaders holding political power, none of this looked quite so convincing and it seemed at least as likely that the problems and the temptations of dealing with political problems reduced the military competence of officers who took power away from politicians.

In the Commonwealth military officers in west-African countries proved particularly ready to see themselves as the answer to political problems, and some of the time they were reacting against political leaders who had outstayed their welcome and were holding on to power by illegal means. Most people believed Albert Margai had escaped defeat in the Sierra Leone election of 1967 only by fraud; the army stepped in, overthrew him, and after a brief interval gave power to Siaka Stevens, who was accepted as the true winner of the election. This was one of the most harmless of military coups, and for ten years Stevens resisted pressure from his supporters to create a one-party state. Eventually he gave way on this, but he retired peacefully after a further seven years in office. His chosen successor lacked his popularity and in the early 1990s an attempt to get back to multi-party democracy was frustrated by a military coup and the country was then dragged into civil war, partly by the disturbances in her eastern neighbour Liberia; and an election in 1996 reduced the problems rather than solving them. In Gambia, a country which exists simply as part of the valley of the river Gambia, the durable President Jawara survived one military coup by negotiating a project of union with the much larger French-speaking country of Senegal, which surrounds it entirely except for the narrow stretch of shore where the river flows into the sea. Subsequently he escaped from this union and continued to win contested election after contested election until, thirty years after he came to power, he was overthrown by an almost casual mutiny among soldiers complaining about not being paid, who held on to power until 1996.

In Ghana and Nigeria the armed forces appeared to have become much more permanently committed to involvement in politics. During the Nigerian civil war of the late 1960s the army naturally thought of itself as the defender of national unity and even when the war was over General Gowon saw himself as indispensable. Eventually in 1975 he was overthrown by officers who were more ready to consider civilian rule once a constitution had been worked out to reduce to a minimum the risk of further attempts at secession. Under the careful guidance of General Obasanjo a system was created which divided into smaller states the large regions which had been the basis of the federation at independence, and rules for a qualified majority were set up to make sure that a party or presidential candidate would have to draw support from a range of different states. This constitution started well enough in 1979, helped by prosperity encouraged by steadily rising oil prices, but tension developed when oil prices began to drop. In 1983 another military *coup d'état* again displaced civilian rule and the new military leadership began an unedifying round of promises of elections at some point which receded steadily into the future, compounded by a rush to divert the nation's oil revenues into their own bank accounts.

Compared with this record even the military men of Ghana looked honest and restrained. Nkrumah had won widespread admiration in Africa and in the rest of the world during the struggle for independence but, once in power, his government quickly spent the country's currency reserves, partly on overambitious investment projects and partly on enriching the politicians in office, and it then set up a one-party state to eliminate criticism. In 1966 the army overthrew him and, when it handed power back to an elected politician in 1969, this looked like a coup in support of democracy. But the army had acquired a taste for intervention; in 1972 it seized power again and retained it until 1979 when Flight-Lieutenant Rawlings, an airman of Scottish and Ewe descent, turned out the other military leaders and used his position to arrange civilian elections. This arrangement did not last: Rawlings was not satisfied with the new government and in 1982 he carried out a second coup and made himself head of the government. He slowly diluted the military aspects of his regime by bringing civilians into his government and allowing regional elections, and eventually in 1992 held a reasonably open presidential election in which he stood and was elected.

Military men in the rest of Africa were less ambitious. Amin's overthrow of Obote in 1971 began a brutal period of social disintegration, which it was hoped had been ended when he attacked Tanzania and was defeated and driven into exile. After a brief interval elections were held and Obote returned to power in 1980, though his second period of power was at least as unsatisfactory as his first had been. His defeated rival, Musaveni, organized a National Resistance Movement for guerrilla warfare; the regular army was not able to resist and by 1985 Obote had been forced out. Within a few months Musaveni was firmly in power, though he did pay Obote the compliment of retaining the legislation he had passed in 1967 to set up a one-party state. Kenyatta's prestige gained in the struggle for Kenyan independence kept his position secure until his death in 1978 and his vice-president and successor, the former leader of the non-Kikuyu Kenya African Democratic Union, Daniel arap Moi, was able to stay in office even longer. He was sometimes clearly afraid that a combination of popular discontent and military ambition would lead to his downfall and defended his position by setting up a one-party state, though he was obliged by international pressure to dismantle part of his structure of power at the beginning of the 1990s. Both Kenyan leaders were understood to have enriched themselves in office and to have let their supporters benefit as well.

Just to the south, in Tanzania, Nyerere maintained a more frugal way of life suited to a very poor country, and while he did stay in office for twenty years he was one of the very few leaders of an independence movement to set an example of withdrawing gradually from office rather than straining everybody's patience by hanging on until death or a *coup d'état* brought a new government to power in difficult circumstances. He did select his own successor, Ali Hassan Mwinyi, who was chosen mainly to consolidate the union of Tanganyika and Zanzibar that had been brought about soon after independence, and Mwinyi retained power in a free election in 1995 that served to give expression to some of the tension in the relationship between the island and the mainland. In Zambia Kaunda stayed in office too long for his own good and in 1990 was forced by popular discontent to agree to a multi-party election in which he was defeated the following year after almost thirty years in office. A grimmer version of the same story was played out in Malawi: Banda remained president so long that he outlived his faculties and was propped up in the post by a group of hangers-on who had done too well out of holding office to want to give it up, and had done too much to retain power to be able to relinquish it safely. After independence Zimbabwe moved towards a one-party state; Mugabe, as the leader of the Mashona majority, saw the dangers of internal division and believed that party conflicts would make them worse, so attempts to set up opposition parties ran into legal and extra-legal difficulties. Further south, problems were even more deeply affected by the presence of South Africa. Swaziland remained an old-fashioned enough monarchy to ignore the problem, but in Lesotho and Namibia the prestige gained by resistance to South Africa naturally led to the dominance of national leaders who discouraged opposition, though in Lesotho, Jonathan, the national leader who used resistance to South Africa to expand his own power, was overthrown by an army coup (assisted by South Africa) in 1986.

Some of the same difficulties in running multi-party democracy could be seen in the Asian countries of the Commonwealth. The army in Pakistan had been among the very first to displace an elected government in the name of efficiency and a belief that it represented the real will of the people, and the attitude of mind that led to the 1958 coup survived the collapse of the policy of West Pakistan predominance. The armies of the new countries of Pakistan (the old West Pakistan) and Bangladesh took much the same view of their position as Ayub Khan had done. In the years immediately after the 1971–2 war the two victors in the 1970 elections, Bhutto in Pakistan and Mujibur Rahman in Bangladesh, remained in office but in 1975 Mujibur Rahman was tempted by the idea of a one-party state, and the army intervened to stop him: he was killed in a military coup, and General Zia ur Rahman became President. Bhutto survived slightly longer but when the Pakistan elections of 1975 seemed to produce no clear result the army felt called on to seize power. General Zia ul-Haq made himself President and had Bhutto put on trial (and subsequently executed) for a political murder. Both military presidents acknowledged that free elections and a return to civilian rule would be the ultimate objective of their policies, but they advanced in this direction very slowly, held elections in which handicaps were placed upon opposition parties, and made it clear that their armies would judge the validity of any elections in which their candidates lost. After the assassination of Zia ur-Rahman in 1981 there was a brief civilian interlude and a return to military rule under General Ershad.

The Indian subcontinent was perhaps no more devoted to the political emancipation of women than other parts of the world, but its readiness to allow family claims to decide the leadership of political parties gave women opportunities they could not often obtain elsewhere. From 1986 onwards Zia ul-Haq was under pressure from political demonstrations led by Bhutto's daughter Benazir. When he was killed in an air crash in 1988 there was no alternative claimant to power and she became Prime Minister. The army kept a hostile eye on her government and overthrew her in 1990 after a short period in office in which perhaps the most noteworthy event was that Pakistan returned to the Commonwealth in 1989. She returned to the work of agitating for multi-party democracy, and in 1993 she returned as Prime Minister and seemed to have succeeded against all the odds. Ershad's regime in Bangladesh was also under criticism in the late 1980s; very few people believed that his party's electoral success in 1988 had been gained by fair means and in 1990 popular demonstrations forced him to resign. In the elections that followed in 1991 the widow of Mujibur Rahman and the widow of General Zia ur-Rahman stood as representatives of the two different streams in the politics of Bangladesh: the widow of Zia ur-Rahman was successful but people did not feel certain that democratic rule was secure and, when she was re-elected in 1996, popular pressure forced her to concede a new election under impartial caretaker control.

In south-eastern Asia neither Malaysia nor the two colonies that had declined to be merged into it, Singapore and Brunei, set up completely democratic systems of government. Brunei remained a monarchy with a king rich enough from the country's oil revenues to live splendidly and maintain a personal style of rule rather like that of Saudi Arabia. In Singapore Lee Kwan Yew (who, under the name of Harry Lee, had led the independence movement of the 1960s) maintained a political system in which contested elections were held regularly but opposition parties found administrative difficulties put in their way and opposition politicians ran into trouble with the law more often than might have been expected. The government's record of economic success could be used to justify its limits on political activity; the city's prosperity rose impressively enough, and enough of its wealth was spent on social services to provide arguments for those who contended that the guided or limited democracy set up in some east-Asian countries did more for the people than pure democracy could always manage. Lee Kwan Yew was shrewd enough to begin withdrawing from office and handing over power to trusted followers in the late 1980s and thus reduce the danger associated with rulers who stay too long on the stage.

Singapore's emergence as a separate state had left a large Malay majority in Malaysia, which had to work with a prosperous Chinese minority that dominated economic activity. This led to some restraints on political activity, some of which could easily be seen as a response to the potential division within the country, and some of which seemed to be used by politicians as a way to raise money to finance party activity. Sri Lanka showed what could go wrong, and its example helps explain politicians' readiness to impose restrictions on political freedom. The politics of the mainstream in Sri Lanka were hard-fought and even bitterly contested, with echoes of politics in India in the form of the assassination of a Prime Minister and the succession to the leadership of the party of the Prime Minister's widow, but all this was cut across by the separatist policy of the Tamil minority, located in the east and north of the island. By the 1980s the alienation of this group was sliding into civil war and by 1983 or 1984 organized warfare was occurring in most Tamil areas in the country. The Indian government, who had to bear in mind the sympathy of Tamils at the south of the continent for people on the island who spoke the same language and practised the same religion, did briefly try to establish a peace keeping force but soon realized that there was no peace to keep. Civil war between a majority but exclusive group and a minority that felt excluded and desperate was the disaster feared by several leaders of newly independent nations: the Indian government must have looked at the position in Sri Lanka and wondered whether the religious concerns of the Sikhs in the Punjab, sometimes expressed by violence, might lead to a similar situation.

The Indian government was more successful when it intervened after a coup in the Maldives to restore democracy, but it did not move further across the Indian Ocean when a coup in the Seychelles removed the elected government in 1977, a year after independence. By the early 1990s public pressure and the shift in international feeling away from authoritarian government had brought President René to hold contested elections in which he was re-elected. Further away again across the ocean, though mainly settled by people from India, Mauritius was able to look after its democratic system for itself and in 1982 could say that it was the first African country in which the head of the government had lost an election and given up power peacefully.

The smallest island members of the Commonwealth were relatively free from problems of this sort and handled the problems of independence within a two-party or multi-party system. The islands of the West Indies had had elected assemblies for a long time; obviously things changed in some ways as they moved to universal suffrage and rule by the black majority, but the new voters were perfectly willing to play by the rules of the existing game. Sometimes the vigour and violence of electoral contests rivalled that of eighteenth century England and in the late 1970s and early 1980s Jamaican party politics looked like a rehearsal for civil war, but the only complaint of serious constitutional impropriety came in 1983. The opposition boycotted the election on the grounds that the register was out of date and Seaga's Jamaica National Party government was re-elected with no opposition, a result that seems to have convinced both sides that politics of this unrestrained type would lead to disaster. The People's National Party won the next election, but Manley was distinctly more conciliatory than he had been in an earlier period in office in the 1970s. The stability of the two-party system did not always mean that parties alternated in office; in St Lucia John Compton was Prime Minister for over thirty years, taking office in 1964, winning re-election for fifteen years before independence and going on for a longer period after independence. This was an unusual type of one-party dominance, but elections were held regularly and opposition parties kept going gallantly if unsuccessfully.

The democratic tranquillity of most of these small territories in the West Indies and the Pacific owed a great deal to the fact that there were no deep divisions within the population. In Guyana and in Fiji politics were embittered by the after-effects of the immigration of Indians brought in to help with the sugar cultivation which had been the economic backbone of the two colonies under British rule. In the 1980s the Indians in Fiji were increasing in numbers to a point where they would soon become a majority of the population, and they gained ground electorally; in 1987 native Fijian army officers carried out two successive military coups which placed them in a position to draw up a constitution which would return a good deal of power to the old-established local chiefs. The second coup was carried out at the time of the biannual Commonwealth conference, and the Commonwealth was able to express the mounting distaste among its members for military seizures of power because the new Fijian government declared its country a republic and, according to precedents going back to the 1940s, would have needed at this point to reapply for membership. It was quite clear that it would not have been accepted, though the rejection would have reflected the dislike of the Indian government for a regime organized explicitly to discriminate against Indian immigrants as much as any general repudiation of all military regimes. The military government took the steps to return to civilian rule that were to be seen in a number of similar regimes at the end of the 1980s, but its readiness to change its approach was probably encouraged by a decline in the immigrant population as Indians left for less unwelcoming countries.

As British Guiana moved towards independence in the mid-1960s, with the new name Guyana, the British government became concerned that power was going to fall back into the hands of Dr Jagan. His electoral strength rested on the support of the Indian population which had come to the sugar plantations in the nineteenth century; in London and Washington he was feared as a potential ally of the Soviet Union because of his Marxist views. The British government picked out Forbes Burnham, the leader of the older-established part of the electorate who were descended from African slaves, as a safe man who would remain within the Western alliance system, and set up a system of proportional representation which served to make sure that he became Prime Minister in 1964. As a matter of global strategy, this approach was successful, but Burnham was no more ready to share power and acknowledge the rights of the opposition than the most ruthless Marxist would have been. He steadily strengthened his grip on power, and eventually became Life-President, a post he held until his death in 1985. His successor Desmond Hoyte dismantled this authoritarian structure and in 1992 accepted defeat in an election which returned the resilient Dr Jagan to office.

The small states which were free from deep internal divisions were also those which most often retained the British monarch as their head of state. Possibly moves towards a republican system, and in particular to one with a strong or executive president, were most likely to be inspired by a feeling of concern about the stability of the country and a belief that a strong personality at the centre, with a great deal of power, would reduce the dangers of disintegration. A certain type of nationalism underlay republicanism as well; Australia, which had not had a military *coup d'état* since 1808, had no fears of instability to make it begin serious consideration of a republican constitution in the 1990s. Support for the change was not enough to save the Labour government from defeat in 1996, but it was not clear if the result showed attachment to the British monarchy or an acceptance of the idea that Australia was a nation of the Pacific combined with a recognition that the countries to the north of Australia, from Japan to Tonga to Thailand, seemed as content with their constitutions as any people in the last years of the century and were perfectly willing to treat monarchies as valuable symbols.

Independence and Democracy

Imperial expansion had itself been inspired by a blend of political ideas that fused nationalism and loyalty to the monarch. The England of Elizabeth I was more conscious of itself as a nation than most areas of the world have been until very recent decades, and that national spirit took Elizabeth as one of its dominant symbols much as imperial expansion at its most assertive in the late nineteenth century took the Queen-Empress as one of its symbols, although Queen Victoria was not nearly as directly concerned in forming policy as Elizabeth had been. To this strong national consciousness the British added considerable political sophistication: representative institutions, the use of federal political systems to unite colonies when possible, and the care taken to reconcile financial and political objectives all showed that British imperial politicians deserved their success. They made relatively little effort to apply this skill to developing a unified system of rule for the empire, and the evidence suggests that they would not have got far if they had tried.

Conceivably the British Empire might, at the end of the nineteenth and the beginning of the twentieth century, have been turned into an organization much more closely unified for tariff and foreign policy and perhaps specific events such as the Liberal election victory in Britain in 1906 changed the course of events decisively. Developments after 1918 seem to be the inevitable working out of forces that were already visible, and even the creation of a different type of organization at the beginning of the century might have done very little to affect the final emergence of independent sovereign states. Very few of the people who wanted to change the late-Victorian empire saw nationalism in the colonies as an enemy, and yet in a generation or two nationalism turned out to be incompatible with imperial unity or vitality. Prudently, the British did not try very hard to resist this; nationalism gained ground partly because Britain was less strong than before, and so no longer had the magnetic power to convince all her subjects that being part of the British Empire was a great destiny. Loss of power also meant that Britain was less well placed for resisting national movements: rebellions had broken out in the past and could be checked easily enough because they never commanded anything like united support in a colony. Admiration for British technical skill or political enlightenment, loyalty to rulers seen as legitimate political superiors, and inertia had all meant that the government could resist local discontent with ease and with a good deal of support from local sources of strength. If they had not had this local strength their position would soon have been abandoned; support from Britain could have triumphed over local revolts if that had been thought worthwhile, but it was difficult to see much reason or need to rule over unwilling subjects at great expense.

In many colonies that were on the road to independence the British found that vulnerable sections of society which expected to do badly out of the change wanted imperial rule to go on but, because of their weakness, these supporters could not be useful or effective allies. The colonies which remained to the last were those which stayed attached to Britain because any national desire for independence would be frustrated by the expansionist ambitions of some nearby country. The assistance given to Kuwait in 1962 and to the Borneo section of Malaysia in 1964 had shown that attacks on small ex-colonies with aggressive neighbours would be resisted if possible. When Belize became independent in 1982 it faced some risk of attack inspired by Guatemalan irredentism, but its position was probably made safer later in the same year by the swift defeat inflicted on Argentina when it briefly took over the Falklands Islands: a force of 6,000 men was quickly sent to the south Atlantic and the Argentinian invasion force of 14,000 men was obliged to surrender. This provoked some argument inside Britain about whether the obvious desire of the inhabitants of the islands to remain British should be taken seriously, but the intervention undoubtedly strengthened Britain's position in negotiations about some remaining colonies. Territories such as Gibraltar (and, some of its inhabitants would say, Northern Ireland) remained British possessions because the population reckoned that independent existence was no more possible for them than it had been for nineteenth-century Canada. Independence might be pleasant, but British rule was preferable to the only real alternative.

In Hong Kong neither independence nor continued British rule seemed possible; the original island acquired in 1842 and the Kowloon district added in 1860 were expanded in 1898 to about twelve times their previous size when Britain obtained the New Territories from China on a 99-year lease, and its was reckoned that when the lease came to an end the original slip of land would become untenable. The British government negotiated an agreement that would return the whole of Hong Kong, old and new territories, to China in 1997 if China undertook to allow the existing economic system—a very successful type of capitalism—to continue for fifty years after the colony returned to China. In 1984 an agreement for the transfer of the colony in 1997 was worked out easily enough; the nominally Communist government of China was moving so rapidly towards freedom for economic enterprise, controlled by a government restrained by no electoral system at all, that the system of government in China differed surprisingly little from the old imperial system in Hong Kong of a nominated legislative council and freedom for business enterprise. But when John Major became Prime Minister in 1990 he looked for ways of strengthening the hand of the Hong Kong government in the period leading up to 1997. After being re-elected in 1992 he sent a new Governor with parliamentary experience to take steps in this direction in the final five years of British rule, and the new Governor set out to provide a much more democratic electoral base for the legislative council. The Chinese government was annoyed that the British government was changing the Hong Kong constitution so substantially after making the agreement to return the colony to China, and said that it would reverse the changes after 1997. Politically active people in Hong Kong argued that the British arrangements did not do enough to give the local population the right to determine its own future; the turnout in the 1995 Hong Kong election was low enough to give some support to the argument of the 'old China hands' that people were not very interested in democracy, but those who did vote were overwhelmingly in favour of party leaders who wanted more respect for the political rights of the people of the colony. As 1997 drew closer it seemed that the shift towards establishing democratic institutions might do no more than produce a period of friction when the colony was taken over. A good many people in Hong Kong took steps to obtain the legal documentation that would let them enter countries such as Canada which welcomed immigrants, and the population hoped that China would not want to disturb economic prospects or that it might want to show that it observed the treaties it had made, possibly to win back the people of the large and prosperous island of Taiwan by showing them that reconciliation could be carried out harmoniously. In any case it was clear that prosperous business leaders in Hong Kong would have to work out some form of accommodation with the Chinese government if they wanted to survive.

Everywhere else, people expected to be able to choose national independence over imperial rule and the option of national independence was normally taken up with an enthusiasm that the British had no desire or real power to resist. A referendum in Bermuda in 1995 produced a substantial majority who voted to continue colonial status, probably to reassure the outside world of the safety of the tourist and banking arrangements on which the island depended for its prosperity. The British government accepted this unusual decision but most of the time it encouraged colonies to move towards independence, devising federations in the familiar style when this step seemed likely to create a new state with a better chance of survival. Whether independence was practicable remained in doubt in some cases: the Commonwealth had produced so many small states, mainly because the British in their days of maritime supremacy had occupied numerous islands and small strips of coastline for their harbours, that they might almost have seemed designed to put temptation in the way of some future expansionist. The forces of nationalism that had led to independence inhibited such changes, and the example of larger colonies which had to wrestle with the problems of conflicting nationalisms, or potential nationalisms, within a single state did not encourage newly independent states to enter federations as willingly as the Colonial Office had set them up in the past. It could be argued that small states would not have had problems if other countries had been willing to observe the theories of self-determination which had been proclaimed in the late twentieth century with no thought of any other considerations. The logical limitations of self-determination were tested in 1983 when a *coup d'état* took place in the island of Grenada; the Prime

Minister was assassinated and the people who had killed him took over the government. The United States intervened to frustrate this, and retained control of the country until free elections could be held. There was something to be said for discouraging the murdering of Prime Ministers, and yet people did argue that assassination was a matter of local rather than international concern.

By the late 1980s both military governments and one-party states were clearly becoming less acceptable than they had been a few years earlier, and the idea of self-determination was no longer treated as a reason why countries should be free from pressure to mend their ways. Military rulers moved towards holding elections, although in some cases they expected to retain by a free vote the power they had first gained by other means; one-party states found that international pressure, sometimes expressed through the direction of foreign aid or by financial constraints, popular discontent, and increasing acceptance of the idea that multi-party democracy was the best method of controlling the government, made their position harder and harder to maintain. In the Communist world the one-party system collapsed almost everywhere. In 1989 and 1990 the states of eastern Europe escaped from Soviet control and held multi-party elections as soon as they could. In 1991 and 1992 the Soviet Union itself broke up and Russia, Ukraine and most of the successor states then held contested elections. Communist parties had to adapt to the new system except in China where the one-party state used armed force to resist pressure from crowds of demonstrators in Tiananmen Square in the capital, and reasserted its old style of authority in political affairs.

Changes like this in the outside world encouraged Commonwealth countries to examine the policies some of them had been following since the great move to independence around 1960. In 1991 the new British Prime Minister John Major came to the Harare conference in a better position for negotiating than his predecessor had enjoyed for several years. The issue of apartheid in South Africa was being solved peacefully as a result of internal reform, the memory of Thatcher's isolation was dying down and the British government felt prosperous enough to write off about £500m. pounds of debts to the smaller and more impoverished countries. Very few Commonwealth governments had possessed either the recklessness or the apparently abundant economic prospects which had enabled a number of Third World countries to run up totally unmanageable debts in the late 1970s, but the remission of debt was a welcome relief that strengthened the hand of the British government as it pressed successfully for a declaration of policy that would commit the Commonwealth to such values as the rule of law and the rights of citizens and of opposition parties that would have been taken for granted thirty years earlier. Attempts to entrench these rights at the time of independence would have been seen as imperial distrust of a colony's capacity to run its own affairs; by the 1990s it was harder to deny the need for some such statement of policy. The largest and the smallest of Commonwealth countries had run democratic systems reasonably success-fully, but a substantial minority of countries large enough to make nation-building a difficult process had run into serious trouble. In some cases people who wanted to avoid the difficulties and possible loss of office that go with democracy had taken advantage of the situation to make their power uncontrollable, but they had a genuine problem of which to take advantage. At the Harare conference the leaders of Zimbabwe and Malay-sia offered some opposition to the declaration of policy, and suggested that the debts had been remitted in order to buy support for it. Their concern was explicable enough; they had to rule countries in which, quite apart from any questions raised by imperial rule, the divisions of Malay and Chinese, or of Mashona and Matabele, forced them to face the problem of a well-defined minority group that might regain a position of dominance and a majority that was anxious to make any such change impossible. They could have pointed out that in Northern Ireland Britain had been faced with a problem of a minority and a majority divided along lines which defied ordinary political adjustment, and that giving unfettered political authority to the Ulster majority between 1920 and 1970 had not led to tranquillity. But the alternatives to democracy tried since the 1960s were unattractive enough for the Harare Declaration to be accepted as Commonwealth policy, and the consequences of the improvements visible at the end of the 1980s worked themselves out as more and more governments recognized that they ought to let their opponents state their case and put it to the electorate.

The military rulers of Nigeria, like several others, had undertaken to hold elections and return power to civilian hands. But when Chief Abiola, a politician unwelcome to them, looked like winning the election to be held in 1993, the military rulers cancelled it and set out to make their power more permanent. Later in the year General Abacha, understood to have been the power behind the throne for ten years, came out into the open as ruler of the country. This breach of public undertakings and of newly proclaimed principles pushed Commonwealth countries in the direction of offering some condemnation of the Nigerian government, but it might have avoided censure if it had tried to attract as little attention as possible until after the 1995 conference. The Nigerian army felt it had a particular mission to protect the unity of the country as it had done in the civil war of the late 1960s. It regarded with deep hostility the organizers of a campaign to protect the position and status of the oil-rich Ogoni region and, when four Ogoni supporters of the central government were assassinated, it seized a number of suspects, put nine of them (including the novelist Saro-Wiwa who had been taking an important role in the Ogoni struggle) hastily on trial and had them executed while the conference was meeting. The Commonwealth leaders must have felt that Nigeria had gone out of its way to show that it would not pay any attention to their calls for clemency for the Ogoni suspects and that it was unlikely to take seriously requests for a speedy return to civilian government. They decided that Nigeria's membership of the Commonwealth should be suspended for two years, to see how its government responded to pressure, and went on to indicate that it would be expelled at the 1997 conference if its respect for the political rights of the population had not improved. It was hard to see substantial ways in which Commonwealth countries could force Nigeria to pay attention to their strong feelings, but they certainly were committing themselves to democratic values much more unequivocally than had been the case in the decades immediately after independence.

Conflict between Nigeria and the Commonwealth on another issue became a possibility when Cameroon became a member. In 1919 the German colony of Kamerun had been divided into a large French mandate territory and two small British mandates on the eastern border of Nigeria. At independence in 1961 the northern British trust territory (the United Nations term for mandated territory) joined Nigeria, while the French and the southern British trust territories were united as Cameroon, with the largest population and national income of all the members of the French Community or *Francophonie* south of the Sahara. At the beginning of the 1990s it began negotiating for Commonwealth membership, and while there were doubts about its status as a one-party state, it became a member of the Commonwealth in 1995 on the basis that it was making proper progress towards democracy. While its main European links were with France, English was recognized as an official language; its position was a little like that of Canada, an old-established member of the Commonwealth which had in addition joined the *Francophonie*. By the time Cameroon became a member it was involved in a border dispute with Nigeria which could leave Commonwealth countries wondering whether they ought to support it against Nigeria. The closest parallel to Cameroon, as a country of which one part had once been under British rule, was Somalia, which seemed unlikely to reach even a minimum level of democratic acceptability for many years. The admission of Mozambique in 1995, which took place partly because of its President's approval of the British government in the 1980s, but mainly because all six of the countries with which it had a common land frontier were members of the Commonwealth, was specifically stated to be unique, and of course the admission of a country which had never had any connection with British rule did open up the possibility of an indefinite expansion of membership. Short of this, Ireland or Fiji, which had once been members of the Commonwealth, or Burma which had been a British colony but had never been a member of

the Commonwealth, were much the most likely candidates for membership
in the foreseeable future.

British expansion had created a couple of dozen small states, with uncertain futures, and perhaps a couple of dozen larger countries, some of them
faced with internal problems resulting from the imperial fusing of political
units. Many of the small states were islands with boundaries fixed by the
sea; the frontiers of the larger states were more often the result of British
diplomacy. Both types of state had been shaped by British influence during
the formative years in which they turned into nations, and in many cases
appeared to want good, though not overwhelmingly close, relations with
Britain to go on into the future. These new nations varied so much in their
attitude and their prospects that it was impossible to make any general
statement about them: they illustrated the diversity and the lack of rigorous
planning about the British Empire, and perhaps even showed that an attempt to apply a consistent policy to such different times and places and
people would have defeated itself. The imperial past fairly clearly left more
of an impression on these countries than on Britain; in some cases they
would not have existed at all without imperial involvement, and in most
cases they had been led to a form of government they would perhaps not
have developed without external pressure. The pressure need not necessarily have come from Britain; for most of the 400 years in which European
ideas were spread around the world the Spanish Empire was larger than the
British. But in the event British influence had shaped a large part of the
world without providing so much opportunity for the outside world to have
much effect on Britain. In the years from 1956 to 1976 Britain showed some
signs of shock at the loss of empire, confused and muffled though the sense
of it might be. By the 1990s Britain was no doubt willing to be seen as a
power of importance in the world, but did not depend on memories of
empire for this, thought more in terms of the European Union than the
Commonwealth, and was untroubled by the fact that Queen Elizabeth II
and her government in London ruled less land than her predecessors had
done for hundreds of years.

BIBLIOGRAPHY

The British Empire has probably been served by its historians as well as could have been hoped, but it is a difficult subject to reduce to a manageable shape; it covers a long period of time, touches on the history of several dozen countries, and raises highly divisive questions about whether it was a good or a bad thing. Four stages can be seen in the development of writing, favourable or unfavourable, about the empire: some books from the period of imperial dominance are still useful, several others were written while the evolution of colonies of white settlement and continued subordination of the other colonies was still taken for granted, many show the influence of the idea that the multi-racial Commonwealth ought to be the subject of a certain amount of self-congratulation, and a few books already accept the fact that the British Empire now ranks with such creatures of the past as the Athenian Empire and the Holy Roman Empire.

Almost all of the eight-volume *Cambridge History of the British Empire* (1929–59), edited by J. Holland Rose and others, was written in the second period, as the volumes for events before 1783, for Canada, for South Africa, for Australia and New Zealand, and the two volumes for the British period of Indian history all appeared between 1929 and 1939. Two other volumes, one published in 1940 and the other in 1959, discussed the system of imperial government and the interconnections between the different parts of the empire. The writers paid relatively little attention to the old-established colonies in the West Indies, the very substantial territories in Africa taken over after 1870, or the vast collection of little bits and pieces from Ascension Island to Fiji that made up the full diversity of the empire. The Oxford University Press and the University of Minnesota Press are now producing a series with the general title of 'Europe and the World in the Age of Expansion' which sets out to cover all European imperial activity: volume 2, Holden Furber, *Rival Empires of Trade in the Orient* (1976), volume 8, Henry Wilson, *The Imperial Experience in Sub-Saharan Africa since 1870* (1977), and volume 9, W. D. McIntyre, *The Commonwealth of Nations* (1977) are the most relevant, though of course all of them except McIntyre's very useful volume include a good deal about other empires.

While a multi-volume multi-author history can be cumbersome, a single volume by a single author is liable to be too short for this immense subject and probably reveals unevenness in the author's knowledge of it. At the most ambitious level of all, D. K. Fieldhouse, *The Colonial Empires* (1966) sets out to cover all the empires from 1700 to 1960. Anyone writing a one-volume history of the British Empire is bound to be grateful to previous writers who have been brave enough to try to tell the whole story from Elizabeth I to Elizabeth II. C. Carrington, *The British Overseas* (1950, partially revised 1968) is a substantial study, though at some points the overseas activity of people from the British Isles is not the same as the history of the empire. G. S. Graham's *A Concise History of the British Empire* (1970), which is copiously and pleasantly illustrated, and J. Bowle's *The Imperial Achievement* (1977) are rather smaller but make similar attempts to tell the whole story. All three volumes read a little like favourable obituaries for the empire.

The idea that there was a first British Empire before 1783 and a second one afterwards was stated in its most sophisticated form in V. T. Harlow, *The Founding of the Second British Empire* (2 vols., 1952–65), a book which was ready to admit that some features of the 'second' empire could be seen before 1783. A good many authors have gone on from that argument to treat the post-1783 empire as a unit of study with little in common with the earlier phase. The title of A. L. Burt's *The Evolution of the British Empire and Commonwealth from the American Revolution* (1956) puts the whole argument. Nicholas Mansergh's *The Commonwealth Experience* (1969) begins a little later, taking Lord Durham's Report as its starting-point, but it too expressed the mid-twentieth-century view that the second empire was better than the first because it had turned into the Commonwealth. J. Morris's imperial triptych, *At Heaven's Command* (1973), *Pax Brittanica* (1968), ansd *Farewell the Trumpets* (1978) accepts this view some of the time, but it is more of a collection of anecdotes and brilliant evocations of bygone scenes from 1815 to the present than a piece of coherent analysis. W. D. McIntyre, *Colonies into Commonwealth* (1966) is a smaller scale and very manageable post-1783 history, stating the evolution-of-empire-into-commonwealth approach, though there are signs in the Preface to the 1974 edition that he may have some doubts about it. B. Porter, *The Lion's Share* (1975) starts later still, after the development of responsible government, and devotes more space to China than to Canada in a slightly uneasy attempt to fit the empire into a solution of Marx-and-water. A. P. Thornton has written a crisp account of the way that people, especially in Britain, thought about their imperial power; *The Imperial Idea and its Enemies* (1959) must take some of the responsibility for the modern fashion of writing imperial history in the language of epigram and paradox. One recent book deals with the pre-1783 British Empire: Angus Calder's *The Revolutionary Empire* (1981) may over-compensate for the neglect of English activity in Scotland and Ireland in previous books, but it does treat earlier overseas activity as worth attention in its own right, even if intellectual fashion sometimes reminds him to add that of course it was all very deplorable.

Part of the difficulty of writing general histories of the empire is that so many things were going on in different places at the same time, but writing a history of one country involves a slight risk that its history as a section of the empire will be treated as a prelude to independence, without much concern about its links with the rest of the empire. This is a natural way to write national history, but it is not a good basis for imperial history. The two volumes on India in the Cambridge History of the British Empire series avoided this as far as possible, by serving also as the last two volumes of the Cambridge History of India, and a new edition (1958) brought the second volume down to the end of British rule. The *Oxford History of India*, originally by V. A. Smith, has been extensively re-written by P. Spear, and the 1981 edition brings the story down to the 1975 emergency. R. C. Majumdar and others, *An Advanced History of India* (1967) is shorter and in some ways more up-to-date. V. P. Anstey's *The Economic Development of India* (1951 edn.) deals with a large subject from a somewhat pro-British point of view. Standard histories of the colonies of white settlement are being written. The *Oxford History of South Africa* (2 vols., 1969–74), edited by M. Wilson and L. Thompson, has not given universal satisfaction, but at least the complaints come from both Left and Right. The *Oxford History of New Zealand* (1981), edited by W. H. Oliver with B. R. Williams, has been received more quietly. Shorter, single-author volumes may be preferred: T. R. H. Davenport, *A Short History of South Africa* (1978) and K. Sinclair, *A History of New Zealand* (1969 edn.) may meet the need. It is not yet easy to choose a substantial general history of Australia; Manning Clark's *A History of Australia* (5 vols., 1962–) has brought the story down to the Anzacs at Gallipoli, but it is so distinctively personal that it may be safe as well as shorter to start with *A New History of Australia* (1974), edited by F. K. Crowley. The volumes of the Centennial History of Canada which are directly relevant to imperial history are mentioned in the notes on appropriate chapters, and all the volumes in the series are important for students of Canadian (as distinct from imperial) history. W. L. Morton's *The Kingdom of Canada* (1963)and K. W. McNaught's *The History of Canada* (1970) are very useful and relatively recent single-volume histories.

Some very useful histories deal with a whole region rather than picking out a single country. A. C. Burns, *A History of the British West Indies* (1965 edn.) does leave the impression that it may be hard to bring this region together and that its unity may be merely linguistic. J. H. Parry and P. M. Sherlock, *A Short History of the West Indies* (1956) take another possible approach to this region, looking at the whole of it and going well beyond the bounds of the British Empire. Anyone writing about Africa is faced with the same choice, on a much larger scale, of sticking to the English-speaking, formerly British countries or trying to tell the whole history of Africa. There is a useful *History of* [formerly British] *East Africa* (3 vols., 1963–76) edited by R. Oliver, G. Mathew, and others, but the general histories try more often to break down the barriers between the European empires and between their successor states: J. D. Fage, *Introduction to the History of West Africa* (1969 edn.), M. Crowder, *West Africa under Colonial Rule* (1968), R. Oliver and J. D. Fage, *A Short History of Africa* (1968 edn.), R. Oliver and A. Atmore, *Africa since 1800* (1972 edn.), and J. D. Fage, *A History of Africa* (1978) all take this approach, and show signs of wanting to push it in a pan-African direction which seems at least as optimistic as anything said by the advocates of closer Commonwealth unity.

In other regions, in which the unity of the area is not a question to raise quite as many problems of current politics, E. Monroe, *Britain's Moment in the Middle East 1914–1956* (1963), W.P. Morrell, *Britain in the Pacific Islands* (1960), and D. G. E. Hall, *A History of South East Asia* (1955) are all reasonably successful at bringing together the history of a number of different countries.

The Dictionary of National Biography is a very useful work of reference in its own right, containing lives of people from all over the empire, and it has in addition inspired a range of companion productions. The *Australian Dictionary of Biography* and the *Dictionary of Canadian Biography* published their first volumes in 1966; both are making good progress though neither is complete yet, and *The Dictionary of South African Biography* was launched in 1968 and is also doing well. For New Zealand, readers must still rely on G. H. Schofield's two-volume *Dictionary of New Zealand Biography* (1940). *The Dictionary of American Biography* (20 vols., 1928–37) gives many lives from the colonial period, which made up over half of the time-span covered by the work.

Some helpful biographies were written in the great burst of activity of the 1960s.

J. E. Flint's *Books on the British Empire and Commonwealth* (1968) is short but that is not always a disadvantage. A great deal more can be found in *The Historiography of the British Empire-Commonwealth* (1966), edited by R. Winks, though perhaps it should be noted that, despite the title, it is made up of essays that select and discuss useful books to read – it does not devote much attention to the different ways in which imperial history is written. The volumes of 'The Bibliography of British History', which the American Historical Association and the Royal Historical Association have been working to encourage for many years, include long and useful chapters about work on imperial history: the relevant volumes are Conyers Read, *1485–1603* (1959 edn.), which naturally contains less imperial material than the others; G. Davies and M. F. Keeler, *1603–1714* (1970 edn.); S. Pergellis, *1714–1789* (1951); L. M. Brown and I. Christie, *1789–1851* (1977); and H. J. Hanham, *1851–1914* (1976). *The Colonial Office List* has changed its name several times since it first came out in 1862 and is now *The Commonwealth Year Book*, but it has continued to provide a good deal of political, social, and economic information about British colonies and members of the Commonwealth every year. Up to 1947 *The India Office List* has information on India and its dependencies, perhaps including more detail on ceremonies and on salaries than anyone except the most deeply involved reader could want.

Books are mentioned only once in this bibliography, but many books of general concern are also of particular usefulness for a specific chapter; and it may also be helpful to look back to see what has been noted as useful reading for earlier chapters.

Chapter 1

One obvious example of a book that can be useful when looking at some later chapters is K. E. Knorr, *British Colonial Theories 1570–1850* (1944). A. L. Rowse, *The Expansion of Elizabethan England* (1955) puts expansion across the ocean into the context of a society that was advancing aggressively in a number of directions. J. A. Williamson, *The Age of Drake* (1952 edn.) is a rousing introduction to the subject and a useful reminder of the way people used to feel about the empire. T. K. Raab, *Enterprise and Empire* (1967) shows who supported the various types of overseas activity that were going on, and G. Bridenbaugh, *Vexed and Troubled Englishmen* (1968) discusses the considerable emigration up to 1640. C. M. Andrews, *The Colonial Period of American History* (4 vols., 1935–8) is the classic account of British colonies in America, but Perry Miller, *Errand into the Wilderness* (1956) is useful for redressing the imbalance that may be caused by Andrews's lack of enthusiasm for the role of religion in colonization. G. L. Beer, *The Origins of the British Colonial System* (1908) explains how governments thought things ought to be arranged, and large parts of W. L. Scott, *The Constitution of Joint Stock Companies to 1720* (3 vols., 1910–12) explain how business men in England actually arranged things. P. Griffiths, *A Licence to Trade* (1974) gives a brief and simple account of the joint stock (or 'chartered') companies, and their effect on imperial development. K. N. Chaudhuri, *The English East India Company* (1965), shows what the Company did in the first, pepper-dominated stage of its career. E. Thompson and G. Garratt, *The Rise and Fulfilment of British Rule in India* (1934) is worth mentioning here, though it obviously covers a long period of time; and it is worth noting that the book concentrates on trade up to 1760 and then turns away to follow the political story as if trade had ceased to matter. C. M. Cipolla, *Guns and Sails in Early European Expansion* (1965) explains why Europeans were able to assert their power in the Indian Ocean so successfully. D. B. Quinn, *England and the Discovery of America 1481–1620* (1974) is an up-to-date account of English exploration, for which it makes some fairly high claims.

Chapter 2

Some interesting continuities can be seen in writers' work. K. N. Chandhuri's *The Trading World of Asia and the English East India Company* (1978) is a very scholarly account, full of well-digested information, of what the company did in the second, textile-dominated stage of its career. G. L. Beer, *The Old Colonial System* (1912) shows how an elaborate pattern of regulation developed in lines laid down in the Navigation Acts. L. W. Labaree, *Royal Government in America* (1930), challenged the idea that the royal governors were incompetent and argued that they were criticized simply as part of the political conflict. More recently S. S. Webb, in *The Governors General 1569–1681* (1979; more volumes to come) has argued that they can be understood only in terms of their military background. The trading aspects of activity in Africa emerge very clearly in K. G. Davies, *The Royal African Company* (1957), which leads naturally across the Atlantic to C. Bridenbaugh, *No Peace Beyond the Line* (1972), an account of the settlement of the British West Indies which picks up speed with the establishment of slavery as the basis of the economy. A. P. Thornton's *West-Indian Policy under the Restoration* (1956) shows how hard it was for the London government to get its orders obeyed. Some of the most original thought – not always well expressed – about trade and its effect in shaping a society can be found in H. A. Innis's analysis of early Canadian development in *The Cod Fisheries* (1954 edn.) and *The Fur Trade* (1956 edn.). Some of these things are easier to follow in E. E. Rich, *The History of the Hudson's Bay Company* (2 vols., 1958–9), and this can be compared with a western Canadian's account in A. S. Morton's *History of the Canadian West to 1870–71* (1939).

Chapter 3

Several of the books already mentioned throw their light forward to the eighteenth century. For a clear-cut new start J. H. Parry, *Trade and Dominion* (1971) is a wide-ranging and well-informed general history. For one part of the trading background, John Carswell's *The South Sea Bubble* (1961) gives so clear an account of the great speculation that it leaves the reader feeling, however briefly, that it is all comprehensible. The view of the British constitution taken here is roughly that of John B. Owen in *The Rise of the Pelhams* (1957). E. E. Williams, *Capitalism and Slavery* (1964 edn.) has come to win some grudging respect, but not acceptance. Among the books that hold the field in its place is R. Anstey, *The Atlantic Slave Trade and British Abolition* (1975), which rehabilitates the philanthropists as well as giving a great deal of information about how the trade worked. The British trade was meant to stock the sugar plantations, and the operation of the industry is covered in R. B. Sheridan, *Sugar and Slavery* (1974). The trade depended on naval strength, which is sketched in Parry's *Trade and Dominion*, C. C. Lloyd, *The Nation and the Navy* (1965) and in an older and more technically informative book, R. Albion,

Forests and Sea-power 1652–1862 (1926). L. Sutherland studies the British end of another area of expansion in *The East India Company in 18th Century Politics* (1952). For quite a lively account of the Company's emergence as a force in Indian politics M. Edwardes, *The Battle of Plassey and the Conquest of Bengal* (1963) is useful if traditional. O. Sherrard, *Lord Chatham* (3 vols., 1952–8) is a substantial life of the man who, more than any other, turned the British Empire from a coastal system into a force to penetrate the interior, though people who want to look at the coastline can find out about part of it in W. S. MacNutt, *The Atlantic Provinces 1712–1857* (1965).

Chapter 4

L. H. Gipson's immense *The British Empire before the American Revolution* (15 vols., 1936–70) concentrates on events after 1763, though it begins a little earlier, and provides a solid foundation for reading about the period. R. Koebner, *Empire* (1961), also begins earlier – much earlier – but its most direct reference to British problems is at this point; it takes the different uses of the word 'empire' and follows them down the centuries. Koebner wished the American War of Independence had not taken place and argues things would have gone better if political leaders had used the word 'empire' more skilfully. What actually happened can be followed in E. S. and H. M. Morgan, *The Stamp Act Crisis* (1963 edn.), which leads on to questions studied in a joint Anglo-American study, I. R. Christie and B. W. Larabee, *Empire and Independence 1760–76* (1976). Christie has also written a fairly brief *Crisis of Empire* (1966), and C. Bridenbaugh (mentioned at the beginning of American colonial history) ends it with *The Spirit of '76* (1976). For the two great areas of empire that remained after the War of Independence, R. Coupland, *The Quebec Act* (1925) deals with a piece of legislation that pointed in several ways to the future, and Hilda Neatby, *Quebec: The Revolutionary Age* (1966) shows how the colony responded to the great transformation; and for India P. J. Marshall's *East India Fortunes* (1976) shows what happened in the first generation after conquest, his *Impeachment of Warren Hastings* (1965) shows part of the way this phase of imperial rule was ended, and his *Problems of Empire: Britain and India 1757–1813* (1968) gives an account of the British ascent to power. B. H. Misra's *The Central Administration of the East India Company 1773–1834* (1960) is concerned, despite its title, almost exclusively with arrangements in India, but does give a great deal of information about what the British were doing when they were ruling but not fighting battles.

Chapter 5

Although repeating titles ought to be avoided V. T. Harlow's *the Founding of the Second British Empire* (2 vols., 1952–65), which directs attention to the Indian and Pacific Oceans, must be mentioned here. And at the far end of the Pacific is Australia, some of whose problems are examined in a very stimulating way in G. Blainey's *The Tyranny of Distance* (1966), a book whose interest in transport suggests answers to problems in many other parts of the world. By its standards B. C. Fitzpatrick's *British Imperialism in Australia* (1939) is rather over-simplified because of the author's readiness to see Australians as naïve and unfortunate puppets who were constantly being victimized by Englishmen who insisted on lending them money. Undoubtedly money was lent; L. H. Jenks, *The Migration of British Capital to 1875* (1938 edn.) is still a good introduction to the early stages of the process. Two useful general histories of Canada start here: G. Craig, *Upper Canada 1784–1841* (1963) and F. Ouellet, *Lower Canada 1791–1840* (1980); and a more interpretive work, D. G. Creighton's *The Commercial Empire of the St. Lawrence* (1937) argues that Canadian history should be seen in terms of geographical unity rather than division. G. S. Graham, *Empire of the North Atlantic* (1950) puts Canada in a wider perspective; and the naval implications are examined in P. M. Kennedy's *The Rise and Fall of British Naval Mastery* (1976). That mastery led to expanding trade, an important part of which is studied in M. E. Edwards, *The Growth of the British Cotton Trade* (1967). Economic and political aspects of empire are often left strictly separate: Philip Mason's *Men Who Ruled India* (2 vols., 1953–4) is exhilirating but says practically nothing about economic affairs. The British connection with Egypt really began in the Napoleonic era and John Marlowe, *Anglo-Egyptian Relations 1800–1953* (1965 edn.) chooses a good starting-point. Philip Curtin, *The Image of Africa 1780–1850* (1964) explains why Britain took little interest in Africa in the early nineteenth century, and P. Denoon, *Southern Africa since 1800* (1972) argues that Africans still determined the fate of the land at the time the British arrived. Helen Taft Manning, *British Colonial Government 1782–1820* (1933) emphasizes administrative change in the colonies rather than in Britain.

Chapter 6

The London end of British colonial administration is covered in D. M. Young, *The Colonial Office in the early 19th Century* (1963). Expansion owed at least as much to technical as to administrative change, and techniques are discussed in D. Headrick, *The Tools of Empire* (1981). The economic aspects of nineteenth-century empire are reduced to statistical order in A. H. Imlah's *Economic Elements in the Pax Britannica* (1958), and the theory behind British economic policy in the years after 1815 is examined in B. Semmel, *The Rise of Free Trade Imperialism* (1970), and the absence of any strictly economic case for ending slavery is explained in S. Drescher, *Econocide* (1977). An empire-wide development is discussed in B. Thomas, *Migration and Economic Growth* (1973 edn.), and D. Charnwell, *The Long Farewell* (1981) examines emigration to Australia in greater detail. The regulation of emigration is the starting-point of O. Macdonagh's *A Pattern of Government Growth* (1961), which is really a study of British administrative history. Australian problems are looked at in B. Fitzpatrick's *The British Empire in Australia* (1949 edn.) and in J. J. Eddy, *Britain and the Australian Colonies 1818–31* (1969), and the romantic idea of the Australian response to difficulty is presented in Russel Ward, *The Australian Legend* (1965 edn.). Two biographies by M. H. Ellis, *Macarthur* (1955) and *Macquarrie* (1958) tell a good deal of the early history of New South Wales – the case for each man is presented skilfully, but at least one of the books must have got the story wrong. The end of this phase of Australian development is presented in J. M. Ward's *Earl Grey and the Australian Colonies* (1958); Ward has also put forward an ambitious argument about *Colonial Self-Government 1759–1856* (1976), showing how politicians thought people in the colonies should enjoy the rights of Englishmen, but perhaps overestimating the powers of eighteenth-century kings. Other views of British policy at the time of the move to responsible government can be found in W. P. Morrell, *British Colonial Policy in the Age of Peel and Russell* (1930) and in P. Bloomfield's highly eulogistic biography *Edward Gibbon Wakefield* (1961). J. M. S. Careless, *The*

Union of the Canadas 1841–57 (1967) covers the establishment of responsible government in Canada. Further west, J. S. Galbraith's *The Hudson's Bay Company as an Imperial Factor* (1957) is a good account of the history of the Canadian frontier; and his *Reluctant Empire* (1963) shows British thrift fighting against South African expansionism in the first half of the century. W. M. Macmillan's *Bantu, Boer and Briton* (1929) tells an earlier version of this story and shows more willingness to believe that missionaries could have an effect in politics. G. S. Graham, *Great Britain in the Indian Ocean* (1967) explains the maritime basis of British power in the east. E. Stokes, *The English Utilitarians in India* (1959) examines the closest thing to a theory about empire that the imperial rulers ever had. S. Runciman, *The White Rajahs 1841–1946* (1960) is a good pro-Brooke account of how to build a family empire, and P. Adams, *Fatal Necessity* (1977) gives the latest synthesis of the reasons for the British take-over of New Zealand. For a general account of imperial development with a very heavy commitment to the Commonwealth ideal, P. Knaplund's *Gladstone and the British Imperial Policy* (1927) is still worth attention.

Chapter 7

The latest popular account of the Indian Mutiny is C. Hibbert's *The Great Mutiny* (1978); it suffers badly from the author's fear of maps. R. C. Majumdar, *The Sepoy Mutiny and the revolt of 1857* (1963 edn.) concludes that it was not a nationalist movement, though it must be added that the book sets very high standards for people to qualify as nationalists. S. C. Ghosh, *Dalhousie in India* (1975) and R. J. Moore, *Sir Charles Wood's Indian Policy 1853–1866* (1966) are good accounts of what the rulers were doing. P. Harnetty, *Imperialism and Free Trade* (1972) suffers from the author's inability to understand how any honest man could be in favour of free trade. W. L. Morton's *The Critical Years 1857–1873* (1964) is a good general history of the years of Canadian confederation, but not as gripping as D. G. Creighton's *John A. Macdonald* (2 vols., 1952–5), and this author's *The Road to Confederation* (1964) is also worth attention. C. P. Stacey, *Canada and the British Army* (1936) explains much more about imperial relations than the title suggests. G. F. G. Stanley, *The Birth of Western Canada* (1961 edn.) takes up a story with deeper roots than is sometimes realized. South African history in this period has not aroused much interest but C. M. de Kiewiet, *British Colonial Policy and the South African Republics* (1929) and *The Imperial Factor in South Africa* (1937) present the background for the activity of later decades. W. Pember Reeves, *The Long White Cloud* (1950 edn.) presents an account of the early decades of New Zealand history after colonization by a man who did a good deal to shape it. The period of greatest British detachment from imperial affairs is discussed in C. A. Bodelson, *Studies in Mid-Victorian Imperialism* (1924) and R. L. Schuyler, *The Fall of the Old Colonial System* (1945); more recently B. Semmel showed the argument between two opposing ideals of empire in the most acute form in *The Governor Eyre Controversy* (1962); and J. W. Cell, *British Colonial Administration in the mid-19th Century* (1970) provides some facts to show what the British were actually doing with their empire.

Chapter 8

For the last twenty years dicussion of Britain's role in the 'scramble for Africa' has been dominated by R. Robinson and J. Gallagher's *Africa and the Victorians* (1961).

and there is a useful study of the argument in *The Robinson and Gallagher Controversy* (1976) edited by W. R. Louis. A different view about Britain's approach before the 'scramble' is presented effectively in C. C. Eldridge, *England's Mission 1868-1880* (1973), and the idea of a turning-point from the absence of interest in the 1860s to the activity of the 1870s is pinpointed by W. D. McIntyre, *The Imperial Frontier in the Tropics 1865-1875* (1967). W. D. Hargreaves is working on the partition of West Africa: *Prelude to the Partition of West Africa* (1963), *West Africa Partitioned 1885-9* (1974), and there are more to come. There is a good life of *Sir George Goldie* (1960) by J. E. Flint. Rhodes has been attacked from so many irreconcilable points of view that there is something to be said for starting with the authorized biography, J. E. Lockhart and C. M. Woodhouse, *Rhodes* (1963), though it is something of a case for the defence. W. Giffard and W. R. Louis have edited two useful collections of essays, *Britain and Germany in Africa* (1967) and *France and Britain in Africa* (1972). W. G. Hynes's argument in *The Economics of Empire* (1979) that commerce, not investment, underlay British expansion deserved a little more elaboration than he was able to give it. J. E. Tyler, *The Struggle for Imperial Unity 1868-1895* (1938) is still a good introduction to the problems of imperial federation, and C. Berger's *The Sense of Power* (1970) shows the appeal of the idea to a self-governing colony. J. E. Kemble, *The Colonial and Imperial Conferences 1887-1911* (1967) discussed the main constitutional innovation of the period. The standard work for Canadian history is P. B. Waite, *Canada 1874-1896* (1971); H. A. Innis wrote an early and gritty *History of the Canadian Pacific Railway* (1925) which repays a bit of trouble; and R. A. Preston's *Canada and 'Imperial Defence' 1867-1919* (1967) covers some interesting topics even if it is a little too inclined to tell the story as a struggle for colonial freedom. In a quite different context A. Seal, *The Emergence of Indian Nationalism* (1968) explains what a complicated issue that struggle can be. It may be worth looking at some of the men who ran the colonial system: J. K. Chapman, *Lord Stanmore* (1964) and J. Rutherford, *Sir George Grey* (1961) are lives of men with varied service as colonial governors; and the *Sowing* (1960) volume of L. S. Woolf's autobiography gives the view of a man who decided that being married to Virginia Stephens was better than helping to rule the empire.

Chapter 9

To a greater extent than usual, books recommended for the previous chapter are relevant here as well. However, R. V. Kubicek, *The Administration of Imperialism* (1969) shows just how small were the resources that the British devoted to running their empire. To introduce a new African colony, J. S. Galbraith's *Crown and Charter* (1974) is useful for the early history of Rhodes's acquisition, and R. Blake's *History of Rhodesia* (1977) is a full-length history of Southern Rhodesia almost to the end of white rule. For slightly further north in Africa, H. H. Johnston, *The Story of my Life* (1923) is in some ways the best autobiography by any active 'man on the spot', and there is also a good biography, R. Oliver's *Sir Harry Johnston* (1957). There is a bigger and better life of an even more important imperial ruler, M. Perham's *Luggard* (2 vols., 1956–60). Another important imperial ruler, Lord Cromer, put his view firmly but impersonally in *Modern Egypt* (2 vols., 1980 – the author is sometimes listed as Evelyn Baring). The Egyptian diplomatic problem is discussed in G. N. Sanderson, *England Europe and the Upper Nile 1882-1899* (1965). Further east S. R. Mehrotra, *The Emergence of the Indian National Congress* (1971) is very useful and his *India and the Commonwealth 1885–1929* (1965) provides more than might have been expected. F. Swettenham, *British Malaya* (1906) is an instructive account by a man who did a good deal to make Malaya British – it reminds readers that people may gain an empire by being aggressive, but they do not do it by being stupid. More recently K. G. P. Tregoning, *History of Modern Malaya* (1964) and *Under Company Rule* (1965), which is about Sabah, provide histories of two of the colonies that went to make up modern Malaysia. R. M. Burden, *King Dick* (1955) is a life of Seddon, who was once described as the only Prime Minister of New Zealand to deserve a biography. Moving to a very general level, the essays in D. A. Low, *Lion Rampant* (1975), deal with a variety of the problems of the period of imperial rule.

Chapter 10

M. Beloff's *Imperial Sunset 1897–1921* (1969) covers almost the same time-span as this chapter. The period starts with the Boer War and on this subject the most recent book is Thomas Pakenham, *The Boer War* (1979), perhaps more interested in military history than is fashionable in academic circles but useful on other things as well. *The Theory of Capitalist Imperialism* (1967), edited by D. Fieldhouse, gives a short but adequate introduction to the argument. Many of the facts are still best organized in H. Feis, *Europe the World's Banker* (1930). The aftermath of the Boer War can be followed in L. M. Thompson, *The Unification of South Africa* (1960) and, over a longer stretch of time, in W. K. Hancock, *Smuts* (2 vols., 1962–8). The problems confronting those who wanted imperial unity were explained at the time by R. Jebb in his *Studies in Colonial Nationalism* (1905), and the resolution of the problem can be seen in R. M. Dawson, *The Development of Dominion Status 1900–1936* (1937). G. Bennett, *Kenya* (1963), and M. Crowder, *West Africa Under Colonial Rule* (1968) explain what the British did about some of the places they acquired during the 'scramble for Africa', and B. Porter, *Critics of Empire* (1968) presents the arguments of those who wanted imperial rule to be improved. S. Koss, *Morley at the India Office* (1969) is a useful account of a piece of restrained Liberal reform. J. M. Brown, *Gandhi's Rise to Power 1915–1922* (1974) is a very rational work of demythologizing. A. Rumbold, *Watershed in India 1914–1922* (1979) accepts the importance of this period in Indian history, but argues that the British in India could have held on to power if opinion in Britain had not changed decisively.

Chapter 11

C. Cross, *The Fall of the British Empire* (1968) shows how hard it was to write on this subject when people had only just realized that the empire had fallen. A good many of the developments in British imperial policy are covered in P. S. Gupta's very useful *Imperialism and the British Labour Movement* (1975). It naturally emphasizes Indian affairs between the two world wars, and this can be followed up in B. R. Nanda, *Mahatma Gandhi* (1958) and *The Nehrus, Motilal and Jawaharlal* (1962), and there is a fuller if slightly uncritical *Jawaharlal Nehru* (2 vols., 1975–9) by S. Gopal, J. M. Brown, *Gandhi and Civil Disobedience* (1977) continues the work of explaining what Gandhi actually did; R. J. Moore's *The Crisis of Indian Unity* (1974) is concerned with the independence movement rather than the problems of the Muslims, but is still worth attention. B. R. Tomlinson, *The Political Economy of the Raj*

1914–1947 (1979) shows how Britain's economic connection with India declined in the first half of the twentieth century. I. Drummond, *British Economic Policy and the Empire 1919–1939* (1972) gives some very mild approval to the policy of imperial preference. Anyone who is bored by *William Lyon Mackenzie King* (3 vols., so far, 1958–) can reflect that this may not be the fault of the authors, R. M. Dawson and B. Neatby, and can turn to E. Page, *Truant Surgeon* (1963) for a very interesting autobiography by a politician who was at the centre of Australian affairs throughout the period between the wars. The diplomacy of the Commonwealth has recently been studied by R. F. Holland in *Britain and the Commonwealth Alliance 1918–1939* (1981).

Chapter 12

This period is close enough to the present day to mean that there has not been much time to open up archives or to produce serious books based on them. Most of the books inevitably are the product of the period of lavish expressions of goodwill for the future: there is a little of this in J. D. B. Miller's *The Commonwealth in the World* (1965), a little in J. Garner's *The Commonwealth Office 1925–1968* (1978), and a fair amount, from a firmly centre-left position, in J. Strachey's *The End of Empire* (1959). On the other hand D. Goldsworthy's *Colonial Issues in British Politics 1945–1961* (1970) is a straightforward piece of contemporary history, which is also written from a centre-left point of view. The great multi-volume collection of documents on the arrival of Indian independence which Nicholas Mansergh is editing has a title, *The Transfer of Power* (1970–), which might possibly lead readers to overlook an interesting memoir by an important participant, *The Transfer of Power in India* (1957) by V. P. Menon. The diary of another participant is available: *Wavell: The Viceroy's Journal* (1973) has been edited by P. Moon. The emergence of Pakistan is discussed from many points of view in *The Partition of India* (1970), edited by C. H. Philips and M. D. Wainwright. The first steps taken on the imperial side towards arranging African independence, which were made around the Second World War, are examined in R. D. Pearce, *The Turning Point in Africa 1938–1948* (1982), and were explained more or less at the time by one of the men in charge, Andrew Cohen, in his *British Policy in Changing Africa* (1959). The African side of the story can be seen in R. I. Rotberg, *The Rise of Black Nationalism in Central Africa* (1965) or in politicians' autobiographies: O. Awolowo's *Awo* (1960) or K. Nkrumah's *The Autobiography of Kwame Nkrumah* (1957), which can be balanced by reading the account of one of his officials, G. Bing's *Reap the Whirlwind* (1968). Elsewhere, R. Clutterbuck's *The Long, Long War* (1967) describes the successful counter-insurgency operation that dominated Malayan history between 1948 and 1962, and K. Sinclair tried to show in his *Walter Nash* (1977) that New Zealand had had another Prime Minister who was worth a biography.

Chapter 13

Scholarly works on the last stages of empire are not numerous, and perhaps they never will be, but some of the participants have published memoirs. H. Macmillan's autobiography, especially volumes 5, *Pointing the Way* (1972) and 6, *At The End of the Day* (1973) are informative in a good debating style. The conflict in central Africa can be followed from various points of view in N. Fisher, *Iain Macleod* (1973),

R. Welensky, *Welensky's 4,000 Days* (1965), and C. Alport, *The Sudden Assignment* (1965). M. Meredith's *The Past is another Country* (1979) brings the story of Rhodesia almost to the end of white rule, with heavy emphasis on the last years. W. P. Kirkman, *Unscrambling an Empire 1956–1966* (1966) is a very good attempt to keep up with the events of the period of most rapid decolonization. M. Blundell, *So Rough a Wind* (1964) is a memoir by a Kenya settler and politician who came to see the need for decolonization. R. Symonds, *The British and their Successors* (1966), was written at a time when people were perhaps a little more cheerful about the prospects facing the successors than was later the case. H. Wilson, *The Labour Government 1964–1970* (1971) is a rather day-to-day account of what he did while he was Prime Minister and shows that he managed to squeeze a great deal of Commonwealth business into his crowded official life.

ADDENDUM

The two major scholarly presses reversed their approaches to standard histories: Cambridge, in the past the great exponent of multi-volume histories in which each volume contained work by several hands, launched its *New Cambridge History of India* (1987–), covering the period from the Moghals to the present in thirty-two volumes, of which about half will be devoted to the period of British rule, and entrusted each volume to a single author. Oxford, which had normally asked a single author to write each volume when it produced a multi-volume series, embarked upon a five-volume *History of the British Empire*, written by a platoon of authors and edited by W. R. Louis, to appear in 1998. At a more popular level Lawrence James's *The Rise and Fall of the British Empire* (1994) gave some support to the idea that single-volume histories of the empire are often more favourable to it than more detailed studies. Two useful pieces of background material were published: Christopher Bayly edited an *Atlas of the British Empire* (1989), which integrated maps and other illustrations into an account of the Empire which recognized geography as well as history; and Andrew Porter produced an *Atlas of British Overseas Expansion* (1991) which was more strictly concerned with detailed maps. At the level of scholarly presentation of original documents, the completion in 1987 of the immense *Constitutional Relations between Britain and India: The Transfer of Power*, edited by N. Mansergh and E. W. E. Lumby, is worth attention.

Bernard Bailyn revised some of the earlier parts of the story in his *Peopling of British North America* (1986). A new analysis of the changes in the Empire in the late eighteenth century was provided by Bayly in his *Imperial Meridian* (1989), and the pains and penalties of transportation to Australia were described very graphically by Robert Hughes in *The Fatal Shore* (1986). The thesis of Hobson's *Imperialism* was taken up in two books: L. Davis and R. Huttenback argued in their *Mammon and the Price of Empire* (1988) that in the second half of the nineteenth century owning an empire involved most people in Britain in large costs for imperial defence on behalf of people in colonies of white settlement, which made the empire safe for upper-class investors from the south of England; while P. J. Cain and A. G. Hopkins gave this line of reasoning a more general application in their *British Imperialism* (1993), which contended that the main thrust of British imperial involvement could best be understood over the centuries by analyzing the overseas transactions of the City of London.

Thomas Pakenham made a determined attempt to provide an easily comprehensible account of *The Scramble for Africa* (1991); and Cecil Rhodes continued to attract attention: a good life by B. Roberts and a very good one by R. Rotberg appeared in 1988. T. Eddy and D. Schreuder produced *The Rise of Colonial Nationalism* (1988), Lord Beloff's *Imperial Sunset* (1987–9) described the last decades of the Empire, and the diplomatic history of the years between the wars was described by A. Clayton in his *The British Empire as a Superpower* (1986). J. D. Hargreaves moved on from the nineteenth century to write *Decolonisation in Africa* (1988) and T. R. H. Davenport brought his *Short History of South Africa* up to the release of Mandela in 1990 (1991).

TABLES

I. Wheat Imports by place of origin (000s of hundredweights)

Britain was a habitual but not a constant importer of wheat in the early 19th century; 1836 was the last year in which she was a net exporter of wheat.

	Russia	Germany/ Prussia	Canada	USA	Argentina	India	Australia
1846	888	1,560	297	742			
1870	10,629	3,348	2,838	13,182			
1890	19,389	1,101	1,128	17,201	2,810	9,112	3,058
1913	5,011		21,788	34,068	14,756	18,766	10,183
1937	8,123		34,257	3,492	15,472	6,274	22,389
1950			49,217	8,955			5,989
1965			57,514	7,744	12,818		15,253

For most of the period covered by this table British domestic production fluctuated around 72,000 bushels which (allowing for the difficulties of conversion) is about 40,000 thousands of hundredweights.

Figures from B. R. Mitchell and P. Deane, *Abstract of British Historical Statistics* (Cambridge, 1962), 100–2 and 204, and B. R. Mitchell and H. G. Jones, *Second Abstract of British Historical Statistics* (Cambridge, 1971), 62.

II. Raw Materials for Textiles by place of origin (millions of lb. weight)

	British wool	Total Wool Imports	of which: Australia	New Zealand	South Africa	Total Cotton Imports
1780	90	1.8				6.8
1790	90	3.2				31.4
1810	100	10.9				132
1820	110	9.8	0.1			120
1840	125	49.4	9.7			459
1850	135	74.3		39.0		588
1860	145	148.4		59.2	16.6	1,084
1890	138	633	323.1	95.6	87.2	1,664
1910	143	803.3	314.5	189.7	104.3	1,632
1930	119	786.5	257.0	174.7	158.2	1,272
1950	58	708.5	383.6	180.1		1,200
1965	83	560.7	181.6	135.3		614

Figures from Mitchell and Deane, op. cit., 178–9 and 192–4; and Mitchell and Jones, op. cit., 90 and 93.

III. British Imports, with special attention to coffee, tea, and sugar (figures in £s)

	Coffee	Sugar	Tea	Largest other item or items when relevant
1700	36,000	668,000	14,000	647,000 wine
1750	75,000	1,270,000	482,000	481,000 tobacco
1800	398,000	4,301,000	1,510,000	1,848,000 raw cotton
1850	3,172,000	9,787,000	5,051,000	21,531,000 raw cotton 12,290,000 corn
1900	2,500,000	19,200,000	10,700,000	58,900,000 grain and flour
1950	11,000,000	80,100,000	57,400,000	203,700,000 meat; and nine other categories were larger than sugar
1965	14,800,000	94,600,000	107,500,000	591,700,000 oil; and sixteen other categories were larger than sugar

Figures from Mitchell and Deane, op. cit., 288–301, and Mitchell and Jones, op. cit., 131–4.

IV. British Exports and Imports (exports include re-exports; figures in £1,000s)

	Asia	Africa south of Sahara	Thirteen Colonies	(rest of) British North America	British West Indies	Rest of World
1710 imports	248	14	250	14	781	2,098
exports	126	69	204	13	205	5,285
1750 imports	1,104	29	815	46	1,516	3,578
exports	509	161	1,313	63	547	8,725
1800 imports	4,942	97	2,358	393	7,369	10,926
exports	2,860	1,099	7,886	976	4,087	18,208

(exports include re-exports; figures in £1,000,000s)

	India (Republic of India)	Africa south of Sahara	USA	British North America/ Canada	British West Indies	Australia	New Zealand	Rest of World
1854 imports	10.7	4.8	29.8	7.1	7.6	4.3	0.1	92.6
exports	9.6	2.9	22.3	6.3	4.0	13.0	0.4	60.5
1900 imports	27.4	8.4	138.8	22.2	1.8	23.8	11.6	287.3
exports	31.0	21.6	37.4	9.6	4.7	23.6	5.9	216.5
1950 imports	98.3	271.1	211.4	180.2	127.4	219.7	133.9	1,367.5
exports	97.2	286.6	127.4	128.4	37.9	256.8	86.8	1,237.8
1965 imports	128.3	604.7	671.4	338.2	98.7	219.5	208.2	3,362.1
exports	116.4	558.2	514.7	208	98.9	284.4	126.1	2,994.1

Figures from Mitchell and Deane, op. cit. 310–26 and Mitchell and Jones, op. cit. 136–40.

Tables

V. Estimates for British Gross National Product and for total Overseas Investment at selected dates

	Gross National Product	Overseas Investment
	(all figures in £m.)	
1700	90	
1760	140	
1780	185	
1801	232	
1815		10
1821	291	60
1855	636	248
1871	1,015	763
1886	1,136	1,576
1913	2,265	3,990
1937	4,616	3,754
1946	9,458	2,329
1964	29,373	10,000

The gross national product figures are taken in money terms, with no alteration for changes in prices; these changes would not really be important until the 20th century, when it could be estimated that prices in 1964 were five times the 1913 level. But the changes between 1700 and 1900 never came to anything like this, though the 1801 figure may be slightly inflated by the price rise of the Napoleonic Wars.

However, correcting for price changes over three centuries makes very little sense; the pattern of consumption changed so much in the period that the comparison would be rather misleading. On the other hand, a comparison to show what multiple of the gross national product had been invested overseas may be useful.

The figures are taken from Mitchell and Deane, op. cit., 366–8; A. M. Imlah, *Economic Elements in the Pax Britannica* (1958), 74–8; the 1965 budget speech and chapter 2, 'The Eighteenth Century Origins', of W. A. Cole and P. Deane, *Origins of British Economic Growth 1688–1959* (1969 edn.). A slight problem here is that the Cole and Deane figures seem to start from a point rather higher than the £50m. of the Gregory King estimate for 1688 would lead one to expect.

VI. Emigration

The British Empire was the scene of a good deal of transfer of population. It is hard to express this at all precisely, but estimates have been made for the period between the two world wars.

75m. estimated British stock in US in 1930

6.63m. white population of Australia in 1933
(almost all British)
subdivided 39 per cent Church of England
(probably mainly English)
18 per cent Roman Catholic
(probably mainly Irish)
11 per cent Presbyterian
(probably mainly Scots)

5.38m. British stock in Canada in 1931
subdivided 50 per cent English
24 per cent Scots
22 per cent Irish

0.29m. in the Crown Colony of Newfoundland in 1933

1.48m. white population of New Zealand in 1936
subdivided 40 per cent Church of England
9 per cent Methodist
(both probably mainly English)
25 per cent Presbyterian
(probably mainly Scots)
13 per cent Roman Catholic
(probably mainly Irish)

2m. white population of South African in 1936
subdivided 57 per cent Dutch Reformed Church
(almost entirely Dutch, though
it might include a few Scots)
19 per cent Church of England
4.5 per cent Presbyterian
9 per cent other Protestants
4.75 per cent Roman Catholic
(these four groups mainly British)
4.75 per cent Jewish
(mainly German)

0.5m in India

0.01m. in the West Indies

58,000 in Southern Rhodesia in 1938

21,000 in Kenya in 1930

These figures are taken from C. Carrington, *The British Overseas* (1949), 508–10.

(*continued overleaf*)

Any totals based on these figures would be dominated by the American figures, and they are the least reliable because they are the furthest back in time of origin. The problems of this type of statistics are brought out in *The Economics of International Migration* (1958), ed. Brinley Thomas. On p. 65 the figures for British emigration adopted in this book are set out: between 1815 and 1914 20m. people left the British Isles, of whom 13m. went to the United States. But it should be noted that on pp. 136–7 the estimate is offered that 8.5m. people came from the British Isles to the United States betwen 1790 and 1914, 4.5m. from Ireland and 4m. from the rest of the country.

A number of people also moved from India, with results that were one or even two orders of magnitude smaller. It has been studied by Hugh Tinker in *A New System of Slavery* (1974), though he tends to overstate its importance. (For instance, he says of the Indians, 'It was their labour, along with British capital and expertise, that created the overseas wealth of Britain' (p. xiii). In practice British overseas wealth was in countries like the United States, Canada, and Australia that did not admit Indians.) So Tinker's figures, taken from pp. 278, 363, and 370–8, are unlikely to be understated. They are:

> 0.75m. in Ceylon (1920s)
> > Burma and Malaya had annual migratory populations
> > from India, but no estimate of numbers is given
> 265,000 in Mauritius (1922)
> 267,000 in British Guyana (1921)
> 160,000 in South Africa (1927)
> 122,117 in Trinidad (1921)
> 18,610 in Jamaica (1921)
> 5,000–10,000 in East Africa (1901)

Between the wars the total population of the British territories in and around the Caribbean was about 2.25m. Subtracting the 0.5m. from India and Britain mentioned above, about 1.75m. remain as descendants of Africans brought across the Atlantic as slaves. Obviously this figure, like so many others, ignores the effects of mixed descent.

VII. Territories of the British Empire

Present name of state or colony if still part of the Commonwealth; or name at time of leaving Empire or Commonwealth	The former names of countries that change their names and stay in the Commonwealth (not listed in col. 5) are given here. Those that have left the Commonwealth (listed in col. 5) are given their original names in col. 1 and the new name is given here, in square brackets	Date of acquisition (See note at end of table)	Date of autonomy: that is, the highest level of self-government accessible at the time listed: responsible government, dominion status or membership of the Commonwealth. If no date is given here or in col. 5, the territory is still a colony	Date of ending relationship with Empire or Commonwealth (or period of absence)
Aden	[South Yemen]	1839		1967
Anguilla		1650		
Antigua and Barbuda		1632	1981	
Australia, formed in 1900 from				
New South Wales		1788	1852–6	
Queensland		1859	1859	
South Australia		1835	1852–6	
Tasmania	Van Dieman's Land	1825	1852–6	
Victoria		1851	1852–6	
Western Australia		1829	1890	
Australian External Territories		from 1788 onwards		
Bahamas		1529	1973	
Bangladesh	East Pakistan until separation		1972	

VII. Territories of the British Empire (cont.)

Present name of state or colony if still part of the Commonwealth; or name at time of leaving Empire or Commonwealth	The former names of countries that change their names and stay in the Commonwealth (not listed in col. 5) are given here. Those that have left the Commonwealth (listed in col. 5) are given their original names in col. 1 and the new name is given here, in square brackets	Date of acquisition (See note at end of table)	Date of autonomy: that is, the highest level of self-government accessible at the time listed: responsible government, dominion status or membership of the Commonwealth. If no date is given here or in col. 5, the territory is still a colony	Date of ending relationship with Empire or Commonwealth (or period of absence)
Barbados		1625	1966	
Belize	British Honduras	1638–1862	1982	
Bermuda		1609		
Botswana	Bechuanaland	1884	1966	
British Antarctica		1819–32		
British Indian Ocean Territories		1815		
British Somaliland	[(part of) Somalia]	1884–7		1960
British Virgin Islands		1672		
Brunei		1888	1983	
Burma	*[Myanmar]*	1826–85		1948
Cameroon	The British trust territory of Southern Cameroons joined Cameroon in 1961		1995	

Canada, formed 1867–1949 from British Columbia including Vancouver Island		1793–1826	1866	
Canada East	Lower Canada, Quebec	1763	1848	
Canada West	Upper Canada, Ontario	1763	1848	
New Brunswick		1713	1854	
Nova Scotia including Cape Breton Island		1713–63	1847	
Newfoundland		1497–1713	1855	
Prince Edward Island		1763	1854	
Rupert's Land and North West Territories		1670–1826	1870	
Cayman Islands		1670		
Cyprus		1878	1960	
Dominica		1763	1978	
Egypt		1882–1914		1922
Falklands Islands		1833		
Fiji		1874	1970	1987
Florida (east and west)		1763		1783
Gambia		1661–1713	1965	
Ghana	Gold Coast	1821–1901	1957	
Gibraltar		1704–13		
Grenada		1763	1974	
Guyana	British Guiana	1796–1815	1966	
Heligoland		1807–14		1890
Hong Kong				
India		1757–1842	1947	
Ionian Islands		1815		1864
Iraq		1918–23		1932

VII. Territories of the British Empire (cont.)

Present name of state or colony if still part of the Commonwealth; or name at time of leaving Empire or Commonwealth	The former names of countries that change their names and stay in the Commonwealth (not listed in col. 5) are given here. Those that have left the Commonwealth (listed in col. 5) are given their original names in col. 1 and the new name is given here, in square brackets	Date of acquisition (See note at end of table)	Date of autonomy: that is, the highest level of self-government accessible at the time listed: responsible government, dominion status or membership of the Commonwealth. If no date is given here or in col. 5, the territory is still a colony	Date of ending relationship with Empire or Commonwealth (or period of absence)
Ireland	[Irish Free State]	1169–1606	1921	1949
Jamaica		1655–70	1962	
Kenya		1887–95	1963	
Kiribati	Gilbert Islands	1892–1918	1979	
Lesotho	Basutoland	1868	1966	
Malawi	Nyasaland	1889–91	1964	
Malaysia, formed in 1963 from Malaya		1786–1909	1957	
Sabah		1862	1963	
Sarawak		1841–1946	1963	
Maldives		1887	1965	
Malta		1800–14	1964	
Mauritius		1815	1968	
Minorca		1708–13		1782–3
Montserrat		1632		
Mozambique	no previous links		1995	

Namibia	South West Africa	1919	1990	
Nauru		1919	1968	
New Zealand		1840	1852	
Nigeria		1861–1903	1960	
Pakistan	separated from India	1947		1972–89
Palestine	[Israel]	1917–23		1948
Papua New Guinea formed in 1945–6 from				
New Guinea		1915–9		
Papua	British New Guinea	1884		
Pitcairn		1838–87		
St Christopher, Nevis		1624–8	1983	
St Helena, Ascension and Tristan da Cunha		1661–1816		
St Lucia		1814	1979	
St Vincent and the Grenadines		1627??	1979	
Seychelles		1814	1976	
Sierra Leone		1787	1961	
Singapore		1819–24	1963–5	
Solomon Islands		1893–1900	1978	
South Africa formed in 1910 from				1961–94
Cape Colony		1795–1815		
Natal		1843		
Orange Free State		1854–1902		
Transvaal [South African republic]		1852–1902		
Sri Lanka	Ceylon	1815	1948	
Sudan		1898		1954

VII. Territories of the British Empire (*cont.*)

Present name of state or colony if still part of the Commonwealth; or name at time of leaving Empire or Commonwealth	The former names of countries that change their names and stay in the Commonwealth (not listed in col. 5) are given here. Those that have left the Commonwealth (listed in col. 5) are given their original names in col. 1 and the new name is given here, in square brackets	Date of acquisition (See note at end of table)	Date of autonomy: that is, the highest level of self-government accessible at the time listed: responsible government, dominion status or membership of the Commonwealth. If no date is given here or in col. 5, the territory is still a colony	Date of ending relationship with Empire or Commonwealth (or period of absence)
Surinam	[Dutch Guiana, Suriname]	1651		1668
Swaziland		1890–1902	1968	
Tanzania formed in 1964 from				
Tanganyika		1919	1963	
Zanzibar		1870–90	1963	
'The Thirteen Colonies'	[The United States of America]			1776
Connecticut		1636–62		
Delaware		1702		
Georgia		1732		
Maryland		1632–4		
Massachusetts		1629		
New Hampshire		1680		

New Jersey, divided for a time into east and west		1664		
New York		1664		
North Carolina		1670–1729		
Pennsylvania		1681		
Rhode Island		1635–63		
South Carolina		1670–1729		
Virginia		1607		
Tonga		1900	1970	
Transjordan	[Jordan]	1917–23		1946
Trinidad and Tobago		1802–15	1962	
Turks and Caicos Islands		1638		
Tuvalu	Ellice Islands	1892–1918	1978	
Uganda		1888–95	1962	
United Kingdom formed in 1707 and 1800 from England and Wales				
Scotland				
Ireland		The English constitution after 1688 was what Lord Durham had in mind when he spoke of 'responsible government'		
Vanuatu	New Hebrides	1887–1960	1980	
Western Samoa		1919	1961–70	
Zambia	Northern Rhodesia	1889–1900	1964	
Zimbabwe	Southern Rhodesia	1888–93	1980	

Index

Printed in the United Kingdom
by Lightning Source UK Ltd.
136216UK00001B/37/P

9 780198 731337